Eva Conrad, *San Bernardino Valley College*   Mark Rafter, *Chaffey College*

THE INTEGRATOR

FOR

ESSENTIALS OF PSYCHOLOGY

Josh R. Gerow

▶ *Some great news for psychology professors…*

You may already know that *Essentials of Psychology* is accompanied by an outstanding supplements package (we wouldn't pass it on to you any other way). But there is one component that you probably have not heard of. It's called THE INTEGRATOR, and it begins on the next page of this special instructor's edition.

▶ *We've cut your prep time in half.*

THE INTEGRATOR is what we like to call a supplement's supplement. It's a reference tool designed to help you better coordinate the instructional resources of the *Essentials of Psychology* package to best support your teaching style. Want to enhance your lecture on and class discussion of "The Brain?" There's no need for additional research. Consult THE INTEGRATOR. Wondering what videos most clearly reinforce the unit on "Personality?" Why read through summaries of all our video selections? Check THE INTEGRATOR.

As you will soon see, there's no end to the help THE INTEGRATOR will give you or the time it will save you; and when you turn the page you'll note that it's placement couldn't be more handy.

2

THE INTEGRATOR

The instructional resources illustrating key concepts in each chapter are organized by text chapters. The page numbers in the column to the right refer to pages in the Instructor's Resource Kit. The resources available to you are arranged in the following categories:

• Chapter Overview

Learning Objectives and a **Chapter Outline** are included for each chapter.

• Lecture Enhancements

Lecture Supplements - Additional information designed to provide background for lectures.

Biographical Profiles - Sketches of key psychologists, briefly tracing their contributions to the field.

Timeline - Overviews of the people and events that have shaped research and theory within the subfields of psychology.

Additional Readings

• Activities

Demonstrations - Step-by-step descriptions of effective demonstrations including handouts formatted for easy reproduction.

APA Publications - Selected demonstrations and articles from three APA publications relevant to teaching introductory psychology: *Activities Handbook for the Teaching of Psychology*, *Teaching of Psychology* (a journal), and *Teaching a Psychology of People: Resources for Gender and Sociocultural Awareness*.

Journey Software - This unique software package provides students with full-color graphic modules in experimental research, learning, developmental psychology, and psychological assessment. Available for IBM and Macintosh computers.

Critical Thinking Exercises - Activities for students that require application, analysis and synthesis of concepts rather than mere memorization. Can be used as in-class or take-home assignments.

• Audio-Visual Support

The **Transparencies** and **Laserdisc** (*Psychology Encyclopedia III*) are accompanied by a comprehensive list of contents. Contact your HarperCollins representative for more information on these support materials.

Telecourse Programs - Brief descriptions of each of 26 half-hour programs in the *Discovering Psychology* and *Psychology: The Study of Human Behavior* telecourse series as well as other relevant telecourse series.

Video Modules - Video clips, ranging in length from 50 seconds to eight minutes, have been drawn from the telecourse *Psychology: The Study of Human Behavior* (HarperCollins *Video Briefs*) and from *The Brain* and *The Mind* series. These clips include experiments, interviews, documentary footage, and dramatic examples of concepts discussed in the text. Ask your HarperCollins representative for support materials for any of the video module sets.

Films and Videos - Annotated descriptions of a variety of films and videos. Includes date of film, running time, and distributor.

4

Chapter 1
The Nature of Psychology

• Audio-Visual Support

Chapter 2
Biological Bases of Behavior

Instructor's Resource Kit Page

• Chapter Overview

• Lecture Enhancements

Lecture Supplements

Paul Piene Broca
Franz Joseph Gall
Stephen Jay Gould
Johan Gregor Mendel
Wilder Graves Penfield
Roger Sperry
Edward Osborne Wilson

• Activities

Demonstrations

Activities Handbook for the Teaching of Psychology
Journal: *Teaching of Psychology*
Teaching a Psychology of People: Resources for Gender and Sociocultural Awareness

Critical Thinking Exercises

• Audio-Visual Support

CHAPTER 3
HUMAN DEVELOPMENT

Instructor's Resource Kit Page

• Chapter Overview

• Lecture Enhancements

• Activities

• Audio-Visual Support

Chapter 4
Sensory Processes

Instructor's Resource Kit Page

• **Chapter Overview**

• Lecture Enhancements

• Activities

• Audio-Visual Support

Chapter 5
PERCEPTION AND CONSCIOUSNESS

• Audio-Visual Support

CHAPTER 6
LEARNING

Instructor's Resource Kit Page

• Chapter Overview

• Lecture Enhancements

Albert Bandura
Konrad Lorenz
Ivan Petrovich Pavlov
Burrhus Frederic Skinner
Edward Lee Thorndike

• Activities

• Audio-Visual Support

Chapter 7
Memory

• Audio-Visual Support

CHAPTER 8
HIGHER COGNITIVE PROCESSES

Instructor's Resource Kit Page

• Chapter Overview

• Lecture Enhancements

• Activities

• Audio-Visual Support

Video Modules

Films and Videos

Chapter 9
Motivation and Emotion

Instructor's Resource Kit Page

• Chapter Overview

• Lecture Enhancements

• Activities

• Audio-Visual Support

Films and Videos

CHAPTER 10
PERSONALITY: THEORIES AND ASSESSMENT

Instructor's Resource Kit Page

• Chapter Overview

• Lecture Enhancements

23

• Activities

• Audio-Visual Support

CHAPTER 11
HEALTH AND STRESS

Instructor's Resource Kit Page

• Chapter Overview

• Lecture Enhancements

Lecture Supplements

• Activities

• Audio-Visual Support

Chapter 12
ABNORMAL PSYCHOLOGY: PSYCHOLOGICAL DISORDERS

Instructor's Resource Kit Page

• Chapter Overview

• Lecture Enhancements

• Activities

• Audio-Visual Support

CHAPTER 13
TREATMENT AND THERAPY FOR PSYCHOLOGICAL DISORDERS

Instructor's Resource Kit Page

• Chapter Overview

• Lecture Enhancements

• Activities

Demonstrations
In-Class RET   490
In-Class Behaviorism   490

APA Publications   491
Activities Handbook for the Teaching of Psychology

Critical Thinking Exercises
A Quick Quiz   493
What Type of Psychotherapy?   495

• Audio-Visual Support

Telecourse Programs
Discovering Psychology   498
      Program 22 Psychotherapy
Psychology: The Study of Human Behavior   498
      Program 22 Approaches to Therapy
      Program 23 Therapy Choices

Video Modules
HarperCollins *Video Briefs*   498
      "Skills Training for Schizophrenics"
      "Three Faces of Therapy"
      "Psychoanalytic Approach"
      "Humanistic Approach"
      "Cognitive-behavioral Approach"
      "Family Systems Approach"
The Mind Video Modules   499
      "Mood Disorders: Medication and Talk Therapy"
      "Treating Depression"
      "Treating Drug Addiction: A Behavioral Approach"

Films and Videos
Abnormal Psychology: The Psychoses   499
Addiction and the Family   499
Anyplace But Here, Parts 1 and 2   499
The Autistic Child: A Behavioral Approach   500
Behavior Therapy: An Introduction   500
Carl Rogers Conducts an Encounter Group   500
Harry: Behavioral Treatment of Self-Abuse   500
Madness and Medicine, Parts 1 and 2   500
Otto: The Behavioral Perspective   500
Otto: The Phenomenological Perspective   500
Otto: The Psychoanalytic Perspective   500
Otto: The Social Perspective   500

Chapter 14
SOCIAL PSYCHOLOGY

Instructor's Resource Kit Page

• Chapter Overview

• Lecture Enhancements

• Activities

• Audio-Visual Support

Chapter 15
Applied Psychology:
I/O, Environmental, and Sports Psychology

Instructor's Resource Kit Page

• Chapter Overview

• Lecture Enhancements

• Activities

• Audio-Visual Support

ESSENTIALS OF PSYCHOLOGY

CONCEPTS AND APPLICATIONS

JOSH R. GEROW

**Indiana University-Purdue University
at Fort Wayne**

HarperCollinsCollegePublishers

To Nancy, Evelyn, Leslie, and Josh IV

Acquisitions Editor: Anne Harvey/Catherine Woods
Developmental Editor: Paula Fitzpatrick
Project Coordination, Text, and Cover Design: PC&F, Inc.
Art Direction: Teri Delgado
Cover Illustration: Robbie Marantz/The Image Bank
Photo Researcher: Sandy Schneider
Production Manager: Willie Lane
Compositor: PC&F, Inc.
Printer and Binder: Von Hoffman Press, Inc.
Cover Printer: The Lehigh Press, Inc.

For permission to use copyrighted material, grateful acknowledgment is made to the copyright holders on pp. 581–583, which are hereby made part of this copyright page.

ESSENTIALS OF PSYCHOLOGY: CONCEPTS AND APPLICATIONS

Copyright © 1993 by HarperCollins College Publishers

Library of Congress Cataloging-in-Publication Data

Gerow, Josh R.
    Essentials of psychology / Josh R. Gerow.
        p. cm.
    Includes bibliographical references and index.
    ISBN 0-673-46656-6 (student ed.) ISBN 0-673-46779-1 (instructor's ed.)
    1. Psychology.   2. Psychology, Applied.   I. Title.
BF121.G428   1993   93-13033
150—dc20   CIP

92 93 94 95 9 8 7 6 5 4 3 2 1

Brief Contents

Contents

Preface

I realize that my name is on the cover of this book, and I am quite willing to take responsiblility for this text. I am also quite willing to acknowledge that writing a textbook is a collaborative effort. It requires the loving support of family and friends. It requires the skilled craftsmanship of editors, designers, illustrators, and production people. It also requires the thoughtful guidance of colleagues willing to read early manuscript drafts and offer style and content suggestions.

For this text, input from colleagues has been particularly critical. I am convinced that if anyone were to write an introductory psychology textbook that adequately addressed all of the interests and desires of the psychologists who might use it, that text would be well over 2,000 pages long! As authors, we psychologists all seem to have our "favorite topics" that we feel should be included in an introductory text.

Fortunately, HarperCollins assembled a team of colleague-reviewers who shared my vision for this text. The basic idea was to prepare a brief, inexpensive text that presented the *essential concepts* of psychology, to present them clearly and fully, and to show how these concepts can be *applied* in everyday life. Hence our title: *Essentials of Psychology: Concepts and Applications.* An equally important goal was to build into the text as many features as possible to help the student appreciate and remember those concepts and applications. Although we wanted to build study-learning aids into the book, we wanted to do so in a way that would not interrupt the flow of the text itself. We wanted to avoid "clutter." In this regard, I believe we have succeeded.

▶ Features of This Text

Because we see the pedagogical learning aids as so important, we have built a large number into the text itself. They include:

▼ **"Introduction: Using Psychology to Study Psychology"** fully details procedures for *effective how-to-study techniques.*

▼ Chapter **"Outlines"** provide a quick and easy overview of what is to come.

▼ Chapter **"Previews"** describe more fully the material to be covered in the chapter and demonstrate why psychologists care about this material, and why you as a student should care as well.

▼ **Boldface key terms** and **Marginal Glossary** highlight important terms and concepts; provide definitions in the text, in the margin (to aid review) and again in an endmatter Glossary.

▼ **"Before You Go On"** questions provide a "marker" for distributing one's practice or study time and an opportunity for interim summarizing. Answers are provided in the Chapter "Summary."

▼ **"Psychology in the Real World"** boxes describe an application of material in the chapter in real-world situations.

▼ **"Thinking Critically About..."** sections encourage you to think critically about the information in the chapter and to relate that information to your own personal experiences.

▼ The chapter **"Summary"** restates the major ideas presented in the chapter in an abbreviated form and provides answers to the "Before You Go On" questions.

▼ **"Practice Tests" and answers** provide a final review of material from the chapter in an objective test format as well as examples of what to expect on exams. Answers are provided in annotated form, fostering the learning-review process.

▶ Supplements to Accompany the Text

For the Instructor

▼ **The Integrator.** Uniquely bound-in to the front of the Instructor's copy. Thirty-one pages are screened for easy identification. Contains complete cross-referencing guide to the entire package.

▼ **Instructor's Resource Kit.** Conveniently packaged in a 3-ring binder. Comprehensive manual features many lecture enhancements including in-class demonstrations, time lines, biographical profiles, and critical thinking exercises for students. Detailed references to video, film and software are included.

▼ **Test Bank.** Contains 100 class-tested and peer-reviewed multiple choice and 10 essay questions per chapter.

▼ **TestMaster Computerized Test Bank.** Software allows instructor to edit existing questions and add new questions. Available in IBM and MAC versions.

▼ **Introductory Transparency Package.** Over 100 4-color acetates. Many illustrations come directly from our Psychology Laserdisc.

▼ **LectureShell.** Detailed chapter outlines that appear in Instructor's Resource Kit and in the Study Guide, available for IBM computers. Instructors can edit outlines and create customized lecture notes.

▼ **Psychology Encyclopedia III Laserdisc.** State-of-the art media presentation, combining still photos, computer art, and moving images from all areas of psychology. Accompanied by a detailed Instructor's Guide which includes a bar code directory.

For the Student

▼ **Study Guide.** Shrinkwrapped with the text at no extra cost to the student. Features 3 multiple-choice practice tests per chapter as well as chapter outline, learning objectives, and study tips.

▼ **SuperShell Computerized Tutorial.** Interactive tutorial program for IBM computers. Provides immediate correct answers to drills, practice exercises. Provides running score for student. Available for IBM-PC's and compatibles.

▼ **Journey.** Gives students hands-on experience dealing with psychological experiments. Full-color graphics in many areas such as learning, memory, development. Available in IBM and MAC.

Acknowledgments

Those colleague-reviewers who had a direct impact on this text are:

Allen R. Branum
South Dakota State University, South Dakota

Glenda Brewer
Rose State College, Oklahoma

Roy Cohen
Mesa Community College, Arizona

Joseph R. Ferrari
Cazenovia College, New York

Richard Florio
Passaic County Community College, New Jersey

Jim Hail
McLennan Community College, Texas

Stan Kary
St. Louis Community College at Florissant Valley, Missouri

David Klein
Stark Technical College, Ohio

Gloria M. Lewis
Tennessee State University, Tennessee

John F. Lindsay, Jr.
Georgia College, Georgia

Kurt Mahoney
Mesa College, Arizona

David R. Murphy
Waubonsee Community College, Michigan

Carrol Perrino
Morgan State University, Maryland

Garry W. Piggrem
Devry Institute of Technology, Ohio

Sandra Stuebner
Chandler-Gilbert Community College, Arizona

Ed Valsi
Oakland Community College, Michigan

Anthony A. Walsh
Salve Regina University, Rhode Island

Marcia Wehr
Santa Fe Community College, Florida

Cecilia K. Yoder
Oklahoma City Community College, Oklahoma

TELEFOCUS GROUP:

Jim Hail
McLennan Community College, Texas

Stan Kary
St. Louis Community College at Flouissant Valley, Missouri

Jack Kirschenbaum
Fullerton College, California

David Klein
Stark Technical College, Ohio

Tom Lombardo
University of Mississippi, Mississippi

David Murphy
Waubonsee Community College, Illinois

Cecilia K. Yoder
Oklahoma City Community College, Oklahoma

Those colleague-reviewers who contributed to *Psychology: An Introduction, 3/e,* from which much of the content of this text was derived are: Michael Aamodt, Radford University; Sharon Akimoto, University of Utah; Mark Alcorn, University of Northern Colorado; Gary Bothe, Pensacola Junior College; Thomas Brothen, University of Minnesota; Robert Brown, Georgia State University; Bill Buskist, Auburn University; Roy Cain, Pan American University; Charlotte Callens, Prince George Community College; James Calhoun, University of Georgia; Karen Christoff, University of Mississippi; Philip Compton, Ohio Northern University; Richard T. Comstock, Monroe Community College; Alfrieda Daly, Rutgers University; Marc DesLauriers, Kansas City Community College; George Diekhoff, Midwestern State University; David Donovan, Northwestern University; Sherry Ellis, Virginia Commonwealth University; Warren Fass, University of Pittsburg/Bradford; William Filbert, Dodge City Community College; John Flanagan, Eastern Kentucky University; Donald Foshee, Valdosta State University; Margaret Fulton, Edison Community College; David Geary, University of Missouri; Judy Gentry, Columbus State Community College; Robert Gentry, College of Charleston; Fredrich Gibbons, Iowa State University; Bryan Gibson, University of Utah; William Gibson, Northern Arizona State; John Goodwyn, School of the Ozarks; Susan Goodwyn, University of California/Davis; Paula Goolkasian, University of North Carolina; William Gray, University of Toledo; Larry Gregory, New Mexico State University; Bruce Hill, Triton College; Wendy James-Alderidge, Pan American University; Philip Langer, University of Colorado; Robert MacAleese, Spring Hill College; Marian Miller, Psychological Service Association; Daniel D. Moriarty, University of San Diego; Arthur Mueller, Community College of Baltimore; Dennis Nagi, Hudson Valley Community College; James Pate, Georgia State University; Carrol S. Perrino, Morgan State University; Virginia Philo, State University of New York/Albany; John Pinto, Morningside College; Lillian Range, University of Southern Mississippi; Robert Riesenberg, Raymond Walters College; Ernst E. Roberts, El Paso Community College; Aaron Roy, Ashland College; Robert Seibel, Pennsylvania State University; Paul Sheldon, Villanova University; Frank Sjursen, Shoreline Community College; Randall Smith, Ouachita Baptist University; Roy Smith, Mary Washington College; Leo Spindel, Centennial College; Dalmus A. Taylor, Wayne State University; Laura Thompson, New Mexico State; Roscoe Thornthwaite, Pembroke State University; Ann Weber, University of North Carolina; Lisa Whitten, State University of New York/Old Westbury; Clair Wiederholt, Madison Area Technical College; Robert Wiley, Montgomery College; Cynthia Willis, Kansas State University; Richard Willis, University of Pittsburg; Randall Wright, Ouachita Baptist University; Cecilia K. Yoder, Oklahoma City Community College.

I would also like to thank reviewers of the First and Second Editions: Robert Ahlering, Central Missouri State University; Roger Allen, North Central Michigan College; Lou Banderet, Northeastern University; Alan Benton, University of Illinois, Circle Campus; Linda Berg-Cross, Howard University; John Best, Eastern Illinois University; Elaine Blakemore, Indiana University—Purdue University at Fort Wayne; Tom Blakemore, Indiana University—Purdue University at Fort Wayne; Walter Bobkiewicz, Oakton Community College; Cynthia Brandau, Belleville Area Community College; Lynn Brokow, Portland Community College; Gary Brown, Kellogg Community College; William Calhoun, University of Tennessee, Knoxville; Edward Clemmer, Emerson College; Donald Cusumano, St. Louis Community College; William O. Dwyer, Memphia State University; Sandra Edwards, Auburn University; Barbara Engler, Union County College; Jody Esper, Valparaiso University; Terence Fetterman, West Valley College; Linda Flickinger, St. Clair County Community College; Cynthia Ford, Jackson State University; James Frost, Cuyahoga Community College; E. Scott Geller, Virginia Polytechnic Institute; David Griese, SUNY Farmingdale; Ernest Gurman, University of Southern Mississippi; Donald Hall, Radford University; Al Heldt, Grand Rapids Junior College; Sandra Holmes, University of Wisconsin, Stevens Point; Christine Jazwinski, St. Cloud State University; Carl Johnson, Central Michigan University; Leon Keys, Ferris State College; Linda Leal, Eastern Illinois University; Paulette Leonard, University of Central Arkansas; Ken LeSure, Cuyahoga Community College; Earl Magidson, Kennedy King College; Willie Manning, Clayton State College; Cynthia Marshall, Skyline College; Sue Martel, Cleveland State Community College, Cleveland, Tennessee; Terry Maul, San Bernardino Valley College; Rick McNeese, Sam Houston State University; Karla Miley, Black Hawk College, Quad-Cities Campus; Hal Miller, Brigham Young University; James Nelson, Parkland College; Steve Nida, Franklin University; Faye Tyler M. Norton, Charlottesville, Virginia; Radha Parker, University of Central Arkansas; Martin Pearlman, Middlesex County Community College; Donald Ragusa, Bowling Green State University; Daniel W. Richards III, Houston Community College; Joel Rivers, Indiana University—Purdue University at Fort Wayne; Joan Rosen, Miami-Dade Community College, South; Steve Rosengarten, Middlesex County Community College; Connie Sanders, University of Tennessee; Michael Scoles, University of Central Arkansas; Fred Shaffer, Northeast Missouri State University; Freddie Shannon, Wayne County Community College; Raymond Shrader, University of Tennessee; W. S. Terry, University of North Carolina, Charlotte; Thomas Tighe, Moraine Community College; Kathy Trabue, Ohio State University; Walter Vernon (deceased), Illinois State University; Wayne Von Bargen, Psychological Service Associates—Fort Wayne, Indiana; Phyllis Walrad, Macomb Community College; Paul Watson, University of Tennessee; Don Welti, Northern Kentucky University; Ursula White, El Paso Community College; Linda Wickstra, St. Louis Community College; Jeffrey Wilson, Indiana University—Purdue University at Fort Wayne; Paul Wilson, Park Center—Fort Wayne, Indiana; Mike Zeller, Mankato State University.

Anne Harvey, psychology acquisitions editor for HarperCollins, was the first and most steadfast to see the real purpose and goal of this book. To her I owe special thanks. Others at HarperCollins who saw to it that my often vague ideas and concepts turned into the book you hold in your hands include developmental editor, Paula Fitzpatrick; senior marketing manager, Barbara Cinquegrani; project editor, Cindy Funkhouser.

Josh R. Gerow

Using Psychology to Study Psychology

▲ **Factors Affecting the Learning Process**

▲ **Time Management for Today's College Student**

▲ **Learning in the Classroom**

▲ **The Importance of Textbook Study**

▲ **Preparing for Exams**

▲ **If All Else Fails, "SQ3R"-IT**

▲▲▲▲▲▲▲

Over the years, psychologists have studied many things, most of which, I hope that eventually you will agree, are practical and relevant to our everyday lives. Among the things that psychologists have investigated are the factors that influence efficient and effective studying behaviors. It seems appropriate to introduce some of the advice that comes from this research now, before we get started. I do firmly believe that if you can put this advice into practice, your performance in this course will benefit directly. We'll return to many of the points raised in this introduction later—mostly in our discussion of learning and memory. As we go along, I'll also point out how some of the features of this book can make your study of psychology easier.

▶ Factors Affecting the Learning Process

How people learn, and how they can learn more effectively are concerns that predate psychology. They are concerns that can be traced to ancient times. What has always surprised me is that after all these hundreds of years, the list of factors known to have a direct and significant impact on learning (academic learning in particular) is really quite short.

As we review this advice on study skills, remember that effective study habits are not developed for their own sake, but to make learning more efficient. You don't go to college to study; you go to college to learn.

▶ Set Goals and Motivate Yourself to Reach Them

We are all aware that we *can* learn some things by accident, without really intending to do so. Our most efficient learning, however, takes place when we intend to learn, when we make a conscious, concerted effort to acquire new information. In a way, this is saying that it helps to be motivated to learn. And we can motivate ourselves to learn. One thing that helps is to establish goals.

Difficulties in learning often arise when college students do not have clear goals. They may not have the foggiest notion of why they are in college in the first place, and can find no particular reason for doing well in their classwork. Therefore, it is a good idea to clarify in your own mind just why you are in college, why you are taking an introductory course in psychology, and why it is important to you (not to someone else) to do well in the course.

▶ Make the Material You Are Learning Meaningful

If you have never studied French, you would certainly find it easier to learn a list of twelve English words than to memorize a list of twelve French words. The reason is quite clear: You know what the English words mean; they make you think of other words; you can associate them with other things; you can imagine what they look like, how they are used, and so on. The French words strike you as nonsense. You cannot relate to them in a meaningful way.

This example can be generalized to many other areas. The learning of any new information is made easier to the extent that the information can be made meaningful, personal, and useful. To a large degree, this means fitting the new information in with your past experiences and future plans. To help you in this endeavor, I've included many examples of the application of the psychological concepts introduced in the text. The catch is that many of *my* examples are particularly meaningful to *me*. This may help you somewhat, but the best thing for you to do is to try to generate your own examples.

▶ Practice, Practice, and Practice Some More

In Chapter Six we will *define* learning to be the result of practice. Practice or rehearsal is an integral part of learning. Learning is NOT something that happens automatically. Acquiring new information involves working with the material, studying it, practicing it. The more you practice material, the better it will be retained. I'll have more to say about the quality of practice in a minute, but for now: *With regard to practice, more is better than less.*

In addition, how you distribute practice time is extremely important. The research on this point is very clear: Overall efficiency is improved when study time is interrupted with occasional rest breaks. For most students and most courses, the recommended schedule is 45 minutes of study followed by a 15-minute rest break. So take short breaks. Get up and stretch, take a stroll, get a drink of water, and so on. But be careful—15 minutes of study followed by 45-minute breaks isn't going to work.

The value of spaced or distributed study is one reason why you will find that I have inserted a number of **Before You Go On** sections in each chapter. They provide a cue as to where a good place might be to take a break. To sit down and study a whole chapter straight through, without a break, is tough to do, and not a very efficient use of your time.

▶ *Get Feedback on Your Learning*

A person with little knowledge of how his or her learning is progressing will be at a distinct disadvantage compared to a person who is informed. The process involved is what psychologists call "knowledge of results," or feedback. Imagine trying to learn how to shoot basketball free throws while blindfolded. With no information about how you are doing or where the ball is going, there's little reason to suspect that you'll ever get to be very good. The same argument holds true for any kind of learning.

Some of the feedback that you get in college comes when your instructor evaluates your work. Use returned exams and papers as feedback. Review them. Note errors you have made. Decide how your learning/study habits can be changed to minimize errors in the future.

You can provide yourself with important—and less costly—feedback. Test yourself on the material you are studying. Self-testing should be an ongoing process, but it is particularly useful as exams approach. For this course, you have two readily available means of providing yourself with feedback or knowledge of results: the **Before You Go On** questions in the text and the **Student Study Guide** that accompanies the text.

▶ *Give Yourself Rewards for Learning*

One of the most practical principles in psychology is that one's actions are often shaped by their consequences. Simply put, behaviors that are rewarded (later we'll say *reinforced*) tend to get repeated whenever possible.

We all know the satisfaction that comes when our goals are attained. That great, exhilarating feeling of doing well on a quiz, term paper, or lab report will go a long way to insure your doing well again. Now, as a college student, many of your rewards will come from instructors, friends, and/or family members. However, you can't always depend on rewards from others to maintain your studying. Try to develop the habit of providing rewards for yourself for work well done. Study hard for 45 to 50 minutes. Then reward yourself for putting in the honest effort. (And by so doing, distribute your study time.) Do something that will make you feel good. It is likely that you will be surprised at how something so simple can have such a significant impact on your behavior.

▶ *Think Critically about What You Are Learning*

To be of any use, the learning that occurs in the context of a college course should involve more than the simple memorization of facts. It should foster or enhance one's ability to think critically about the subject matter. This is particularly true of a psychology course.

Many of us have a tendency to accept without question what we are told by people we perceive to be experts. I am here and now challenging you to do otherwise. To be sure, I believe that the information I have included in this text is as accurate and honestly presented as such information can be. But do not accept what is said here (or any place else) without thinking—critically—about that information. To think critically doesn't mean just to be negative. More than anything else, it means to question, in your own mind, from your own point of view, in the context of your own experience, what is being presented. In a way thinking critically about what is presented here is an important way to make the information meaningful. And we know that that helps learning.

What sorts of questions should you ask about the ideas presented in your psychology class? There are many. Here are just a few suggestions. Where did this information or conclusion come from? On what sort of research was it based? Are there other ways in which this observation can be explained? Does this information fit my own personal experience? In what ways might this conclusion be biased? Given this information, what other possibilities come to mind? In order to help you think about the material presented in the text, there is a special section at the end of each chapter called **Thinking Critically About**. . . . As the name suggests, these questions do not have just one "best" answer. They simply raise issues worth thinking about, or points to ponder.

▶ *Work to Improve Your Performance*

Let's make an important distinction. Learning is a process that takes place inside an individual. We cannot see it as it occurs. We cannot measure it directly. We can only infer learning from performance. You may think that your little nephew can play a tune on the piano. He's told you that he has learned to do so. If you really needed to know if he had learned that tune, what would you do? You would ask him to demonstrate what he has learned. You would ask him to perform. A similar situation exists in the college classroom.

Put simply, learning involves acquiring new information, while performance involves retrieving that information when it is needed. And justifiably or not, it is your performance—based on what you've learned—that is evaluated. Your performance, not your learning, earns your grades in the classroom, or your raise or promotion in the workplace. So to do well in a college class is a two-phase process. First you must learn the required material and then you must be able to retrieve it from memory when it is needed. In the next few pages, I'll elaborate on these general principles of learning by giving specific advice on how to get more out of class, how to use your textbook more effectively, and how to prepare for exams.

▶ *Time Management for Today's College Student*

Here's a reality that causes problems for many of us: There are only 168 hours in each week. For many students, academic success is often a direct reflection of the extent to which these 168 hours are managed.

"Non-traditional" students were once thought of as students who were older, employed outside the home at least on a part time basis, and living at home with household and family responsibilities. On many college campuses today, including my own, this description fits so many students that calling them "non-traditional" just doesn't seem appropriate. It is for this sort of student, however, that issues of time management are most critical.

A very standard rule of thumb is the advice that one should schedule 3 hours of study each week for every hour spent in class. Introductory psychology courses usually meet for about 3 hours a week, which means that the average student should begin a semester planning to spend *9 hours a week studying psychology*—in addition to going to class! Most of my students laugh when I tell them about this rule of thumb, but they also recognize that if they could or would study that much, they would have no trouble doing well in my class.

The short of it is that if you want to succeed as a college student, you are going to have to schedule time (and a place) for studying as surely as schedule time for sleep, meals, your job, taking out the trash, or driving the kids to their soccer games.

One area of time management over which you have significant control is the number of classes in which you enroll each term. Here's what I tell my academic advisees: "Take your time. Enroll only in the number of classes you honestly feel that you can handle. Some day you will graduate, and no one—a potential employer or graduate school committee—is going to ask you how long it took for you to graduate. What they probably will ask you is how well you did—your grades. It seems to me much more reasonable to take 6 or 7 years to graduate with As and Bs than to rush through in 4 years with Cs."

▶ Learning in the Classroom

"But I never missed a class!" is the claim teachers often hear from students who have not done well on an exam, and who have not learned the difference between attending a class and taking an active part in class. The difference has a great effect on how well students learn. Just going to class, although a step in the right direction, seldom does anyone very much good.

▶ Prepare for Class

It is always easier to listen to and understand information you are somewhat familiar with than it is to listen and try to understand totally unfamiliar information. To be sure, few lectures and class activities are designed to be about something you knew before you took the class. The material will have to be somewhat new; that is what you are paying for. But if you prepare and plan carefully, lectures and class discussions will not seem totally alien.

Once the term is under way, preparing for class will be relatively easy. You will have had time to "feel out" your instructor and develop a sense of what will be happening in class. At least you should have reviewed recent lecture notes and previewed the text. Perhaps the most important thing to do is to familiarize yourself with the vocabulary that might come up in class. If you're familiar with the vocabulary before you get to class, your listening for ideas and concepts will be easier because you will not have to think about new words. You will then have a chance to concentrate, organize what is being said, and summarize your thoughts in coherent notes.

Most good listening is a matter of attitude. To be an effective listener, you must be in the proper frame of mind. As you take your seat, you have to rid your mind of thoughts of the trivial activities of the day. You cannot do a good job of listening to a lecture if you are thinking about last night's date or this afternoon's lunch. You can't contribute to a discussion if all you want to talk about is last weekend's game. You must be thinking about psychology. Get your mind warmed up. What's the instructor going to talk about today? What contributions will you be expected to make? How will today's class fit in with what you've already learned? How can you relate this material to your own personal experience? When you find yourself totally surprised at what is being said in class, you have not prepared correctly.

▶ Develop Your Listening Skills

Listening is an active process in which you relate what is being said to what you already have stored in your memory. It is a matter of taking in new information, organizing, and storing it in such a way that it can be used again at some later time. Given the large amounts of information headed toward you in the classroom, this active listening process will require considerable concentration on your part.

We don't often think of it as such, but listening is a skill, a skill that can be developed just like bicycle riding, typing, or reading. Proficiency in listening can be increased through practice. Listening in class for new and useful information is different from listening to casual conversation or your favorite radio station. This is because a larger portion of the information will involve new or technical vocabulary, and because you will be expected to recall the information at some later time (on exams). Every time you listen in class you are practicing a basic learning skill.

▶ Take Useful Notes

Class attendance and careful listening are important because lectures are presented to you only once. Therefore, you will need some written record of the information presented orally in class to study and review later. Good lecture notes written in your own words are as valuable as a summarized and organized compilation of classroom instruction.

There is a large body of research devoted to note-taking skills. For now, we will consider just two basic principles you can use—principles that will help you learn psychology or any other discipline.

Principle 1: Select and Organize the Material Presented to You. It will soon become apparent to you, if it isn't already, that there is no way that you can write down everything your instructor says in class. Actually, this can be an advantage. Note-taking should be an active process of selecting and organizing the information you write down. Although it generally is better to take too many notes than it is to take too few, you must be an active listener who participates in class—not just a mechanical writer.

The notes that you take will be your notes. Put them in a form that you can use. Except for technical terms and new vocabulary, use your own words. In this way, your notes will be more meaningful to you when you review them. Copying information is not learning it.

You should develop some shortcuts—alternatives to writing everything out in longhand. The key here is flexibility. Feel free to abbreviate. But abbreviate only if you will be able to understand your own symbols and notes when you go back to study later. Illegible or incoherent notes are worse than useless: You have wasted valuable listening time taking them.

You should also be aware that there will be times when it is best not to take any notes at all. Participating in a class discussion or asking questions may provide you with the sort of information that you will remember best.

Once again, one of the best ways to learn new material is to get involved, to work with it and make it personal.

Principle 2: Edit and Review Your Notes. Once class is over, only part of your work is done. During the class period you have been listening, selecting, organizing, participating, thinking, and writing. Now you should go back over your written record of the class. This is best accomplished in three stages.

(1) Immediately after class while the material is still fresh in your mind, review your notes, fill in gaps, underline for emphasis, note unclear sections that will require further work, and use the margins in your notebook to add information you simply did not have time to record. (2) Several times a week as part of your study for each course, continue the editing process. Use your textbook, other notes, outside readings, or consult with your instructor for correct spellings, missing details, and the like. (3) An important stage in reviewing your notes should occur after each examination in a course. Go back and critically evaluate your own notes. To what extent did they help? How can they be improved? Did you write too much? Too little? Was the format the best one possible?

▶ The Importance of Textbook Study

For any class you take, you will find that there is more information stored in your textbook than could ever be presented in class. Since this is the case, learning how to get information from your text is one of the most important skills you can acquire in college. This is not to devalue the role of your instructor or class attendance. Instructors update text material, interject personal experience and points of view, and emphasize what they believe to be the most important sections of assigned readings. Here are a few general ideas to guide your study of textbooks.

▶ Prepare for Textbook Study

Because textbook study is so important, you should develop expectations about the material in the chapter by reading the chapter preview, skimming the summary, and by glancing at the headings, subtitles, and illustrations. Before you actually begin reading/studying the text, you should have a series of questions in mind. If nothing else, you should begin your assault on a text chapter with questions such as: "What in the world is *this* all about?" "How can this be of any use to me?" "How can I relate any of this to what I already know?" "How is this material going to show up on our next classroom exam?"

▶ Read Your Textbook Differently from Other Books

Perhaps the most significant insight about textbook study is that it is quite different from casual reading. Reading the chapter is not studying. Studying is a process in which you must become personally involved. Studying a text requires a great deal more concentration and mental effort than does reading for pleasure. What is the author trying to say? What are the major ideas? What evidence supports those ideas? What are the minor points? How can the material be related to what you already know—from personal experience, previous reading, or classroom lectures? How will this information show up on a test?

There are times while studying when you should look up from the book, pause, and consider what you have just read. You should be able to quickly summarize in your own words what you have just read. Here's another reason why we have included **Before You Go On** sections within each chapter of this book. If you cannot answer the questions provided in these sections, there is little point in going further. Go back over the section you've just read. Speed may be fine, but speed without comprehension is a waste of time.

Effective textbook study is a skill that can be learned by anyone, but it will not be learned automatically. It takes hard work and practice to develop textbook study skills. The rewards for your work, however, will be almost immediate.

▶ Make Textbook Study an Active Process

There is no doubt that you must be mentally active and alert while studying so that you can search, question, and think. This text and its accompanying Study Guide have been designed to facilitate active studying. *If you have not done so yet, please go back now and read the section of the Preface titled "Features of this Text."*

Underlining in textbooks has become a common practice. Unfortunately, it often is misused. The purpose of underlining is to highlight or emphasize particular passages of the text so that essential points of a chapter can be reviewed by simply restudying underlined passages. The mistake that many students make is to underline too much. When 80 percent of a page is underlined for emphasis, the remaining 20 percent usually appears more striking.

You can increase the value of your textbook for studying by using the margins of the text for your personal notations. Make your text a storehouse of references. Cross-reference textbook material with information in your notes. If it's your book, use it—write in it.

▶ Preparing for Exams

Few occasions are quite as pleasant as the one you experience when you walk into class to take a big exam fully prepared, confident that you know the material and that you are going to do well. I also know from personal experience how absolutely miserable it feels to face an exam unprepared, doomed before you begin, unable to understand, much less answer, the first question. The key lies in being fully prepared. Proper preparation for exams helps to furnish the kind of positive reinforcement that education is meant to provide. Preparing for exams is not an easy process. It invoves scheduling your time, self-testing your progress, and continuous, active review.

▶ Rule 1: Prepare on a Daily Basis—Don't Cram

In almost every case, you will be notified of upcoming examinations well in advance. Often, scheduled exams are noted on the course outlines distributed on the first day of class. Most of your exams come as no surprise to you. The secret to good exam performance is that daily preparation is needed.

To be truthful, preparing daily is not an easy task. It's difficult to sit down today to study for an exam that won't take place for three more weeks. With so much time before the exam, it seems that there will be plenty of opportunity for studying later.

On the other hand, daily preparation is not all that special. It involves the sort of things I mentioned above. Preparing for and carefully listening in class is daily preparation, as is taking good notes and editing and reviewing them soon after class. A crucial step in preparing for exams is to make a complete, realistic schedule. If you study your textbook on a regular basis, you won't have to consider cramming for exams.

▶ Rule 2: Find Ways to Test Yourself

As examination day approaches, you will want some indication of just how well your studying has been progressing. To be most effective, this self-testing must begin well in advance of any examination date. There are many different techniques for evaluating your own achievement, all of which involve constructing, taking, and "grading" your own test on assigned material before your instructor does. For example, if you think that you may have to identify the important structures of the eye, then draw a picture of one, labeling all of the structures that you can think of, then check your drawing with the one in your book. If you know that your next exam will ask for the definitions of new terms and concepts, see how many you can write out on your own.

Once again, you should find two features of this text particularly helpful: the **Before You Go On** sections, which include questions for every major section of every chapter, and (2) the **Test Yourself** sections, which are found at the end of each chapter.

I am personally quite convinced that self-testing is the one single best thing you can do to prepare for classroom exams. Perhaps I'm soft-hearted, but I tend to believe those students who come to me after a test and say—with teary eye and quivering lip—"But I read the book, over and over." They probably did. They probably learned a lot of psychology in the process, and that is certainly a good thing. But classroom tests do not measure what you have learned. They measure what you can remember. Students often spend too much time putting information into memory, and too little time getting information out of memory, which is what is being tested.

Imagine that you have just finished studying the section on the history of psychology in Chapter One of this book. I'd like to think that that material is presented clearly and in a form that is easy to understand. Let's say you agree with me. Having read this section, you can honestly say to yourself, "Okay, I understand all that. I appreciate something of psychology's history. I learned something." Now comes the crucial part. Now you have to ask yourself, "How is this going to show up on the classroom exam?" You've got at least three things you can do. (1) You can check the Test Yourself sections at the end of each chapter, or (2) You can check the *Student Study Guide* to see how it tests over the material you've just read, or (3) You can pretend that you are the instructor, and *you* can make up some practice items. This last possibility is probably the best of the three because it actively involves you in the process, even though it takes a bit of time to develop the skill of test item writing.

▶ Rule 3: Build Learning by Reviewing

If you have maintained a schedule of daily preparation, and have consistently evaluated your own performance, you should be able to approach examination day with confidence. There is no way that everything you'll need to know for an exam can be assimilated the night before. You simply cannot understand and digest large amounts of material hours before an exam. However, it is well worth your time to review the material that is to be on the exam. To review means "to look at again." You should certainly review just before an exam. But a more helpful procedure is to review on a regular basis throughout the term. You constantly should be reviewing what you've learned. Research evidence and common sense tell us that most forgetting occurs soon after learning. Frequent review, however, can improve retention significantly.

▶ A Final Word on Exam-Taking

When you take an exam, you are being asked to perform on the basis of what you have learned. Although the effects of anxiety on *learning* are subtle, the effects of anxiety on *performance* are well known. Your performance will be poor if you become overly anxious, upset, and uptight—even if you have learned the material reasonably well. Just realizing that anxiety may reduce your efficiency does little to help. Anxiety is very difficult to eliminate by sheer force of willpower. The most effective way to reduce anxiety is to deal with its cause. If you have conscientiously applied yourself to the job of preparing for an exam, you should have reduced, if not eliminated, the most common cause of test anxiety. If being overly nervous about taking exams becomes a source of concern for you, consider talking to someone in the counseling center, learning lab, or psychology department who can help you with this problem. (We'll also discuss related issues in Chapter 11 when we bring up strategies for dealing with stress.)

▶ If All Else Fails, "SQ3R"-It

In this last section, I simply want to take the ideas we have been talking about and recast them in a slightly different way. Nearly half a century ago a teacher by the name of Francis Robinson described a strategy for studying that he called the **SQ3R Method.** The method has two features that highly recommend it: (1) It is quite simple. (2) It works. Although you are sure to recognize that there is nothing new here, thinking about your studying in this way may be helpful. SQ3R can be rewritten, S-Q-R_1-R_2-R_3. All we have to do is to see what these letters stand for.

S = Survey. The idea here is to anticipate what you are about to study by looking ahead, reading the chapter **Preview**, skimming the **Summary**, and quickly glancing through the chapter. The plan is to get an overview what is going to come up during your reading and studying.

Q = Question. [As you might have guessed, this is the one point of the five in the list that I feel is most important.] The idea is to continually ask yourself questions about what you are reading. If nothing else, stop from time to time and ask what I call *The Universal Study Question.* The Universal Study Question is: "Whaaa?"—in the sense of: "What did I just read about?" As it happens, you get considerable help with this book because we're going to keep asking you questions in the **Before You Go On** sections.

R1 = Read. Once you've surveyed and questioned, the time has come to get to it and read the text. Remember: Don't try to sit down and read the entire chapter from beginning to end. Go for smaller sections—space or distribute your practice.

R2 = Recite. We usually think of reciting in terms of performing out loud— as in a "recital." In this instance, you needn't be so literal. The basic idea is to "talk to yourself" about what you're reading. Having surveyed the chapter, you've formed some questions, and are now reading the chapter. By "recite" we mean that the time has come to answer those questions. Really. Go ahead and try to answer the **Before You Go On** questions, for example. Yes, in this book answers to **Before You Go On** questions are provided in the **Summary**. But don't just turn back there and read MY answer. Try to provide an answer on your own first.

R3 = Review. See, we *have* been through all this, haven't we? By review, Robinson meant what we meant when we talked about reviewing earlier. You should plan to schedule time to go back over your notes, back over the text, testing yourself anew each time. Just because you "knew" the answer to a question yesterday, doesn't mean that you know it today. To find out: review.

The Nature of Psychology

▲▲▲▲▲▲▲

Test-taking really *can* be a learning experience—even when your score on the test does not have an impact on your grade. So let's start off your study of psychology with a short true-false quiz. At least this is a test that you can grade for yourself—answers are provided on page 41. As much as anything else, this little quiz will give you a sense of the sorts of issues that we'll be discussing for the next few hundred pages. So, give it your best shot: Is each statement either true or false?

T F 1. Most psychologists are engaged in scientific research on the mind—how people feel and what they think.

T F 2. Because there is such a strong correlation between income level and depression, we can conclude that being poor causes depression.

T F 3. If a person's left side is paralyzed due to a stroke, it is because there is damage to the left side of the brain.

T F 4. Everybody dreams every night, usually several times each night.

T F 5. When awake and alert, the average adult can attend to about 12 events at the same time.

T F 6. In daylight, red is the easiest color to see.

T F 7. Cats can see in complete darkness.

T F 8. People can be hypnotized against their will.

T F 9. Principles of learning that apply to rats and dogs seldom can be applied to the learning experiences of humans.

T F 10. The fear of snakes, bees, and/or the dark is unlearned or instinctive.

T F 11. Rote repetition is an inefficient process for remembering information.

T F 12. People who take a long time to learn something generally remember what they have learned better than those who learn quickly.

T F 13. A preschool child with a very high IQ (say, 140) will almost certainly be an outstanding college student.

T F 14. Stress is an unavoidable fact of life.

T F 15. To suffer from at least one psychological disorder during adolescence is normal in today's society.

T F 16. Most sexual problems among adult humans are related to levels of their sex hormones.

T F 17. Most people in psychiatric hospitals or institutions are there because they are a danger to others.

T F 18. People with schizophrenia have "split personalities."

T F 19. If you are in danger or in trouble, you are more likely to get help if there are many people around instead of just a few.

T F 20. People with psychosomatic disorders suffer from physical symptoms that are imaginary.

How do you think you did? The truth is, this is not an easy quiz. Many of these statements sound like common sense, yet are false. Indeed, one of the things that you'll learn about psychology is that some of what we know does conform to common sense, but a lot of it does not.

▶ Preview

"Why do I feel this way?" "Why did he *do* that?" "How can she possibly believe anything so strange?" Questions such as these are fundamental to the human species. Questions about feelings, thoughts, and behaviors have challenged theologians and philosophers for thousands of years. Since the nineteenth century, these issues have been at the center of the science of psychology. In Chapter 1, our aim is to describe the essential nature of this young science.

Once we have defined psychology, we'll take a brief look at some of the major events and contributors to its past, for psychology did not just spring forth, full-blown, a few years ago. By examining a bit of its history, we can better appreciate the nature of psychology as we know it now. Once we've reviewed some history, we'll take a slightly different perspective. We'll deal with two related questions: (1) What are the goals of psychology; that is, what is it that psychologists are trying to do? (2) What are the methods that psychologists use to reach their goals?

This chapter ends with a very brief discussion of some of the abiding themes and threads that have been central to psychology throughout the years. These themes are overarching areas of concern and interest within psychology. What makes them "threads" is that we will find them interwoven throughout the rest of our discussion. In fact, we often will be reminded of the points raised in this introductory chapter as we progress through the rest of this book.

▶ Defining Psychology

psychology the scientific study of behavior and mental processes

Psychology is the science of behavior and mental processes. This is a fairly common definition—one that millions of psychology students before you have committed to memory. If there is a problem with this definition, it's that it is somewhat sterile; it doesn't tell us very much about what psychologists actually study or how they go about it. We'll take the rest of this chapter, and in fact the rest of this book, to fill in the details in an attempt to make this definition more meaningful. First, let's see what it means to say that psychology is a science that studies behavior and mental processes.

▶ Psychology Is a Science

There are many ways to find out about ourselves and the world in which we live. Some of what we believe we have taken as a matter of faith ("There is a God"—or "there isn't."). Some understanding has come through tradition, passed on from previous generations, accepted simply because "they said it is so." Some of what we believe we credit to "common sense" ("You beat a dog often enough and sooner or later it will get mean."). Some of the insights that we have about ourselves and the human condition we have taken from art, literature, poetry, and drama. Psychology, however, claims that there is a better way to come to an understanding of its subject matter: by applying the values and methods of science.

science an organized body of knowledge gained through application of scientific methods

If psychology claims scientific status for itself, we should have some appreciation of what qualifies a discipline to be a science. Most simply put, we can say that a **science** is an organized body of knowledge gained through application of scientific methods. So to qualify as a science, a discipline has to demonstrate two things: (1) an organized body of knowledge, and (2) the use of scientific methodology.

scientific methods systematic procedures of discovery that include observation, description, control, and replication

hypothesis tentative proposition or explanation that can be tested and confirmed or rejected

Over the years, psychologists have accumulated a great deal of information about their subject matter. To be sure, we still can ask many interesting and important questions for which we have no good answers. Not having all the answers can be frustrating at times, but that is part of the excitement of psychology; there are still so many questions to be answered. The truth is, however, that psychologists *have* learned much about their subject matter. What is known is quite well organized. You have in your hands one version of the organized collection of knowledge that is psychology.

What we know in psychology we have learned through the application of **scientific methods,** which we may define as systematic procedures of observation, description, control, and replication. To explain something scientifically is often a matter of ruling out alternative explanations. The basic process goes something like this: The scientist (psychologist) makes observations about her or his subject matter (behavior and/or mental processes). [Perhaps you notice that some students get better grades on psychology tests than do others and that there seems to be a relationship between where students sit and the grades they get.] On the basis of one's observations, a **hypothesis** is developed. A hypothesis is a tentative explanation of a phenomenon that can be tested and then either supported or rejected. In a way, a hypothesis is an educated guess about one's subject matter. [You may hypothesize that intelligent, well-motivated students tend to sit as close to the front of a classroom as they can.]

After formulating a hypothesis, the scientist observes and describes relevant events again. These observations are then analyzed to see if the hypothesis was well founded. Alternative hypotheses or explanations are examined also. [You might see if you can find IQ test scores (or SAT scores, or grade point averages) for the students in your class, and then keep careful records of where students choose to sit. If students in the front of the room *do* earn high test grades, is there any possible explanation other than your hypothesis?] The results of one's investigation are then communicated to others who may test them further. [Do smart, well-motivated students tend to sit near the front in other classes?]

In science, a hypothesis may be rejected or it may be supported, but it cannot be "proven" (as true). This is because no matter how much support one finds for one's hypothesis, there may be alternative hypotheses (as yet unthought of) that will do a better job of explaining observed phenomenon. We'll have much more to say about the particulars of scientific methods as they are used in psychology later in this chapter.

Before You Go On
▼▼▼▼▼▼▼▼▼▼

Why may we make the claim that psychology is a science?

▶ The Subject Matter of Psychology

Skimming through the pages of this book should convince you that listing everything that psychologists study would not be very instructive. Our list would be altogether too long to be useful. However, it is fair to suggest, as our definition does, that the subject matter of psychology is behavior and mental processes. Let's explore a bit more fully just what that means.

Psychologists study behavior. By **behavior** we mean what organisms do; how they act, react, and respond. Some of the behaviors of organisms are observable and—at least potentially—can be measured. If I am concerned

behavior what an organism does; an action of an organism that can be

publicly verifiable the agreement (verifiability) of observers (public) that an event did or did not take place

cognitions the mental processes of knowing, perceiving, thinking, and remembering

affect the feelings or mood that accompany an emotional reaction

operational definition a definition of a concept given in terms of the methods (or operations) used to measure that concept

Figure 1.1

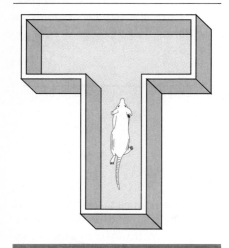

▲ *A rat in a T–maze. Determining whether a rat turns left or right may necessitate operationally defining what we mean by "turn."*

with whether a rat will press a lever under some circumstance, I can observe its behavior directly. If I wonder about Susan's ability to draw a circle, I can ask her to do so, and observe her efforts. Observable, measurable behaviors such as lever-pressing and circle-drawing have an advantage as the subject matter of a science because they are **publicly verifiable.** In other words, several observers (public) can agree on (verify) the behavior of the organism being studied. We can all agree that the rat did or did not press the lever or that Susan drew a circle, not a triangle. Events, including behaviors, that can be publicly verified have greater credibility in science.

When psychology first emerged as a separate discipline late in the nineteenth century, it was defined as the science of *mental processes,* or the science of consciousness. Mental processes can be divided into two types: cognitions and affect. **Cognitions** include perceptions, beliefs, thoughts, ideas, and the like. *Cognitive* processes include such activities as perceiving, thinking, understanding, and remembering. On the other hand, **affect** refers to one's feelings, mood, or emotional state.

Here we have a scheme that we will encounter repeatedly: The **ABC's** that comprise the subject matter of psychology. That is, the subject matter of psychology may be taken to be **A**ffect, **B**ehavior, and **C**ognition. To fully understand someone at any given time, we have to understand what they are feeling (**A**), what they are doing (**B**), and what they are thinking (**C**).

In general terms we say that psychologists study what organisms do, how they feel, and what they think. Psychologists often find it useful, and occasionally necessary, to define their subject matter in terms of the operations or procedures they use to measure it. When they do so, they are using **operational definitions.**

For example, let's say we are interested in the conditions under which a rat turns left, rather than right, in a maze (Figure 1.1). It seems like a relatively simple matter to determine the direction that a rat turns in a maze. But exactly what will constitute a turn? Will sticking its nose around the corner be taken as a turn? What if it gets most of its body around the corner and then scoots back? Does the rat's tail have to make it all the way around? As silly as it may sound, you may have to operationally define *a turn in the maze* by specifying just how you intend to measure it.

What if we wanted to compare the behaviors of hungry and nonhungry rats in the same maze. How do we know when a rat is hungry? How will we define *hungry rat?* We can offer an operational definition, specifying that—at least for our study—a hungry rat is one that has been deprived of food for 24 hours. (We also may operationally define a hungry rat as one that has lost 15 percent, or 20 percent of its normal body weight.)

There are some limitations with operational definitions. They may *oversimplify* truly complex concepts. For example, we might operationally define *intelligence* in terms of how we are going to measure it—with some psychological test. But surely there is more to what we mean by intelligence than a score on a single test. On the other hand, operational definitions specify *exactly* how we are going to measure the behavior or mental process we are studying, and, as a result, they help us communicate accurately with others. We will see many examples of operational definitions in this text.

Before You Go On
▼▼▼▼▼▼▼▼▼

What is the subject matter of psychology?

What are operational definitions?

16 ▲ Chapter 1 The Nature of Psychology

▲ Because we cannot observe a person's intelligence directly, we may choose to operationally define intelligence as "that which an IQ test measures."

✄ ▶ *Psychological Approaches Past and Present*

No two psychologists approach their subject matter in exactly the same way. As individuals, psychologists bring their own experiences, expertise, values, and prejudices to the study of behavior and mental processes. This is true today, and it always has been the case. In this section we can add to our definition of psychology by considering some of the major approaches that have evolved throughout its history.

▶ *Psychology's Roots in Philosophy and Science*

Psychology did not simply appear full-blown as the productive, scientific enterprise that we know today. Most of the questions that engage psychologists today can be traced to the beginnings of history. But seeking answers to one's questions about behavior and mental processes in a casual way is quite different from looking for such answers in a systematic, formal way. The formal roots of psychology can be found in both philosophy and science.

Philosophy. We credit philosophers for suggesting that it is reasonable to seek explanations of human behaviors at a human level. After all, most of the earliest explanations tended to be largely at the level of God—or the gods. If someone were smarter than you, well, it was because God willed it that way. If someone suffered from fits of terrible depression that could not be attributed to any obvious cause, it was because that someone had offended the gods. What philosophers did was to convince us that we might be able to explain why people did what they did and felt and thought as they did without constant reference to God's intentions in the matter.

Although earlier philosophers made important contributions, we begin our discussion with the French philosopher René Descartes (1596–1650). Descartes liked to think about the nature of thinking. As he "lay abed of a morning thinking" he wondered how the body and mind functioned to produce the very process he was then engaged in—thinking.

▲ René Descartes

▲ *John Locke*

interactive dualism Descartes's position that a separate body and mind influence each other and are thus knowable

British empiricists philosophers (including Locke) who claimed, among other things, that the contents of mind come from experience

Descartes's main contribution was that he envisioned the human body to be rather like a piece of intricate machinery. If the body was composed essentially of tubes and gears and valves and fluids, then its operation must be subject to natural, physical laws, and those laws could and should be discovered. Descartes went further to suggest that humans possess more than just a body. They have "souls" or minds. He thought it likely that the mind also functions through the actions of knowable laws, but getting at these laws would be difficult. Here's where Descartes had a truly important insight. We *can* learn about the mind, and the laws under which it operates, because the mind and the body *interact* with each other. We call Descartes's position **interactive dualism**: "dualism" because the mind and the body are separate entities, and "interactive" because they each influence each other. So we have with René Descartes the real possibility that we might be able to understand the mind, how it works, and how it interacts with the body.

Nearly 100 years later, across the English Channel, a group of British thinkers brought the part of philosophy concerned with the workings of the mind very close to what was soon to become psychology. This group got their start from the writings of John Locke (1632–1704). Locke was sitting with some friends after dinner one evening discussing philosophical issues when it became clear that no one in the group really understood how the human mind comes to understand anything, much less complex philosophical questions. Locke thought that by their next meeting, he could provide the group with a short explanation of the nature of human understanding. What was to have been a simple exercise took Locke many years to complete, and provided philosophers with a whole new set of ideas and theories to consider.

Locke, and those who followed his initiative, are known as **British empiricists**. Their major concern was how we come to represent the world "out there" in the internal world of the mind. Others (including Descartes) had asked this very question before, and many had assumed that we are born with certain basic ideas, notions about ourself, the world, and, of course, God. Locke and the other empiricists thought otherwise. They believed that we are born with our minds empty, essentially like blank slates. (The notion of the mind as a blank slate, or *tabula rasa*, was not new with Locke; it had been introduced as far back as Aristotle (384–322BC)). So how does the mind come to be filled with all its ideas, thoughts, and memories? To this question Locke answered, "In one word, from *experience*."

Philosophers had focused attention on the mind: how it worked, what contents it held, where those contents (ideas) came from, how ideas could be manipulated, and how the mind and the body could influence each other. Philosophers had raised some very intriguing questions. Could the methods of science provide some answers to the philosophers' questions?

Science. During the nineteenth century, natural science was progressing on every frontier. By the middle of the century, Charles Darwin (1809–1882) had returned from his lengthy sea voyage on *HMS Beagle,* and in 1859 he published *The Origin of Species,* which reported observations from his trip and spelled out the details of evolution. Few non-psychologists were ever to have as much influence on psychology as did Darwin. What Darwin did for psychology was to confirm that the human organism was part of the natural world of animals, special through no particular divine intervention. Darwin also made it clear that the different species of this planet are, in a nearly infinite number of ways, related to one another. The impact of this reality, of course, is that what we discover about the nature of the tree sloth or the ground squirrel or the rhesus monkey may enlighten us about ourselves.

▲ *Charles Darwin*

▲ *Herman Von Helmholtz*

The mid-1800s found physiologists coming to a better understanding of how the human body functions. By then it was known that nerves carry electrical messages to and from different parts of the body, and that the nerves serving vision are different from those that serve hearing and the other senses, and different too from those that activate muscles and glands. Of all the great physiologists of the nineteenth century, the one whose work is most relevant to the beginning of psychology is Hermann von Helmholtz (1821–1894). Although a physician by trade, von Helmholtz's true love was pure science, the laboratory, and research. He developed an interest in matters that were clearly psychological. He performed experiments and wrote theories on how the nervous system is involved in some behaviors, on how long it takes to react to stimuli, on how we process information through our senses, on how we experience color, and on similar issues of a psychological nature. But in the mid-1800s there was no psychology—at least not a formal, recognized science as we know it today.

By the late nineteenth century, psychology's time had come. Philosophy had become intrigued with mental processes, the nature and the sources of ideas, and with the contents of the mind. Physiologists had begun to focus attention on the nervous system, on sensation and perception, and were doing so using scientific methodology. Biologists were raising questions about relationships between humans and other species, and how mental processes might help us to adapt and to survive. What was needed was someone with a vision to unite these interests and these methods and to establish a separate discipline. Such a person was Wilhelm Wundt.

▲ *Wilhelm Wundt (center) and students in the Leipzig laboratory.*

structuralism the school of psychology (associated with Wundt and Titchener) interested in the elements and structure of the human mind

Before You Go On
▼▼▼▼▼▼▼▼▼

In what way did the philosophies of Descartes and Locke prepare the way for psychology?

In what way did the science of Darwin and von Helmholtz influence the emergence of psychology?

✴▶ Psychology Begins: The Early Years

It is generally claimed that psychology "began" in 1879 when Wilhelm Wundt (1832–1920) officially opened his laboratory at the University of Leipzig. Wundt had been educated to practice medicine and had studied physiology. At Heidelberg University he served as a laboratory assistant to the great Helmholtz. He also held an academic position in philosophy. Wundt was a scientist/philosopher with an interest in such psychological processes as sensation, perception, attention, word associations, and emotions.

Wundt wanted to find out how the mind worked. He wanted to be able to carefully and systematically describe its contents. What are the basic elements of mental life? What is the nature of ideas, of images, of feelings, of sensations? For Wundt, psychology was the scientific study of the mind, of consciousness. Because of his focus of attention on the structure of the human mind, Wundt's variety of psychology was called **Structuralism.** Wundt was a scientist who left nothing to chance. His hypotheses concerning the structure and nature of conscious experience were to be tested and then retested in his laboratory under carefully controlled conditions.

introspection a technique in which one examines one's own mental experiences and reports them in the most fundamental, basic terms

▲ *Edward B. Titchener*

▲ *William James*

functionalism an approach to psychology emphasizing the study of the mind and consciousness as they help the organism adapt to the environment

One of Wundt's most successful students was an Englishman, Edward B. Titchener (1867–1927), who left the laboratory in Leipzig to open his own at Cornell University in Ithaca, NY. Titchener championed the cause of Wundt's structuralism, and extended some of Wundt's methods.

Titchener refined **introspection**, a method for studying consciousness first used in Wundt's laboratory. Introspection literally means to look within. Titchener trained many students to do just that—to look into their own mind and report what they saw. Titchener trained students because he did not believe that just anybody could introspect with accuracy and consistency— two hallmarks of good science. Introspectors were to avoid using common words or labels for the objects they observed. Thus a banana was not to be described as "a banana," but it was to be described as it was experienced in consciousness, in very basic terms, such as "yellowness" and "smoothness," for example. The technique was used in experiments where introspective descriptions of experiences were recorded over and over as stimuli were modi- fied under different conditions. Try as they might, even the well-trained stu- dents of Wundt's and Titchener's laboratories could not "hold consciouness still" and reliably describe its contents. Introspection is no longer considered to be a valid scientific method.

About the same time that Wundt's and Titchener's laboratories were flourishing, an American philosopher at Harvard University, William James (1842–1910), began to take issue with the sort of psychology that was being practiced there. James never thought of himself as a psychologist, although he taught classes on the subject and in 1890 published a wonderful text- book, *Principles of Psychology*. William James did agree that psychology should rightfully study the mind and consciousness. He defined psychology as "the science of mental life," a definition very similar to Wundt's. On the other hand, he thought that the German-trained psychologists were off base trying to discover the contents and structure of the human mind. William James argued that consciousness cannot be broken down or analyzed into elements. Consciousness is dynamic, a stream of events, personal, changing, and continuous. Psychology should be concerned not with the structure of the mind, but with its function. The focus of study should be on the practi- cal *uses* of the mind and mental life. In this regard, James was responding to the lead of Darwin. To survive requires that members of a species adapt to the environment. How does the mind function to help an organism adapt and survive in the world?

James's practical approach to psychology found favor in North Amer- ica, and a new approach emerged, initially at the University of Chicago. Psychologists continued to focus their scientific study on the mind, but now emphasized the useful, adaptive functions of the mind. As a result, we refer to this approach as **Functionalism.** It was well established by the 1920s. Functionalist psychologists relied on experimental methods, con- tinued to use introspection (although they were much less rigid than Titchener about how to do so), and they introduced the study of animals to psychology—reflecting the influence of Darwin. In fact, one character- istic of functionalism was its willingness to be open to a wide range of topics—so long as they were in some way related to mental life, adapta- tion, or had practical application. As a result, we can trace the origin of child, abnormal, educational, social, and industrial psychology to early functionalism.

As bright young scientists were drawn to psychology, new academic departments and laboratories began to prosper. Scientific psychology was well under way—as the scientific study of the mind, its structures and/or its functions.

Before You Go On
▼▼▼▼▼▼▼▼▼

When and where did psychology "begin" and whom do we credit with formally establishing the discipline?

Briefly describe the first approaches that psychologists took toward their subject matter.

▶ *Psychoanalysis*

Sigmund Freud (1856–1939) was born in what is now Czechoslavakia, moving to Vienna with his family when he was 4 years old. He remained a resident of Vienna until the Nazi invasion in 1938, when he moved to England, where he died the next year.

Freud was trained in medicine, but his intellectual love was science and research. He practiced as a physician out of economic necessity, and became intrigued with what were then called "nervous disorders." Freud was struck by how little was known about these disorders, and as a result, chose to specialize in psychiatry.

Freud was not a laboratory scientist; he performed few experiments. Most of his insights concerning the nature of the mind came from his careful observations of his patients and of himself. Structuralism, the psychology of Wundt and Titchener, and most academic psychologists of his day, concentrated on the nature of the conscious mind. Freud added a new dimension to psychological theorizing. He claimed that one's mental processes and behaviors are subject to forces of which we are not aware: our unconscious mind. Many of our behaviors are expressions of instinctive strivings, he claimed.

Not only did Freud study and write about the nature of personality and its development, but he also put his thoughts into practice in the diagnosis and treatment of psychological disorders. The approach to

▲ *Sigmund Freud*

psychoanalysis the form of psychotherapy associated with Freud, aimed at helping the patient gain insight into unconscious conflicts

psychology that traces its origins to Sigmund Freud is called **psychoanalysis.** We'll have ample opportunity to discuss the many and varied contributions of Freud in later chapters. We will refer to Freud in our discussions of child psychology, memory, consciousness, personality theory, and psychotherapy.

▶ *Behaviorism*

John B. Watson (1878–1958) was born on a farm in South Carolina. After graduating from nearby Furman University, Watson enrolled as a graduate student in psychology at the University of Chicago. He had read about psychology as an undergraduate, and thought that Chicago—where many of the leading functionalists were teaching—would be the best place to study. He was soon disappointed. It seems that he had little talent for introspection, and he developed little sympathy for attempts to study consciousness with scientific methods. Even so, he stayed on as a psychology major, studying the behavior of white rats.

▲ *John B. Watson*

With his Ph.D. in hand, at the age of 29, Watson moved to Johns Hopkins University in Baltimore, where he nearly single-handedly changed the nature of psychology. Watson argued that if psychology were to become a mature, productive science, it had to give up its preoccupation with the mind and conscious or unconscious mental activity. Psychology should concentrate on the observation and measurement of events. It should give up the study of the mind and focus on *behavior:* hence the name of a new approach to psychology—**behaviorism.**

behaviorism an approach to psychology emphasizing the overt, observable, measurable behavior of organisms

Neither Watson nor the behaviorists that followed him ever claimed that people do not think, have ideas, or form mental images. What he did say was that such processes were not the proper subjects of scientific investigation. Science must focus on those events that observers can measure and agree upon, and behavior fits the bill. No one else, after all, can share your thoughts, your ideas, or your images. Watson argued that we ought to make psychology as rigorously scientific as possible. Watson once referred to behaviorism as "common sense grown articulate. Behaviorism is a study of what people *do*" (Watson, 1926, p. 714).

No one following Watson has epitomized the behaviorist approach to psychology more than B. F. Skinner (1904–1990). Skinner spent a long and productive career in psychology trying to demonstrate that we can predict and control the behaviors of organisms by studying relationships between their observable responses and circumstances under which those responses are made.

Skinner simply avoided any reference to the internal states of his subjects, be they rats, pigeons, or people. What mattered for Skinner is how behaviors are modified by changes in the environment. Behaviorists would not address the question of "why" a rat turns left in a maze by talking about what the rat wanted or what the rat was thinking at the time. Rather, they would try to specify the environmental conditions (e.g. the presence of food) under which a rat is likely to make left turns. For more than fifty years, Skinner consistently held to the argument that psychology should be defined as "the science of behavior" (Skinner, 1987).

The truth is that in the 1990s we can find little left of the approaches to psychology taken by Wundt and Titchener. We can see in the diversity of psychology today many of the issues raised by Functionalism. Behaviorism and psychoanalysis—to varying degrees and in different varieties—are still with us. Now we will look briefly at some of the other approaches to psychology that are also still in evidence today.

▲ *B. F. Skinner*

▲ Carl Rogers

humanistic psychology an approach to psychology emphasizing the person or self as a central matter of concern

▲ Abraham Maslow

gestalt whole, totality, configuration; where the whole (gestalt) is seen as more than the sum of its parts

▲ Max Wertheimer

Before You Go On
▼▼▼▼▼▼▼▼

Briefly summarize Psychoanalysis and Behaviorism as approaches to psychology.

▶ Humanistic Psychology

An approach we call **humanistic psychology** arose in many respects as a reaction against behaviorism *and* psychoanalysis. Its original leaders were Carl Rogers (1902–1987) and Abraham Maslow (1908–1970). Humanistic psychologists take the position that the individual or the self should be the central concern of psychology. It is their argument that we need to focus on the "person" in psychology. If we only attend to stimuli in the environment and overt responses to those stimuli, we're leaving the person out of the middle—and that's dehumanizing. Such matters as caring, intention, concern, will, love, and hate are real phenomena, worthy of scientific investigation whether they can be directly observed or not. Any attempt to understand people without considering such processes will be doomed. Humanistic psychologists also tend to emphasize the possibility of personal growth and achievement. Freudian reliance on instincts as even partially responsible for human action was too controlling. Our biology notwithstanding, we are—or can be—in control of our own destinies. Taking this approach led Maslow to develop a theory of human motivation (see Chapter 9) and Rogers to develop a system of psychotherapy (see Chapter 13).

▶ Gestalt Psychology

In the first quarter of this century a group of German scientists was taking an approach to psychology that was different from that of Wundt, James, Freud, *or* Watson. Under the leadership of Max Wertheimer (1880–1943), this approach became known as Gestalt Psychology. **Gestalt** is one of those words that is difficult to translate literally into English. Roughly, it means "whole," or "totality." If you can see the big picture, if you can focus on the forest and not the individual trees, you have formed a gestalt. Indeed, it was the big picture of perception that most intrigued the Gestalt psychologists.

Gestalt psychologists argued against trying to analyze perception, or consciousness into separate entities. To do so would be to destroy the very nature of what was being studied. "The whole is *more* than the sum of its parts," they said. When we look at a drawing of a cube, we don't see lines and angles and surfaces. We combine these elements to form a whole, a gestalt, which we recognize as a cube. When we look at a banana we see a banana and not yellowness or smoothness, no matter what Titchener's introspectionists might want to tell us.

Among other things, Gestalt psychologists examined the factors that determine which of many stimuli we attend to. They developed principles to describe how we organize the world we perceive, how we form meaningful gestalts from bits of our sensory experience. The Gestalt psychologists claimed that some basic, set ways of perceiving the world are innate and unlearned. That is, *everything* in the mind need not come through experience as Locke had argued. We see the world as three dimensional; we attend to contrasts between adjacent stimuli; stimuli in motion tend to grab our

▲▲▲▲▲▲▲▲▲▲▲▲▲▲▲

What Psychologists Do

In the real world, psychologists work in many places: colleges and universities, hospitals, mental health centers, private practice, counseling centers, government agencies, schools, business and industry, and elsewhere (in this order). The work that psychologists do in these settings varies considerably from psychologist to psychologist. Can we provide a reasonable overview of what psychologists do?

The largest professional organization of psychologists, the American Psychological Association, or APA, lists over 40 divisions or specialty areas to which its members belong. What follows is a short list that combines many of the APA divisions into broader categories. A danger inherent in lists like this one is that someone may infer that it provides a ranking in some order of importance. None is intended.

Physiological—biological psychology is concerned with the interactions among body activity, behavior, and mental processes for a range of organisms, including humans. This is the subfield most concerned with structures and functions of the brain and the role it plays in our behavior. When we ask, "Why did I do (or feel or think) that?" psychologists who take this approach will look first to physiological, genetic and biochemical explanations.

Developmental psychology is concerned with the physical and psychological development of the individual from conception through death. Most developmental psychologists focus primarily on the childhood years, while others attend to adolescence, adulthood, old age, or take a broader life-span approach.

Educational—instructional psychology is devoted to a study of learning and memory and to the application of what we know about these processes in real-life situations. In both academic and business settings, educational and instructional psychologists often serve as consultants to improve training and educational programs.

Clinical psychology includes those whose concern is with the psychological well-being of the individual. The training of clinical psychologists provides them with the means to diagnose and treat persons

attention; large stimuli appear to us closer than small ones. Why? The Gestalt psychologists would say, "because"—because that's the way we were born to see, and learning or experience have little to do with it.

Before You Go On
▼▼▼▼▼▼▼▼▼▼

What is the major thrust of the humanistic approach in psychology?

What does "gestalt" mean?

What area of psychology was of major concern to the Gestalt psychologists?

withpsychological disorders. Clinical psychology is by far the largest sub-field in psychology. When combined with counseling psychology (below), it accounts for nearly 60 percent of all psychologists.

Counseling psychology is very much like clinical psychology. Counseling psychologists, however, tend to serve persons with less severe and less chronic disorders. They are more likely to be involved in such processes as grief counseling for disaster victims, divorce counseling, or short-term work with college students who are having adjustment problems.

Health psychology is one of the newer subfields. Health psychologists are committed to the notion that one's physical health is (or can be) affected by psychological variables and vice versa. Finding ways to minimize behaviors that have an adverse affect on one's health is typical of the activities of the health psychologist.

Cognitive psychology includes those psychologists who investigate the basic processes of the mind: perception, learning, memory, and thinking. There are specialty areas within cognitive psychology. Psycholinguists, for example, are interested in language—how it is acquired, produced, perceived, and interpreted.

Psychometrics involves the development and use of psychological tests and the statistical interpretation of data. Psychological testing is big business in our society, particularly in educational and business settings.

Social psychology reflects the observation that most organisms live in the company of others. The interactions among the behavior of individuals is the general concern of social psychologists. Predictably, this area has many subfelds also, reflecting interests in sex roles, attitudes, prejudice, group conflict, conformity, and the like.

Industrial-organizational (I/O) psychology is defined largely by the work setting of the psychologist. Some I/O psychologists are concerned with marketing and advertising, some with group productivity or consumer satisfaction, some with the design of equipment, and others with personnel decisions; still others focus on helping those who suffer from the stress of the workplace.

Many psychologists would claim that they do not fit any of these categories. Others might claim that they fit two or more. The very diversity of psychology is one of the things that makes it such an exciting field.

► *Modern Approaches*

We have noted that when scientists are faced with a concept that is difficult to define in abstract terms, they often rely on operational definitions. Here is an operational definition of psychology: *Psychology is what psychologists do.* I'm not proposing this as a serious definition of psychology, but there is something to be said for it. One of the things that you'll be learning about in this course is the wide range of things that psychologists do. In a sense, this course and this text provide a definition of psychology. If you were to ask me what psychology is, I might answer, "Everything in this book—and more." But, for now, let us summarize some of the activities of psychologists. This summary is found in the Box labeled "Psychology in the Real World: What Psychologists Do."

In general terms, we can say that contemporary psychologists have two interrelated goals. One is the goal of the science of psychology: to use scientific methods to understand the subject matter of psychology—behavior and mental processes. The second is the goal of application: to apply that understanding of behavior and mental processes in the real world. We will have ample opportunity to discuss the application of psychology throughout this text, particularly in the chapter on the treatment of mental disorders. For now, let's concentrate on the methods that psychologists use to understand their subject matter. Although psychologists use many different techniques, we can consider psychological methods in three categories: observational, correlational, and experimental.

▶ Observational Methods in Psychology

Before we can understand and explain what people do, we must first make valid observations of what people do. As it happens, there are several ways in which psychologists make observations and several steps that they can take to ensure that their observations are valid.

▶ Naturalistic Observation

naturalistic observation the method of observing and noting behaviors as they occur naturally

As its name implies, the method called **naturalistic observation** involves carefully and systematically watching behaviors as they occur naturally—without any involvement from the observer. There is a strong logical appeal to the argument that if you are trying to understand what organisms do in real life, you should simply watch them while they are doing it, noting their behaviors and the conditions under which those behaviors occur.

As logically appealing as naturalistic observation may sound, it does present a few difficulties that need to be acknowledged. For one thing, if we truly do want to observe people (or any other organism for that matter) *the way they naturally act,* then we must make sure that they do not realize that we are watching them. As you know from your own experience, people may act very differently from "normal" if they think they are being watched. You may do all sorts of things in the privacy of your home that you would never do if you thought that someone was watching you. This issue was first raised back in the 1930s in a series of studies of the job performance of workers in a factory that made telephone equipment. It seemed that many workers improved their productivity simply because they thought that their behaviors were being observed. The phenomenon is called the "Hawthorne Effect" after the name of the factory in which the study was done. (See pp. 504–505 for a full discussion of the Hawthorne studies.)

observer bias the interference of the researcher's own motives, expectations, and past experiences interfere with the objectivity of experimental observations

A second potential problem is **observer bias:** Observers should not let their own motives, expectations, and experiences interfere with the objectivity of their observations. It might be very difficult for a researcher to be objective in her observations of children in a playschool setting if she constantly compares their behaviors to those of her own two children. One solution to the problem of observer bias is to have observers note behaviors as they occur without full knowledge of the particular relationships that are under investigation in the research study. Another protection against bias is to check the reliability of observations by using several observers, and only relying on those that can be verified by a number of observers.

A third potential problem with naturalistic observation is often more difficult to deal with. The behaviors you want to observe may not be there when you are. For example, if you are interested in conformity and want to observe people conforming naturally, in the real world, just where would you go? Where are you likely to observe conformity happening naturally? There may be some environments in which conformity behaviors are more likely to occur than others. But there is no guarantee that during any particular day, or week, or month, the people you are watching will provide any evidence of conformity at all. If you start manipulating a situation so that people are more likely to conform, you are no longer doing *naturalistic* observation.

Even with these potential problems, naturalistic observation has proven to be useful for providing descriptions of actual behaviors in the real world. Note that this method cannot *explain* the behaviors being observed, but it can *describe* what is happening. Adequate descriptions can then give rise to hypotheses that can be tested to see if we can explain what has been observed.

Before You Go On
▼▼▼▼▼▼▼▼

What is naturalistic observation?

List some of the potential problems that can arise with this method.

▶ Surveys

survey a means of collecting observations from a large number of subjects, usually by interview or questionnaire

When we want to make observations about a large number of subjects, we may use a **survey** method. Doing a survey amounts to asking many people the same question or set of questions. The questions may be asked in person, or in a telephone interview, or in the form of a written questionnaire. Survey studies yield data that would be difficult to gather otherwise.

If we wanted to know if there were a relationship between income level and the type of automobile one drives, or television programs that one watches regularly, we could ask about these issues in a survey of a large number of people. Surveys can tell us what large portions of the population think and feel and can provide insights about preferences for products or services (or political candidates). If the staff of the cafeteria on your campus *really* wanted to know what students preferred to eat, they could survey a sample of the student population. Textbook publishers often survey psychology instructors to see what they would like to have included in the books that they use. As it happens, they seldom survey psychology students. We'll make this text something of an exception then, by referring you to the back of the book (pp. 601–602), where you will find a survey from the publisher (and me) asking for your reactions to what you have read this term. Getting this survey information from you will help us design better texts in the future.

sample the portion of a larger population chosen for study

A critical aspect of observations made from survey data is the size and representativeness of the **sample** that is surveyed. A sample is a subset or a portion of a larger population that is chosen to be studied. We would like to be able to extend our observations beyond those subjects we survey in our sample. If we cannot, we say that we have used a "biased sample." Textbook publishers who survey only instructors at small liberal arts colleges, or cafeteria managers who survey only students attending morning classes, may be using a biased sample, and their data may not generalize to the intended population—that is, the larger, complete pool of subjects from which the sample was drawn.

▶ Case Histories

case history an intensive, usually retrospective, detailed study of some aspects of one (or a few) individual(s)

The **case history** method provides yet another sort of information. In the case history method, one person—or a small sample of persons—is studied in depth, often over a long period of time. Using this method usually involves an intense and detailed examination of a wide range of issues. The method is usually retrospective, which means that we start with some given situation that exists today and go back in time to see if there is any relationship between today's state of affairs and previous experiences or events. We may use interviews and/or psychological tests as a means of collecting our data.

As an example, let's say that we are interested in Mr. X, a known child abuser. Our suspicion (hypothesis) is that Mr. X's own childhood experiences might be related to his present status as a child abuser. We talk to Mr. X at length and interview his family and his friends—those who knew him as a child—trying to form some retrospective picture of Mr. X's childhood. If we find some clues (e.g. Mr. X was punished with severe spankings, or he missed class at school significantly more often than other children) we may then explore the early childhood experiences of other known child abusers, looking to find common experiences that might be related to the fact that they abuse children now that they are adults. Note that case history data can be subject to bias. Mr. X may choose to tell me only what he thinks I want to hear, or I may "hear" only that part of his story that confirms my hypothesis.

I have always been intrigued by the choices that college students make when they decide on a major course of study. (Perhaps this is because when I started college I was a chemistry major!) Why do some students major in psychology, while others choose mathematics or music? Perhaps the case history method could provide some insights about the choice of a college major. How would we proceed? We'd choose a sample of students from each major, and ask them a number of (hopefully) penetrating questions about their experiences, listening for things that all students of one major had in common, but that were different from the experiences of those who opted for other majors.

As we shall see, Freud based most of his theory of personality on his intensive examination of the case histories of his patients (and himself). An advantage of the case history method is that it can provide us with a wealth of detailed information about a few cases. A disadvantage is that we have to be particularly careful when we try to generalize our findings beyond those individuals we have chosen to study.

Now that we have reviewed some of the ways in which psychologists make careful, reliable, observations, we need to see how these observations can be translated into useful psychological laws or principles.

Before You Go On
▼▼▼▼▼▼▼▼▼

How can surveys and case history studies be used to help us understand behavior and mental processes?

▶ Correlational Methods in Psychology

Observations about people's behaviors, or thoughts, or feelings often provide interesting insights in their own right. How many people in the U. S. and Canada smoke cigarettes? What do most people think about abortions performed during the first trimester of pregnancy? How do people feel about Sylvester Stallone making yet another *Rambo* movie? As interesting

correlation a statistical technique used to determine the nature and extent of the relationship between two measured responses

correlation coefficient a number that indicates the nature (+ or –) and the strength (0 to 1) of the relationship between measured responses

or informative as they may be, observations become scientific laws only when they are related consistently to other observations. **Correlation** is a statistical procedure that we can use to assess the nature and the degree to which sets of observations are lawfully related. To say that observations are correlated is to say that they are related to each other (co-related).

As an example, let's say that we are interested in whether or not there is a relationship between reading ability and performance in introductory psychology. First, we need operational definitions for the responses in which we are interested. That is, how will we measure reading ability and performance in introductory psychology? *Performance in introductory psychology* isn't difficult to deal with. We'll take that to mean the total number of points earned by a student on classroom exams over the course of the semester. *Reading ability* is a little more difficult. What do we mean by reading ability? We could design a test of our own to measure those behaviors that we think reflect reading ability, but it turns out that we're in luck. There are many tests of reading ability already available. We decide to use the Nelson Denny Reading Test, or the NDRT (Brown, 1973).

Now we're ready to collect some data (make our observations). We'll give a large group of students our reading test (the NDRT). Once the tests are scored we have one large set of numbers. At the end of the semester, we add up all the points earned by each of our students and we have a second set of numbers. So for each student in our study we have a pair of numbers—one indicating reading ability and one indicating performance in the psychology course. From here on out, our method is more statistical than it is psychological.

We enter our pairs of numbers into a calculator or a computer. A series of arithmetic procedures is applied—there are prescribed formulae for these calculations that need not concern us here. The result of the calculations is a single number, the **correlation coefficient**. The value of a correlation coefficient can be any number between –1.00 and +1.00. What does that mean? How can one number be the basis for a scientific law? In truth, it takes some experience to be comfortable with the interpretation of correlation coefficients, but we can make some general observations.

First, let's deal with the sign of the correlation coefficient, which can be positive (+) or negative (–). A positive coefficient tells us that our two responses are related to each other and that high scores on one response are associated with high scores on the other. It also tells us that low scores on one measure are associated with low scores on the other. Most correlations with which we are familiar are of this positive type—the correlation between SAT scores and college grade point averages, for example. In our example, if a student does well on the reading test, she will probably do well in an introductory psychology course. Those students who do poorly on the reading test are likely to earn lower grades in the psychology course. We can make these predictions only if our two sets of measured responses are positively correlated. As it happens, there is evidence that such is the case (Gerow & Murphy, 1980). Figure 1.2A shows what a graph of the scores from our example might look like, showing a positive correlation. This example shows us the major use of correlations: If we determine that two responses are correlated, we can use our observation of one response to make predictions about the other.

What if our calculations result in a correlation coefficient that is a negative (–) number? Here too we have a useful rules. We can use scores of one response to predict scores of the other. But, when the correlation coefficient is negative, we know that the relationship between our two measured responses is inverse, or upside down. With negative correlation coefficients, high scores on one response predict *low* scores on the other. If we measured body size and looked to see if it were related to gymnastic ability, we might very well find a negative correlation: Large body size is associated with poor gymnastic ability, while small body sizes (low scores) are associated with good gymnastic ability (high scores). If these two sets of observations are negatively correlated, we can still use body size to predict gymnastic ability. Figure 1.2B shows data depicting the possible relationship between gymnastic ability and body size, a negative correlation.

What if our correlation coefficient turned out to be zero, or nearly so (say, 0.0003)? In this case, we would have to conclude that the two sets of observations that we have made simply are not related to each other in any consistent, lawful way. Let's say that I worked from the faulty notion that intelligence is a function of brain size, and that one's head size tells us how big a person's brain is. If I were to measure the head size of a large number of students and also measure grade point average (attempting to show a lawful relationship between intelligence and grades), I would find that the calculations for the correlation coefficient would result in a number very close to zero. As correlations approach zero, predictability decreases. Figure 1.2C completes our set of examples by showing what a graph of data from two sets of unrelated measures would look like.

What about the numerical value of the correlation coefficient? Again, it takes some practice to get used to working with numbers such as −.46, +.5, and +.002. For now, let us just say that *the closer we get to the extremes of +1.00 or −1.00, the better or stronger the relationship between the responses we have measured.* That is, as our correlation coefficient approaches +1.00 or −1.00 (say, +.84 or −.93), we will have increased confidence in our ability to predict one response knowing the other. The closer our coefficient gets to zero (say, −.012 or +.004), the weaker the relationship and the less useful it is for making predictions. I should also mention that the confidence that we have in our correlations is in large part determined by the number of observations that are used in our calculations. In

Figure 1.2

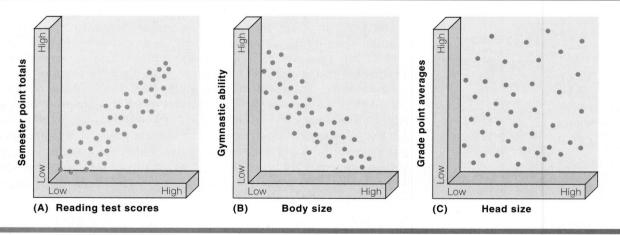

(A) Reading test scores

(B) Body size

(C) Head size

▲ *Positive, negative, and zero correlation. (A) A graph depicting the reading test scores and semester point totals earned by 40 students. These data indicate a positive (+) correlation between the two measured responses. As reading test scores increase, so do semester point totals. (B) A graph depicting the body size and gymnastic ability of 40 students. These data indicate a negative (−) correlation between the two measured responses. As body size increases, gymnastic ability decreases. (C) A graph depicting head size and grade point averages earned by 40 students. These data indicate a zero (0) correlation between the two measured responses. There is no relationship between head size and grade point averages.*

general, the larger the sample—the more observations we have made—the greater the confidence we can put in our correlation coefficient.

As you read through this text, you'll encounter many studies that use a correlational analysis of measured observations. It is important, then, that you keep in mind two important points about correlations. (1) *Cause- and-effect conclusions are inappropriate for correlational studies.* Even if two responses are well correlated with each other, we cannot claim that one causes the other. For some reason, this point seems difficult to remember. Sometimes logic overwhelms us. It does make sense that an inability to read will actually cause some students to do poorly in an introductory psychology class, where reading is so important. Yes, it makes sense. *But* if all we have to guide us is the fact that reading ability and grades are correlated, we can make no statement at all about cause and effect—all we can say is that they are related. (2) Our second point is also easy to lose sight of from time to time. *Even when two responses are well correlated with each other, we cannot make predictions for individual cases.* As I said, reading ability and introductory psychology grades *are* positively correlated. By and large, more often than not, students who read well, do well in the course and students who do not read well tend to do poorly. So, *in general,* we can use reading test scores to predict grades, but we have to allow for exceptions. A few poor readers may do very well indeed, and a few excellent readers may still fail the course. Exceptions are to be expected. In fact, the further from +1.00 or −1.00 our correlation coefficient is, the more exceptions we can expect. Statements of correlation hold true only "by and large," "generally," "in the long run," or "more often than not."

Before You Go On

▼▼▼▼▼▼▼▼▼

What data are needed to calculate a correlation coefficient?

How does a correlation coefficient tell us about the relationship between two measured responses?

▶ Experimental Methods in Psychology

experiment a series of operations used to investigate relationships between manipulated events (independent variables) and measured events (dependent variables), while other events (extraneous variables) are eliminated

Most of what we know in psychology we have learned by doing **experiments**. Experiments involve a set of operations used to investigate relationships between manipulated events and measured events, while extraneous events are controlled or eliminated. In the abstract, that's quite a mouthful! The actual procedures are not that difficult to understand. In fact, like all other methods in psychology, experiments involve making observations.

▶ The Basic Procedures

One of the important things about experiments is they are intended to discover cause-and-effect relationships. With experiments we are no longer content to discover that two measured observations are simply related; now we want to be able to claim that—at least to some degree—one is caused by the other. To see if such a claim can be made, an experimenter manipulates one variable to see if that manipulation causes any measurable changes in another variable. A variable is simply something that can vary—an event that can take on different values. Experimental methods are described in terms of variables.

independent variables events in an experiment that are manipulated by the experimenter that are hypothesized to produce changes in responses

dependent variables responses measured in an experiment whose values are hypothesized to depend upon manipulations of the independent variable

extraneous variables factors in an experiment that need to be minimized or eliminated so as not to affect the relation between the independent and the dependent variable

Let's start with a terribly simple example. You may have correlation data that tells you that amount of studying and points earned on a test are correlated. What you'd like to demonstrate now is that studying causes (or, at least is part of the cause) of higher grades on tests. The conditions or events that an experimenter manipulates are **independent variables**. [You have some students study a textbook before being tested on a chapter, while other students read a newspaper instead of studying. Amount of studying is your independent variable.] Those events or conditions that the experimenter measures are **dependent variables**; their value should *depend* on the experimenter's manipulation of independent variables. [You give all your subjects the same test on the chapter, and grade the test.] The hope is that the manipulation of the independent variable will cause changes in the dependent variable—changes predicted by one's hypothesis. [Your hypothesis is that those subjects who studied will earn higher scores on your test.]

If there *are* changes in the measured dependent variable, the experimenter would like to claim that these changes are due *solely* to the influence of the manipulated independent variable. In order to make such a claim, it must be shown that all other variables that might have influenced what is being measured have been controlled or eliminated. These factors that need to be eliminated from consideration are often called **extraneous variables** (extraneous means "not essential" or "irrelevant"). [If the group of subjects who studied did do better on your test, is there any other factor that might have accounted for the observed difference, other than the amount of studying?] So, to do an experiment, one manipulates independent variables, measures dependent variables, and eliminates or controls the effects of extraneous variables. This is not as confusing as it may sound on first reading. Going over a couple of examples will help.

After a few quizzes in your biology class you notice that the student sitting right in front of you is consistently scoring higher than you are—not by much, but by enough to be aggravating. You ask this student how she does it, and she tells you that she has "a system" that she learned in high school. To help remember a series of otherwise unrelated concepts, she weaves the terms together to form some sort of story. Recalling the story is relatively easy, and can be used to help her recall terms for her quizzes. This system sounds sensible to you, and you decide to do an experiment to test if there is a cause and effect relationship here. (This is a decision that was also made in 1969 by Gordon Bower and M. C. Clark.)

You get some volunteers from your introductory psychology class and divide them into two groups. One group (A) is asked to memorize a list of ten unrelated nouns. They are left on their own to learn the list. The other group (B) is asked to memorize the very same list of nouns, but they are told about the scheme of tying the words together to form a meaningful story, and they are told to try to use this strategy in learning the list.

You've manipulated the memorizing process, so whether or not learners are told to use a certain strategy is your *independent variable*. You believe that this variable will have an effect on memory. How will you measure this to see if it is so? What will be your *dependent variable*? You ask your students to return three weeks later. At that time you ask them all to "write down as many of the words as you can recall from the list you learned three weeks ago." Thus, your dependent variable is the average number of words recalled three weeks later. When you look at your data, you discover that, on the average, Group A recalls 3.5 words of the original 10, and Group B (those that made up a story) recall 8.2 words correctly. It seems that a strategy of generating a story *is* useful in memorizing words. It seems to cause better recall.

What are the possible extraneous variables in this experiment? These are factors that might have affected the average recall of our two groups of students over and above what was manipulated (memorization strategy). (It should be clear that these factors should have been considered before you actually did the experiment.) For one thing, we need to be certain that the students in our two groups are of essentially the same ability to begin with. It would not do if the students in Group A were mostly poor, struggling students while those in Group B were all honor students. It also is obviously the case that both groups of learners need to be presented with identical materials to be learned—and the list of words needs to be presented in the same way to both groups.

The short of it is—and this is a very important point—when we are done with our experiment and find differences in our dependent variable, we want to be able to claim that these differences are due to our manipulation of the independent variable, and to nothing else. In fact, it is the extent to which extraneous variables are anticipated and eliminated that determines the quality of an experiment. Figure 1.3 reviews the steps in our example experiment.

Figure 1.3

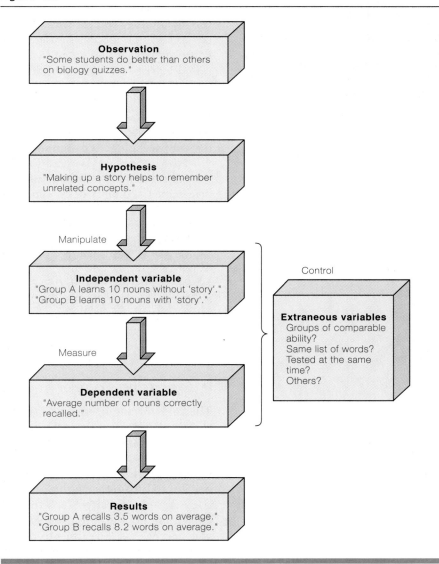

▲ *The stages involved in our example experiment illustrating the different types of variables.*

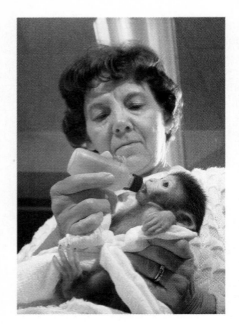

▲ When studying behavior and mental processes, psychologists often find it convenient, if not necessary, to use nonhuman animals in their research.

Suppose you believe that a stimulating environment during early childhood improves intellectual functioning at adolescence. You propose to do an experiment to support your hypothesis. You have two groups of newborn children, with 20 in each group. One group will be raised for three years in a very stimulating environment filled with toys and games, bright wallpaper and pictures in the nursery, and many adults around every day. The other group of 20 children will be reared in isolation, in quiet, empty rooms, with only their basic biological needs attended to. *Wait a minute!* This sort of experimental manipulation is unethical and would be out of the question. You wouldn't isolate and deprive a group of children this way—particularly if your hypothesis is that doing so would have negative consequences.

This problem provides an example of an experiment that you might want to do with rats. Rats could be raised in cages that provide differing amounts of stimulation. When the rats approach maturity, you could test their ability to negotiate mazes or learn a variety of responses. Early exposure to stimulation would be the independent variable, and scores on your tests of learning ability would be the dependent variables.

One advantage of using rats in experiments is that extraneous variables usually are easy to deal with. You seldom have to be concerned with previous experience, inherited differences, parental influences, and the like (all of your rats have a known and very similar genetic history, and all have been raised in very similar conditions). The problem with using rats is obvious. Even if you do demonstrate your point with rats, you then have to argue that the data you have collected for rats is applicable to humans. As we'll see, in many cases this argument is not difficult to make, and with the advantage of ease of control, we can see why the use of nonhuman organisms in psychology is commonplace.

Now that we've covered the basic procedures involved in experiments, we can examine in a little more detail some of the considerations that often determine the quality of an experimental method.

Before You Go On

▼▼▼▼▼▼▼▼▼

What is the essence of doing an experiment?

Define independent, dependent, and extraneous variables in the context of an experiment.

▶ Exercising Control

The value of an experimental finding depends on the researcher's ability to eliminate or control the influence of extraneous variables. The most difficult extraneous variables to deal with involve the past experience of the subjects. This was the case in our example experiment on a memorizing strategy. In a typical experiment, the independent variable is manipulated by presenting one group of subjects with a treatment (such as a hint about how to memorize a list of words) while withholding that treatment from another group. Subjects in both groups are then tested for any effect. By definition, subjects who receive some treatment constitute the **experimental group**. An experiment may have any number of experimental groups. Our example used just one. Subjects who do not receive an experimental treatment are in a **control group**. Experiments usually have one control group; in our example, this was Group A, students who received no hint about how to memorize the words.

experimental group participants in an experiment who receive a treatment or manipulation—there may be more than one such group in an experiment

control group participants in an experiment who do not receive any experimental treatment or manipulation

random assignment the selection of members of a population in such a way that each has an equal opportunity to be assigned to any one group

baseline design a method in which subjects' performance with an experimental treatment is compared with performance without that treatment (the baseline)

To ensure that control and experimental groups begin an experiment on an equal footing, you could do one of a number of things. You could try to match the groups on the variable of interest. In our example, you might have done this by giving all your subjects a recall test before the experiment and then assigned them to either Group A or Group B so that the average scores on this test were close to equal.

A more common technique would be to place subjects into groups by **random assignment**, which means that each participant in the research has an equal chance of being assigned to any one of the groups that you are using. If assignment is truly random, then honor students would be equally likely to be in either of the groups—the one that does or the one that doesn't get a hint about weaving the words into a story. But remember, that matching or randomly assigning subjects is something that must be considered before the experiment is actually begun.

Another method for dealing with the differing past experiences of subjects is a **baseline design**. Although there are a number of such designs, they each amount to arranging things so that each subject serves in both experimental and control group conditions. Imagine, for example, that you wished to determine if a certain drug causes a decrease in the reaction time required for a subject to respond to a signal. With a baseline design, you would first measure the reaction time of persons without giving them the drug (a baseline measure). Then you would check the reaction times of the same persons after they were given the drug. Changes in their reaction time (your dependent variable) could then be attributed to the drug (your independent variable). You could then check the subjects' reaction times again, after the effects of the drug wears off, to see if the time it takes to respond to the signal behavior returns to the baseline.

Before You Go On

▼▼▼▼▼▼▼▼▼

How do random assignment and baseline designs help to minimize error in psychological experiments?

▶ Ethics in Psychological Research

Ethical and moral concerns affect all the sciences. Ethical issues usually center on the application of knowledge. We know how to split the atom; should we build a bomb? We can manufacture effective insecticides; should we use them? We can devise means to render people infertile; should we? We can use machinery to keep people alive indefinitely; would this be right? We can bury radioactive waste; where should we?

The relation of ethics to psychology is a unique one. As with all sciences, ethical considerations are very important in the application of knowledge, be it in diagnosis, therapy, counseling, training, or whatever (these we'll deal with in later chapters). In psychology, ethical considerations are often central in the *gathering* of information. After all, the objects of study are living organisms. Their physical and psychological welfare must be protected as we investigate their behaviors and mental processes. Psychologists have been concerned with the ethical implications of their work for a long time. The American Psychological Association has regularly revised and published *Ethical Principles of Psychologists* for practitioners and researchers alike. The most recent version was amended in 1989 and published in 1990.

We'll deal very briefly with a few of the issues these guidelines address with regard to research.

As the investigator plans an experiment, the degree to which subjects will be put at risk should be assessed. What are the potential physical or psychological dangers that might accompany participation? Even if potential risks are deemed to be slight, they need to be considered and balanced in the light of what good might come from the experiment. Researcher Gregory Kimble put it this way, "Is it worth it? Do the potential benefits to science and eventually to animal and human lives justify the costs to be extracted here and now?" (1989, p. 499). Seldom will any one psychologist have to make the ultimate decisions about the potential benefits/risks of research. Advisory committees of researchers, familiar with the techniques and the problems of the proposed research, will have to approve it before the project begins.

What are some other ethical issues related to research in psychology?(1) The subject's confidentiality must be guaranteed. Often, the subject's name is not used, replaced instead with an identification number. In a research project, no matter what you are asked to do or say, you should be confident that no one will have access to your responses but the researchers. (2) Participation in research should be totally voluntary. There are no circumstances under which you should feel that you must participate in psychological research. Volunteers should be allowed the option of dropping out of any research project, even after it has begun. For example, college students *cannot* be offered extra credit to participate in psychological research unless there are other options for earning the same amount of extra credit. (3) Subjects should participate in experiments only after they have given their informed consent. Subjects must know what the potential dangers of participation are going to be, why the project is being done, and what is expected of them. For example, no one can have access to your college records (GPA or entrance exam scores, etc.) without your specific knowledge and approval. Obviously, some deception may be required when doing experiments, and is (almost) always required when using naturalistic observation. Even so, the amount of deception needs to be balanced with the promise of the outcome of the research. (4) Subjects should be **debriefed** after the experiment has been completed. That means that the true nature of the project and its basic intent should be explained fully to all those who participated in it. Subjects also should be informed of the results of the project when they become available.

Published ethical guidelines for the use of animals in research also are quite stringent. Only experts trained and experienced in animal care and housing should have responsibility for laboratory animals. Those experts must then provide training to all others who work with the animals in the proper, humane treatment of the animals under their care. Every effort must be made to minimize discomfort, illness, and pain of animals. Putting animals in a situation where they might experience injury, pain or stress is acceptable *only* if no other procedure is available, and when the goal is justified by its prospective scientific, applied, or educational value. As with human subjects, there are usually review committees that must approve the design of any research using nonhuman subjects, where the major concern is the ethical, humane, protection of the animals.

debrief to fully inform a subject about the intent and/or hypotheses of one's research once data have been collected

Before You Go On
▼▼▼▼▼▼▼▼▼▼

Describe four ethical issues that must be considered when doing psychological research.

▶ Important Themes and Threads

Psychologists have learned a great deal about the behaviors and the mental processes of organisms. Some of the observationss that psychologists have made seem so important, so general in their application, that they deserve special mention. The themes and threads listed here are so basic, so well established, that they are essentially part of our definition of psychology. In every chapter that follows you will recognize a reflection of these ideas.

▶ *An Organism's Nature and Nurture Interact*

How much of who we are—our affect, behavior, and cognition—is the result of our inheritance, our biological *nature*? And how much of who we are reflects the influences of our environment, our learning experiences, our *nurture*? Is intelligence largely inherited (nature) or due to one's experience (nurture)? Is aggressiveness inborn (nature), or learned (nurture)? Does alcoholism reflect innate nature, or is it an acquired reaction to events in the environment?

Early observers realized that questions about one's nature and nurture were not either/or questions. What we will see repeatedly, in many different contexts, is that behavior and mental processes result from an *interaction* of inherited genetic factors and environmental influences. In this context, interaction is a difficult concept. We'll extend our understanding as we go along. For now, just remember that any psychological characteristic is not the result of *either* heredity *or* experience alone, but reflects the extent to which these forces have influenced each other. As one researcher put it, ". . . most behavioral traits appear to be influenced by many genes, each with small effects, [and] behavior is substantially influenced by nongenetic factors" (Plomin, 1990). Here's another way to say the same thing: "For all psychological characteristics, inheritance sets limits on, or creates a range of potentials for development. Environment determines how near the individual comes to developing these potentials" (Kimble, 1989).

▶ *Things Are Not Always as They Seem*

phenomenology the study of events as they are experienced by the individual

The deceptively simple and classic notion I'm referring to here actually has a name: **phenomenology**. Phenomenology has to do with the study of events *as they are experienced by the individual* (not as they occur "in reality"). As you might imagine, we can easily get involved in some fairly deep philosophical discussions here, but we need not. What we need to appreciate, and what we need to keep an eye out for as we go along, is the notion that we each attend to, interpret, and remember (i.e., experience) different aspects of the same world.

Here's a very simple, classic example of what I'm talking about, attributed to the philosopher John Locke (1632–1704). Imagine that you have before you three pails of water. The water in the pail on your left is really quite hot, the water in the pail on your right is nearly ice cold, and the water in the center pail is about body temperature. You put your left hand into the hot water and your right hand into the cold. Then, after a minute or two, you place both hands in the center pail of water. What is its temperature? How does the water feel? To your left hand (which had been in the hot water), the water seems quite cool, while to your right hand (which had been in the cold water) the very same water now feels warm. Well, what *is* the temperature of the water in the center pail? Is it cool or is it warm? Now a physicist may come along and measure the temperature of the water in that center pail with astonishing accuracy. But we're not interested in the physics of the water. We're interested in the psychology of your *experience* of the water, and we may—with something of a smile—report that the water in the center pail is both warm *and* cool. What matters is, not the physical temperature of the water in the center pail, but rather your comparative experience of that water.

Here's another example (from Bruner & Goodman, 1947). Children are given the opportunity to change the size of a small circle. They are asked to make the circle exactly the same size as a quarter. Almost all of the children consistently overestimate the size of the coin. But what is more interesting is that poor children overestimate the size of the quarter to a significantly greater degree. To the poorer children, quarters seem *much* larger than they actually are.

This theme has practical relevance in many areas of psychology. It will show up most clearly in our discussion of sensation and perception, where we will see that what we perceive often depends more on what we want to perceive or expect to perceive than on what is "really there." A quick study of Figure 1.4 will give you an idea of what I mean.

▶ For Many Questions in Psychology There Are No Simple Answers

We alluded to this observation earlier when we claimed that there are many good questions in psychology for which there are as yet no good answers. For some questions we have answers with which almost all psychologists agree. On the other hand, for others we don't even have reasonably accept-

Figure 1.4

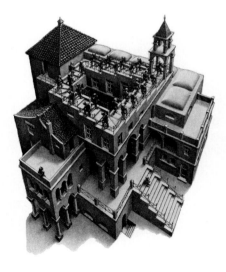

▲ (A) The highlighted letter is neither an A or H. It is interpreted to be one or the other based on our experience with the English language. (B) What do you see? This ambiguous drawing may be an old woman or a young Victorian lady depending on the context in which it is viewed. (C) Are the figures marching up or down the stairs? A careful inspection of these figures will reinforce the point that "things are not always as they seem."

able hypotheses. What you are going to encounter in your study of psychology is that complex phenomena often have complex explanations.

As an example, let's briefly anticipate a discussion we'll have later when we cover psychological disorders. What causes schizophrenia? For the moment, let us simply acknowledge that schizophrenia is one of the most devastating and debilitating of all the psychological disorders, afflicting approximately 2.5 million in the United States today. What causes the distortions in the way a person feels, thinks and acts that is schizophrenia? The truth is that we just don't know. We have a number of hypotheses, and each holds some promise. Part of the answer is genetic; schizophrenia does tend to run in families. Part of the answer is biochemical; the brains of persons with schizophrenia do not function in the same way as the brains of those who do not have schizophrenia. Part of the answer is environmental, or situational; stress and some experiences can bring on symptoms and/or at least make symptoms worse than they would be otherwise. So what causes schizophrenia? Answer: a number of interacting factors, some genetic, some physiological, some environmental, perhaps all operating at the same time. And so it goes for virtually *all* of our behaviors and mental processes.

The main point of this theme in psychology is that if you are looking for simple answers to explain your own behavior or the behavior of someone else, you're bound to be disappointed. Disappointed you may be, but please do not be discouraged. Behaviors and mental processes are complex, and explaining them is going to take a certain degree of complexity. Complexity in itself should not be worrisome. Behaviors and mental processes generally have multiple causes. Our challenge is to discover them.

▶ Psychology Has Practical Application in the Real World

We might get an argument from biologists, chemists, physicists, geologists, and even some astronomers, but I am quite willing to make the claim that no science has more practical application in the real world than does psychology. In everyday life, people can get by without thinking about physics or geology or biology; but they cannot get by without thinking *psychologically*. They must take into consideration a multitude of sensations, perceptions, memories, feelings, and consequences of their own actions if they are going to prosper, or even survive. As you read about psychology on the following pages, you should always be on the lookout for how the topic you're reading about can be put to use in your own life.

Here's an example you can put to use right now. When we get into our discussion of learning and memory, we'll make the point that material is easier to learn and easier to remember if it is meaningful. So one of your jobs as a learner—as a student in a beginning psychology class—is to make the material about which you are learning as meaningful as possible. What that means (among other things, of course) is that part of your job is to find ways in which you can personally relate to the issues you are reading about. In psychology, finding such relevance is usually easy. After all, the subject matter of psychology is the behavior and mental processes of organisms—and that includes you and me.

As we approach the twenty-first century it is becoming increasingly obvious to most of us that the physical health of the planet Earth is in jeopardy (*e.g.,* Brown et al., 1990). Overpopulation, the "Greenhouse Effect," the erosion of the ozone layer, overused landfills, acid rain, the pollution of ground water, and air pollution are just some of the issues with which psychologists are becoming involved. The problem for psychology is how to turn "global issues," such as the loss of the tropical rain forests, into "local actions" that have real and immediate impact on individuals. Some of the

▲ One application of psychology in the real world is the development of programs to change people's behavior in ways that benefit the physical environment.

problems that face the planet today just seem overwhelming—beyond the resources of individuals. They are not. Most of the problems our environment faces today have been caused by the actions (and the feelings, and the cognitions) of individuals. Some of the problems have accumulated their effects over a long periods of time, but each is ultimately the result of decisions made by individuals. Now the challenge is to apply psychology to improve the chances of the planet's very survival (Saegert & Winkel, 1990).

Before You Go On

What does it mean to say that an organism's nature and nurture interact?

What does "phenomenology" mean in psychological terms?

Why do there tend to be few simple answers in psychology?

In what way can we claim psychology to be one of the most applied of all the sciences?

Thinking Critically about the Nature of Psychology

I mentioned in the *Introduction* that one of your goals as a student of psychology, should be to learn to think critically about psychological issues. This requires time and practice, and does not always result in one, sure, absolute, best answer. At the end of each chapter I will provide you with a short list of questions to ponder. Taking the time to reflect on these questions will help you to organize and remember the material presented in the chapter. It will also make you a better "consumer" of psychology.

1. Is psychology the only science that studies behavior and mental processes? Surely psychology is not the only science that cares about people and

what they do or feel or think. In what ways are psychology the same as or different from anthropology or sociology or economics?

2. We often say that if we understand something, we can make predictions about it. In fact, to demonstrate that we understand someone, we may be asked to predict what that person will do in certain situations. If we understand someone and can make predictions about that person, does it follow that we can control that person?

3. If a magazine were to report that Brand X is the most "trouble-free car in the world," how do you suppose "trouble-free" has been operationally defined?

4. Is it possible to be a religious person and a psychologist at the same time?

5. I often claim that "81.746 percent of what we know in psychology today, we have learned in the last 30 years." I'm not really serious when I say that, but how *could* we determine how much has been learned in psychology in the last 30 years, or 20 years, or 10 years?

6. Because all that I know about the relationship between reading ability and performance in introductory psychology reflects what I know from doing correlations, I cannot make any cause-and-effect statements about this relationship. If I hypothesized that students' reading level actually caused them to get the grades that they do, how would I find out if I were right?

7. You hear an ad on television that claims that in a "taste test," LOXO COLA was compared to two nationally-known brands, and LOXO COLA was "preferred nearly 2 to 1." What extraneous variables might be having an influence on this result?

8. Is there ever any justification for using nonhuman animals in psychology experiments? Why or why not?

NOTE: Answers to the True-False Quiz with which we began this chapter: Except for items #4, 11, and 14, these statements are essentially false.

Summary

▼▼▼▼▼▼▼▼▼▼▼▼▼▼▼▼▼▼▼▼▼▼▼▼▼

Why may we make the claim that psychology is a science? We may claim scientific status for psychology because it meets two criteria: It has an organized body of knowledge and it uses scientific methods. *Pages 14–15*

What is the subject matter of psychology? The subject matter of psychology is behavior and mental processes: affect, behavior, and cognition. *Pages 15–16*

What are operational definitions? Operational definitions define concepts in terms of the techniques, or operations, used to measure those concepts. *Page 16*

In what way did the philosophies of Descartes and Locke prepare the way for psychology? Both René Descartes and John Locke directed the attention of philosophy to the study of the mind—how it interacts with the body and how it acquires information, and they did so without reference to religious issues. *Pages 17–18*

In what way did the science of Darwin and von Helmholtz influence the emergence of psychology? Charles Darwin (from biology) and Hermann von Helmholtz (from physiology) brought scientific and experimental methods to bear on questions that were essentially psychological in nature. *Pages 18–19*

When and where did psychology "begin" and whom do we credit with formally establishing the discipline? We credit Wilhelm Wundt for having founded psychology at the University of Leipzig in 1879. *Page 19*

Briefly describe the first approaches that psychologists took toward their subject matter. Wundt and Titchener used experiments and introspection to study the mind or consciousness, particularly its contents and structure. Following the suggestions of William James, the functionalists were also concerned with the mind and mental activity, but focused on the adaptive usefulness or function of consciousness. *Pages 19–20*

Briefly summarize psychoanalysis and behaviorism as approaches to psychology. Behaviorism (associated with Watson and Skinner) holds that the subject matter of the science of psychology should be measurable and observable—thus, we should study behavior, not the mind. Psychoanalysis (associated with Freud and his followers) asserts that behaviors and mental processes are often under the influence of basic drives and unconscious forces. *Pages 21–22*

What is the major thrust of the humanistic approach in psychology? Humanistic psychology (associated with Rogers and Maslow) focuses on the self or the person, emphasizing internal processes and the poten-

tial for growth and development. As such, this approach can be seen as a reaction against behaviorism and psychoanalysis. *Page 23*

What does "gestalt" mean? Gestalt means whole, totality, or configuration. *Page 23*

What area of psychology was of major concern to the Gestalt psychologists? *Gestalt* psychologists focus their study on factors that influence the selection and organization of perceptions. *Page 23*

What is naturalistic observation? Naturalistic observation involves the careful, systematic, reliable observation of behaviors as they occur naturally. *Page 26*

List some of the potential problems that can arise with this method. Use of naturalistic observation requires that (1) the subjects not be aware of the fact that they are being observed, (2) the observers' biases not influence the observations, and (3) patience be exercised in the search for those behaviors that occur infrequently. *Page 26*

How can surveys and case history studies be used to help us understand behavior and mental processes? Surveys provide a few responses (observations) from very large samples of respondents, whereas case history studies tend to provide detailed and specific information (observations) about just a few subjects. In either case, one may discover relationships among the responses observed. *Pages 27–28*

What data are needed to calculate a correlation coefficient? In order to calculate a correlation coefficient, one needs to measure two responses of the same group of subjects, yielding a set of paired observations or measurements. *Page 29*

How does a correlation coefficient tell us about the relationship between two measured responses? Positive correlation coefficients tell us that high scores on one response are associated with (and predict) high scores on the other response and that low scores on one response are associated with (and predict) low scores on the other. Negative correlations tell us that the two responses are inversely related with high scores on one measure associated with low scores on the other. Correlation coefficients of or near zero tell us that our measured responses are not coordinated in any way. The closer the coefficient is to the extremes of +1.00 or –1.00, the stronger the relationship between the responses, but in no case can one infer a cause-and-effect relationship from correlational data. *Pages 28–31*

What is the essence of doing an experiment? An experiment involves manipulating independent variables, measuring dependent variables, and minimizing the effects of extraneous variables. *Pages 31–32*

Define independent, dependent, and extraneous variables in the context of an experiment. Independent variables are hypothesized to have an effect on some mental process or behavior. To see if such is the case, one looks for changes in some measured dependent variable that are consistent with changes in the manipulated independent variable. Before a claim of a cause-and-effect relationship between the independent and dependent variables, all other events (extraneous variables) that could have affected the dependent variable must have been controlled or eliminated. *Page 32*

How do random assignment and baseline designs help minimize error in psychological experiments? Random assignment of subjects to experimental or control conditions of an experiment assures that each subject has an equal opportunity to be in any experimental treatment. Any preexperimental differences among subjects should thus balance out over groups. With baseline designs, the same subjects serve in both experimental and control conditions, thus serving as their own controls. *Page 35*

Describe four ethical issues that must be considered when doing psychological research. Subjects in psychological research must have their confidentiality maintained. They should give informed consent before voluntarily participating in the research and should be debriefed about the project when it is over. Above all,

the investigator should consider whether potential risks in the research are offset by the present or future value of the results that may come from the research. Similar considerations are given to the use of animals in research. *Pages 35–36*

What does it mean to say that an organism's nature and nurture interact? It means that who we are—our affects, behaviors, and cognitions—jointly reflect characteristics that we have inherited as well as experiences that we have had in our environments. Both our nature and our nurture are important, yet neither is sufficient to explain the source of an organism's behaviors or mental processes. *Page 37*

What does "phenomenology" mean in psychological terms? The position of phenomenology asserts that in many cases what matters to an individual most is not so much what happens as what that individual has noticed. In other words, what is perceived is often more important than what "actually" was. *Pages 37–38*

Why do there tend to be so few simple answers in psychology? Because psychologists study the complex phenomena of behavior and mental processes of organisms, we find that there are few simple answers to our questions. Behaviors and mental processes are usually caused by a multitude of interacting physical, biological, psychological, and social factors. *Pages 38–39*

In what way can we claim psychology to be one of the most applied of all the sciences? Psychology is a very relevant and applied field of study because the major focus of its study is the mental processes and behaviors of people. *Pages 39–40*

1.1 When a researcher develops a tentative explanation for some phenomenon that can be tested and then rejected or supported, that researcher has developed   a) a scientific method.   b) a theoretical case history.   c) a hypothesis.   d) an experimental method. *Page 15*

1.2 In the context of research studies, what can scientific methods do for us?   a) They can lead us to reject hypotheses that are not true.   b) They can tell us which results are likely to be popular.   c) They can prove that one hypothesis is the best to explain a given phenomenon.   d) They can help us decide which of a number of research issues ought to be investigated next. *Page 15*

1.3 True or False: Science is the only way for humans to gain insights about the nature of human behavior. *Page 14*

1.4 Which of the following provides the best statement of psychology's subject matter?   a) what people do, both normally and abnormally   b) the actions of organisms when they are stimulated   c) the mental activity and behaviors of organisms   d) what people think about the things that affect them. *Page 15*

1.5 To say that psychologists study affect is to say that part of the subject matter of psychology is   a) thoughts, beliefs, and knowledge.   b) underlying biological or physiological factors.   c) behaviors, actions, and reactions.   d) emotions, feelings, and moods. *Page 15*

1.6 Which of these is LEAST publicly verifiable?   a) how many times a pigeon pecks a disk   b) the time it takes a rat to run through a maze   c) the content of a person's dream   d) a student's performance on a classroom exam. *Page 16*

1.7 When psychology emerged as a separate discipline, it did so because it had combined   a) energy and matter.   b) scientific methods with philosophical questions.   c) cognitive processes with affect.   d) mental processes with behavior. *Page 16*

1.8 René Descartes and John Locke deserve mention in a discussion of the history of psychology because   a) predicted that the science of psychology would be popular and successful.   b) believed that human actions could be explained without relying on God or religion for explanations.   c) realized the importance of the spinal cord for human behavior.   d) applied scientific methods to issues of human nature and human understanding. *Page 17*

1.9 If I were to show you a bunch of grapes and ask you to describe your inner, private experience in the most basic and fundamental terms, I would be using the method of   a) introspection.   b) psychophysics.   c) dualism.   d) functionalism. *Page 18*

1.10 What did John Locke and Wilhelm Wundt share in common?   a) a basic interest in the nature of consciousness and the contents of the mind   b) a deep belief in the truth of Darwin's theory of evolution   c) a reliance on the methods of science to support their claims and hypotheses   d) all of the above. *Page 20*

1.11 True or False?   The first psychology laboratory was opened in the late 1800s by Sigmund Freud in Vienna. *Page 19*

1.12 About when in its history did psychology become known as "the science of behavior?"   a) when Wundt opened his laboratory in Leipzig   b) when Titchener went to direct the laboratory at Cornell   c) when James was teaching psychology at Harvard   d) when Watson was Chair of the department at Johns Hopkins. *Page 22*

1.13 True or False?   Sigmund Freud's laboratory began doing experiments on psychoanalysis in the 1920s. *Page 21*

1.14 Who is most likely to have made the statement, "Psychology should focus on the person, the self in all its aspects as it interacts with the fabric of experience"?   a) a behaviorist psychologist   b) a Freudian psychologist   c) a Gestalt psychologist   d) a humanistic psychologist. *Page 23*

1.15 Each of the following is true with regard to naturalistic observation EXCEPT   a) Organisms may not behave naturally if they believe they are being observed.   b) The behaviors in which the observer is interested may occur infrequently.   c) We can only observe the behaviors of organisms in social situations, when they interact with others.   d) The expectations, motivation, and past experiences of the observer may bias his or her observations. *Page 26*

1.16 Which of the following questions provides the best candidate for a study using naturalistic observation: a) Are nightmares more common after eating pizza?   b) How do chess players develop their strategies?   c) Do third-grade boys tend to play with girls or boys at recess?   d) What are the effects of a tranquilizer on memory tasks? *Page 26*

1.17 Most of Freud's theories and therapy derived evolved from the use of the _____ method.   a) case history   b) correlational   c) experimental   d) survey. *Page 28*

1.18 True or False?   Surveys will involve more subjects than will case history studies. *Page 27*

1.19 Which of the following correlation coefficients indicates a relationship between two responses where we can most confidently predict one response knowing the other?   a) +.56   b) +.0002   c) −.71   d) −2.34. *Page 29*

1.20 A correlation between which of these pairs is most likely to be negative?   a) high school GPAs and college GPAs   b) scores on a typing test and typing skills   c) number of cigarettes smoked daily and the likelihood of developing lung cancer   d) amount of light in a restaurant and the price of a meal there. *Page 29*

1.21 True or False?   Positive correlations are more useful than negative correlations. *Page 30*

1.22 The quality or value of an experiment depends mostly on   a) the extent to which extraneous variables have been controlled or eliminated.   b) the number of independent variables that have been manipulated.   c) the extent to which the dependent variables are correlated with each other.   d) whether humans or nonhumans have been used as experimental subjects. *Page 33*

1.23 If you want to experimentally test the usefulness of a new drug for the treatment of psychological disorders, the independent variable in your experiment will be: a) the extent to which patients show improvement after using the drug.   b) the amount of drug administered to the patients.   c) the types of psychological disorders being treated.   d) other forms of therapy or drugs the patients are receiving at the same time. *Page 32*

1.24 True or False?   When we do an experiment, we wish to be able to claim that differences in our measured dependent variable depend on our manipulations of the independent variable and nothing else. *Page 32*

1.25 A major advantage of a baseline design is that   a) all subjects serve in both control and experimental conditions.   b) it takes much less time to do.   c) they are more appropriate for human than for nonhuman subjects.   d) subjects need not be debriefed when the experiment is over. *Page 35*

1.26 True or False?   Potentially harmful research in psychology typically has been approved by some committee or board of review. *Page 36*

Chapter 2 ▼▼▼▼▼ # The Biological Bases of Behavior

▲▲▲▲▲▲▲

You are walking down the hall late at night in your bare feet, when—Ouch! You've stepped on a tack. Soon, you are hopping around on one foot, trying to grab the other, and rapidly becoming furious at whoever it was who left a tack on the hallway floor. The whole scene lasts about two minutes. What was involved in producing this experience? The answer is: a series of incredibly complex biological processes—processes that you probably did not care about at the time. Roughly, here's what happens, with some intriguing questions in brackets:

• As your injured foot jerks up off the floor, your arms flail out so that you can maintain your balance. [What stimulated the muscles of my leg to pull up my foot? How do my arms know what to do to keep me balanced?]

• You realize that your foot hurts. [Where does that realization occur? In my brain?]

• To be more specific, the point of the tack punctures the sole of your foot and stimulates a nerve cell. [What does it mean to say that a nerve cell is stimulated? What kind of nerve cell reacts to tacks? For that matter, what *is* a nerve cell?]

• The cell that is stimulated by the tack sends a message to other nerve cells. [Wait a minute! What do you mean "message?" How do messages get from one nerve cell to another?]

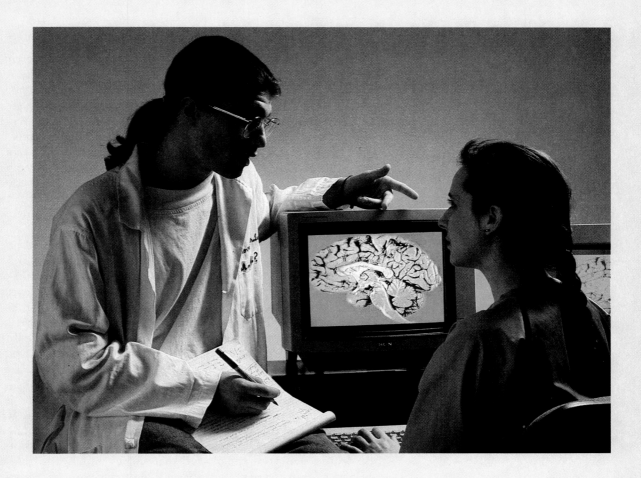

- Messages now race up your leg to the base of the spinal cord. [Why to the spinal cord? What does the spinal cord look like? What does it do?]

- Once in the spinal cord, messages now go in two different directions: up to the brain and back down to the muscles in your leg. [How do the messages get to my brain? For that matter, how do they get to my leg? Do they go to my brain first?]

- Messages from the spinal cord to your leg stimulate muscles to lift your leg quickly off the floor. At the same time, those messages to your brain are being interpreted. [Do you mean to say that my leg lifts up off the floor without my brain even thinking about it? Doesn't my brain have to control that movement?]

- You identify the source of your pain as a tack. Still hopping on one foot, you wonder who left the tack on the hall floor, and start to get angry. [But to recognize a tack implies that I'm using my memory and remember what a tack is. Where are memories stored in the brain? Are there separate parts of the brain involved in emotions like anger?]

Even in a stimulus-response chain of events as simple as stepping on a tack, a remarkable series of physiological and biochemical reactions takes place. Ultimately, all of our behaviors and mental processes—from the simple blink of an eye to profound and abstract thought—are no more and no less than the integrated reactions of our nervous systems.

▲ *The genetic transmission of physical traits is often reflected in the extent to which children resemble their parents.*

gene the basic mechanism of hereditary transmission; that which gets passed from one generation to the next

chromosome literally, "colored body"; that tiny, threadlike structure found in 23 pairs in human cells that carry genes

▶ *Preview*

We have seen that psychology is a science that has many different subfields and that uses a variety of methods. This chapter reflects the reality that regardless of one's approach to psychology, one must understand at least the basics of the biology and physiology of the organism being studied. Our aim is not to become amateur biologists or physiologists. We have two major concerns. One is with the nature of genetic transmission of characteristics from one generation to the next. This transmission is not a simple matter, but because so much of who we are reflects our genetic history, we ought to be aware of some of the basic issues involved. Our second concern is with the structures and functions of the nervous system. It is the central nervous system—the brain and the spinal cord—that is most intimately involved in behavor and mental processes.

We will start off with an overview of some of the general principles of genetics, introducing some vocabulary and looking at the relationships between genetics and behavior. Then we'll begin our discussion of the nervous system, taking a building-block approach. We'll describe the individual nerve cell and see how these cells interact with one another and with other cells, and we'll discuss how the billions of nerve cells in our bodies work together to form the major human nervous systems. We'll then move on to consider the spinal cord. Finally, we'll get to the focal point of the chapter: the human brain.

Discussions of genetics and of the structures and functions of the central nervous system occasionally sound rather impersonal, as if we were talking about some strange mass of gooey tissue in a glass jar. What you'll need to do from time to time is remind yourself that we're talking about *your* neurons, *your* spinal cord, and *your* brain—and mine too. As you read these words, it is your spinal cord that carries impulses to the muscles in your arm to turn the page, your brain that directs your eyes to move across the page, your brain that processes impulses from your eyes, your brain that seeks understanding, and your brain that monitors your heart rate and keeps you breathing while you read.

▶ *Genetics and Psychology*

The science of genetics studies how traits and characteristics are passed from one generation to the next. Its focus is on heredity. For thousands of years, humans have engaged in the selective breeding of all sorts of plants and animals. Some dogs have been bred to be "lap dogs" and good pets, while others have been bred to retrieve or to do field work with livestock. Ages ago, it was discovered that when meaty bulls mated with meaty cows, the resulting calves tended to be meaty also. Rose growers have been creating new varieties of flowers for centuries through selective breeding. To some degree, it always has been appreciated that children tend to be more like their parents, and like each other, than anyone else; that many traits, both physical and psychological, seem to "run in families."

The science of genetics began at about the time of the U. S. Civil War, when a monk, Gregor Mendel discovered one of the mechanisms of heredity as he studied the selective breeding of the lowly pea. What Mendel discovered was the **gene**, the basic actor in hereditary transmission. The genes that Mendel assumed to exist (at the time there was no way he could actually *see* one) are located on microscopically tiny structures called **chromosomes**, which means colored (chroma) body (soma). Chromosomes are found, in pairs, in the nucleus of every single cell in a living organism.

dominant gene a gene that carries a trait that will be expressed regardless of the gene it is paired with

recessive gene a gene that carries a trait that will be expressed only if it is paired with another similiar recessive gene

The nucleus of every human cell contains 23 pairs of chromosomes, *except* for the sex cells (the sperm in males, the ovum in females) which hold only half of each of the 23 possible pairs. At conception, the male and female sex cells unite to produce a new cell, producing a new mixture of 23 chromosome pairs (and, hence, genes), half from the father and half from the mother.

If both parents contribute a gene that is responsible for some physical characteristic (say, blue eyes), then their child will have blue eyes. If both parents contribute a gene that results in brown eyes, their child will develop brown eyes. The story starts to get interesting when one parent contributes a gene that develops blue eyes while the other parent contributes a gene that develops brown eyes. Here's where the idea of a dominant gene and recessive gene becomes relevant. A **dominant gene** is one whose characteristics will show up regardless of the gene paired with it. With eye color, the gene for brown eyes is dominant, so a child who inherits a gene for brown eyes from either parent, will have brown eyes. A **recessive gene**, on the other hand, expresses its characteristic only when it is paired with another, similar recessive gene. With eye color, the gene for blue eyes is recessive, so a child who inherits a gene for blue eyes from either parent will have blue eyes only if another gene for blue eyes is inherited from the other parent. Perhaps Figure 2.1 will help.

When we discuss the genetic transmission of physical traits, we often use eye color as an example. This is because the coloration of the human eye is one of the few noticeable characteristics that actually can be accounted for by just a couple of known genes. (Even eye color can be a complicated matter of gene interaction.) Many genes express their characteristic only if *other genes* are present also. There are a few other complications that also deserve mention. One is that genes do not literally create any characteristic directly. For example, a gene for brown eyes does not "make brown eyes," but causes a certain chemical to be manufactured during the early stages of development which *has the effect of* producing brown eyes. We do not inherit characteristics; we inherit genetic codes which, in turn, produce particular chemicals which, in turn produce noticeable characteristics.

Figure 2.1

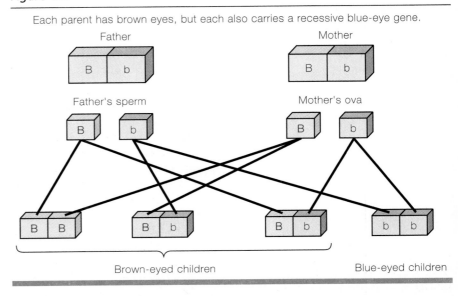

Each parent has brown eyes, but each also carries a recessive blue-eye gene.

▲ *Genetic transmission of dominant/recessive traits. Here, two brown-eyed (B) parents each carry a recessive blue-eyed gene (b). Only a child who receives the recessive gene (b) from both parents will, in fact, have blue eyes.*

Another complication is that the effects of some genes need time to pass before they are expressed. For example, a type of baldness called "male-pattern baldness" is inherited in a straightforward fashion. Obviously, the observable consequences of this "gift" of heredity take time to be expressed. A third complication is that even characteristics that are determined primarily by genetic transmission require some environmental influence for those traits to be evidenced. Consider why I happen to be 6'4" tall. A lot of it has to do with the fact that both of my parents were taller than average, and that on both sides of *their* families there were a number of relatives who were tall also. There happened to have been a good number of genes that promote tallness around, and I got some of them. But, that I am 6'4" tall also reflects the fact that I was, and continue to be, well fed and cared for. My environment, in other words, allowed those genes to be expressed close to their full potential. Had I *not* been well fed, or had I been raised in an impoverished environment, I might not have grown to my present height.

Our inherited physical characteristics have a considerable impact on how we think, feel, and behave. What we call "self-image" is, in many ways, determined by traits that are more physical than psychological. Deciding to invest extracurricular time in the basketball team is an option that seldom occurs to people who happen to be considerably shorter than average. Similarly, whether you are male or female is largely a genetic matter, and one of considerable importance to you, no doubt. When psychologists ask about who you are as a person, at least some of the answer must be given in terms of genetically determined physical characteristics. But we inherit chromosomes and genes which, in turn, produce certain chemicals. We do not inherit our mother's talent for music, our father's aggressiveness, or Aunt Tillie's mental illness. We inherit chemicals, not behaviors.

In fact, there is evidence that many of our behaviors, skills, and emotional reactions are influenced by genetic factors. In truth, most of this evidence is indirect, but we are now at a point in time when we cannot find any human endeavors that are not to some degree influenced by one's genetic constitution. Some genes seem able to predispose us—in complex ways—to be more or less likely to do, think, or feel as we do. As it happens, we will be back over this ground many times in the following chapters as we cover different psychological characteristics.

Of all the structures we inherit, none is more remarkable than the complexly interacting set of cells that comprise our nervous systems. It is to that aspect of our biological being that we now turn, focusing first on the single nerve cell, or neuron.

Before You Go On

What are some of the basic concepts involved in any discussion of the genetic transmission of physical characteristics?

What is it that we inherit from our parents?

▶ The Neuron

neuron a nerve cell, the basic building block of the nervous system that transmits neural impulses

Our study of the nervous system begins at the level of the single nerve cell, which is called a **neuron**. Neurons are microscopically small and exist throughout our nervous systems by the billions. They are so tiny and complex that estimating their number is very difficult, if not absurd. To give you an idea of the sizes and numbers we're talking about, there are about *125 million* specialized neurons on the back, inside surface of each human eye, and about *100 billion* neurons in the human brain (Hubel, 1979; Kolb, 1989).

▶ The Structure of Neurons

We may not be sure about snowflakes, but it is a sure bet that no two neurons are identical. There is no such thing as a typical neuron, but most do have a number of structures in common. Figure 2.2 illustrates these common features, and Figure 2.3 illustrates what a few neurons actually look like.

One structure that all neurons are certain to have is a **cell body**. The cell body is the largest concentration of mass of the neuron. It contains the nucleus of the cell, which contains the genetic information that keeps the cell functioning.

Extending away from the cell body are several tentaclelike structures called **dendrites,** and one particularly long structure called the **axon.** Our drawing in Figure 2.2 is very much simplified, showing only a few dendrites, when in a mature neuron there may be thousands. Typically, dendrites reach out to receive messages, called neural impulses, from other neurons. These impulses are then sent along to the cell body and on down the axon toward other neurons, or to muscles or glands. Some axons are quite long—as much as two or three feet long in the spinal cord. It is generally true, then, that within a neuron, impulses travel from dendrite to cell body to axon, and most of the trip will be made along the axon.

The neuron illustrated in Figure 2.2 has a feature not found on all neurons. The axon of this neuron has a cover or sheath of **myelin.** Myelin is a white, fatty material found on about half of the neurons in an adult's nervous system. It is myelin that allows us to tell the difference between the gray matter (dendrites, cell bodies, and unmyelinated axons) and the white

cell body the largest mass of a neuron, containing the cell's nucleus, and which may receive neural impulses

dendrites branchlike extensions from a neuron's cell body where most neural impulses are received

axon the long, taillike extension of a neuron that carries an impulse away from the synapse

myelin a white, fatty covering found on some axons that serves to insulate and protect them, while increasing the speed of impulses

Figure 2.2

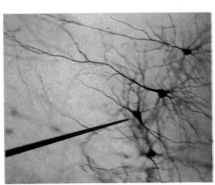

▲ *A photograph of neurons taken through a powerful microscope.*

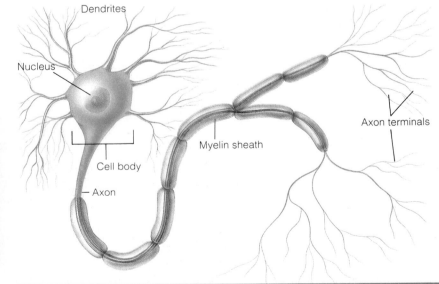

▲ *A typical neuron with its major structures.*

matter (myelinated axons) we see so clearly when we look at sections of nervous system tissue. Myelin is not yet developed at birth—it develops and adheres to axons as the nervous system matures. Myelin serves a number of useful functions. It serves to protect the long delicate axon. It acts as an insulator, keeping the activity of one neuron separate from those that happen to be nearby. Myelin serves to speed impulses along the length of the axon. We tend to find myelin sheaths on axons that carry impulses relatively long distances throughout the body.

Whether they are myelinated or not, axons end in a branching series of bare end points called **axon terminals**. It is at axon terminals that neurons communicate with other neurons. The spreading axon terminals and the large number of dendrite extensions allow one neuron to interact with hundreds or even thousands of other cells. To quickly review: within a neuron, impulses typically travel from the dendrites to the cell body, to the axon (which may be myelinated) and ultimately to the axon terminals.

Here's a far-reaching observation about neurons, particularly those in our brains: Virtually no neurons are generated after we are born. We are born with more neurons than we will ever have again. In fact, we are born with about twice as many neurons as we'll ever use. What happens to the rest? They just die off, or we actively kill them (by a number of means, including physical damage, or more commonly with drugs such as alcohol). Bryan Kolb (1979), of the University of Lethbridge in Canada, gives us this analogy. During normal development, the brain is "constructed" in a manner rather like that in which a statue is chipped away from a block of granite. Rather than building up the finished product one small piece at a time, more material than what one needs is made available. Then, what is needed and/or used is retained, and the rest dies away. Here's a related reality: in order to have those billions of neurons in our brains at the time of birth, brain cells must be generating at a rate of approximately 250,000 per minute(!) while the brain is being formed *before birth* (Cowan, 1979). There are implications about prenatal care in this observation, which we'll explore in Chapter 3.

The fact that when neurons die they are not replaced with new ones makes neurons rather unique among cells. We're constantly making new blood cells to replace lost ones. If we didn't, we could never donate a pint of blood. Skin cells are constantly being replaced by new ones. You rinse away skin cells by the hundreds each time you wash your hands. Neurons are different; once they're gone, they're gone forever. As it happens, we are often in luck, however, because *the functions* of lost neurons can be taken over by other, surviving neurons. It is to the function of neurons that we turn next.

Before You Go On
▼▼▼▼▼▼▼▼▼

What are the major structures of a neuron?

What is myelin, and what is its function?

▶ The Function of Neurons

The function of a neuron is to transmit neural impulses from one place in the nervous system to another. Let's start with a working definition: A **neural impulse** is a sudden and reversible change in the electrical charges within

---

axon terminals the series of branching end points of an axon where one neuron communicates with the next in a series

neural impulse a sudden and reversible change in the electrical charges within and outside the membrane of a neuron, which travels from the dendrite to the axon end of a neuron ion an electrically charged (either + or –) chemical particle

resting potential the difference in electrical charge between the inside of a neuron and the outside when it is at rest (–70mV)

action potential the short-lived burst of a change in the difference in electrical charge between the inside and the outside of a neuron when it fires (+40 mV)

and outside a neuron that travels down a neuron when it fires. Now let's see what all that means.

Neurons, as living cells, are filled with and surrounded by fluids. Only a thin membrane (rather like a skin) separates the fluids inside a neuron from fluids outside it. These fluids contain tiny chemical particles called **ions**. Chemical ions carry a very small electrical charge, either positive (+) or negative (–). These electrically-charged ions float around in all the fluids of the body, but are heavily concentrated in the nervous system. And it's no great mystery where ions come from: They come from the foods and liquids we eat and drink that are dissolved by our digestive system.

Neurons that are just lying around not doing anything are said to be neurons at rest, although "at rest" doesn't seem an accurate description. This is because a tension develops between the electrical charge of ions trapped *inside* the neuron and the charge of ions trapped *outside* the neuron. A state of balance would exist if the positive and negative electrical charges on both sides of the neuron's membrane were equal. But this is not the case. When it is "at rest," the inside of the neuron has a negative (–) charge compared to the positive (+) charge of the fluids on the outside of the neuron. Hence the tension (and why "at rest" is not very descriptive). The positive and negative ions are drawn or attracted toward each other, but they cannot become balanced because of the neuron's membrane, which separates them. This imbalance of electrically charged chemical particles makes each neuron at rest like a tiny battery, holding a small electrical charge, called a **resting potential**. The electrical charge of a neuron at rest is about 70 millivolts (mV). To be more precise, we should say that the resting potential of a neuron is –70 mV, because we measure the inside relative to the outside, and the inside of the neuron is where we have the concentration of negative ions. If this sounds at all mysterious to you, think about a common D-cell battery of the sort you use in a flashlight. It too has two aspects, one positive, the other negative. The electrical charge that is possible with one of these batteries is usually about 1500 mV, much greater, of course, than that of a tiny neuron.

When a neuron is stimulated to fire, or to produce an impulse, the electrical tension of the resting potential is released. Suddenly and quickly, the polarity of the nerve cell changes. For a very brief instant (about 1/1000 of a second) at one point along the length of the neuron, the electrical charge within the cell becomes more *positive* than the area outside the cell. The whole "charge" of the battery changes instantaneously. This new charge is called the **action potential** or neural impulse. The electric potential is now about +40 mV, the positive sign indicating that the inside of the neuron is now more positive than the outside. Then, in a few thousandths of a second, the neuron returns to its original state. The tension redevelops. It is ready to fire again.

To repeat, what happens is something like this. When at rest, there is a difference between the electrical charge inside and outside a neuron (the inside being more negative). When the neuron fires, the difference suddenly reverses, so that the inside is slightly more positive. Then the tension of the restiing potential returns again (see Figure 2.4).

It is important to note that when an impulse travels down a neuron, *nothing* physically moves from one end of the neuron to the other. The only movement of physical particles that takes place is that of electrical ions moving in and out of the neuron through its membrane. What travels "down a neuron" is *where* this action potential takes place—where the release of tension of the resting potential occurs. The story of how impulses travel between neurons is just as remarkable, but quite different from the story of how impulses travel within neurons.

Figure 2.4

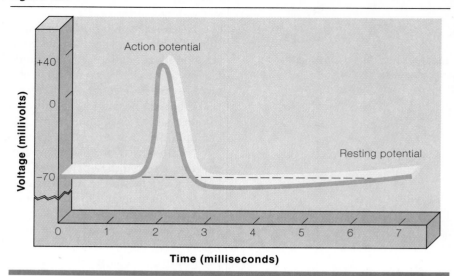

▲ Changes in electrical potential that occur during the firing of a neuron. Note that voltage is negative (–70 millivolts) when the neuron is at rest, and positive (+ 40 millivolts) during the firing of the impulse. Note, too, that the entire process lasts but a few milliseconds.

Before You Go On
▼▼▼▼▼▼▼▼▼▼

What is the basic process involved when a neuron fires?

▶ From One Cell to Another: The Synapse

synapse the general location where an impulse is relayed from one neuron to another by means of neurotransmitters

vesicles the small containers, concentrated in axon terminals, that hold neurotransmitter molecules

neurotransmitters chemical molecules released at the synapse that will, in general, either excite or inhibit neural impulse transmission

synaptic cleft the space between the membrane of an axon terminal and the membrane of the next neuron in a sequence

The general location where an impulse is relayed from one neuron to another is called the **synapse.** Here's what happens there.

At the very end of an axon are many branches called axon terminals (refer back to Fig. 2.2). Throughout the neuron, but concentrated in the axon terminals, are incredibly small containers called **vesicles.** These vesicles hold complex chemicals called **neurotransmitters.** When a neural impulse reaches the axon terminal, the vesicles at the very end, near the membrane, open and release the neurotransmitter they have been holding. Released from their vesicles, the neurotransmitter floods out into the **synaptic cleft,** a tiny space between two neurons. The two neurons involved do not touch; they are separated by the synaptic cleft. Once in the synaptic cleft, some neurotransmitter molecules move to the membrane of the next neuron where they may fit into "receptor sites" and enter the membrane. See Figure 2.5.

Then what happens? Actually, any number of things. Let's look at a few. The most reasonable scenario is that the neurotransmitters flood across the synaptic cleft, enter into receptor sites in the next neuron, and by so doing, excite that next neuron to release the tension of its resting potential and fire a new impulse down to its axon terminals. There, neurotransmitter chemicals are released from vesicles, cross the synaptic cleft and stimulate the next neuron in the sequence to fire. In fact, this *is* the case, when the neurotransmitter is an *excitatory* chemical. It simply stimulates the next neuron in a sequence to fire.

Figure 2.5

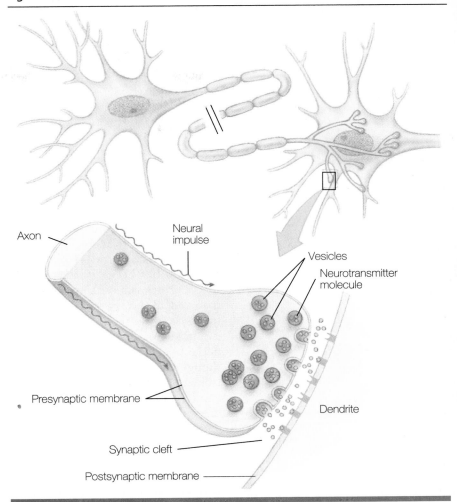

Axon

Neural impulse

Vesicles

Neurotransmitter molecule

Presynaptic membrane

Dendrite

Synaptic cleft

Postsynaptic membrane

▲ *A synapse, in which transmission is from upper left to lower right. As an impulse enters the axon terminal, vesicles release neurotransmitter chemicals through the presynaptic membrane into the synaptic cleft. The neurotransmitter then stimulates the postsynaptic membrane of the next dendrite.*

As it happens, there are many neurons throughout our nervous systems that contain neurotransmitters that have the opposite effect. When they are released, they flood across the synaptic cleft and work to prevent the next neuron from firing. We refer to these neurotransmitters as *inhibitory*. So that brings up another possibility. An impulse may race down a neuron, release a neurotransmitter into the synaptic cleft which floods across to the membrane of the next neuron and as a result, *nothing may happen!* In fact, nothing *will* happen unless there is sufficient excitatory neurotransmitter chemical to activate an impulse in the next neuron.

Not long ago, it was believed that neurons produce and release one of just two neurotransmitters; excitatory and inhibitory. We now realize that this view is much too simplistic. Although one neuron produces and releases just one neurotransmitter, we know of nearly 60 different neurotransmitters today, and it is virtually certain that there are many others that have yet to be discovered. We'll be discussing them many times later in a variety of contexts, but for now we ought to at least briefly note a few of the better-known neurotransmitters.

Acetylcholine (usually pronounced uh-**see'**-til-**koh"**-leen), or *ACh,* can be found throughout the nervous system. It is usually excitatory in its action. ACh is found in the brain, but most commonly works in synapses between motor neurons and muscle tissue cells. When it is released into the synapse, it stimulates the muscle cells to contract. The variety of food poisoning called botulism acts to blocks the release of acetylcholine and thus causes paralysis (as does the drug curare). In fact, some poisons (the venom of the Black Widow spider, for instance) have just the opposite effect, causing excess ACh to be released, which may result in muscle contractions or spasms so severe as to be deadly. As we shall see, acetylcholine is also implicated in normal memory function and is thus a prime object for research on memory problems such as those found in Alzheimer's disease.

Norepinephrine and *dopamine* are related in the sense that both seem to be involved in mood regulation. When there is too much norepinephrine in a person's brain and/or spinal cord, the result is often a feeling of arousal, anxiety, agitation, and the like. (One of the things that cocaine does is to increase the the release of norepinephrine, leading to a state of agitation and a "high" mood state.) Too little norepinephrine in the brain has been linked to feelings of depression. Dopamine is one of the neurotransmitters that most intrigue psychologists. It seems to be involved in a very wide range of psychological functioning. Either too much or too little dopamine within the nervous system seems to produce a number of different effects, depending primarily on which system of nerve fibers is involved. Dopamine has been associated with some of the thought and mood disturbances of some of the psychological disorders (schizophrenia in particular), and with impairment of movement—not enough dopamine and we find difficulty in making voluntary movements; too much and we find involuntary temors. Some pathways in the brain in which we find dopamine acting as a neurotranmitter are areas that have been the focus of research trying to find a physiological basis for reward or reinforcement.

Endorphins (plural because there seem to be several of them) are our natural pain suppressors. They are inhibitory neurotransmitters that block pain messages to the brain. By and large, what we call our pain threshold—our ability to tolerate levels of pain—is a function of the production of endorphins (Watkins & Mayer, 1982). With excess endorphins, we feel little pain; a deficit in endorphins results in more experienced pain. Surely, we'll return to this story later in more detail (see p. 150).

As you can imagine, we could continue this list through several more neurotransmitters, but for now it is the basic idea of what they do that matters: They excite or inhibit the transmission of neural impulses throughout the nervous system, and that excitation or inhibition can have significant effects on our thoughts, feelings, and behaviors.

Finally, it is important to be clear about one thing: Neural impulse transmission is seldom a matter of one neuron simply stimulating one other neuron that in turn stimulates yet one more. Remember that any neuron may have hundreds or thousands of axon terminals and synapses. Any one neuron, then, has the potential for exciting or inhibiting (or being excited by or inhibited by) many other neurons.

Before You Go On
▼▼▼▼▼▼▼▼

Summarize neural impulse transmission at the synapse.

▶ Nervous Systems: An Overview

Now that we have a sense of how neurons work individually and in combination, let's step back for a moment to consider the broader context in which they function. Behavior and mental activity generally require large numbers of integrated neurons working together in complex organized systems. Figure 2.6 shows how these systems are related to each other.

The first major division of the nervous system is determined wholly on the basis of anatomy. The **central nervous system (CNS)** includes all of the neurons found in the spinal cord and brain. In many ways, this system of nerves is the most complex and the most intimately involved in the control of our behavior and mental processes. The **peripheral nervous system (PNS)** is composed of all the neurons in our body NOT in the CNS—that is, the nerve fibers in our arms, face, fingers, intestines, and so forth. Neurons in the peripheral nervous system carry impulses either *from* the central nervous system to the muscles and glands (on *motor neurons*), or they carry impulses *to* the CNS from receptor cells (on *sensory neurons*).

central nervous system (CNS) those neurons in the brain and spinal cord

peripheral nervous system (PNS) those neurons not found in the brain or spinal cord, but in the peripheral organs of the body

Figure 2.6

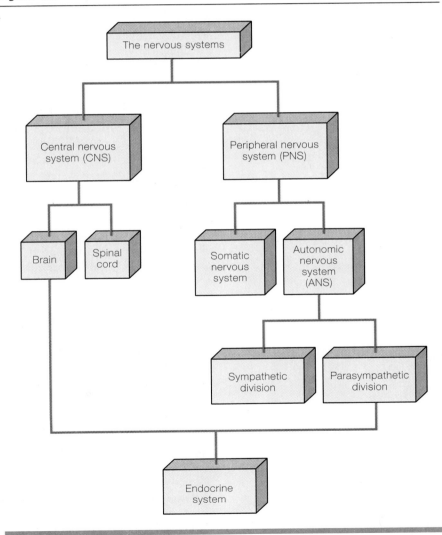

▲ *The organization of the human nervous systems.*

somatic nervous system sensory and motor neurons outside the CNS that serve the sense receptors and the skeletal muscles

autonomic nervous system (ANS) those neurons of the PNS that activate the smooth muscles and glands

sympathetic division (of the ANS) those neurons involved in states of emotionality

parasympathetic division (of the ANS) those neurons involved in the maintenance of states of calm and relaxation

endocrine system a network of glands that secrete hormones directly into the bloodstream

hormones A variety of chemical compounds, secreted by the glands of the endocrine system, many of which have effects on behavior or mental states

The peripheral nervous system is divided into two parts, based on the part of the body being served. The **somatic nervous system** includes those neurons outside the CNS that serve the muscles and that pick up impulses from the major sense receptors—the eyes and ears, for example. The other component of the PNS is the **autonomic nervous system (ANS)**, where "autonomic" means essentially the same thing as "automatic." The fibers of the ANS are involved in activating the smooth muscles (such as those of the stomach and intestines) and the glands. The ANS also provides feedback to the CNS on the activity of these internal processes.

Because the autonomic nervous system is so involved in emotional response, we'll return to it again in that context. For now, we simply note that the ANS is made up of two parts also, the **sympathetic division** and the **parasympathetic division**. These two divisions commonly work in opposition to each other, the former being active when we are in states of emotional excitement or under stress, and the latter becoming active when we are relaxed and quiet.

There is another system depicted in the overview of Figure 2.6—the **endocrine system**. The endocrine system can be influenced by the central nervous system, and can influence CNS activity, but *it is not a system of nerves*. It is an interconnected network of glands that has its effect on behavior through the secretion of chemicals called **hormones** into the bloodstream. Curiously, many of the hormones produced by the endocrine system are chemically very similar to neurotransmitters and have many of the same overall effects. The endocrine system's glands and hormones are controlled by both the brain and by the autonomic nervous system, which is why we have drawn it as we have in Figure 2.6. I've also included mention of the endocrine system here because its overall function is very similar to that of all the nervous systems: to transmit information from one part of the body to another. Nervous systems do so through the transmission of neural impulses; the endocrine system uses hormones sent through the bloodstream. The endocrine system is slower to react, but many of its effects are longer lasting. Most of the endocrine system's involvement in our behavior occurs in states of emotion and motivation, and we'll return to this system in the context of these topics.

There is good reason to separate out all of these different organizations of neurons. It's not just an academic exercise. It helps make a very complex system easier to deal with, and it reminds us that not all neurons in our body are there doing the same thing for the same purpose at the same time. But we have to keep in mind that the outline of Figure 2.6 is very simplified to this extent: All of the nerve fibers in each of the different systems have profound influences on each other. They are not at all as independent as our diagram might imply.

Now we are ready to begin our discussion of the structures and functions of the human central nervous system. Given its relative simplicity, we'll begin with the spinal cord.

Before You Go On

▼▼▼▼▼▼▼▼

Name the different human nervous systems, and indicate how they are related to each other.

► The Spinal Cord

As we have seen, the central nervous system consists of the brain and the spinal cord. In this section, we'll consider the structure and the function of the spinal cord, reserving our discussion of the brain for later. Now, as we look at the spinal cord, for the first time we clearly can see the role of the central nervous system in behavior.

► The Structure of the Spinal Cord

The spinal cord is a massive collection of neurons within the spinal column that looks rather like a section of rope or thick twine. It is surrounded and protected by the hard bone and cartilage of the vertebrae. Sometimes it is difficult to remember that the spinal cord itself is made up of soft, delicate nerve fibers living just inside our backbone.

A cross-section view of the spinal cord is illustrated in Figure 2.7. There are only a few structural details that need mention. These details will become relevant shortly, when we talk about spinal cord function. Note that the spinal cord itself—the neurons of the CNS—is located in the middle of the spinal column that reaches from your lower back to high in your neck, just below your brain. Then note that the nerve fibers that enter and leave the spinal cord do so from the side, not the front or back. Neurons and nerve fibers that carry impulses to the brain or spinal cord are called "sensory neurons" or fibers. Sensory neurons and their impulses enter the spinal cord on dorsal roots (dorsal means "toward the back"). Neurons and nerve fibers that carry impulses *from* the brain or spinal cord to muscles and glands are called

Figure 2.7

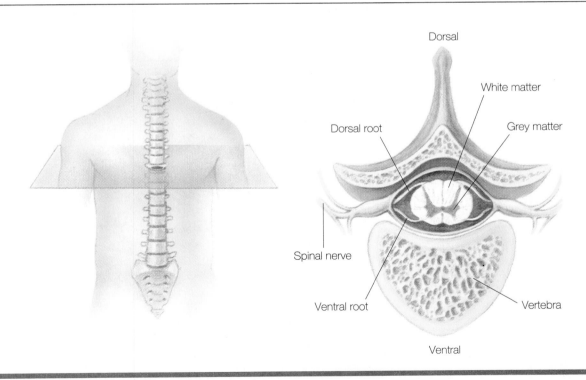

▲ *A cross-sectional view of the spinal cord showing dorsal and ventral roots and gray matter and white matter.*

"motor neurons" or fibers. Impulses that leave the spinal cord on motor neurons do so on ventral roots (ventral means "toward the front"). Neurons *within* the central nervous system are called "interneurons."

Also notice that the center area of the spinal cord itself is made up of dark gray matter, rather in the shape of a butterfly, while the outside area is light, white matter. Remember, this means that the center portion is filled with cell bodies, dendrites, and unmyelinated axons, while the outer section is filled with myelinated axons. Both of these observations about the spinal cord's structure provide keys to understanding its function.

▶ The Function of the Spinal Cord

The spinal cord has two major functions, one of which is to transmit neural impulses rapidly to and from the brain. Whenever sensory impulses originate below the neck and go to the brain, they do so through the spinal cord. When the brain transmits motor impulses to parts of the body below the neck, those impulses first travel down the spinal cord.

Impulses to and from different parts of the body leave and enter the spinal cord at different levels (impulses to and from the legs, for example, enter and leave very near the base of the spinal cord). If the spinal cord is cut or damaged, the consequences can be disastrous, resulting in a loss of feeling from the part of the body served and a loss of voluntary movement (paralysis) of the muscles in the region. Quite clearly, the higher that damage takes place, in the spinal cord, the greater will be the resulting losses.

The second major function of the spinal cord is the **spinal reflex**. Spinal reflexes are very simple and automatic behaviors that occur without conscious, voluntary action of the brain. To understand how these reflexes work, follow along with the drawing in Figure 2.8. Here we have yet another drawing of the spinal cord to which we've added a few features.

spinal reflex an automatic, involuntary response to a stimulus that involves sensory neurons carrying impulses to the spinal cord, interneurons within the spinal cord, and motor neurons carrying impulses to muscles

Figure 2.8

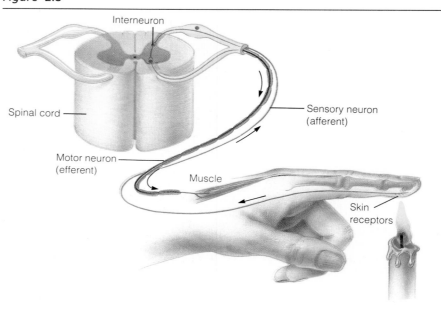

▲ *A spinal reflex. Stimulation of the receptor in turn stimulates sensory neurons, interneurons, and motor neurons. Impulses also ascend to the brain through tracts in the white matter.*

Let's trace your reaction to having your fingertip placed over the flame of a candle (we'll assume that you're blindfolded at the time). Receptor cells in your fingertip respond to the flame, sending neural impulses racing along sensory neurons, through a dorsal root and into the spinal cord. Then, two things happen at the same time. Impulses rush up the ascending pathways of the spinal cord's white matter to your brain, and impulses also travel to interneurons and go right back out of the spinal cord (through a ventral root) on motor neurons to your arm and hand, where muscles are stimulated to contract, and your hand jerks back from the flame.

Here is a simple reflex. Impulses travel *in* on sensory neurons, *within* on interneurons, and *out* on motor neurons. We're now clearly involved with behavior. We have an environmental stimulus (here, a flame), activity in the central nervous system (neurons in the spinal cord), and an observable response (hand withdrawal).

There are a couple of observations to make about reflexes of the type depicted in Figure 2.8 before we go on. First, the fact that neural impulses enter the spinal cord and immediately race to the brain is not indicated in the drawing. As you know very well, in a situation like the one depicted, you may jerk your hand back "without thinking about it," but very soon thereafter you are well aware of what has happened, that awareness occurs in the brain, not the spinal cord. It is also the case that some reflexes are more simple than the one in Figure 2.8 in that no interneurons are involved. That is, sensory neurons may form synapses directly with motor neurons inside the spinal cord—which is what happens in the familiar knee jerk reflex. On the other hand, you should realize that the total complex pattern of behaviors involved in having one's finger burned in a flame would actually involve many more than just three or four neurons.

Before You Go On
▼▼▼▼▼▼▼▼

Why does spinal cord injury sometimes cause paralysis?

Describe the major features of a spinal reflex.

▶ "Lower" Brain Centers

There are many different ways in which we could organize our discussion of the brain. We'll choose a very simple one and divide the brain into two parts: the cerebral cortex; and everything else, which I'm calling lower brain centers. Because the cerebral cortex does so many important things (such as initiating voluntary movements, storing memories, interpreting sensory inputs, and other activities we'll review shortly), this division is a reasonable one.

The lower brain centers are "lower" in two ways. They are physically located below the cerebral cortex, and they are the brain structures to develop first, both in an evolutionary sense, and within the developing human brain. They are the brain structures we most clearly share with other animals. You should not think of these lower centers as being unimportant. As we will soon see, our very survival depends on them. You can use Figure 2.9 as a guide to locate the different structures as we discuss them.

▶ The Brain Stem

As you look at the spinal cord and brain, you really can't tell where one ends and the other begins. There is no abrupt division line separating these

Figure 2.9

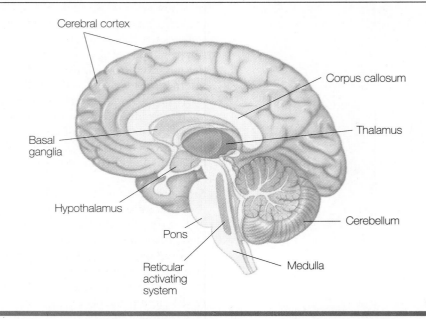

▲ *The major structures of the human brain. Note the orientation of the "lower" brain centers–the medulla, pons, cerebellum, and reticular activating system.*

brain stem the lowest part of the brain, just above the spinal cord, comprised of the medulla and the pons

medulla an area of the brain stem that monitors breathing and heart rate, and where most cross laterality occurs

nuclei small collections or bundles of neural cell bodies

cross-laterality the process of nerve fiber scrossing over the brain stem so that the left side of the body sends impulses to and receives impulses from the right side of the brain

pons a brain stem structure forming a bridge between the brain and the spinal cord

two parts of the central nervous system. Just above the spinal cord there is a slight widening of the cord that suggests that we're into brain tissue. Here, are two important structures that together form what we call the **brain stem**—the medulla and the pons.

The very lowest structure in the brain is the **medulla**. In one sense, the medulla acts like the spinal cord: Its major functions involve involuntary reflexes. There are many small structures called **nuclei** (actually, they're collections of neural cell bodies) within the medulla. These nuclei control such functions as reflexive eye and tongue movements. For example, you don't have to think about blinking your eye as something rushes toward it; your medulla will produce that eye blink reflexively.

The medulla also contains nuclei that control breathing reflexes and that monitor the muscles of the heart to keep it beating rhythmically. We *can* exercise some voluntary control over the nuclei of the medulla, but only within certain limits. The medulla controls our respiration, but we *can* override the medulla and hold our breath. We cannot, however, hold our breath until we die (as children occasionally threaten). We can hold our breath until we lose consciousness, which is to say until we give up higher-level voluntary control, and then the medulla picks up where it left off, and breathing continues.

It is at the level of the medulla that nerve fibers to and from the brain cross over from left to right and vice versa. By and large, the left side of the brain receives impulses from and sends impulses to the right side of the body. Similarly, the left side of the body sends impulses to and receives messages from the right side of the brain. This process of crossing fibers from one side of the body to the opposite side of the brain is called **cross-laterality,** and it takes place in the brain stem.

Just above the medulla is a structure called the **pons**. (The pons is one structure—there is no such thing as a pon.) Primarily, the pons serves as a bridge (which is what "pons" means in Latin), relaying sensory messages from the spinal cord up to higher brain centers and reversing the relay for motor impulses coming down. The cross-laterality that begins in the medulla continues in the pons.

Before You Go On

▼▼▼▼▼▼▼▼

Name the two brain stem structures, indicate where they are located, and describe what they do.

▶ The Cerebellum

cerebellum a spherical structure at the lower rear of the brain involved in the coordination of bodily movements

Your **cerebellum** (literally, "little brain") is about the size of your closed fist. It is more or less spherical in shape and is positioned right behind your pons, tucked up under the base of your skull. The cerebellum itself looks like a small brain. Its outer region (its cortex) is very convoluted, meaning that the tissue there is folded in upon itself, creating many deep crevices and lumps.

The major function of the cerebellum is to smooth and coordinate rapid body movements. Most intentional, voluntary movements originate in higher brain centers (usually, the motor area of the cerebral cortex), and are only coordinated by the cerebellum. Because of the close relationship between body movement and vision, many eye movements originate in the cerebellum.

Our ability to casually stoop, pick a dime off the floor, and slip it into our pocket involves a complex series of movements made smooth and regular by our cerebellum. When athletes train a movement, such as a golf swing or a gymnastic routine, we sometimes say that they are trying to "get into a groove," so that their trained movement can be made simply and smoothly. In a sense, such athletes are training their cerebellum.

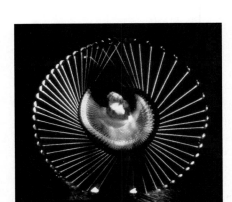

▲ *Learning to make a golf swing smooth and consistent may involve training the cerebellum.*

Few of our behaviors are as well-coordinated as are the movements required to make speech sounds. Next time you're talking to someone, try considering just how quickly and effortlessly your lips, mouth, and tongue are moving—thanks to your cerebellum. Damage to the cerebellum disrupts fine, coordinated movements. Speech becomes slurred; one may shake and stagger when walking. In fact, a person with cerebellum damage may appear to be quite drunk. (On what region of the brain do you suppose alcohol has a direct and noticeable effect? The cerebellum, of course.)

tremors involuntary, trembling, jerky movements

Damage to the cerebellum may disrupt motor activity in other ways. If the outer region of the cerebellum is damaged, a person may suffer jerky **tremors,** or involuntary trembling movements, when he or she tries to move (called "intention tremors"). Damage to inner areas of the cerebellum leads to "tremors at rest," where the limbs and/or head may shake or twitch even when the person tries to remain still.

Before You Go On

▼▼▼▼▼▼▼▼

Where is the cerebellum located, and what is its major function?

▶ The Reticular Activating System (RAS)

reticular activating system (RAS) a network of nerve fibers extending from the brain stem to the cerebrum that is involved in maintaining levels of arousal

The **reticular activating system (RAS)** is hardly a brain structure at all. It is a complex network of nerve fibers that begins down in the brain stem and works its way up through and around other structures all the way to the top portions of the brain.

Exactly what the reticular activating system does and how it works remain something of a mystery. As its name implies, the RAS is involved in determining our level of activation or arousal. It influences whether we're awake and attentive, sound asleep, or at some level in between. Electrical stimulation of the RAS can produce patterns of brain activity associated with being awake and alert. Lesions of the RAS cause a condition of constant sleep in laboratory animals (Lindsley et al., 1949; Moruzzi and Magoun, 1949). In a way, the reticular activating system acts like a valve allowing sensory messages to pass from lower centers up to the cerebral cortex or shutting them off partially or totally. What we don't know yet is just how the RAS does what it does, and what stimulates it to produce the effects that it does.

▶ The Limbic System

limbic system a collection of structures, including the amygdala and septum, which are involved in emotionality; and the hippocampus, involved in forming long-term memories

The **limbic system** is a collection of structures rather than a single unified one. It is of utmost importance in controlling the behaviors of nonhuman animals, which do not have as large or well-developed a cerebral cortex as humans. The limbic system controls many complex behavioral patterns that we usually think of as instinctive. The location of the limbic system, and its constituent parts are presented in Figure 2.10.

Within the brain, parts of the limbic system are involved in the display of emotional reactions. One center in the system, the *amygdala*, produces reactions of rage and/or aggression when stimulated, while the *septum* has the opposite effect, reducing the intensity of emotional responses when it is stimulated. The impact of the amygdala and septum on emotional reactions is quite immediate and direct in nonhumans. In humans, it is more subtle, reflecting the influence of other brain centers.

Another center in the limbic system, called the *hippocampus*, is less involved in emotion and more involved with the forming of memories. People with a damaged hippocampus are often unable to "move" experiences into permanent memory storage. They can remember events for short periods of time. They also may be able to remember events from the distant past, but only if those events occurred before the hippocampus was damaged.

Figure 2.10

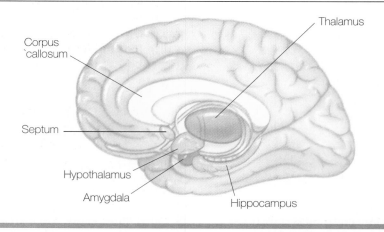

▲ *A number of small structures make up the limbic system, including the amygdala, septum, hypothalamus, and hippocampus.*

▶ The Hypothalamus

hypothalamus a small structure near the limbic system in the center of the brain, associated with feeding, drinking, temperature regulation, sex, and aggression

The **hypothalamus** is often considered to be a part of the limbic system. It is located near the limbic system, and it too is involved in our motivational and emotional reactions. Among other things, it influences many of the functions of the endocrine system, which, as we have seen, is involved in emotional response.

The major responsibility of the hypothalamus seems to be to monitor critical internal bodily functions. It has centers (*nuclei* again) that control feeding behaviors. It is sensitive to the amount of fluid in our bodies and indirectly gives rise to the feeling of being thirsty. The hypothalamus also acts as a thermostat, triggering a number of automatic reactions should we become too warm or too cold. This structure also is involved in aggressive and sexual behaviors. It acts as a regulator for many hormones. Recently, the hypothalamus has been implicated as having a direct role in the development of homosexual orientations (LeVay, 1991)—an implication we'll return to later (p. 318). To be sure, we'll discuss the hypothalamus again in several contexts, when we study needs, motives, and emotions in later chapters.

▶ The Thalamus

thalamus the last sensory relay station; it sends impulses to the appropriate area of the cerebral cortex

The last structure to discuss as a lower brain center is the **thalamus**. It is positioned right below the cerebral cortex and is intimately involved with its functioning.

Many impulses from the cerebral cortex to lower brain structures, the spinal cord, and eventually out to the peripheral nervous system pass through the thalamus. Overcoming the normal function of the medulla (by voluntarily holding our breath, for example) involves messages that pass through the thalamus. The major role of the thalamus, however, involves the processing of information from the senses.

In handling incoming sensory impulses, the thalamus collects and directs sensory messages to the appropriate areas of the cerebral cortex. Sensory messages from our lower body, our eyes, ears, and other senses (except for smell, which has its own special pathway) pass through the thalamus. For example, it is at the thalamus that nerve fibers from the eyes are sorted out and projected to the back of the cerebral cortex.

Before You Go On
▼▼▼▼▼▼▼▼▼

Indicate the location, and briefly describe the major function of: the RAS, the limbic system, the hypothalamus, and the thalamus.

▶ The Cerebral Cortex

cerebral cortex (or cerebrum) the large, convoluted outer covering of the brain that is the seat of cognitive functioning and voluntary action

The human brain is a homely organ. There's just nothing very pretty about it. When we look at a human brain, the first thing we are likely to notice is the large, soft, lumpy, creviced outer covering of the **cerebral cortex** ("cortex" means outer bark, or covering). The cerebral cortex (sometimes called the cerebrum, or just the cortex) of the human brain is significantly larger than any other brain structure. Indeed, it is the complex and delicate development of the cerebral cortex that makes us uniquely human. It is our center for the processing and storage of information about the world in which we live and is the starting place for virtually all of our voluntary action.

▶ *Lobes and Localization*

Figure 2.11 presents two views of the cerebral cortex, a top view and a side view. You can see from these illustrations that the deep folds of tissue of the human cerebral cortex provide us with markers for dividing it into areas. The most noticeable division of the cortex can be seen in the top view, where we can see the very deep crevice that runs down the middle from front to back, dividing it into the left and right **cerebral hemispheres.**

A side view of a hemisphere (Fig. 2.11 shows us the left one) allows us to see the four major divisions of the cerebral cortex that are found in each hemisphere. These divisions are referred to as *lobes* of the brain. The **frontal lobes** are the largest and are defined by two large crevices. The **temporal lobes** are located at the temples, with one on each side of the brain. The **occipital lobes,** at the very back of the brain, are defined somewhat arbitrarily, with no large crevices setting them off, and the **parietal lobes** are wedged in behind the frontal lobes and above the occipital and temporal lobes.

We have learned much about what normally happens in the different regions of the cerebral cortex. Scientists have mapped out what goes on in most of the cortex, but many of the details of cerebral function are yet to be understood. There are three major areas that have been mapped: *sensory areas,* where impulses from our sense receptors are sent; *motor areas,* where many of our voluntary movements originate; and *association areas,* where higher mental processes are thought to occur. We'll review each of these areas in turn, referring to Figure 2.12, where general locations are indicated.

Sensory Areas. Let's review for just a minute. Receptor cells (specialized neurons) in our sense organs respond to stimuli in the environment. These cells then pass neural impulses along sensory nerve fibers, eventually to the cerebral cortex. Senses in our body below our neck send impulses first to the spinal cord, then up the spinal cord, through the brain stem and thalamus, and beyond. After they leave the thalamus, impulses from our senses go to a particular **sensory area,** depending on which sense is involved.

cerebral hemispheres the two halves of the cerebral cortex, separated by a deep fissure running from front to back

frontal lobes the largest of the cerebral lobes, located in front of the central fissure and above the lateral fissure

temporal lobes the lobes of the cerebrum, located at the temples

occipital lobes the cerebral lobes at the very back of the brain

parietal lobes the lobes of the cerebrum found behind the frontal lobes, in front of the occipital lobes, and above the temporal lobes

sensory areas those areas of the cerebral cortex that receive impulses from our sense receptors

Figure 2.11

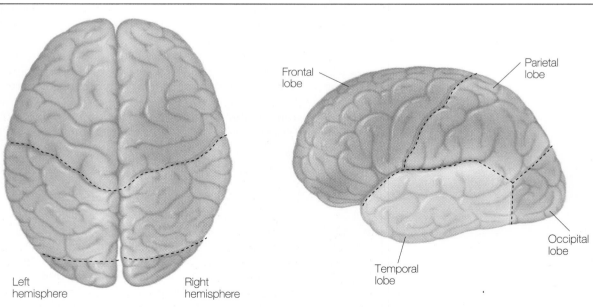

Left hemisphere   Right hemisphere

Frontal lobe   Parietal lobe   Occipital lobe   Temporal lobe

▲ *The human cerebral cortex is divided into the left and right hemispheres, which in turn are divided into four lobes that house various functional areas.*

Figure 2.12

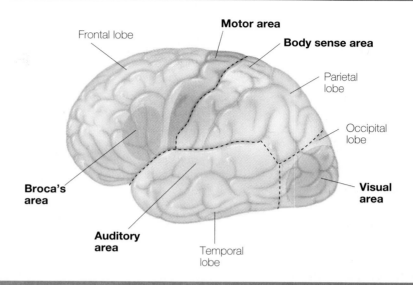

▲ *The human cerebral cortex areas of localization.*

Reflecting their relative importance to us, large areas of the cerebral cortex are involved with vision and hearing. Virtually the entire occipital lobe processes visual information (the "visual area" in Fig. 2.12). Auditory (hearing) impulses end up in large centers ("auditory areas") in the temporal lobes.

Our body senses (touch, pressure, pain, and so on) from different parts of our body send impulses to a strip at the very front of the parietal lobe (the "body sense area" in Fig. 2.12). Within this area of the parietal lobe we can map out specific regions that correspond to different parts of the body. When we do so, we find that some body parts—the face, lips, and fingertips, for example—are overrepresented in the body sense area of the cerebral cortex, reflecting their high sensitivity. (In other words, some parts of the body, even some very small ones, are processed in larger areas of the cortex than are other parts of the body.)

This is a good place to remind ourselves of the concept of *cross-laterality* (p. 62). Cross-laterality refers to the fact that information from senses on the left side of the body crosses over to the right side of the brain, and vice versa, with this crossing occurring in the brain stem. When someone touches your right arm, that information ends up in your left parietal lobe. A tickle to your left foot is processed by the right side of your cerebral cortex.

Motor Areas. We have already seen that some of our actions—at least very simple and reflexive ones—originate in our central nervous system below the cerebral cortex. Although some lower brain centers may be involved, it is still fair to say that most voluntary activity originates in the cerebral cortex—in strips at the very back of our frontal lobes. These **motor areas** (remember, there are two of them, left and right) are directly across the central fissure from the body sense areas in the parietal lobe (see Fig. 2.12). I need to make the disclaimer that the actual, thoughtful decision making process of whether or not one *should* move probably occurs elsewhere, almost certainly further to the front of the frontal lobes.

As is the case for sensory processing, we find that some muscle groups (such as those that control movements of the hands and mouth) are processed by disproportionately larger areas of cerebral cortex.

motor areas the strips at the back of the frontal lobes that control voluntary movement

As you know, we also find cross-laterality at work with the motor area. It is your right hemisphere's motor area that controls the movements of the left side of your body. Someone who has had a cerebral stroke (a disruption of blood flow in the brain that results in the loss of neural tissue) in the left side of their brain will have impaired movement of their right side.

Association Areas. Once we have located the areas of the cerebral cortex that process sensory information and originate motor responses, we've still got a lot of cortex left over. The remaining areas of the cerebral cortex are called **association areas.** There are three of them in each hemisphere: the frontal, parietal, and temporal. Exactly what happens in these association areas is not well understood.

There is considerable support for the idea that it is in our association areas that so-called higher mental processes occur. The frontal association

association areas the areas of the frontal, parietal, and temporal lobes in which higher mental processing occurs

---

Psychology in the Real World

▲▲▲▲▲▲▲▲▲▲▲▲▲▲▲

Who Left the Tack on the Hallway Floor?

Do you remember at the beginning of this chapter, I raised some questions about the underlying physiological processes that occur if you were to step on a tack? Now that we've been through most of our discussion of the central nervous system, this may be a good time to see how many of those questions we can answer.

The point of the tack punctures the sole of your foot and stimulates a nerve cell. *What does it mean to say that a nerve cell is stimulated? What kind of nerve cell reacts to tacks? For that matter, what IS a nerve cell?* Nerve cells, or neurons, are living cells that transmit impulses by releasing a tension that builds up between electrically charged chemical ions. When neurons are at rest (not stimulated), negatively charged ions are concentrated inside the neuron, and positive ions are concentrated outside the neuron. Neurons can be stimulated to release their potential and transmit impulses in many different ways. Some specialized neurons respond directly to physical stimulation. The neurons that carry impulses from our senses (such as pain) to our nervous system are called sensory neurons.

The cell that is stimulated by the tack sends a message to other nerve cells. *Wait a minute! What do you mean "message?" How do messages get from one nerve cell to another?* Saying that neurons send "messages" is a casual way of saying that they transmit impulses, changes in electrochemical potentials that travel from dendrite end to the axon end. Once at the end of the axon, impulses have reached the synapse, where the nature of impulse transmission changes. At the synapse, neurotransmitters are released from vesicles held in axon endings. The neurotransmitters then travel across the synaptic cleft to the next neuron, stimulating it to fire.

Messages now race up your leg to the base of the spinal cord. *Why to the spinal cord? What does the spinal cord look like? What does it do?* The spinal cord is one part of the central nervous system, a mass of neurons that looks rather like a piece of rope, extending from your lower back up to the base of your brain. One of the functions of the spinal cord is to provide a quick route to and from the brain, which is one reason why impulses enter there.

areas are involved in a number of such processes. As Pierre-Paul Broca (1824–1880) discovered more than a century ago, most language and speech behaviors are localized in the frontal association area. Damage to the very front of the frontal lobes often interrupts or destroys the ability to plan ahead, to think quickly, or to think things through.

In this context, we should remind ourselves not to get too carried away with cerebral localization of function. Let's not fall into the trap of coming to believe that separate parts of the cerebral cortex operate independently and have the sole responsibility for any one function. This is a point that neurologist Marcel Kinsbourne makes this way: "There are no discontinuities in the brain. No independent channels traverse it; nor is its territory divisible into areas that house autonomous processors" (1982, p. 412). This will be particularly important to keep in mind as we now look at the division of the cerebral cortex into right and left hemispheres.

Once in the spinal cord, messages now go in two different directions: up to the brain and back down to the muscles in your leg. *How do the messages get to my brain? For that matter, how do they get to my leg? Do they go to my brain first?* Impulses get to your brain by racing up nerve fibers in the white matter of your spinal cord. They'll pass through several structures, including the pons and the thalamus, on their way to your cerebral cortex. Neurons that carry these impulses are called interneurons because they are within the central nervous system. Once into the gray matter of the spinal cord, impulses also race back down to your leg to muscles there on motor neurons or motor fibers. These impulses do not go to the brain first—they are involved in a spinal reflex.

Messages from the spinal cord to your leg stimulate muscles to lift your leg quickly off the floor. At the same time, those messages to your brain are being interpreted. *Do you mean to say that my leg lifts up off the floor without my brain even thinking about it?* That's right. This is a spinal reflex action for which your brain is quite unnecessary. *Doesn't my brain have to control that movement?* No, at least not the original movement of jerking your foot up. True, most movements, certainly our voluntary, conscious movements do originate in the brain—usually at the very back of our frontal lobes of the cerebral cortex, in fact.

You identify the source of your pain as a tack. Still hopping on one foot, you wonder who left the tack on the hallway floor, and start to get angry. *Ah, but to recognize a tack implies that I'm using my memory and remember what a tack is. Where are memories stored in the brain? Are there separate parts of the brain involved in emotions like anger?* Yes, recognizing that you've stepped on a tack does require memory, and we are quite sure that memories are stored in the brain—although we're not at all sure just how. More than that, it is most likely that memories are stored in those parts of the cerebral cortex we call association areas. There are many areas of the brain that become involved in emotionality. Perhaps of primary concern is the collection of structures called the limbic system.

And here's one more: *Suppose I stepped on that tack with my right foot, to which side of the brain would impulses be sent?* This is an easy one, isn't it? Given the cross-laterality that occurs in the brain stem the left side of your cerebral cortex would be first to know about the tack.

Before You Go On
▼▼▼▼▼▼▼▼

Given a side view of the brain, locate the four lobes of the cerebral cortex.

Locate the primary sensory, motor, and association areas of the cerebrum, and describe what happens there.

▶ The Two Cerebral Hemispheres

Even the ancient Greeks knew that the cerebral cortex was divided into two hemispheres. That there should be a division of the cerebral cortex into two halves seems quite natural. After all, we have two eyes, arms, legs, lungs, kidneys, and so forth. Within the last 30 years, interest in this hemispheric division has heightened as we have accumulated evidence that each half of the cerebral cortex may have primary responsibility for different mental functions.

In most humans, the left hemisphere of the cerebral cortex is usually the larger of the two halves, contains a higher proportion of gray matter, and is probably the dominant hemisphere (more active in more tasks). We already noted that the language center is housed in the left cerebral hemisphere. At least this is true for virtually all right-handed people. For some, but not all, left-handers, language may be processed primarily by the right hemisphere.

Because humans are so language-oriented, not much attention was given to the "lowly" right hemisphere; but, a remarkable surgical procedure first performed in the 1960s provided us with new insights about the two cerebral hemispheres (Sperry, 1968; 1982; Springer & Deutsch, 1981).

Normally, the two hemispheres of the cerebral cortex are richly interconnected by a series of fibers called the **corpus callosum** (which can be seen in Figure 2.10). Through the corpus callosum, one side of our cortex remains in constant and immediate contact with the other. Separating the functions of the two hemispheres is possible, however, through a surgical technique called a **split-brain procedure** which is neither as complicated nor as dangerous as it may sound. The procedure amounts to destroying the corpus callosum's connections between the two hemispheres. The surgery was first tried on humans in 1961 by Joseph Brogan in an attempt to lessen the severity of the symptoms of epilepsy. As an irreversible treatment of last resort, the split-brain procedure was found to be very successful.

Most of what we know about the activities of the cerebral hemispheres we have learned from split-brain subjects, both human and animal. One thing that makes this procedure remarkable is that under normal circumstances, split-brain patients behave quite normally. Only in the laboratory can we see the results of having made the hemispheres of the cerebral cortex function independently (*e.g.*, Gazzaniga & LeDoux, 1978; Hellige, 1983). To be sure, all of the answers aren't in, but we can draw some tentative conclusions.

Experiments with split-brain patients confirm that speech production is a left hemisphere function in a great majority of people (again, virtually all right handers). Suppose you have your hands behind your back. I place a house key in your left hand, and ask you to tell me what it is. Your left hand feels the key. Impulses travel up your left arm and the spinal cord, and cross over to your *right* cerebral hemisphere—remember cross-laterality. You can readily tell me that the object in your hand is a key because your brain is intact. Your right hemisphere passes information about the key to

corpus callosum a network of nerve fibers that interconnect the two hemispheres of the cerebrum

split-brain procedure a surgical technique of severing the corpus callosum, causing the two hemispheres to operate independently

your left hemisphere, and your left hemisphere directs you to say, "It's a key." Now suppose that your corpus callosum is severed (you are a split-brain subject). Now you cannot answer my question, even though you understand it perfectly. Why not? Your right brain knows that the object in your left hand is a key, but without a corpus callosum, it has no way to inform the left hemisphere, where your speech production apparatus is located. You *would* be able to point out the key from among other objects placed before you, under the direction of the right cerebral hemisphere. Once your eyes saw you do so, they would communicate that information to your left hemisphere, and now it too would know, and tell us, what your right hemisphere knew all along!

A major task of the left hemisphere then is the production of speech. But before we go any further, we need to pause and caution against over-interpretation. (Remember what I said in the *Introduction* about thinking critically?) When results from split-brain studies were first made known, many people—psychologists and non-psychologists alike—rushed to premature conclusions. What we now believe is that virtually no behavior, virtually no mental process, is the simple and single product of just one hemisphere (*e.g.,* Hellige, 1990). It is more reasonable to say that one hemisphere dominates the other, or is the primary processing area, for certain actions. For example, the left hemisphere is dominant in the perception and interpretation of speech. *But* some language processing seems to be more the responsibility of the right hemisphere. The right hemisphere is more involved in the processing of common phrases and clichés, such as "How do you do?" or "Have a nice day!" (*e.g.,* Kempler & Van Lancker, 1987).

Granted that we have to be careful and shouldn't *overinterpret*, what are some of the activities that are processed *primarily* in one hemisphere or the other? We've seen that the left hemisphere can be given credit for most of our language skills, and given our reliance on language, that's no small matter. Simple arithmetic tasks of calculation also seem to be primarily a left brain function. Indeed, the left hemisphere often has been credited with

▲ *A major task of the left hemisphere of the cerebral cortex is the reception and production of language and speech.*

▲ There is evidence that creativity, particularly for drawing and spatial relations, is largely a function of the right hemisphere of the cerebral cortex.

the processing of information in an analytical, one-piece-at-a-time sort of way, although the data here are a bit tenuous (Hellige, 1990, p. 59).

What then of the right hemisphere? The best evidence is that the right hemisphere dominates in the processing of visually presented information (Bradshaw & Nettleton, 1981; Kosslyn, 1987). Putting together a jigsaw puzzle, for instance, uses the right hemisphere more than the left. Skill in the visual arts (painting and drawing, for example) is associated with the right hemisphere more than the left. The right hemisphere is also credited with being more involved in our emotionality—both interpreting emotional stimuli and expressing emotional reactions. Consistent with the hypothesis that the left hemisphere tends to be analytic and sequential in dealing with information, the right is thought to be better able to grasp the big picture, see the overall view of things, and to be somewhat more creative.

Even these few possibilities are intriguing. There is little doubt that there are differences in how the two sides of the cerebral cortex process information. But the differences are slight, and many remain controversial. In fact, we are finding that the more we study hemispheric differences, the more we tend to find similarities. It seems that any special programs or courses that claim to be designed to train or educate one side of our brains to the exclusion of the other are misguided, no matter how well-intentioned they may be.

Before You Go On

▼▼▼▼▼▼▼▼▼

What is a split-brain procedure, why has it been done on humans, and what have we learned from it?

Briefly summarize the different functions of the left and right cerebral hemispheres of the human brain.

▼▼▼
Thinking Critically about Psychology

1. Think back to the opening story about stepping on a tack. This scenario might be of interest to different sorts of professionals: medical researchers, biochemists, physicists, and architects who design hallways, just to name a few. How many different professionals can you think of who could have some interest in the process of stepping on a tack on a hallway floor? What particular point of view does each bring to his or her interest? How is the interest or approach of a psychologist different from that of the others?

2. How many ways can you think of from your own experience to support the hypothesis that claims: "To say that a characteristic is largely or even totally inherited does not mean that that characteristic cannot be changed by influences of the environment."?

3. Let's anticipate a discussion we'll be having soon: Suppose it turns out that Asian-American students in the United States consistently outscore other students on tests of academic achievement and IQ tests. What, if anything, does this tell us about the genetics of intelligence? Are Asian-Americans intellectually superior to other Americans? And, of course, we have to add: "Why or why not?"

4. How do you suppose that scientists have learned so much about the intricate workings of the neural impulse and impulse transmission at the synapse?

5. What would happen if someone were to take a drug that delivered extra amounts of inhibitory neurotransmitter substance to the synapses of the nervous system? What if someone took a drug that stopped neurons from releasing excitatory neurotransmitters in the first place? Do such drugs exist?

6. What happens to neurotransmitter chemicals once they perform their function?

7. Can you review each of the structures of the spinal cord and brain that has been introduced in this chapter and indicate what would happen if that structure were either stimulated or destroyed?

8. If you wanted to begin an education/training program that "fully trained all aspects of the human brain," what sorts of training exercises would you include in your program? For example, how would you "train" the left and the right hemispheres of the cerebral cortex?

9. As it happens, the physical size of one's brain seems to have little to do with what we normally call "intelligence." Why doesn't it? What aspect of the brain does?

Summary

▼▼▼▼▼▼▼▼▼▼▼▼▼▼▼▼▼▼▼▼▼▼▼▼▼▼▼▼▼▼▼▼▼

What are some of the basic concepts involved in any discussion of the genetic transmission of physical characteristics? Physical characteristics are inherited to the extent that genes, carried on chromosomes, are passed from the sex cells of parents to the child. Each cell in the body contains 23 pairs of chromosomes in its nucleus (except the sex cells, which contain only 23 single chromosomes). Genes may be *dominant,* which means that the trait they carry necessarily will be expressed, or *recessive,* in which case they must be paired with another similar recessive gene in order to be expressed as a trait (review Fig. 2.1). *Pages 48–50*

What is it that we inherit from our parents? In discussing the inheritance of physical or psychological traits, we always need to keep in mind that we directly inherit only genes, not behaviors or abilities or traits of any kind. *Pages 49–50*

What are the major structures of a neuron? There are three major structures: the *cell body,* which houses the nucleus of the cell, a number of *dendrites,* which usually receive neural impulses, and an *axon,* which carries impulses away from the cell body. *Page 51*

What is myelin, and what is its function? The axons of some neuron are covered by a white, fatty myelin sheath that insulates and protects the delicate axon and speeds impulses along the axon. Even myelinated axons end with a set of bare, branching axon terminals. *Pages 51–52*

What is the basic process involved when a neuron fires? When a neuron fires, a tension created by an imbalance of electrically charged chemical ions is quickly released. When a neuron is NOT firing, or is at rest, the inside of the neuron is more negatively charged than is the outside (a resting potential of –70mv). At the point where the impulse occurs, this polarity changes, and the inside of the neuron becomes momentarily positive compared to the outside (an action potential of +40mv). *Pages 52–53*

Summarize neural impulse transmission at the synapse. At the synapse, an impulse triggers the release of neurotransmitter chemicals, which flood across the synaptic cleft to the membranes of adjacent neurons. If sufficient quantities of neurotransmitter is released, either new impulses will be excited, or the process will be inhibited. *Page 53*

Name the different human nervous systems, and indicate how they are related to each other. See Figure 2.6. The major division is into CNS and PNS, where the CNS is divided into the brain and the spinal cord and

the PNS is divided into the somatic and autonomic (ANS) nervous systems. The ANS is further divided into the sympathetic and parasympathetic divisions. The endocrine system is a network of glands that, under the direction of the brain and the ANS, secretes hormones into the bloodstream which, in turn, influence behavior and mental processes. *Pages 57–58*

Why does spinal cord injury sometimes cause paralysis? If the spinal cord is damaged, impulses originating in the brain to move parts of the body cannot get past the damaged area to stimulate the appropriate muscles, resulting in paralysis. *Pages 59–60*

Describe the major features of a spinal reflex. In a spinal reflex, impulses enter the spinal cord on sensory fibers, may form a synapse with interneurons, and then exit the spinal cord on motor fibers to activate a muscle response. At the same time, impulses are sent to the brain on fibers in the spinal cord's white matter. *Pages 60–61*

Name the two brain stem structures, indicate where they are located, and describe what they do. The brain stem is made up of the medulla, at the very base of the brain, which controls several important reflexes, monitors heart rate and breathing, and is where most cross-laterality occurs, and the pons, just above the medulla, which acts like a bridge, passing impulses between the spinal cord and the brain. *Pages 61–63*

Where is the cerebellum located, and what is its major function? The cerebellum is located at the base of the brain and is most involved in the smoothing and coordinating of rapid muscular movements. *Page 63*

Indicate the location, and briefly describe the major function of: the RAS, the limbic system, the hypothalamus, and the thalamus. The RAS (or reticular activating system) extends from the brain stem through the middle of the brain to the cerebral cortex and is involved in maintaining levels of arousal. The limbic system, just above the brain stem, is involved in emotional expression (the amygdala and septum in particular) and the transfer of information to long-term memory (the hippocampus). The hypothalamus, which is near the limbic system, is involved in such reactions and responses as feeding, drinking, sex, aggression, and temperature regulation. The thalamus, located just below the cerebral cortex, is a final relay station for sensory impulses that it projects up to the appropriate parts of the cerebrum. *Pages 63–64*

Given a side view of the brain, locate the four lobes of the cerebral cortex. The location of the frontal, temporal, parietal, and occipital lobes can be reviewed in Figure 2.11. *Pages 66–69*

Locate the primary sensory, motor, and association areas of the cerebrum, and describe what happens there. Figure 2.12 shows the location of these areas. The sensory areas of the cerebral cortex (visual, auditory, and body sense) receive impulses (through the thalamus) from our senses. Voluntary motor activity is initiated in the motor areas, and cognitive processes, such as memory, thinking, and problem solving, are thought to occur in the so-called association areas. *Pages 66–69*

What is a split-brain procedure, why has it been done on humans, and what have we learned from it? The split-brain procedure severs the fibers of the corpus callosum, the structure that carries impulses back and forth between the two cerebral hemispheres. The procedure, then, allows the hemispheres to operate independently. It is used as a treatment of last resort for epilepsy. *Page 70*

Briefly summarize the different functions of the left and right cerebral hemispheres of the human brain. Although one hemisphere may dominate another in some cases, seldom does one have total and complete control of any important brain function. However, it is safe to say that language and speech are usually processed in the left hemisphere, while visual, spatial information is usually processed in the right. Also possible, but less certain, is the left hemisphere's dominance in simple calculations and the sequential, analytical processing of information, while the right hemisphere is thought to be more involved with the "big picture," with the visual arts, and with emotionality. *Pages 70–72*

2.1 At conception, human sex cells combine to create a new cell that contains   a) 23 genes.   b) 23 pairs of genes.   c) 23 chromosomes.   d) 23 pairs of chromosomes. *Page 49*

2.2 Blue eye coloration in humans is a recessive trait, which means that a blue-eyed child   a) must have two blue-eyed parents.   b) must have one blue-eyed parent, either mother or father.   c) must have received genes for blue eyes from both parents.   d) must have received genes for blue eyes from only one parent, either mother or father. *Page 49*

2.3 Which statement most reasonably summarizes the contributions of heredity and the environment in shaping human traits?   a) The environment cannot change or influence genetic predispositions.   b) Human traits are completely determined by environmental influences.   c) Genetic predispositions and experiences in the environment interact to produce human traits.   d) About half of all human traits are determined by inheritance and about half are determined by the environment. *Page 50*

2.4 Of the following structures, which is likely to occur in neurons in the greatest number?   a) dendrites   b) nuclei   c) axons   d) cell bodies. *Page 51*

2.5 Myelin sheaths serve a number of different functions. Which of these is NOT something that myelin does?   a) It insulates axons from nearby neurons.   b) It helps to speed up neural impulses.   c) It contains the neurons's genes and chromosomes.   d) It protects the delicate axon from physical damage. *Page 52*

2.6 If a neuron dies: a) a new neuron will be created to take its place.   b) the result will be paralysis.   c) its function may be replaced by the action of other neurons.   d) the psychological experience will be a slight sensation of pain. *Page 52*

2.7 True or False?   Myelinated neurons carry impulses faster than do unmyelinated neurons. *Page 52*

2.8 True or False?   The number of neurons in our brains gradually increases from birth until they begin to die off in old age. *Page 52*

2.9 When a neuron is "at rest,"   a) it has no electrical charge.   b) the inside of the neuron has a negative charge compared to the outside.   c) it is in the process of "firing" or transmitting an impulse   d) chemical ions are racing in and out of the neuron through its membrane. *Page 53*

2.10 When an impulse moves down, or along, a neuron, what physically moves from one end of the neuron to the other?   a) the chemical ions   b) the neural membrane   c) the fluids within the neuron   d) nothing. *Page 53*

2.11 Although there are many specific neurotransmitters, we can classify them in terms of their action as being either   a) central or peripheral.   b) sensory or motor.   c) excitatory or inhibitory.   d) axonic or dendritic. *Page 56*

2.12 The action of neurotransmitters at the synapse is basically a(n) _____ process.   a) electrical   b) mechanical   c) chemical   d) psychological. *Page 54*

2.13 Of the following, which nervous system is most intimately involved in our experience of emotionality?   a) the peripheral nervous system   b) the parasympathetic nervous system   c) the somatic nervous system   d) the sympathetic nervous system. *Page 58*

2.14 When we look at a cross-section of the spinal cord, we clearly see areas that are made up of white matter. In this white matter we have   a) the location where reflexes occur.   b) fibers going to and from the brain.   c) dorsal roots, but few, if any, ventral roots.   d) the part of the spinal cord that controls our emotions. *Page 60*

2.15 In a spinal reflex, neural impulses enter the spinal cord on: a) motor neurons.   b) ascending tracts or fibers.   c) sensory neurons.   d) descending tracts or fibers. *Page 61*

2.16 True or False?   The correct sequence of events in a spinal reflex may be summarized as: In on sensory neurons, within on interneurons, and out on motor neurons. *Page 61*

2.17 As one travels up through the brain from the spinal cord, the first brain structure to be encountered would be the   a) corpus callosum.   b) basal ganglia.   c) medulla.   d) thalamus. *Page 62*

2.18 Which of the following is best associated with the medulla?   a) thinking or problem solving   b) breathing reflexes   c) sensory projections to the cerebral cortex   d) muscle coordination. *Page 62*

2.19 Cross laterality occurs in the   a) spinal cord.   b) brain stem   c) limbic system.   d) base of the cortex. *Page 62*

2.20 If someone were to cut your pons, the result would be that you would be   a) blind.   b) unable to control your emotions   c) unable to store information in memory.   d) paralyzed from the neck down. *Page 62*

2.21 True or False? As the human organism develops, the first brain structure to develop is the most important: the cerebral cortex. *Page 61*

2.22 Speaking requires many different, interrelated areas of the brain. Which lower brain center is involved in coordinating the muscles that produce speech sounds? a) the right frontal lobe b) the limbic system c) the medulla d) the cerebellum. *Page 63*

2.23 If I were to electrically stimulate the reticular activating system of a sleeping cat, the result would be that the cat would a) no longer demonstrate normal emotional responses. b) die. c) begin to make small twitching movements, indicative of dreaming. d) wake up. *Page 64*

2.24 A railroad worker by the name of Phineas Gage survived an accident in which an iron bar was thrust through his head, destroying brain tissue. One result of the accident was that Gage had much less control of his emotional reactions, which suggests that the accident cut tissues between his cerebral cortex and his: a) limbic system. b) corpus callosum. c) medulla. d) cerebellum. *Page 64*

2.25 Which lower brain center is most clearly involved in our experience of being thirsty? a) the hypothalamus b) the hippocampus c) the amygdala d) the septum. *Page 65*

2.26 The brain structure that sends, or projects, sensory impulses to the appropriate area of the cerebral cortex is the a) thalamus. b) projectorator. c) medulla nuclei. d) sense area of the parietal lobe. *Page 65*

2.27 Our body senses (touch, pressure and so on) are largely processed in the front of the _____ lobe of the cerebral cortex. a) occipital b) parietal c) temporal d) frontal. *Page 67*

2.28 Most of the neurons located in the gray matter at the center of the spinal cord are: a) myelinated neurons. b) sensory neurons. c) motor neurons. d) interneurons. *Pages 59–60*

2.29 True or False? Visual information is processed in the occipital lobe of the cerebral cortex. *Page 67*

2.30 A person has had a split-brain operation to separate her left and right cerebral hemispheres. She is blindfolded. A paper clip is placed in her LEFT hand and we ask her to tell us what we have placed there. She will a) tell us that the object is a paper clip and can point to it when it is placed on a table with other objects. b) have no idea what the object is. c) be unable to tell us what it is at first, but can point to it when it is placed on a table with other objects. d) respond just as if we had placed it in her right hand. *Pages 70–71*

2.31 True or False? Someone whose corpus callosum has been severed in a split-brain operation probably will have to be hospitalized or closely supervised for the rest of his or her life. *Page 70*

Human Development

In her book *Word Associations of Young Children*, Doris Entwistle of Johns Hopkins University, claimed that young children produce word association responses of a different sort than do older children and adults (Entwistle, 1966). I was intrigued by her findings and decided to measure how long it took children to produce associations. The procedure was simple: Present a stimulus word, have a child respond with the first thing that came to mind, and note how long it took the child to make a response.

Having secured the cooperation of a number of nursery schools in the area, two undergraduate research assistants went off to collect data. I could not go with them on the first day because I had a class to teach. When I met the assistants upon their return, they were frustrated and upset. When I asked how everything had gone, one student said, "It was awful! The darn kids wouldn't do it! It was just a mess!" I became very paternalistic and reassured the assistants, "Now, now, don't worry, Dr. Gerow will go with you tomorrow and everything will be all right." It wasn't. My assistants were right. To a large degree, the darned kids wouldn't do it.

I approached a 4-year-old with a proposition. "Hi. How are you? Let's play a game, okay? Would you like to play a game with words?" My first discovery was that 8 percent of the children simply did not want to play. They just walked away and went back to their sandbox or some other activity. When children did agree to "play," they did some most peculiar things. I gave my simple instructions: "I'm going to say a word, and then you tell me the first word that my word makes you think of. Okay? My first word is *black*." After a moment's pause, a subject responded, "My Mommy has a black dress and she wears it to church sometimes."

"Okay, that's fine," I'd say, "but next time tell me only one word. Don't tell me a story. For example, if black makes you think of your Mommy's dress, just say 'dress,'

okay?" I gave the next word on the list. "The next word is *happy*." "Dress," the child quickly responded. "No, no. You have to tell me what HAPPY makes you think of." "Oh, I'm happy when we have ice cream for dessert."

Some children demonstrated that they were learning their alphabet. "What's the first thing you think of when I say *black*?" The response: "Bee." To *man* the reponse was "em," and so on. Some children responded with sounds I didn't even know how to record. In response to *black*, one child responded with a series of "buh-buh-buh" noises. To *happy* the response was "hap-hap-puh-puh-puh."

I eventually included more than 300 children in this study, just to see how children *would* respond to my little "word game." Most of the responses produced by the children were nonword responses.

With the word association procedure, we have one of the easiest, most straightforward techniques in all of psychology. But "playing the game" is a task that some children may do with their own set of rules, and others may simply not be ready to play the game at all. I had failed to account for the level of cognitive development of my subjects. The point of all this is that doing even simple experiments with children is often not as simple as it sounds (a slight variation on one of our themes from Chapter 1). If children do not understand the instructions of the experimenters, results may be misleading at best. To study the behavior of young children scientifically requires that we be particularly clever—or exceedingly patient. Experiments may not work at all, and other research methods, such as naturalistic observation, may be needed. To a degree, similar problems arise throughout our study of human development.

Now that we have some idea about the nature of psychology and the biological bases of behavior, we can turn to developmental psychology, which will provide us with an overview of many psychological processes. Throughout this chapter we will be discussing matters of sensation, perception, learning, memory, and socialization. We'll return to each of these topics in subsequent chapters.

From conception to death, human beings share certain developmental events that unite us as one species. As we have already noted, it is also true that each of us is unique—different from everyone else. Developmental psychologists are interested in the common patterns of our development and growth, *and* they care about the ways in which we differ throughout our lives. In this chapter we will use "growth" and "development" to mean slightly different things. "Growth" refers to simple enlargement—getting bigger. A child demonstrates growth by becoming taller or heavier. "Development," on the other hand, implies a differentiation of structure or function. Something "develops" when it appears for the first time, and remains. Thus, we say that the nervous system develops between week 2 and 8 after conception.

We tend to think that a person's development begins at birth. In fact, development begins much earlier—at conception, and with the first division of one cell into two. This chapter will consider factors that influence the development of the human organism across the lifespan. We will begin with an examination of the course of development from conception to birth—the *prenatal period* of development. Then we'll turn our attention to children—development from birth to puberty.

Growth and development do not end with childhood. We continue to develop throughout adolescence and adulthood. Most of the changes that reflect our later development are more gradual and subtle than those that occur in childhood. They may be more difficult to observe, but they are no less significant. In our discussion of adolescence, we will examine various definitions of adolescence; discuss the physical, mental, and social development of adolescents; and sample some issues of concern to contemporary psychologists. The psychology of adult development is a comparatively recent area of research and theory. We will arbitrarily divide adulthood into three segments—early adulthood, middle adulthood and late adulthood—and will examine some psychological milestones that are related to each of these periods.

Throughout this chapter we will be discussing human development in terms of developmental stages or periods and critical events. It is easy to be impressed with the apparent orderliness and predictability of human development. We must always remember not to take all of this too literally. Orderly sequences of development emerge from examining averages and pregressions *in general*. Developmental trends and stages are like so many other things: If one looks hard enough, they can be found. But the individual differences we see around us constantly remind us that for any one person—child, adolescent, or adult—many of our generalizations may not hold true. The orderliness of human development may exist only in the eyes of the observer.

▶ *Prenatal Development: Influences before Birth*

conception the moment when the father's sperm cell unites with the mother's ovum to produce a zygote

Human development begins at **conception**, when the father's sperm cell unites with the mother's ovum. At that time, 23 chromosomes from each parent pair off within a single cell. We have in that one action the complete transmission

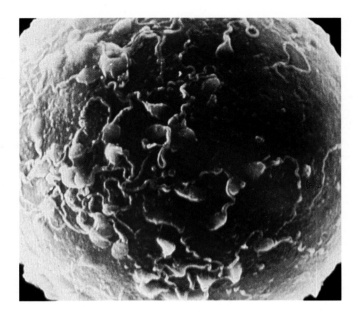

▲ *At conception, as pictured here, the egg cell unites with the sperm cell. During this time, the zygote receives all of its inherited characteristics.*

of all inherited characteristics. [You might want to review the basics of genetics and heredity on pages 48–50 in Chapter 2.]

Within the next 30 hours or so, that one cell will divide and become two. In 3 days, there may be about a dozen cells; after 5 days, there will be slightly more than 100 (Moore, 1982; Torrey & Feduccia, 1979). No one knows how many cells the average human organism has at birth, and few are willing to even hazard a guess; to say "more than a trillion" is probably a conservative estimate (Moore, 1982).

The period from conception to birth is called the **prenatal period** of development. Until recently, this period of human development received only minor attention from psychologists. We now recognize that many events that can have lifelong consequences occur during this very sensitive period.

▶ *Physical Aspects of Prenatal Development*

Prenatal development is divided into three different stages or periods: the stages of the zygote, embryo, and fetus. These stages are not all of the same length, and each is characterized by its own landmarks and events.

The stage of the **zygote** is the shortest of the prenatal stages, from conception until approximately 2 weeks later, when the zygote becomes implanted in the wall of the uterus. The ovum usually is fertilized as it moves along the fallopian tubes from the ovaries, where ova (the plural of ovum) are stored and released, one at a time, at approximately 28-day intervals. It typically takes the zygote about 7 days to travel down the fallopian tube to the uterus, and another 7 days to become firmly attached there (Figure 3.1). At this point, the zygote has grown to include hundreds of cells, and for the first time it is clear that all the cells are not exact replicas of one another. Some of the cells, for example, develop to form the protective placenta, while others form the umbilical cord that ultimately will supply nourishment to the developing organism.

Once implantation is complete, the stage of the zygote is over, and the organism has entered the stage of the embryo. This stage lasts about six weeks, from week 2 to week 8. During this period, the embryo develops rapidly. Early on, we can differentiate three types of cells: those that will

prenatal period the period of development from conception to birth

zygote the one-cell product of the union of the sperm and ovum at conception

Figure 3.1

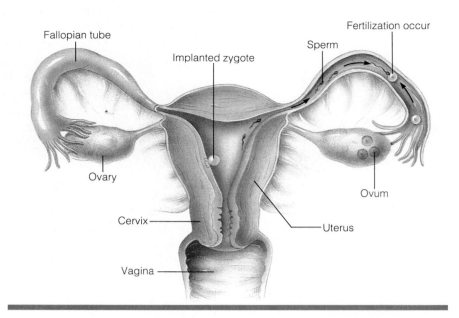

▲ *The female reproductive organs, indicating where fertilization and implantation take place.*

become the nervous system, the sense organs, and the skin; those that will form the internal organs; and those that will form the muscles, skeleton, and blood vessels. By the end of this stage, we can identify the face area, eyes, ears, fingers, toes, and male or female genitals. That is, not only do the cells increase in number, but they also differentiate further.

It is during this stage—more conservatively, within the first three months—that the unborn is most sensitive to environmental influences. It seems that if there are going to be problems (e.g., birth defects), they are most likely to develop during this critical period. If the heart, hands, eyes, and ears, for example, do not become differentiated and develop during this period, there will be no way to compensate later. As it happens, the central nervous system is at risk throughout prenatal development—particularly so in weeks 3 through 6.

Two months after conception, the stage of the embryo draws to a close. The inch-long embryo now has enough of a primitive nervous system to respond to a light touch with a simple reflex movement.

The final period of prenatal development is also the longest, the stage of the **fetus**, which includes months 3 through 9. The organs of the body continue to increase in complexity and size, and they begin to function. The arms and legs move spontaneously by the end of the third month. In two more months, these movements will be strong enough for the mother to feel them. At the end of the fifth month, the fetus is approximately 10 inches long. Internal organs are developed, but not to the point of sustaining life outside the uterus. The brain has developed, but neurons within it have not formed many synapses.

Development and growth continue throughout the last few months of pregnancy. The most noticeable change—certainly most noticeable to the mother—is the significant increase in weight and overall movement of the fetus. Sometime during the seventh month, most fetuses have reached the point of **viability**. This means that if they were forced to do so, they could

fetus the developmental period from week 8 until birth

viability the ability to survive without interference or intervention

survive and continue to develop without medical intervention if they were born prematurely. During its last few weeks in the uterus, the growth of the fetus slows. Its movements may be more powerful, but overall activity is also slowed due to the cramped quarters in which the fetus finds itself. After nearly 270 days, the fetus is ready to enter the world as a newborn.

Before You Go On
▼▼▼▼▼▼▼▼▼

Briefly summarize the three stages of prenatal development.

▶ Environmental Influences on Prenatal Development

In most cases, development of the human organism from zygote to embryo to fetus follows the plans of the genes—heredity providing the blueprint for prenatal development. As prenatal development takes place, however, the human organism is not immune to environmental influences.

"Until the early 1940s, it was generally accepted that human embryos were protected from environmental agents by their fetal membranes and their mother's abdominal walls and uterus" (Moore, 1982, p. 140). It was then discovered that birth defects often resulted when a pregnant woman contracted rubella (or German measles). Twenty years later, it was a well-established fact that many drugs taken by a pregnant woman have measurable effects on the development of the embryo and fetus. It is now common knowledge that during the very rapid period of prenatal development, even small environmental disturbances can have serious and lasting consequences. Most of the external influences on prenatal development that we know about are those that tend to have negative consequences.

Never meant to be taken literally, the old expression "You are what you eat" does have some truth to it. By the same token, before we are born, we are what our mothers eat. When pregnant women eat poorly, the unborn may share in the consequences. Maternal malnutrition often leads to increases in miscarriages, stillbirths, and premature births. At best, we can expect the newborn child of a malnourished mother to be similarly malnourished (*e.g.*, Lozott, 1989).

It is also the case that vitamin and mineral deficiencies affect the prenatal organism (Bratic, 1982). For example, a mother's calcium deficiencies affect the development of bones and teeth in the fetus. But as is the case for many nutrients, it may very well be the mother who suffers most. That is, if there are inadequate supplies of calcium in the mother's system, "the fetal need for calcium will be met at the expense of the mother" (Hughes & Noppe, 1985, p. 140).

There is ample evidence that smoking has harmful effects on the smoker. Smoking by pregnant women has harmful effects on their unborn children (Frazier, et al., 1961; Fribourg, 1982; Jacobson, 1984). Exactly how smoking affects the fetus is not known for certain, but we do know that cigarette smoking is a cause of retarded prenatal growth (Golbus, 1980). Mothers who smoke a pack a day or more double the chances of having a low-weight baby. Smoking mothers more frequently have miscarriages, stillbirths, and babies who die soon after birth than do mothers who do not smoke (Frazier, et al., 1961; Golbus, 1980).

Alcohol is perhaps the most commonly abused of all drugs, and it can be injurious to unborn children. Alcohol is quickly passed through the umbilical cord from the mother to the fetus. The effects can be stunning.

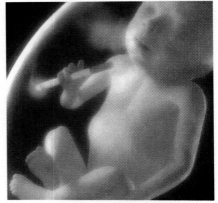

WOULD YOU GIVE A CIGARETTE TO YOUR UNBORN CHILD?

YOU DO EVERY TIME YOU SMOKE!

AMERICAN CANCER SOCIETY

▲ *Studies reveal that women who smoke during pregnancy increase significantly their chances of having miscarriages, stillbirths, low-weight babies, and babies who die shortly after birth.*

fetal alcohol syndrome a cluster of symptoms (*e.g.,* low birth weight, poor muscle tone, intellectual retardation), associated with a child born to a mother who was a heavy drinker of alcohol during pregnancy

Heavy drinking (e.g., 3 ounces of liquor, or 3 glasses of wine or beer per day) significantly increases the chance of having smaller babies with retarded physical growth, poor coordination, poor muscle tone, intellectual retardation, and other problems, collectively referred to as **fetal alcohol syndrome** (Jones et al., 1973; Mattson, Barron & Riley, 1988). In the 1970s, it was believed that a social drink or two had no particular lasting effect on prenatal development. The best advice now seems to be total abstinence (Abel, 1981; 1984; Barr et al., 1990; Kolata, 1981).

There is little doubt that mothers who use or abuse drugs such as heroin or cocaine (including "crack") during pregnancy cause many complications for their unborn children. At best, such children enter the world with low birth weights (putting them at risk for many other complications), difficulty regulating their sleep/wake cycles, and symptoms of fetal alcohol syndrome (perhaps because their mothers *also* abused alcohol) (Finnegan, 1982). At worst, they are born addicted themselves and must—within days of birth—suffer the pains of withdrawal (Adler, 1989; Chasnoff, et al., 1989; Finnegan, 1982). Mothers using illegal drugs often fail to get adequate medical care during their pregnancy, perhaps out of fear of discovery. A question as yet unanswered is what the long-term consequences of maternal drug abuse and addiction during pregnancy will be for the children involved.

Some drugs taken by the mother during her pregnacy seem to have no noticeable effect on the developing child—penicillin, for example (Golbus, 1980). Some have predictable effects that are not life-threatening. The antibiotic tetracycline, for example, when passed to the developing fetus is deposited in the teeth and bones, coloring them yellow. Other prescription drugs may have devastating effects. One example is the drug thalidomide, routinely prescribed in Europe in the early 1960s as a mild tranquilizer and treatment for nausea associated with pregnancy. Thalidomide children, as they are called, developed shortened, malformed limbs, or no limbs at all, and very often were mentally retarded.

Also in the 1950s and 1960s, many women who had problems during earlier pregnancies were given the drug DES (diethylstilbestrol) to reduce the likelihood of miscarriage. This synthetic hormone is now believed to be related to cervical cancer in the *daughters* of women who had taken the drug years earlier. Even the sons of women who received DES are now found to have higher than normal rates of infertility (Stenchever, et al., 1981). The bottom-line advice again seems very clear: Pregnant women should use drugs of any sort only with great care, and only after consultation with their physicians.

There is a certain logic that tells us that a mother's emotional health can affect her unborn baby. There is even some logic to the physiology of the argument. As we shall see, emotionality is accompanied by many hormonal changes, and these changes may have some influence on the development of the embryo or fetus. It is also the case that when a pregnant mother is under stress, the blood flow in her body is, at least for a short while, diverted from the uterus to other organs, reducing the amount of oxygen available to the prenatal organism (Stechler & Halton, 1982).

▲ Babies born to mothers who used crack cocaine during their pregnancy enter the world at great risk for numerous physical and psychological disabilities

Before You Go On
▼▼▼▼▼▼▼▼▼▼

Briefly review the impact of diet, drugs, and stress on prenatal development.

Physical and Motor Development in Childhood

childhood the period of human development between birth and puberty (the onset of adolescence)

neonate the newborn, from birth to age 2 weeks

Now we turn our attention to development in **childhood**, that period between birth and adolescence. In this section, we'll focus on the physical growth of children and note the orderly sequence of the development of their motor responses—their abilities to do things with their bodies. We'll begin by considering some of the abilities of the newborn infant.

As recently as 20 years ago, textbooks on child psychology seldom devoted more than a few paragraphs to the behaviors of the **neonate**—the newborn through the first 2 weeks of life. It seemed as if the neonate did not do much worth writing about. Today, most child psychology texts devote much more space to discussing the abilities of newborns. It is unlikely that over the past 20 years neonates have gotten smarter or more able. But psychologists have—they have devised better ways of assessing the abilities of neonates.

A careful examination of babies reveals that they are capable of a wide range of behaviors. Almost all of these behaviors are reflexive—simple, unlearned, involuntary reactions to specific stimuli. Many of the neonate's reflexive responses serve a useful purpose. Some do not seem to have any survival value, but even these are important to know about because they can be used as diagnostic indicators of the quality of the neonate's development, particularly the development of the nervous system. There are more than a dozen reflexes that can be observed and measured (for strength and duration, for example) in the newborn child (see Figure 3.2).

Parents trying to keep their young children in properly fitting clothes know how quickly children can grow. In their first three years, children's height and weight normally increase at a rate never again equaled. Although changes in size and motor skills are rapid, they tend to be orderly and follow a prescribed pattern. It is with that pattern that we are concerned here.

One of psychology's most reliable observations is that individuals differ. No two children can be expected to grow at the same rate or develop control over their bodies at the same time. Bill may walk unaided at the age of 10 months. Joanne may not venture forth on her own until she's 13 months old. Differences between children are often as great as their similarities.

Figure 3.2

REFLEXES OF THE NEONATE

Name	Stimulus	Response	Age when disappears
Moro	Loud sound, or sudden loss of support	Arms and legs thrown outward; fingers spread; then, with fists clenched arms and legs pulled back	4–6 months
Rooting	Light stroke on cheek	Head turns toward stimulus; mouth opens; sucking begins	3–4 months
Sucking	Object (e.g., nipple) inserted in mouth 3–4 cm.	Rhythmic sucking and mouth movements	variable
Grasping	Rod pressed in palm	Close fist and grasp firmly	3–5 months
Walking/ stepping	With feet just touching surface, baby moved forward	Coordinated rhythmic stepping movements	2–4 months
Babinski	Stroke sole of foot from heel to toes	Small toes spread; big toe raised	9–12 months
Tonic neck	With baby on its back, turn head to one side	Arm and leg on that side thrust outward, while other arm and leg drawn in to body	3–4 months
Swimming	Place infant in water	Rhythmic swimming movements	4–6 months

▲ *Whether a child begins to walk at 10 months or 13 months, he or she will still follow the same sequence of sitting, crawling, and then walking.*

Regardless of the *rate* of motor development, there are regularities in the *sequence* of motor development. The development of some common motor skills is summarized in Figure 3.3. There are two important things for you to notice about Figure 3.3: The sequence of events is very regular, but *when* each behavior develops includes a range of ages that should be considered as normal. The sequence and timing of the events in this figure hold equally for boys and girls. In these basic motor skills there are no sex differences.

The regularity of physical growth and development seems to be guided by two different "principles." (1) *Cephalocaudal sequencing:* a child's growth and bodily control proceed from top to bottom, or from head to upper torso to lower body. For example, childrens' heads and upper torsos develop before their trunks and lower bodies; hands and arms can be manipulated before feet and legs can. (2) *Proximodistal sequencing:* a child's growth and body control proceed from the center core to the extremities; from the internal organs to the arms and legs to the hands and feet to the fingers.

Before You Go On

▼▼▼▼▼▼▼▼▼

Why do we care about neonatal reflexes?

What general observations can we make about physical growth and motor control in childhood?

Figure 3.3

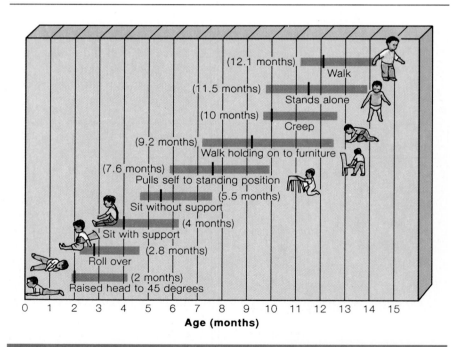

▲ *The sequence of human motor development. Each bar represents the age at which 25 percent of children engage in a behavior (left end) to the age at which 90 percent of children engage in that behavior (right end). Also indicated is the age at which 50 percent of children show the behavior. (After Frankenburg & Dodds, 1967.)*

▶ Sensory and Perceptual Development in Childhood

One of the reasons psychologists used to think that newborn children couldn't do much was that it was commonly believed that newborns could not sense or perceive very much. We now understand that neonates respond to a range of stimuli in their environments. To varying degrees, all human senses function at birth, having developed in order: touch, body position, balance, taste, smell, hearing, and vision (Gibson, 1987; 1988; Hall & Oppenheim, 1987).

The neonate's ability to sense even subtle changes is quite remarkable. However, there *are* limitations. The ability of the eyes to focus on an object, for example, does not develop fully until the child is about 4 months old. The neonate can focus well on objects held at a distance of one to two feet, but everything else appears blurred or out of focus. This means that even the newborn can adequately focus on the facial features of the person cradling or feeding the newborn. Visual acuity—the ability to discern detail—shows at least a three- to fourfold improvement during the first year (Aslin & Smith, 1988).

An issue that has been of considerable interest to psychologists is just when the perception of depth and distance develops. Even newborns have some simple reactions to depth. They will close their eyes and squirm away if you rush an object toward their face (Bower, Broughton & Moore, 1971).

In the late 1950s, two Cornell University psychologists, Eleanor Gibson and Richard Walk (1960), constructed an apparatus to test the depth perception of very young children. The *visual cliff*, as it is called, is a deep box covered by a sheet of thick, clear Plexiglas. It is divided into two sides, one shallow, one deep. The deep and shallow sides are separated by a center board (see Figure 3.4).

Gibson and Walk discovered that 6-month-old children would not leave the center board to venture out over the deep side of the box, even to get to their mothers. By crawling age, therefore, the child seems able to perceive depth *and* to make an appropriate response to it.

It seems likely that the perception of depth develops before the age of 6 months—and almost certainly before the development of a fear of heights. When neonates (who obviously can't crawl) are placed on the Plexiglas over the deep side of the visual cliff, their heart rates decrease, indicating that at least they notice the change in visual stimulation (Campos, et al., 1978). When 7-month-old infants are placed over the deep side of the visual cliff, their heart rates *increase*. The increase in heart rate is taken as indicating fear, a response that develops after the ability to detect depth (Bertenthal & Campos, 1989; Campos, 1976). So it seems that in some rudimentary form, even a neonate may sense depth, but reacting appropriately to depth may require experiences and learning that come later.

What about the other senses? Newborn infants can hear very well. They can direct their attention to the source of a sound, even a faint one. Wertheimer (1961) reports a study demonstrating sound localization in a newborn between three and ten *minutes* after birth! (The child moved her eyes to the left or right in response to a loud clicking sound.) Sounds probably don't *mean* much to neonates, but they can respond differently to sounds of different pitch and loudness. Even 3-day-old newborns are able to discriminate the sound of their mother's voice from other sounds (DeCasper & Fifer, 1980; Kolata, 1987; Martin and Clark, 1982).

Newborns can also respond to differences in taste and smell. They can discriminate among the four basic taste qualities of salt, sweet, bitter, and

Figure 3.4

▲ The visual cliff was designed to determine if depth perception is innate or learned. By the time they can move about, most infants will avoid the "deep" side of the apparatus.

sour. They display a distinct preference for sweet-tasting liquids. Although they are unable to use it then, the sense of smell seems to be established before birth. Right after birth, neonates respond predictably—drawing away and wrinkling their noses—to a variety of strong odors.

In summary, a wide range of sensory and perceptual capabilities is available to the newborn child. The neonate may require some time to learn what to do with sensory information that it acquires from its environment, but many of its senses are operational. What the newborn makes of the sensations it receives will depend upon the development of its mental or cognitive abilities. This is the subject that we turn to now.

Before You Go On
▼▼▼▼▼▼▼▼

Summarize the basic sensory capacities of the neonate.

▶ Cognitive and Social Development in Childhood

Cognitive processes enable us to find out about and understand ourselves and the world around us. In this section, we'll look at how these skills develop throughout childhood, beginning with the cognitive capacities of the newborn. Our major focus will be the theories of Jean Piaget. Then we'll consider development from a more social perspective, considering the psychosocial theory of Erik Erikson and Lawrence Kohlberg's theory of moral development. We'll end this topic with a brief section on the development of social attachments. (The development of another cognitve skill, language, will be addressed in Chapter 8).

▶ The Cognitive Abilities of the Neonate

As we have seen, reflex reactions can help neonates survive. For long-term survival, however, neonates must learn to adapt to their environments and profit from their experiences. Neonates have to begin forming memories of their experiences and learn to make discriminations among the many stimuli with which they are presented. Are these cognitive processes possible in a baby just a couple of days or weeks old? In a number of specific ways, the answer seems to be yes.

Friedman (1972) has reported a demonstration of what we might call memory in neonates only 1 to 4 *days* old. Babies were shown a picture of a simple figure, say a checkerboard pattern, for 60 seconds. Experimenters recorded how long the baby looked at the stimulus pattern. After the same pattern was shown over and over again, the baby appeared to be bored and gave it less attention. When a different stimulus pattern was introduced, the baby stared at it for almost the full 60 seconds of its exposure.

So what does this have to do with memory? The argument is that for the neonate to stare at the new stimulus, it must have formed some memory of the old one. Otherwise, how would it recognize the new pattern as being new or different? In fact, if the new stimulus pattern was very similar to the old one, the baby would not give it as much attention as it would if it were totally different. It is as if a cognitive judgment was being made about the distinctiveness of the new stimulus and the old (remembered) ones.

In talking about recognizing patterns, we should mention the research of Robert Fantz (1961, 1963). Fantz presented newborn children with pairs of visual stimuli. In most pairs, one stimulus was more complex than the other. As the babies lay on their backs, looking up at the stimuli, the experimenters could note which one of the two stimuli received the most attention from the child. In almost every case, a preference was shown for the more complex stimulus pattern.

This in itself is interesting and difficult to explain. The major finding is that babies could at least discriminate between the two stimuli. That attention equals "preference" is more of an assumption than a research finding. Fantz also discovered that even newborn infants show a distinct preference for (choose to attend to) drawings of a human face. They chose the face pattern as the focus of their attention no matter what it was paired with. These results have been confirmed by other researchers who have demonstrated that infants can even discriminate among facial expressions displaying different emotional states, looking more at facial expressions of joy than of anger, for instance (Malatesta & Isard, 1984).

Before You Go On
▼▼▼▼▼▼▼▼▼

Cite an example of research evidence demonstrating a cognitive reaction in neonates.

▶ Piaget's Theory of Cognitive Development

The physical growth and development of a child is remarkable. Even more impressive are the increases in cognitive and intellectual abilities that occur during childhood. By the time the human reaches adolescence, she or he has acquired an enormous stockpile of information. More than just learning facts, the child comes to appreciate how to learn. Strategies for survival and success begin to develop in childhood (Siegler, 1983).

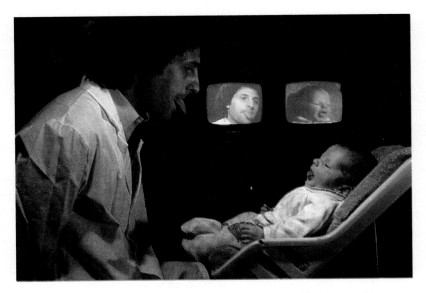

▲ *Babies often imitate facial expressions they see, as this 23-day-old newborn is doing.*

▲ Jean Piaget

schema a system of organized general knowledge, stored in long-term memory, that guides the encoding and retrieval of information

assimilation the process of adding new material or information to an existing schema

accommodation in Piaget's theory, the process of altering or revising an existing schema in the light of new information

sensorimotor stage in Piaget's theory, from birth to age 2 years, when a child learns by sensing and doing

Accounting for *how* children's intellectual skills change is a difficult business. It is important to be able to describe the changes that occur, but it is more important to be able to specify the principles that underlie cognitive development (Siegler, 1989). The theory that has attracted the most attention in this regard is that of the Swiss psychologist Jean Piaget (1896–1980), and it will be the focus of our discussion (Piaget, 1948, 1954, 1967).

In Piaget's theory, cognitive development centers on the formation of **schemas,** or organized mental representations of the world that have predictable behavioral consequences. Organizing the world into a network of schemas is a process that can be found in all children, claimed Piaget. For example, children develop a schema for "daddy," for "mommy," for "eating breakfast," and for "bedtime." The function of schemas is to aid the child in adapting to the demands and pressures of the environment. Schemas are formed by experience.

Forming mental representations of the environment involves two basic processes, assimilation and accommodation. **Assimilation** involves taking on new information and fitting it into an existing schema. Children develop a rather complex schema for mealtime, for instance. When, for the first time, they are taken to "eat out" at a fast-food restaurant, new information will have to be added to the mealtime schema. In fact, as you learn about new and different things that psychologists do, we may say that information is being assimilated into your schema for "psychology."

Accommodation involves changing or revising existing schemas in the face of new experiences, not just adding to them. As children are shifted away from the bottle to strained foods, to chunkier foods, to regular food, they must accommodate their schemas for efficient feeding—what used to work in the past doesn't work any longer. Learning that mommy and daddy won't *always* come running when one cries may require accommodation.

Piaget proposed that as children assimilate new ideas into existing schemas and modify or accommodate old ones, they progress through four stages of development: the sensorimotor stage, the preoperational stage, the concrete operations stage, and the formal operations stage. Determining precisely when each stage begins or ends is not always possible, since two adjacent stages may overlap and blend for a while. Even so, each stage is characterized by its own schemas, cognitive methods, insights, and abilities.

Sensorimotor Stage. (Ages 0 to 2 years.) For children younger than 2, language is not an effective means of finding out about the world. Children of this age are unable to discover much about their world by asking questions about it or by trying to understand long-winded explanations. Explaining to a 10-month-old baby *why* it shouldn't chew on an electrical cord is likely to be an unrewarding piece of parental behavior. In this **sensorimotor stage,** children discover by *sensing* (sensori-) and by *doing* (motor). A child may come to appreciate that a quick pull on a dog's tail (a motor activity) reliably produces a loud yelp (a sensory experience), perhaps followed in turn by parental attention.

One of the most useful schemas to develop in the sensorimotor stage is that of *causality.* Infants come to the realization that events sometimes have knowable causes and that some behaviors cause predictable reactions. Pushing a bowl of oatmeal off the high chair causes a mess and gets Mom's attention: If *A,* then *B*—a very practical insight.

Another important discovery that occurs during this developmental stage is that objects can exist even when they are not immediately in view. Early in this stage, an object that is out of sight is more than out of mind. It ceases to exist for the child. By the end of the sensorimotor period, children have learned that objects can exist even if they are not physically present,

object permanence the appreciation that an object no longer in view can still exist and reappear later

and children can anticipate their reappearance. This awareness is called **object permanence** (see Figure 3.5).

One of the skills that best characterizes the sensorimotor period of development is that of imitation. So long as it is within the baby's range of abilities, a baby will imitate almost any behavior it sees. A cognitive strategy has developed, one that will be used for a lifetime: trying to imitate the behaviors of a model.

Before You Go On
▼▼▼▼▼▼▼▼▼

How are schemas formed during the sensorimotor stage?

What characterizes this stage of development?

Preoperational Stage. (Ages 2 to 6 years.) By the end of the sensorimotor stage, a child recognizes that he or she is a separate, independent person in the world. Throughout most of the preoperational stage, a child's thinking is self-centered, or **egocentric**. According to Piaget, the child has difficulty understanding life from someone else's perspective. In this stage, the world is very much *me, mine,* and *I* oriented.

egocentric to be characterized by self; by "me" and "mine" and "my point of view"

Perhaps you have seen two preschool children at play. They are right next to each other, one playing with a truck, the other coloring in a coloring book. They are jabbering at each other and take turns, but each is oblivious to what the other is saying:

> *Jill: "This sure is a neat truck!"*
> *Leslie: "I think I'll paint the sky a kinda purple."*
> *Jill: "I'm gonna be a truck driver some day."*
> *Leslie: "But if I make the sky a kinda purple, what'll I make the trees?"*
> *Jill: "Maybe I'll drive a milk truck. Broooom!"*
> *Leslie: "I know, blue."*

Such exchanges, called *collective monologues,* demonstrate the egocentrism of children's thinking in this stage.

In the **preoperational stage**, not only do we find egocentric thought, but we also see that children begin to develop and use symbols—usually in the

preoperational stage in Piaget's theory, from age 2 years to 6 years, when a child begins to develop symbolic representations but cannot manipulate them; also characterized by egocentricity

Figure 3.5

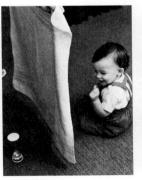

▲ *The older infant has developed the concept of object permanence. The infant sees the toy and even when it is blocked from view, he realizes it is still there and crawls under the blanket to get it.*

form of words to represent concepts. But at this stage, children do not appreciate how to manipulate those symbols in a consistent, rule-governed way, which is why it is referred to as *pre*operational. It's not until the end of this period that they can play "word games," or understand why riddles about someone throwing a clock out of a window in order to "see time fly" are funny. It is similarly true that children at this stage of development have great difficulty with many "abstract" concepts, such as those involved with religious beliefs. Manipulating concepts, even abstract concepts, comes in the next stage of development.

Before You Go On
▼▼▼▼▼▼▼▼▼

In Piaget's theory, what best characterizes the preoperational stage of development?

concrete operations stage in Piaget's theory, from age 7 years to 12 years, when concepts can be manipulated, but not in an abstract fashion

conservation in Piaget's theory, an appreciation that changing the physical properties of an object does not necessarily change its essence

Figure 3.6

▲ *In a demonstration of the concept of "conservation of volume," a child in Piaget's preoperational stage of cognitive development will claim that there is more liquid in the tall beaker than there is in the short one, even when the amounts of liquid are, in fact, equal.*

Concrete Operations Stage. (Ages 7 to 12 years.) In the **concrete operations stage**, children develop many concepts *and* show that they can manipulate those concepts. For example, they can classify things: balls over here, blocks over there, plastic soldiers in a pile by the door, and so on. Each of these items is recognized as a toy, ultimately to be put away in the toy box and not stored in the closet, which is where clothes are supposed to go. Thus, it is in this period that we may say that rule-governed behavior begins. The concrete objects of the child's world can be classified, ranked, ordered, or separated into more than one category.

A sign of the beginning of the concrete operations stage is an ability to solve conservation problems. **Conservation** involves the cognitive awareness that changing the form or the appearance of something does not necessarily change what it really is. Many experiments convinced Piaget that the ability to demonstrate conservation marked the end of the preoperational stage of development. Figure 3.6 shows a test for conservation of *volume.* We can show the conservation of *size* by giving two, equal-sized balls of clay to a 4 year old. One is then rolled into a long cigar shape, and the child will now assert that it has more clay in it than the ball does. A 7 year old will seldom hesitate to tell you that each form contains the same amount of clay. The 7 year old has moved on to the next stage of cognitive development.

As its name suggests, in the concrete operations stage, children begin to operate on (use and manipulate) concepts and ideas. Those manipulations are still very concrete, however, very much tied to real objects in the here and now. For example, an 8 year old can easily be expected to find her way to and from school, even if she throws in a side trip or two along the way. What she will have a hard time doing is *describing* just how she did so. Drawing a sensible map is difficult for her. If she actually stands on the corner of Maple Street and Oak Avenue, she knows where to go next. Dealing with the concrete reality, here and now, is fairly easy. Dealing with such knowledge in abstract terms is what is difficult.

Before You Go On
▼▼▼▼▼▼▼▼▼

What cognitive skills might we expect from a child in the concrete operations stage of development?

formal operations stage in Piaget's theory, ages older than 12 years, when one can generate and test abstract hypotheses, and think as an adult, where thinking follows rules

Formal Operations Stage. (Ages over 12 years.) The logical manipulation of abstract, symbolic concepts does not appear until the last of Piaget's stages—**formal operations.** The key to this stage, usually begun at adolescence, is abstract, symbolic reasoning. By the age of 12 years, most children can develop and then mentally test hypotheses—can work through problems in their minds.

It is only at the stage of formal operations that youngsters are able to reason through hypothetical problems: "What if you were the only person in the world who liked rock music?" "If nobody had to go to school, what would happen?" Similarly, children are now able to deal with questions that are literally contrary to fact: "What if Richard Nixon were still president of the United States?" The stages of Piaget's theory and the cognitive milestones associated with each are summarized in Figure 3.7.

Before You Go On

What cognitive ability characterizes the stage of formal operations?

▶ Reactions to Piaget

There can be no doubt of the importance of Piaget's influence on the study of the cognitive abilities of children. His observations, insights, and theories about intellectual development spanned decades. On the other hand, there has been a quantity of research that has brought into question some of Piaget's basic ideas. The two major criticisms of Piaget's theory are that (1) the borderlines between his proposed stages are much less clearcut than his theory suggests, and (2) Piaget significantly underestimated the cognitive talents of preschool children (Flavell, 1982, 1985; Gelman, 1978).

Figure 3.7

PIAGET'S STAGES OF COGNITIVE DEVELOPMENT

1. ***Sensorimotor stage* (birth to age 2 years)**
   "Knows" through active interaction with environment
   Becomes aware of cause-effect relationships
   Learns that objects exist even when not in view
   Imitates crudely the actions of others
2. ***Preoperational stage* (ages 2 to 6 years)**
   Begins by being very egocentric
   Language and mental representations develop
   Objects are classified on just one characteristic at a time
3. ***Concrete operations stage* (ages 7 to 12 years)**
   Develops conservation of volume, length, mass, etc.
   Organizes objects into ordered categories
   Understands relational terms (e.g., bigger than, above)
   Begins using simple logic
4. ***Formal operations stage* (ages over 12)**
   Thinking becomes abstract and symbolic
   Reasoning skills develop
   A sense of hypothetical concepts develops

For example, the egocentrism said to characterize the preoperational preschool child may not be as obvious as Piaget would have us believe. In one study (Lempers, et al., 1977), children were shown a picture that was pasted inside a box. They were asked to show the picture to someone else. Not only did they do so, but in showing the picture, they turned it so that it would be right-side up to the viewer. Every child over 2 years of age indicated such an appreciation of someone else's point of view. Also, there is considerable evidence that object permanence may be neither universal nor consistently found in any one child—it depends on how you test for it (Harris, 1983).

Even Piaget's well-researched notion of conservation may not be such an obvious indicator of cognitive development as was once thought. When experimenters pour liquid from a short beaker into a tall one, a 5 year old probably will say that the taller beaker now holds more liquid—evidence of a failure to conserve in the preoperational stage. If the *child* actually does the pouring from one beaker to the other, as opposed to just watching, even 5 year olds show definite signs of conservation and recognize that the amount of liquid is the same in both containers (Rose & Blank, 1974).

Another criticism is that Piaget's theory, focusing from the start on a stage approach, gives little attention to the impact of language development. Piaget had little to say about the smooth and gradual increase in the capacity of a child's memory. Just because a child of any age *can* demonstrate some cognitive skill is no guarantee that the child normally *does* use that skill in her or his daily activities.

So it seems that some of Piaget's observations and assumptions have come under attack. This is to be expected in science. In fact, one of the most important contributions of Jean Piaget was that he developed a theory of the cognitive development of children (based on the observations of very few children) that was so rich, so detailed, so thought-provoking, that it will continue to challenge researchers for years to come.

Before You Go On
▼▼▼▼▼▼▼▼▼

Cite two criticisms of Piaget's theory of cognitive development.

▶ Erikson's Theory of Psychosocial Development

Erik Erikson is a psychologist who, like Piaget, proposed a stage theory of human development (1963; 1965; 1968). Unlike Piaget, his theory focuses on more than cognitive development, although this aspect is included. Erikson's theory is based on his observations of a wide range of people of different ages. As we'll see, his theory extends from childhood through adolescence into adulthood. Many of his observations had more of a cross-cultural basis than did Piaget's. Erikson chose to focus on the *social* environment, which is why his theory is referred to as "psychosocial."

Erikson's theory lists eight stages of development through which an individual passes. These stages are not so much periods of time as they are a series of conflicts, or crises, that need to be resolved. Each of the eight stages can be referenced by a pair of terms that indicates the nature of the conflict that needs to be resolved in this period of development.

As a stage theory, Erikson's implies that we naturally go through the resolution of each conflict or crisis in order and that facing any one type of crisis usually occurs at about the same age for all of us. Figure 3.8 is a summary of each of Erikson's eight stages of development. Also included are very brief descriptions of how each crisis might be resolved.

▲ Erik Erikson

Figure 3.8

ERIKSON'S EIGHT STAGES OF DEVELOPMENT

Approximate age	Crisis	Adequate resolution	Inadequate resolution
0–1½	Trust vs. mistrust	Basic sense of safety	Insecurity, anxiety
1½–3	Autonomy vs. self-doubt	Perception of self as agent capable of controlling own body and making things happen	Feelings of inadequacy to control events
3–6	Initiative vs. guilt	Confidence in oneself as initiator, creator	Feeling of lack of self-worth
6–puberty	Competence vs. inferiority	Adequacy in basic social and intellectual skills	Lack of self-confidence, feelings of failure
Adolescent	Identity vs. role confusion	Comfortable sense of self as a person	Sense of self as fragmented; shifting, unclear sense of self
Early adult	Intimacy vs. isolation	Capacity for closeness and commitment to another	Feeling of aloneness, separation; denial of need for closeness
Middle adult	Generativity vs. stagnation	Focus on concern beyond oneself to family, society, future generations	Self-indulgent concerns; lack of future orientation
Later adult	Ego-integrity vs. despair	Sense of wholeness, basic satisfaction with life	Feelings of futility, disappointment

After Erickson, 1963

One of the major strengths of Erikson's view is that it covers the entire life span. While Piaget focused mainly on the stages of development of children, Erikson extended his views to late adulthood. For now, we'll just describe Erikson's first four crises, but we will return to his theory later.

During one's first year of life, according to Erikson, one's greatest struggle centers around the establishment of a sense of trust. There's just not much that a newborn can accomplish on its own. If its needs are met in a reasonable fashion the child will develop a sense of safety and security, optimistic that the world is a predictable place. If the child's needs are not adequately met, what develops is a sense of mistrust—of insecurity and frustration.

During the period of *autonomy vs. shame and doubt*, what emerges most plainly is a sense of self-esteem. The child begins to act independently and to dress and feed itself. Physically more able, the child can be seen to strive off on its own, exploring ways of assuming personal responsibility. Frustration at this level of development leads to feelings of inadequacy and doubts of one's self-worth.

From ages 3 years to 6 years we have Erikson's period of *initiative vs. guilt*. Now the challenge is to develop as a functioning, contributing member of social groups, particularly the family. If the child is encouraged to do so, he or she should develop a strong sense of initiative, a certain joy of trying new things. Without such encouragement, the child is likely to feel guilty, resentful, and lacking in self-esteem.

The final childhood period, *industry vs. inferiority*, lasts from about age 6 years to puberty. During this period of choices, the child is challenged to move beyond the safety and comfort of the immediate family unit. Now the major thrust of development is "out there" in the neighborhood and the school. Children have to at least begin to acquire those skills that will enable them to become fully functioning adults in society. If the child's efforts of industry are constantly belittled, criticized, or ignored, he or she may develop a sense of inadequacy and inferiority, and remain dependent upon others even into adulthood.

▶ Kohlberg's Theory of Moral Development

How children acquire the capacity to judge between right and wrong is a process of development that has received considerable attention (Darley & Shultz, 1990; Vitz, 1990). Piaget included moral development in his theory, arguing that morality is closely related to one's cognitive awareness (Piaget, 1932). Lawrence Kohlberg has proposed a theory that focuses on moral development (1963, 1969, 1981, 1985). Kohlberg's is a theory of stages, of progressing from one stage to another in an orderly fashion. Kohlberg's data base comes from responses made by young boys who were asked a number of questions about stories that involve some moral dilemma. A commonly cited example of such a story concerns whether or not a man should steal a drug in order to save his wife's life after the pharmacist who invented the drug refuses to sell it to him. Should the man steal the drug; why or why not?

This method lead Kohlberg to propose three major levels of moral development, with two stages (or "orientations") at each level. The result is the six stages of moral development, which are briefly summarized in Figure 3.9. A child who says, for example, that the man should not steal the drug to save his wife's life because, "He'll get caught and be put in jail," would be at the first, preconventional level of moral reasoning because the prime interest of the child is simply with the punishment that comes from breaking a rule. A child who says that the man should steal the drug because "it will make his wife happy, and most people would do it anyway," is reflecting a type of reasoning at the second level because the judgment is based on a blindly accepted social convention, and social approval matters as much or

Figure 3.9

KOHLBERG'S STAGES OF MORAL DEVELOPMENT

Level 1	**Preconventional morality**	
	1. Obedience and punishment orientation	Rules are obeyed simply to avoid punishment; "If I take the cookies, I'll get spanked."
	2. Naive egotism and instrumental orientation	Rules are obeyed simply to earn rewards; "If I wash my hands, will you let me have two desserts?"
Level 2	**Conventional (conforming) morality**	
	3. Good boy/girl orientation	Rules are conformed to in order to avoid disapproval and gain approval; "I'm a good boy 'cause I cleaned my room, aren't I?"
	4. Authority-maintaining orientation	Social conventions blindly accepted to avoid criticism from those in authority: "You shouldn't steal because it's against the law, and you'll go to jail if the police catch you."
Level 3	**Postconventional morality**	
	5. Contractual-legalistic orientation	Morality is based on agreement with others to serve the common good and protect the rights of individuals; "I don't like stopping at stop signs, but if we didn't all obey traffic signals, it would be difficult to get anywhere."
	6. Universal ethical principle orientation	Morality is a reflection of internalized standards; "I don't care what anybody says, what's right is right."

more than anything else. The argument that, "no, he shouldn't steal the drug for a basically selfish reason, which in the long run would just promote more stealing in the society in general," is an example of moral reasoning at Kohlberg's third level, reflecting complex, internalized standards.

Research tells us that the basic thrust of Kohlberg's theory has merit (Rest, 1983) and that it has crosscultural application, at least at the lower stages (Edwards, 1977; Snarey, 1987). Problems with the theory also exist, however. For one thing, there is little evidence that many people (including adults) operate at the higher stages of moral reasoning described by the theory (Colby & Kohlberg, 1984). This is particularly true in cultures that emphasize group or communal membership rather than individuality, such as the Israeli kibbutz or tribal groups in New Guinea (Snarey, 1987). On the other hand, some evidence shows that children are quite capable of making involved moral judgments at a much younger age than Kohlberg would predict—perhaps by the age of three (Kagan & Lamb, 1987). Another problem is that Kohlberg argued that progress from stage to stage is irreversible, and such is not always the case (Darley & Shultz, 1990).

A rather strong argument has been raised against Kohlberg's theory as it applies to women (Ford & Lowery, 1986; Gilligan, 1982). All of Kohlberg's original data came from the responses of young boys, remember. Later, when young girls were tested, some studies seemed to suggest that girls showed slower moral development when compared to boys. Carol Gilligan's argument is that the moral reasoning of females is neither slower nor faster so much as *different* from the reasoning of males. Males, concerned with rules, justice, and an individual's rights, simply approach moral dilemma problems differently than do females, who are characteristically more concerned with caring, personal responsibility, and interpersonal relationships (Gilligan, 1982). Gilligan's book has brought a new slant to research on morality and value development in general. The issue is not a judgmental one in the sense of trying to determine if males are more or less moral in their thinking than females. The question is whether or not females and males develop different styles of moral reasoning and/or different types of moral behaviors. And this is a question for which final answers are not yet available. In fact, most studies show that any differences between men and women in resolving moral conflicts is really quite small (Darley & Schultz, 1990; Donneberg & Hoffman, 1988; Mednick, 1989; Walker, 1989).

Before You Go On
▼▼▼▼▼▼▼▼▼

Briefly summarize the stages of Kohlberg's theory of moral development.

▶ Adolescence

As I was reviewing the literature on the psychology of adolescence, I was constantly reminded of an observation we made back in Chapter 1: "For many questions in psychology, there are no simple answers." Take for example, the semingly straightforward question, "What are the defining characteristics of the stage of development we call 'adolescence'?"

Adolescence is clearly a period of transition—from the dependence of childhood to the independence of adult life. It is very difficult, however, to specify exactly when adolescence begins or when it ends. There are several choices.

puberty the stage of physical development at which one becomes capable of sexual reproduction

We may choose to define adolescence in biological terms. In that case, adolescence begins with **puberty** (sexual maturity and a readiness to reproduce) and ends with the end of physical growth—usually late in the teen years. A person's sexuality and physical growth surely do have psychological implications, but there are other ways of defining adolescence.

A more psychological perspective emphasizes the development of the cognitions, feelings, and behaviors that characterize adolescence. This approach views adolescence "as a psychological process occurring within the individual" (Forisha-Kovach, 1983, p. 8). Psychological approaches emphasize the development of problem-solving skills, and an increased reliance on the use of symbols, logic, and abstract thinking. Such perspectives stress the importance of identity formation, and a developing sense of self.

We also may consider adolescence from a more social perspective by examining the role of adolescents in society (Kett, 1977). These approaches generally define adolescence in terms of being in-between; not yet an adult, but no longer a child (Peterson & Ebata, 1987). In this context, adolescence usually lasts from the early teen years through one's highest educational level, when the individual is thought to enter the adult world. In this case, we see that the limits of adolescence may presently be changing as more young people opt to go on to college right after high school, still maintaining contact with and dependence on family and other support groups developed during the teen years.

adolescence the developmental period between childhood and adulthood, often begun at puberty and ending with full physical growth, generally between the ages of 12 and 20

Actually, whether we accept a biological, psychological, or social view of adolescence, we usually are talking about people who are between the ages of approximately 12 and 20. For the sake of our discussion, we will define **adolescence** as that period of development begun at puberty and lasting through the teen years. This is fairly close to the definition chosen by Anne Peterson for her review of adolescent development. She decided to focus on the second decade of life (Peterson, 1988).

One of the intriguing issues in the psychology of adolescence today is how to characterize the period in a general way. Is adolescence a period of personal growth, independence, and positive change? Or is adolescence a period of stress, turmoil, rebellion and negativism?

The view that adolescence should be characterized in terms of turmoil, storm, and stress is the older of the two, attributed to G. Stanley Hall (who wrote the first textbook on adolescence in 1904) and to Anna Freud (who applied Freudian theory to adolescents (A. Freud, 1958)). This position claims that normal adolescence involves the experience of all sorts of difficulties of adjustment. Anna Freud wrote, "To be normal during the adolescent period is by itself abnormal" (1958, p. 275). Thus, in this view, "Adolescents may be expected to be extremely moody and depressed one day and excitedly 'high' the next. Explosive conflict with family, friends, and authorities is thought of as commonplace" (Powers, Hauser & Kilner, 1989, p. 200).

Over the past 25 years, psychologists have come to appreciate that such a characterization of adolescents is inappropriate. Adolescence is not to be considered a period of great emotional distress that, with time, one outgrows. As we'll see, the teen years can present considerable pressure and conflict that require difficult choices. Sometimes teenagers do react to the pressures of their own adolescence in maladaptive ways. Adolescence does require change and adjustment, but those changes and *adjustments are usually made in psychologically healthy ways* (Garbarino, 1985; Manning, 1983; Offer & Offer, 1975; Peterson & Ebata, 1987; Rutter, et al., 1976). The picture of the troubled, rebellious, uncooperative adolescent is no doubt based on real experience, but is more often a reflection of a stereotype.

How might adolescence be defined from a physical, psychological, and social point of view?

▶ Physical Changes in Adolescence

The onset of adolescence generally is marked by two biological or physical changes. First, there is a marked increase in height and weight, known as a **growth spurt**, and second, there is sexual maturation or puberty.

The growth spurt of early adolescence usually occurs in girls at an earlier age than it does in boys. Girls begin their growth spurt as early as 9 or 10 years of age and then slow down at about age 15. Boys generally show their increased rate of growth between the ages of 12 and 17 years. Indeed, males usually don't reach their adult height until their early 20s, whereas girls generally attain their maximum height by their late teens (Roche & Davila, 1972; Tanner, 1981). Figure 3.10 provides one way to represent the adolescent growth spurt in graphic form.

growth spurt a marked increase in both height and weight that accompanies the onset of adolescene

Figure 3.10

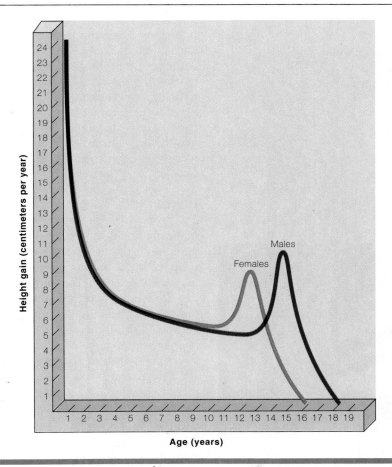

Age (years)

▲ *Females begin their main growth spurt around age 10, while the growth spurt in males does not begin until about age 12. In general, males will grow faster and for a longer period of time than females. (After Tanner, Whitehouse & Takaishi, 1966.)*

At least some of the challenge of early adolescence is a direct result of the growth spurt. It is not uncommon to find increases in weight and height occurring so rapidly that they are accompanied by real, physical growing pains, particularly in the arms and legs. Unfortunately, the spurt of adolescent growth seldom affects all parts of the body uniformly. Thirteen- and 14-year-old boys often appear incredibly clumsy and awkward as they try to coordinate their large hands and feet with the rest of their body. One of the most noticeable areas of growth in boys is that of the larynx and vocal cords. As the vocal cords lengthen, the pitch of the voice is lowered. To the embarrassment of many a teenage boy, this transition is seldom a smooth one, and he may suffer through months of a squeaking, crackling change of pitch right in the middle of a serious conversation (Adams, 1977; Adams & Gullotta, 1983).

puberty the stage of physical development at which one becomes capable of sexual reproduction

With the onset of **puberty**, there is a significant increase in the production of the sex hormones. Boys seldom know when their own puberty begins. For some time they have experienced penile erections and nocturnal emissions of seminal fluid. Biologically, puberty in males begins with the appearance of live sperm, and most males have no idea when *that* happens—such determinations require a laboratory test.

menarche a female's first menstrual period, often taken as a sure sign of the beginning of adolescence

In females, puberty is quite noticeable. It is indicated by the first menstrual period, called **menarche**. With puberty, adolescents are ready, in a biological sense, to reproduce. Perhaps more important than the physical changes themselves are the psychological reactions of the adolescent and others to these physical changes (Peterson, 1988, p. 593).

Many boys and girls reach puberty before or after most of their age mates, and are referred to as early or late bloomers. Reaching puberty well before or after others of one's age may have some psychological effects, but few are long-lasting. A girl who enters puberty early probably will be taller, stronger, faster, and more athletic than other girls (and many of the boys) in her class at school. She is more likely to be approached for dates, have more early sexual encounters, and marry at a younger age than her peers. She may have problems with her self-image, particularly if she puts on extra weight and shows marked breast development (Conger & Peterson, 1984; Crockett & Peterson, 1987). There also is a small but consistent advantage with regard to objective measures of intellectual functioning (Newcombe & Dubas, 1987).

Because of the premium put on physical activity in boys, the early-maturing boy is at a greater advantage than the early-maturing girl. He will have more dating and sexual experiences than his age mates, which will raise his status among his peers. He also will have a better body image and higher self-esteem (Peterson, 1988).

For teenagers of both sexes, being a late bloomer is more negative *at the time* than is being an early bloomer (Gross & Duke, 1980). There is some evidence (*e.g.,* Jones, 1957) that late-maturing boys may carry a sense of inadequacy and poor self-esteem into adulthood. Late maturity for girls seems to have little long-term negative consequence. Some feel, at least in retrospect, that being a late bloomer was an advantage because it allowed them to develop a wide range of broadening interests, rather than becoming "boy crazy" like so many of their peers in early adolescence (Tobin-Richards, et al., 1984).

Summary generalizations are often dangerous, but we may suggest that (1) early maturity is more advantageous than late maturity, at least at the time of adolescence, and (2) boys profit from early maturity more than do girls, but also may suffer more long-term consequences from late maturity.

▲ Adolescence can bring with it a number of challenges, including how to deal effectively with acne.

▲ One of the challenges of adolescence is identity formation. Who am I? What kind of a person am I to be? What shall be my values? What will I do with my life as I give up my dependence on others?

identity crisis the struggle to define and integrate one's sense of self and what one's attitudes, beliefs, and values should be

Before You Go On
▼▼▼▼▼▼▼▼

Briefly describe the physical changes that accompany the beginning of adolescence.

▶ Some Challenges of Adolescence

Adolescence is a developmental period that is marked by the stage of formal operations in Piaget's theory of cognitive development and by the stage of identity formation in Erikson's psychosocial theory. According to Piaget, an adolescent is able to think abstractly and to imagine, to think about what *is,* and to ponder what *might be.* This new, higher level of cognition often gets turned toward self-analysis, toward a contemplation of one's self in a social context (Keating, 1980). In this section, we'll examine a few issues that present specific challenges to the adolescent: identity formation, egocentrism in the adolescent, drug use, and adolescent sexuality.

Identity formation. Adolescents often give the impression of being great experimenters. They experiment with hairstyles, music, religions, drugs, sexual outlets, fad diets, part-time jobs, part-time relationships, and part-time philosophies of life. In fact, it may appear that most of a teenagers' commitments are made on a part-time basis. They are busily trying things out, doing things their own way, off on a grand search for Truth.

The perception of adolescents as experimenters is not without basis. It is consistent with the view that one of the major tasks of adolescence is the resolution of an **identity crisis**—the struggle to define and integrate the sense of who one is, what one is to do in life, and what one's attitudes, beliefs, and values should be. "Who am I?" "What am I going to do with my life?" Needless to say, these are not trivial questions. A person's search for his or her identity may lead to conflicts. Some of these conflicts may be resolved very easily, some continue into adulthood.

For Erik Erikson (1963), the search for identity is the fifth of eight stages of psychosocial development (see Figure 3.8). For many young people, adolescence brings very little confusion or conflict in terms of attitudes, beliefs, or values. Many teenagers are willing to accept without question the values and sense of self that they began to develop in childhood.

For many teenagers, however, the conflict of identity is quite real. They have a sense of giving up the values of parents and teachers in favor of new ones—their own. Physical growth, increased sexuality, and perceived societal pressures to decide what they want to be when they "grow up" may lead to what Erikson calls *role confusion.* Wanting to be independent, to be one's own self, often does not fit in with the values of the past, of childhood. Hence, the teenager tries to experiment with different possibilities in an attempt to see what works out best, occasionally to the dissatisfaction of bewildered parents.

Before You Go On
▼▼▼▼▼▼▼▼

Summarize the adolescent's search for identity as described by Erikson.

adolescent egocentrism self-centered cognitions, plus the belief that one is the center of the others' attention

Egocentrism in the Adolescent. According to Piaget, egocentrism, a focusing on oneself and an inability to take the point of view of others, can be found in children during the stage of preoperational thought (between the ages of 2 and 6). David Elkind (1967, 1981, 1984) uses the term in a slightly different way. In **adolescent egocentrism,** not only do individuals engage in self-centered thinking, but they also come to believe that virtually everyone else is thinking about them too. Because they now can think abstractly, adolescents begin to think about the thoughts of others and have a tendency to believe that they are the focus of others' attention. Needless to say, adolescent egocentrism leads to a heightened sense of self-consciousness.

Elkind says there are two manifestations of adolescent egocentrism. For one thing, teenagers often feel that they are "on stage," performing. They become convinced that when they enter a room, everyone is watching them and making judgments about everything, from what they are wearing to how their hair is styled. Now, in truth, it may be that no one is watching, but the adolescent believes that they are. Elkind calls this the construction of an *imaginary audience,* which may be explanation enough for the extreme self-consciousness of many young teens (Elkind & Bowen, 1979).

Adolescents often tend to overemphasize their own importance. They are, after all, the focus of their own attention, and given their imaginary audience, they feel that they're the focus of everyone else's attention as well. As a result, they tend to develop some rather unrealistic cognitions about themselves, which Elkind calls *personal fables.* These are "stories" about themselves that teenagers generate, often on the basis of irrational beliefs. They come to believe (egocentrically) that no harm can come to *them. They* won't become addicted after trying a drug at a party. *They* won't get pregnant. *They* won't get AIDS. *Their* driving won't be affected by alcohol. These sorts of beliefs can be dangerous, of course, and they can trigger considerable parental anxiety.

Before You Go On
▼▼▼▼▼▼▼▼▼

What is adolescent egocentrism, and how is it expressed?

▲ *Facing the challenge of drug use is a struggle for many adolescents.*

Drug Use by Adolescents. There is simply no doubt that many adolescents experiment with drugs. Many use drugs on a regular basis, and many abuse drugs. Smoking (45%) and drinking (56%) lead the list of drug-related activities that teenagers have tried at least once. Nearly 30 percent have tried illicit, or illegal, drugs (usually marijuana) (National Institute on Drug Abuse, 1987). Very few high school students have ever tried heroin, but in 1987, as many as 15 percent tried cocaine at least once (Millstein, 1989).

In fact, the use of illicit drugs is on the decline. Both use and abuse figures showed a slow but steady decline throughout the 1980s. The use of cocaine, for example, dropped in 1988 from the previous year's 15 percent to 12 percent (Landers, 1989). The use of most drugs by high school seniors increased between the mid-1970s and the 1981–1982 school year, but since then there has been a (gradual) reduction in drug use (Oetting & Beauvais, 1990). Perhaps more importantly, attitudes about the use of drugs are also becoming more negative among teenagers (Newcomb & Bentler, 1989). It is still the case that the use of drugs "remains very high, with 92% of [high school] seniors having had some experience with alcohol, and 66% using it in the past month. Regarding abuse, 5% were daily drinkers and 37.5% reported at least one occasion of heavy drinking (five or more drinks in a row). About one-fifth of seniors were daily cigarette smokers" (Newcomb & Bentler, 1989). [I should mention that even though alcohol and tobacco may be classified as licit or legally available drugs, their purchase and/or use by minors *is* illegal in most states.] Surveys aso indicate that, among high school students, there are no racial differences in drug use or abuse (Oetting & Beauvais, 1990).

What do all these statistics mean? For one thing, they mean that drug use and abuse among adolescents certainly deserve our strict attention, but at the same time, drug use among teenagers is *not* greater than it is for adults—and it *is* on the decline.

Jonathan Shedler and Jack Block, researchers at the University of California at Berkeley, recently reported on a study of adolescent drug use and psychological health that is bound to affect the way we view drug use among teenagers (1990). The subjects in this investigation were 101 18-year-olds who had been under study since they were 3 years old. Based on reports of their drug use, the subjects were divided into three groups: (1) *abstainers* (N=29), who had never tried any drug, (2) *experimenters* (N=36), who had used marijuana "once or twice, or a few times," and who tried no more than one other drug, and (3) *frequent users* (N=20), who reported using marijuana frequently and tried at least one other drug. (Sixteen subjects could not be placed into any of these three categories.) There were no socioeconomic or IQ differences among the groups.

The major findings of this study had to do with personality characteristics of the 18-year-olds in each group. *Frequent users* were found to be generally maladjusted, alienated, deficient in impulse control, and were "manifestly distressed." The *abstainers* were found to be overly anxious, "emotionally constricted," and lacking in social skills. These same results were apparent when the researchers examined records from when the same subjects were 7 and 11 years old. By and large the *experimenters* were found to be better adjusted and psychologically "healthier" than either of the other two groups.

The authors of this study have stated their strong concern that their research may be misinterpreted to indicate "that drug use might somehow improve an adolescent's psychological health" (p. 628). Clearly, this interpretation would be in error! These are correlational data from which no conclusion regarding cause-and-effect is justified (see Chapter 1, p. 31). While drug use among adolescents is, and should be, a matter of great concern, there is evidence to suggest that we need not get hysterical about infrequent, occasional drug use among teenagers. In a review of substance use and abuse among teenagers, Newcomb and Bentler (1989) put it this way:

> ▲ "Not all drug use is bad and will fry one's brain (as the commercials imply). Such claims as reflected in the national hysteria and depicted in media advertisements for treatment programs, repeat the failed scare tactics of the past. All drug abuse is destructive and can have devastating consequences for individuals, their families, and society. The difference or distinction lies in the use versus abuse of drugs" (p. 247).

To summarize again: adolescents do use and do abuse drugs, both licit drugs (e.g., alcohol and tobacco) and illicit drugs (e.g., marijuana and cocaine). At least the use of illicit drugs does seem to be decreasing, and we can say that drug use is no greater among teenagers than among adults. Thus, we cannot point to drug use to support the contention that adolescence is a time of special turmoil and distress. Now let's move from one touchy subject to another; from teenage drug use and abuse to teenage sexuality.

Psychology in the Real World

▲▲▲▲▲▲▲▲▲▲▲▲▲▲

What Can Be Done About Teenage Suicide?

The death of any young person is a tragic and sad occurrence. When that death is the result of suicide, our emotional reaction becomes magnified. As a final solution to perceived problems, suicide is certainly final, but it solves little.

In the real world, suicide among adolescents is real and present danger. Suicide is now the second leading cause of death among adolescents (behind accidents) (Brent et al., 1988). The number of suicide attempts by teenagers is on the increase, with estimates ranging as high as 300 percent *increase* since 1960. More than one million adolescents harbor serious thoughts of suicide each year (Peck, 1982).

There are two obvious questions. (1) Why do adolescents attempt suicide? and (2) What can be done to prevent teenage suicide? Let's deal with causes first. Bem Allen (1987) tells us that there are three levels of factors that may lead to adolescent suicide. The following summarizes his case:

A. **Predisposing Factors (general background variables)**
   1. *Family*: Family problems such as divorce, poor communication, imposition of many restrictions, and alcohol use within the family
   2. *Peers*: Isolation, or peer relations in conflict
   3. *Birth Trauma*: (surprisingly) difficulty at or soon after birth
   4. *Personal Factors*: Low self-esteem; drug/alcohol use; loss of boy/girlfriend; lack of confidant; depression; sex (most attempts are by females, but most successful attempts are by males)
   5. *Technological Advance*: Technology provides an ever-increasing number of choices, but not necessarily the means to make the best choice, leading to helplessness, perhaps despair
   6. *Acceptance of Suicide*: Exposure may lead to desensitization, making it an acceptable alternative
   7. *Moblity and Rootlessness*: Fosters a lack of long-term relationships

B. **Predictors (diagnoses from psychological testing)**
   1. *Depression*: Many measures of depression are related to suicide, but suicide need not be premised on depression.

Before You Go On
▼▼▼▼▼▼▼▼▼

Briefly summarize the data on drug use and abuse in adolescence.

Adolescent Sexuality. Going through puberty is a very personal, private, and potentially confusing process. Large doses of sex hormones enter the bloodstream, stimulating the development of secondary sex characteristics: In males, the neck and shoulders expand, hips narrow, facial and body hair begins to sprout, and the voice crackles and then lowers in pitch. In females, the breasts begin to develop, the hips broaden and become more rounded, and the shoulders narrow. All of this takes time, of course, but then puberty is more of a process than a single event.

As personal and private as her or his sexuality may be for the teenager, discussions of adolescent sexuality often revolve around statistics— impressive and

2. *Locus of Control*: A reliance on the belief that one's life is under the control of outside forces, including "fate" and "chance"
3. *Hopelessnesss:* May be more important than depression, perhaps even the cause of observed depression

C. Precipitating Events (factors that lead directly to suicide attempts)
1. *Clustering* : Implies that suicide is virtually "contagious," seems to be of recent vintage; perhaps conveys the notion that suicide is acceptable or "the thing to do." Why suicides tend to occur in clusters is a mystery.
2. *Independent Traumatic Events:* Things beyond the control of the individual, such as: death of a close friend or relative, parental divorce, loss of confidant through no fault of the individual, sudden economic setback
3. *Nonindependent Events:* Events initiated by the suicidal individual, such as: drug or alcohol consumption, acquisition of a lethal weapon, pregnancy out of wedlock, the disruption of close relationship(s)

To the extent that this list is accurate, it is very helpful to have a sense of the background factors that may lead to suicide attempts. But the more pressing issue may be: What can be done to stem the tide of teenage suicide? Allen (1987) suggests a number of things, and most revolve around *education*. First, we must all realize that suicide among teenagers IS a real problem, and we must bring discussions of suicide out into the open. (However, that at the same time we should not lose sight of the point made repeatedly in the text that *by far* most teenagers adjust effectively to their own adolescence and never give suicide serious thought.) In addition, we must all learn the signs and symptoms of impending suicide. Peers must be educated to be good and open listeners and to suggest therapy and professional help for acquaintances and friends who may be contemplating suicide. When one considers the cost in terms of grief, as well as in terms of lost human resources, there is ample reason for our commitment to efforts to mount a national campaign against suicide.

occasionally depressing statistics. What do the statistics tell us about the sexual behaviors of adolescents?

One of the first large-scale studies of teenage sexual practice was that of Sorenson (1973) who found that by the time they are 19 years old, more than half the females (57%) and almost three-quarters of the males (72%) reported having sexual intercourse. These data are consistent with those found in other, more recent and larger surveys (Coles & Stokes, 1985; Hofferth & Hayes, 1987; Zelnik & Kantner, 1980). A report from the Centers for Disease Control (CDC) released in early 1991 tells us that premarital sexual activity among adolescent females has risen in the last two decades —with a sharp increase since 1985. The survey from the CDC reports that nearly twice as many female teenagers (51.5%) had engaged in premarital sex by their late teens in 1988 compared to 1970 (28.6%). The largest relative increase occurred among those girls 15 years of age. When the report was released, the chief of the behavioral studies section of the CDC, Sevgi Aral, was quoted as saying that, "This is really important because it happened during a time when we thought we were doing so much in terms of

▲ *Dealing with their emerging sexuality is a difficult challenge for many teenagers.*

health education and AIDS prevention." Sexual activity is also increasing slightly among boys (Landers, 1990). The conflict for teenagers is that while biology says that they are ready for sexual behaviors and pregnancy, our culture tells them that they are not, even though that same culture promotes sexuality in advertising, clothing styles, and movies and television.

Most teens do not "plan" to become sexually active; it just "happens" (Chilman, 1983). One study (Coles & Stokes, 1985), indicates that about 60 percent of the males, but only 23 percent of the females "felt glad" about their first intercourse (34% of the males and 61% of the females reported feeling "ambivalent"). These data mirror those of Darling and Davidson (1986) who report that 67.4 percent of the males in their survey were "psychologically satisfied after their first sexual experience," while only 28.3 percent of the females in the study shared that satisfaction.

With all this sexual activity among adolescents, it is not surprising that teenage pregnancy has surfaced as a major social problem. There are a number of ways of looking at the data. We can note that this year more than half a million babies will be born to adolescent mothers (Kisker, 1985). Nearly two-thirds of the white mothers of those babies will be unmarried, and virtually all of the black mothers (97%) will be single (Furstenberg, Brooks-Gunn & Chase-Lansdale, 1989). Girls in the United States younger than 15 are *five times more likely* to give birth than are young girls from any other developed country for which data are available (Landers, 1987). In 1980, nearly 10,000 babies were born to mothers *age 14 or younger!* Note that so far we are talking about babies, not pregnancies. What of those teenage mothers who have miscarriages or abortions? Hayes (1987) claims that approximately 400,000 teenage pregnancies end in abortion each year. It is difficult to assess the true number, but estimating teenage pregnancies at well over a million a year is probably not far off (Auletta, 1984; Millstein, 1989; Zelnick & Kantner, 1980).

The physical, psychological, and financial costs of teenage pregnancy to individuals, families, and society are very high. The child of a teenage mother is certainly a baby at risk. Teenage mothers face innumerable hurdles—among other things, they are much more likely to drop out of school (Hayes, 1987; Hofferth & Hayes, 1987). But remember, most adolescents do not plan to become pregnant. More than anything else, teenage pregnancy may reflect a poor understanding of sexuality. For example, a significant number do not believe that they can become pregnant the first time

▲ *When adolescents become parents, both the parents and their child face numerous problems.*

they have intercourse, and teenagers hold negative attitudes about the use of contraceptives (Morrison, 1985).

The statistics reviewed here are impressive and depressing. Sexually active adolescents number in the millions. Many adolescents are woefully ignorant of the consequences of their own sexual behaviors. Those for whom sexual activity results in pregnancy number in the hundreds of thousands. But again, let's not lose sight of the fact that *most* teenagers *do not* have unwanted pregnancies. Many adolescents know a lot about sex. Dealing effectively with one's sexuality is never easy. It is but one of the challenges that we must address as we pass through adolescence.

Before You Go On
▼▼▼▼▼▼▼▼▼

What evidence supports the notion that adolescents are a sexually active group?

Briefly summarize the data on teenage pregnancy.

▶ Adulthood

The changes that occur during our adult years may not seem as striking or dramatic as those that typify our childhood and adolescence, but they are no less real. Many of the adjustments that we make as adults may go unnoticed as we accommodate to physical changes and psychological pressures. An adult's health may become a concern for the first time. Psychological and social adjustments must be made to marriage, parenthood, career, the death of friends and family, retirement, and, ultimately, one's own death.

Our adult lives end with death, but when adulthood begins is not easy to say. Legally, adult status is often granted by governments—at age 18 for some activities, at age 21 for others. Psychologically, adulthood is marked by two phenomena that at first seem almost contradictory: (1) *independence*, in the sense of taking on responsibility for one's actions and no longer being tied to one's parents, and (2) *interdependence*, in the sense of building new commitments and intimacies in interpersonal relationships.

Following the lead of Erikson (1968) and Levinson (1974, 1986), we'll consider adulthood in terms of three overlapping periods, eras, or seasons: early adulthood (roughly ages 18 to 45), middle adulthood (approximately ages 45 to 65), and late adulthood (over 65). Presenting adult development in this way may mislead us, so we should be careful. Although there is support for the notion of developmental stages in adulthood, these stages may be better defined by the individual adult than by the developmental psychologist (Datan, et al., 1987). In fact, some psychologists find little evidence for any orderly transitions in the life of adults (Costa & McCrea, 1980; McCrea & Costa, 1984), while others find significant sex differences in what determines the stage or status of one's adult life (Reinke, et al., 1985).

▶ Early Adulthood

If anything marks the transition from adolescence to adulthood, it is choice and commitment independently made. The sense of identity fashioned during adolescence now needs to be put into action. In fact, the achievement of a strong sense of self by early adulthood is an important predictor of the success of intimate relationships later in adulthood (Kahn, et al., 1985). With the attainment of adult status, there are new choices to be made. Advice may be sought from elders, parents, teachers, or friends, but as adults, individuals make their own choices. Should I get married? Should I stay single? Perhaps I should live with someone. Who? Should I get a job? Which one? Do I need more education? What sort of education? How? Where? Should we have children? How many? When? Many of these issues are first addressed in adolescence, during identity formation. But for the adult, these questions are no longer abstract. They are very real questions that demand some sort of response.

Levinson calls early adulthood the "era of greatest energy and abundance and of greatest contradiction and stress" (1986, p. 5). In terms of our physical development, we are at something of a peak during our 20s and 30s, and we're apparently willing to work hard to maintain that physical condition (McCann & Holmes, 1984; Shaffer, 1982). Young adulthood is also a season for finding our niche, working through the aspirations of our youth, raising a family. On the other hand, it is a period of stress, taking on parenthood, finding and keeping the "right" job and keeping a balance among self, family, job, and society at large. Let's take a brief look at two decision making processes of young adulthood, the choice of mate and family, and the choice of job or career.

It is Erikson's claim (1963) that early adulthood revolves around the basic choice of *intimacy versus isolation*. Failing to establish close, loving, or intimate relationships may result in loneliness and long periods of social isolation. Marriage is certainly not the only source of interpersonal intimacy, but it is the first choice for most Americans. More young adults than ever are postponing marriage plans, but fully 95 percent of us do marry (at least once). In fact, we're more likely to claim that happiness in adulthood depends more on a successful marriage than any other factor, including friendship, community activities, or hobbies (Glenn & Weaver, 1981).

Beyond establishing an intimate relationship, becoming a parent is generally taken as a sign of adulthood. For many, parenthood has become more a matter of choice than ever before because of more available means of contraception and new treatments for infertility. Having one's own family helps foster the process of *generativity* that Erikson associates with middle adulthood. This process reflects a growing concern for family and for one's impact on future generations (Chilman, 1980). Though such concerns may not become central until one is over 40, parenthood usually begins much sooner.

There is no doubt that having a baby around the house significantly changes established routines, often leading to negative consequences (Miller & Sollie, 1980). The freedom for spontaneous trips, intimate outings, and privacy is in large measure given up in trade for the joys of parenthood. As parents, men and women take on the responsibilities of new social roles—that of father and mother. These new roles in adulthood add to the already established roles of being a male or a female, a son or a daughter, a husband or a wife, and so on. Choosing to have children (or at least choosing to have a large number of children) is becoming less popular (Schaie & Willis, 1986). Although many people still regard the decision not to have children as basically selfish, irresponsible, and immoral (Skolnick, 1978), there is little evidence that such a decision leads to a decline in well-being or life satisfaction later in life (Beckman & Houser, 1982; Keith, 1983).

By the time a person has become a young adult, it is assumed that he or she has chosen a vocation or life's work. With so many possibilities to choose from, this decision is often a difficult one to make. Selection of a career is driven by many factors; educational requirements, family influence, and the

▲ *Having a baby around requires new parents to make adjustments to their daily lives. As a result, they find themselves staying at home more often.*

potential for earnings are just three. In fact, many young adults are dissatisfied with their initial choice(s) (Rhodes, 1983; Shertzer, 1985).

Jeffrey Turner and Donald Helms (1987) claim that choosing a career path involves seven identifiable stages. Let's review their list:

1. Exploration: There is a concern that something needs to be done, a choice needs to be made, but alternatives are poorly defined, and plans for making a choice are not yet developed. This period is what Daniel Levinson (1978) calls "formulating a dream."

2. Crystallization: Some actual alternatives are being weighed, pluses and minuses are associated with each possibility, and although some are eliminated, a choice is not made.

3. Choice: For better or worse, a decision is made. There is a sense of relief that at least one knows what one wants, and an optimistic feeling that everything will work out develops.

4. Career clarification: The individual's self-image and career choice are meshed together. Adjustments and accommodations are made. This is largely a matter of fine tuning one's initial choice, "I know I want to be a teacher; now what do I want to teach, and to whom?"

5. Induction: The career decision is implemented. This presents a series of potentially frightening challenges to one's own values and goals.

6. Reformation: One finds that changes need to be made if one is to fit in with fellow workers and do the job as one is expected to do it.

7. Integration: The job and one's work become part of one's self, and one gives up part of self to the job. This is a period of considerable satisfaction.

If someone were to make the wrong career decision, it is most likely to happen in the third stage of choosing a career path, but probably won't be recognized until the fourth or fifth stage. In such cases, there is little to do but begin again and work through the process, seeking the self-satisfaction that comes at the final stage. Unfortunately for many, "starting over" can be troublesome, and occasionally even an impossible thing to do. When this is the case, the person is often stuck with making the best of whatever possibilities do exist.

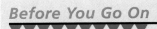

Before You Go On
▼▼▼▼▼▼▼▼

What developments may be said to characterize early adulthood?

▶ Middle Adulthood

As the middle years of adulthood approach, many aspects of one's life become settled. By the time most people reach the age of 40, their place in the framework of society is fairly well set. They have chosen their lifestyle and have grown accustomed to it. They have a family (or have decided not to). They have chosen what is to be their major life work or career. "Most of us during our 40s and 50s become 'senior members' in our own particular worlds, however grand or modest they may be." (Levinson, 1986, p. 6).

The movement to middle adulthood involves a transition filled with reexamination (Levinson, et al., 1974; Sheehy, 1976). During the middle years, one is forced to contemplate one's own mortality. One's "middle-age spread," loss of muscle tone, facial wrinkles, and graying hair are evident each day in the mirror. At about the age of 40, sensory capacities begin to diminish. Most people in this stage now notice obituaries in the newspaper where more and more people of the same age are listed every day.

For some people, the realization that time is running out produces something of a crisis, even approaching panic. But, by and large, the notion of a "midlife crisis" is mostly myth (Costa and McCrae, 1980; Farrell and Rosenberg, 1981). *For most, middle age is a time of great satisfaction and true opportunity* (Rossi, 1980).

Robert Havighurst (1972) says there are seven major tasks that one must face in the middle years:

1. *Accepting and adjusting to the physiological changes of middle age:* Although there certainly are many physical activities that middle-aged persons can engage in, they sometimes must be selective or must modify the vigor with which they attack such activities.

2. *Reaching and maintaining satisfactory performance in one's occupation:* If career satisfaction is not attained, one may attempt a mid-career job change. And, of course, changing jobs in middle age can be more a matter of necessity than choice. In either case, the potential for further growth and development or for crisis and conflict exist.

3. *Adjusting to aging parents:* This can be a major concern, particularly for "women in the middle" (Brody, 1981) who are caring for their own children and parents at the same time. In spite of widespread opinions to the contrary, individual concern and responsibility for the care of the elderly has not deteriorated in recent years (Brody, 1985). In fact, 80 percent of all health care for the elderly is provided by the family.

4. *Assisting teenage children to become happy and responsible adults:* During the middle years of adulthood, parents see their children mature through adolescence. Helping prepare them for adulthood (leaving the nest) becomes a task viewed with ambivalence.

5. *Achieving adult social and civic responsibility:* This task is similar to what Erikson calls the crisis of *generativity vs. stagnation.* People shift from thinking about all that they have done with their life to considering what they will do with what time is left for them and how they can leave a mark on future generations (Erikson, 1963; Harris, 1983).

6. *Relating to one's spouse as a person:* and (7) ***Developing leisure-activities:*** Although all seven of these tasks are clearly related and interdependent, this is particularly true of these last two. As children leave home and financial concerns diminish, there is more time for one's spouse and for leisure. Taking advantage of these changes in meaningful ways provides a challenge for some adults whose whole lives previously have been devoted to children and career.

Before You Go On
▼▼▼▼▼▼▼▼

What are some of the issues typically faced during the middle years of adulthood?

▲ *By middle adulthood most people have chosen careers and lifestyles and have more time for leisure activities.*

▶ Late Adulthood

The transition to what we are here calling late adulthood generally occurs in our early to mid-60s. Perhaps the first thing we need to acknowledge is that persons over the age of 65 comprise a sizable and growing proportion of the population in the United States. More than 30.4 million Americans were in this age bracket (by1988), and the numbers are increasing by an average of 1,400 per day (Fowles, 1990; Kermis, 1984; Storandt, 1983). This is an increase of 18% since 1980, compared to an increase of 7% for the under-65 population. By the year 2020, Americans over 65 will make up nearly 20 percent of the population (Eisdorfer, 1983). Because of the coming of age of the "baby boom" generation, by the year 2030, there will be about *66 million* older persons in the Unites States (Fowles, 1990).

ageism discrimination or negative stereotyping formed solely on the basis of age

Ageism is the discriminatory practice or negative stereotyping that is formed solely on the basis of age. Ageism is particularly acute in our attitudes about the elderly (Kimmel, 1988). One misconception about the aged is that they live in misery. Sensory capacities are not what they used to be. But, as Skinner (1983) suggested, "If you cannot read, listen to book recordings. If you do not hear well, turn up the volume of your phonograph (and wear headphones to protect your neighbors)." Many cognitive abilities suffer with age, but others are developed to compensate for most losses (Salthouse, 1989). Some apparent memory loss may reflect more of a choice of what one chooses to remember rather than an actual loss. There is no doubt that mental speed is reduced, but the accumulated experience of years of living can, and often does, far outweigh any advantages of speed (Meer, 1986).

Children have long since "left the nest," but they're still in touch, and now there are grandchildren with whom to interact. Further, the children of the elderly have themselves now reached adulthood and are more able to provide support for aging parents. In fact, only about 5 percent of Americans over the age of 65 live in nursing homes (Fowles, 1990; Harris, 1975; 1983).

Many individuals dread retirement, but most welcome it as a chance to do those things they have planned on for years (Haynes, et al., 1978). Many people over 65 become *more* physically active after retiring from a job where they sat at a desk all day long.

Although we often assume that old age necessarily brings with it the curse of poor health, in 1987 only 31 percent of the respondents over age 65 claimed poor health to be a serious problem. That may sound like a high percentage, but it compares to 7 percent in the 18 to 54 age range and 18 percent in the 55 to 65 age range. So although health problems *are* more common, they are not nearly as widespread or devastating as we might think. (I should also note that poor health among the elderly is related to income and educational levels. For example, elderly persons with incomes below $5000 are much more likely to report having serious health problems. Once again reminding ourselves of the nature of correlational data, we can argue that at least some of the elderly may have low incomes because of their poor health, as well as vice versa.)

One scheme that developmental psychologists are finding useful is to divide those over age 65 into two groups: the *young-old* and the *old-old*. This distinction is not made on the basis of one's actual age, but on the basis of psychological, social, and health characteristics (Committee on an Aging Society, 1986; Neugarten & Neugarten, 1986). The distinction reinforces the notion that aging is in itself not some sort of disease. The young-old group is the large majority (80–85 percent). They are described as "vigorous and competent men and women who have reduced their time

▲ *Many people who reach late adulthood use the time very productively. They look forward to visits with their grandchildren and continue to be active in organizations, such as a senior legislature.*

investments in work or homemaking, are relatively comfortable financially and relatively well educated, and are well-integrated members of their families and communities" (Neugarten & Neugarten, 1989).

The concept of "successful aging" has been with us for some time, however, it is a concept that seldom gets much attention. John Rowe and Robert Kahn (1987) would have us do no less than to change the entire focus of our study of human aging, particularly aging late in life. Most research has focused on *average* age-related losses and deficits. Rowe and Kahn claim that, "the role of aging per se in these losses has often been overstated and that a major component of many age-associated declines can be explained in terms of life style, habits, diet, and an array of psychosocial factors extrinsic to the aging process" (p. 143).

What goes unnoticed is the variability in adjustments made by older persons and the real possibility of aging "successfully." The argument is that the declines, deficits, and/or losses of the elderly are not the result of advanced age, but of factors over which we can exercise some control. The major contributors to decline in old age are poor nutrition, smoking, alcohol consumption, inadequate calcium intake, not maintaining a sense of autonomy and control over one's life circumstances, and lack of social support (so long as the support does not erode self-control). Attention to these factors may not significantly lengthen the life span, but should extend what the authors call the "health span, the maintenance of full function as nearly as possible to the end of life" (p. 149). Recent research tells us, for example, that maintaining close family relationships and involvement in effective exercise programs predict successful aging (Clarkson-Smith & Hartley, 1989; Valliant & Valliant, 1990).

Of the two sure things in life, death and taxes, the former is the surer. There are no loopholes. Dealing with the reality of our own death is the last major conflict or crisis that we face in life. As it happens, many people never have to deal with their own death in psychological terms. These are the people who die young or suddenly, from natural or accidental causes. But many individuals do have the time to contemplate their own death, and this usually takes place in late adulthood.

Much attention was focused on the confrontation with death in the popular book *On Death and Dying* by Elisabeth Kübler-Ross (1969, 1981). Her description of the stages that one goes through when facing death was based on hundreds of interviews with terminally ill patients who were aware that they were dying. Kübler-Ross suggests that the process takes place in five stages: 1. *Denial*—a firm, simple avoidance of the evidence; a sort of, "No, this can't be happening to me" reaction. 2. *Anger*—often accompanied by resentment and envy of others, along with a realization of what is truly happening; a sort of "Why me? Why not someone else" reaction. 3. *Bargaining*—a matter of dealing, or barter, usually with God; a search for more time; a sort of "If you'll just grant me a few more weeks, or months, I'll go to church every week; no, every day" reaction. 4. *Depression*—a sense of hopelessness that bargaining won't work, that a great loss is imminent; a period of grief and sorrow both over past mistakes and what will be missed in the future. 5. *Acceptance*—a rather quiet facing of the reality of death, with no great joy or sadness; simply a realization that the time has come.

It turns out that the Kübler-Ross description is an idealized one. Many dying patients do not fit this pattern at all (Butler & Lewis, 1981). Some may show behaviors consistent with one or two of the stages, but seldom all five (Schultz & Alderman, 1974). There is some concern that this pattern of approaching death may be viewed as the "best" or the "right'" way to go about it. The concern here is that caretakers may try to force dying people into and through these stages, instead of letting each face the inevitability of death in his or her own way (Kalish, 1976; 1985).

Although elderly people may have to deal with dying and death, they are generally less morbid about it than are adolescents (Lanetto, 1980). In one study (Kalish, 1976), adults over 60 did more frequently think about and talk about death than did the younger adults surveyed. However, of all the adults in the study, the oldest group expressed the least fear of death, some even saying they were eager for it.

Before You Go On

▼▼▼▼▼▼▼▼▼

Briefly summarize some of what we know about the elderly.

▼▼▼

Thinking Critically about Human Development

1. Without getting into whether you think it is "right" or "wrong," and given our discussion of prenatal development, what sort of information, if any, could psychologists provide that could help a person resolve conflicts about abortion? That is, is there anything that psychologists —as psychologists—could add or should add to the national policy debate on abortion?

2. Most of the data we have on the environment's impact on prenatal development comes from studies in the United States. What possibilities do you see for investigating prenatal development by examining the practices of other countries and other cultures?

3. How would you define "thinking" in a neonate, and what evidence would you have to generate to demonstrate whether neonates think?

4. To what extent should early childhood education programs be based on the results of research by developmental psychologists? For example, if we

now know that even neonates can demonstrate basic learning and memory skills, should we start sending newborns to school?

5. What reasons might you provide for the "gap" that seems to exist between the world of the teenager and the world of parents. Why do adolescents seem to feel a need to reject the values—and the music—of the previous generations? Now the REAL question: Do adolescents reject the values and/or the music of the previous generation? Why are we so ready to believe that they do?

6. What does your own experience as an adolescent tell you about that stage of development in terms of the abnormal being normal for adolescents?

7. If there is no such thing as a mid-life crisis, why do so many people seem to act as if there were?

8. As the population of the United States and Canada continues to become older and older, what changes in policy, at a local and national level, do you see as being helpful?

9. How do different cultures view and treat the elderly in their societies?

Summary

▼▼▼▼▼▼▼▼▼▼▼▼▼▼▼▼▼▼▼▼▼▼▼▼▼▼▼▼▼▼▼▼▼▼▼▼

Briefly summarize the three stages of prenatal development. Prenatal development begins at conception and ends at birth. This period is divided into three stages: the stage of the zygote (conception to 2 weeks), at which time the zygote becomes implanted in the uterus; the stage of the embryo (week 2 to week 8), during which there is rapid growth and differentiation of developing cells; and the stage of the fetus (month 3 until birth), during which the organs begin to function. *Pages 82–83*

Briefly review the impact of diet, drugs, and stress on prenatal development. A mother's diet and use of drugs have potentially profound effects on prenatal development. Malnutrition in the mother, or deficiencies of specific vitamins or minerals, are usually shared by the embryo or the fetus. Smoking and alcohol use during pregnancy have well-documented negative effects. The rule of thumb is to avoid drugs of any sort unless prescribed by a physician. Research on the effects of stress has not produced clear-cut results. *Pages 83–84*

Why do we care about neonatal reflexes? Even though some neonatal reflexes seem to have no particular survival value for the infant, they give us an idea of the adequacy of physical development. *Page 85*

What general observations can we make about physical growth and motor control in childhood? Although the age at which motor abilities develop varies considerably from child to child, the sequence is quite regular and predictable. Review Figure 3.4 for the ages at which some motor behaviors tend to develop. Growth and development also follow two patterns, (1) cephalocaudal, from head to torso to feet, and (2) proximodistal, from center to extremities. *Pages 85–86*

Summarize the basic sensory capacities of the neonate. The neonate's senses function reasonably well right from birth. The eyes can focus well at arm's length, although they will require a few months to focus over a range of object distances. Rudimentary depth perception seems to be present even in the neonate, but improves considerably within the first year. Hearing is quite good, as are the senses of taste, smell, and touch. *Page 87*

Cite an example of research evidence demonstrating a cognitive reaction in neonates. Recently we have come to appreciate that neonates can exhibit memory. They will attend to a new and different visual pattern after coming to ignore a familiar one, showing an appreciation of the difference between familiar and new. They show definite preferences for complex visual patterns over simple ones, and seem to prefer (attend to) visual representations of the human face. *Page 89*

How are schemas formed during the sensorimotor stage? During the sensorimotor stage of cognitve development, the child learns to develop new schemas (assimilating new information and accommodating old concepts) through an active interaction with the environment—by sensing and doing. *Page 90*

What characterizes this stage of development? The baby begins to appreciate cause-and-effect relationships, imitates the actions of others, and develops a sense of object permanence. *Pages 90–91*

In Piaget's theory, what best characterizes the preoperational stage of development? Egocentrism is a cognitive reaction that occurs during the preoperational stage of development. The child becomes very *me* and *I* oriented, unable to appreciate the world from the perspective of others. In addition, children begin to develop and use symbols, in the form of words, to represent concepts. *Pages 91–92*

What cognitive skills might we expect from a child in the concrete operations stage of development? In the concrete operations stage of development, a child organizes concepts into classes or categories and begins to use simple logic and to understand relational terms. The cognitive skills of conservation are not acquired until the end of the period. Conservation involves understanding that the form of something (rolling out a ball of clay, or pouring liquid from one container to another) does not change its essential nature or quality. *Page 92*

What cognitive ability characterizes the stage of formal operations? The essential nature of the formal operations stage of cognitive development is the ability to think, reason, and solve problems symbolically, in abstract, rather than concrete, tangible form. *Page 93*

Cite two criticisms of Piaget's theory of cognitive development. (1) There is little evidence that abilities develop in a series of well-defined, sequential stages. (2) Preschool children in particular seem to have more cognitive strengths than Piaget suggested. *Page 93*

Describe the first four stages of development according to Erikson. (1) Trust vs. mistrust, whether the child develops a sense of security or anxiety; (2) autonomy vs. shame and doubt, whether the child develops a sense of competence or doubt; (3) initiative vs. guilt, whether the child gains confidence in his or her own ability or develops a sense of inadequacy; and (4) industry vs. inferiority, whether the child develops a sense of confidence in intellectual and social skills or a sense of failure and a lack of confidence. *Page 95*

Briefly summarize the stages of Kohlberg's theory of moral development. Kohlberg proposes that the sense of morality develops through three levels and six stages. First, one decides right from wrong on the basis of avoiding punishment and gaining rewards (preconventional morality), then on the basis of conforming to authority or accepting social convention (conventional morality), and finally on the basis of one's understanding of the common good, individual rights, and the internalization of standards (postconventional morality). Although much of the theory has been supported by research, there is little evidence that many individuals reach the higher levels of moral reasoning, and there may be serious deficiencies in applying the theory equally to men and women. *Page 96*

How might adolescence be defined from a physical, psychological, and social point of view? Adolescence may be defined in a number of different ways. Physically, it begins with puberty (the attainment of sexual maturity) and lasts until the end of one's physical growth. Psychologically, it is defined in terms of the cognitions and feelings that characterize the period, searching for identity and abstract reasoning. Socially, it is a marginal period of transition, coming between childhood and adulthood, and is defined in terms of how the adolescent is viewed by others. *Page 98*

Briefly describe the physical changes that accompany the beginning of adolescence. Two significant physical developments mark adolescence: a spurt of growth, seen at an earlier age in girls (9 to 15) than in boys (12 to 17); and the beginning of sexual maturity, a period called puberty. That is, as adolescents, individuals are for the first time physically prepared for sexual reproduction. *Pages 99–100*

Summarize the adolescent's search for identity as described by Erikson. The search for one's identity—a sense of who one is and what one is to do with one's life—is, for Erikson, the major crisis of adolescence. Most teenagers do develop such a sense of identity, while some enter adulthood in a state of role confusion. *Page 101*

What is adolescent egocentrism, and how is it expressed? When youngsters engage in adolescent egocentrism they think mostly about themselves and come to believe that everyone else is thinking about them also. It is demonstrated by the creation of an *imaginary audience* when the adolescent comes to feel that everyone is watching and that they are "on stage," performing for and being noticed by others. This form of egocentrism also leads to the creation of *personal fables* when the individual develops unrealistic, storylike cognitions in which harm can come only to others. *Page 102*

Briefly summarize the data on drug use and abuse in adolescence. Most teenagers have experimented with drugs (mostly alcohol, tried by 92 percent of high school seniors), and a disturbing number use drugs quite frequently; however the use of illicit drugs is clearly on the decline. One recent study demonstrated that among frequent users, experimenters, and abstainers, the experimenters evidenced the fewest psychological problems as 18-year-olds. *Pages 102–103*

What evidence supports the notion that adolescents are a sexually active group? By the time they are 19 years old, more than half of all females and nearly three-quarters of all males report having had sexual intercourse. Sexual activity is on the rise for both males and females. First sexual encounters most often "just happen," without planning or forethought. *Pages 105–106*

Briefly summarize the data on teenage pregnancy. Over 1 million teenagers will become pregnant this year. Slightly more than half these pregnancies will result in live births. About two-thirds of white teenage mothers are unmarried, and virtually all black teenage mothers are unmarried. *Page 106*

What developments may be said to characterize early adulthood? Early adulthood (roughly ages 18 to 45) is a period characterized by choices and commitments independently made. One assumes new responsibilities and is faced with a series of difficult decisions concerning career, marriage, and family. For Erikson, the period is marked by the conflict between intimacy and social relationships on the one hand and social isolation on the other. *Page 108*

What are some of the issues typically faced during the middle years of adulthood? In many ways, middle adulthood (roughly ages 45 to 65) defines a period first of reexamination and then of settling down to one's life goals. Entering into the period may be troublesome for some, but most find middle age a period of great satisfaction and opportunity. The individual comes to accept his or her own mortality in a number of ways. The tasks or issues of middle age involve occupation, aging parents and growing children, social and civic responsibilities, and one's spouse and leisure time. *Pages 110–111*

Briefly summarize some of what we know about the elderly. There are now more than 30 million Americans over the age of 65, and the number of elderly is growing steadily. Although there are often sensory, physical, and cognitive limitations forced by old age, only 21 percent of elderly people rate health problems as a major concern. Although some elderly are isolated and lonely, fewer than 5 percent live in nursing homes, and only 8 percent consider themselves lonely. Older people are naturally concerned about death, but they are neither consumed nor morbid about it. With good nutrition, the development of a healthy lifestyle, proper social support, and the maintenance of some degree of autonomy and control over one's life, "successful aging" can become more common. *Pages 112–114*

3.1 How many cells does it take to form a zygote? a) 2 b) 23 c) 23 pairs, or 46 d) more than one trillion. *Page 81*

3.2 At which stage, or at what point is the developing human at greatest risk, of physical defects? a) as a zygote b) during the stage of the embryo c) as a growing fetus d) during the birth process *Page 82*

3.3 An organism is said to be viable when a) its brain is fully developed. b) it can survive without medical intervention. c) it is at least 270 days old. d) it can no longer be influenced by toxins or poisons from the environment. *Pages 82–83*

3.4 Each of these can have a negative effect on the developing organism. Which is most commonly the most negative? a) the mother's inability to gain weight during her pregnancy b) inadequate calcium intake during pregnancy c) taking antibiotics such as penicillin or tetracycline during pregnancy d) alcohol abuse during pregnancy. *Page 83*

3.5 True or False? The fetal alcohol syndrome includes the likelihood of mental or intellectual retardation. *Page 84*

3.6 The behaviors of the neonate can be described as a) learned or acquired. b) essentially useless. c) difficult to observe. d) largely reflexive. *Page 85*

3.7 True or False? Most neonatal reflexes have no apparent survival value. *Page 85*

3.8 Which statement concerning physical or motor growth and development in young children (younger than age 5) is TRUE? a) Physical growth in this period is slower than it has been earlier, or than it will be later. b) Growth and development occur at the very same rate for all normal, healthy children. c) Development and control begin at the extremities of the body and move inward, toward the trunk. d) Although rates of development vary, the sequence of development is very similar for all children. *Page 86*

3.9 Which sensory capacity or ability is probably the WEAKEST in a 6-month old child? a) the perception of depth and distance b) the sense of balance and body position c) the ability to discriminate among sounds d) the visual perception of faces. *Page 87*

3.10 One way to show that a newborn has a cognitive ability is to show that a) it uses reflexes regularly. b) all newborns follow the same sequence of development. c) newborns respond differently to new and previously experienced stimuli. d) virtually all of its senses are functioning at birth. *Page 88*

3.11 On what basis are Piaget's stages of development determined? a) the actual age of the child b) whether the child uses assimilation or accommodation c) the extent to which the child is egocentric or social d) how schemas are formed or modified with experience. *Page 90*

3.12 Melonie is 9 years old. She easily can get to school and back, a distance of six city blocks. On the other hand, she has great difficulty telling you just how she manages to make the trip to school and back each day. Melonie is probably in Piaget's _____ stage of cognitive development. a) sensorimotor b) preoperational c) concrete operations d) formal operations. *Page 92*

3.13 True or False? In forming his theory of cognitive development, Piaget seems to have underestimated the cognitive skills of very young, preschool children. *Page 93*

3.14 Of these, which is the biggest difference between Piaget's theory and Erikson's theory of development? Erikson's theory a) relies less on the notion of stages. b) was based on experiments, not observations. c) is more relevant for boys than for girls. d) describes development throughout the lifespan. *Page 95*

3.15 What we call "self-esteem," or one's sense of self worth is most critically important in which of these stages of Erikson's theory? a) trust vs. mistrust b) autonomy vs. shame and doubt c) initiative vs. guilt d) industry vs. inferiority. *Page 95*

3.16 Kohlberg's theory of development focuses primarily on the development of a) cognitive representations, called schemas. b) strategies that children use to learn. c) morality and the sense of right and wrong. d) how children and adolescents interact with each other. *Page 96*

3.17 True or False? Carol Gilligan has argued that with regard to moral development, there are sex differences in what is considered to be right or moral and what is considered to be wrong or immoral. *Page 97*

3.18 Which observation concerning adolescence is most valid? a) It is a stage or period through which many individuals never pass. b) It is a period defined in terms of stress, turmoil, and abnormality. c) It is a period through which most people pass in psychologically adaptive ways. d) It is virtually the only period for which the beginning and end of the period are defined in biological terms. *Page 98*

3.19 True or False?   Most adolescents are seriously troubled, rebellious, and uncooperative. *Page 98*

3.20 Which observation concerning menarche is TRUE? a) It is found more commonly in boys than in girls.   b) It occurs just before one's adolescence ends.   c) It generally occurs two or three years after puberty begins.   d) It is produced or triggered by the release of sex hormones. *Page 100*

3.21 Which observation concerning adolescent drug use is TRUE?   a) Adolescents experiment with and use drugs more than adults do.   b) Adolescents are more likely to use illicit/illegal drugs than licit/legal ones.   c) Both the use and abuse of drugs by adolescents has declined in the last decade.   d) Adolescents who have never used drugs experience fewer adjustment problems than those who have experimented with drugs. *Page 102*

3.22 True or False?   Any sort of use or experimentation with drugs by adolescents is bound to have long-term negative effects. *Page 103*

3.23 The best estimate of the number of teenagers who will become pregnant this year is approximately: a) 50,000.   b) 100,000.   c) 400,000. d) 1,000,000. *Page 106*

3.24 Which of the following "explanations" for teenage pregnancy is LEAST acceptable or LEAST reasonable?   a) Teenagers are ignorant about their own sexuality.   b) Many teenagers want to start their own families.   c) Teenagers have negative attitudes about contraceptive use. d) Pregnancies simply happen "by accident," without intention. *Pages 106–107*

3.25 What two concepts, taken together, characterize the beginning of adulthood?   a) independence and interdependence   b) death and dying c) growth and development   d) assimilation and accommodation. *Page 107*

3.26 For Erikson, early adulthood is best characterized in terms of   a) competency vs. inferiority. b) ego-identity vs. despair.   c) intimacy vs. isolation.   d) generativity vs. stagnation. *Page 108*

3.27 True or False?   Most young adults are unhappy or dissatisfied with their first career choices. *Page 109*

3.28 True or False?   Most Americans experience a real midlife crisis accompanied by the realization that "time is running out" and they may not get to do all they want to do. *Page 110*

3.29 Which of the following best characterizes the elderly in the United States?   a) Most (more than 50%) require supervision of the sort found in nursing homes.   b) Most (more than 50%) are preoccupied with thoughts of their own death. c) Most (more than 75%) are vigorous and competent.   d) Most (nearly 65%) list poor health as a serious problem. *Page 112*

Sensory Processes

▲▲▲▲▲▲

Remember this: The stimulus for vision is light. Now that you've stored that little tid-bit away, let me ask you a question. "What is the color of a barn that has been painted with 'red paint'?"

Even if you figure that there's a catch to this question, you must have a strong desire to answer that the color of a barn that has been painted red is, in fact, red. If this weren't a psychology textbook, and if I weren't being very very picky, you would be correct. But I want to be picky, and I want you to start thinking about how we process information about the world around us, so I'm going to argue that that barn is not really red. It isn't green or any other color. A barn that has been painted with red paint is black if it's anything at all. *Black!* Where did I get that bizarre notion? I did say I was going to be picky. In fact, you can't see the barn at all!

I can say that you do not see the barn because your eyes do not respond to barns—or cows or horses or red paint for that matter. What you see when you see a "red barn" is the light reflected from the barn—not the barn itself. Remember: The stimulus for vision is *light*.

Now if the farmer who owns the barn paints it red, the light that hits it and is reflected off it into your eyes gives rise to the experience of what we call red. (That's a psychologist saying that the barn will look red.) The barn reflects red light (and absorbs and diffuses all other colors of light) because the farmer painted it with a chemical that has the ability to reflect red light. There are other chemicals that have the property of reflecting yellow light, or blue light. If the farmer had covered the

barn with such chemicals then the barn would appear yellow or blue, but only because it was reflecting those lights into your eyes (the stimulus for vision is light).

In fact, paint (or crayons, or dyes, or any pigment) is itself without color. Color is a property of light. Pigment is a chemical that absorbs some colors of light while reflecting others. In this sense, paint has no color. If you doubt the truth of this, go to the hardware store and buy a small can of chemical labeled RED PAINT. Take the can into the closet, close the door, turn off the light, and open the can. What do you see? Right. You don't see anything. You certainly don't see anything red. You don't see any color. Color belongs to light, not to paint.

Note that I could continue this silliness into a discussion of all of our other senses as well as light and vision. We may *say* that we hear a churchbell in the distance, but what we are really "hearing" are the vibrations of air against our eardrum that we have come to associate with churchbells. What we really "taste" are molecules of chemicals on our tongue that we associate with cheeseburgers. We don't "feel" a pat on the back so much as we respond to pressure stimulations of receptors in our skin. The psychology of sensory processes is all about how stimuli in the environment produce responses within us.

▶ Preview

This chapter begins our discussion of memory. We are born into this world knowing very little about it. As newborns, we do have several important reflexes, and we are able to start learning quickly. But our minds—our memories—are pretty empty. By the time we are adults, our memories are packed with infomation, some of it critically important (What is edible; what isn't?), some of it comparatively trivial (What's the difference between hard rock and punk rock?). A centrally important question for many psychologists is how all that information gets processed into our memories. How do we find out about ourselves and the world in which we live? Answers to this question begin here, with a consideration of sensation.

Sensation involves converting physical energy from the environment into the neural energy of our nervous system. It is the process of getting the world "out there" into the world of our experience. Memories are stored in our brains, and our brains respond only to neural impulses, not to lights, sounds, odors, tickles, or other stimuli from the environment. The psychology of sensation deals with how our different senses manage to do what they do.

The chapter will begin with some general observations about how our senses work. We'll discuss how we assess the sensitivity of our senses and introduce the concept of sensory adaptation. Then we'll deal with vision. Most of our coverage of the senses, will be spent on vision, because vision provides us with a great deal of information about the world, and because we simply know more about vision than we do the other senses. Then we'll briefly review each of the other senses, examining the nature of the relevant stimuli, and discussing the relevant sense organ and sense receptors.

▶ A Few Basic Concepts

Before we get into how our sense organs convert physical energy from the environment into neural energy, we ought to consider a few important concepts. We begin with one of the oldest subfields in psychology, psychophysics.

▶ Sensory Thresholds

Psychophysics is the study of the relationships between the physical attributes of stimuli and the psychological experiences that they produce. At a simple level, we can say that the techniques of psychophysics have been designed to assess the sensitivity of our senses, allowing us to answer such questions as: "Just how good *is* your hearing after all these years of playing bass in a rock band?" On a more theoretical level, we can think of psychophysics as providing a means of systematically relating the outside *physical* world to the inner *psychological* world. Now the question we just asked may be recast to sound like: "How much of a change in the actual, physical intensity of this sound will it take for you to hear, or experience, a difference in loudness?" Psychophysical methods are designed to measure sensory thresholds, both absolute thresholds and difference thresholds.

Absolute Thresholds. Imagine the following simple experiment. You are seated in a dimly lighted room, staring at a small box. The side of the box facing you is covered by a sheet of plastic. Behind the plastic is a light bulb. I can decrease the physical intensity of the light bulb to the point where you cannot see it at all. I can increase the light's intensity so that you can see it very clearly. I also have many intensity settings between these extremes. My

sensation the process of receiving information from the environment and changing that input into nervous system activity

psychophysics the study of the relationship between physical attributes of stimuli and the psychological experiences they produce

basic question is: At what point of *physical* intensity will the light first become visible to you?

Common sense tells us that there should be some physical intensity below which you cannot see the light and above which you can. That point would be your absolute threshold. The term *threshold* here means the same thing that it means in other contexts—a point of crossing over. (You cross the threshold of a door as you move from outside to inside, or vice versa.) Threshold is clearly related to *sensitivity*, but in an inverse sort of way. As threshold levels decrease, we say that sensitivity increases. The lower the threshold of a sense receptor, the more sensitive it is.

Now let's return to our imaginary experiment. I repeatedly vary the light's intensity, and ask you to respond "Yes, I see the light," or "No, I don't see the light," depending on your experience. (In this experiment, I will not allow you the luxury of saying that you don't know or aren't sure.)

When this experiment is actually done, we discover something that at first seems strange. There are many intensities of the light for which your responses are inconsistent over a number of presentations of the very same light intensity. In other words, there are intensities of light to which you sometimes respond "yes" and sometimes say "no," even though the actual, physical intensity of the light is unchanged!

In reality, there just isn't very much that is absolute about absolute thresholds at all. They keep changing from moment to moment, reflecting small, subtle changes in the sensitivity of our senses. (They also reflect such factors as momentary shifts in our ability to pay attention.) Figure 4.1 shows (A) what we might like to happen in an experiment like the one we've just described, and (B) what actually does happen in such an experiment.

absolute threshold the physical intensity of a stimulus that one can detect 50 percent of the time

Because there are no truly "absolute" measures of sensory sensitivity, psychologists resort to the following definition of **absolute threshold**: the physical intensity of a stimulus that a subject reports detecting 50 percent of the time. That is, intensities below threshold are detected less than 50 percent of the time, while intensities above threshold are detected more than 50 percent of the time. This complication occurs for all our senses, not just for

Figure 4.1

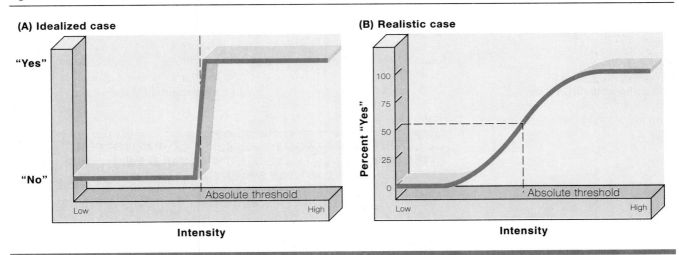

▲ *Determining absolute threshold values. (A) The idealized case, in which there is a point before which the stimulus is never detected and after which it is always detected, and (B) the realistic case, where absolute threshold is the intensity of stimulation that is detected 50 percent of the time.*

vision. I would have the same general result if I tested your ability to detect sounds, smells, touches, or tastes.

So what good is the notion of an absolute threshold? For one thing, as a measure of sensitivity, absolute threshold levels can be used to discover if one's senses are operating properly and detecting low levels of stimulation (which is what happens when you have your hearing tested). Engineers who design sound systems know about absolute thresholds—speakers that do not reproduce sounds above threshold levels aren't of much use. Warning lights must be designed to be well above absolute threshold if they are to be of any use to us. How much perfume is required for it to be noticed? How low must you whisper so as not to be overheard in a classroom? Do I smell natural gas in the house, or is it my imagination? Unless stimulus intensity exceeds absolute threshold levels, they may not be experienced (sensed) at all. As it happens, our sense receptors are remarkably sensitive, as the oft-quoted examples in Figure 4.2 attest.

Before You Go On

How is the process of sensation defined?

What is psychophysics?

What is an absolute threshold, and how is it related to the sensitivity of our senses?

difference threshold the minimal difference in some stimulus attribute, such as intensity, that one can detect 50 percent of the time

Difference Thresholds. We don't often encounter situations that test our ability to detect very low-intensity stimuli. However, we often *are* called upon to detect differences among stimuli. The issue here is not if stimuli can be detected, but if they are in some way *different* from each other. A **difference threshold** is the smallest difference between stimulus attributes that can be detected. As you may have guessed, we have the same complication here that we have when we try to measure absolute thresholds. To slight degrees, one's difference threshold for any attribute tends to vary from moment to moment. So again we say that to be above one's difference threshold, differences between stimuli need to be detected more than 50 percent of the time.

Here is an example. I present you with two tones. You can hear them both (they're both above your absolute threshold), and report that they seem equally loud. If I gradually increase (or decrease) the intensity of one of the tones, I will eventually reach a point where you can just barely notice a difference between the loudness of the two tones. This **just noticeable difference (j.n.d)** is defined

just noticeable difference (j.n.d.) the smallest detectable change in some stimulus attribute, such as intensity

Figure 4.2

EXAMPLES OF ABSOLUTE THRESHOLD VALUES FOR FIVE SENSES (I.E., THESE STIMULI WOULD BE NOTICED AT LEAST 50 PERCENT OF THE TIME)

Vision	a candle flame seen from a distance of 30 miles on a clear, dark night
Hearing	the ticking of a watch under quiet conditions from a distance of 20 feet
Taste	I teaspoon of sugar dissolved in 2 gallons of water
Smell	one drop of perfume in a three-room apartment
Touch	the wing of a bee dropped on your cheek from a height of one centimeter

(From Galanter, 1962.)

as the amount of change in a stimulus that makes it just noticeably different from what it was. This as essentially the same thing as a difference threshold.

The concept of just noticeable difference is relevant in many contexts. A parent asks a teenager to "turn down that stereo!" The teenager reduces the volume, but not by a j.n.d. from the parent's perspective, and trouble may be brewing. Does the color of the belt match the color of the dress closely enough? Can anyone tell the difference between expensive ingredients in the stew and cheaper ones?

Signal Detection. We recognize that sensory thresholds are not fixed. They vary from moment to moment and therefore are defined in terms of probability. This amounts to saying that the sensitivity of our senses changes. It changes because of momentary shifts in attention and because of the random electrical activity of the nerve cells in our sensory systems.

When we are asked if a stimulus is present, what we really are being asked to do is to judge whether or not we can detect a signal against a background of other stimuli and randomly changing neural activity called *noise*. Thinking about threshold determination in this way involves the basics of **signal detection theory**. The theory takes the position that stimulus detection is the process of deciding if a signal exists against a background of noise (Green & Swets, 1966).

According to this theory, the absolute threshold can be influenced by many factors in addition to the actual sensitivity of one's senses. We have seen that random nervous system activity needs to be accounted for. So do the individual's attention, expectations, and biases. For example, in a study to determine absolute threshold, subjects are simply more likely to say that they detect a stimulus than they are to say that they don't (Block, 1965). Other subjects may be overly cautious, not saying "Yes" until they are absolutely sure that the stimulus in question has been presented.

Remember the basics of the absolute threshold study with which we began our discussion of psychophysics? I had a light in a box. I changed the intensity of the light and asked whether you could see it. Your absolute threshold was taken to be the intensity of the light to which you responded

signal detection theory the view that stimulus detection is a matter of decision making, of separating a signal from background noise

▲ *The trading floor at the Chicago Board of Trade provides a challenging environment in which to test signal detection theory.*

"Yes" 50 percent of the time. Signal detection theory simply asks us to consider *all* of the factors that might have prompted you to say "Yes" at any exposure of the light. What might some of these factors be? One would be the amount of other light available in the room. Wouldn't you be more able to detect the signal of my light in a room that was totally dark as opposed to a room in which all of the standard lights were on? What if I had offered you a reward, say $5, for each time you correctly detected the light. Wouldn't you tend to say "Yes" often, whether you were really sure of yourself or not? By the same token, if I were to fine you $1 each time you said "Yes" when the light was not really on, might you not become very conservative, saying "Yes" only when you were very sure? Might we not expect a difference in your patterns of saying "Yes" and "No" depending on whether we tested you in mid-morning or late in the day, when you were tired?

Signal detection procedures try to take into account such factors as background noise (e.g. amount of other light in the room), level of attention, and subject bias in the determination of sensory thresholds. The result is a better, clearer picture of sensory sensitivity.

▶ *Sensory Adaptation*

We need to introduce one more general concept that applies, to varying degrees, to each of our senses. **Sensory adaptation** is a process by which sensory experiences decrease with the continued exposure to a stimulus.

Many common experiences provide us with examples. When we first jump into the pool or the lake, the water feels very cold, but after only a few minutes, we adapt and are reassuring our friends to "Come on in; the water's fine." When we first walk into a house where cabbage is cooking, the odor is nearly overwhelming, but soon we adapt and do not notice it at all. When the compressor motor of the refrigerator first turns on, it seems to make a very loud noise, one that we soon do not notice at all—until the motor *stops* and silence returns to the kitchen. Sensory adaptation again.

There is an important psychological point hidden in these examples. It is that the ability to detect the presence of a stimulus depends largely on the extent to which sense receptors are being newly stimulated or have to some degree already adapted. In other words, sense receptors respond to *changes* in stimulation. The constant stimulation of a receptor leads to adaptation, and less of a chance that that stimulation will be detected.

There is an exception to this usage of the term *adaptation*. Have you thought of it? What happens when you move from a brightly lit area to a dim place? Perhaps you enter a dark movie theater on a sunny afternoon. At first you can barely see anything at all. But in a few minutes, you are seeing reasonably well. What do we say happened? We say that you have "adapted to the dark." Here we are using the term adaptation in a different way. **Dark adaptation** refers to the fact that with time spent in the dark, our visual receptors actually become *more* sensitive to what little light is available. In terms of threshold, we say that our threshold for light intensity *decreases*, because—as you recall—the lower our threshold, the more sensitive our sense receptors.

sensory adaptation the process in which our sensory experience tends (in most cases) to decrease or diminish with continued exposure to a stimulus

dark adaptation the process by which our eyes become more sensitive to light as we spend time in the dark

Before You Go On
▼▼▼▼▼▼▼▼▼

What is a difference threshold, or j.n.d.?

Briefly summarize the basic ideas of signal detection theory.

What is sensory adaptation?

▶ The Stimulus for Vision: Light

As you will recall from our opening section: *Light is the stimulus for vision.* **Light** is a wave form of radiant energy. That means that light *radiates* from its source in the *waves* (which we call light waves). Light waves have three major physical characteristics that are related to psychological experience: wave amplitude, wavelength, and wave purity.

▶ Wave Amplitude (Intensity)

One of the ways in which light energy may vary is in its intensity. When we think about light traveling in the form of waves of energy, differences in intensity correspond to differences in the **wave amplitude** of light. The amplitude of a wave is represented by its height. You can refer to Figure 4.3 and assume that the two waves in the drawing represent two different light waves. One of the physical differences between light (a) and light (b) is in the height of the waves, or wave amplitude.

The amplitude of a wave represents a light's *physical* intensity. Our psychological experience of intensity is what we call **brightness**. The difference between a dim light and a bright light is due to the difference in wave amplitude. Of the two lights in Figure 4.3, (a) has the higher amplitude and thus would be seen as the brighter light. Switches that control the brightness of some light fixtures are in essence controlling the amplitude of light waves.

▶ Wavelength

A second physical characteristic of waves of energy (such as light waves) is **wavelength**, which is the distance between any point in a wave and the corresponding point on the next cycle—from peak to peak, for example. In Figure 4.3, one difference between waves (a) and (b) is their wavelength, where (a) has the longer wavelength. Although it is difficult to imagine distances so tiny, we *can* measure the length of a light wave. Our unit of measurement is the **nanometer (nm)**, which is equal to one billionth of a meter or one millionth of a millimeter!

As it happens, there are many forms of radiant energy that travel in waves. However, the human eye responds only to radiant energy that has a wavelength between (roughly) 380 and 760 nanometers. This is the range of light waves that makes up what we call the visible spectrum. Wave forms of energy with wavelengths shorter than 380nm (such as X-rays and ultraviolet rays) are so short that they do not stimulate the receptors in our eyes, and they go unnoticed. Wave forms of energy with wavelengths in excess of 760nm (microwaves and radar are two examples) do not stimulate the receptor cells in our eyes either.

Wave amplitude determines our experience of brightness. Wavelength is the attribute of light that determines the **hue** (color) we perceive. As light waves increase in length from the short 380nm wavelengths to the long 760nm wavelengths, our experience of them changes—from violet to blue to green to yellow-green to yellow to orange to red along the color spectrum (see Figure 4.4, which also presents some of the invisible varieties of radiant energy in wave form).

A source of radiant energy with a 700 nanometer wavelength will be seen as a red light. In fact, that's what a red light *is*. (A bright red light has a high amplitude, and a dim red light has a low amplitude, but both have 700nm wavelengths.) As we can see from Figure 4.4, if a light had waves 550nm long, it would be seen as a yellow-green light, and so on. (Note that yellow-green is a single hue produced by a given wavelength of light

---

light a radiant energy that can be represented in wave form with wavelength between 380 and 760 nanometers

wave amplitude a characteristic of wave forms (the height of the wave) that indicates intensity

brightness the psychological experience associated with a light's intensity or wave amplitude

wavelength a characteristic of wave forms that indicates the distance between any point on the next cycle of the wave

nanometer (nm) one millionth of a millimeter, the unit of measurement for the wavelength of light

hue the psychological experience associated with a light's wavelength

---

Figure 4.3

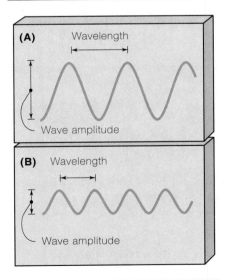

▲ Representations of light waves differing in wavelengths and wave amplitude. See text for explanation of how these physical characteristics are related to our psychological experience of light.

Figure 4.4

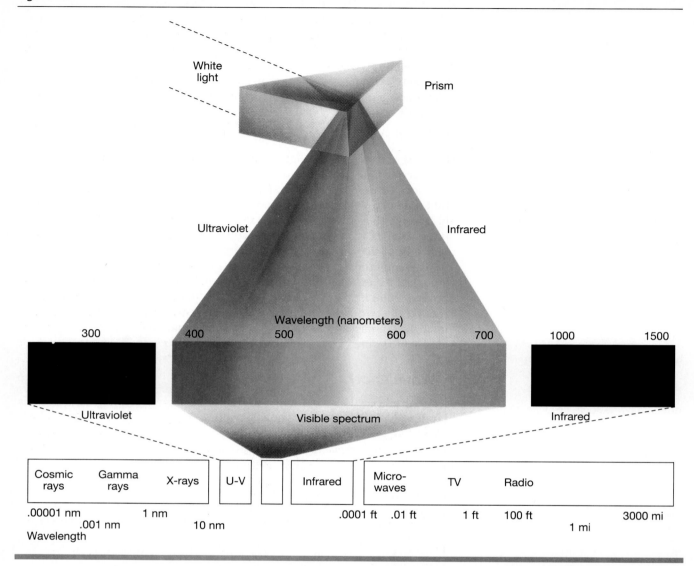

▲ *The spectrum of electromagnetic energy in wave form of which light is but a small segment. Here we see that light is energy with a wavelength between 380nm and 760nm. As wavelength increases, our experience of light changes to produce a "rainbow."*

(550nm). It is *not* some sort of combination of yellow and green. We simply have no other name for this hue, so we call it yellow-green.)

▶ Wave Purity

Imagine a light of medium amplitude with all its wavelengths exactly 700 nanometers long. The light would appear to be of medium brightness. And because the wavelengths are all 700nm, it would appear red. More than that, it would appear as a pure, rich red. We call such a light **monochromatic** because it is made up of light waves all of one (mono) length or hue (chroma). In truth, we seldom see such lights outside the laboratory, because producing a pure, monochromatic light is expensive.

monochromatic literally one colored; a pure light made up of light waves all of the same wave length

saturation the psychological experience associated with the purity of a light wave, where the most saturated lights are monochromatic and the least saturated are white light

white light a light of the lowest possible saturation, containing a mixture of all visible wavelengths

Even the reddest of lights that you and I see in our everyday experience have other wavelengths of light mixed in along with the predominant 700nm red. (If the 700nm light wave did not predominate, the light wouldn't look red at all.) Even the red light on top of a police car has some violet and green and yellow wavelengths of light in it.

The physical purity of a light determines the psychological experience that we call **saturation**. Pure, monochromatic lights are the most highly saturated; their hue is rich and obvious. (Think of lights that are highly saturated as being so filled—saturated—with the one wavelength that there isn't room for any other.) As more and more different wavelengths get mixed into a light, it becomes lower and lower in saturation—and it starts to look pale and washed out.

What do we call a light that is of the lowest possible saturation; a light that contains a random mixture of wavelengths of light? By definition, it is **white light**. It is something of a curiosity that white light is in fact as *impure* a light as possible. A pure light has but one wavelength; a white light contains many wavelengths.

True white light is as difficult (and as expensive) to produce as is a pure monochromatic light. Fluorescent light bulbs produce reasonable approximations, but their light contains too many wavelengths from the short (or blue-violet) end of the spectrum. Light from regular incandescent light bulbs contain too many light waves from the orange and red end of the spectrum (even if we paint the inside of the bulb with white paint). A prism can take a beam of white light—sunlight is an approximation—and break it down into its various parts, giving us the experience of a rainbow of hues. Where did all those hues come from? They were there all along, mixed together the white light.

We have seen that three physical characteristics of light influence the nature of our visual experience. Wave amplitude determines brightness; wavelength determines hue; and wave purity determines saturation. These relationships are summarized in Figure 4.5.

Before You Go On

▼▼▼▼▼▼▼▼

In what ways do the major physical characteristics of light waves of energy (amplitude, length, and purity) affect our psychological experience of light?

Figure 4.5

THE PHYSICAL CHARACTERISTICS OF LIGHT WAVES INFLUENCE OUR PSYCHOLOGICAL EXPERIENCE OF LIGHT.

Physical Characteristic	Psychological Experience
Wave amplitude (intensity)	Brightness
Wavelength	Hue
Wave purity	Saturation

► The Eye

Vision involves changing light wave energy into the energy of the nervous system. This transformation takes place in the eye. Even so, most of the structures of the eye have little to do with the actual process of energy conversion; their function is to focus the images that enter the eye on the layer of cells that responds directly to light waves.

► Structures That Focus Visual Images

Using Figure 4.6 as a guide, let us trace the path of light as it passes through the eye, ultimately to produce a visual experience. Light first enters through the **cornea**. The cornea is the tough, round, virtually transparent outer shell of the eye. Those of you who wear contact lenses float them on your corneas. The cornea serves to protect the delicate structures behind it, and starts to bend the entering light waves in order to focus an image on the back surface of the eye.

Having passed through the cornea, light then travels through the **pupil**, an opening in the **iris**. The iris is the part of your eye which is pigmented, or colored. When we say that someone has blue, brown, or green eyes, we are referring to the color of their iris. The iris expands or contracts, changing the size of the pupil. This is a reflex reaction, not something you can control by conscious effort. Contractions of the iris that change pupil size are most commonly made in response to the level of light present—opening the pupil wide when only small amounts of light are present and reducing its size (protectively) in response to high-intensity lights. Increasing pupil size is also one of the automatic responses that occurs with heightened levels of emotionality—an adaptive reaction to let in as much light as possible.

After the pupil, the next structure light encounters is the **lens**. As in a camera, the main function of the lens of the eye is to focus a visual image. The lens changes shape to bring an image into focus—becoming flatter when we try to focus on an object at a distance and becoming rounder, when we try to view something up close. This, too, is largely a reflex. Obviously, lenses are not normally as hard as glass or they wouldn't be able to

cornea the outermost structure of the eye, which protects the eye and begins to focus light waves

pupil the opening in the iris that changes size in relation to the amount of light available and emotional factors

iris the colored structure of the eye that reflexively opens or constricts the pupil

lens the structure behind the iris that changes shape to focus visual images in the eye

Figure 4.6

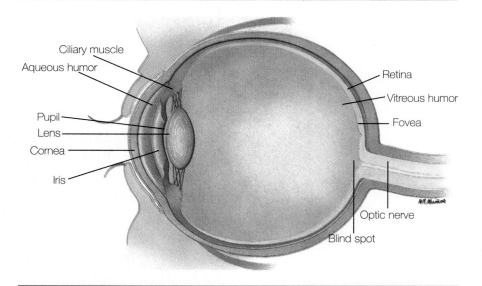

▲ *The major structures of the human eye.*

change their shape. (With age, our lenses tend to harden, making it difficult to focus and requiring that we use corrective lenses to help out.)

ciliary muscles small muscles attached to the lens that control its shape and focusing ability

accommodation in vision, the process in which the shape of the lens is changed by the ciliary muscles to focus an image on the retina

Some very powerful little muscles control the lens. They are called **ciliary muscles,** and they push on the lens or relax in order to change its shape. The process by which the ciliary muscles change the shape of the lens is called **accommodation.** It is often the case that an image does not focus as it should, either because of the shape of the lens or the eye itself or a failure of accommodation. It is also sometimes the case that a healthy lens and functioning ciliary muscles still can't get an image to focus because of the shape of the eyeball itself. The result is nearsightedness or farsightedness. Figure 4.7 shows examples of what happens in these cases.

Figure 4.7

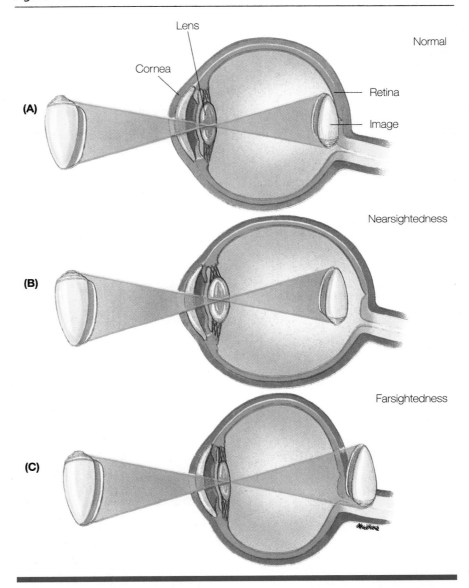

▲ *Sightedness. (A) Normal vision, where the inverted image is focused by the cornea and lens in the retina. (B) Nearsightedness, where the focused image falls short of the retina because the eyeball is too rounded. (C) Farsightedness, where the focused image falls beyond the retina because the eyeball is too short or the lens too flattened.*

aqueous humor watery fluid found in the space between the cornea and the lens that nourishes the front of the eye

vitreous humor the thick fluid behind the lens of the eye that helps keep the eyeball spherical

retina layers of cells at the back of the eye that contain the photosensitive rod and cone cells

photoreceptors light-sensitive cells (cones and rods) of the retina that convert light energy into neural energy

rods photosensitive cells of the retina that are most active in low levels of illumination and do not respond differentially to different wavelengths of light

cones photosensitive cells of the retina that operate best at high levels of illumination and are responsible for color vision

There is a space between the cornea and the lens filled with a clear fluid called **aqueous humor**. This humor (which means "fluid") provides nourishment to the cornea and the other structures at the front of the eye. If the fluid cannot easily pass back out of this space, pressure builds within the eye, causing distortions in vision or, in extreme cases, blindness. This disorder is known as *glaucoma*.

There is another, larger space *behind* the lens that is also filled with a fluid or humor. This fluid is called **vitreous humor**. It is not nearly as watery as aqueous humor. It is thick and filled with tiny structures that give it substance. Its major function is to keep the eyeball rounded.

▶ The Retina

So far we've listed several structures of the eye, each important in its own way, but none of them doing much more than allowing light waves back through the eye to other structures, usually in more focused form. It is at the **retina** that vision begins to take place. It is here that light energy is changed into neural energy.

The retina is a series of layers of specialized nerve cells at the back surface of the eye. These cells are specialized neurons, and in a sense should be thought of as part of the brain. The location of the retina and its landmarks are shown in Figure 4.6, while Figure 4.8 shows the retina in more detail.

To describe the retina, let's move from the back of the eye out toward the front. The layer of cells at the very back of the retina are the receptor cells for vision or **photoreceptors**. It is here at this level that light wave energy is changed into neural impulses.

As it happens, there are two types of photoreceptor cells: **rods** and **cones**. They are aptly named, because they look like small rods and cones. Their ends or tips respond to light wave energy and begin a neural impulse.

Figure **4.8**

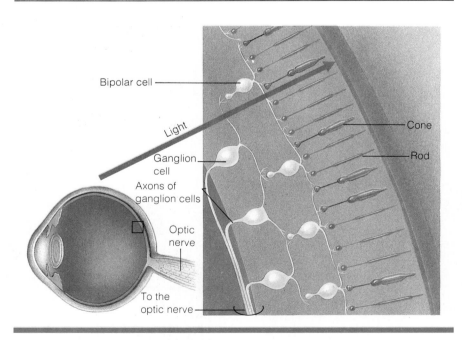

▲ *The major features of the human retina.*

optic nerve a fiber composed of many neurons, which leaves the eye and carries impulses to the occipital lobe of the brain

fovea the region at the center of the retina, comprised solely of cones, where acuity is best in daylight

blindspot a small region of the retina, containing no photoreceptors, where the optic nerve leaves the eye

These impulses travel down the rods and cones and pass on to (form a synapse with) other cells, also arranged in layers.

At these layers of nerve cells there is considerable combination and integration of neural impulses. Each rod and each cone does not have a single direct pathway to the cerebral cortex of the brain. Impulses from many rods and cones are combined right in the eye (by *bipolar cells* and *ganglion cells*, among others). Fibers from ganglion cells gather together to form the **optic nerve**, which leaves the eye and starts back toward other parts of the brain.

Notice again the arrow in Figure 4.8 that indicates the direction of the light entering the retina. It is drawn correctly. Yes, light waves first pass through all those layers of cells, past all those nerve cells, to reach the tips of the rods and cones where they are transformed into neural impulses. It would seem to make more sense to point the light-sensitive tips of the rods and cones out toward the incoming light, yet virtually all mammalian retinas are constructed in the manner shown in Figure 4.8.

The two main features of the retina shown in Figure 4.6 are the **fovea** and the **blindspot**. There are no rods in the fovea, only cones, which are tightly packed together. It is here at the fovea that our ability to discern detail (acuity) is best—at least in reasonably high levels of illumination. If you were to try to thread a needle, you'd want to focus the image of the needle and thread directly on the fovea.

The blindspot of the retina is where the nerve impulses from the rods and cones, having passed through all those other layers of cells, exit the eye. At the blindspot, there are no rods and cones—there's nothing there but the optic nerve threading its way back deeper into the brain. Because there are no rods or cones, there is no vision here, which is why this area is called the blindspot. Figure 4.9 provides you with a way to locate your own blindspot.

Before You Go On
▼▼▼▼▼▼▼▼▼▼

List the major structures of the eye, and describe the function of each.

Figure 4.9

▲ *Finding your blindspot. (A) Close your right eye and stare at the cross. Hold the page about a foot from your open eye. Move the page until the star falls on your blindspot and disappears. (B) Close your right eye and stare at the cross. Hold the page about a foot from your left eye and move the page until the break in the line falls on your blindspot. The line will look unbroken.*

▶ More on Rods and Cones

Let's go back now and deal with the fact that the human eye contains two distinctly different photoreceptor cells. Both rods and cones exist in our retinas, but they are not there in equal number. In one eye, there are approximately 120 million rods, but only 6 million cones, that is, rods outnumber cones approximately 20 to 1.

Not only are rods and cones found in unequal number, but they are not evenly distributed throughout the retina. Cones are concentrated in the center of the retina, at the fovea. Rods are concentrated in a band or ring surrounding the fovea, out toward the periphery of the retina. These observations have led psychologists to wonder if the rods and cones of our eyes have different functions.

In fact, we claim that cones function best in medium to high levels of illumination (as in daylight) and are primarily responsible for our experience of color. On the other hand, our rods operate best under conditions of reduced illumination. They are more sensitive to low-intensity light. However, our rods do not discriminate among wavelengths of light, which means that rods do not contribute to our appreciation of color.

Some of the evidence supporting these claims can be verified by our own experiences. Don't you find it difficult to distinguish different colors at night or in the dark? The next time you are at the movies eating some pieces of candy that are of different colors, see if you can tell them apart without holding them up to the light of the projector. You won't be able to tell a green piece from a red one because they all appear black—a problem if you happen to have a favorite flavor. You can't discriminate colors well in a dark movie theater because you are seeing them primarily with your rods, which are very good at seeing in the reduced illumination of the theater but which don't differentiate among different wavelengths of light. Note, however, that you have little difficulty making out the colors of the images being projected on the screen. This is simply because that light is intense enough (bright enough) to stimulate the cones of your fovea, giving rise to the experience of different colors.

If you are looking for something small outside at night, you'll probably not see it if you look directly at it. Imagine that you're changing a tire along the roadside at night. You're replacing the wheel and can't find one of the lug nuts that you know is there someplace in the gravel. If you were to look at it directly, the image of the nut would fall on your fovea. Your fovea is made up almost entirely of cones. Cones do not operate well in relative darkness, and you'll not see the nut. To have the best chance of finding it, you'll have to get the image of the nut to fall on the periphery of your eye where your rods are concentrated.

One of the reasons why nocturnal animals (such as many varieties of owl) see well in low light is because their retinas are packed with rods. Such animals usually have no fovea, or have fewer cones and are demonstrably colorblind. (How you might test the color vision of an owl is discussed in Chapter 6.)

Let's mention just one other piece of evidence that supports the idea that our rods and our cones are essentially providing us with two different types of vision. Let's take a closer look at what happens during dark adaptation, the process by which our eyes become more sensitive as we spend time in the dark (p. 126).

Figure 4.10 is a graphic representation of the dark adaptation process. It shows us that with time spent in the dark, our sensitivity increases, or our threshold decreases. At first, we see only very bright lights (say, the light reflected from the movie screen); then we can see dimmer lights (those

▲ Many nocturnal animals see well in the dark because of a high concentration of rods in their retinas

reflected from people in the theater), and then still dimmer ones (reflected from pieces of candy perhaps) as our threshold drops. As Figure 4.10 indicates, the whole process takes about 20 to 30 minutes.

But there is something strange going on. The dark adaptation curve is not a smooth one. At about the 7-minute mark, there is a change in the shape of the curve. This break in the curve is called the *rod-cone break*. At first—for 6 to 7 minutes—both rods *and* cones increase their sensitivity (the first part of the curve). But our cones are basically daylight receptors, not cut out for seeing in the dark; and after that first few minutes, they have become as sensitive as they are going to get. On the other hand, the rods keep lowering their threshold, or continue to increase their sensitivity (represented by the part of the curve after the "break").

Now that we've reviewed the nature of light and the eye, the stimulus and receptor for vision, we'll finish our discussion of the sensory process of vision by examining how our cones provide us with the experience of color.

Figure 4.10

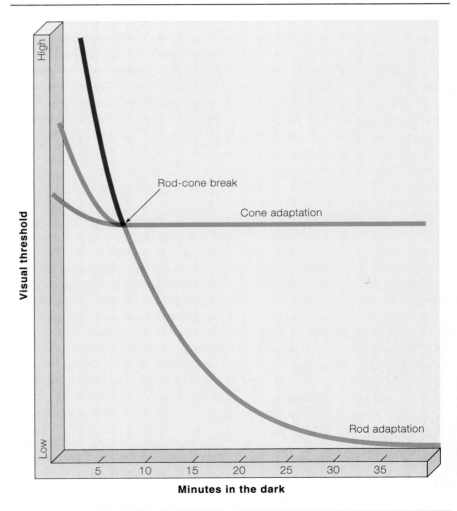

▲ *The dark adaptation curve. At first, both rods and cones lower thresholds, or increase sensitivity. After 6–8 minutes, the cones have become as sensitive as possible; adaptation then is due to the rods alone.*

Why can we claim that rods and cones provide us with two different kinds of visual experience?

▶ Color Vision and Color Blindness

Explaining how the eye codes or responds to different intensities of light is not too difficult. High-intensity lights cause the more rapid firing of neural impulses than do low-intensity lights. It is also sensible that high-intensity lights stimulate more cells to fire than do lights of low intensity. How the eye codes different wavelengths of light to produce different experiences of hue or color, however, is another story. To be honest about it, I should say that psychologists really don't know exactly how the process occurs. There are many theories of color vision that have received research support. Two were proposed many years ago. As is often the case with competing theories that try to explain the same phenomenon, both are probably partially correct.

The older of the two theories of how we code color is the *trichromatic theory*. It was first proposed by Thomas Young very early in the nineteenth century and was revised by Hermann von Helmholtz about 50 years later. As its name suggests, the *tri*chromatic theory proposes that the eye contains three separate and distinct receptors for color.

Although there is considerable overlap, each receptor responds best to one of three *primary hues* of light: red, green, and blue. These hues (or colors of light) are primary because by the careful combination of the three, all other colors can be produced. You see this in action everyday on your television screen. The picture on your TV screen is made up of a pattern of very small dots, each one being either red, green, or blue. From these three wavelengths alone, all other colors are constructed, or integrated. (Don't get confused with the primary colors of *pigment*, which are red, yellow, and blue. These are the three primary colors of paint, or dye, or pastel, etc. that can be mixed together to form other colors of pigment. Our eyes respond to light, not to pigment.)

Because the sensitivities of the three receptors overlap, when our eyes are stimulated by a nonprimary color, say orange, the orange-hued light will stimulate each receptor to varying degrees so as to produce the sensation or experience of orange. What gives this theory credibility is that *there really are* such receptor cells in the human retina. Obviously, they are cones (which are responsible for color vision). The relative sensitivity of these three cone systems is shown in Figure 4.11.

Ewald Hering thought that the Young-Helmholtz theory left a good bit to be desired, and in 1870 he proposed a theory of his own. This theory has come to be called the *opponent-process theory*. Hering's position is that there are three *pairs* of visual mechanisms that respond to different wavelengths of light. One mechanism is a blue-yellow processor, one a red-green processor, and the third deals with black-white differences.

Each mechanism is capable of responding to *either* of the two hues that give it its name, but not to both. That is, the blue-yellow processor can respond to blue *or* yellow, but can't handle both at the same time. The second mechanism responds to red *or* green, but not both. The third codes brightness. The members of each pair work to oppose each other, giving the theory its name. If blue is excited, then yellow is inhibited. When red is excited, green is inhibited. A light may appear to be a mixture of red and

Figure 4.11

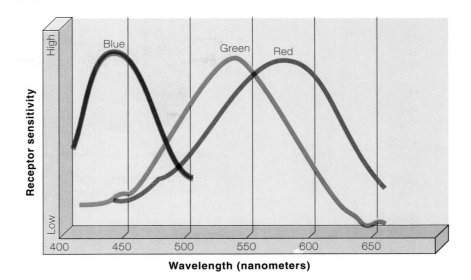

▲ *The relative sensitivities of three different kinds of cones to light of different wavelengths. Note that although there is considerable overlap, each cell is maximally sensitive to different wavelengths (or colors).*

yellow, but cannot be seen as a mixture of blue and yellow, because both blue and yellow cannot be excited at the same time. (It is difficult to imagine what a "reddish-green" or a "bluish-yellow" would look like, isn't it? Can you picture a light that is bright and dim at the same time?)

The opponent-process theory may at first appear overly complicated, but there are some strong signs that Hering was on the right track. In the first place, excitatory-inhibitory mechanisms such as he proposed for red- green, blue-yellow, and black-white have been found. As it happens, they are not at the level of rods and cones in the retina (as Hering thought), but at the layer of the ganglion cells (Figure 4.8) and also in an area of the thalamus.

Some support for Hering's theory comes from our experiences with *negative afterimages*. If you stare at a bright green figure for a few minutes and then shift your gaze to a white surface, you'll notice an image of a red figure. Where did that come from? The explanation is: While you were staring at the green figure, the green component of the red-green process fatigued because of all the stimulation it was getting. When you stared at the white surface, both the red and green components of the process were equally stimulated, but because the green component was so fatigued, the red predominated, producing the experience of seeing a red figure. (Figure 4.12 provides an example for you to try.)

We also have evidence to support both theories of normal vision that comes from the study of persons with color vision defects. Defective color vision of some sort occurs in about 8 percent of males and slightly less than 0.5 percent of females. Most cases are clearly genetic in origin. It makes sense that if cones are our receptor cells for the discrimination of color, then people with a deficiency in color discrimination should have a problem with their cones. Such logic is consistent with the Young-Helmoltz theory of color vision.

For the most common of the color vision deficiencies *(dichromatism)* there is a lack of a particular type of cone. For instance, those people who are "red-green color-blind," have trouble telling the difference between red

Figure 4.12

▲ *To illustrate the experience of color fatigue, stare at the green figure for 30 seconds, and then shift your gaze to a completely white surface. You should see the same figure, but it will appear red because the green receptors are fatigued. Now try the same experiment with the blue figure. What color do you see when you shift your gaze?*

and green (a problem for stop lights, except that red is always on the top or on the left). People with this sort of colorblindness also have trouble distinguishing yellow from either red or green. Notice that the deficiency is not in actually seeing reds or greens. It is in distinguishing reds and greens from other colors. Put another way, someone who is red-green colorblind can clearly see a bright red apple; it just looks no different from a bright green apple.

Some color vision defects can be traced to defects in the cones of the retina. But damage to cells higher in the visual pathway—more toward the cerebral cortex—are implicated in some rare cases of color vision problems. When such problems do occur, there are losses for both red and green or losses for yellow and blue, color pairings predicted by the opponent process theory (*e.g.*, Schiffman, 1990).

Because there are cone cell systems that respond differentially to red, blue, and green light, we cannot dismiss the trichromatic theory. Because there are cells that operate the way the opponent-process theory predicts, we cannot dismiss this theory either. Well, which one is right? Both. Our experience of color probably depends upon the interaction of different cone cells *and* different opponent-process cells within our visual pathway. This is the sort of complication that reminds us of the theme I mentioned back in Chapter One—that simple questions sometimes have complex answers.

Before You Go On
▼▼▼▼▼▼▼▼▼▼

Summarize the trichromatic and the opponent-process theories of color vision.

▶ Hearing

Hearing (more formally, *audition*) provides us with nearly as much useful information about our environment as vision does. One of its main roles is its involvement in our development of language and speech. Without hearing, these uniquely human skills are difficult to acquire.

▲ *Sound is a series of pressures of air that produce vibrations of the eardrum.*

Figure 4.13

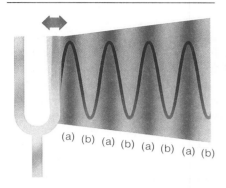

▲ *Sound waves are produced as air pressure is spread by the tine of a tuning fork vibrating to the right (a) and left (b). The point of greatest pressure is the high point of the wave; least pressure is indicated by the low point of the wave.*

loudness the psychological experience correlated with the intensity, or amplitude, of a sound wave

decibel scale a scale of experience of loudness in which 0 represents the absolute threshold and 140 is sensed as pain

▶ The Stimulus for Hearing: Sound

The stimulus for vision is light; for hearing, it is sound. Sound is a series of pressures of air (or some other medium, such as water) that beat against our eardrum. We can represent these pressures as sound waves. As a source of sound vibrates, it pushes air against our eardrums. Figure 4.13 shows how we may depict sound as a wave form of energy.

As for light waves, there are three major physical characteristics of sound waves—amplitude, frequency (the inverse of wavelength), and purity—and each of them is related to a different psychological experience. We'll briefly consider each in turn.

Wave Amplitude (Intensity). The amplitude of a sound wave depicts its intensity—the force with which the air strikes our eardrums. The physical intensity of a sound determines the psychological experience of **loudness**. The higher its amplitude, the louder we perceive a sound to be. Soft, quiet sounds have low amplitudes (see Figure 4.14).

Measurements of the physical intensity of sound are given in units of force per unit area (which is really pressure). Loudness is a psychological characteristic. The **decibel scale** of sound intensity has been constructed to reflect *perceived* loudness. Its zero point is the lowest intensity of sound that can be detected, or the absolute threshold. Our ears are very sensitive receptors and respond to very low levels of sound intensity. (In fact, if our ears were much more sensitive, we could hear molecules of air bouncing against our eardrums.) Sounds that are louder than those produced by jet aircraft engines, or fast-moving subway trains (around 120 decibels) are experienced

Figure 4.14

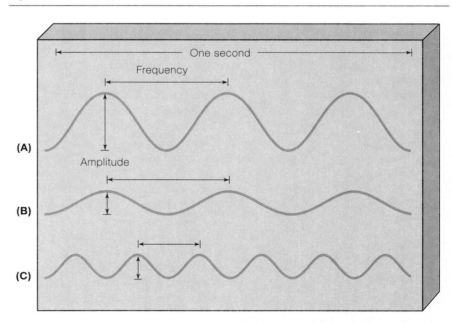

▲ *How the physical characteristics of sound waves influence our psychological experiences of sound. (1) Though waves (A) and (B) have the same frequency, wave (A) has a higher amplitude and would be experienced as a louder sound. (2) Though waves (B) and (C) have the amplitude, wave (C) would be experienced as having a higher pitch because of its greater frequency.*

hertz (Hz) the standard measure of sound wave frequency that is the number of wave cycles per second

pitch the psychological experience that corresponds to sound wave frequency and gives rise to high (treble) or low (bass) sounds

timbre the psychological experience related to wave purity by which we differentiate the sharpness, clearness, or quality of a tone

Figure 4.15

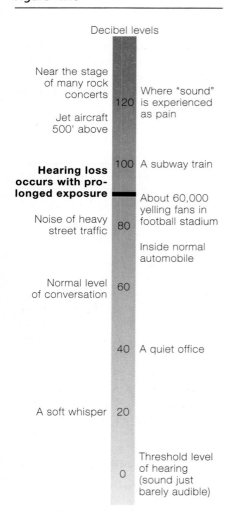

▲ Loudness values in decibel units for various sounds.

more as pain than as sound. Figure 4.15 shows decibel levels for some of the sounds we might find in our environment.

Wave Frequency. When we discussed light, we noted that wavelength was responsible for our perception of hue. With sound, we talk about *wave frequency*—the number of times a wave repeats itself within a given period of time. Sound wave frequency is measured in terms of how many waves of pressure are exerted every second. The unit of sound frequency is the **Hertz**, abbreviated **Hz.** If a sound wave repeats itself 50 times in one second, it is a 50Hz sound; 500 repetitions is a 500Hz sound, and so on. Waves of different frequency are shown in Figure 4.14, where you can see the relationship between wavelength and frequency.

The psychological experience corresponding to sound wave frequency is **pitch.** Pitch is our experience of how high or low a tone is. The musical scale represents differences in pitch to the human ear. Low frequencies correspond to low, bass sounds, such as those produced by foghorns or tubas. High-frequency vibrations give rise to the experience of high-pitched sounds, such as the musical tones produced by flutes or the squeals of smoke alarms.

Just as the human eye cannot respond to all possible wavelengths of radiant energy, so the human ear cannot respond to all possible sound wave frequencies. A healthy human ear responds to sound wave frequencies between 20Hz and 20,000Hz. If air strikes our ears at a rate of less than 20 times per second, we don't hear it as sound. Vibrations faster than 20,000 cycles per second usually cannot be heard either—at least by the human ear. Many animals, including dogs, *can* hear sounds with frequencies above 20,000Hz, such as those produced by dog whistles.

Wave Purity. A third characteristic of sound waves is wave purity (its opposite is called complexity). You'll recall that we seldom experience pure, monochromatic lights. Pure sounds are also uncommon in our everyday experience. A pure sound would be one in which *all* of the waves from the sound source were vibrating at exactly the same frequency. Such sounds can be produced, of course, and tuning forks produce reasonable approximations, but most of the sounds we hear every day are complex sounds, composed of many different sound wave frequencies.

A tone of middle C on the piano is a tone of 256Hz. (Again, this means that the source of the sound, here a piano wire, is vibrating 256 times per second). A *pure* 256Hz tone is composed of sound waves (vibrations) of only that frequency. As it happens, the middle C of the piano has many other wave frequencies mixed in with the predominant 256Hz wave frequency. (If the 256Hz wave did not predominate, the tone wouldn't sound like middle C.)

The psychological quality of a sound, reflecting its degree of purity, is called **timbre.** For example, each musical instrument produces a unique variety or mixture of overtones, so each type of musical instrument tends to sound a little different from all others. If a trumpet, a violin, and a piano were each to play the same note (say that middle C of 256Hz), we could still tell the instruments apart because of our experience of timbre. (In fact, one instrument may produce different timbres, depending on how it is played.)

With light, we found that the opposite of a pure light was white light— a light made up of all the wavelengths of the visible spectrum. Again, the parallel between vision and hearing holds up. Suppose I have a sound source that can produce all the possible sound wave frequencies. I produce a random mixture of these frequencies from 20Hz to 20,000Hz. What would

Figure 4.16

THE PHYSICAL CHARACTERISTICS OF LIGHT AND SOUND WAVES AFFECT OUR PSYCHOLOGICAL EXPERIENCES OF VISION AND HEARING AS ILLUSTRATED IN THIS TABLE.

Physical Characteristic	Psychological Experience for Vision	Psychological Experience for Hearing
Wave amplitude	Brightness	Loudness
Wavelength or frequency	Hue	Pitch
Wave purity or mixture	Saturation	Timbre

that sound like? Actually, it would be a buzzing noise. The best example would be the sound that one hears when a radio is tuned in between stations (and as it happens, FM works better than AM). This soft, whispering, buzzing sound, containing a range of many audible sound frequencies, is useful in masking or covering other unwanted sounds. A random mixture of sound frequencies is called **white noise**, just as we called a random mixture of wavelengths of light *white light*.

The analogy between light and sound (and between vision and hearing) is striking. Both types of stimulus energy can be represented as waves. In both cases, each of the *physical* characteristics of the waves (amplitude, length or frequency, and purity or complexity) is correlated with a *psychological* experience. All of these relationships are summarized in Figure 4.16.

> **white noise** a sound composed of a random assortment of wave frequencies from the audible spectrum

Before You Go On

▼▼▼▼▼▼▼▼▼

What are the three major physical characteristics of sound, and which psychological experiences do they produce?

▶ The Ear

Deep inside the ear, the energy of sound wave pressures is converted into neural impulses. As with the eye, most of the structures of the ear simply transfer energy from without to within. Figure 4.17 is a drawing of the major structures of the human ear. We'll use it to follow the path of sound waves from the environment to the receptor cells for sound.

The outer ear is called the **pinna**. Its main function is to collect sound waves and funnel them through the auditory canal toward the **eardrum**. Air waves beat against the eardrum (the tympanic membrane), setting it in motion, so that it vibrates at the same rate as the sound source. Once the eardrum is vibrating back and forth, the sound moves deeper inside the ear.

There are three very small bones (collectively called *ossicles*) in the middle ear. These bones are, in order, the **malleus, incus, and stapes**. Because of their unique shapes, these bones are sometimes referred to as the *hammer*, *anvil*, and *stirrup*. These bones pass the vibrations of the eardrum along to the *oval window*, another membrane like the eardrum, only smaller. As the ossicles pass the sound vibrations along to the oval window, they also amplify them, increasing their force.

> **pinna** the outer ear, which collects and funnels sound waves into the auditory canal toward the eardrum

> **eardrum** the outermost membrane of the ear; it is set in motion by the vibrations of a sound and transmits vibrations to the ossicles

> **malleus, incus, and stapes** (collectively, *ossicles*) three small bones that transmit and intensify sound vibrations from the eardrum to the oval window

Figure 4.17

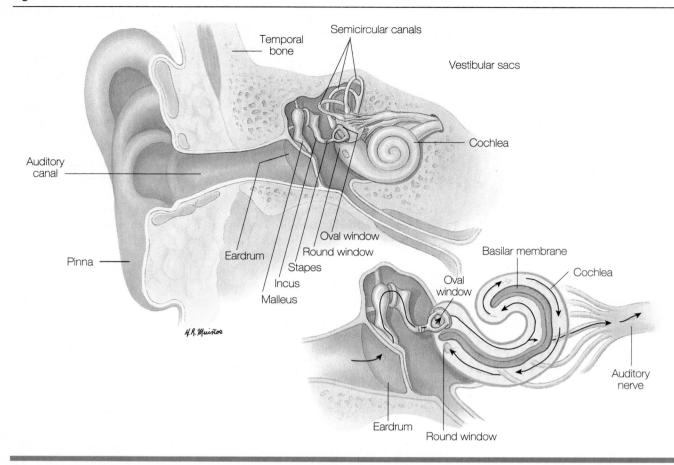

Temporal bone
Semicircular canals
Vestibular sacs
Cochlea
Auditory canal
Pinna
Eardrum
Oval window
Round window
Stapes
Incus
Malleus
H.R. Muiñoe
Basilar membrane
Cochlea
Oval window
Auditory nerve
Eardrum
Round window

▲ *The major structures of the human ear.*

cochlea part of the inner ear where sound waves become neural impulses

basilar membrane a structure within the cochlea that vibrates and thus stimulates the hair cells of the inner ear

hair cells the receptor cells for hearing, located in the cochlea, stimulated by the vibrating basilar membrane; they send neural impulses to the temporal lobe of the brain

When sound is transmitted beyond the oval window, the vibrations are in the *inner ear*. The main structure of the inner ear is the **cochlea** a snail-like structure that contains the actual receptor cells for hearing. As the stapes vibrates against the oval window, a fluid inside the cochlea is set in motion at the same rate.

When the fluid within the cochlea moves, the **basilar membrane** is bent up and down. This membrane is a small structure that runs just about the full length of the cochlea. Hearing takes place when very tiny **hair cells** are stimulated by the vibrations of the basilar membrane. Through a process not yet fully understood, the mechanical pressure of the basilar membrane on the hair cells starts a neural impulse that leaves the ear on the auditory nerve, traveling toward the temporal lobe.

Exactly how the basilar membrane and hair cells work together to give rise to the experience of different pitches is still not well understood. One theory suggests that the whole length of the basilar membrane vibrates so as to stimulate hair cells and send impulses to the brain that match the frequency of the sound entering the ear. This is called the *frequency theory*. As it happens, there is evidence that this is (sometimes) the case—when sound frequencie, or pitches, are reasonably low (below 1000Hz). The *place theory*s is an older point of view (associated with von Helmholtz (1863) and Békésy (1953)). It argues that some places on the basilar membrane are more sensitive to particular frequencies of sound than are other places, and thus different hair cells are stimulated as different pitches reach our ear. As was the case for theories of color vision, the best course of action for us is to say that both theories are partially correct, but neither is any better than the other; to a degree, they are both right.

So it is in the ear that the physical energy of sound is transduced into the neural energy that gives rise to a psychological experience in the brain. Most of the structures of the ear are responsible for amplifying and directing waves of pressure to the hair cells in the cochlea, where the neural impulse begins.

Before You Go On

▼▼▼▼▼▼▼▼▼

Summarize how sound wave pressures pass through the different structures of the ear.

▶ The Chemical Senses

Taste and smell are referred to as chemical senses because the stimuli for both of them are molecules of chemical compounds. For taste, the chemicals are dissolved in liquid (usually the saliva in our mouths). For smell, they are dissolved in the air that reaches the smell receptors high inside our noses. The technical term for taste is *gustation*; for smell, *olfaction*.

If you have ever eaten while suffering from a head cold that has blocked your nasal passages, you realize the extent to which our experiences of taste and smell are interrelated. Most foods appear to lose their taste when we cannot smell them. This is why we differentiate between the *flavor* of foods (which includes such qualities as odor and texture) and the *taste* of foods. A simple test demonstrates this point very nicely. While blindfolded, eat a small piece of peeled apple and a small piece of peeled potato, and see if you can tell the difference between the two. You shouldn't have any trouble making this discrimination. Now hold your nose very tightly and try again. Without your sense of smell to help you, discrimination on the basis of taste alone is very difficult.

▶ Taste (Gustation)

Our experience of the flavors of foods depends so heavily on our sense of smell, texture, and temperature that we sometimes have to wonder if there is any sense of taste alone. Well, there is. Taste seems to have four basic psychological qualities: sweet, salty, sour, and bitter. You should be able to generate a list of foods that produce each of these basic sensations. Most foods derive their special taste from a unique combination of the four basic taste sensations. Have you noticed that it is more difficult to think of examples of sour and bitter tasting foods than it is to think of sweet and salty ones? This reflects the fact that we usually don't like bitter and sour tastes and have learned to avoid them.

The receptor cells for taste are located on (*in* might be more precise) the tongue. The receptors for taste are called **taste buds**. We have about 10,000 taste buds, and each one is made up of a number of parts (see Figure 4.18). When parts of taste buds die (or are killed by foods that are too hot, for example) new segments are regenerated. That in itself makes taste a unique sense—as receptor cells, taste buds are essentially nerve cells, and we've

Figure 4.18

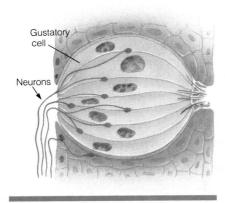

Gustatory cell

Neurons

▲ *Enlarged view of a taste bud, showing how the sensation of taste travels from the gustatory receptor cells to the brain.*

taste buds the receptors for taste located in the tongue

▲ The tip of the tongue is most sensitive to sweet tastes.

already noted that nerve cells are usually not replaced when they die. At the same time, it is true that with age, fewer and fewer taste buds are replaced and one's sensitivity to taste decreases. This may explain why some older people seem to enjoy heavily seasoned or spicy foods when they did not enjoy those foods when they were younger.

Different taste buds respond primarily to chemicals that produce one of the four basic taste qualities. That is, some receptor cells respond best to salts, while others respond primarily to sweet-producing chemicals, like sugars. As it happens, these specialized cells are not evenly distributed on the surface of the tongue. Receptors for sweet are at the very tip; receptors for salty tastes are toward the front; sour receptors are on the sides; and bitter receptors are at the back of the tongue. A vinegar solution right at the tip of the tongue might very well go unnoticed until some of it gets washed over to the side of the tongue. To best savor a lollipop, children learn quickly to lick it with the tip of the tongue. The locations of primary taste receptors are shown in Figure 4.19.

▶ Smell (Olfaction)

Smell often gives us great pleasure—think of the aroma of bacon frying over a wood fire or of freshly picked flowers. It can produce considerable displeasure—consider the smell of old garbage or rotten eggs.

The sense of smell originates in cells located high in the nasal cavity, very close to the brain. We know that the path from these receptors to the brain is the most direct and shortest of all the senses (see Figure 4.20). What we don't understand well is how molecules suspended in air (or some other gas) actually stimulate the small hair cells of the olfactory receptor to fire neural impulses.

We know that the sense of smell is a very important sense for many nonhumans. The dog's sense of smell is legendary. Many organisms emit chemicals, called **pheromones**, that produce distinctive odors. Sometimes pheromones are secreted by cells in the skin, sometimes in the urine, and occasionally from special glands (in some deer, this gland is located near the rear hoof). One purpose that pheromones serve is to mark or delineate one's territory. If you take a dog for a walk around the block and discover that the pooch wants to stop and deposit small amounts of urine on just about every front lawn, that dog is leaving behind a pheromone message that essentially says, "*I* have been here; this is *my* odor; this is *my* turf."

Commonly, pheromones carry sexually-related messages to members of the opposite sex of the same species. Most often that message is roughly translated into, "I am available for sexual activities." The result is that these pheromones attract members of the opposite sex. Knowledge of this relationship can be useful. Japanese beetles are a common garden pest, very difficult to kill (safely) with standard poisons. Traps are now available that contain a small amount of a pheromone attractive to Japanese beetles. The beetles smell the odor the trap gives off, come rushing to investigate, and slide off a slippery plastic platform to their doom in a disposable plastic bag. It is rather gruesome, but it works.

It is likely that pheromone production is related to the sex hormones, even in humans. For example, there is evidence that women who live in close quarters (say in a college dormitory) for a long time soon synchronize their menstrual cycles. It also may be true that humans use pheromones to attract members of the opposite sex (Cutler et al., 1986; Wallace, 1977). If we do, the real effect is probably small, although people who advertise perfumes and colognes would have us think otherwise (*e.g.*, Doty, 1986).

pheromones chemicals that produce an odor used as a method of communication between organisms

Figure 4.19

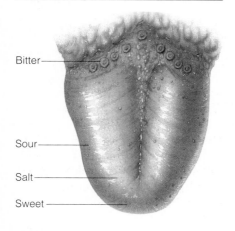

Bitter

Sour

Salt

Sweet

▲ The four primary qualities of taste are experienced in specific areas of the tongue.

Figure 4.20

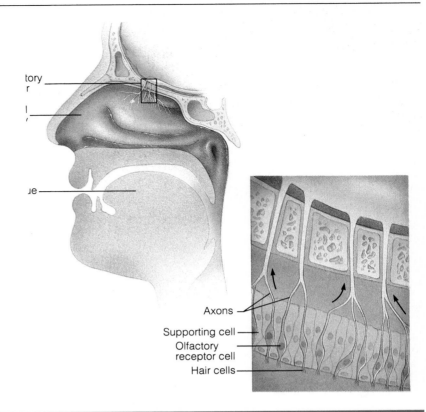

tory
r

l
,

ue

Axons
Supporting cell
Olfactory
receptor cell
Hair cells

▲ *The olfactory system showing its proximity to the brain and the relationship between the sensations of taste and smell.*

Before You Go On
▼▼▼▼▼▼▼▼

Discuss the chemical senses of taste and smell, noting the stimulus and sense receptor for each.

What are the primary qualities of taste?

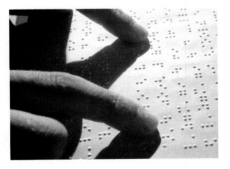

▲ *The tips of the fingers contain many cutaneous receptors for touch or pressure.*

▶ The Skin (Cutaneous Senses)

Most of us take our skin for granted—at least we seldom think about it much. We frequently abuse our skin by overexposing it to the sun's rays in summer or to excess cold in winter. We scratch it, cut it, scrape it, and wash away millions of its cells every time we bathe or shower.

Figure 4.21 is a diagram of some of the structures found in an area of skin from a hairy part of the human body. Each square inch of the layers of our skin contains nearly 20 million cells, including many sense receptors. Some of the skin receptors have *free nerve endings*, while some have some sort of small covering over them. We call these latter cells *encapsulated nerve endings*, of which there are many different types. It is our skin that gives rise to our psychological experience of touch or pressure and of warmth and cold. It

The (Subliminal) Devil Made Me Do It

The concept of subliminal perception has interested and frustrated psychologists for more than forty years. The first thing to recognize is that "limen" is the Latin word for "threshold." Because *sub* means "below," *subliminal perception* literally means "below threshold perception." What we have here is an apparent contradiction, referring to our ability to perceive something that is below our ability to perceive it! The idea is intriguing—that somehow we can be influenced by stimuli of which we are not consciously aware.

Picture this. You are sitting in a theater watching a movie. Bruce Willis is about to jump from a building just before it explodes. Suddenly, there on the screen, in great big letters, is a message: "BUY COKE," followed shortly by another, "HOW ABOUT SOME POPCORN?" If this sort of interruption actually occurred, you'd probably be upset, leave the theater, and demand your money back. You paid to see a movie, not a series of commercial messages. But what if the messages embedded in the movie were *so* brief and/or *so* dim as to be below your absolute threshold for vision? You don't even realize they are there. Can they still influence your behavior?

When we ask the question this way, the answer is a clear and resounding, "No." Although the implications for misuse are clear, it's almost a shame that subliminal perception in this sense doesn't work. Wouldn't it be useful *if we could* reduce shoplifting by imbedding anti-shoplifting messages into the background music in retail stores? Wouldn't it be wonderful *if we could* earn more money, or improve our study habits, or become more self-confident *with no effort,* by simply listening to audio tapes or watching video tapes into which subliminal messages had been inserted? But, again, these tapes do not work—at least they do not work through anything like subliminal perception. Many people claim to have been helped by such tapes. Perhaps they have been. But, the best explanation is that when people genuinely believe that the tapes will help, and have invested a good deal of time and money in them, they rather easily can convince themselves that the tapes are of value (Balay and Shevrin, 1988; Dixon, 1971; Duncan, 1985; Vokey and Read, 1985).

The possibility that subliminal messages can have direct and potentially devasting effects on behavior was a major issue in a Reno, Nevada courtroom during the summer of 1990. CBS Records and the English heavy-metal band Judas Priest were charged with directly causing the deaths of two young men, Raymond Belnap, age 18 and James Vance, age

would be very convenient if each of the different types of receptor cells within the layers of our skin independently produced a different type of psychological sensation, but such is not the case. Indeed, one of the problems in studying the skin senses, or *cutaneous senses,* is trying to determine which cells in the skin give rise to the different sensations of pressure and temperature. We can discriminate between a light touch and a strong jab, and among vibrations, tickles, and itches. Again, a simple proposal is that there are different receptors in the skin responsible for each different sensation. Unfortunately, this proposal is not supported by the facts. Although *some*

20. On December 23, 1985, these two men each turned a loaded shotgun to his face and pulled the trigger. Vance died immediately. Belnap destroyed his face, but survived the blast. He died in 1988 due to complications following a drug overdose. The Nevada trial centered on the allegation that CBS and Judas Priest were responsible for the "wrongful" death of Vance and Belnap because they had "intentionally and recklessly" imbedded subliminal messages on one of their records—a favorite of Belnap and Vance, one they were listening to that day in December, 1985. The messages were suicidal in nature ("Let's be dead!" "Do it. Do it."), the prosecution claimed. As it happened, the judge found for the defendants. Both of the victims were described as very troubled young men who had a long history of drug use and abuse. Ironically, however, the judge in the case (Judge Jerry Whitehead) ruled that there *were* "subliminals" on the recording, but that they were not placed there intentionally! The judge did go on in his 68-page ruling to declare that he had heard no evidence that subliminal messages could have had the effect of causing anyone to commit suicide, or any act like it. (And Judas Priest decided to call their next concert tour: "Subliminal Criminals.") In Chapter One I made the point that psychology has practical application in the real world. Occasionally that application is somewhat bizarre.

Is it then true that stimuli presented at levels slightly below one's absolute threshold can have *no* effect? No, that's too strong a statement. Although subliminally presented messages are not going to get you to get up from your TV set and march down to the store to buy some new type of snack food, there *is* evidence that to some degree we may be sensitive to stimuli that are below absolute threshold levels. Here's one example of this sort of evidence.

A subject sits in front of a small screen. A word is flashed on the screen so dimly and briefly that the subject does not report seeing the word. Let's say the word is "EASTER." Now two words are presented on the screen that the subject *can* see clearly. The task is to choose the word related in some way to the word that was not seen. Let's say the choice words in this example are "Bunny" and "Pencil." Even when subjects claim they are just guessing, they choose "Bunny" significantly more frequently than chance would predict. If the subliminal prompt were "PEN," not "EASTER," then they would tend to choose "Pencil." It is as if the initial subliminally presented word somehow influences their choice (*e.g.*, Cheeseman and Merikle, 1984; Dixon, 1971, 1981; Fowler, et al., 1981).

So there seems to be evidence that some stimuli below the levels of our absolute thresholds of detection can have some discernible impact on us. On the other hand, there is no evidence that subliminal messages can directly influence actual behaviors in any meaningful way.

types of receptor cells are more sensitive to *some* types of stimuli, current thinking is that our ability to discriminate among different cutaneous sensations is due to the combination of responses that the many receptor cells have to different types of stimuli.

By carefully stimulating very small areas of the skin, we can locate areas that are particularly sensitive to temperature. We are convinced that warm and cold temperatures each stimulate different locations on the skin. Even so, there is no consistent pattern of receptor cells found at these locations, or temperature spots. That is, we have not yet located specific receptor cells

Figure 4.21

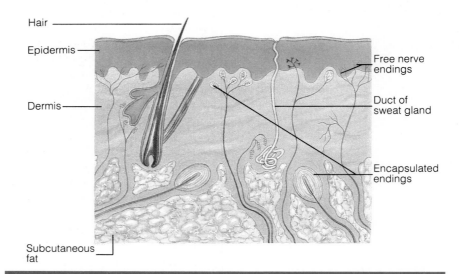

Hair
Epidermis
Dermis
Free nerve endings
Duct of sweat gland
Encapsulated endings
Subcutaneous fat

▲ *A patch of hairy skin, showing the different layers of the skin and the various nerves.*

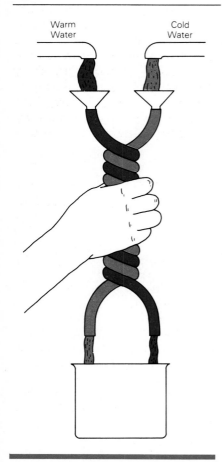

Warm Water   Cold Water

▲ *A demonstration that our sensation of hot may be constructed from the sensations of warm and cold. Even if you know the coiled tubes contain only warm and cold water, when you grasp the tubes they will feel hot.*

Figure 4.22

for cold or hot. As a matter of fact, our experience of hot seems to come from the simultaneous stimulation of both warm and cold spots. A rather ingenious demonstration shows how this works. Cold water is run through one metal tube and warm water is run through another tube. The two tubes are coiled together (see Figure 4.22). If you were to grasp the coiled tubes, your experience would be one of *heat*—the tubes would feel hot even if you knew that they weren't.

Before You Go On

▼▼▼▼▼▼▼▼▼

What are the cutaneous senses, and what are the transducers for each?

▶ The Position Senses

Another sensory capacity we often take for granted is our ability to detect how and where our bodies are positioned in space. Although we seldom worry about it, we quickly can become aware of how our bodies are positioned in regard to the pull of gravity. We also get sensory information about where different parts of our body are in relation to each other. We can tell if we are moving or standing still. And unless we are on a roller coaster, or racing across a field, we usually adapt to these sensory messages quickly and pay them little attention.

Most of the information about where we are in space comes through our sense of vision. If we want to know just how we are oriented in space, all we have to do is look around. But notice that we *can* do the same sort of thing even with our eyes closed. We have two systems of position sense over

vestibular sense the position sense that tells us about balance, where we are in relation to gravity, and acceleration or deceleration

kinesthetic sense the position sense that tells us the position of different parts of our bodies and what our muscles and joints are doing

and above vision. One, the **vestibular sense**, tells us about balance, where we are in relation to gravity, and acceleration or deceleration. The other, the **kinesthetic sense**, tells us about the movement or position of our muscles and joints.

The receptors for the vestibular sense are located on either side of the head, near the inner ear. Five chambers are located there: three semicircular canals and two vestibular sacs. (Their orientation was shown in Figure 4.17.) Each of these chambers is filled with fluid. When our head moves in any direction, the fluid in the semicircular canals moves, drawn by gravity or the force of our head accelerating in space. The vestibular sacs contain very small solid particles that float around in the fluid within the sacs. When these particles are forced against one side of the sacs, as happens when we move, they stimulate hair cells that start neural impulses. Overstimulation of the receptor cells in the vestibular sacs or semicircular canals can lead to feelings of dizziness or nausea, reasonably enough called *motion sickness.*

Most receptors for our kinesthetic sense are located in our joints, while some information also comes from muscles and tendons. Kinesthetic receptors sense the position and movements of parts of the body. Impulses from these receptors travel to our brain through pathways in our spinal cord. They provide excellent examples of reflex actions. As muscles in the front of your upper arm (your biceps) contract, the corresponding muscles in the back of your arm (triceps) relax for you to bend your arm at the elbow. How fortunate it is that our kinesthetic receptors, operating reflexively through the spinal cord, take care of these details without our having to manipulate consciously all the appropriate muscular activity. In fact, about the only time we realize that our kinesthetic system is functioning is when it stops working well, as when our leg "falls asleep" and we have trouble walking.

Before You Go On
▼▼▼▼▼▼▼▼▼

What are our position senses, and how do they operate?

▶ Pain: A Special Sense

Our sense of pain is a curious and troublesome one for psychologists interested in sensory processes. Pain, or the fear of it, can be a very strong motivator; we do all sorts of things to avoid it. Pain is unpleasant, but at the same time, it is terribly useful. Feelings of pain alert us to problems occurring somewhere within our bodies, warning us that steps need to be taken to remove the source of pain. Without a sense of pain, a person might very well die of a burst appendix. Our feelings of pain are private sensations—they are difficult to share or describe to others (Verillo, 1975).

Just what *is* pain? What causes the sensation of pain? What are its sense receptors? At present, we really don't know. Many stimuli can cause pain. Very intense stimulation of virtually any sense receptor can produce pain. Too much light, very strong pressures on the skin, excessive temperatures, very loud sounds, and even too many "hot" spices can all result in our experiencing pain. But as we know, the stimulus for pain need not be intense. Under the right circumstances, even a light pin prick can be very painful.

▲ *Rollercoaster rides provide considerable stimulation to the vestibular sense.*

▲ *The gate-control theory developed by Ronald Melzack (pictured here) and Patrick Wall proposes that pain centers in the brain are responsive to stimulation from nerve fibers that "open the gate" and allow for the sensation of pain.*

gate-control theory the theory of pain sensation that argues that there are brain centers that regulate the passage of pain messages from different parts of the body to the brain

Our skin seems to have many receptors for pain, but pain receptors can also be found deep inside our bodies—consider stomach aches, lower back pain, and headaches. Pain is experienced in our brains, but pain is the only "sense" for which we can find no one specific center in the cerebral cortex.

A theory of pain that still attracts attention from researchers (most of it supportive, some not) is Melzack and Wall's **gate-control theory** (1965; Melzack, 1973). It suggests that our experience of pain happens not so much at the level of the receptor (say, in the skin), but within the central nervous system. The theory proposes that a gate-like structure in the spinal cord responds to stimulation from a particular type of nerve—one that "opens the gate" and allows for the sensation of pain by letting impulses on up to the brain. Other nerve fibers can offset the activity of the pain-carrying fibers and "close the gate" so that pain messages are cut off and never make it to the brain.

There are several situations in which this theory of opening and closing a gate to pain seems reasonable. One of the things that happens when we are exposed to persistent pain is that certain neurotransmitters—*endorphins*—are released in the brain (Hughes, et al., 1975; Terenius, 1982). Endorphins (plural because there may be a number of them) naturally reduce our sense of pain and generally make us feel good. When their effects are blocked, pain seems unusually severe. Endorphins stimulate nerve fibers that go to the spinal cord and effectively close the gate that monitors the passage of impulses from pain receptors.

One situation that seems to fit the gate-control theory is abnormally persistent pain. Some patients who have received a trauma to some part of their body (through accident or surgery, for example) continue to experience extreme pain even after the initial wound is completely healed. Abnormal pain is also found in the so-called "phantom limb" pain, experienced by some (about 10 percent) of amputees. These patients continue to feel pain in an arm or leg, even after that limb is no longer there. How can this be?

Figure 4.23

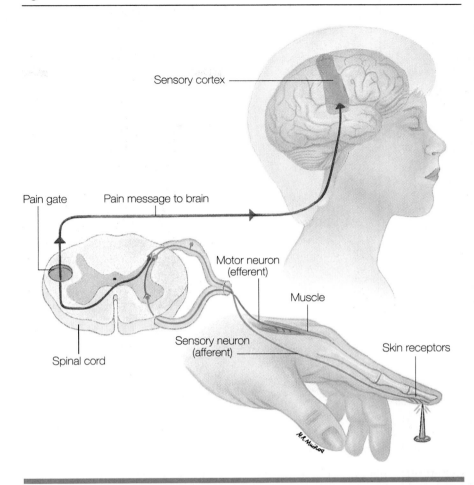

Sensory cortex

Pain gate   Pain message to brain

Motor neuron (efferent)

Muscle

Pain gate

Spinal cord

Sensory neuron (afferent)

Skin receptors

▲ *How the gate-control theory of pain works. A stimulus on the skin initiates neural impulses that enter the spinal cord and rush through a "pain gate" to the brain. Many mechanisms (including the release of endorphins through acupuncture) can act to close the gate, at least to some degree, thus reducing the experience of pain by the brain.*

Recent thinking is that the severe trauma of amputation overloads and destroys the function of important cells in the spinal cord that normally act to close the gate for pain messages, leaving the pain circuits uninhibited (Gracely, Lynch & Bennett, 1991; Laird & Bennett, 1991).

Think of some of the other mechanisms that are useful in moderating the experience of pain. Hypnosis and cognitive self-control (just trying very hard to convince yourself that the pain you're experiencing is not that bad and will go away) *are* effective (Litt, 1988; Melzack, 1973). That pain can be controlled to some extent by cognitive training is clear from the success of many classes aimed at reducing the pain of childbirth. The theory is that psychological processes influence the gate-control center in the spinal cord. We also have ample evidence that **placebos** can be effective in treating pain. A placebo is a substance (perhaps in pill form) that a person *believes* will be effective in treating some symptom, when, in fact there is no active pain-relieving ingredient in the substance. When subjects are given a placebo that they genuinely believe will alleviate pain, endorphins are released in the

placebo an inactive substance that works because a person has to come to believe that it will be effective

brain which, again, help to close the gate to pain-carrying impulses (Levine, et al., 1979).

Another process that works to ease the feeling of pain, particularly pain from or near the surface of the skin, is called "counterirritation." The idea here is to stimulate forcefully (not painfully, of course) an area of the body *near* the location of the pain. Dentists have discovered that rubbing the gum near where a novacaine needle is to be inserted significantly reduces the patient's experience of the pain of the needle. Again, as you might have guessed, the logic is that all the stimulation from the nearby rubbing action serves to close the pain gate so the needle has little effect. And speaking of needles, the ancient oriental practice of acupuncture can also be tied to the gate-control theory of pain. We don't know yet just why acupuncture works as well as it does when it is effective, (there are cases where it doesn't work well at all), but these usually involve patients who are skeptics and "don't believe in" acupuncture. (That observation suggests that at least some of acupuncture's benefits derive from its function as a placebo.) But the really important aspect may be its function as a counterirritant. There also is evidence that acupuncture releases endorphins in the brain. Perhaps each or all of these functions serve the major purpose of controlling pain by closing off impulses to the brain.

Before You Go On

▼▼▼▼▼▼▼▼▼

What produces the sensation of pain?

What is the gate-control theory of pain?

▼▼▼
Thinking Critically about Sensory Processes

1. One of the concerns of psychophysics is determining the sensitivity levels (we call them threshold values) for the various senses. In an experiment to determine your absolute threshold for brightness, I ask you to tell me if you can see a light located at the other end of a small room. You are to say simply "Yes" or "No." What factors other than the actual intensity of the light itself may influence your responses? (These are the factors of concernin signal detection theory.)

2. A student—we'll call him Bob—does poorly on his first semester of college work. Over the holidays, Bob buys a subliminal tape advertised as being able to improve his memory. The next semester Bob's grades are significantly higher, an increase he readily attributes to the wonderful subliminal tape he has been using. What other factors might have contributed to Bob's change in performance?

3. Bob (again) does very well on a surprise test in his physics class and claims that he "knew" the test was coming because he had dreamed about it the night before. Bob's now quite convinced that he has ESP, or extrasensory perception which, among other things, involves the perception of information without that information passing through the senses (hence, "extra" sensory). How can we test whether Bob or anyone else has such powers of ESP? What other factors might have accounted for Bob's good fortune?

4. Here are a few questions to which psychologists do have answers, although they involve more information than we usually get into at the introductory level. What do you think? Why are some emergency vehicles (and tennis balls and golf balls) painted yellow-green? Why are the lights on top of police cars and along airport runways and taxiways blue? How could you determine if a dog is more or less colorblind than a cat?

5. Consider for a few minutes the experiences of persons who have some sensory limitation. Can people who are blind from birth dream in pictures? If a person deaf from birth were to have his or her hearing restored, could he or she recognize the voice of a friend? What would it be like to have no sensation of pain at all?

Summary

▼▼▼▼▼▼▼▼▼▼▼▼▼▼▼▼▼▼▼▼▼▼▼▼▼▼▼▼▼▼▼▼▼▼▼

How is the process of sensation defined? Sensation is the first step in information processing. It involves converting physical energy from the environment into the energy of the nervous system. This conversion takes place at our senses. *Page 122*

What is psychophysics? Psychophysics is the subfield of psychology that attempts to specify the nature of the relationships between physical stimuli and the psychological experience of those stimuli. Psychophysical methods can be used to determine the sensitivity of one's senses. *Page 122*

What is an absolute threshold and how is it related to the sensitivity of our senses? An absolute threshold is the intensity of a stimulus that can be detected 50 percent of the time. The lower one's threshold for any sense, the more sensitive that sense is; thus, sensitivity and threshold are inversely related. *Page 123*

What is a difference threshold, or j.n.d.? A difference threshold is the value of the difference between stimuli that are detected to be just noticeably different (j.n.d.). *Page 124*

Briefly summarize the basic ideas of signal detection theory. Signal detection theory considers threshold in terms of detecting a signal against a background of noise; the subjects' biases, motivation, and attention are also considered. *Page 125*

What is sensory adaptation? Sensory adaptation is the phenomenon in which our senses become less and less sensitive to stimuli that are constantly presented to us. An exception is dark adaptation, where our eyes actually become *more* sensitive to stimulation with increased time in the dark. *Page 126*

In what ways do the major physical characteristics of light waves of energy (amplitude, length, and purity) affect our psychological experience of light? Wave amplitude determines our experience of the light's brightness; wavelength determines our experience of hue; and wave purity determines a light's degree of saturation, from the extreme of a pure, monochromatic light to the lowest saturation, called white light. *Page 127*

List the major structures of the eye, and describe the function of each. Before light reaches the retina, it passes through several structures whose major function it is to focus an image on the retina. In order: light passes through the cornea, the pupil (or opening in the iris), aqueous humor, lens (whose shape is controlled by the ciliary muscles), and vitreous humor. Then, at the retina, after passing through layers of neural fibers that combine and integrate visual information (*e.g.,* ganglion and bipolar cells), light reaches the photosensitive rods and cones which are the sense receptor cells for vision. Neural impulses that originate at the rods and cones, are collected at the optic nerve and exit the eyeball at the blindspot. *Pages 130–133*

Why can we claim that rods and cones provide us with two different kinds of visual experience? Cones, which are concentrated in the fovea, respond best to medium to high levels of illumination ("daylight") and respond differentially to different wavelengths (or hues or colors). While rods, concentrated in the peripheral retina, do not discriminate among hues, they do respond to relatively low levels of light. Evidence for this point of view comes from common experience, the examination of the retinas of nocturnal animals, and data on dark adaptation. *Pages 134–135*

Summarize the trichromatic and the opponent-process theories of color vision. These theories attempt to explain how the visual system codes different wavelengths of light, the process that gives rise to our experience of color. The trichromatic theory (associated with Young and von Helmholtz) claims that there are three different kinds of cones, each maximally sensitive to just one of the three primary colors—red, green, or blue. The opponent-process theory (associated with Hering) claims that there are three pairs of mechanisms involved in our experience of color: a blue-yellow processor, a red-green processor, and a black-white processor. Each of these can respond to either of the characteristics that give it its name, but not to both. There is anatomical and physiological evidence that supports both these theories, some of which comes from our understanding of why some people have defects in color vision. *Pages 136–138*

What are the three major physical characteristics of sound, and which psychological experiences do they produce? Like light, sound may be represented as a wave form of energy with three physical characteristics: wave amplitude, frequency, and purity (or complexity). These in turn give rise to the psychological experiences of loudness, pitch, and timbre. *Pages 139–141*

Summarize how sound wave pressures pass through the different structures of the ear. Most of the structures of the ear (the pinna, auditory canal, eardrum, malleus, incus, stapes, and oval window) intensify and transmit sound wave pressures to the fluid in the cochlea. Motions of this fluid cause vibration of the basilar membrane, which in turn stimulates tiny hair cells to transmit neural impulses along the auditory nerve to the temporal lobes of the brain. *Page 142*

Discuss the chemical senses of taste and smell, noting the stimulus and sense receptor for each. The senses of taste (gustation) and smell (olfaction) are very interrelated. They are referred to as the chemical senses because both respond to chemical molecules in solution. The receptors for smell are hair cells that line the upper regions of the nasal cavity. For taste, the receptors are cells in the taste buds located in the tongue. *Pages 143–144*

What are the primary qualities of taste? Taste appears to have four primary qualities: sweet, sour, bitter, and salty. *Page 143*

What are the cutaneous senses, and what are the receptor cells for each? The cutaneous senses are our skin senses: touch, pressure, warm, and cold. Specific receptor cells for each identifiable skin sense have not yet been localized, although they no doubt include free nerve endings and encapsulated nerve endings, which most likely work together in different combinations. *Pages 145–148*

What are our position senses, and how do they operate? One of our position senses is the vestibular sense, which, by responding to the movement of small particles suspended in a fluid within the vestibular sacs and semicircular canals, can inform us about orientation with regard to gravity or accelerated motion. Our other position sense is kinesthesis, which, through receptors in our muscles and joints, informs us about the orientation of parts of our body. *Pages 148–149*

What produces the sensation of pain? A wide variety of environmental stimuli can give rise to our experience of pain, from high levels of stimulus intensity, to light pin-pricks, to internal stimuli of the sort that produce headaches. There seems to be no one receptor for the pain sense. *Pages 149–150*

What is the gate-control theory of pain? This theory assumes the existence of a gate-control mechanism in the spinal cord that either blocks or sends impulses carrying information about pain to the brain. Given the gate-control theory of pain, anything that can block the passage of pain impulses (*i.e.*, close the gate) will control our experience of pain. *Page 150*

4.1 The major thrust of psychophysics is the search for   a) lawful relationships between events in the world and our experiences of those events.   b) the basic or elemental particles of thought that make up human consciousness.   c) ways to relate how we feel (affect) to the way we think (cognition) and the way we behave.   d) the physiological or biological processes that allow us to sense the world as we do. *Page 122*

4.2 If a sound is determined to be below your absolute threshold   a) you will never hear that sound.   b) that sound enters your unconscious mind only.   c) you will hear that sound less than 50 percent of the time.   d) you cannot tell if it is different from other sounds. *Page 123*

4.3 Signal detection theory suggests that determining sensory threshold values (for brightness, let us say)   a) is virtually impossible.   b) is largely a matter of recognizing detection to be a decision making process.   c) requires a subject to detect whether two signals are the same or different.   d) can only be done in a very dark room. *Page 125*

4.4 The notion of sensory adaptation suggests that what we tend to experience most readily are   a) lights and smells, not sounds and tastes.   b) stimuli that have remained the same for a long time.   c) objects and events that we are used to or have adapted to.   d) changes in level and/or type of stimulation. *Page 126*

4.5 True or False?   If a stimulus is above your absolute threshold, you will detect it every time it is presented. *Page 123*

4.6 Wavelength is to hue as wave amplitude is to   a) color.   b) brightness.   c) purity.   d) saturation. *Page 127*

4.7 Which of the following is NOT technically possible?   a) a bright, monochromatic light with 550nm wavelengths   b) a light with 700nm and 400nm wavelengths mixed together   c) a light that is both bright and of low saturation at the same time   d) a highly saturated white light of medium brightness. *Page 129*

4.8 Where in the eye are light waves converted into neural impulses?   a) the lens and ciliary muscles   b) the blindspot and optic nerve   c) the rods and cones   d) the aqueous and vitreous humors. *Page 132*

4.9 The amount of light that strikes the eye will most noticeably affect the: a) cornea.   b) iris.   c) lens.   d) vitreous humor. *Page 130*

4.10 True or False?   If someone is nearsighted or far-sighted, he or she most obviously has a problem with his or her retina. *Page 131*

4.11 If we want to identify a small object at night, in low levels of illumination, the most sensible thing to do (other than making more light available) is to have the image of the object fall on the   a) fovea.   b) blindspot.   c) periphery, away from the fovea.   d) optic nerve. *Page 134*

4.12 When we plot a curve that shows how our eyes become more sensitive to the dark, the curve is not a smooth, regular one, but shows a "break" at about the 7-minute mark. This break occurs because   a) the cones have now stopped adapting to the dark.   b) the retina changes its orientation after 7 minutes in the dark.   c) at that point, our ability to see color increases markedly.   d) the rods have reached a point where they can no longer continue to increase their sensitivity. *Page 135*

4.13 True or False?   Because they operate best at low levels of illumination, our rods give us the most information about the colors of objects in our environments. *Page 134*

4.14 True or False?   In the human retina, there are many more cones than there are rods. *Page 134*

4.15 The Young-Helmholtz theory of color vision proposes that there are specially sensitive receptors for wavelengths of light that correspond to the primary colors of: a) red, green, and yellow.   b) black and white.   c) red, orange, yellow, green, blue, and violet.   d) blue, green, and red. *Page 136*

4.16 The stimulus for audition is   a) electromagnetic energy in wave form.   b) pressures of a medium vibrating against the ear.   c) chemicals that are dissolved in the air or in a liquid.   d) the cochlea of the inner ear. *Page 139*

4.17 As sound waves increase in their frequency, our experience is that   a) the sound gets louder.   b) what used to be sound becomes painful.   c) we hear more overtones.   d) the pitch of the sound gets higher. *Page 139*

4.18 Wave amplitude of light is to brightness as wave amplitude of sound is to   a) loudness.   b) pitch.   c) hue or color.   d) timbre. *Page 139*

4.19 A sound made up of a random assortment of audible wave frequencies would sound like   a) a pure, electronically produced sound.   b) white noise.   c) human speech.   d) a musical chord, or harmony. *Page 141*

4.20 True or False?   The human ear hears as sound the vibrations of a medium that cause the eardrum to vibrate at rates between 20Hz and 20,000 Hz. *Page 140*

4.21 True or False?   The decibel scale provides a measure of the perceived loudness of sounds. *Page 139*

4.22 As sound waves approach the human ear, they are first collected by the   a) pinna.   b) cochlea.   c) basilar membrane.   d) oval window. *Page 141*

4.23 The receptor cells for sound are   a) waves of air pressure.   b) ossicles.   c) cochlea.   d) hair cells. *Page 142*

4.24 The technical name for one's sense of taste is: a) flavor.   b) gustation.   c) biochemical transduction.   d) olfaction. *Page 143*

4.25 True or False?   Neural impulses from sense receptors in our nose do not go to the brain. *Page 144*

4.26 Pheromones are   a) hormones that produce sexual behaviors in nonhumans.   b) chemicals whose odors are related to territoriality and sex.   c) neurotransmitters involved in the chemical senses.   d) the actual sense receptors for both taste and smell. *Page 144*

4.27 What cutaneous stimulation leads to our experience of heat?   a) the simultaneous stimulation of warm and cold receptors   b) the continuous stimulation of free nerve endings   c) above-threshold stimulation of heat-receptor cells   d) intermittent stimulation of encapsulated nerve endings. *Page 145*

4.28 Which sense informs us about the position of our bodies with respect to gravity?   a) the vestibular sense   b) the kinesthetic sense   c) the cutaneous sense   d) the gravitational sense. *Page 149*

4.29 If there is such a thing, the "gate" in Melzack and Moore's gate-control theory controls our experience of   a) arousal or excitement.   b) pain.   c) temperature and other skin senses.   d) balance. *Page 150*

4.30 True or False?   Receptors for pain are found only in or near the skin. *Page 150*

Chapter 5 ▼▼▼▼▼ Perception and Consciousness

▲▲▲▲▲▲

I have never had the nerve to try this classroom demonstration—I've always thought it would be too dangerous. However, when I was a graduate student I had the opportunity to observe it. The demonstration is something of a classic now, and it has been replicated in many forms.

I was able to find a seat at the back of the introductory psychology class, unnoticed by the more than 600 students who had filed into the lecture hall. The instructor entered the room from a side door at the front and began his lecture on the basic principles of sensation and perception. After a few minutes, the class settled down to taking notes and listening to the lecture about the importance of paying attention. The room had become very quiet.

Suddenly, a screaming student burst through the large double doors at the rear of the lecture hall. I recognized him as the professor's graduate assistant, but no one else in the class knew who he was or what he was doing. I felt that he overacted a bit as he stomped down the center aisle of the lecture hall, yelling the foulest of obscenities at the professor, "Dr. X, you failed me for the last time, you *&%@#% so-and-so. You're going to pay for this you *%&$#@*!" Needless to say, the class was stunned. Everyone gasped as the student leaped over the lectern to grab the professor.

The student and the professor struggled briefly, and then suddenly—in clear view of everyone—there was a bright, chrome-plated revolver! Down behind the lectern they fell. **BANG!** The sound of a gunshot filled the room. No one moved; the students sat frozen to their seats. The graduate student raced out the same side door through which the professor had entered just a few minutes earlier. The professor lay sprawled out on the floor, moaning loudly. (It was now *his* turn for some overacting.)

Still no one moved. Six hundred students sat stunned in their seats. At just the right dramatic moment, the professor slowly drew himself up to the lectern, and in a

calm, soft voice said, "Now, I want everyone to take out a pencil and some paper and write down exactly what you saw."

I'm sure I need not describe all the results of this demonstration. You can guess what happened. I never did read all 600 descriptions of the events that took place in class that day, but I did help to summarize the responses. It was impressive. The "enraged" graduate student was described as being from 5'4" to 6'3" tall and weighing between 155 and 225 pounds. Although there was some agreement, one would have a difficult time coming up with a single physical description of the suspect in this shooting.

The most remarkable misperception that took place had to do with the gun. As I watched the professor take his place at the front of the class before he began to lecture, i was sure that he had blown the demonstration. I clearly saw him remove the pistol from his suitcoat pocket and place it on top of his lecture notes. When the "crazed student" crashed into the room, the professor reached down, grabbed the gun and pointed it at the student as he came charging down the center aisle. In fact, the student *never* had the gun in his hands. The professor had it all along. The first move the student made was to grab the wrist of the professor and point the gun toward the floor. It was the professor who fired the shot that startled us all. *Fewer than 20 students of the 600 in class that day reported seeing these events the way they actually occurred.* The experiences of those students were affected by many factors besides what actually happened in class that morning. In this chapter, we focus on perception and the factors that influence this basic psychological process.

► Preview

perception the cognitive process of selecting, organizing, and interpreting

Now that we have a general idea of how our senses work, we can move on to consider what happens next as we process information about the world. As we have seen, the psychology of sensation is concerned with how our different senses manage to do what they do. **Perception** deals with the selection, organization, and interpretation of stimuli, it can be a complex, active, and even creative cognitive process. You can think of these interrelated processes this way: Our senses present us with information about the world, while perception represents (re-presents) that information, often flavored by our motivational states, our emotions, our expectations, and our past experiences. That is, we create our perceptions of reality based on more than just the information provided by our senses.

consciousness our awareness or perception of the environment and of our own mental processes

In this context, we also can consider issues related to consciousness. In general, **consciousness** refers to our awareness of the environment and of our own mental processes. To be fully conscious is to be awake, aware, alert, and attentive. The extent to which we are aware or conscious of ourselves and our environment will influence how—and the extent to which—we can process information. This is why I have chosen to put our discussion of consciousness here in this chapter.

We begin the chapter with some general observations about perception and consciousness and then move on to discuss several related topics. First, we'll deal with perceptual selectivity ("paying attention"), a defining characteristic of consciousness. Second, we'll consider issues of perceptual organization or why we tend to experience some stimuli as "belonging together." Having discussed selection and organization, we'll examine some processes we often take for granted: our perception of depth and distance, and the constancy of our perceptions over time and over a variety of situations. We'll end our coverage of perception and consciousness by considering a few situations in which our normal perception or awareness is altered, changed, or distorted. We'll see how consciousness changes when it is affected by sleep, hypnosis, and drugs.

► The Nature of Perception and Consciousness

We have defined perception as an active cognitive process involving the selection, organization, and interpretation of stimuli. As we go through this chapter, it will become clear to you that perception is a psychological process very much related to both sensation and to memory; it helps us make sense of the multitude of stimuli that bombard us at at every moment. By giving meaning to sensory input, it readies that information for storage in memory. Similarly, the processing of the information provided by our senses requires that we rely on memories already stored away. Thus, perception may be thought of as a two-way bridge between information from the world around us and information as stored in memory.

We have defined consciousness as the perception or awareness of the environment and one's own mental processes. Consciousness, then, is a state of mind—the active awareness of all thoughts, feelings, memories, and perceptions.

How then can we characterize human consciousness? One of the first to try systematically was William James, nearly 100 years ago (James, 1890; 1892; 1904). For James, there were four basic characteristics of normal waking consciousness.

1. Consciousness is always *changing*. Consciousness doesn't hold still. It cannot be held in the mind for study. "No state once gone can recur and be identical with what was before," James wrote (1892, p. 152). He also wrote, "Consciousness, then, does not appear to itself chopped up in bits. Such words as 'chain' or 'train' do not describe it fitly as it presents itself in the first instance. It is nothing jointed; it flows. A 'river' or 'stream' is most naturally described. In talking about it hereafter, let us call it the stream of thought, of consciousness. . ." (James, 1890, p. 243).

2. Consciousness is a *personal* experience. Consciousness does not exist without an individual to have it. My consciousness and yours are separate and different. You may try to tell me about your state of mind, your consciousness, but I will never be able to appreciate it fully.

3. Consciousness is *continuous*. There are no gaps in our awareness. We really can't tell where one thought leaves off and another begins. Again, James' metaphor of a 'stream of consciousness' is appropriate.

4. Consciousness is *selective*. Awareness is often a matter of making choices, of selectively attending to or focusing on some aspect of experience while ignoring others. "We find it [consciousness] always doing one thing, choosing one out of several materials so presented to its notice, emphasizing and accentuating that and suppressing as far as possible all the rest" (James, 1890, p. 139).

It will soon become clear, if it isn't already, that each of the features that James attributed to consciousness hold equally well for perception. Our perceptions of the world are always changing (the way we interpret things today may be quite different from yesterday). Our perceptions are personal (what you perceive and what I perceive, even in the same situation, may be very different). Our perceptions are continuous (we do not "know" when our mental processes shift from sensation to perception to memory and back again). Our perceptions are selective (our senses provide us with too much information to attend to). We'll begin our discussion of perception with this idea: Perception is a process of selecting information from the environment.

Before You Go On

▼▼▼▼▼▼▼▼▼

Define "perception" and "consciousness."

What, according to William James, are the four major features of consciousness?

▶ Perception

Imagine that you are at a party, engaged in a dreadfully boring conversation with someone you've just met. Suddenly, it occurs to you that wearing your new shoes was not a good idea—your feet hurt. You are munching on an assortment of tasty appetizers. Music blares from a stereo. Aromas of foods, smoke, and perfume fill the air. There must be at least 50 people at this party, and you don't know any of them. Your senses are being bombarded simultaneously by all sorts of information: sights, sounds, tastes, smells, even pain. Suddenly, you hear someone mention your name. You redirect your attention, for the moment disregarding the person talking right in front of you.

▲ *We often attend to stimuli that are different, or that contrast with other nearby stimuli.*

contrast the extent to which a stimulus is in some physical way different from other surrounding stimuli

▶ *Perceptual Selectivity: Paying Attention*

What determines which of many competing stimuli attract our attention? In fact, there are many variables that influence our selection of stimuli from the environment. They can be divided into two types: *stimulus factors* and *personal factors*. By stimulus factors, I mean those characteristics of stimuli that make them more compelling (or attention-grabbing) than others, no matter who the perceiver is. By personal factors, I am referring to those characteristics of the person, the perceiver, that influence which stimuli get attended to. We'll start by considering stimulus factors.

Stimulus Factors in Selectivity. The most common and important stimulus factor in perceptual selection is **contrast**, the extent to which a given stimulus is physically different from other stimuli around it. One stimulus can contrast with other stimuli in a variety of ways. For example, we are more likely to attend to a stimulus if its *intensity* is different from the intensities of other stimuli. Generally, the more intense a stimulus, the more likely we are to select it for further processing.

Simply put, a shout is more compelling than a whisper; a bright light is more attention-grabbing than a dim one. Notice that this isn't always the case. The context in which a stimulus occurs makes a difference. A shout may be more compelling than a whisper—unless everyone is shouting; then it may very well be the soft, quiet, reasoned tone that gets our attention. When faced with a barrage of bright lights, a dim one may be the one we process most fully.

The same argument holds for the stimulus characteristic of physical *size*. Typically, the bigger the stimulus, the more likely we are to attend to it. There is little point in erecting a small billboard to advertise your new restaurant. You'll want to construct the biggest billboard you can afford in hopes of attracting attention. Although it may not hold true for billboards, contrast effects are such that when we are faced with many large stimuli, one that is smaller may be the one to which we attend. It seems to me that the easiest player to spot on a football field is the placekicker, who tends to be much smaller than the other players, and who usually does not wear as much protective padding.

A third physical dimension that may determine perceptual selectivity, and for which contrast is relevant, is *motion*. Motion is a powerful factor in determining visual attention. A bird in flight is much easier to see than a bird sitting in a bush. In the fall, walking through the woods, you may come close to stepping on a chipmunk before you notice it, so long as it stays still —an adaptive response of camouflage that chipmunks do well. But if that chipmunk makes a dash to escape, it is easily noticed scurrying across the leaves. Once again, the *contrast* created by movement is important.

Although intensity, size, and motion are three physical characteristics of stimuli that readily come to mind, there are many others. Indeed, any way in which stimuli may contrast (be different) or can determine which stimulus we attend to. (A very small spot can easily grab one's attention if it is right in the middle of a solid yellow tie.) This is why we have printed important terms in **boldface type** throughout this book—so you will notice them and attend to them as important stimuli.

There is another stimulus characteristic that can determine attention, but for which contrast is really not relevant, and that is *repetition*. Simply put: the more often a stimulus is presented, the more likely it is that it will be attended to—everything else being equal, of course. Instructors who want to get across an important point will seldom mention it just once, but will repeat it. (Most students recognize that generally there is a high correlation between the importance of a piece of information and how often it is brought up in class.) This is why we have repeated the definitions of those important terms in the text, in the margin, *and again* in the glossary at the end of the book.

Think again of the billboard you're going to erect to advertise your restaurant. No matter how large or bright it is, and even if you have managed to build motion into it, you will be well advised to erect as many billboards as you can if you want to get the attention of as many people as possible. The people who write and schedule television commercials want you to attend to their messages, and repetition is obviously one of their main techniques.

To summarize, there are many ways in which stimuli may differ—brightness, size, motion, color, pitch, and loudness, for example. The greater the contrast between any one stimulus and the others around it, the greater the likelihood that that stimulus will capture or draw our attention. And, everything else being equal, the more often a stimulus is presented, (at least up to a point) the greater the likelihood that it will be perceived.

Before You Go On
▼▼▼▼▼▼▼▼▼

What stimulus factors determine the selection of perceptions?

Personal Factors in Selectivity. Sometimes, attention is determined not so much by the physical characteristics of the stimuli present, but by the characteristics of the perceiver. For example, imagine that two students are watching a football game on TV. Both are presented with identical stimuli from the same television screen. One asks, "Did you see that tackle?" The other responds, "No, I was watching the cheerleaders." The difference in perception here is not one that we can attribute to the nature of the stimuli, since both students received the very same sensory information from the same TV. The difference is due to characteristics of the perceivers, which we are calling *personal factors.* Although there are many personal factors that can determine the selection of our perceptions, we can categorize them as being a function of motivation, expectation, and/or past experience.

Imagine that the two students watching the football game on TV are avid supporters of the two teams involved. One is a fan of the Chicago Bears; the other is a staunch backer of the Los Angeles Rams. Our TV viewers may have a small wager on the outcome of this important game. Suppose that the Bears win the hard-fought game with a last second field goal. Now, both students have watched exactly the same game on the same TV, but which of the two is more likely to have perceived the officiating of the game as fair, honest, and above reproach? Which student is more likely to have seen the game as "one of the poorest refereed games ever"? The perception of the officiating may depend on who won, who lost, and the motivation of the perceiver. In large measure, the viewers, like all spectators, tended to see what they *wanted* to see. You might not be surprised to learn that research confirms this very scenario (Hastorf & Cantril, 1954).

It is true that we often perceive what we want to perceive, and it is equally true that we often perceive what we *expect* to perceive, whether it's really there or not. Similarly, we often do not notice stimuli when they *are* present simply because we didn't expect them. When we are psychologically prepared to perceive something, we say that we have formed a **mental set.** Notice that we can also develop a mental set *not* to perceive something.

mental set a predisposed (set) way to perceive something; an expectation

Figure 5.1

▲ Our mental set affects our perception. How many "the"s did you see when you first glanced at this simple figure? Why?

Take a second and quickly glance at the message in Figure 5.1. What did the message say? (If you've seen this before, you'll have to try it with someone who hasn't.) Many people claim that the message is PARIS IN THE SPRING. In fact, there are two THEs in the triangle—PARIS IN THE THE SPRING. People familiar with the English language and with this phrase do not expect there to be two *the*s right next to each other. Following their mental set, they report perceiving only one. Other people may develop a different mental set. Their line of reasoning may be something like: "This is a psychology text, so there's probably a trick here someplace, and I'm going to find it." In this instance, skeptics get rewarded. There *is* a trick, and if their mental set was to find one, they did so. Note that this example makes the point that sometimes our expectations not only affect what we perceive, but they also affect what we don't perceive. In other words, if you don't expect something to happen, if you're not "looking for it," you may miss it.

We will see later (Chapter 8) that an inability to change a mentally set way of perceiving a problem may interfere with our finding a solution to that problem. What we call "creative" problem solving often is only a matter of perceiving aspects of a problem in new, unique, or unexpected ways. Thus, even as complex a cognitive process as problem solving often hinges on basic perceptual processes.

Have you noticed that when we say that paying attention is due to motivation and expectation, we are claiming that what we perceive is often influenced by our past experiences. Much of our motivation comes from our past experiences. For example, the two folks watching the football game between Chicago and Los Angeles were not born fans of those two teams. Their allegiances reflect their past experiences. Similarly, expectations develop from past experiences. We are likely to expect to perceive, or be set to perceive, what we have perceived in the past in similar circumstances. Perhaps a personal example will make clear what I mean here.

I once took a course in comparative psychology that examined the behaviors of nonhuman organisms. One of the co-teachers of the course was an ornithologist (a scientist who studies birds). One of the requirements of the course was to participate in an early morning outing to go bird watching. The memory is very vivid to this day: Cold, tired, clutching my thermos of warm coffee, I slopped through the marshland looking for birds, as the sun was just rising. After 20 minutes of this unpleasantness, our instructor had identified 10 or 11 different birds. I wasn't quite certain, but I thought I had spied a duck. I didn't know just what sort of duck it was, but I did think that I had seen a duck. Now the differences in perception between my instructor and me that cold, wet morning could be explained in terms of motivation (he *did* care much more than I); but mostly, I suspect, his ability to spot birds so quickly reflected his experience. He knew where to look and what to look for.

Before You Go On

▼▼▼▼▼▼▼▼▼

What personal factors are involved in perceptual selectivity?

▶ Perceptual Organization

As we have seen, one of our basic perceptual reactions to the environment is to select for processing certain stimuli from among those that strike our receptors. Then we must organize the bits and pieces of experience that are presented to our senses into meaningful, organized wholes. We don't really hear the individual sounds of speech; we organize them and perceive them as words and phrases and sentences. Our visual experience is not one of tiny bits of color and light and dark, as recorded at the retina, but of identifiable objects and events. We don't perceive a pat on the back as responses from hundreds of receptors in our skin.

Perceptual organization was a process of special interest to the Gestalt psychologists. As you recall from Chapter 1, **gestalt** is a German word that means something like "configuration" or "whole." One forms a gestalt when one sees the overall scheme of things. If you have a general idea of how something works or can appreciate the general nature of something without overly attending to details, you have formed a gestalt.

One of the most basic principles of Gestalt psychology is that of the **figure-ground relationship**. Of all the stimuli in your environment at any one time, those that you attend to and group together are said to be *figures*, while all the rest become the *ground*. As you focus your attention on the words on this page, they form figures against the ground (or background, if you prefer) formed by the rest of the page. When you hear your instructor's voice during a lecture, that voice is the figure against the ground of all the other sounds in the room. Figure 5.2 provides a couple of examples of the figure-ground relationship.

The Gestalt psychologists were interested in factors that influenced our attention to stimuli in the environment. They were also intrigued by how the process of perception enabled us to group and organize stimuli together to form meaningful gestalts. As was the case for perceptual selection, there are *several* factors that influence how we organize our perceptual worlds. Again, let's consider stimulus factors and personal factors separately.

Stimulus Factors in Organization. By stimulus factors, we are referring to characteristics of stimuli that help us organize them into a figure or gestalt. We will consider five: proximity, similarity, continuity, common fate, and closure.

gestalt whole, totality, configuration; where the whole (gestalt) is seen as more than the sum of its parts

figure-ground relationship the Gestalt psychology principle that stimuli are selected and perceived as figures against a ground or background

Figure 5.2

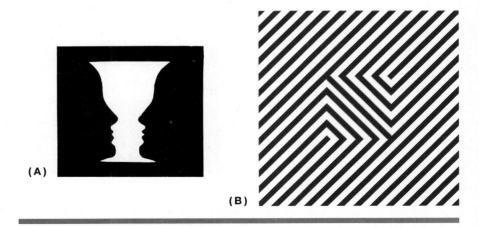

(A)

(B)

▲ *(A) A classic reversable figure-ground pattern. What do you see here? A white vase or a birdbath? Or do you see two black profiles facing each other? Can you clearly see both figures at the same time? (B) After a few moments' inspection, a small square should emerge as a figure against the ground of diagonal parallel lines.*

proximity the Gestalt principle of organization that asserts that stimuli will be perceived as belonging together if they occur together in space or time

similarity the Gestalt principle of organization that says that stimuli will be perceived together if they share some common characteristic(s)

continuity the Gestalt principle of organization that claims that a stimulus or a movement will be perceived as continuing in the same smooth direction as first established

1. *Proximity.* Glance quickly at Figure 5.3(A). Without giving it much thought, what did you see there? A bunch of Xs, yes; but more than that, there were two separately identifiable groups of Xs, weren't there? The group of eight Xs on the left seems somehow separate from the group on the right, while the Xs within each group seem to go together. This illustrates what the Gestalt psychologists called **proximity** or *contiguity*. What this means is that events that occur close together in space, or in time, are generally perceived as belonging together as part of the same figure. In Figure 5.3(A), it's difficult to see the Xs as falling into four rows or four columns. They just belong together as two groups of eight Xs each.

Proximity operates on more than just visual stimuli. For example, sounds that occur together in speech are perceived as going together to form words or phrases. In written language there are physical spaces between words on the printed page; with spoken language there are (usually) very brief pauses between words. Thunder and lightning usually occur together, the sound of thunder following shortly after our experience of the lightning. And as a result of our experience of thunderstorms, it's rather difficult to even think about lightning without also thinking about thunder.

2. *Similarity.* Now glance at Figure 5.3(B) and describe what you see there. We have a set of Xs and Os that clearly are organized into a pattern. The usual way to organize these stimuli is to see them as two columns of Xs and two of Os. Perceiving rows of alternating Xs and Os is very difficult. This drawing demonstrates the Gestalt principle of **similarity**. Stimulus events that are in some way alike or have properties in common tend to be grouped together in our perception—a "birds of a feather are perceived together" sort of thing. Australian koalas are perceived (and thought of) by most of us as "bears" because to us, they look more like bears than anything else. As it happens, they're not. They are related more to kangaroos and wallabies than to bears.

3. *Continuity.* The principle of **continuity** (called *good continuation* by some) suggests that we tend to see things as ending up consistent with the

Figure 5.3

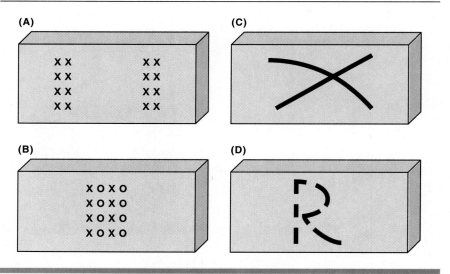

▲ *(A) These Xs are organized as two groups, not four rows or columns, because of* **proximity**. *(B) Here we see two columns of Os and two of Xs because of similarity. (C) We tend to see this figure as two intersecting lines, one straight and one curved, because of continuity. (D) This figure is perceived as an R—which it is not—because of closure.*

way they started off. Figure 5.3(C) illustrates this point with a simple line drawing. The clearest, easiest way to organize this drawing is as two separate but intersecting lines: one straight, the other curved. It's difficult to imagine seeing this figure any other way.

Very often our perceptions are guided by a logic that says, for example, "Lines that start out straight, should continue straight." The Gestalt principle of continuity also may account for some of the ways we organize our perceptions of people. Aren't we particularly shocked when a young man who was an award-winning honor student throughout high school suddenly does poorly at college and flunks out? That's not the way we like to view the world working. We wouldn't be nearly as surprised to find that another student, who barely made it through grade school and high school, fails to pass at college.

common fate the Gestalt principle of organization that says that we group together all the elements of a scene that move together in the same direction at the same speed

4. *Common Fate.* **Common fate** describes our tendency to group together in the same figure those elements of a scene that appear to move together in the same direction and at the same speed. Common fate is a lot like continuity, but for moving stimuli. Remember that chipmunk sitting motionless on the leaves in the woods? So long as both the chipmunk and the leaves stay still, the chipmunk won't be noticed. But when it moves, the moving parts of the chipmunk all move together—sharing a common fate— and we see it clearly scurrying away.

5. *Closure.* Perhaps the most commonly encountered Gestalt principle of organization is called **closure**. This is our tendency to fill in gaps in our perceptual world. Closure provides an excellent example of my point that perception is an *active* process. It underscores the notion that we constantly seek to make sense out of our environment—whether that environment presents us with sensible stimuli or not. Closure is illustrated by Figure 5.3(D). At a glance, anyone would tell you that this figure is the letter R, but, of course, it is not. That's not the way anybody makes an R. It may be the way we perceive an R due to closure.

closure the Gestalt principle of organization that asserts that we tend to perceive incomplete figures as whole and complete

Closure occurs commonly during our everyday conversations. Just for fun some day, tape record a casual conversation with a friend. Then try to write down exactly what was said during the conversation. A truly faithful transcription will reveal that many words and sounds were left out. Even though they were not actually there as stimuli, they were not missed by the listener because he or she filled in the gaps (closure) and understood what was being said.

subjective contours the perception of a contour (a line or plane) that is not there, but is suggested by other aspects of a scene

A phenomenon that many psychologists believe is a special case of closure is our perception of **subjective contours,** in which arrangements of lines and patterns enable us to see figures that are not actually there. Now if that sounds just a bit spooky, look at Figure 5.4 where we have two examples of subjective contour. In Fig. 5.4(A) you can "see" a solid triangle that is so clearly there it nearly jumps off the page. The triangle is in front of the other patterns on the page, and seems even whiter than the page itself. There is no accepted explanation for subjective contours (Bradley & Dumais, 1975; Coren, 1972; Kanizsa, 1976; Rock, 1986), but it does seem that they provide good examples of our perceptual processes filling in gaps in our perceptual world in order to provide us with sensible information.

Personal Factors in Organization. We can cover the personal factors that influence perceptual organization rather quickly, because they are the same as those that influence selection: motivation, expectation, and past experience. We perceive stimuli as going together, as forming a gestalt, because we want to, because we expect to, and/or because we have perceived them together in the past.

Figure 5.4

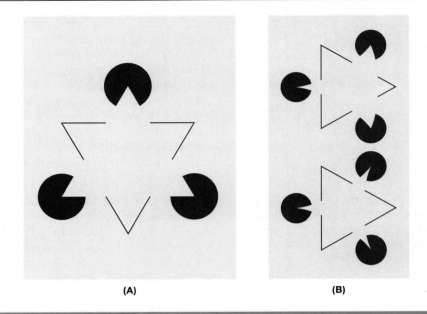

(A)   (B)

▲ *Examples of subjective contours.*

Think back to my description of the classroom demonstration at the beginning of the chapter—an apparently crazed student rushes into a class, a gun comes into view, goes off, the professor falls to the floor. A key issue was the perception of the gun. Perceptual selectivity was *not* the issue. All the students attended to the gun. What was significant about this scenario was the students' perception of where the gun came from. Virtually everyone "organized" that gun into the hands of the student. No one was *mentally set* for or expected the professor to have a gun in class. Certainly no one *wanted* to see their professor with a gun. Hopefully, no one had ever *experienced* a professor bringing a gun to class. (Seeing crazed students with guns is not a common experience either, but with television and movies, it's certainly a more probable one. In fact a sadly similar and deadly experience did occur in the fall of 1991 at the University of Iowa.) This demonstration will come up again when we discuss ways in which our memories can be distorted, thus reinforcing our point that perception and memory are very much related.

How we perceive—judge, interpret, organize—a stimulus is often flavored by how we perceive other stimuli presented at about the same time. In other words, a very important factor in how we organize our perceptions is the *context* in which they are perceived. We seldom make perceptual judgments in a vacuum. Figures are usually presented in a given context. Context often affects what we expect to perceive or think we have perceived.

Figure 5.5 provides two examples of the effect of context on visual perception. In Figure 5.5(A), is the highlighted stimulus the letter H or the letter A? In fact, by itself, it isn't a very good example of either. But in the proper context—given our past experience with the English language—that same stimulus may appear to be an A *or* an H.

Figure 5.5(B) is Edwin Boring's (1930) classic *ambiguous figure*. When looked at one way, the drawing depicts a young lady, in Victorian-style clothing, a large feather in her hat, looking away from the viewer. Looked at another way, the same picture shows an old woman, chin tucked down into her collar, hair down to her eyes, with a rather large wart on her nose.

Figure 5.5(A)

THE CAT SAT BY THE DOOR.

▲ *Is the highlighted letter A or an H? In fact, it is neither and can be interpreted as one or the other only on the basis of context and our past experience with the English language.*

Figure 5.5(B)

▲ *This perceptually ambiguous draw-ing can be interpreted in different ways depending on the context in which it is viewed. Do you see a young woman or an old woman? (After Boring, 1930).*

retinal disparity the phenomenon in which each retina receives a different (disparate) view of the same three-dimensional object

Figure 5.6

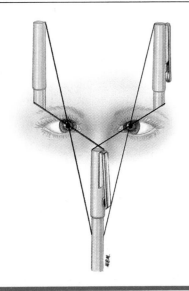

▲ *When looking at one object, the right eye sees a different image than the left eye due to retinal disparity. This disparity gives us a cue that the object we are viewing is three-dimensional.*

If I had shown you a set of pictures of young men and women dressed in Victorian costume, as if they were at a grand ball, and *then* presented Figure 5.5(B), you almost certainly would have seen the young lady. In the context of a series of pictures of old, poorly dressed men and women, you probably would have organized the very same line drawing to depict the old woman. Things are not always as they seem.

How we organize our experience of the world depends on a number of factors. Our perception that some stimuli in our environments go together with other stimuli to form coherent figures is a process influenced by the proximity or similarity of the events themselves, by our interpretations of closure and continuity, by the context in which those stimuli appear, and by our own personal motives, expectations, and past experiences.

Before You Go On
▼▼▼▼▼▼▼▼▼

List stimulus and personal factors that determine how we organize stimuli in perception.

▶ The Perception of Depth and Distance

We have noted that perception is a more complex cognitive process than the simple reception of information that we call sensation. Perception requires that we select and organize stimulus information; it also involves actively recognizing, identifying, and assigning meaning to stimuli.

One of the ways in which we interpret a visual stimulus is to note not only *what* it is that we are seeing, but *where* it happens to be. We perceive the world as three-dimensional. So long as we are paying attention (surely a required perceptual process), we don't run into buildings or fall off cliffs. We know with considerable accuracy just how far we are from objects in our environment. What is remarkable and strange about this ability is that the light reflected from objects and events in our environment falls on *two*-dimensional retinas. The depth and distance in our world is not something we directly *sense;* it is something we *perceive.*

The ability to judge depth and distance accurately is an adaptive skill that plays an important role in determining many of our actions. Our ability to make such judgments so well reflects the fact that we are simultaneously responding to a large number of clues or cues to depth and distance. Some of these cues are built into the way our visual systems work and are referred to as *ocular cues,* while others, called *physical cues,* have more to do with our appreciation of the physical environment itself.

Ocular Cues. Some of the cues we get about distance and depth reflect the way our eyes work. Cues that involve both eyes are called binocular cues (*bi* means two); cues that only require one eye are called monocular cues (*mono* means one).

Binocular cues result from the fact that our eyes are separated. For example, when we look at a nearby three-dimensional object, each eye gets a some-what different view of it. Hold a pen with a clip on it about twelve inches away. Rotate the pen until the clip can be viewed by the right eye, but not the left. (You can check that out by closing one eye then the other as you rotate the pen.) Now each eye (retina) is getting a different (disparate) view of the same object. This phenomenon is called **retinal disparity**. It is a powerful cue that what we are looking at must be solid or three-dimensional. Otherwise, each eye would see the same image, not two disparate ones. See Figure 5.6.

convergence the tendency of the eyes to move toward each other as we focus on objects up close

accommodation in vision, the process in which the shape of the lens is changed by the ciliary muscles

Figure 5.7

▲ *Although we know that the sides of the road are parallel, they appear to come together in the distance, an example of linear perspective.*

Figure 5.8

▲ *A house on a stick: the failure of linear perspective in a child's drawing.*

Convergence is the name we give to the action of our eyes turning in toward each other when we view something up close. Convergence reflects the fact that we "know" how our eyes are aligned in our heads, even if we seldom pay much attention to it. As we gaze off into the distance, our eyes aim out in almost parallel fashion. As we focus our view on objects that are close to us, our eyes come together, or converge, and we simply interpret that convergence as an indication that what we are looking at is close to us. Convergence is also illustrated in Figure 5.6.

The rest of the cues we'll consider are monocular. (Even the physical cues listed below are monocular cues because they can be appreciated by persons who see with but one eye.) A unique monocular cue to distance—at least relatively short distances—is **accommodation**. This process, you'll recall, is the changing of the shape of the lens, by the ciliary muscles, to focus images on the retina. When we focus on distant objects, accommodation flattens our lens, and when we focus on nearby objects, our lens gets rounder or fatter, thanks to the action of the ciliary muscles. Although the process is reflexive and automatic, our brain reacts to the activity of our ciliary muscles in terms of the distance of an object from our eyes. That is, our brain "knows" what our ciliary muscles are doing to focus an image and interprets these actions in terms of distance. Accommodation does not function as an effective cue for distances beyond arm's length because the changes in the activity of the ciliary muscles in such cases are too slight to be noticed. But, after all, it is within arm's length that accurate decisions about distance are most critical.

Physical Cues. The physical cues to distance and depth are those we get from the structure of our environment. These cues are sometimes called *pictorial* cues because they are used by artists to create the impression of three-dimensionality on a two-dimensional canvas or paper. Here are some of the most important.

1. *Linear perspective* (see Figure 5.7). As you stand in the middle of a road, looking off into the distance, the sides of the road, which you know to be parallel, seem to come together in the distance. Drawing with this cue obviously takes some time and experience to develop. Have you ever seen a child's drawing of a house that looked something like Figure 5.8? There are the roof, the chimney (with smoke, of course), the windows, the door, and the front sidewalk. Because the child *knows* that the sidewalk is as wide at the street as it is by the door, it is drawn as two parallel lines. The result looks like a house on a stick. Only later the child will come to appreciate the usefulness of linear perspective and will make the sidewalk appear wider in the foreground at the street.

2. *Interposition* (see Figure 5.9). This cue to distance reflects our appreciation that objects in the foreground tend to cover, or partially hide, objects in the background, and not vice versa. One of the reasons that I know that people sitting in the back of a room are farther away from me than people sitting in the front row is information that I get from interposition. People (and other objects) in the front partially block my view of the people sitting behind them.

3. *Relative size* (see Figure 5.10). This is a commonly used clue to our judgment of distance. As it happens, very few stimuli in this world change their size. Lots of things get nearer or farther away from us. So, everything else being equal, we tend to judge the object that produces the larger retinal image as being closer to us. This may sound like a silly thing to do, but have a friend hold an object up very close to your closed eye. We'll imagine your

Figure 5.9

▲ *Interposition occurs when objects in the foreground partially cover objects that are farther away.*

Figure 5.10

▲ *Although all these hot air balloons are about the same size, those in the distance appear much smaller because the image that they cast on our retinas is smaller.*

Figure 5.11

▲ *Gradiants of texture provide cues to distance so we can see more details of objects that are close to us.*

friend is holding an apple. When you open your eye, all you see is "red." At first, you may not even experience the object in front of your eye as an apple. Now have your friend slowly move the apple away from you. As the apple is moved away, the image of that apple on your retina gets smaller and smaller. If your friend moves far enough, you eventually may lose sight of the apple altogether. Now you know that apples do not shrink, and you interpret the reduction in retinal size as a cue to distance—as retinal size gets smaller, the object is moving away.

4. *Texture gradient* (see Figure 5.11). Standing on a gravel road, looking down at your feet, you clearly can make out the details of the texture of the roadway. You can see individual pieces of gravel. But as you look on down the road, the texture gradually changes, details giving way to a smooth blending of a textureless surface. We interpret this gradual change (which is what *gradient* means) in texture as indicating a gradual change in distance.

5. *Patterns of shading* (see Figure 5.12). Drawings that do not use shading look flat and two-dimensional. Children eventually learn that if they want their pictures to look lifelike, they should shade in tree trunks and apples and show them as casting shadows. Two-dimensional objects do not cast shadows, and how objects create patterns of light and shade can tell us a great deal about their shape and solidity.

6. *Motion parallax* (see Figure 5.13). This rather technical sounding label names something with which we are all familiar. The clearest example may occur when we are in a car, looking out a side window. Even if the car is going at a modest speed, nearby utility poles and fence posts seem to race by. Objects farther away seem to be moving more slowly, and mountains or trees way off in the distance seem not to be moving at all. This difference in apparent motion is known as motion parallax. By the way, observation of this phenomenon during a train ride in 1910 was what first got Max Wertheimer interested in what evolved into Gestalt psychology.

Before You Go On
▼▼▼▼▼▼▼▼

Name and describe some of the cues that provide us with information about depth and/or distance.

▶ Perceptual Constancies and Illusions

There are a variety of *perceptual constancies*—stable patterns of perceiving the world—that help us organize and interpret the stimulus input we get from our senses. It is because of this stability that we can recognize a familiar object as being the same regardless of how far away it is, the angle from which we view it, or the nature of the light reflected from it. You can recognize your textbook whether you view it from a distance or close up, straight on or from an angle, in a dimly or brightly lit room, or in blue, red, or white light. If it were not for perceptual constancies, every individual sensation might be perceived as a new experience, and little if anything would appear familiar.

Constancies. We've already mentioned the role of *size constancy* in helping us judge how far away we are from an object. A friend standing close to us may fill our visual field. At a distance, the image of that same person may

Figure 5.12

▲ *Patterns of light and shadow provide us with information about the three-dimensionality of objects in our environment.*

Figure 5.13

▲ *As we move through the environment, stationary objects near us seem to whiz by very quickly, while objects that are farther away seem to move by us more slowly. This cue to distance is called motion parallax.*

illusion a perception that is at odds with (different from) what we know as physical reality

take up only a fraction of our visual field. The size of the image on our retina may be significantly different, but we know very well that our friend hasn't shrunk but simply has moved farther away.

Shape constancy refers to our perception that solid objects tend to maintain their shape even though they may produce different retinal images. Shape constancy can be demonstrated with any familiar object. As you look at the door from different positions in the room, the shape of the image of the door on your retina changes radically (Fig. 5.14). Closed, it appears to be a rectangle; partially open, the image is that of a trapezoid; from the edge, the retinal image is essentially that of a straight line. Regardless of the retinal image, because of shape constancy, you still see the object as a door.

Due to *brightness constancy*, the apparent relative brightness of a familiar object is perceived as being the same regardless of the actual type or amount of light under which the object is viewed. The white shirt you put on this morning may be sensed as gray when you pass through a shadow, or as dark and black as night falls, but it is still perceived as a white shirt, in no way darker than it was this morning. The same is true for color perception. If you know that you put on a white shirt this morning, you'd still perceive it as white even if I were to shine a red light on it. The light waves reflected from the shirt into your eyes would be associated with the experience of red, but you would still know the shirt was white and perceive it as white. Someone else, who didn't know any better might perceive your shirt as red, but you'd see it as a white shirt in a red light because of color constancy.

Illusions. By now, you appreciate that the relationship between the real world and our perception of it is tenuous at best. What we perceive often is flavored by many factors beyond physical stimuli that impinge on our sense receptors. We've seen a number of applications of this theme. The interaction between physical reality and our psychological experience can be appreciated clearly when we consider illusions. We define **illusions** as "experiences in which our perceptions are at odds with what we know as physical reality."

A number of very simple—and very compelling geometrical illusions are presented in Figure 5.15. Consider Figure 5.15(A). This drawing depicts the *vertical-horizontal illusion*. Figure 5.15(B) is the same illusion but in slightly

Figure 5.14

▲ *Though we see four different images, we know we are looking at a door because of the shape constancy.*

Figure 5.15

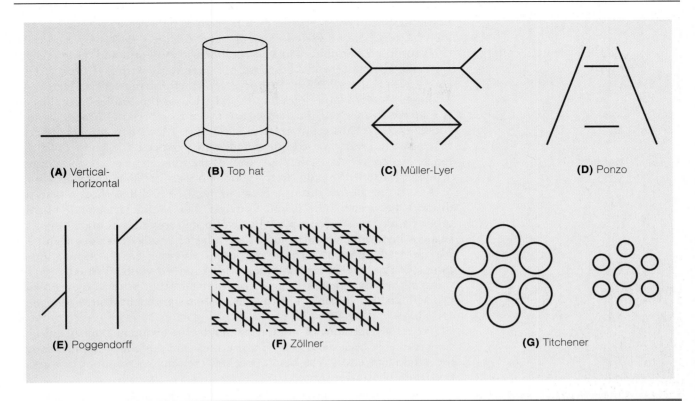

(A) Vertical-
horizontal

(B) Top hat

(C) Müller-Lyer

(D) Ponzo

(E) Poggendorff

(F) Zöllner

(G) Titchener

▲ *A few geometrical illusions. In each case you* know *the answer, but the relevant questions are: (A) Are the vertical and horizontal lines the same length? (B) Is the brim as wide as the hat is tall? (C) Are the two horizontal lines the same length? (D) Are the two horizontal lines the same length? (E) Are the two diagonals part of the same line? (F) Are the diagonal lines parallel? (G) Are the two center circles the same size?*

more meaningful terms. Are the lines in Figure 5.15(A) the same length? Yes, you know they are—we're talking about illusions here. But, do they *appear* to be the same length? No, they do not. The vertical line seems significantly longer than the horizontal one. The hat in Figure 5.15(B) seems to be considerably taller than it is wide. The illusion is inescapable.

Notice that the vertical-horizontal illusion "works" even after you have measured the two lines to confirm that they are the same length. They *still* don't look equal. I've seen this illusion in many forms for many years, yet every time I see it, I'm taken in by it. This is one of three fundamental facts about illusions: They do not depend on our ignorance of the situation.

A second fact about illusions is that they do not "occur" at the retina. Figure 5.15(C) is the well-known *Müller-Lyer illusion,* named after the man who first drew it. The top line would continue to appear longer than the bottom one even if the two (equal) lines were presented to one eye, and the "arrow-like vanes" were presented to the other. A third fact about illusions is that their effects do not depend upon movements of the eye. Illusions appear vividly even when they are flashed before the eyes so quickly there is no opportunity to scan the presented image (Gillam, 1980).

Illusions of the sort presented in Figure 5.15 are not new. Scientists have been searching for reasonable explanations for illusions for well over

100 years. How do geometrical illusions give rise to perceptions, to visual experiences that are at odds with the physical reality detected by the eyes? Frankly, we can't say. Several factors seem to be working together to create illusions. The effects of illusions depend largely on how we perceive clues to the size of objects in a three-dimensional world and on inferences we make about the world based on our experience with it (Coren & Girgus, 1978; Gillam, 1980; Gregory, 1977; Hoffman, 1983). Here's an example. A reasonable-sounding explanation of the Müller-Lyer illusion is that the "vanes" of the arrows are taken to represent corners, as in a room. To see what I mean, refer to Figure 5.16(A). When corners are near to us or far away, we are presented with perspective cues to their distance. Hence, we "see" the "arrows" of the illusion as edges and corners (Gregory, 1963). Sounds pretty good, doesn't it? Then, why in Figure 5.16(B) do we see the distance between points A and B as shorter than the distance between points B and C, when they are in fact equal? On the other hand, there are people who live in cultures that contain very few straight lines, much less corners. The Zulus of South Africa are such people (at least those that have not been "Westernized.") Among other things, Zulus live in circular huts with rounded roofs. Virtually everything in their experience is curved or rounded. Zulu people do experience the Müller-Lyer illusion, but to a much less significant degree (Gregory, 1977).

There are illusions of motion as well as the common geometrical illusions we have been discussing. Two of these are the phi phenomenon and the autokinetic effect. The basic concept is the same: perceptions that are at odds with physical reality.

The **phi phenomenon** can be illustrated with just two lights. If two equally bright lights of the same color flash on and off alternately, it is very

phi phenomenon the visual illusion of the apparent motion of stationary lights flashing on and off in sequence

Figure 5.16

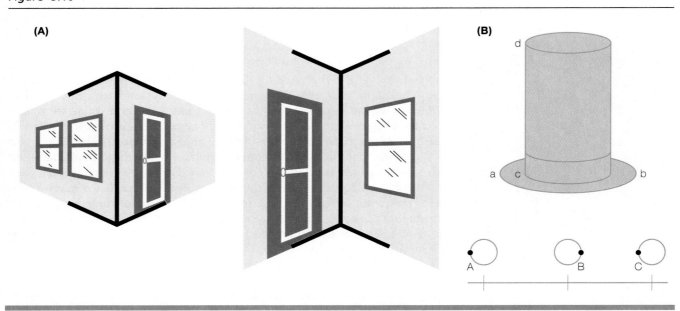

(A)

(B)

▲ *(A) One attempt to "explain" the Müller-Lyer illusion as the representation of edges and corners. (B) A variant of the Müller-Lyer illusion. The distance from A to B is equal to the distance from C to D. The explanation in terms of edges and corners no longer seems reasonable.*

autokinetic effect the visual illusion of apparent motion in which a stationary pinpoint of light in an otherwise dark environment appears to move

Figure 5.17

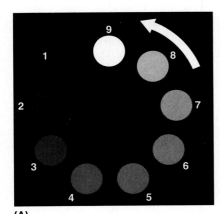

(A)

(B)

▲ (A) The rapid consecutive flashing of these stationary lights will appear to be a single light traveling in a circle due to the phi phenomenon. (B) Though these lights are stationary, the rapid consecutive lighting of them creates an illusion of motion.

easy to see them as one light moving back and forth. Look at Figure 5.17(A). Imagine that each small circle represents a stationary light bulb. One at a time, each light flashes on for a fraction of a second. The lights come on in order—Light 1, then 2, then 3, and so on. If the lights flash on and off fast enough, an observer will perceive a single light traveling in a circular path. This phenomenon accounts for the apparent movement of lights in theater marquees or in large signs (Fig. 5.17(B)). The arrow may look like it is moving through space, even though we know that it is securely fastened to the wall. Perhaps you recognize this as a subset of the Gestalt principle of closure: We fill in the gaps between the flashing stimuli and see them as moving. We'll encounter this phenomenon again in our discussion of sensory memory (pp. 231–232).

The **autokinetic effect** is the apparent movement of a pinpoint source of light in an otherwise darkened environment. You might want to demonstrate this illusion for yourself. To do so, you'll need a large room that you can darken completely. Get a good flashlight and cover the lens with black paper or tape so that no light escapes. Poke a very small hole in the paper or tape covering so that only a small pinpoint of light can be seen. Now secure the light at one end of the room, with the hole pointed out toward the center of the room. Turn off all the lights except for your flashlight. Within seconds a strange thing happens as you stare at that point of light: It starts to move and float around.

Psychologists do not have a complete explanation for this phenomenon. The most commonly accepted view is that the apparent movement is produced by very small head and body movements (*e.g.*, Pola & Matin, 1977; Post & Leibowitz, 1985). As you try to focus on the light, your eyes, head, and even your body move slowly—which causes the light to cast an image that moves across your retina. Because the image moves across your retina and you are not conscious of your body moving, you perceive the light as moving.

The autokinetic illusion can be a problem for pilots or ships' captains who must navigate at night with only a single distant beacon or light source as a guide. With no other frame of reference but that one light source, the light will appear to move, making it difficult to determine exactly where it is. For the same reason, military pilots in World War II had difficulty maintaining flight formations at night when the only way they could tell where they were in the formation was to make judgments based on small lights on the wingtips of adjacent aircraft. The solution to this problem was to replace the constant light with a flashing one. We also may experience the autokinetic effect when we try to stare at a single star (or planet) in the early evening sky. With no other context to provide a background, we may perceive the stationary star as moving.

The main instructional point about illusions, whether of geometry or of motion, is that they remind us that perception is a process at a higher level than simple sensation. Perception involves the organization and interpretation of the information we get from our senses, and that things are not always as they seem.

Before You Go On

▼▼▼▼▼▼▼▼

Name and discuss four types of perceptual constancy. What are two illusions of motion and how are they produced?

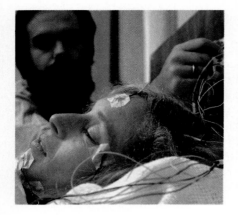

▲ *Subjects in sleep labs provide scientists with information about humans during sleep. By hooking the subjects to EEGs, scientists can study the activity of the brain during sleep.*

insomnia the chronic inability to get to sleep and to get an adequate amount of sleep

electroencephalograph (EEG) an instrument used to measure and record the electrical activity of the brain

electromyograph (EMG) an instrument used to measure and record muscle tension/relaxation

alpha activity an EEG pattern associated with quiet relaxation and characterized by slow wave cycles of 8 to 12 per second

▶ "Altered States" of Perception and Consciousness

So far in our discussion, we have assumed that we have been talking about individuals who are awake and alert—fully conscious. For the remainder of this chapter, we'll take a different perspective and examine consciousness when its nature has been altered. By definition, if we are in an altered state of consciousness, our perception of ourselves and our environment will be in some way changed. We will first discuss an altered state of consciousness that is quite normal: sleep. (Altered states of consciousness need not be weird or bizarre.) Then we'll examine two means of altering consciousness that require voluntary, deliberate action: hypnosis and the use of drugs.

▶ Sleep and Dreams

Sleep alters consciousness by reducing alertness, awareness, and perception of events occurring around us. Sleep is a normal process, yet it is one we do not understand well. We are seldom aware or conscious of our own sleeping, even though we may spend more than 200,000 hours of our lifetime asleep.

Just as the level or degree of our awareness varies during the day, so does our sleep vary in its level or quality from night to night and throughout the night.

Stages of Sleep. How do we know when someone is asleep? Self-reports of sleeping are notoriously unreliable. A person who claims that he or she "didn't sleep a wink last night," may have slept soundly for several hours. It may be that some people who claim they have **insomnia** (a chronic inability to get to sleep and to get an adequate amount of sleep) actually dream that they are awake and then remember their dreams (Dement, 1974).

Our best, most reliable indicators of sleep are physiological measurements, usually of brain activity and muscle tone. The **electroencephalograph** (EEG) is an instrument that measures and records the electrical activity of the brain. It does so through small electrodes that are pasted onto the scalp. The process is slightly messy, but it is in no way painful. The **electromyograph** (EMG) similarly produces a record of a muscle's activity, tone, or state of relaxation.

When you are in a calm, relaxed state, with your eyes closed, but not yet asleep, your EEG pattern shows a rhythmic cycle of brain waves called **alpha activity**. In this presleep stage, we find relatively smooth EEG waves cycling 8 to 12 times every second. If, as you sit or lie there, you start worrying about an event of the day, or start trying to solve a problem, the smooth alpha waves become disrupted and are replaced by an apparently random pattern of heightened electrical activity typical of what we usually find in wakefulness.

As you drift from relaxation into sleep, your brain waves change, as alpha waves give way to the stages of sleep. The EEG tracings of sleeping subjects reveal that sleep can be divided into four different stages (Bobély, 1986). As we describe these four stages, you can refer to Figure 5.18, which shows the EEGs of a subject in each of the stages of sleep. These tracings were chosen because they best illustrate each of the four stages. Actual EEG tracings are not always this clear.

Stage 1. This is a very light sleep from which you can be easily aroused. The smooth, cyclical alpha pattern disappears, replaced by the slower *theta waves* (3–7 cycles per second). The amplitude (or magnitude)

Figure 5.18

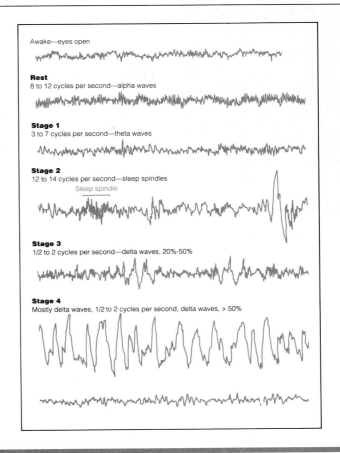

Awake—eyes open

Rest
8 to 12 cycles per second—alpha waves

Stage 1
3 to 7 cycles per second—theta waves

Stage 2
12 to 14 cycles per second—sleep spindles
Sleep spindle

Stage 3
1/2 to 2 cycles per second—delta waves, 20%-50%

Stage 4
Mostly delta waves, 1/2 to 2 cycles per second, delta waves, > 50%

▲ *The EEG records of sleeping subjects illustrate the brain wave activity associated with the different stages of sleep.*

of the electrical activity also lessens considerably. At the same time, your breathing is becoming more regular, and your heart rate is slowing and blood pressure is decreasing. This stage does not last very long—generally less than 10 minutes. Then, you start to slide into Stage 2 sleep.

Stage 2. In this stage, the basic EEG pattern is similar to Stage 1—low amplitude with no noticeable wavelike pattern. The difference is that we now see what are called *sleep spindles* in the EEG record. These are brief, high-amplitude bursts of electrical activity that occur with regularity (about every 15 seconds or so). You're really getting off to sleep now, but still can be easily awakened.

Stage 3. Now you're getting into deep sleep. There is a reduction in the brain's electrical activity. Now we can clearly make out *delta wave* activity in your EEG. Delta waves are high, slow waves (from 0.5 to 3 cycles every second). In Stage 3, delta waves constitute between 20 and 50 percent of your EEG pattern. Your internal functions (temperature, heart rate, breathing) are lowering and slowing. It is difficult to wake you now.

Stage 4. Now you're in deep sleep. Your EEG record is virtually filled with slow delta waves, recurring over and over again (as opposed to Stage 3, where delta waves comprise only a portion of your brain wave activity). At this point, readings from an electromyogram indicate that your muscles

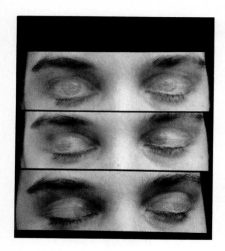

▲ The rapid eye movements of REM sleep are captured in this double exposure photograph.

REM sleep rapid eye movement sleep during which vivid dreaming occurs, as do heightened levels of physiological functioning

have become totally relaxed. About 15 percent of your night's sleep will be spent in this stage of deep sleep.

It usually takes about an hour to go from Stage 1 to Stage 4. How long it actually takes will, of course, depend somewhat on how tired you are and the physical conditions that surround you. We'll assume a nice, quiet, dark room, with a comfortable and familiar bed. After an hour's passage through these four stages, the sequence reverses itself. You go back through Stage 3, then to Stage 2, but before going through the cycle again, something truly remarkable happens. Your eyes start to move rapidly under closed eyelids.

Before You Go On
▼▼▼▼▼▼▼▼▼

What are the EEG and the EMG?

Briefly describe the four stages of sleep.

▶ REM and NREM Sleep

In the early 1950s, Nathaniel Kleitman and Eugene Aserinsky made quite a discovery—that as sleeping subjects began their second cycle into deeper levels of sleep, their eyes darted back and forth under their closed eyelids (Aserinsky and Kleitman, 1953). This period of *r*apid *e*ye *m*ovement is called **REM sleep.** When sleeping subjects are awakened during REM sleep, they usually (about 85% of the time) report that they are having a vivid, storylike dream. When awakened during sleep periods that are not accompanied by rapid eye movements (NREM sleep), reports of dreams are significantly fewer and much more fragmented (Kleitman, 1963). At first it was believed that eye movements during REM sleep were being made as the dreamer literally viewed, or scanned, images produced by the dream. It turns out that a dreamer's eye movements are unrelated to the content of his or her dream. Eye movements are produced instead by a cluster of cells in the brain stem (Hobson, 1977; Kiester, 1980).

REM sleep patterns occur throughout the night, normally lasting from a few minutes to half an hour. About 90 to 120 minutes each night is spent "REMing." During these REM periods, we are probably dreaming. As one goes through a night's sleep, REM periods tend to become longer and dreams more vivid. Dream time seems well correlated with real time. That is, if subjects are awakened after five minutes of REM sleep, they report that they had been dreaming for about five minutes. If they are left to REM for 20 minutes, they report that they have had a longer dream (Dement & Kleitman, 1957).

Everyone REMs. Everyone dreams. Some of us may have difficulty remembering what we have dreamed when we awake in the morning, but we can be sure that in the course of a normal night's sleep, we have dreamed several times. (There's no great mystery why we don't remember our dreams any better than we do. Most of our dreams are quite ordinary, boring and forgettable. Unless we make some conscious effort to do so, we seldom try to store dream content in our memories so that they can be recalled later.)

The normal pattern of REM occurrences is presented in Figure 5.19, from research by William Dement (1974). Notice in this figure that during the course of a night's sleep, one *does not necessarily pass through all of the stages of sleep in an orderly fashion.* That is, in some cycles, stage 3 may be passed over completely; in another cycle, stage 4 may be absent. Indeed,

Figure 5.19

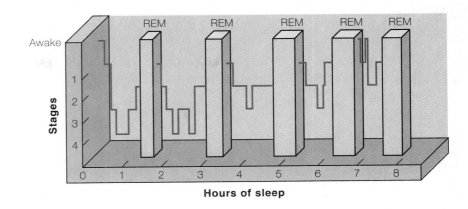

▲ *The typical sequence of sleep stages during a typical night of a young adult. Notice the recurring REM sleep throughout the night.*

toward the end of our sleeping, we tend not to return to the deep sleep of stage 4 between REM cycles. If you refer back to Figure 5.18, you will find an EEG tracing typical of the sort found during REM sleep. Note that it looks very much like the tracing indicating wakefulness.

Although we're sure that everyone does dream, we're not sure *why* everyone dreams. Some theories have their basis in the writings of Sigmund Freud (1900), who believed that dreaming allows us the opportunity to engage in fantasy and wish fulfillment of a sort that would probably cause us discomfort or embarrassment if we entertained such thoughts while we were awake. Freud saw dreams as a pathway (a *royal road*, as he called it) to the discovery of the content of our unconscious mind—content that otherwise might be kept from conscious awareness.

More modern theories of the function of REM sleep and dreaming tend to emphasize the physiological activity that occurs during this phase of sleep. One hypothesis argues that REM sleep helps the brain consolidate memories of events that occurred during the day. In one study, for example, subjects were less able to recall stories they read before they went to bed if

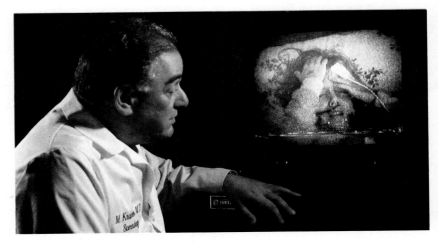

▲ *Dreams can be disruptive. Here, a five-year-old child suffering from nightmares followed by severe headaches is videotaped and studied by a psychiatrist.*

their REM sleep was interrupted during the night (Tilley & Empson, 1978). Another intriguing notion is that dreams (and our recall of them) represent convenient cognitive "explanations" for what may be simple random activity in our brains. That is, if the area of the brain associated with the movement of our legs becomes active while we are asleep, our brain will "manufacture" a reasonable story (a dream) that involves our running, or kicking, or in some way using our leg muscles (Hobson & McCarley, 1977).

Dreaming isn't the only thing that happens during REM sleep. From the outside, a sleeper in REM sleep seems quiet and calm, but on the inside there is quite a different story. One noticeable change is a muscular immobility—called **atonia**. The paralysis of atonia is not caused by a tensing of muscles, but because centers in the brainstem keep the muscles from acting (Chase & Morales, 1990). This state of immobilization is occasionally interrupted by slight muscle "twitches" (which you may have observed if you've watched a sleeping dog that appears to be chasing some imaginary rabbit in its dream). Some people do not demonstrate normal atonia and thrash about wildly during REM sleep—a disorder reasonably called *REM sleep disorder* (Mahowald & Schenck, 1989).

In many ways, the REM sleeper is very active, even though he or she may be oblivious to (or not conscious of) most external stimulation. During REM sleep there is usually an excitement of the sex organs, males having a penile erection, females having a discharge of vaginal fluids (although this latter finding is not as common). Breathing usually becomes shallow and rapid. Blood pressure levels may skyrocket, and heart rates increase, all while the subject lies "peacefully" asleep. Because all this physiological activity is going on, REM sleep is sometimes referred to as *paradoxical sleep*. There doesn't appear to be very much quiet and peaceful about it at all. These changes take place regardless of what the subject is dreaming about. It matters little whether one is dreaming about lying on the beach getting a tan, enjoying some sexual encounter, or engaging in hand-to-hand combat; physiologically, the reactions are the same.

atonia muscular immobility, associated with REM sleep, caused by the total relaxation of the muscles

▲ *Hypnosis is an altered state of consciousness that one enters voluntarily. It has been used for a variety of purposes, including treatment of some psychological and physical disorders.*

hypnosis an altered state of consciousness characterized by an increase in suggestibility, attention, and imagination

Before You Go On
▼▼▼▼▼▼▼▼▼▼

What are REM and NREM sleep?

What occurs during REM sleep?

▶ Hypnosis

Now that we have reviewed some of the evidence and theories of the altered state of consciousness called sleep, we can turn to those states that require some effort to attain. **Hypnosis** is characterized by (1) a marked increase in suggestibility, (2) a focusing of one's attention, (3) an exaggerated use of imagination, (4) an inability/unwillingness to act on one's own, and (5) an unquestioning acceptance of distortions of reality (Hilgard & Hilgard, 1975). There is little truth to the belief that being hypnotized is like going to sleep. In fact, few of the characteristics of sleep are to be found in the hypnotized subject. EEG patterns, for example, are significantly different.

Hypnosis has been used, with varying degrees of success, for a number of different purposes. As you know, it is used as entertainment, as a show business routine where members of an audience are hypnotized—usually to do silly things in public. Hypnosis has long been seen as a method of gaining

Psychology in the Real World

Why Can't I Get a Good Night's Sleep?

A good night's sleep is a wonderful and apparently necessary thing. Some people have no difficulty sleeping and seem to be able to sleep through anything. Others experience problems, either in getting to sleep in the first place or during sleep itself. Perhaps as many as 10 million Americans suffer from sleep disturbances that persist and disrupt their lives. As is the case for so many psychological processes, we often take sleep for granted until we experience some abnormality of sleep. Here, we'll briefly review three types of sleep disorder.

Insomnia. At some time or another, each of us has suffered from a bout of insomnia—an inability to fall asleep and/or stay asleep when one wants to. When we experience insomnia, we usually know why. We may be excited or worried about something that is going to happen the next day. We may have overstimulated our autonomic nervous system with drugs, such as the caffeine in coffee and tea. Actually, most people who chronically (regularly) suffer from insomnia haven't the slightest idea why they are unable to get a good night's sleep.

An interesting finding from the sleep laboratory is that many people who *believe* that they are not getting any sleep are, in fact, sleeping much more than they think. The phenomenon is called *pseudoinsomnia*, and the argument is that such people spend a number of dream episodes each night dreaming that they are awake and trying to get to sleep. Then, in the morning, they remember their dreams and come to believe that they haven't slept at all. Pseudoinsomnia can usually be cured simply by demonstrating to patients that they are getting a good night's sleep, as indicated by their EEG records.

Prescribing sleeping pills, or using over-the-counter medications to treat insomnia may cause more problems than it solves. The pills (sedatives or depressants) may have a positive effect for a while, but eventually, dosages have to be increased as tolerance builds. When the drugs are discontinued, a rebound effect makes it even more difficult to get to sleep than it was before. Generally, insomnia is not considered a disease in any sense, but is taken as a symptom—probably of anxiety and/or depression.

Narcolepsy. Narcolepsy involves going to sleep, even during the day, without the intention of doing so. Sleep occurs in "sleep attacks," lasting from 5 to 30 minutes. The strangest thing about these sleep attacks is that they tend to be attacks of REM sleep. The person quickly falls asleep and then almost immediately begins dreaming. Narcoleptics generally skip over the initial, gradual staging of sleep. They go very quickly into REMing. The biggest problem with narcolepsy (in addition to the embarrassment it may cause) is that narcoleptic sleep attacks are sometimes accompanied by the total relaxation of muscle tone that is also associated with REM sleep (Dement, 1974; Lucas, et al., 1979). The danger involved in suddenly going to sleep and losing muscle control during one's daily activities is obvious.

Sleep apnea. Apnea means a sudden stop in breathing. If we stop breathing when we are awake and conscious, we can do something about it. We can exercise conscious, voluntary control over our breathing. We cannot do so, however, when we are asleep. Sleep apnea involves patterns of sleep during which breathing stops entirely. Usually episodes are short and long-term dangers are few. When apnea episodes are longer—say a minute or two—carbon dioxide in the lungs builds to such a level that the sleeper is awakened, draws a few gasps of air, and returns to sleep, perhaps oblivious to what just happened.

For reasons not clearly understood, sleep apnea appears most commonly in obese, middle-aged males. Sleep apnea also is a prime suspect in the search for a cause of Sudden Infant Death Syndrome, or SIDS for short. In this syndrome, young infants, apparently without any major illness, but sometimes with a slight cold or infection, suddenly die in their sleep. Such sudden death occurs in about two infants per thousand.

access to memories of events not in immediate awareness. Hypnosis also has been used as a treatment for a wide range of psychological and physical disorders. In this section, we'll provide answers, as best we can at the moment, to some common questions about hypnosis.

1. ***Can everyone be hypnotized?*** No, probably not. Susceptibility to hypnosis varies rather widely from person to person. Contrary to popular belief, you cannot be hypnotized against your will, which is why we say that one enters a hypnotic state voluntarily, although I acknowledge that some hypnotists do claim that they can hypnotize anyone under the right conditions—which is why I hedged and said "probably" not.

2. ***What best predicts who can be easily hypnotized?*** Although not everyone can be easily hypnotized, some people are excellent subjects, can readily be put into deep hypnotic states, and easily learn to hypnotize themselves (Hilgard, 1975; 1978). A number of traits are correlated with hypnotizability. The most important factor seems to be the ability to engage easily in daydreaming and fantasy, to be able to "set ordinary reality aside for awhile" (Lynn & Rhue, 1986; Wilkes, 1986, p. 25). Other positively related traits include suggestibility and a certain degree of passivity or willingness to cooperate, at least during the session. Another intriguing notion is that persons who were punished often in childhood, or are avid readers, runners, or actors are good subjects. The logic is that these people have a history of self-induced trance-like states (to escape punishment, to focus, and become absorbed in the task at hand), which makes them more likely to be hypnotized (Hilgard, 1970).

3. ***Can I be made to do things under the influence of hypnosis that I would be embarrassed to do otherwise?*** Next to being unknowingly hypnotized, this seems to be the greatest fear associated with hypnosis. Again, the answer is *probably* no. Under the influence of a skilled hypnotist, you may do some pretty silly things and do them publicly. Under the right circumstances, you might do those very same things without being hypnotized. It is unlikely that you would do under hypnosis anything that you would not do otherwise. It is also true that under certain (unusual) circumstances, people can do outrageous—and dangerous—things, which is why hypnosis should be used with caution.

4. ***Are hypnotized subjects simply more open to suggestions, or is their consciousness really changed?*** This question does not get a clear yes or no answer either. The issue is in dispute. Some believe that hypnosis is really no more than a heightened level of suggestibility (Barber, 1972; Spanos & Barber, 1974). Others believe it to be a special state, separate from the compliance of a willing subject. When hypnotized subjects are left alone, they maintain the condition induced by their hypnosis. Those not hypnotized, but simply complying as best they can with an experimenter, revert quickly to normal behaviors when left alone (Hilgard, 1975; Orne, 1969).

5. ***Can hypnosis be used to alleviate pain—real, physical pain?*** Yes. It won't (can't) cure the underlying cause, but it can be used to control the feeling of pain. If a subject is a good candidate for hypnosis in the first place, there is a good chance that at least a portion of perceived pain can be blocked from conscious awareness (Hilgard & Hilgard, 1975; Long, 1986).

6. ***Is a person in a hypnotic state in any sense aware of what she or he is doing?*** Yes, but in a strange way. It seems that within the hypnotized subject is what Hilgard calls a "hidden observer" who may be quite aware of what is going on. In one study (Hilgard & Hilgard, 1975), a subject was hypnotized and told that he would feel no pain as his hand was held in a

container of ice water (usually very painful). When asked, the subject reported feeling very little pain, just as expected. The hypnotic suggestion was working. The Hilgards then asked the subject if "some part of him" was feeling any pain and to indicate the presence of such pain by using his free hand to press a lever (or even to write out a description of what he was feeling). Even though the subject continued to *report verbally* no feeling of pain, the free hand (on the behalf of the "hidden observer") indicated that it "knew" there was considerable pain in the immersed hand.

7. *Can I remember things under hypnosis that I couldn't remember otherwise?* Probably not, although there is no more hotly contested issue with regard to hypnosis than this. In the everyday sense of "Can you hypnotize me to remember my psychology material better for the test next Friday?" the answer is "Almost certainly not." (Sorry.) I might be able to convince you under hypnosis that you had better remember your psychology and lead you to *want* to remember your psychology, but there is no evidence that hypnotic suggestion can *directly* improve your ability to learn and remember new material. In the more restrictive sense of "I don't recall all the details of the accident and the trauma that followed. Can hypnosis help me recall those events more clearly?" the answer is less definite. When we get to our discussion of memory (Chapter 7), we'll see that distortions of memory in recollection easily can occur in normal states. In hypnotic states, the subject is suggestible and susceptible to distortions in recall furnished by the hypnotist (even assuming that the hypnotist has no reason to cause distortions). To the extent that hypnosis can reduce feelings of anxiety and tension, it may help in the recollection of anxiety-producing memories. The evidence is neither clear nor convincing on this issue in either direction. What of the related question, "Can hypnosis make me go back in time (regress) and remember what it was like when I was only 3 or 4 years old?" Here, I'm afraid, we *do* have a clear-cut answer, and the answer is: No. So-called "age-regression" hypnotic sessions have simply not proven to be valid (*e.g.*, Nash, 1987).

Hypnosis does alter one's consciousness, does open one to suggestions of the hypnotist, can be used to treat symptoms (not their underlying causes), and can distort one's view of reality. However, we are learning that it is neither mystical nor magical; there are limits to what hypnosis can do.

Before You Go On
▼▼▼▼▼▼▼▼▼

What is hypnosis?

What changes in consciousness does it produce?

Who can be hypnotized?

▶ *Altering Consciousness with Drugs*

In this final section, we'll discuss some of the chemicals that alter consciousness by inducing changes in our perception, mood, and/or behavior. Because they can alter basic psychological processes, these chemicals are referred to as **psychoactive drugs**.

Drugs have been used for centuries for the purpose of altering states of consciousness. No reasonable person would take a drug because he or she expected to have a bad, negative, unpleasant experience. Psychoactive drugs are taken—at least initially—to achieve a state of consciousness that the

psychoactive drug a chemical that affects psychological processes and consciousness

user considers to be good, positive, pleasant, even euphoric. As we all know, however, the use of drugs often has seriously negative outcomes. In this regard, there are a few terms that will be relevant for our discussion. Although there is not complete agreement on how these terms are used, for our purposes, we'll use the following definitions.

1. **Dependence.** (a) When continued use of a drug is required to maintain bodily functioning (physical dependence), or (b) when continued use of a drug is believed to be necessary to maintain psychological functioning at some level (psychological dependence). *"After a hard's day work, I just need a couple of martinis to relax."*

2. **Tolerance.** A condition in which the use of a drug leads to a state where more and more of it is needed to produce the same effect. *"I used to get high with just one of these; now I need three."*

3. **Withdrawal.** A (usually extreme) negative reaction, either physical or psychological, that results when one stops taking a drug.

4. **Addiction.** An extreme dependency, physical or psychological, in which signs of tolerance and painful withdrawal are usually found. *"No way I'm gonna give it up no matter what. It feels too good, and it hurts too much without it."*

One other distinction we should make is that between drug use and **drug abuse.** The dividing line here is not sharp and clear, of course, but we feel that we are dealing with abuse when we find (1) a lack of control as evidenced by frequent intoxication, and continued use, even given the knowledge that one's condition will deteriorate, (2) a disruption of interpersonal relationships and/or difficulties at work that can be traced to drug usage, and (3) signs that maladaptive drug use has continued for at least one month (American Psychiatric Association, 1987). Hidden in this distinction is the observation that drug use may not have negative consequences; drug abuse will.

There are many psychoactive drugs. We'll focus on four different types: stimulants, depressants, hallucinogens, and (separately) marijuana. Not only will we describe the effects of using these drugs, but we will also address briefly the consequences of their abuse.

Stimulants. Chemical **stimulants** do just that—they stimulate or activate the nervous system. They produce a heightened sense of arousal, creating an increase in general activity and an elevation of mood.

Caffeine is one of the most widely used of all stimulants. It is found in a number of foods and drinks (chocolate, coffee, and tea) as well as many varieties of painkillers. It is also an ingredient in many soft drinks. In moderate amounts, it seems to have no dangerous or life-threatening effects. At some point, a mild dependence may develop. Although it is not yet known precisely how caffeine does so, it temporarily increases metabolism (the process of converting food into energy), resulting in a burst of energy. It also seems to block the effects of some inhibitory neurotransmitters in the brain (Julien, 1985).

After excessive or lengthy use, giving up sources of caffeine can result in the pain of withdrawal. If you drink a lot of coffee and cola drinks during the week, but take a break from them on the weekend, you may experience the headaches of caffeine withdrawal. There is usually a rebound sort of effect when caffeine intake is stopped. For example, you may drink many cups of coffee to help stay awake to withstand an all-night study session, but within a few hours after you stop ingesting the caffeine, you may rebound and experience a streak of mental and physical fatigue—right at exam time!

drug abuse a condition defined by lack of control, disruption of interpersonal relationships or difficulties at work, and a history of maladaptive drug use for at least one month

stimulants drugs (such as caffeine, cocaine, and amphetamines) that increase nervous system activity

Nicotine is another very popular stimulant, usually taken by smoking and absorption by the lungs. Nicotine is carried from the lungs to the brain very quickly—in a matter of seconds. There is no doubt that nicotine is a stimulant of central nervous system activity, but it also relaxes muscle tone slightly, which perhaps explains in part the rationalization of smokers who claim that they can relax by having a cup of coffee and a cigarette. Nicotine seems to have its stimulant effect by activating excitatory synapses in both the central and peripheral nervous systems (McKim, 1986).

Many individuals develop a tolerance to nicotine, requiring more and more of it to reach the desired state of stimulation. Indeed, beginning smokers generally cannot smoke more than one or two cigarettes without becoming ill. The drug often leads to dependency. In 1989, then Surgeon General C. Everett Koop declared cigarette smoking an addiction, claiming it the single most preventable cause of death in our society, accounting for more than one-sixth of all the deaths reported in 1985 (DeAngelis, 1989). How addictive nicotine (or perhaps any other drug) becomes may depend primarily on how quickly it enters the brain. That is, people who take many quick deep puffs when smoking may become addicted more easily to nicotine than will people who take slow, shallow puffs (Bennett, 1980).

Cocaine is a naturally-occurring stimulant derived from leaves of the coca shrub (native to the Andes mountains in South America). The allure of cocaine and its derivative "crack" is the rush of pleasure and energy that it produces when it first enters the bloodstream, either through the mucous membranes when inhaled as smoke ("freebasing"), through the nose as a powder ("snorting"), or directly through injection as a liquid. A cocaine "high" doesn't last very long—15 to 20 minutes is typical.

There are many physiological reactions that result from cocaine use. It elevates blood pressure and heart rate. Cocaine blocks the reuptake of two important neurotransmitters. That means that once these neurotransmitters have entered a synapse, cocaine will prohibit their being taken back into the neuron from which they have been released. The end result is that, for some period of time at least, excessive amounts of these neurotransmitters are available in the nervous system. The two neurotransmitters in question are *norepinephrine,* which acts in both the central and peripheral nervous system to provide arousal and the sense of extra energy, and *dopamine,* which acts in the brain to produce feelings of pleasure and euphoria.

It seems that some of the physiological effects of cocaine use are very long-lasting, if not permanent, even though the psychological effects last but a few minutes. Not only is the rush of the psychological reactions to cocaine or "crack" short-lived, but these reactions are followed by a period of letdown approaching depression. As the user knows, one way to combat letdown and depression is to take more of the drug. This vicious cycle leads to dependency and addiction. Cocaine is such a powerfully addictive drug that many individuals can become both psychologically and physically dependent upon its use after just one or two episodes. Cocaine addiction tends to run in families to such an extent that current research is exploring the hypothesis that there is a genetic basis for cocaine addiction.

Amphetamines are synthetically manufactured chemical stimulants that usually come in the form of capsules or pills under many street names, such as "bennies," "uppers," "wake-ups," "cartwheels," "dexies," or "jellie babies." In addition to blocking reuptake, amphetamines actually cause the release of excess dopamine and norepinephrine. However, their action is considerably slower and somewhat less widespread than is that of cocaine. Once the amphetamine takes effect, users feel alert, awake, aroused, filled with energy, and ready to go. Unfortunately, such results are short-lived and illusory. The drug does not create alertness so much as it masks fatigue,

▲ *"Crack" cocaine is often ingested in smoke.*

which ultimately will overcome the user when the drug wears off. It now seems clear that these are not the only effects of amphetamine use; it has a direct effect on the cardiovascular system, causing irregular heartbeat and increased blood pressure, for example (McKim 1986). You've heard it before, but it's true: speed (yet another name for amphetamines) does kill.

Before You Go On
▼▼▼▼▼▼▼▼▼▼

What are stimulant drugs, and what are their effects?

depressants drugs (such as alcohol, opiates, heroin, and barbiturates) that slow or reduce nervous system activity

Depressants. In terms of their effect on consciousness, **depressants** are the opposite of stimulants. They reduce one's awareness of external stimuli, slow bodily functioning, and decrease levels of behavior. The reaction that one gets to depressants depends largely on how much is taken. In small doses, they can produce relaxation, a sense of freedom from anxiety, and a loss of stifling inhibitions. In greater amounts, they can produce sedation, sleep, coma, or death.

Alcohol is doubtless the most commonly used of all depressants and has been in use for thousands of years. In many ways, alcohol is the most dangerous of all drugs, largely because of its popularity and widespread use. More than two-thirds of Americans drink alcohol on a regular basis, and more than $36 *billion* per year is spent on distilled spirits alone (Mayer, 1983). More than that, it is estimated that between 10 and 15 percent of the adult population of North America are alcohol *abusers* (Mayer, 1983; The National Council on Alcoholism, 1978). Nearly $600 million in federal funds are spent each year in attempts to study, prevent, and/or treat alcohol abuse (Nathan, 1983). Over $30 *billion* of lost productivity in the United States alone is attributed to alcohol-related problems (Quayle, 1983). Alcohol is certainly the most deadly of drugs. In the summer of 1990, the Centers for Disease Control released a study indicating that well over 100,000 deaths a year in the United States could be attributed directly to alcohol consumption. The potentially devastating effects of alcohol consumption by pregnant women is also well documented (see Chapter 3, p. 84).

Perhaps the first thing to remember about alcohol is that it *is* a depressant. Some individuals may feel that they are being stimulated when they begin to drink alcohol, but their nervous system is actually being depressed, or slowed. Alcohol increases urination, leading to an overall loss of fluids. It affects vision by making it more difficult to detect dim lights. There is no

▲ *The behavioral impact of many drugs often depends on dosage. With too much alcohol, one may lose consciousness altogether.*

doubt that alcohol affects mood, leading to feelings of friendly elation as levels rise and of anger, depression, and fatigue as alcohol levels drop.

The specific effects of alcohol on the drinker usually reflect a number of interacting factors. What matters most is the amount of alcohol that gets into a person's bloodstream. The amount of alcohol is absorbed (blood alcohol level) at any one time is affected by how much one drinks and by how fast the alcohol can get into the bloodstream, which in turn is affected by what else happens to be in the stomach at the time. Drinking on an empty stomach may be more dangerous than drinking while or after eating, because the alcohol will be more quickly absorbed. In most states, 1/10 percent alcohol in the bloodstream is enough to define someone as legally intoxicated. At this level, brain activity is so affected that decision making is distorted and motor coordination is impaired (both are the sorts of skills usually required to drive safely).

Opiates, such as morphine and codeine, are also called "analgesics" because they can be used to reduce or eliminate sensations of pain. It was for this purpose that they were first commonly used. In small doses, they create feelings of well-being and ease, relaxation, and a trancelike state. Unlike alcohol, they seem to have little effect on motor behavior. The catch (once again) is that they produce very strong dependence and addiction. Their removal results in extreme pain and depression.

Heroin is an opiate, originally (in the 1890s) derived from morphine, but thought not to be as addictive—a notion soon proven wrong. Dependency and addiction grow rapidly. As with other drugs, the addictive nature of heroin may be related to its very rapid entry into the brain. (Methadone, used in some treatment programs for long-term heroin users, is a drug with many of the chemical properties of heroin and many of the same psychological effects. A difference is that methadone is slow to reach the brain and tends not to produce heroin's predictable "rush," which makes it less addictive.)

The effects of heroin (above whatever pain-killing use it may have) seem to be most related to the users emotional state and mood. Unlike alcohol or the opiates, it seldom produces hallucinations or thought disturbances. But as increased amounts of heroin become needed to produce the desired euphoria, tolerance builds—and increased dosages of heroin can cause breathing to stop, often for long enough periods that death results.

Barbiturates are synthetically produced sedatives. There are many types and varieties. All slow nervous system activity in small amounts producing a sense of calm and tranquility and higher doses producing sleep or coma. Some barbiturates are addictive, producing strong withdrawal symptoms when their use is discontinued. All will produce dependency if used with any regularity. As is generally the case, once an addiction develops, conquering it is very difficult

Before You Go On
▼▼▼▼▼▼▼▼▼

What are depressant drugs, and what are their effects?

hallucinogens drugs (such as LSD) whose major effect is the alteration of perceptual experience and mood

Hallucinogens. Of the psychoactive drugs, **hallucinogens** have the most unpredictable effects on consciousness. One of the main reactions to these drugs is the formation of hallucinations, usually visual. That is, users often report seeing things when there is nothing there to see, or they see things in ways that others do not. Hallucinations of hearing, smell, touch, and taste are possible but much less common.

LSD (lysergic acid diethylamide) is a potent and popular hallucinogen. Psychologically, LSD raises levels of emotionality and can change perception profoundly, usually producing vivid visual hallucinations. One of the first steps in the discovery of how LSD works was finding that levels of a certain neurotransmitter called serotonin increased when LSD was given to animals (Jacobs and Trulson, 1979; Jacobs, 1987). In itself, this was not surprising, because LSD (and similar hallucinogens, such as mescaline) has a chemical composition similiar to that of serotonin. LSD acts on serotonin receptor sites, acting as if it were a neurotransmitter. And very small doses (measured in only millionths of a gram) can produce major behavioral effects.

The changes in mood that take place under LSD are commonly extreme exaggerations of the users present mood. Note that this is yet another example of how perceptions—even distorted perceptions that result from drug use—can reflect one's experience, motivation, and mental set. From the start, this has been viewed as one of the dangers of LSD. Some people are drawn to drugs like LSD because things are not going well for them. Perhaps they are depressed and becoming hopeless. They think that LSD might help cheer them up. In fact, it may worsen their mood, resulting in a "bad trip," by exaggerating the feelings they had when they took the drug.

Before You Go On

▼▼▼▼▼▼▼▼

What are hallucinogenic drugs, and what are their effects?

▶ Marijuana—A Rather Special Case

Marijuana is a consciousness-altering drug that we'll consider as a special case, because it doesn't fit neatly into any of the three categories we've used so far. In some ways, marijuana acts as a depressant. In small dosages, its effects are similar to those of alcohol: decreased nervous system activity and depression of thought and action. In higher doses, marijuana acts as if it were a hallucinogen, producing hallucinations and alterations in mood.

Marijuana is produced from the hemp plant (Cannabis sativa), which was the source of most of the rope manufactured for sailing ships in the 18th century. It was an important crop in the American colonies, grown by George Washington, among other notables. As a source of raw materials for twine and rope, the plants were farmed in great numbers throughout the midwest during World War II. A hardy plant, many of the remnants of those cannabis farms of the early 1940s can still be found in Illinois and Indiana where every summer, adventurers come in search of yet another profitable—albeit illegal—harvest.

The active ingredient in marijuana is the chemical compound THC (tetrahydrocannabinol). Although marijuana, in large doses, has been found to increase overall levels of some neurotransmitters, it is not known just how it produces this effect. There do not seem to be any specific receptor sites at synapses for THC; at least, none have been found yet.

The most debatable aspect of marijuana use involves the results of moderate to heavy long-term use. People are tired of hearing this response (users in particular), but the evidence just isn't in yet. The data are more suggestive than definitive. Marijuana seems to cause bronchitis and other lung ailments (usually associated with smoking, but with marijuana, even more so). It may have genetic implications (it may produce chromosomal abnormalities—in nonhumans, at least). It may adversely affect the body's immune system and white blood cells. Its use can impair memory function, affecting memories of recent events in particular. Its use has predictably negative effects when taken during pregnancy, resulting in smaller babies, increased numbers of miscarriages, and other problems (Grinspoon, 1977; Julien, 1985).

Before You Go On
▼▼▼▼▼▼▼▼▼

What is the active ingredient in marijuana, and what effects does it produce?

▼▼▼
Thinking Critically about Perception and Consciousness

1. How many different stimuli can you attend to at the same time? How many different stimuli can you attend to within a 10-second interval? What factors influence your answers to these questions?

2. If what we choose to perceive (attend to) and how we organize what we perceive are influenced by so many factors over and above the stimuli themselves (factors such as motivation, mental set, and past experience, for example), why do we place so much weight on the value of eyewitness testimony in our court system?

3. To what extent (and how) does one's native language influence the way in which he or she perceives the world? To what extent, and in what ways, is one's perception of the world a reflection of one's culture?

4. When you look at a piece of motion picture film, you see nothing moving there. The film is just a series of still photos. Why then does the projection of that film lead us to believe that we are seeing actual motion?

5. People see a film of two cars making contact. They are asked to judge the speed of the two cars involved. The judgment of the cars' speed depends in large measure on how the question is phrased. Some are asked, "How fast were the cars going when they contacted each other?" Others are asked "How fast were the cars going when they collided?" Others are asked the same question with "collided" replaced by terms such as "bumped together" or "smashed into each other." Everybody sees the same film, but their judgments reflect the way in which the question is asked. Why?

6. In Chapter 1 I made the point that "Things are not always as they seem." Well, if things are not always as they seem, *whom* or *what* are we to believe?

7. Can we determine why people dream what they dream? If so how?

8. Different organisms have different sleep-wake cycles. (That is, within one day's time, people tend to sleep for about 8 hours and be awake for about 16 hours. Such is not the case for other animals. Rabbits and sheep, for example, sleep only for a few hours, while lions sleep much longer than humans do.) What could account for the differences in sleep-wake cycles among different species?

9. Once people realize that drugs are no good for them, or could even kill them, why don't they just stop using them?

Summary

▼▼▼▼▼▼▼▼▼▼▼▼▼▼▼▼▼▼▼▼▼▼▼▼▼▼▼▼

Define "perception" and "consciousness." In processesing information, perception is the cognitive process that intervenes between sensation and memory. It is the active process of selecting, organizing, and interpreting stimuli. Consciousness is somewhat more difficult to define. We say that consciousness is the awareness of the environment (which makes it very related to perception) and the awareness of our own mental processes. *Page 160*

What, according to William James, are the four major features of consciousness? According to William James, consciousness can be characterized as changing, personal, continuous, and selective. *Page 161*

What stimulus factors determine the selection of perceptions? Of all the information that stimulates our receptors, only a small portion is attended to or selected for further processing. One set of factors that affects which stimuli will be attended to concerns the characteristics of the available stimuli themselves. We are more likely to attend to a stimulus if it *contrasts* with others around it (where contrast may be in terms of size, intensity, motion, or any other physical characteristic). Up to a point, the simple *repetition* of a stimulus also increases the likelihood that it will be attended to. *Page 162*

What personal factors are involved in perceptual selectivity? The selection of stimuli is partly based on characteristics of the perceiver, such as motivation, expectation (mental set), and past experience. *Pages 163–164*

List stimulus and personal factors that determine how we organize stimuli in perception. The perceptual organization of stimuli depends in part on the characteristics of the available stimuli, such as proximity, similarity, continuity, common fate, and closure. The personal factors that affect perceptual organization are the same as those that affect selection: motivation, mental set, and past experience. *Page 169*

Name and describe some of the cues that provide us with information about depth and/or distance. We are able to perceive three-dimensionality and distance even though we sense the environment with a two-dimensional retina because of the many cues with which we are provided. Some have to do with the visual system itself and are called ocular cues, such as retinal disparity (each eye gets a different view of a three-dimensional object), convergence (when we look at something up close our eyes turn inward), and accommodation (our lenses change shape to focus images at different distances). Other cues come from the environment, including the physical cues of linear perspective (parallel lines seem to come together in the

distance), interposition (near objects partially block our view of more distant ones), relative size (everything else being equal, the smaller a stimulus, the farther away we judge it to be), texture gradients (details of texture can be seen clearly up close and gradually less clearly in the distance), patterns of light and shade, and motion parallax (as we move by stationary objects, those close to us seem to move past us more rapidly than those objects in the distance. *Pages 169–170*

Name and discuss four types of perceptual constancy. Perceptual constancies bring stability and order to our perceptual world. With size constancy, we perceive familiar objects as remaining the same size even when the size of their retinal images changes. Similarly, shape constancy refers to the stability of our perception of an object's shape regardless of the shape of its retinal image. With brightness and color constancy, we are able to perceive an object's true color or brightness regardless of the intensity or wavelength of the light that is actually reflected from it. *Page 172*

What are two illusions of motion and how are they produced? The perception of motion when there is none is an example of an illusion. The phi phenomenon is such an illusion and can be demonstrated by flashing a series of lights on and off in sequence, giving the appearance of one light in motion. The autokinetic effect occurs when a stationary point of light is perceived as moving in an otherwise darkened environment. *Pages 174–175*

What are the EEG and the EMG? The EEG (electroencephalograph) is an instrument that measures the general pattern of electrical activity in the brain, and is the most common indicator of the stages of sleep. The EMG (electromyograph) measures muscle tone or tension and may be used as another indicator of sleep. *Page 176*

Briefly describe the four stages of sleep. In addition to a state of relaxed wakefulness, characterized by EEG alpha waves, we say there are four stages of sleep: (1) light sleep with low-amplitude, slow theta waves; (2) sleep showing low-amplitude EEG waves with sleep spindles present; (3) a level where delta waves enter the EEG pattern, and (4) deep sleep, with more than 50 percent delta wave activity. *Pages 176–177*

What are REM and NREM sleep? REM sleep is rapid eye movement sleep, and it occurs four to seven times per night. NREM means sleep without rapid eye movements. *Page 178*

What occurs during REM sleep? Several events occur during REM sleep, most noticeably vivid, storylike dreams. During REM sleep we find loss of muscle tone (atonia), excitement of sexual organs, rapid breathing, and increased heart rate and blood pressure. During NREM sleep one progresses through the four stages of sleep, accompanied by little dream activity. *Page 180*

What is hypnosis? Hypnosis is an altered state of consciousness into which one enters voluntarily; it is characterized by an increase in suggestibility, a strict focusing of attention, an exaggeration of imagination, a reduction of spontaneous activity, and an unquestioning acceptance of distortions of reality. *Page 180*

what changes in consciousness does it produce? By definition, those listed in the answer above to the previous question. *Page 180*

Who can be hypnotized? Not everyone can be hypnotized. Those who can be most readily hypnotized are persons who easily engage in fantasy and daydreaming and who show signs of suggestibility and a willingness to cooperate with the hypnotist. *Page 182*

What are stimulant drugs, and what are their effects? Stimulants are psychoactive drugs such as caffeine, nicotine, cocaine, and amphetamines. Their basic effect is to increase the level of nervous system activity and to elevate mood, almost always by affecting the activity of the neural synapse, (usually) increasing the levels of the neurotransmitters norepinephrine and dopamine. With heavy use, tolerance may develop, as may dependence and addiction. *Page 184*

What are depressant drugs, and what are their effects? The depressants include such drugs as alcohol, heroin, and a variety of synthetic barbiturates. All depressants slow nervous system activity, reduce the awareness of external stimuli, and in small doses may alleviate feelings of nervousness and anxiety. In large doses, however, they produce sedation, sleep, coma, or death. Tolerance, dependence and/or addiction may result from the use of these drugs. *Page 186*

What are the hallucinogenic drugs, and what are their effects? Hallucinogens are drugs that alter mood and perception. LSD is an example. They get their name from their ability to induce hallucinations. *Page 187*

What is the active ingredient in marijuana, and what effects does it produce? The active ingredient in marijuana is the chemical compound THC. Listing its short- and long-term effects is difficult because of contradictory evidence. It is at least as dangerous as smoking cigarettes and it is illegal. Of more concern is long-term, heavy use. Here marijuana use has many of the negative effects that we associate with long-term alcohol use: impaired judgment and reflexes, unrealistic mood, and poor coordination. Marijuana may have adverse effects on the body's immune system and has been implicated in a range of negative consequences when taken during pregnancy. *Page 188*

5.1 Which psychologist was MOST interested in matters relating to consciousness?   a) E. B. Titchener   b) William James   c) John B. Watson   d) Wilhelm Wundt. *Page 160*

5.2 James claimed that consciousness has four characteristics. Which of the following was NOT one of these? Consciousness is always   a) selective.   b) stable.   c) continuous.   d) personal. *Pages 160–161*

5.3 Of the following, it is most reasonable to classify perception as a _____ process.   a) motivational   b) learned   c) cognitive   d) sensory. *Page 161*

5.4 Of these factors that determine attention, which is most general in that it may include each of the others?   a) size   b) contrast   c) motion   d) intensity. *Page 162*

5.5 True or False?   Perception is such a fundamental process that it is independent of—or not influenced by—such "higher" processes as memory or motivation. *Page 161*

5.6 If you and I were standing next to each other at a party, and if someone behind us were to mention my name, I might turn around and attend to what was going on, while you might not even realize that my name had been mentioned. This would demonstrate the role of _____ in perceptual attention.   a) repetition   b) mental set   c) contrast   d) past experience. *Page 162*

5.7 When we say that someone is likely to perceive something that they expect to perceive, we are saying that: a) figures and grounds are often confused.   b) some stimuli are innately more attention-grabbing than others.   c) our motivational states often direct our attention.   d) we can form a mental set that influences our attention. *Page 163*

5.8 We tend to hear the individual speech sounds of a word as organized together and separate from the sounds of other words largely because of the Gestalt organizational principle of   a) proximity.   b) novelty.   c) continuity.   d) similarity. *Page 166*

5.9 The appearance of subjective contours can be seen as a special case of the Gestalt principle of: a) proximity.   b) similarity.   c) common fate.   d) closure. *Page 167*

5.10 True or False?   Common fate is a Gestalt organizational principle that is applicable for objects in motion. *Page 167*

5.11 What makes our perception of the world as being three dimensional remarkable is that   a) it is a skill or ability found only in humans.   b) it is a perception that has no particular survival value.   c) images of the world are inverted by the lens of the eye to appear upside-down.   d) the retina records visual experiences in only two dimensions. *Page 169*

5.12 Which of the following cues to depth or distance is referred to as binocular?   a) accommodation   b) motion parallax   c) linear perspective   d) retinal disparity. *Page 169*

5.13 Objects in the foreground close to us partially cover or hide more distant objects, which is the physical cue to distance called: a) perspective.   b) interposition.   c) texture gradient.   d) relative size. *Page 170*

5.14 True or False?   Motion parallax is an example of a common illusion of motion—seeing motion where there is none to be perceived. *Page 171*

5.15 The phiphenomenon is   a) a variety of extrasensory perception, or ESP.   b) one of the cues we have for judging depth and distance.   c) an illusion of motion when there isn't any.   d) one of the things that happens when figure and ground get confused. *Page 174*

5.16 Visual illusions   a) involve the perception of objects and/or events that are not really there in the physical world, but are imagined   b) no longer have their effect once you know that you are dealing with an illusion.   c) are not noticed if they are flashed before the eyes too quickly for the subject to scan the image.   d) provide examples of perceptual experiences that are at odds with, or different from, physical reality. *Page 175*

5.17 To enter an "altered state of consciousness"   a) is to change one's perception of one's self and the environment.   b) is to have strange, weird, or bizarre experiences.   c) is something that one cannot do voluntarily or on purpose.   d) requires that the individual remain awake and aware. *Page 176*

5.18 Delta waves are most common and most evident in an EEG record when a subject is: a) relaxed, but not quite asleep yet.   b) in the middle of a dream.   c) thinking about something, perhaps a problem.   d) in the deepest stage of sleep. *Page 177*

5.19 True or False?   The most reliable indicator of sleep is the self-report. *Page 176*

5.20 We know that, by definition, your eyes move when you are in REM sleep. What happens to your EEG record?   a) It shows that your muscles are tense and immobile.   b) It appears that you might be awake.   c) It is filled with cyclical alpha wave patterns.   d) It shows a preponderance of delta waves. *Page 179*

5.21 Which of the following is most likely to occur during REM sleep?   a) Your muscles will become totally relaxed.   b) You will be dreaming about some (sexual) fantasy.   c) You will wake up as soon as the REM period is over.   d) Your heart rate and blood pressure will decrease significantly. *Page 180*

5.22 With regard to hypnosis, which statement is most clearly TRUE?   a) There is no good way to predict who can be hypnotized.   b) Under hypnosis anybody can be made to do anything.   c) Hypnosis can ease the experience of real physical pain.   d) When under hypnosis, one has no idea what he or she is doing. *Page 182*

5.23 True or False?   Hypnosis can help us remember details of traumatic or anxiety-producing events. *Page 183*

5.24 All drugs that alter one's state of consciousness are known as   a) psychoactive.   b) hallucinogenic.   c) illicit (or illegal).   d) uppers or downers. *Page 183*

5.25 What one word best differentiates drug abuse from drug use?   a) legality   b) maladaptive   c) psychological   d) amount. *Page 184*

5.26 Worldwide, the most common chemical stimulant is   a) heroin.   b) nicotine.   c) alcohol.   d) caffeine. *Page 184*

5.27 True or False?   Stimulants, depressants, and hallucinogens influence cognition, but do not influence affects or behavior. *Page 183*

5.28 True or false?   Alcohol, taken in the proper dosage, is a stimulant to thinking. *Page 186*

Chapter 6
▼▼▼▼▼

Learning

▲▲▲▲▲▲▲
_____

There were approximately 25 students enrolled in the Psychology of Learning class that met every Monday, Wednesday, and Friday morning from 9:00 to 9:50. The instructor was a dynamic lecturer. The topic for the week was the process called operant conditioning. After describing the procedures and stressing the importance of operant conditioning in our everyday lives, the instructor suggested that the students try to use operant conditioning to change the behavior of someone they knew.

The choice was an easy one. Following the learning class, most of the students moved across the hall for a class in child psychology. It was a larger class, with as many as 75-80 students in attendance on a good day. The professor in the child psychology class had a very boring lecture style: He simply read his notes to the class. Every day he would go through the same ritual. He would find his place in his notes, check the time on his pocket watch, and then read to the class for 50 minutes. While what he was reading was no doubt high-quality psychology, the students thought that his classroom style left much to be desired.

The 25 or so students from the learning class decided to reward the professor for doing what they wanted him to by smiling, looking attentive, and appearing to take many notes. When the professor did what the students did not want him to do, they would look away, appear bored, and stop taking notes.

The project began on a Wednesday. When the students assembled after class that day, they realized they weren't very well organized. They hadn't specifically defined just *what* it was they were to reward. They only knew that they wanted the professor to stop reading to them. They thought the professor was looking up from his notes a bit more than usual, but because they did not have a good baseline for comparison, they couldn't be sure.

After their first "failure" on Wednesday, the students did get some results on Friday. By the end of the class, the professor *was* looking up more than usual, and he was moving about in his chair. Monday's class brought a real breakthrough: The professor rose from the chair! From time to time he would sit down again (only to be ignored), and he would not give up physical contact with his notes. He was still reading, but occasionally he would stand to do so.

On the first Wednesday: virtually nothing. The following Friday: some movement. The next Monday: standing. By the following Friday, about halfway through the class period, the professor was standing in the corner of the room; notes still on his desk, he was talking to the class about child psychology.

Think about that. In just five days these students had lifted a professor from his chair and placed him in the corner! The students had no doubt that within 10 minutes they could have moved their professor from one corner to the other. All this was done simply by rewarding some behaviors with attention and by ignoring other behaviors—and in fewer than five sessions. The class was impressed.

This is a true story. I was one of those 25 students, and I was very impressed indeed. The sight of our instructor leaning back in the corner of our classroom just talking about child psychology is still a vivid memory. The end of this story is not a happy one. When our professor got to the corner, we could control ourselves no longer. We started laughing, and our instructor demanded to know what was going on. When he was told, he did not take kindly to our little experiment and went back to reading his notes to us. If you try this exercise, please be careful in choosing the subject of your experiment and the behaviors you want to control.

Learning affects how we perceive the world, how we interact with it as we grow and develop, how we form social relationships, how we change during a course of psychotherapy. The human organism is poorly suited to survive in the world without learning. If we are to survive, not to say prosper, we must profit from our experiences.

In this chapter, we'll begin by defining learning. Then we'll concentrate on a simple form of learning: classical conditioning. Most of our descriptions of classical conditioning will be based on Ivan Pavlov's work with salivating dogs. Once we have the basic principles in hand, we'll consider why classical conditioning is so important to all of us and how the procedures of classical conditioning can be applied regularly in our daily lives. We'll also review how psychologists today view classical conditioning, discovering as we do so that some of Pavlov's original assumptions may not have been correct.

Following our discussion of classical conditioning, we will move on to operant conditioning—the type of learning described in our opening story. The basic premise of operant conditioning is that behaviors are influenced by the consequences they produce. Learning is a matter of increasing the rate of responses that produce positive consequences and decreasing the rate of responses that lead to negative consequences. In this section, we will discuss the nature of reinforcement.

We'll end the chapter by considering the role of the learner in the learning process. Both classical and operant conditioning focus on the nature of environmental stimuli and observable responses. What we call "cognitive approaches" to learning tend to emphasize the mental processes (cognitions) of the organism involved in the learning task. A good deal of your own learning as a student can be thought of in this way. You have altered your cognitions on the basis of your experiences. You have acquired many new cognitions, and some of these new or altered ideas may never be expressed in actual behavior.

▶ A Definition of Learning

learning demonstration of a relatively permanent change in behavior that occurs as the result of practice or experience

Let's begin with a definition. We say that **learning** is demonstrated by a relatively permanent change in behavior that occurs as the result of practice or experience. This is a rather standard definition, but it raises a few important points that we should explore.

When we say that learning is *demonstrated by* changes in behavior, we are saying that learning (like many other psychological processes) cannot be observed directly. In a literal sense, there is no way that I can directly observe or measure what you have learned. All I can measure is your performance or behavior. To determine if you have learned something, I must ask you to perform and then make inferences about your learning on the basis of your performance. Sometimes I may be wrong.

For example, you may learn all there is to know about the psychology of learning for your next exam. But just days before the exam, someone you care about becomes seriously ill. As a result, you don't get much sleep. With your resistance weakened, you develop a sinus infection and catch the flu. When you come to class to take your exam, you feel miserable, have a high fever, can't concentrate, and fail the exam. Your instructor now may infer (incorrectly in this case) that you haven't learned very much about learning. On the other hand, there may be someone else in class who hasn't studied at all and has learned very little. But the exam is of the multiple-choice type, and she correctly guesses the answers to 90 percent of the questions. Your instructor might infer (incorrectly again) that this student has learned a great deal.

▲ Changes in behavior that are due to learning can be traced to practice or experience. Tigers learn to sit and stand on stools. They learn behaviors that are at odds with what may come naturally for tigers.

One way to express the point we're making here is to say that what is learned is a *potential,* or predisposition, to respond. Because what is learned is simply potential, we will not recognize that learning has taken place until that potential is realized in behavior.

Learned changes in behavior are characterized as *relatively permanent.* This means that they are not fleeting, short-lived or cyclical changes, such as those due to fatigue or temporary shifts in motivation. On the other hand, learned changes in behavior need not be expected to last for a lifetime.

Imagine, for example, the change in typing behavior that occurs—even for a skilled typist—between 8:00 AM on a Monday morning and 10:00 AM that same morning. There is likely to be an improvement in typing behavior that we really ought not attribute to learning but to what is called *warm-up.* That skilled typist may not type quite so well toward the end of the day—a change in behavior we might better attribute to fatigue than to forgetting. These are important changes in behavior, but they are not due to learning. Learned changes are relatively permanent.

We have another phrase in our definition to remind us that there are other, often important, changes in behavior that do not result from learning. We say that learned changes in behavior result from *practice* or *experience.* For one thing, this phrase reminds us that some changes may be due to maturation (i.e., heredity). That birds fly, that salamanders swim, or that humans walk has more to do with genes and physical development than with learning. This phrase also serves to remind us that any changes in our behaviors due to automatic physiological reactions, such as sensory adaptation, are not learned. When we enter a darkened theater, we don't "learn" to see in the dark. Our vision improves and our behaviors change as our eyes adapt to the lighting in the theater—an unlearned reaction requiring neither practice nor previous experience.

One final point about the nature of learning is worth mentioning. We often fall into the habit of thinking that learning is necessarily a good thing. Clearly, it isn't always so. We can learn bad, ineffective habits as readily as we learn good, adaptive ones. For example, no one I know ever claimed to enjoy the first cigarette that he or she smoked, yet many people have learned the habit, which is hardly an adaptive one.

If we combine these ideas, we come up with our definition: Learning is demonstrated by (or inferred from) a relatively permanent change in behavior that occurs as the result of practice or experience. We begin our discussion of learning by considering two varieties of learning called *conditioning.* Although conditioning and learning are not technically synonymous terms, they can be used interchangeably. We will follow common usage here and agree to call the most basic, fundamental types of learning "conditioning."

Before You Go On
▼▼▼▼▼▼▼▼▼

How do we define learning?

▲ Ivan Pavlov (seated) watches a dog in one of his laboratory's testing chambers.

▶ Classical Conditioning

When we think about learning, we generally think about such activities as memorizing the Bill of Rights, studying for an exam, or learning to *do* things, like ice skate. But our study of learning begins in the laboratory of a Russian physiologist who taught dogs to drool in response to tones.

reflex an unlearned, automatic response that occurs in the presence of specific stimuli

classical conditioning learning in which an originally neutral stimulus comes to elicit a new response after having been paired with a stimulus that reflexively elicits that same response

unconditioned stimulus (UCS) in classical conditioning, a stimulus (for example, food powder) that reflexively and reliably evokes a response (the UCR)

unconditioned response (UCR) in classical conditioning, a response (for example, salivation) reliably and reflexively evoked by a stimulus (the UCS)

orienting reflex the simple, unlearned response of orienting toward, or attending to, a new or unusual stimulus

habituation in classical conditioning, a simple form of learning in which an organism comes to ignore a stimulus of no consequence

Psychology was just emerging as a science late in the nineteenth century. When Ivan Pavlov, a physiologist, studied the basic processes of digestion—work for which he was awarded the Nobel Prize in 1904. Focusing on the salivation reflex in dogs, Pavlov knew that he could produce salivation in his subjects by forcing food powder into their mouths. A **reflex** is an unlearned, automatic response that occurs in the presence of a specific stimulus. Every time Pavlov presented them with food, his dogs salivated.

Pavlov's reputation in psychology stems from the fact that he pursued something not so simple as reflexive responses. He noticed that occasionally, his dogs would salivate *before* the food was put in their mouths. They would salivate at the very sight of the food or even at the sight of the laboratory assistant who delivered the food. With this observation, Pavlov went off on a tangent that he pursued for the rest of his life (Pavlov, 1927; 1928). We now call the phenomenon he studied **classical conditioning**—a type of learning in which an originally neutral stimulus comes to elicit a response after having been associated with another stimulus. In the abstract, that may not make much sense. But as we go through the process step by step, I think you'll appreciate that the process is simple and straightforward.

To demonstrate classical conditioning, we first need a stimulus that consistently produces a predictable response. The relationship between this stimulus and the response it evokes is usually a natural, unlearned, reflexive one. Here is where Pavlov's food powder comes in. When the food powder is presented, the salivation reliably follows. Because there is no learning involved here, we call the stimulus an **unconditioned stimulus** (UCS) and the response that it elicits an **unconditioned response** (UCR). So now we have a UCS (food powder) producing a UCR (salivation).

To get classical conditioning under way, we need a *neutral stimulus* that elicits a minimal response or a response of no interest. For this neutral stimulus, Pavlov chose a tone produced by a simple tuning fork.

At first, when a tone is sounded a dog *will* respond. It will, among other things, perk up its ears and try to orient toward the source of the sound. We call this response an **orienting reflex**. After a while, however, the dog will get used to the tone and essentially will ignore it. Technically, we call this process **habituation** and say that the dog "habituates" to the tone. Habituation is itself a simple variety of learning—essentially, the dog learns *not* to orient toward the tone.

Now we are ready to go. We have two stimuli—a tone that produces a minimal response of no particular interest and food powder that reliably produces salivation.

Neutral Stimulus	⟶	"no response"
(a tone)		(no salivation)
UCS	⟶	UCR
(food powder)		(salivation)

Once we get our stimuli and responses straight, the rest is easy. The two stimuli are paired. That is, they are presented at about the same time—the tone first, then the food powder. The salivation occurs automatically in response to the food powder. So we have a neutral stimulus, then a UCS, which is followed by a UCR, or tone-food-salivation.

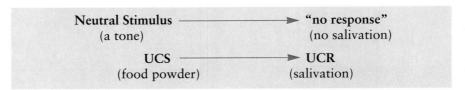

| Neutral Stimulus | + | UCS | ⟶ | UCR |
| (a tone) | | (food powder) | | (salivation) |

conditioned stimulus (CS) in classical conditioning, an originally neutral stimulus (for example, a tone) that, when paired with a UCS, comes to evoke a new response (a CR)

conditioned response (CR) in classical conditioning, the learned response (for example, salivation) evoked by the CS after conditioning

Each pairing of the stimuli may be considered a conditioning *trial*. If we repeat this procedure a number of times (a number of trials) conditioning, or learning, takes place. We find a relatively permanent change in behavior as a result of this experience. After a number of trials, when we present the tone by itself, the dog salivates, something it did not do before. The dog now salivates not just in response to the food powder, but also in response to the tone. Clearly, the tone is no longer "neutral." Because of conditioning, it produces a response, so we now call the tone a **conditioned stimulus (CS)**. To keep the salivation response that it elicits separate from the salivation we get in response to the food powder, we call it a **conditioned response (CR)**, indicating that it has been conditioned, or learned.

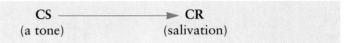

Let's review this again: (1) We start with two stimuli—the neutral stimulus, which elicits no response, and the UCS, which elicits the UCR. (2) We repeatedly present the two stimuli together. (3) We find that when we present the CS alone, it now elicits a CR.

One thing you must realize is that the same stimulus, say, a tone, can be either a neutral stimulus (before learning occurs), or a conditioned stimulus (when it elicits a learned response). Similarly, the same response, say, salivation, can be either an unconditioned response (if it is elicited without learning) or a conditioned response (if it is elicited as the result of learning).

If you have a pet at home, you've no doubt seen this process in action. If you keep your pet food in the same cabinet all the time, you may note a full range of excited, anticipatory behaviors by your pet every time you open that cabinet door. The open cabinet door (CS) has been repeatedly paired with the food within it (UCS), now producing the same sort of reaction (CR) that was originally reserved only for the food.

Soon we'll look at how classical conditioning influences human reactions, but before we go on, let's make it clear that classical conditioning is not something that only occurs in dogs and cats. You, too, demonstrate a classically conditioned salivation response (particularly when you're hungry) when you see pictures or smell the aromas of your favorite foods. If you respond with anxiety at the sight of your instructor entering the classroom with a stack of exam papers, you are demonstrating a classically conditioned response.

Before we examine some of the procedures associated with classical conditioning, there are two technical points to make. These two points serve to remind us that even fundamental psychological processes are not quite as simple as they first appear. First, the CR seldom reaches the strength of the UCR no matter how many times the CS and the UCS are paired. For example, in Pavlov's demonstration, we never get as much saliva in response to the tone (salivation as a CR) as we originally got in response to the food powder (salivation as a UCR). Second, *how* the conditioned stimulus and the unconditioned stimulus are paired *does* matter. There are many ways in which two stimuli can be presented at about the same time (*e.g.*, simultaneously, or UCS then CS, or CS then UCS, with varying time intervals in between). Only one method works best: the CS first, followed shortly (within a second) by the UCS, or *tone-food-salivation* again. I tell my classes that classical conditioning is basically a matter of "ding-food-slobber."

▶ Classical Conditioning Phenomena

Now that we've covered the basics of classical conditioning, we can consider some of the details that go along with it, for example, some of the procedures developed in Pavlov's laboratory. We'll first go through the steps involved in an actual classical conditioning procedure. Just to keep terminology firmly in mind, I'll continue to refer to the original Pavlovian example of salivating dogs.

The stage of classical conditioning during which the strength of the CR increases—where a dog acquires the response of salivating to a tone—is called **acquisition**. When conditioning begins, the conditioned stimulus (CS) does not produce a conditioned response (CR)—which is why we referred to it as a "neutral stimulus" at this point. After a few pairings of the CS and UCS together (conditioning trials), we can demonstrate the presence of a CR. To do that, of course, we'll have to present the conditioned stimulus (CS) by itself. Now we find that there is some saliva produced in response to the tone presented alone. The more trials of the CS and UCS together, the more the dog will salivate in response to the tone when it is presented alone. Over repeated trials, the increase in CR strength (here, the amount of saliva in response to the tone) is rather rapid at first, but soon starts to slow and eventually levels off. The first part of Figure 6.1 illustrates the acquisition phase of a classical conditioning demonstration.

Assume that we now have a dog producing a good deal of saliva at the sound of a tone. Continuing to present the CS + UCS pair adds little to the amount of saliva we get when we present the tone alone. Suppose that we now go through a series of trials during which the CS (the tone) is presented but is *not* paired with the UCS (no more food powder). The result of this procedure is that the CR will weaken. As we continue to present the tone alone, the dog provides less and less saliva. If we keep it up, the dog will eventually stop salivating to the tone. This process is called **extinction**, and we say that the CR has extinguished.

It would appear that we are right back where we started. Because the CR has extinguished, when we present the tone, our dog does nothing—at least it no longer salivates. Let's give our dog a rest and return it to the kennel for awhile. When the dog is returned to the laboratory and the tone is sounded, the dog salivates again! Not a lot, perhaps, but the salivation does return. Since it recovers automatically, or spontaneously, we call this phenomenon **spontaneous recovery**. Extinction and spontaneous recovery are also illustrated in Figure 6.1.

Spontaneous recovery takes place after extinction and following a rest interval. This fact which indicates two things: First, one series of extinction trials may not be sufficient to eliminate a conditioned response. Because of the possibility of spontaneous recovery, in order to get our dog to stop salivating altogether, we may have to run a series of extinction trials. Second, what is happening during extinction is not literally forgetting, at least not in the usual sense. It seems that the response is not forgotten so much as it is *suppressed*. That is, the learned salivation response is still there, but it is not showing up in performance during extinction; which is why it can (and does) return later, in spontaneous recovery.

acquisition the process in classical conditioning by which the strength of the CR increases with repeated pairings of the CS and UCS

extinction the process in classical conditioning by which the strength of the CR decreases with repeated presentations of the CS alone (without the UCS)

spontaneous recovery the phenomenon in classical conditioning in which a previously extinquished CR returns after a rest interval

Figure 6.1

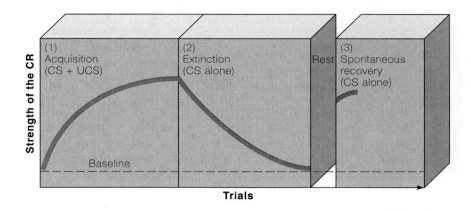

▲ The stages of conditioning. (1) Acquisition is produced by repeated pairings of the CS and the UCS. The strength of the CR increases rapidly at first and then more slowly. (2) Extinction is produced by presenting the CS without the UCS. The strength of the CR decreases. (3) After a rest interval, spontaneous recovery produces a partial return of the CR.

Before You Go On
▼▼▼▼▼▼▼▼▼▼

In classical conditioning, what are acquisition, extinction, and spontaneous recovery?

generalization the phenomenon in operant conditioning in which a response that was reinforced in the presence of one stimulus appears in response to other similiar stimuli

discrimination the process in operant conditioning of differential reinforcement wheerin one stimulus is reinforced while another stimulus is not

Figure 6.2

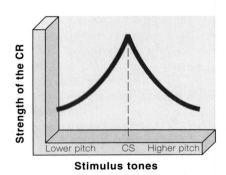

▲ Generalization. Presenting stimuli other than the CS may produce a CR. How much CR is produced depends on the similarity between the new stimulus and the original CS.

During the course of conditioning, assume that we consistently use a tone of a given pitch as the conditioned stimulus. After repeated pairings of this tone with food powder, a dog now salivates when the tone is presented alone.

What will happen if we present a different tone, one that the dog has not heard before? The dog will salivate in response to it also. This response will not be as strong as the original CR (there may not be as much saliva)—how strong depends on how similar the new tone is to the original CS. The more similar it is to the original, the more saliva will be produced. This process is called **generalization**, and we say that a conditioned response will generalize to other new, yet similar stimuli.

This is a powerful process. It means that an unconditioned stimulus need not be paired with all possible conditioned stimuli. If you choose an average, or midrange, CS, the conditioned response will automatically generalize to many other similar stimuli. A graph of this process is shown in Figure 6.2. Imagine that a young boy is bitten by a large black Labrador retriever. Originally, this dog was a neutral stimulus, but having been associated with the pain of a bite, the dog (a CS) is now feared by the boy (a CR). Is it not predictable that the boy's conditioned fear will generalize to other large, black dogs—and, to a lesser extent, to small gray ones?

So if a dog is conditioned to salivate to a tone of middle pitch, it will also salivate to higher and lower tones through generalization. What if we do not want it to? What if we want our dog to salivate to the CS alone and *not* to other tones? We would use **discrimination** training, a process in which an organism learns to make a CR in response to only one CS, but not to other stimuli. In a sense, discrimination is the opposite of generalization. To demonstrate discrimination training, we would present a dog with many

▲ Until they are classically conditioned otherwise, many children enjoy playing with spiders, snakes, bugs, and caterpillars.

tones, but would pair the UCS food powder with only one of them—the CS we want the dog to salivate to. We might, for example, pair the food powder with a tone of middle C. A lower tone, say A, would also be presented to the dog, but *would not* be followed by food powder. At first, there probably would be some saliva produced in response to the A tone (generalization). Eventually, however, our subject would learn to discriminate and would no longer salivate to the A tone.

Before You Go On

▼▼▼▼▼▼▼▼▼

In classical conditioning, what are generalization and discrimination?

▶ The Significance of Classical Conditioning: What about People?

It is time to leave our discussion of dogs, tones, salivation, and Pavlov's lab. We need to turn our attention to the practical application of all of this. We can find examples of classically conditioned human behaviors everywhere.

Conditioned Emotional Responses. One of the most significant aspects of classical conditioning is its role in the acquisition of emotional responses to stimuli in our environment. There are very few stimuli that naturally, or instinctively, elicit emotional responses. Yet think of all those things that *do* directly influence how we feel.

For example, very young children seldom seem afraid of spiders, plane rides, or snakes. (Some children actually seem to enjoy them.) Now consider how many people you know who *are* afraid of these things. There are many stimuli in our environments that cause us to be afraid. There also are stimuli that produce within us feelings of pleasure, calm, and ease.

What scares you? What makes you feel relaxed and at ease? Why? Might you feel particularly upset or distressed in a certain store because you once had an unpleasant experience there? Might you happily anticipate a vacation at the beach because of a very enjoyable vacation you had there as a child? Do you shudder at the sight of a police car—or a pile of exam papers? Do you smile at the thought of a payroll envelope? In each of these cases, we are talking about classical conditioning. (To be fair, I must say that not all our learned emotional reactions are acquired through classical conditioning alone. As we shall see, there are other possibilities.)

When I was a senior in high school, I had surgery on my nose. (A clumsy child, I had broken it a number of times.) I won't bore you with all the gory details. Suffice it to say that the surgery, done under local anesthetic, was painful and altogether unpleasant. That surgery was performed many years ago, but to this day, when I visit a hospital I get a slight ache in my nose! Now, I know better. I know that the pain is just "in my head," but my nose still hurts! What is happening here is that I am being reminded of some relatively permanent classical conditioning. The CS of hospital sights, sounds, and odors was paired with the UCS of an operative procedure that caused a UCR of pain and discomfort. This pairing, which lasted for a number of days, led to the establishment of a CR of discomfort associated with the CS of the hospital. Note that this conditioned response *generalized* to other hospitals, not just the one in which the surgery was performed. And the conditioned response has obviously lasted a long time.

Advertising provides us with many examples of classical conditioning designed to change the way we feel about products or services. How many

▲ *Words mean different things to different people. For example, young children who have pleasant experiences with dogs will probably have pleasant thoughts and feelings about dogs as they grow older.*

times have you seen TV ads showing healthy, good-looking young people having a great time—at the beach playing volleyball, riding bicycles down mountain trails, swinging on ropes over cool streams, and so on—while drinking large amounts of Brand X. All those attractive, "fun" stimuli are designed to make us "feel good." The intent of pairing "fun" stimuli (here the UCS) with Brand X (the CS) is to have us acquire a "feel good" response (CR) to the beverage being advertised.

Before You Go On
▼▼▼▼▼▼▼▼

What sort of responses are most readily influenced by classical conditioning?

The Case of "Little Albert." Let's take a rather detailed look at a famous example of the conditioning of an emotional response. In 1920, John Watson (yes, the founder of behaviorism) and his student assistant, Rosalie Rayner, published a summary article on experiments they performed with "Little Albert." Albert's experiences have become quite well known. Even though Watson and Rayner's report of their own work tended to oversimplify matters a bit (Samuelson, 1980), the story of Little Albert still provides a good model for the classical conditioning of emotional responses.

Eleven-month-old Albert was given many toys to play with. Among other things, he was allowed to play with a live white rat. Albert seemed to enjoy the rat—he certainly showed no signs of fearing it. Then conditioning began. One day, just as Albert reached for the rat, one of the experimenters (Rayner) made a sudden loud noise by striking a metal bar with a hammer. The loud noise was frightening—that much Watson and Rayner had established two months earlier during initial observations of Albert in the laboratory. At least Albert made responses that Watson and Rayner felt indicated fear.

After repeated pairings of the rat and the noise, Albert's reaction to the rat underwent a relatively permanent change. Albert would at first start to reach out toward the rat, then he would recoil and cry, often trying to bury

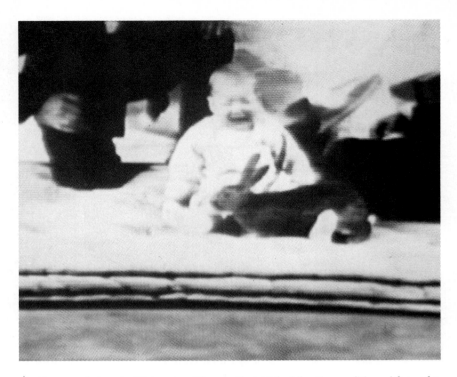

▲ *It seemed clear to Watson and Rayner that Little Albert's conditioned fear of a white rat had generalized to a brown rabbit.*

his head in his blanket. He was clearly making emotional responses to a stimulus that did not elicit those responses before it was paired with sudden loud noises. This sounds like classical conditioning: The rat is the CS and the loud sudden noise is the UCS that elicits the UCR of a fear response. After repeated pairings of the rat and the noise (the CS and UCS), the rat elicits the same sort of fear response (or CR). Figure 6.3 presents a diagram of the procedures used to condition Little Albert to be afraid of a white rat.

Watson and Rayner then went on to demonstrate that Albert's fear of the white rat *generalized* to all sorts of other stimuli: a dog, a ball of cotton, and even a mask with a white beard and mustache. In a number of instances, however, Watson and Rayner did not test for generalization as they should have. They occasionally paired the loud noise (UCS) with new stimuli before testing to see what the reaction might be (Harris, 1979).

Several issues have been raised concerning Watson and Rayner's research on learned fear—not the least of which is the unethical treatment of poor little Albert. It is unlikely that anyone would attempt such a project today. Watson had previously argued (1919) that emotional experiences of early childhood could affect an individual for a lifetime, yet here he was purposely frightening a young child (and without the advised consent of his mother). Although his acquired fears would have extinguished eventually, Albert's mother removed him from the hospital before Watson and Rayner had a chance to undo the conditioning. They were convinced that they could remove Little Albert's fear (by pairing the rat with pleasant stimuli), but as fate would have it, they never got the chance.

Even with these technical disclaimers, it's easy to see how the Little Albert demonstration can be used as a model for describing the development of fear and other emotional responses. When they began, Albert did not respond fearfully to a rat, cotton, or a furry mask. After pairing a neutral stimulus (the rat) with an emotion-producing stimulus (the loud noise), Albert appeared afraid of white, furry, fuzzy objects.

Figure 6.3

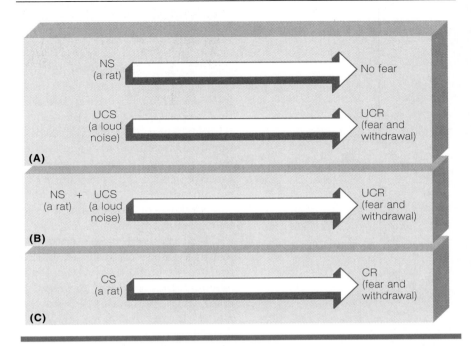

▲ *Conditioned fear in "Little Albert" as an example of classical conditioning.*

Before You Go On

▼▼▼▼▼▼▼▼▼▼

Briefly summarize the Little Albert experimental demonstration.

▶ *Rethinking What Happens in Classical Conditioning*

As you read about classical conditioning, you may very well get the idea that what we are describing here is only of historical interest. After all, most of our discussion has dealt with procedures and phenomena associated with Pavlov's laboratory at the turn of the century. Interest in classical conditioning did not end with Pavlov's lab, however. In fact, classical conditioning continues to be a very active area of research in experimental psychology (Domjan, 1987; Rescorla 1987; 1988; Spear, 1990).

Psychologists today are interested in understanding the precise mechanisms of classical conditioning and the factors that influence the effectiveness of the procedure.

Pavlov believed—as did generations of psychologists after him—that *any* stimulus paired with an unconditioned stimulus could serve as a conditioned stimulus. It's easy to see how psychologists came to this conclusion. A wide variety of stimuli *can* be paired with food powder, and as a result come to elicit a salivation response.

We now see conditioning in a much broader light. Conditioning is now viewed as the learning of relationships that exist among events in the world. Conditioning is seen as an active search for sensible ways to represent the environment, a search for information that one stimulus gives about another (Rescorla, 1988; Spear, et al., 1990).

There are two lines of research that suggest that one cannot present *any* stimulus with an unconditioned stimulus and expect conditioning to result. One research program is associated with Robert Rescorla, the other with Leon Kamin. Let's deal with Rescorla's data first (1968; 1987).

A rat can be conditioned to fear the sound of a tone by presenting that tone and consistently following it with a mild electric shock. Assume that we present a second rat with a tone, occasionally following it with a mild shock. But for this rat, we also simply present the shock from time to time *without the preceding tone*. This rat might receive several shocks without a preceding tone, but it will have as many tone-shock pairings as our first rat. Will this second rat demonstrate any conditioned response to the tone when the tone is presented alone? No, it won't. Even though this rat experienced the same number of tone-shock pairings, there will be no conditioning.

A related phenomenon can be found in Kamin's research (1968; 1969). In a demonstration of a phenomenon called *blocking*, rats are shocked (UCS) at the same time a noise (CS) is presented. Classically conditioned fear of the noise is readily established. The rats are then given a number of trials in which the noise *and* a light are paired with the UCS of a shock. Although the light (now presented with the noise) is paired with the shock many times, no conditioned fear of the light can be found. The rats had already learned that noise is a good predictor of shock; the light is redundant or unnecessary.

In both of these cases and others (*e.g.,* Miller & Spear, 1985; Pearce & Hall, 1980; Rescorla & Wagner, 1972), it seems that what matters most in determining whether or not a stimulus will act as a CS is *the extent to which that stimulus provides useful information or predicts or signals the occurrence of another stimulus.* In the basic Pavlovian demonstration, the tone was highly informative: Every time the tone was presented, food powder followed, and in this case the tone served as an effective CS. In Rescorla's experiments, we see that if a tone does not predict the onset of shock (if some shocks occur without a tone), then that tone will not serve as a CS no matter how many times it is paired with the UCS. In Kamin's experiments, we see that because the rats had already learned that the noise predicted the onset of shocks, adding the light as a potential CS provided no additional useful information and hence was ineffective.

If we can talk about rats representing their environment by learning which stimuli are likely to signal other stimuli, isn't it reasonable to consider classical conditioning in humans in the same way? We experience a pleasant, warm feeling when we see a picture of a beach because it is the beach that is best associated with our favorite vacation—not the fact that we happened to have left on a bus. Beaches predict fun and good times; buses don't necessarily. Although Little Albert's fear generalized to many stimuli, Albert developed no particular fear of blankets, even though he was sitting on a blanket each time Rayner created the loud noise that Albert did associate with the rat.

Now that we understand the basics of Pavlovian classical conditioning, we can move next to consider another fundamental form of conditioning that we call operant conditioning.

Before You Go On

▼▼▼▼▼▼▼

Under what circumstances are stimuli likely to serve effectively as CSs?

▲ E. L. Thorndike

operant conditioning changing the rate of a response on the basis of the consequences that result from that response

law of effect (Thorndike's) the observation that responses that lead to "satisfying states of affairs" tend to be repeated, while those that do not are not

Figure 6.4

▲ An operant chamber, or Skinner box.

▶ *Operant Conditioning*

Most of the early research on operant conditioning was done by B. F. Skinner. Although we correctly associate operant conditioning with him, he did not discover it or invent it in any literal sense. The techniques of operant conditioning had been applied both scientifically and casually for hundreds of years before Skinner was born. What Skinner did was to bring that earlier work into the psychology laboratory, where he studied the procedures of operant conditioning with a unique vigor and helped the rest of us realize the significance of the process.

▶ *The Basics of Operant Conditioning*

Operant conditioning changes the probability or rate of responses on the basis of the consequences that result from those responses. Responses that are followed by reinforcers tend to increase in rate; those not followed by reinforcers tend to decrease in rate. Notice that we are simply claiming that past experiences influence present ones. As Skinner put it, ". . . behavior is shaped by its consequences, but only by consequences that lie in the past. We do what we do because of what *has* happened, not what *will* happen" (Skinner, 1989, p. 14).

As it happens, the first clear statement of the essentials of operant conditioning comes not from Skinner, but from E. L. Thorndike (1874–1947). Thorndike's **law of effect** claims that responses are learned when they are followed by a "satisfying state of affairs" (Thorndike, 1911, p. 245). When an organism makes a response and then experiences a satisfying state of affairs (reinforcement), the organism will tend to make that response again. If a response is not followed by a satisfying state of affairs (reinforcement does not occur), then the organism will tend not to make that response again. This seemingly simple observation is also a profound one, because it is true. Our behaviors *are* shaped by their consequences.

One hardly needs special apparatus or a laboratory to observe operant conditioning at work. Imagine a father rushing through a supermarket with his toddler seated in a shopping cart. The child is screaming at the top of his lungs for a candy bar—over and over, echoing throughout the store, "I wanna candy bar! I wanna candy bar!" Father is doing a good (and appropriate) job of ignoring this monstrous behavior until he spies a neighbor coming down the next aisle. The neighbor has her three children with her, and all three are acting like quiet, perfect angels. What's a parent to do? He races by the checkout lanes, grabs a candy bar, and gives it to his child. One does not have to be an expert in child psychology (or operant conditioning) to predict what will happen on the next visit to the store. Screaming "worked" this time, so it will be tried again. Reinforced behaviors tend to recur.

As we did with classical conditioning, we'll use examples from the laboratory to describe the procedures and phenomena of operant conditioning. You should have little difficulty finding examples in your own experience.

The Procedures of Operant Conditioning. To demonstrate operant conditioning in the controlled environment of the laboratory, Skinner built a special piece of apparatus called an operant chamber. Skinner never used the term, and said he didn't like it (Skinner, 1984), but we often call this device a "Skinner box." Figure 6.4 shows a standard operant chamber. The chamber pictured here is designed for rats. The box is empty except for a small lever that protrudes from one wall and a small cup to hold a piece of rat food. Pellets of food are automatically dispensed through a tube into the food cup. Pellets are released one at a time when the lever is depressed.

Treating Fear with Classical Conditioning

We have seen that classical conditioning can be demonstrated in the laboratory, and we have noted numerous examples of classical conditioning in our everyday lives. Now let's explore a way in which psychologists use the procedures of classical conditioning in the real world as a form of psychotherapy.

There are many things in this world that are life-threatening and downright frightening. Being afraid of certain stimuli is often a wise, rational, and appropriate reaction. If, for example, you are walking in the downtown center of a large city late at night and you are approached by three huge thugs dragging motorcycle chains and holding knives, you are likely to feel a reaction of fear.

Occasionally, however, we find people who experience discomforting, distressing fears of stimuli that are not threatening in a real or rational sense. Some people are intensely afraid of riding on elevators, being in small closed-in areas, flying on airplanes, spiders, or the dark. Psychologists say that these people are suffering from a *phobic disorder*—an intense, irrational fear of some object that leads a person to avoid contact with it. There are many possible explanations for how phobic disorders are formed, but one clear possibility, of course, is classical conditioning.

This explanation suggests that an individual experiences an intense and natural emotional response to a powerful, emotion-producing stimulus—perhaps some traumatic event, such as a severe injury, or an accident. When such a stimulus occurs in the presence of another, neutral stimulus, the pairing may result in the formation of a conditioned fear response to the originally neutral stimulus. As a working example, imagine that a youngster at a local carnival becomes separated from his parents, and gets swept away by a large crowd into a tent where clowns are performing. The child is (sensibly) very frightened by the separation from his parents, and after they are reunited, requires considerable reassurance before he settles down. Should we be terribly surprised if this child, even much later as an adolescent or an adult, appears irrationally afraid of carnivals, circuses, or clowns? Not if one believes that classical conditioning can account for the formation of phobic fears.

Sadly enough, phobic disorders are far from uncommon. Best guess estimates place prevalence rates at between seven to twenty percent of the population—that's tens of millions of people (Marks, 1986; Robins, et al., 1984). Phobic reactions seldom extinguish "on their own." Why not? There are a number of reasons, but one is that someone with a phobia is usually successful at avoiding the conditioned stimulus that elicits the fear.

▲ *A phobic fear of heights is one conditioned emotional response that can be lessened with systematic desensitization.*

Now that we have our chamber, we need a subject. If we put a hungry rat into the chamber and do nothing else, the rat occasionally will press the lever. There is very little else for it to do in there. Rats naturally explore their environments and tend to manipulate objects in it. The rate at which the rat presses the lever is called its *base rate* of responding. Typically, a rat will press the lever 8–10 times over the course of an hour.

After a period of observation, we activate the food dispenser so that a pellet of food is delivered every time the lever is pressed. As predicted by Thorndike's law of effect, the rate of the lever-pressing response increases.

Someone with a fear of flying simply may be able to manage by taking a bus or train or by driving. Although there are a number of different techniques that can be used to treat phobic disorders (see Chapter 13, pp. 426–453), one of the most common is based directly on principles of Pavlovian conditioning. The procedure is called *systematic desensitization*, and was introduced over thirty years ago by therapist Joseph Wolpe (1958; 1969; 1981).

In its standard form, there are three stages involved in systematic desensitization. The first thing the therapist does is instruct the client to relax. There are many ways to go about such training. Some procedures use hypnosis, but most simply have the subject relax one foot, then both feet, then one leg, then both, and so on, until the whole body is relaxed. No matter what method is used, this phase generally doesn't take very long, and after a few hours of training at the most, the subject knows how to enter a relaxed state.

The second step is to construct an "anxiety hierarchy"—a list of stimuli that gradually decrease in their ability to elicit anxiety. The most feared, most anxiety-producing stimulus is placed at the top of the list (for our example subject, that might be "clowns," followed by "carnival," circus," "mimes," and so on). Each item that follows elicits less and less fear until, at the bottom of the list, we place stimuli that elicit no fear at all.

Now treatment is ready to begin. The client relaxes completely and thinks about the stimulus lowest on the anxiety hierarchy. The client is then instructed to think about the next highest stimulus, and the next, and so on, all the while remaining as relaxed as possible. As progress is made up the list, toward the anxiety-producing stimuli at the top, the therapist constantly monitors the subject's tension-relaxation level. When anxiety seems to be overcoming relaxation, the person is told to stop thinking about that item on the hierarchy and to think about an item lower on the list.

Notice that what is going on with systematic desensitization is more than just the simple extinction of a previously conditioned fear response. A new response (relaxation) is being acquired to "replace" an old one (fear). The logic is quite obvious. A person cannot be relaxed and anxious at the same time—these are incompatible responses. So, if I pair a stimulus (the CS) with the feeling associated with being relaxed (the UCS), through classical conditioning it will come to produce a reaction of calm (a new CR), not the incompatible response of tension and anxiety (the old CR). For many people, this technique can be effective (*e.g.*, Wilson, 1982). It works best for those anxieties or fears that are associated with easily identifiable, specific environmental stimuli; it works least well for a diffuse, generalized fear (for which hierarchies are difficult to generate).

The rat may reach the point of pressing the lever at a rate of as many as 500 to 600 times per hour. Learning has taken place. There has been a relatively permanent change in behavior as a result of experience.

Here is a little subtlety: Has the rat learned to press the lever? In any sense can we say that we have taught the rat a lever-pressing response? No. The rat knew how to press the lever and did so long before we introduced the food pellets as a reward for its behavior. What it did learn—the change in behavior that took place—was a change in the *rate* of the response, not in the nature of the response *per se*.

What is the essence of operant conditioning?

The Course of Conditioning. Now that we have the basic principles of operant conditioning in mind, let's review how the procedure is applied.

One reality of operant conditioning is that before you can reinforce a response, you have to get that response to occur in the first place. What if you place a rat in an operant chamber and find that after grooming itself, it stops, stares off into space, and settles down, facing away from the lever and the food cup? If your rat never presses the lever, it will never get a pellet. Your apparatus is prepared to deliver a food pellet as soon as your rat presses the lever, but it appears that you may have a long wait.

In such a circumstance, you could use the procedure called **shaping**, or reinforcing *successive approximations* of the response you want to condition.

You have a button that delivers a pellet to the food cup of the operant chamber even though the lever is not pressed. When your rat turns to face the lever, you deliver a pellet, reinforcing that behavior. This is not exactly the response you want, but at least the rat is facing in the correct direction. You don't give your rat another pellet until it moves toward the lever. It gets another pellet for moving even closer to the lever. The next pellet doesn't come until the rat touches the lever.

A reinforcer is delivered each time your rat successively approximates the lever-press response. Eventually the rat will press the lever to deliver a pellet by itself. Shaping is over, and the rat is on its own. In practice, this procedure is not as easy as it may sound. You have to be quick with your reinforcement, and you must be sure that each reinforced response is really closer to the one you ultimately want. Remember that your rat will continue to do whatever it was doing just before its behavior was reinforced. If you are not careful, your rat may be rewarded for running to the lever, or bobbing its head up and down, or turning in circles, instead of pressing the lever.

Once an organism begins to emit the responses you wish to reinforce, the procedures of operant conditioning are simple. Immediately following the desired response, reinforcement is provided. As responses produce reinforcers, those responses become more likely to occur. The increase in response rate that follows reinforcement generally will be slow at first, then become more rapid, and eventually will level off. We call this phase or stage of operant conditioning **acquisition**. Figure 6.5 is a curve depicting the stages of operant conditioning. It is very important to note that the vertical, *y*-axis in this curve is a measure of *rate* of response, not response strength.

Once a rat is responding at a high rate, what happens if reinforcers are withheld? Let's say that because we have reinforced its lever pressing, a rat is pressing a lever at a rate of 550 presses per hour. From now on, however, it will receive no more pellets of food for its efforts—no more reinforcers. What happens is very predictable: The rate of lever-pressing decreases gradually until it returns to the low base rate at which it began. Eventually the lever pressing returns to base rate (not to zero, because it didn't start at zero), and we can say that **extinction** has taken place.

Now let us assume that extinction has occurred, and that the rat has been removed from the operant chamber and returned to its cage for a few days. When we again deprive it of food and return it to the chamber, what will it do? It will go right over to the lever and begin to press it again, and at a high rate. Even though the lever-pressing has gone through extinction—

shaping a procedure of reinforcing successive approximations of a desired response until that desired response is made

acquisition the process in operant conditioning in which the rate of a reinforced response increases

extinction the process in operant conditioning in which the rate of a response decreases as reinforcers are withheld

Figure 6.5

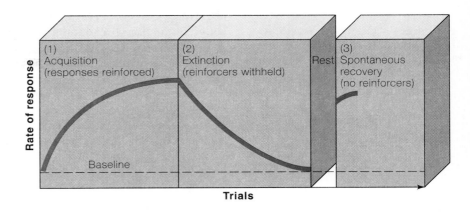

▲ *The stages of operant conditioning. (1) During acquisition, response rates increase when responses are reinforced. (2) In extinction, reinforcers are withheld and the response rate returns to the baseline rate. (3) During spontaneous recovery, an increase in response rate is noted following a rest interval after extinction. The stages here are the same as those found in classical conditioning.*

spontaneous recovery the phenomenon in operant conditioning in which a previously extinguished response returns after a rest interval

the last time we saw this rat in the operant chamber it was not pressing the lever—it will press the lever again after a rest interval. This return of an extinguished response following a rest interval is called **spontaneous recovery**. As was the case in classical conditioning, the significance of spontaneous recovery is that once acquired, an operant response seldom can be eliminated in just one series of extinction trials. Figure 6.5 also shows extinction and spontaneous recovery for operant conditioning.

Before You Go On
▼▼▼▼▼▼▼▼▼

What is shaping, and how does it work?

Describe acquisition, extinction, and spontaneous recovery as they occur in operant conditioning.

---

reinforcement a process that increases the rate or probability of the response that it follows

▶ *Reinforcement*

From what I've said, it should be obvious that reinforcement is a crucial concept in operant conditioning. **Reinforcement** (the administration of a reinforcer) is a process that increases the rate or the probability of the response that precedes it. In this section we'll define what we mean by *reinforcer,* and we'll discuss a number of different types of them. We'll also examine the effects of scheduling reinforcers. We will then move on to consider punishment.

Positive and Negative Reinforcers. What qualifies as an effective reinforcer? What creates that satisfying state of affairs Thorndike claimed is necessary to increase response rate? For a hungry rat in an operant chamber, the answer seems deceptively simple. Here we can ensure that a rat is hungry, and we can confidently predict that the delivery of food will be reinforcing. For people, or for rats who are no longer hungry, the answer may not be so obvious.

reinforcers stimuli that increase the rate or probability of the response they follow

positive reinforcer a stimulus that increases the rate of a response when it is presented after the response is made

negative reinforcer a stimulus that increases the rate of a response when that stimulus is removed after the response is made

Skinner and his students argue that we should define reinforcers operationally. That is, we should define reinforcers only in terms of their effect on behavior. Reinforcers are stimuli. Stimuli that increase the rate or the probability of the response that they follow are **reinforcers.**

At first reading, this logic may sound a bit backward. A reinforcer is a stimulus that increases the rate of those responses that it follows. This line of reasoning suggests that nothing is *necessarily* going to be reinforcing. Reinforcers are defined only after we have noted their effect on behavior and we do not know ahead of time what will or will not produce an increased rate of response. We may have some strong suspicions, based on what has worked in the past, but we will not know for sure until we try.

For many people, money is a powerful reinforcer. What do you suppose would happen if your instructor decided to offer $10 for every test item answered correctly? Such a reinforcement scheme might increase the rate of students' studying behaviors. But, hard as this may be to believe, some students might not be interested. For them, the monetary award would not be at all reinforcing. In that case, it would not lead to an increase in the studying behaviors of those students. Farfetched, perhaps, but the point is that we cannot always tell whether or not a stimulus will be reinforcing until we try it. It is reinforcing *only* if it increases the rate or the likelihood of the response that it follows (Kimble, 1981).

Now that we have a general idea of what a reinforcer is, we can begin to get a bit more specific. A **positive reinforcer** is a stimulus *presented to* an organism that increases (or maintains) the rate of a response that it follows. The term does appear to be redundant: If something is positive, it certainly ought to be reinforcing. Positive reinforcers are often like rewards. Examples include such stimuli as food for hungry organisms, water for thirsty ones, high letter grades for well-motivated students, and money, praise, and attention for most of us.

A **negative reinforcer** is a stimulus that increases (or maintains) the rate of a response that precedes *its removal*. "Negative reinforcer" is a strange term. There is something contradictory about the very sound of it. If something is negative, how can it be a reinforcer? The key word here is *reinforcer* and reinforcers increase the rate of responses. In terms of the law of effect, negative reinforcement must produce some sort of satisfying state of affairs, and that it does. But the reinforcement comes not from the delivery or presentation of negative reinforcers, but from their removal. (It is helpful to remember that reinforce*ment* is a process. You may think of negative reinforcers as being generally unpleasant aversive stimuli, while negative reinforcement is a pleasant outcome.)

So, negative reinforcers are stimuli that increase the probability of a response *when they are removed*. They may include such stimuli as shocks, enforced isolation, and ridicule. They are exactly the sorts of things that an organism would work (respond) to avoid or escape. Note that even though it may not sound like it, "negative reinforcement is highly desirable. If offered negative reinforcement, one should accept the offer. It is always good to have bad things terminated or removed" (Michael, 1985, p. 107).

Remembering that the bottom line in negative reinforcement is that an organism's rate of response increases, here's an example involving a rat: a rat in an operant chamber is shocked (through the metallic floor of the chamber). As soon as the rat presses the lever, the shock is turned off. The lever-press has been reinforced and is likely to increase. Because a painful aversive stimulus was terminated, this is negative reinforcement—and the negative reinforcer is the shock.

You take an aspirin when you have a headache and are reinforced—the pain stops, and you will be likely to try aspirin again the next time you have a headache. When a prisoner is released from prison early, "for good behavior," the good behavior is being reinforced by removing the aversive imprisonment. The process is negative reinforcement.

Before we go on, one more suggestion for understanding positive and negative reinforcement is to think of these processes in terms of plus (+) and minus (−). When using positive reinforcement, one adds (+) a reinforcer. In negative reinforcement one takes away, or subtracts (−) a reinforcer.

Now that we have some of the basics laid down, let's make another distinction between reinforcers, this time between primary and secondary reinforcers. Then, we'll consider how we might schedule the delivery of reinforcers, and the implications of such schedules.

Before You Go On
▼▼▼▼▼▼▼▼▼

Provide an operational definition of reinforcement.

Distinguish between a positive and a negative reinforcer.

Primary and Secondary Reinforcers. Reinforcers are defined in terms of their effect on behavior. Positive and negative reinforcers increase response rates. Now we need to distinguish between primary and secondary reinforcers. At issue here is the extent to which reinforcers are unlearned or acquire their reinforcing capability through learning or experience.

Primary reinforcers do not require previous experience in order to be effective. They are in some way related to the organism's survival and are usually biological or physiological in nature. Food for a hungry organism or water for a thirsty one are common examples. Providing a warm place by the fire to a cold, wet, stray dog involves primary reinforcement.

Secondary reinforcers are often referred to as *learned, acquired,* or *conditioned* reinforcers. There is nothing about them that suggests that they are inherently reinforcing or satisfying in any biological sense, yet they operate to strengthen responses.

Most of the reinforcers that you and I work for are of this sort. Money, praise, high letter grades, and promotions are good examples. Money, in and of itself, is not worth much (the metal variety wears holes in your pockets, and paper money may carry germs). But our previous learning experiences have convinced most of us of the reinforcing nature of money, and it can serve to increase the rate of a wide variety of responses. Among other things, we have learned that money can provide us with access to many other reinforcers, such as food and clothing.

The use of secondary reinforcers—and operant conditioning—can be illustrated by a type of psychotherapy called *contingency contracting* (see pp. 445–446 in Chapter 13). Contingency contracting amounts to setting up a system that provides secondary reinforcers for appropriate behaviors. The system that is established is usually referred to as a "token economy." For example, a child may earn a check mark on the calendar for each day he or she makes the bed (or takes out the trash, or walks the dog, or clears the table, or whatever). The economy hinges on the extent to which the check marks serve as secondary reinforcers. In other words, the child must first learn that a certain number of check marks can be exchanged for something that already reinforces the child's behaviors (*e.g.,* an extra dessert, an hour of playing a video-game, a new toy, etc.). Such techniques, when applied consistently, can be very effective in modifying behavior.

primary reinforcer a stimulus (usually biologically or physiologically based) that increases the rate of a response with no previous experience required

secondary reinforcer a stimulus that increases the rate of a response because of having been associated with other reinforcers; also called conditioned, or learned, reinforcer

continuous reinforcement schedule (CRF) a reinforcement schedule in which each and every response is followed by a reinforcer

intermittent reinforcement schedules reinforcement schedules in which responses are not reinforced every time they occur

Scheduling Reinforcers. In all of our discussions and examples so far, I have implied that operant conditioning requires that a reinforcer be provided after every desired response. In fact, particularly at the start, it probably *is* best to reinforce each response as it occurs. But once response rates begin to increase, there may be good reason for reinforcing responses only intermittently.

The procedure of reinforcing each and every response after it occurs is called a **continuous reinforcement (CRF) schedule.** A problem with CRF schedules is that earning a reinforcer after each response may soon reduce the effectiveness of that reinforcer. For example, once a rat has eaten its fill, food pellets will no longer serve to reinforce its behavior, and the rat will have to be removed from the operant chamber until it becomes hungry again (Skinner, 1956). Another problem is that responses acquired under a CRF schedule tend to extinguish very quickly. Once reinforcers are withheld, response rates decrease drastically.

Alternatives to reinforcing every response are called **intermittent reinforcement schedules.** Simply, these are strategies for reinforcing a desired behavior less frequently than every time it occurs. There are several ways in which one might go about reinforcing responses according to an intermittent schedule. We'll review four such strategies: fixed-ratio, fixed-interval, variable-ratio, and variable-interval schedules. These schedules were devised in the laboratory. In the world outside the laboratory, there are not many good examples of the literal application of intermittent schedules. There are, however, a few "real-life" examples that are fairly close and instructive. Although intermittent schedules do influence the manner in which responses are acquired, their major effects are on extinction. These effects are depicted in Figure 6.6.

With a *fixed-ratio (FR) schedule*, one establishes (fixes) a ratio of reinforcers to responses. In a FR,1:5 schedule, for example, one reinforcer is delivered after every five responses. A 1:10 fixed-ratio schedule for a rat in an operant chamber means that the rat receives a pellet only after it presses the lever 10 times. Piecework is an example of a fixed-ratio schedule: "I'll pay you 25¢ for every 12 gizmos you assemble," or "You'll earn ten points of extra credit for every three book reports you hand in." As you might imagine, there is a high and steady rate of responding under an effective fixed-ratio schedule—the more responses, the more reinforcement. Responses acquired under a FR schedule are more resistant to extinction than those acquired under a CRF schedule.

With a *fixed-interval (FI) schedule*, time is divided into established (fixed) intervals. After each fixed time interval, a reinforcer is delivered when the next response occurs. A FI,30-second schedule, for example, calls for the delivery of a food pellet for the first lever-press a rat makes after each 30-second interval passes. With such a schedule, you know from the start that you won't be dispensing more than two pellets every minute. A common example is employees being paid on a regular interval of, say, every Friday, or once a month. Under an FI schedule, the behavior of the organism shows a characteristic pattern. Response rates decrease considerably just after a reinforcer, but then increase significantly as the time for the next reinforcer approaches. Fixed-interval schedules also produce responses that are resistant to extinction.

Figure 6.6

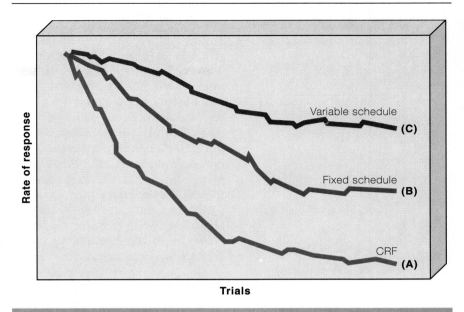

▲ The effects of a schedule of reinforcement on extinction. Three hypothetical extinction curves following operant conditioning under (A) continuous reinforcement (CRF), (B) a fixed schedule, (C) a variable schedule of reinforcement.

There are two variable schedules of reinforcement, the *variable-ratio (VR) schedule* and the *variable-interval (VI) schedule.* From the learner's point of view, these schedules are very much alike. For the VR schedule, one simply varies the ratio of reinforcers to responses. With a VR,1:5 schedule, the experimenter administers one reinforcer for every five responses *on the average,* but always in a different ratio. That is, the first reinforcer may come after five responses, the next after six, the next after nine, the next after one, and so on. On the average, the ratio of reinforcers to responses is 1:5, but the patterning of actual ratios is variable. From the learner's point of view, this is a random schedule. The most commonly cited example of VR reinforcement schedules is gambling devices, such as slot machines. They are programmed to pay off (reinforce) on a variable ratio schedule where the ratios are usually quite large. Not surprisingly, the VR schedule produces a very high rate of responding, and produces responses that are very resistant to extinction.

Variable interval schedules follow the same logic as do variable ratio schedules. For a rat on a VI,30-second schedule in an operant chamber, a food pellet comes following the first lever-press response after a 30-second interval; the next follows the first response after a 50-second interval; then after a 10-second interval, and so on. Here the varied intervals *average* 30 seconds in length. An instructor who wants to keep a class on its toes, studying regularly and attending class consistently, may schedule quizzes on a variable interval schedule. The students learn the quizzes are coming, but they never know when. What we find with VI schedules is a slower, but very steady pattern of performance. If you know when your exams are coming, you may hold off studying until just before they occur. If they are scheduled to occur randomly throughout the semester, you'll keep your studying rate up just in case there's a test scheduled for the next class.

The terminology we have used here is standard, but it is somewhat technical. The main point is that operant conditioning does not require that each response be reinforced. The scheduling of reinforcers will influence the pattern of the learned responses and affects their resistance to extinction.

There is another point that should be made regarding the scheduling of reinforcers that is true regardless of whether one is using a continuous schedule or one of the intermittent schedules. *Reinforcers should come immediately after the desired response.* Delayed reinforcement is likely to be ineffective. I'm not saying that delaying reinforcement destroys the possibility of learning; I'm simply suggesting that in most cases, the more immediate the reinforcer, the better the learning. In one study, for example, pigeons learned to peck at a disk much faster when a food reward was given two seconds after each peck rather than four seconds following a peck, even though in the latter case, they were allowed to eat for twice as long (Rachlin and Green, 1972). The point here is sensible. What if parents buy tickets to the circus to reinforce their son's behavior with the baby-sitter? But the circus is not until Saturday. When the family goes off to the circus Saturday afternoon, what is being reinforced may not be the child's appropriate behaviors of last Tuesday night, but all of his inappropriate behaviors on Wednesday, Thursday, Friday, and Saturday morning.

Before You Go On
▼▼▼▼▼▼▼▼▼▼

Define FR, FI, VR, and VI intermittent schedules of reinforcement.

▶ Punishment

We've talked at length about reinforcement, positive and negative, primary and secondary, and how reinforcers can be scheduled. Let's now consider punishment. What happens with punishment is essentially the opposite of what happens with reinforcement. **Punishment** occurs when a stimulus delivered to an organism *decreases* the rate or the probability of occurrence of the response that preceded it. In common usage, punishment is usually in some way painful—either physically (a spanking) or psychologically (ridicule). It is a painful, unpleasant, aversive stimulus that is presented to an organism after some response is made. If the rate, or probability, of the organism's response then drops, or decreases, we may say that the response has been punished. It may have occurred to you that if punishers *are removed* or *terminated,* the result will be reinforcing—we'd have an example of negative reinforcement.

Determining ahead of time what stimulus will be punishing is often as difficult to do as determining what stimulus will serve as a reinforcer. Once again, one's intention's are quite irrelevant. We only know for sure that something is a punisher in terms of its effect on behavior. For example, we may *think* that we are punishing Richard by sending him to his room because he has begun to throw a temper tantrum. It may be that "in his room" is exactly where Richard would like to be. We may have reinforced Richard's temper tantrum behaviors simply by attending to them. The only way to know for sure is to note the effect on behavior. If Richard's tantrum-throwing becomes less frequent as a consequence of our actions, sending him to his room may indeed be a punishing thing to do.

Is punishment an effective way of controlling behavior? Does punishment work? Yes, it does. Punishment can be an impressive modifier of one's behavior. A rat has learned to press a lever to get a food reinforcer. You now decide that you do not want the rat to press the lever. You pass an electric current through the lever so that each time it is touched, the rat receives a strong shock. What will happen? As a matter of fact, a number of

punishment the administration of a punisher, which is a stimulus that decreases the rate or probability of a response that precedes it

things may happen, but—if your shock is strong enough—there's one thing of which we can be sure: the rat will stop pressing the lever. If punishment is all that effective, why do psychologists argue against its use?

There are potential problems of the use of punishment, even when it is used correctly. And often, it is used incorrectly. Let's review some of what we know about the effective use of punishment (*e.g.,* Axelrod & Apsche, 1983; Azrin & Holz, 1966; Walters & Grusec, 1977).

1. To be effective, punishment should be delivered immediately after the response. The logic here is the same as that for the immediacy of reinforcement. Priscilla is caught in mid-afternoon throwing flour all over the kitchen. Mother counts to ten (good), then says, "Just wait 'til your father gets home." (not so good). For the next three hours, Priscilla's behavior is perfect. When father gets home, what is punished—Priscilla's flour-tossing, or all of her appropriate behaviors that followed?

2. Punishment needs to be administered consistently. If one chooses to punish a certain behavior, it should be punished on every occasion—and often that is difficult to do.

3. Punishment may decrease overall behavior levels. Although an effectively punished response may end, so may other responses as well. Not only will that rat who has been shocked for pressing the bar stop pressing the bar, but it will cower in the corner, doing very little of anything.

4. When responses are punished, alternatives should be introduced. Think about your rat for a minute. The poor thing knows what to do when it is hungry: press the lever. Now it gets shocked for doing so. When the rat is given no alternative response to make in order to get food, it is in a conflict that has no solution, no way out. The result may be fear, anxiety, and even aggressiveness. We say that punishment does not convey any information about what to do; it only communicates what NOT to do. Rubbing your puppy's nose in a "mess" it just made on the livingroom carpet doesn't give the dog much of an idea of what it is supposed to do when it feels a need to relieve itself. Simply try to anticipate its needs and show it where it is supposed to go.

Before You Go On
▼▼▼▼▼▼▼▼

What is a punisher?

How can punishers be used effectively?

▶ Generalization and Discrimination

In classical conditioning, we saw that in the right circumstances, a response conditioned to one particular stimulus could be elicited by similar stimuli. We have a comparable phenomenon in operant conditioning, and again we call it **generalization**—responses that have been conditioned to some specific stimulus may appear in response to similar stimuli.

For example, little Leslie may recieve a reinforcer for saying "doggie" as a neighbor's poodle wanders across the front yard. "Yes, Leslie, good girl. That's a doggie." Having learned that calling the neighbor's poodle a "doggie" earns parental approval, the response is tried again, this time with a German shepherd from down the street. Leslie's operantly conditioned response of "doggie" in the presence of a poodle now generalizes to the German shepherd. The problem is that Leslie may overgeneralize "doggie" to virtually any small, furry four-legged animal and start calling cats and raccoons "doggie"

generalization the process by which a response that was reinforced in the presence of one stimulus appears in response to similar stimuli

discrimination the process of differential reinforcement where in one stimulus is reinforced while another stimulus is not

also. When a child turns to a total stranger and utters "dada," generalization can (usually) be blamed for the embarrassing mislabeling.

The process of generalization can be countered with **discrimination** conditioning. Discrimination learning is basically a matter of *differential reinforcement*. What that means is that only responses made to appropriate stimuli are reinforced, while responses made to inappropriate stimuli are ignored (*note*: by withholding reinforcers, *not* by punishing the response).

To demonstrate how discrimination training works, let's consider a strange question. Are pigeons colorblind? Disregarding for now why anyone would care, how might you go about testing the color vision of a pigeon?

A pigeon can be trained to peck at a single lighted disk in order to earn a food reward. A pigeon in an operant chamber pecks at a lighted disk, and a grain of food is delivered. Soon the pigeon pecks the disk at a high rate.

Let's now present the pigeon with *two* lighted disks. One disk is red and one is green. Otherwise, they are identical: the same shape, brightness, size, and so on. Our basic question is whether or not the pigeon can tell the difference between red and green. We'll make the green disk the (positive) discriminative stimulus. Responses to the red disk will be extinguished, or will not be reinforced. The position of the colored disks is randomly altered. We don't want to demonstrate that the pigeon can tell left from right.

The results of this sort of manipulation are depicted in Figure 6.7. At first, the red and green lighted disks are responded to at an approximately equal rate. But in short order, the pigeon ignores the red disk and pecks only at the green one, for which it receives its reinforcer.

To maintain this behavior, the pigeon must be able to discriminate between the two colored disks. We don't know what red or green look like to a pigeon, but we can conclude that pigeons can tell the difference between the two. This is sensible because the eyes of pigeons contain cones in their retinas, and cones are the receptors for color. Some varieties of owls are virtually without cone cells in their retinas and thus, are color blind. They cannot discriminate between red and green and appear very frustrated in a discrimination learning task based on color.

▲ *A pigeon in an operant chamber with a red disk and a green disk is able to distinguish one from the other.*

Figure 6.7

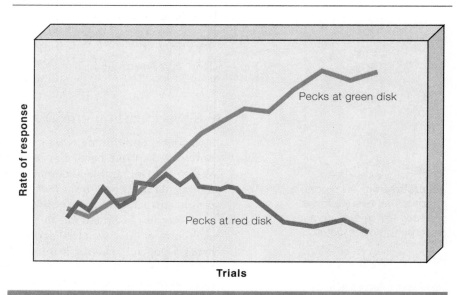

▲ *Discrimination training. Response rates of a pigeon pecking at a green disk and a red disk presented together. Pecks at the green disk are reinforced; those to the red disk are not.*

Please don't think that generalization and discrimination learning in operant conditioning are processes relevant only to very young children and rats and pigeons. Much of our own learning experience involves learning to discriminate when certain behaviors are appropriate and are likely to be reinforced, and when they are inappropriate and are likely to be ignored (at best) or punished. Many of the behaviors that may have been reinforced at a party, you recognize as inappropriate responses in the classroom. You may have learned that it's okay to put your feet up on the coffee table at home, but not at your boss's house.

Before You Go On
▼▼▼▼▼▼▼▼

In the context of operant conditioning, what are generalization and discrimination?

▶ Cognitive Approaches to Learning

Cognitions, as you recall, are mental representations, including knowledge, ideas, and beliefs. Cognitive approaches to learning emphasize changes that occur within an organism's system of cognitions. Cognitive learning involves the acquisition of knowledge or understanding and need not be reflected in overt behavior. You may recognize that we anticipated this approach in the coverage of the work of Rescorla and Kamin on classical conditioning. There we noted that a stimulus acts as an effective conditioned stimulus only when it informs the organism about something happening in its world; as in "when the tone sounds, food will soon follow." Extracting information from real-world experiences is a cognitive experience. In this section, we'll briefly review the work of two theorists who have stressed cognitive approaches to learning: Edward Tolman and Albert Bandura.

▶ Latent Learning and Cognitive Maps

Do rats have brains? Of course they do. Their brains aren't very large, and the cerebral cortex of a rat's brain is small indeed. A more intriguing issue is whether or not rats have minds. Can they figure things out? Can they understand? Can they manipulate cognitions? Surely they can form simple associations. They can learn to associate a light with a shock. They can associate a lever-press response with a reinforcer. Can they do more?

Consider a now-classic experiment performed over 60 years ago by Tolman and Honzik (1930). Even then, it was known that a rat could learn to run through a complicated maze of alleyways and dead ends to get to a goal box where it would receive a food reward. Tolman and Honzik wanted to understand just *what* the rats were learning when they learned to negotiate such a maze. They used three different groups of rats with the same maze.

One group of hungry rats was given a series of exposures to the maze (trials). Each time they ran from the starting point to the goal box, they were given a food reward for their efforts. Over the course of 16 days, the rats in this group showed a steady and predictable improvement in their maze-running. Their rate of errors dropped from approximately nine per trial to just two.

A second group of rats was also given an opportunity to explore the maze for 16 days of trials. They were *not* given a food reward for making it to the end of the maze. The average number of errors made by the rats in this group also dropped over the course of the experiment (from about nine errors per trial down to about six), suggesting that simply being removed

▲ *Edward Tolman*

from the maze provided some measure of reinforcement. Even so, after 16 days, this group was having much more difficulty in their maze-running than was the group being given a food reinforcer.

A third group of rats was allowed to explore the maze on their own for 10 days during which they were *not* given a food reward upon reaching the goal box. Beginning on day 11, a food reinforcer was introduced when they reached the end of the maze. The food was given as a reinforcer on days 11 through 16. The introduction of the food reward had a very significant effect on the rats' behaviors. Over the course of the first 10 days in the maze—without the food—performance showed only a slight improvement. Soon after the food was introduced, their maze running improved markedly. In fact, on days 13 through 16, they made even fewer errors than did the rats who had received the food all along! Figure 6.8 shows the relative performance of these three groups of rats.

Why did that third group of rats perform so much better after the food reward was introduced? Might they have learned something about that maze *before* they received reinforcement for getting to the goal box? Might they have figured out the maze early on, but failed to rush to the goal box until there was some good reason to do so?

Tolman thought that they had. He argued that the food only rewarded a change in the rats' performance, and that the actual learning had taken place earlier. This sort of learning is called **latent learning** because it is, in a sense, hidden and not shown in behavior at the time it occurs.

During those first 10 days in the maze, the rats developed what Tolman called a **cognitive map** of the maze; that is, they formed a mental picture, or representation, of what the maze was like. The rats "knew" about the maze, but until food was provided at the goal box, there was no reason, or purpose, for getting there in any big hurry. This sort of logic led Tolman to

latent learning hidden learning that is not demonstrated in performance until that performance is reinforced

cognitive map a mental representation of the learning situation or physical environment

Figure 6.8

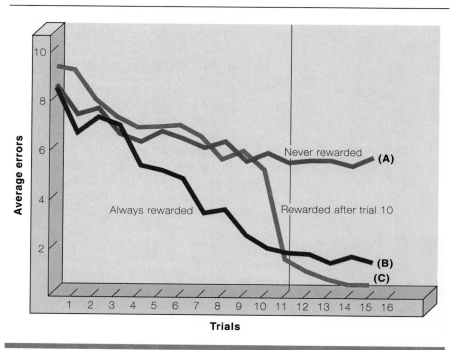

▲ *The performance of rats in a maze that (A) were never rewarded, (B) were rewarded on every trial, or (C) were rewarded only on trials 11-16. (After Tolman & Honzik, 1930.)*

▲ *Albert Bandura*

refer to his approach as *purposive behaviorism* (Tolman, 1932). Introducing the notion of purpose, and drawing a distinction between performance and what was actually learned, tended to focus attention on what was happening to the learner during learning, which was one of Tolman's goals.

This may make sense for rats, but what about people? For one thing, there is the argument that if we can show that cognitive restructuring takes place when *rats* learn, it seems clear that such processes can also occur in *humans*. You should be able to find examples from your own experiences that approximate the latent learning and cognitive maps of Tolman. You may take the same route between home and campus every day. If one day an accident blocks your path, won't you use your knowledge of other routes (a cognitive map) to get where you are going? Although the term *cognitive map* may at first sound strange, aren't there many occasions where the concept can be useful? When you park your car in a new, large parking lot, what do you do as you start walking away from your car? Don't you look around, trying to develop a mental image, or cognitive map of the parking lot and some of its major features? Imagine that you are to meet a friend in a new classroom building on campus. You arrive early, so you stroll around the building for a few minutes. Isn't it likely that your unreinforced, apparently aimless behavior will be useful when you have to locate a room in that building for class the next semester?

Another setting in which we may find Tolman's purposive behaviorism is in athletics. Before the big game, the coaching staff may devise a perfect game plan—a set of ideas or cognitions dealing with what the team should do. In theory, the team members know what they are supposed to do to win (latent learning). But what ultimately will decide the contest is not their understanding, but their performance. In sports, this is called execution. Knowing what to do and doing it are often two different things.

Before You Go On
▼▼▼▼▼▼▼▼▼▼

What is learned when one forms a cognitive map?

What is latent learning?

▶ Social Learning Theory and Modeling

social learning theory the theory that learning takes place through observation and imitation of others

Albert Bandura's approach to learning is also cognitive in nature, but it adds a decidedly social flavor to the process and for that reason is referred to as **social learning theory** (Bandura, 1974; 1977; 1982). His thesis is that learning often takes place through the observation and the imitation of models. What makes social learning theory *social* is the notion that we learn from others. What makes it *cognitive* is that what is learned through observation or modeling are changes in cognition that may never be expressed as behavior nor be directly reinforced.

The classic demonstration of observational learning was reported in 1963 by Bandura, Ross, and Ross. For this demonstration, 96 preschoolers were randomly assigned to one of four experimental conditions. One group of children observed an adult model act aggressively toward an inflated plastic "Bobo" doll toy (Figure 6.9). The adult model vigorously attacked the doll. Children in the second group watched the same aggressive behaviors directed toward the "Bobo" doll, but in a movie, not live and in person. The third group watched a cartoon version of the same behaviors, this time performed by a cartoon cat. Children in the fourth group comprised the control group and did not watch anyone interact with "Bobo" dolls, either live or on film.

Figure 6.9

 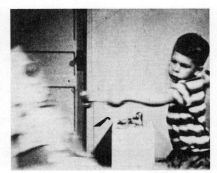 

▲ In Albert Bandura's classic study, children who watched adults behave aggressively toward the "Bobo" doll displayed the same sort of behavior themselves. The children learned aggressive behavior through observation

Then the test began. Each child (tested individually) was given new and interesting toys to play with, but only for a brief time. The child was then led to another room that contained fewer, older, and less interesting toys——including a small version of the inflated "Bobo" doll. Each child was left alone in the room while researchers watched the child's behavior. The children did not know they were being observed.

There was no doubt that the children who had seen the aggressive behaviors of the model—whether live, on film, or in cartoon form—were themselves more aggressive in their play than were the children who did not have the observational experience. Children from each of the first three experimental conditions attacked the "Bobo" doll. What's more, they attacked it in the same vigorous, stereotyped sort of way the model had.

According to social learning theory, the children in the first three groups learned simply by observing. But as we saw with latent learning, the learning was separated from performance. The children had no opportunity to imitate what they had learned (to perform) until they had a "Bobo" doll of their own. The learning that took place during observation was symbolic, or cognitive.

Later studies have shown that reinforcement and punishment *can* play a significant part in observational learning. For example, a new twist was added to an experiment that basically replicated the one just described. The difference was that after attacking the "Bobo" doll, adult models were either rewarded or punished for their behavior. As you might guess, children who saw the model being punished for attacking the doll engaged in very little aggressive behavior toward their own dolls. Children who saw the model's behavior of attacking the doll get reinforced, acted aggressively, imitating the model's behaviors in considerable detail (Bandura, 1965).

The application of this sort of data is straightforward. For example, most of Bandura's research suggests that children can and do learn all sorts of potentially inappropriate behavior by watching TV. Our concern, however, should be reserved for those occasions where inappropriate behaviors are left unpunished. So long as children are exposed to the consequences of the inappropriate behaviors, they will be less likely to imitate them. This logic suggests that it would be most unfortunate for one of a child's TV heroes to get away with murder, much less be rewarded for doing so. Also, reinforced behaviors of valued models are more likely to be imitated than punished behaviors of less valued models (see, for example, Bandura, 1965).

Learning about the consequences of one's behaviors by observing the consequences of someone else's behavior is called **vicarious reinforcement** or **vicarious punishment**. Our own experiences reflect the useful ness of these concepts. Aren't you much more likely to imitate the behaviors of a person who is rewarded for his or her efforts than you are to imitate the

vicarious reinforcement (or punishment) increasing the rate (with reinforcement) or decreasing the rate (with punishment) of responses due to observing the consequences of someone else's behaviors

behaviors of someone who gets punished? A child does not have to burn her fingers in a fire to learn to avoid the fireplace. Watching someone else get burned (or pretending to get burned) will usually suffice (Domjan, 1987).

In fact, learning through observation and imitation is a common form of human learning. Your television on any Saturday provides many examples, particularly if you watch a PBS station. All day long there are people (models) trying to teach us how to paint landscapes, build solar energy devices, do aerobic exercises, improve our golf game, remodel the basement, replace a carburetor, or prepare a low-calorie meal. The basic message is "Here, watch me; see how I do it. Then try it yourself."

Before You Go On
▼▼▼▼▼▼▼▼

Summarize the basic concepts of social learning theory and modeling.

▼▼▼
Thinking Critically about Learning

1. Psychologists say that few, if any, human behaviors are unlearned or instinctive. What would it take to demonstrate a human instinct? In other words, what criteria would we need to show that a human behavior was not learned?

2. Psychologists claim that the stimuli in our environment that produce fearful reactions in us do so largely because of learning—classical conditioning in particular. What stimuli can you think of that elicit fearfulness without the benefit of any previous learning?

3. We've spent a lot of time in this chapter talking about dogs and rats. To what extent are the learning experiences of dogs and rats relevant to the learning experiences of humans?

4. If by some stroke of good fortune, "Little Albert" were still alive, do you suppose that he would still be afraid of white rats and other white, furry things? Why or why not?

5. See if you can find ten examples of advertisers using classical conditioning to try to change your attitude about some product or service. I think you'll be surprised how easy it is.

6. Think about the issue of "awareness" and reinforcement. Can reinforcers work if you don't realize that you're being reinforced? Will reinforcement work if you do realize that someone is purposively reinforcing you? (Think back to the opening story of the psychology professor conditioned to stand in the corner. To what extent was he "aware" of what was happening to him?)

7. We say that gambling devices, such as slot machines are scheduled to "pay off," or reinforce the user's behavior on a variable ratio schedule. Can you imagine what it would be like to find a slot machine programmed to pay off on a fixed ratio schedule? a fixed interval schedule? a variable interval schedule?

8. Psychologists often make the argument that there is no justification for ever using physical punishment (slapping, spanking, etc.) with children. Why would they make such an argument, and if one doesn't use physical punishment, what alternatives are there?

9. How can you apply what you have learned in this chapter to help you study psychology—or any other class you may be taking?

Summary

▼▼▼▼▼▼▼▼▼▼▼▼▼▼▼▼▼▼▼▼▼▼▼▼▼▼▼

How do we define learning? Learning is demonstrated by a relatively permanent change in behavior that occurs as the result of practice or experience. We define "conditioning" similarly, as it is a basic form of learning. *Pages 196–197*

Summarize the essential procedures involved in classical conditioning. In classical, or Pavlovian, conditioning, a neutral stimulus that originally does not elicit a response of interest is paired with an unconditioned stimulus (UCS), one that reflexively and reliably produces an unconditioned response (UCR). As a result of this pairing, the once-neutral stimulus becomes a conditioned stimulus (CS) and elicits a conditioned response (CR) that is the same kind of response as the original UCR. *Page 198*

In classical conditioning, what are acquisition, extinction, and spontaneous recovery? In classical conditioning, acquisition is an increase in the strength of the CR that occurs as the CS and the UCS continue to be presented together, whereas extinction is a decrease in the strength of the CR when the CS is repeatedly presented without being paired with the UCS. Spontaneous recovery is demonstrated by the return of the CR after extinction and then a rest interval. *Page 200*

In classical conditioning, what are generalization and discrimination? In generalization, we find that a response (CR) conditioned to a specific stimulus (CS) will also be elicited by similar stimuli. The more similar the new stimuli are to the original CS, the greater the CR. In many ways, discrimination is the opposite of generalization. It is a matter of learning to make a CR in response to a specific CS that is paired with the UCS, while learning not to make a CR in response to other stimuli not paired with the UCS. *Page 201*

What sort of responses are most readily influenced by classical conditioning? Classical conditioning has its most noticeable effect on emotion and mood, or affect. Most of the stimuli to which we respond emotionally probably have been classically conditioned to elicit those responses. *Page 202*

Briefly summarize the Little Albert demonstration. In the Watson and Rayner 1920 "Little Albert" study, a sudden loud noise (the UCS) was paired with the originally neutral stimulus of a white rat. As a result, Albert came to display a learned fear response (a CR) to the rat. The conditioned fear generalized to similar stimuli. This demonstration has been used to "explain" learned emotional reactions to events in our environment. *Pages 203–205*

Under what circumstances are stimuli likely to serve effectively as CSs? Pavlov and many others believed that any stimulus could serve effectively as a conditioned stimulus if it were paired repeatedly with an unconditioned stimulus (UCS). We now believe this to be an oversimplification. Stimuli that are most effective as CSs are those that most reliably predict or signal the occurrence of the UCS. Stimuli are effective conditioned stimuli only if they provide useful information to the organism, *e.g.,* "a shock is going to follow this tone." *Pages 205–206*

What is the essence of operant conditioning? Operant conditioning is the type of learning in which the rate or probability of a response is changed as a result of its consequences. Reinforced responses increase in rate, while nonreinforced responses decrease in rate. *Page 207*

What is shaping, and how does it work? Shaping is a procedure used in operant conditioning to establish a response that then can be reinforced—that is, to get the response we are interested in to occur in the first place. We shape a response by reinforcing successive approximations to that response. *Page 210*

Describe acquisition, extinction, and spontaneous recovery as they occur in operant conditioning. In operant conditioning, acquisition is produced by reinforcing a desired response so that its rate will increase. Extinction is the phenomenon of decreasing the rate of a response (to return to baseline levels) by withholding reinforcement. After a rest interval, a previously extinguished response will return at a rate above baseline; that is, in the same situation, it will spontaneously return or recover. *Pages 210–211*

Provide an operational definition of reinforcement. In general, reinforcement is a process that increases the rate or probability of the response that it follows. *Page 211*

Distinguish between a positive and a negative reinforcer. A positive reinforcer increases the rate of the response that precedes its presentation. A negative reinforcer increases the rate of the response that precedes its removal or termination. *Page 212*

Compare and contrast primary and secondary reinforcers, providing examples of each. Primary reinforcers are stimuli that are in some way biologically important or related to the organism's survival, such as food for a hungry organism or warm shelter for a cold organism. Secondary reinforcers increase the rate of a response because of the organism's previous learning history. That is, secondary reinforcers, such as praise, money, letter grades, or promotions, are acquired reinforcers. *Page 213*

Define FR, FI, VR, and VI intermittent schedules of reinforcement. Intermittent schedules of reinforcement provide a reinforcer for less than every response. The FR (fixed-ratio) schedule calls for a reinforcer after a set number of responses (*e.g.*, one reinforcer after every five responses). A VR (variable-ratio) schedule randomly changes the ratio of reinforcers to responses, but maintains some given ratio as an average. The FI (fixed-interval) schedule calls for the administration of a reinforcer for the first response following a specified time interval. A VI (variable-interval) schedule calls for a reinforcer for the first response following a time interval whose length is varied. In general, responses reinforced by fixed schedules are more resistant to extinction than are responses that have been reinforced every time (a CRF, or continuous reinforcement schedule). Responses acquired under variable schedules of reinforcement are even more resistant to extinction than those acquired under fixed schedules. *Pages 214–215*

What is a punisher? A punisher is a stimulus that decreases the rate or probability of a response that it follows. *Pages 216–217*

How can punishers be used effectively? Punishers can be effective in suppressing a response when they are strong enough and delivered right after the response to be punished. Fear, anxiety, aggression and an overall suppression of activity may accompany punishment,

which in itself provides no information about what an organism *should* do in a given situation. Punishing one response should therefore be paired with the reinforcement of another, more appropriate response. *Pages 216–217*

In the context of operant conditioning, what are generalization and discrimination? In operant conditioning, generalization occurs when a response reinforced in the presence of one stimulus also occurs in the presence of other, similar stimuli. Discrimination, on the other hand, is a matter of differential reinforcement—reinforcing responses to some stimuli while extinguishing responses to other (inappropriate) stimuli. *Pages 217–219*

What is learned when one forms a cognitive map? According to Tolman, when one forms a cognitive map, one develops a mental representation (or picture) of one's surroundings—an appreciation of general location and where significant objects are located. *Pages 219–221*

What is latent learning? The formation of cognitive maps can be seen as a type of latent learning. That is, latent learning is the acquisition of information (an internal, cognitive process) that may not be demonstrated in performance until later, if at all. *Page 220*

Summarize the basic concepts of social learning theory and modeling. Bandura's social learning theory emphasizes the role of observation of others and imitation in the acquisition of cognitions and behaviors. We often learn by imitating models through vicarious reinforcement and punishment. *Pages 221–223*

6.1 To say that learning is demonstrated by changes in behavior is to suggest that   a) if we cannot remember something, we did not learn it in the first place.   b) some changes in behavior do not last very long, or are cyclical.   c) the only way we can be sure if someone learned something is to ask them.   d) learning is an internal process that is inferred from performance. *Page 196*

6.2 Which of the following ideas is NOT found in our definition of learning?   a) Changes in behavior due to learning must be relatively permanent.   b) learning involves making good and proper adjustments and adaptations to the environment.   c) For changes to be classified as learned, they must result from practice or experience.   d) Learning cannot be measured or observed directly. *Page 197*

6.3 As Pavlov noted, when a dog is first brought to the laboratory, stood on a table, and a bell is sounded, the first thing we will notice is   a) an orienting reflex.   b) an unconditioned stimulus.   c) habituation or acclimation.   d) no response by the dog. *Page 198*

6.4 True or False?   Ivan Pavlov won a Nobel Prize for psychology in 1902. *Page 198*

6.5 True or False?   In a demonstration of classical conditioning, the unconditioned response occurs without any previous learning experience. *Page 198*

The next three items involve the following situation: A dog is exposed to the sound of a bell until it comes to ignore it. Now, soon after the bell is sounded, a shock is delivered to the front left paw of the dog. When it is shocked, the dog quickly lifts its foot. This procedure is repeated 12 times.

6.6 What is likely to be the response when the bell is sounded now?   a) A UCS will occur.   b) A UCR will occur.   c) A CR will occur.   d) Nothing will happen. *Page 198*

6.7 In this example of conditioning, the UCR is ___ and the CR is ___.   a) shock; foot withdrawal   b) shock; a bell   c) a bell; an orienting reflex   d) foot withdrawal; foot withdrawal. *Page 199*

6.8 If the bell were to be sounded alone (no more shock) for a few dozen presentations, what is likely to occur?   a) extinction   b) generalization   c) acquisition   d) spontaneous recovery. *Page 200*

6.9 Which process is essentially the opposite of generalization?   a) discrimination   b) reinforcement   c) acquisition   d) habituation. *Page 201*

6.10 Although each of these responses or behaviors is learned, which most clearly results from classical conditioning?   a) typing or keyboard skills   b) feeling relief at realizing that a class period is about over   c) understanding the difference between a CS and a UCS   d) speaking the language you do rather than a different one. *Page 202*

6.11 With "Little Albert" as their subject, John Watson and Rosalie Rayner demonstrated each of the following EXCEPT: a) generalization.   b) classical conditioning.   c) extinction.   d) a learned and unlearned stimulus for fear. *Page 203*

6.12 A stimulus will serve as a most effective CS if: a) it is repeatedly presented after the presentation of the UCS.   b) it naturally produces an orienting reflex.   c) its presentation reliably predicts the UCS.   d) it is repeatedly paired with an appropriate CR. *Page 206*

6.13 The basic thrust or premise of operant conditioning is that   a) under the proper circumstances, any organism can learn to make any response.   b) organisms learn to make responses that are only in their own best interest.   c) behaviors are shaped or controlled by their consequences.   d) people learn only if they want to learn. *Page 207*

6.14 If operant conditioning is successful, what is most likely to be changed?   a) the rate or probability of a response   b) cognitive representations of the organism   c) the stimuli that produced the learned response   d) the strength or nature of a response. *Page 207*

6.15 True or False?   Skinner stated the law of effect after observing rats (and pigeons) in his operant chambers. *Page 208*

6.16 A rat in an operant chamber is given a pellet of food each time it depresses a lever. After 100 pellets have been provided for lever-pressing, the rat no longer gets a pellet when it depresses the lever. What is most likely to occur?   a) The lever-pressing response will decrease.   b) The rat will become frustrated, anxious, and aggressive.   c) The rat will continue to press the lever at the same rate.   d) The rat's operant rate will spontaneously recover. *Page 210*

6.17 You want to reinforce Mickey for hanging his coat in the closet, but he never does so; he simply drops his coat on the floor as he walks through the door. What procedure would be most effective?   a) physical punishment   b) discrimination learning   c) stimulus generalization   d) shaping. *Page 210*

6.18 True or False?   Shaping is an operant conditioning technique accomplished by the method of successive approximations. *Page 210*

6.19 The major difference between positive and negative reinforcement is whether   a) something is given or taken away   b) rates of responding go up or down.   c) responses are rewarded or punished.   d) reinforcers are innate or learned. *Page 212*

6.20 Which of the following provides the best example of negative reinforcement?   a) paying Billy a dollar for every A or B on his report card   b) having a root canal procedure to ease the pain of a severe toothache   c) spanking Amy for playing with the water in the toilet bowl   d) using play money to modify the behaviors of a retarded child. *Page 212*

6.21 True or False?   Using a "token economy" means that one is using negative reinforcers. *Page 213*

6.22 Using each of the following reinforcement schedules, rats are trained to press levers at a high rate. The lever-pressing of rats trained on a _____ schedule will now extinguish most quickly.   a) continuous   b) fixed-ratio   c) fixed-interval   d) variable-interval. *Page 214*

6.23 Which statement regarding punishment is most justified?   a) Because it creates anxiety, it never should be used.   b) Physical punishment is more effective than psychological.   c) Punishment is only effective if it has been threatened repeatedly.   d) Punishment decreases the rate of responses it follows. *Page 216*

6.24 True or False?   You may punish responses even when you are trying to reinforce them. *Page 216*

6.25 In operant conditioning, discrimination training is mostly a matter of   a) learning right from wrong.   b) discovering the difference between reinforcement and punishment.   c) differential reinforcement.   d) extinction followed by spontaneous recovery. *Page 218*

6.26 In general, cognitive approaches to learning tend to emphasize   a) the interaction of genetics and experience.   b) knowing ahead of time what will serve as a reinforcer.   c) changes inside the organism that may not result in changes in behavior.   d) the role of learning in the acquisition of emotional responses. *Page 219*

6.27 If learning is latent, it is by definition: a) of no value to the learner.   b) not (yet) reflected in behavior.   c) learned, but not remembered.   d) displayed only in social situations. *Page 220*

6.28 True or False?   Because cognitive maps require a certain degree of intelligence, only humans are capable of forming them. *Page 220*

6.29 Of the following, what is it that makes Bandura's social learning theory social?   a) The fact that it is a cognitive approach to learning.   b) The concepts of vicarious reinforcement and/or punishment.   c) It requires that learning result from practice or experience.   d) The fact that it can only be found in humans and not in nonhumans. *Page 221*

Chapter 7 ▼▼▼▼▼ *Memory*

▲▲▲▲▲▲ _____

You have been studying your psychology text for nearly three hours and decide to put into practice what you have been reading about operant conditioning. You decide to reinforce your good, concentrated efforts by having a pizza. Furthermore, you decide to have the pizza delivered. (You just learned this afternoon that Pizza City now delivers free of charge.) Never having called Pizza City before, you have no idea what their telephone number is, so you turn to the yellow pages. You scan the yellow pages looking for their number. There it is: 555-5897. You repeat the number to yourself as you contemplate your choices of toppings—555-5897. Confident that you know the number, you close the phone book and return it to the desk drawer. You easily dial the number without error—555-5897. Buzzz-buzzz-buzzz. Darn, the line's busy! Well, no problem, you'll call back in a minute or so.

Just as you hang up the phone, the front door bell rings. "Now who can that be?" you wonder. It's the paper boy coming to collect for your daily newspaper. He claims that you owe him $11.40 for the past two weeks' deliveries. Discovering that you don't have enough cash on hand to pay for the newspaper *and* the pizza you want to have, you write a personal check for the paper. "Let's see, today's date. What *is* today's date? Oh, yes, April 17th; 4/17. Now, how much did you say I owed you? Oh yes, $11.40—plus a dollar tip comes to $12.40. This is check number 1079; I'd better write that down: check #1079...$12.40...newspaper. There you go; thanks a lot. Have a nice day."

The paper boy leaves. You return to your studying and then suddenly recall that you were going to order a pizza. Only 5 or 6 minutes have passed since you called Pizza City and got a busy signal. Maybe you'll have better luck this time. As you pick up the phone and go to dial Pizza City, however, you cannot for the life of you remember their phone number. Back to the desk drawer; back to the yellow pages to look it up again.

This experience demonstrates the action and a limitation of a common type of human memory. Pizza City's phone number was in your memory—at least it was stored there briefly. You remembered the number long enough to dial it once. But, unable to rehearse the number (and not thinking to write it down for future use), when you needed it again, just a few minutes later, you discovered that the number was no longer accessible. In this chapter, we'll see several examples of how useful, and limiting, this type of "short-term memory" is in our everyday experiences. There are, after all, many pieces of information that we really want to remember only for the "short term," and not store away for great lengths of time.

By the way, right now, without looking back, can you recall the telephone number of Pizza City?

It is nearly impossible to imagine what life would be like without memory. For one thing, this sentence would make no sense. Without your memory, you would have no idea of what a textbook is or why you had it open in front of you. The black patterns of print that you now recognize as words would appear as no more than random marks. In fact, without memory we would have no idea of who we are. All of those things that define us as individuals—feelings, beliefs, experiences, behaviors, moods, and attitudes—are stored away somehow in our memories.

Over the past 30 years, there have been many significant changes in the way that psychologists think about memory. We now are prepared to accept the notion that memory may not be just one unified structure or process; there may be several types or levels of memory processing. Another change in thinking about memory reflects the idea that memory is not simply a passive receptacle of information. The use of memory is now viewed as an active process, whereby information is actively processed into memory, stored there, and then actively retrieved.

We'll begin our discussion by considering how information is processed and stored in three different kinds of memory: sensory memory, short-term memory and long-term memory. Then we will take up the practical matter of retrieval—the process of getting information out of memory once it has been stored there. We'll see how memory retrieval can be measured, as well as the factors that influence whether retrieval is successful.

▶ *Memory: Some Basic Terms*

Memory was once considered simple and straightforward, merely as a passive storehouse of information. There was thought to be just one kind of memory that either worked when we wanted it to (when we remembered), or failed (when we forgot). Using it was seen as an automatic process. Psychologists, following the tradition of the ancient Greeks, viewed memory as being like a block of wax. No one ever really believed we have wax in our heads, but the metaphor seemed workable. Experiences make impressions in the wax. Sometimes the wax is soft and malleable, and the impressions (memory) are good and clear. Sometimes the wax is hard, and memories are only faint and imperfect impressions of one's experiences. The Greeks also recognized individual differences in memory, claiming that some people were born with larger and softer blocks of wax than others (Adams, 1980).

It is now more common to think of memory as the final step in a series of cognitive activities related to information processing. This view of memory claims that complex cognitive processes, such as remembering and forgetting, can be best understood as a series of simpler, associated functions. The basic thrust is as follows: We are born into this world knowing very little about it. By the time we are adults, we know an incredible number of things. Much of the information we have stored away may be trivial and irrelevant, but much of it is essential for survival. How do our minds come to be filled with so much information? As we first noted in Chapter 3, the processing of information begins with sensation, when our sensory receptors are stimulated. Through perception, information from our senses is selected and organized. With memory, we form a record of the information we have processed.

Thus, **memory** can be thought of as the capacity to encode, store, and retrieve information. Using memory is a complex cognitive process involving

memory the cognitive ability to encode, store and retrieve information

encoding the active process of representing, or putting information into memory

storage the process of holding encoded information in memory

retrieval the process of locating, removing, and using information that is stored in memory

three interrelated stages. The first puts information *into* memory, a process called **encoding**. To encode information, stimuli are represented in the nervous system. Encoding is the process of forming a cognitive representation of information. Once that representation is in memory, we then must keep it there. This process is called **storage**. To use stored information, we need to get it out again, a process of **retrieval**. Memory, then, involves the cognitive processes of encoding, storing, and retrieving information.

Modern theories view memory as being more than one simple process. That is, not all of the information that gets into memory necessarily gets encoded or stored in the same way or in the same place. It is useful to think about three different types of memory: sensory memory, short-term memory, and long-term memory. For each type of memory, we'll have the same questions: How does this memory receive information? What is its capacity, or how much information can be held there? What is its duration, or for how long will information be held there without further processing? In what form is information held in this memory?

Before You Go On
▼▼▼▼▼▼▼▼

How do we define memory?

▶ *Sensory Memory*

sensory memory the type of memory that holds large amounts of information registered at the senses for very brief periods of time

Sensory memory stores large amounts of information for very short periods of time (a few seconds or less). The concept of a very brief sensory memory is a strange one, but it has a place in information processing models. All of the information that gets stored in our memories first enters through our senses. Simply put, to be able to recall what a lecturer says, you first must be in class to hear that lecture. In order to remember a drawing from this book, the image of the drawing first must stimulate your visual system. You can't remember the aroma of fried onions if you've never smelled them in the first place.

The basic idea of a sensory memory is that information does not pass directly through our sensory systems; instead, it is held in sensory memory for a brief period of time. Even after a stimulus has left our environment and is no longer physically present, it has left its imprint, having formed a sensory memory.

The *capacity* of sensory memory seems, at least in theory, to be very large indeed. At one time it was believed that we are able to keep as much in our sensory memory as our sense receptors can respond to at one time. Such claims may give sensory memory more credit than it is due. Sensory memory can hold more information than we can attend to, but there may be limits on its capacity.

The practical problem with sensory memory lies in its *duration*. We may be able to get vast amounts of information into our sensory memory, but we cannot keep it there (storage) very long. What *is* the duration of sensory memory? It's difficult to say exactly, but memories stay in sensory storage only very briefly—about 0.5 seconds for visually presented materials (Sperling, 1960; 1963), perhaps for as long as 3 to 10 seconds for orally presented information (Cowan, 1984; Darwin, et al., 1972; Massaro, 1975). It certainly won't be of much help for your next psychology exam to process information to this memory and no further.

Sensory memory is viewed as a rather mechanical or physical type of storage. The information stored there cannot be acted upon. You can't *do* anything with it. Information is *not encoded* in sensory memory—you have to take the information in your sensory memory pretty much as your receptors deliver it. It's as if stimuli from the environment make an impression on our sensory systems and then rapidly fade or are replaced by new stimuli.

Here are two examples that demonstrate sensory memory in action. In a dark area, stand about 20 feet away from a friend who is pointing a flashlight at you. Have your friend swing the flashlight around in a small circle, making about one revolution per second. What do you see? Your experience is that of a circle of light. At any one instant, you're seeing where the light *is,* and you are also experiencing, from your sensory memory, where the light *has just been.* If your friend moves the flashlight slowly, you see a "tail" of light following it, but you won't see a circle any more because the image of the light's position will have decayed from sensory memory. Our experience of motion when we view motion pictures also involves sensory memory. The film being projected is actually made up of a series of still pictures, each one slightly different from the last. Because we can hold a short series of projected pictures in our sensory memories we can construct the impression of motion in our minds.

Does this sound familiar? Someone asks you a question to which your reply is, "Huh? What did you say?" Then, before the person gets a chance to repeat her question, you answer it. (Which may in turn provoke a response such as "Why didn't you answer me in the first place?") Perhaps you didn't clearly hear all of the question that you were asked, but while it was still reverberating (echoing) in your sensory memory, you listened to it again and formed your answer.

As I said, this notion of a sensory memory as the very brief storage of large amounts of minimally processed information is an odd one. There is evidence that sensory memory is a real phenomenon, at least for vision and audition. We may not be aware of its usefulness in any practical sort of way, but perhaps that extra fraction of a second or two of storage in sensory memory provides us with the time we need to attend to information so that we can then move it further along into our memory.

Before You Go On
▼▼▼▼▼▼▼▼▼

Summarize the adolescent's search for identity as described by Erikson.

▶ Short-Term Memory (STM)

Once information gets to sensory memory, where does it go next? Most of it rapidly fades or is replaced by new stimuli. With a little effort, however, we can process material from our sensory memories more fully by moving it to **short-term memory (STM)**. Short-term memory has a limited capacity and, without the benefit of rehearsal, a brief duration.

To encode information into STM requires that we pay attention to it. It can be viewed as something like a workbench or desk top where we can use and manipulate the information to which we pay attention (*e.g.,* Baddeley, 1982). Information can get into STM directly from our sensory memory, or it can be retrieved from our long-term memory. Attending to information moves it into STM. The capacity of short-term memory is limited by our

short-term memory (STM) a type of memory with limited capacity (7 ± 2 bits of information) and limited duration (15-20 seconds)

Figure 7.1

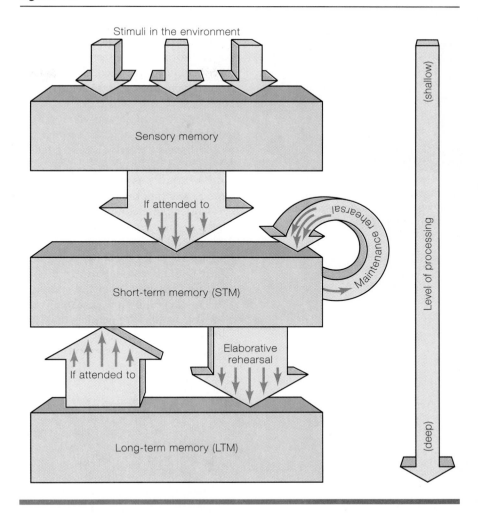

▲ *A simplified model of human memory. See text for description.*

attention span. There are limits on the amount of information to which we can attend in a short period. In Chapter 5, we reviewed many of the factors that guide this process of selective attention.

Figure 7.1 presents a schematic diagram of the model of memory that we are constructing. At the top we have stimuli from the environment impacting on our senses and moving directly into sensory memory. In the middle of the diagram is short-term memory (STM). We see that information from sensory memory *or* from long-term memory can be moved into STM. It will be helpful to refer to this diagram as we continue to expand our model.

Because of its limited duration and capacity, STM sometimes acts like a bottleneck in the processing of information from our senses into long-term storage. Let's see just how limited our short-term memories are.

▶ The Duration of STM

Interest in short-term memory processing can be traced to two experiments reported independently in the late 1950s (Brown, 1958; Peterson & Peterson, 1959). We'll review the Petersons' experiment.

▲ *If we are not interrupted, we can easily hold a telephone number in STM long enough to dial it.*

On a typical trial, a subject is shown three consonants, such as KRW, for 3 seconds. Presenting the letters for 3 seconds assures that they are attended to and, hence, encoded into STM. The person is asked to recall the three letters after retention intervals ranging from 0 to 18 seconds. This doesn't sound like a very difficult task, and it isn't. Anyone can remember three letters for 18 seconds. However, in this experiment, subjects are kept from rehearsing the letters during the retention interval. They are asked to count backward, by threes.

For example, if you were a participant in this sort of experiment, you would be shown a letter sequence, say KRW, and then you immediately would have to start counting backward from, say, 397 by threes, or "397, 394, 391, 388," and so forth. You'd be instructed to do your counting out loud as rapidly as possible. The idea is that the counting task prohibits you from rehearsing the three letters you were just shown.

Under these conditions, your correct recall of the letters depends on the length of the retention interval. If you are asked to name the letters after just a few seconds of counting, you won't do badly. If you have to count for as long as 15 to 20 seconds, your recall of the letters drops to near zero (see Figure 7.2). Because you are distracted by the counting task, and cannot rehearse the letters, they are soon unavailable to you.

This experimental example is not as abstract as it may first appear. All you have to do is remember the little story about ordering pizza from Pizza City at the beginning of this chapter. It presented a somewhat more "real life" example of the Peterson-Brown experiments.

Figure 7.2

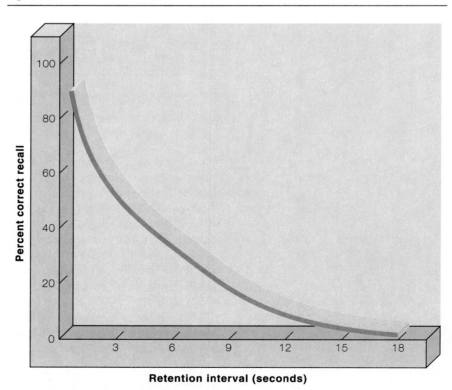

▲ *Recall of letters as a function of retention interval when maintenance rehearsal is minimized. (Peterson & Peterson, 1959)*

▲ *Many mathematical operations require that we use STM to hold information until we can use it in our calculations.*

maintenance rehearsal a process of rote repetition (reattending) to keep information in STM

One way in which we can increase the duration of short-term memory is to rehearse the information stored there. This kind of rehearsal is called **maintenance rehearsal**, and amounts to little more than a simple repetition of the information already in STM. To get material into STM (encoding), we attend to it. By repeating that material over and over (as we might if we wanted to remember a telephone number until we could dial it), we are reattending to it with each repetition.

As a rule of thumb, we can say that unrehearsed material will stay in STM for about 15 to 20 seconds. Experiments like that of the Petersons also tell us is that once in short-term memory, some information may become unavailable almost immediately, and it may take 20 seconds for all of it to be lost. That's better than sensory memory, but short-term memory, by itself, still won't help much when it comes to taking an exam next week.

At least the duration of STM is long enough to allow us to use it in everyday activities. Usually, we only want to remember a phone number long enough to dial it. Seldom do we feel the need to make a permanent record of a telephone number. Using STM in mathematical computations is another good example. Multiply 28 by 6 without paper and pencil. "Let's see. Eight times 6 is 48. Now I have to keep the 8 and carry the 4." Stop right there. Where do you "keep the 8" and where do you store the 4 until it is needed? Right. In your STM. And, for that matter, where did the notion that 8 x 6 = 48 come from in the first place? Where did the notion of what "multiply" means come from? How did *this* information get into STM? Right, again. This is an example of information entering STM, not from the outside through your senses, but from long-term storage (see Figure 7.1 again).

Having discussed the duration of short-term memory, let's deal now with its capacity. Just how much information can we hold in STM?

Before You Go On
▼▼▼▼▼▼▼▼▼

For how long is information stored in STM?

What is required to get material into STM and then keep it there?

chunk a somewhat imprecise concept referring to a meaningful unit of information as represented in memory

▶ The Capacity of STM

In 1956, George Miller wrote a charming paper on "the magical number seven, plus or minus two." He argued that the capacity of short-term memories is very small—limited to just 5 to 9 (or 7 ± 2) bits or "chunks" of information.

In the context of short-term memory, the concept of chunk is actually a technical term. A **chunk** is the representation in memory of a meaningful unit of information. The claim is that we can store approximately 7 ± 2 meaningful pieces of information in STM.

We can easily attend to, encode, and store five or six letters in STM. Holding the letters **YRDWIAADEFDNSYE** in your short-term memory would be quite a challenge. Fifteen randomly presented letters exceed the capacity of STM for most of us. What if I asked you to remember the words FRIDAY and WEDNESDAY? Now keeping just these two simple *words* in STM is very easy—even though they contain (the same) 15 letters. Here, you would be storing just two chunks of (meaningful) information, not fifteen. In fact, you easily could store *50* letters in short-term memory if you recoded them into the one meaningful chunk: "Days of the Week."

▲ *Chunking information together while listening to a lecture is an effective way to store it for later study.*

As we all know, we can readily store a telephone number in our short-term memory. Adding an area code makes the task somewhat more difficult because the 10 digits now come fairly close to the upper limit of our STM capacity. Notice, though, how we tend to cluster the digits of a telephone number into a pattern. The digit series 8694935661 is more difficult to deal with as a simple string than when it is seen and encoded as a phone number: (869) 493-5661 (Bower & Springston, 1970). Re-grouping the digits in this way let's us see them in a new, more meaningful way. So, by chunking bits and pieces of information together, we can add meaningfulness and thus extend the apparent capacity of short-term memory.

At best, short-term memory works like a leaky bucket. From the vast storehouse of information available in our sensory memory, we scoop up some (and not much at that) by paying attention to it and hold it for a while until we either use it, maintain it with rehearsal, move it on to long-term storage, or lose it.

Before You Go On

▼▼▼▼▼▼▼▼▼

How much information can be held in STM?

How can chunking affect the capacity of STM?

▶ How Information Is Represented in STM

The material or information stored in our sensory memory is kept there in virtually the same form in which it was presented. Visually presented stimuli are held as visual memories or impressions, auditory stimuli form auditory memories, and so on. Getting information into STM is not such an automatic process. We first have to attend to the material to encode it into short-term memory. How, then, is information stored or represented in STM?

Conrad (1963; 1964) was one of the first to argue that information is stored in STM with an acoustic code. That means that material tends to be processed in terms of how it *sounds*. Conrad's conclusion was based on his interpretation of the errors that subjects make in short-term memory experiments.

For example, in one experiment, he presented a series of letters to his subjects. The letters were presented *visually*, one at a time, and subjects were asked to recall the letters they had just seen. It was not surprising that many errors were made over the course of the experiment. What *was* surprising was that when subjects responded with an incorrect letter, it was very frequently with a letter that *sounded* like the correct one. For example, if subjects were to recall the letter E and failed to do so, they commonly would recall V, G, or T, or a letter that sounded like the E they were supposed to recall. They rarely responded F, which certainly *looks* more like the E they had just seen than does V, G, or T. (By the way, this was true whether the subjects gave their recall orally or in writing.)

It seems then that using short-term memory is a matter of talking to ourselves. No matter how it is presented, we tend to encode information acoustically, the way it sounds. At least that's what the early evidence suggested. Subsequent research has not changed the view that acoustic coding is the most important method of coding in STM. The possibility does exist, however, that some material may be encoded in STM in other ways—visually or semantically (Cooper & Shepard, 1973; Martindale, 1981; Shulman,

1971; 1972; Wickens, 1973). Perhaps the most we can say is that there is a tendency to rely heavily on the acoustic coding of information in short-term memory, but other codes also may be used.

Before You Go On
▼▼▼▼▼▼▼▼▼▼

How is information encoded (represented) in short-term memory?

▶ Long-Term Memory (LTM)

long-term memory (LTM) a type of memory with virtually unlimited capacity and very long, if not limitless, duration

Long-term memory (LTM) is memory as you and I usually think of it—memory for large amounts of information held for long periods of time. As we did for sensory and short-term memory, we'll begin by considering two basic issues: capacity and duration.

Our own experiences tell us that the capacity of long-term memory is huge—virtually limitless. At times we even impress ourselves with the amount of material we have stashed away in LTM. Just how much material can be stored in human memory may never be measured, but we can rest assured that we will never learn so much that there won't be room for more.

For an example of memory's huge capacity, consider an experiment by Standing, Conezio, and Haber (1970). Over the course of five days, they presented 2500 different pictures to subjects and asked them to remember them all. Even a day or so later, subjects correctly identified, from a new collection of pictures, 90 percent of the ones they had seen before. Standing (1973) increased the number of pictures that subjects viewed to 10,000. (As you can imagine, it took a long time simply to view 10,000 pictures.) Again, subjects later correctly recognized more than 90 percent of them.

There seems to be no practical limit to the amount of information we can process (or encode) into long-term memory. (Getting that information out of our memories when we want it is another matter, which we'll get to shortly.) How long will information stay in LTM once it is there? Assuming that you

▲ *The capacity of our long-term memories seems almost limitless, which is especially apparent when we use LTM to play games such as Trivial Pursuit*®.

remain free from disease or injury, you are likely never to forget some information such as your own name or the words to "Happy Birthday."

At the moment, it is impossible even to imagine an experiment that could tell us with any certainty how long our memories remain stored in LTM. One thing we do know is that we often cannot remember things we know we once knew. The issue is *why*. Do we forget because the information is no longer *available* to us in our long-term memories, just not there any more? Or do we forget because we are unable to retrieve the information from LTM, which implies that it is still available, but somehow not *accessible?* Another problem is, "How can we ever be sure that a memory failure is due to the relevant information being unavailable and hence inaccessible under all conceivable conditions rather than just merely being inaccessible under the prevailing conditions?" (Watkins, 1990, p. 330).

Most psychologists believe that once information is processed into LTM, it stays there until we die. In fact, 84 percent of the psychologists who were asked agreed with the statement: "Everything we learn is permanently stored in the mind, although sometimes particular details are not accessible" (Loftus & Loftus, 1980, p. 410).

How pleasant (or, perhaps, unpleasant) it is to think that everything we ever knew, everything that ever happened to us, is still there someplace, ultimately retrievable if we only knew how to get it out. As intriguing as this view may be, there is reason to believe that it is not totally accurate. A review article by Elizabeth and Geoffery Loftus (1980) raised the issue of the relative permanence of long-term memories. The Loftuses reviewed the data supporting the argument for permanence and found that "the evidence in no way confirms the view that all memories are permanent and thus potentially recoverable" (p. 409). They claim that when we think we are remembering specific memories of the long-distant past, we are often reconstructing a reasonable facsimile of the original information from bits and pieces of our past. That is, when we remember something that happened to us a long time ago, we don't recall the events as they actually happened. Instead, we recall a specific detail or two and then *actively reconstruct* a reasonable story, a process which in itself creates new memories.

Now that we have a sense of long-term memory's capacity and duration of storage, we need to address how long-term memories are formed. We'll also see that there may be different types of LTM.

Before You Go On
▼▼▼▼▼▼▼▼▼

Are long-term memories necessarily permanent?

▶ Encoding in LTM: A Matter of Repetition and Rehearsal

We already have seen how simple repetition (maintenance rehearsal) can be used to keep material active in short-term memory. This sort of rehearsal is also one way to move information from STM to LTM. Within limits, the more one repeats a bit of information, the more likely it will be remembered—beyond the limits of short-term memory. Although there *are* circumstances when this is true, in many cases the simple repetition of information is not sufficient to process it into LTM. No, simply attending to information—the essence of repetition—is an inefficient means of encoding information in long-term memory.

elaborative rehearsal a mechanism for processing information into LTM that involves the meaningful manipulation of the information to be remembered

▲ Basic procedures or techniques, such as those required to ride a bicycle, are stored in procedural memory.

▲ The meanings and correct spellings of words are stored in semantic memory.

procedural memory in LTM, the storage area of stimulus-response associations and skilled patterns of responses

semantic memory in LTM, the storage location for vocabulary, facts, simple concepts, rules, and the like are stored

To get information into long-term memory usually requires that we think about it, reorganize it, form images of it, make it meaningful, or relate it to something already in our long-term memories. To get information into LTM we need to process it more fully. We need **elaborative rehearsal**, to use a term proposed by Craik and Lockhart (1972).

Consider a hypothetical experiment in which subjects are to respond to a list of words in a number of different ways. In one case, they are asked to count the number of letters in each word. In another they are to generate a word that rhymes with the one they are reading, and in a third case they are asked to use each word in a sentence. The logic is that in each case, the words were processed more fully as subjects focused on (1) the simple, physical structure of the words, (2) the sounds of the words as they are said aloud, and (3) the meaning of the words, and their role in sentence structure. In such experiments, as processing increases, so does the recall of the subjects (Cermak & Craik, 1979; Craik & Tulving, 1975).

Before You Go On
▼▼▼▼▼▼▼▼

Contrast elaborative rehearsal with maintenance rehearsal as a means of encoding information into long-term memory.

▶ Are There Different Types of Long-Term Memories?

Our own experiences tell us that the information we have stored in LTM can be retrieved in many different forms. We can remember the definitions of words. We can picture or visualize people and events from the past. We can remember the melodies of songs. We can recall how our bodies moved when we first tried to ski or roller skate. It may be that information in long-term memory is processed by different sub-systems or types of LTM. This notion of different LTM systems is a relatively new one in psychology, and as you might expect, there is no general agreement on just what all of the systems within LTM might be (Johnson & Hasher, 1987). Here, we'll briefly review three possible LTM sub-systems.

Endel Tulving suggests that the information we have stored in LTM is of three different types (1972; 1985; 1986). Although the three can and do interact with each other, they are basically different. One type of long-term memory is called **procedural memory**. Procedural memory enables "organisms to retain learned connections between stimuli and responses, including those involving complex stimulus patterns and response chains, and to respond adaptively to the environment" (Tulving, 1985, p. 387). In this memory, we have stored our recollections of learned responses, or chains of responses, to particular stimuli. Also stored here is our collection of patterned responses that we have learned well, such as how to balance and ride a bicycle, how to type, or how to swing a golf club. The memories we have stored here are generally put into use with virtually no effort. For example, at one time in your life, handwriting was difficult at best, as you strained to form letters and words correctly. But by now, your writing skills or procedures are so engrained in procedural memory that you can retrieve the steps involved almost without thinking.

In **semantic memory** we store all our simple concepts, vocabulary, and rules (including the rules that govern our use of language). Here we have stored

▲ Life experiences, mundane and dramatic, are stored in episodic memory.

episodic memory in LTM, the location where life events and experiences are stored

recall a measure of retrieval in which an individual is given the fewest possible cues to retrieval

our knowledge of ourselves and the world in which we live. In a way, our semantic memories are crammed with facts, both important and trivial, such as:

> *Who opened the first psychology laboratory in Leipzig in 1879?*
> *How many stripes are there on the American flag?*
> *Is "Colorless green ideas sleep furiously" a grammatical sentence?*
> *What do dogs eat?*

If we can answer these questions, we have found those answers in our long-term semantic memories.

The third type or system of memory proposed by Tulving is called **episodic memory**. It is here that we store the memories of our life events and experiences. It is a time-related memory, and in a sense, it is autobiographical. For example:

> *What were you doing the day the Challenger space shuttle exploded?*
> *When and where did you learn how to ride a bike?*
> *How did you spend last summer's vacation?i*
> *What did your dog eat yesterday?*

The answers to these sorts of questions are stored in our episodic memories.

Before You Go On
▼▼▼▼▼▼▼▼▼▼

Name and briefly describe three possible systems or types of LTM.

▶ How to Improve Memory: Factors Affecting Retrieval

It is time to turn to the practical matter of reviewing what can be done to help us remember information better than we do. What sorts of factors influence our ability to retrieve information from our long-term memories? In truth, the list of such factors is not a very long one. We will organize our discussion around four different, but interrelated factors: (1) how memory is measured, (2) how encoding strategies influence later retrieval, (3) how encoding or practice is scheduled, and (4) how interference and repression can adversely affect retrieval. Throughout this discussion we will assume that the to-be-remembered information *is* stored in LTM. That is, we will focus only on potential problems of retrieval, not retention.

▶ Factor I: How We Measure Retrieval

One factor affecting the retrieval of information from long-term memory is how one is asked to go about retrieving it. This is one factor over which you and I seldom have much control. In this section we'll see how measuring retrieval by either direct or indirect means can influence retrieval.

Let's design an example to work with. We have subjects come to the laboratory on a given Tuesday to learn a list of 15 randomly chosen words. Some subjects take longer than others, but eventually all of them learn the list. The subjects then report to the laboratory two weeks later when our basic question is: "How many of the words that you learned two weeks ago do you still remember?" How could we find out?

One thing we could do is ask for simple **recall** of the list of words. To do so, we need only provide our research participants with a blank sheet of paper and ask them to write, in any order, as many of the words from the learned list as they can. (Technically, this is "free recall." If we asked subjects to recall the list in the order in which it was presented, we'd be asking for "serial recall.") For recall, we provide the fewest cues to aid the retrieval. We just specify the information we want and essentially say, "Now go into your long-term memory, locate that information, get it out, and write it down." Let's assume that one subject correctly recalls six words.

Suppose that we furnish our subject with a list of 50 words, including those on the previously learned list. We instruct her to "circle the words on this list that you *recognize* from the list you learned two weeks ago." In this case, we are not asking for recall, but for **recognition**, a retrieval task that requires a subject to identify material learned previously. Isn't it likely that our subject will do better on this task? She *recalled* 6 words of the list, so let's say she *recognizes* 11 words. In a way, we now have a slight dilemma. Should we say that our subject remembered 6 words or 11 words? The answer is, "Both or either." Whether our subject remembered 6 words or 11 words depends on how we asked her to go about remembering.

In virtually all cases, retrieval by recognition is superior to retrieval by recall (e.g., Bahrick, 1984; Brown, 1976; Schacter, 1987). Figure 7.3 provides some clear-cut data in support of this point. With recall, we provide minimal retrieval cues; with recognition, we provide maximum cues and ask the subject to identify a stimulus as being one that she or he has seen before (Mandler, 1980).

recognition a measure of retrieval in which an individual is required to identify as familiar material previously learned

Figure 7.3

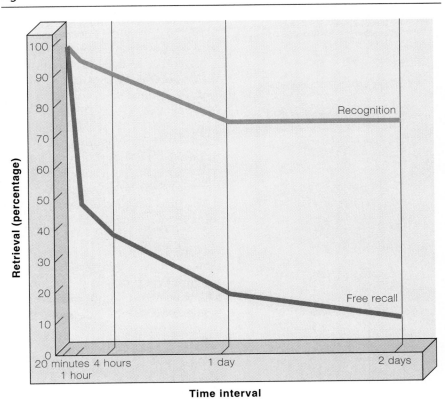

▲ *Two curves demonstrating retrieval for nonsense syllables over a 2-day period. In one case, retrieval is measured with a test for recognition, while the other tests for recall. (From Luh, 1922.)*

▲▲▲▲▲▲▲▲▲▲▲▲▲▲▲

Where do Memories Live?

We may safely assume that memories are stored in our brains. A compelling logic suggests that as information is encoded, stored, and retrieved, there must be changes in the structures or functions of the nervous system. The search for where and how memories are formed within the nervous system is not a new line of research, but within the last decade it has become one of the most exciting and most promising.

Karl Lashley (1890–1958) spent over thirty years trying to find the specific part of the brain in which memories are stored. Lashley taught rats, cats, and monkeys to negotiate all sorts of complex mazes. He then removed, or lesioned (cut) portions of the learner's cerebral cortex. Having destroyed a part of brain, he tested his subjects' memory for the previously learned task. What Lashley found was quite unexpected (1950) and sparked research that still continues. Lashley discovered that specific memories have no specific location in the cerebral cortex. When he looked for a memory area in the brain to lesion, he could not find one. What he found was that the more brain tissue he destroyed, the more impaired the organism's performance, but it *seemed to matter very little where the damage occurred.*

We now recognize some of the limitations of Lashley's studies. For one thing, he studied maze learning—a rather complex set of procedures that involves the interaction of many senses and many muscle groups. Lashley may have been correct about memories for mazes: They may not be stored in any one location. But some memories may be found in certain predictable locations. Individual experiences of sight or sound or touch may be stored in or near the relevant sensory area of the cortex (Squire, 1986; 1987).

Another problem we see in Lashley's work is that it focused only on the cerebral cortex. More recent evidence suggests that lower brain centers are intimately involved in encoding and storing information (*e.g.*, McCormick, et al., 1982; Mishkin & Appenzeller, 1987; Thompson, 1969; 1981; 1986). The lower brain center that has attracted the most attention is the *hippocampus.* Brain surgery on one individual known to us only as "H.M.", prompted this attention (Milner, 1959).

H.M. suffered from epilepsy. For almost 11 years, he experienced an average of one large convulsive attack and several partial seizures each day. It was decided that drastic treatment was needed. Parts of the temporal lobes would be cut, and the hippocampus would be removed from both sides of H.M.'s brain. The surgery was remarkably successful: epileptic seizures became rare. Sensory, perceptual, and intellectual functioning remained intact. But, there were disastrous effects on H.M.'s memory. He could not form new long-term memories. He clearly remembered what he had known before the surgery. Failure to recall events before the surgery would have meant a diagnosis of *retrograde* (backward-acting) *amnesia.*

What if one of the subjects in our hypothetical example came back to the laboratory two weeks after memorizing a list of words and could neither recall nor recognize any of the items? We might be a bit surprised, but we could be wrong if we assumed that our subject retained nothing. What if we ask this subject to relearn the list of 15 words? Two weeks ago it took the subject 10 trials, or presentations of the list, before she learned the words. Now, relearning the same list, we find it takes only seven trials. This is a common finding in memory research.

No, this was not the problem. H.M. had *anterograde* (forward-acting) *amnesia*—the inability to form new long-term memories. H.M. could not form lasting memories for events that occurred after his surgery.

H.M. could read a magazine over and over, responding to it each time as if it were for the first time. When asked what year it was, he would answer "1953"—the year in which his surgery was performed. With great effort, he could memorize a 3-digit number for a short time, but if he were distracted, the number would be lost. After his surgery, H.M. had only a short-term memory. His experiences provide impressive evidence that the hippocampus is involved in the formation of long-term memories (Milner, 1965; Corkin, 1984; Milner, Corkin & Teuber, 1968). Additional research has confirmed that the hippocampus is involved in moving memories from short-term to long-term storage (Mishkin & Appenzeller, 1987; Squire, 1982).

When information is encoded as a memory, changes take place in the central nervous system. In humans, most of those changes occur in the brain, many in the cerebral cortex. What sorts of changes take place as memories are formed? What is changed, and how? You can anticipate my response: Answers to these questions are not yet available, and what hints we do have suggest that the processes involved are incredibly complex.

By the 1970s, the best guess was that evidence for memory formation could be found by examining changes at the synapse (Bartus, et al., 1982; Deutsch, 1973; Kandel & Schwartz, 1982; Matthies, 1989; McNaughton & Morris, 1987). The argument that emerges from the research—most of it done with simple, nonhuman animals—is that with repetition, the flow of impulses across synapses becomes easier and easier, as if synapses become more efficient with practice.

If memories are formed because experience allows certain neurotransmitters to work more effectively at the synaptic level, then what would happen if something disrupted the action of those neurotransmitters? Memories formed at synapses that used those neurotransmitters would be disrupted. The neurotransmitters most often involved in studies like these are acetylcholine (ACh) and serotonin.

A slightly different line of research claims that experience does not increase, or alter in any way, the neurotransmitter released at synapses. What matters, some scientists argue, are changes in the postsynaptic membrane. The most common changes are thought to be increases in the number of effective receptor sites (e.g., Lynch & Baudry, 1984). As synapses are used and used again, the number of receptor sites increases, and this makes for more efficient use of the synapse.

So, what can we conclude for the moment? We can be reasonably sure that forming memories involves making some synaptic transmissions easier than they once were. What remains to be determined is whether changes at the synapse involve changes in the amount of neurotransmitter present, or physical changes in the neuronal membranes involved to allow existing neurotransmitters to function more effectively.

relearning a measure of memory in which one notes an improvement in performance when material is learned for a second time

Relearning almost always takes less effort or time than did original learning, and the difference is attributed to the advantage provided by one's memory of the original learning.

Because relearning does not require that a subject directly retrieve any information from memory, it is referred to as an indirect, or *implicit* test of memory retention (Graf & Schacter, 1985). Implicit tests of memory have become an active area of research in cognitive psychology (Richardson-Klavehn & Bjork, 1988; Roediger, 1990; Schacter, 1987). Among other things, research on implicit memory supports the hypothesis that information may be stored in different types of long-term memory.

Although we may think of the relearning of verbal materials, such as words, as an indirect measure of memory, most tests of implicit retention focus on *procedural memories*. Procedural memories include the storage of "knowing how to go about doing things," such as tying a shoelace, typing, speaking, or riding a bicycle.

Procedural memories may be very resistant to destruction. Patients who suffer from amnesia show significantly poorer performance on explicit tests of memory, such as recall or recognition tasks, but may perform as well as nonamnesic persons on implicit measures of memory (Warrington & Weiskrantz, 1968; 1970). This finding has been replicated many times (see Shimamura, 1986).

What this means is that even in the worst of amnesia cases, some long-term procedural memories may be maintained. Remember the last time you heard about a victim of retrograde amnesia (in which memories of past experiences seem to be forgotten). Typically, we hear about some adult found wandering about, totally unaware of who he is, where he came from, or how he got there. There seems to be no *direct* recollection of any long-term memories. But have you noticed that such amnesia patients *do* demonstrate all sorts of long-term memories? They remember how to talk. They remember how to eat. They remember how to get dressed. They remember, in short, those behavior patterns stored in their procedural memory.

Before You Go On

How do recall and recognition measures affect our assessment of retrieval?

What are implicit tests of retention, and what do they tell us about long-term memory?

▶ Factor II: How We Encode Information

I have made the point before that encoding, storage, and retrieval are interrelated memory processes. In this section, we'll explore the relations that exist between retrieval and encoding. The issue is quite simple: If you do not encode information appropriately, you will have difficulty retrieving it. You cannot recall my mother's maiden name because you never encoded or stored it in the first place. You've never heard my mother's maiden name before, but you *have* had countless encounters with pennies. Can you draw a picture of a penny, locating all of its features? Can you recognize from a set of drawings which one accurately depicts a penny (see Figure 7.4)? In fact, very few of us can correctly recognize a drawing of a penny, and even fewer can recall all of its essential features, nearly 90 percent forgetting that the word "LIBERTY" appears right behind Lincoln's shoulder (Nickerson & Adams, 1979). These retrieval failures do not result from a lack of experience but from a lack of proper encoding. There are three general encoding issues that we'll discuss here, and each is relevant to your study of psychology. We'll cover context effects, meaningfulness, mnemonic devices, and schemas.

The Power of Context. Retrieval tends to be best when the context, or situation, in which the retrieval takes place matches the context that was present

Figure 7.4

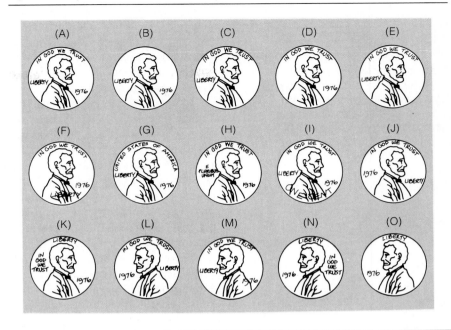

▲ Fifteen drawings of the top side of a penny, testing encoding and retrieval. (Nickerson & Adams, 1979.)

encoding specificity principle the hypothesis that we can retrieve only what we have stored and that retrieval is enhanced to the extent that retrieval cues match encoding cues

at encoding. When cues present at encoding are also present during retrieval, retrieval is enhanced. The **encoding specificity principle** states that we can retrieve only what has been stored, and *how* we retrieve that information depends on how it was encoded in the first place (Flexser and Tulving, 1982; Newby, 1987; Tulving & Thompson, 1973). Recalling the months of the year in alphabetical order is difficult because this is not the order in which they were processed into memory in the first place. The principle suggests that not only do we encode and store particular items of information but we also note and store the context in which those items occur.

Here's a hypothetical experiment (based on Thompson & Tulving, 1973) that demonstrates encoding specificity. Students are asked to learn a list of 24 common words. Half of the students are given cue words to help them remember each item on the list. For the stimulus word "wood," the cue word is "tree," for "cheese," the cue word is "green," and so on for each of the 24 words. The other half of the students receive no cue during their learning (i.e., while encoding). Later, the students are asked to recall as many words from the list as they can. What we discover at recall is that the cue helps those students who had seen it during learning, but it actually decreases the recall for those who had not seen it. If learning takes place without a cue, recall will be better without it.

Here's an application of this research: You should choose one special place for studying. Your kitchen table is probably not a good choice, because that setting is already associated with eating experiences. The context of your kitchen is not a good one for encoding information unless you expect to be tested for retrieval in that same context—which seems highly unlikely. This advice was reaffirmed by a series of experiments by Smith (1979). For example, he had subjects learn material in one room, and then he tested their recall for that material in either the same room or a different one. When a different room—a new context, with different

state-dependent memory the
hypothesis that retrieval can be
enhanced by the extent to which the
state of mind at retrieval matches the
state of mind at encoding

cues—was used for recall, retrieval performance dropped substantially. Simply instructing students to try to remember and think about the room in which learning took place helped recall considerably. (Which means that the best place to study for your next exam is in the room where the exam will be given.)

Context effects are related to what is called **state-dependent memory.** The idea is that to some degree, retrieval depends on the extent to which a person's state of mind at retrieval matches his or her state of mind at encoding (Leahey & Harris, 1989). When learning takes place while a subject is under the influence of a drug, for example, *being similarly under the influence of that drug at retrieval has beneficial effects* (*e.g.,* Eich, et al., 1975; Goodwin, et al., 1969; Parker, et al., 1976). Research by Gordon Bower (Bower, et al., 1978; Bower, 1981) and others suggests that one's mood also may predict retrieval. Using moods (sad or happy) induced by posthypnotic suggestion, Bower found that retrieval was best when mood at retrieval *matched* mood at learning—regardless of whether that mood was happy or sad. This effect seems particularly true for female subjects (Clark & Teasdale, 1985).

There also is evidence that our memories for emotionally arousing experiences are likely to be easier to recall than emotionally neutral events (Thompson, 1982). This may be because emotional arousal increases the levels of certain hormones (adrenalin in particular) that, in turn, (perhaps by increasing glucose levels) help to form vivid memories associated with the emotional arousal (Gold, 1987; McGaugh, 1983). That emotional arousal may help to form particularly vivid memories helps us to understand what Brown and Kulik (1977) call **flashbulb memories.** These are memories of events that are unusually clear and vivid. You may have flashbulb memories of a number of events: your high-school graduation; the funeral of a friend; what you were doing on January 28, 1986, when the space shuttle Challenger exploded, or how you learned of the beginning of the Desert Storm war in the Mideast. Although flashbulb memories *are* particularly clear and vivid, there is little reason to believe that they are necessarily any more complete or any more accurate than any other memories (McCloskey, Wible & Cohen, 1988). They are typically memories of the sort that are stored in episodic LTM. It is also true that if the experienced emotion is extreme, personally-relevant anxiety, the memory of the experience may be even more difficult to recall than normal (See the discussion of repression below, p. 255).

flashbulb memories particularly clear
and vivid memories that are easily
retrieved but not necessarily accurate in
all detail

Before You Go On

▼▼▼▼▼▼▼▼

How does the situation in which one encodes information affect retrieval of that information?

▲ *In order to learn new material students should do whatever they can to make what they are studying meaningful. Asking questions about a new subject and relating it to things that are already familiar add more meaning to the material.*

The Usefulness of Meaningfulness. I have a hypothesis. I believe that I can determine the learning ability of students by noting where they sit in a classroom. The good, bright students tend to choose seats farthest from the door. The poorer, dull students sit by the door, only interested in easily getting in and out of the room. (Although there may be some truth to this, I'm not serious.) To make my point, I propose an experiment. Students seated away from the door are asked to learn a list of words that I read aloud only once. I need a second list of words for those students seated by the door because they've already heard my first list.

The list that my "smart students" hear is: *cat, dog, mother, father, black, white,* and so forth. As I predicted, they have no problem recalling this list after one presentation. The students huddled by the door get my second list: *insidious, tachistoscope, sophistry, flotsam, episcotister*, and so forth. Needless to say, my hypothesis will be confirmed.

This is obviously not a fair experiment. Students sitting by the door will yell foul. My second list of words is clearly more difficult to learn and recall than the first. The words on the first list are shorter, more familiar, and easier to pronounce. However, the major difference between these two lists is the **meaningfulness** of the items—the extent to which they elicit existing associations in one's memory. The *cat, dog, mother* list is relatively easy to remember because each word is meaningful. Each makes us think of many other things, or produces many associations, i.e., these items are easy to elaborate. Words like *tachistoscope* and *episcotister* are more difficult because they evoke few if any associations.

A very important point to keep in mind is that meaningfulness is not a characteristic or a feature built into material to be learned. *Meaningfulness resides in the memory of the learner. Tachistoscope* may be a meaningless collection of letters for many people, but for others, it may be a word rich in meaning, a word with which they can readily form many associations. What is meaningful is a function of our individual experiences.

It follows that one of your tasks as a learner is to do whatever you can to make meaningful the material you are learning. You need to seek out and establish associations between what you are learning and what you already know. You need to rehearse elaboratively what you are encoding so that you can retrieve it later. You need to be prepared to ask yourself a series of questions about what you are studying. What does this mean? What does it make me think of? Does this remind me of something I already know? Can I make this material more meaningful? If you cannot, there is little point in going on to more confusing material. Perhaps you now see a major reason for our including **"Before You Go On"** questions within each chapter.

Before You Go On

▼▼▼▼▼▼▼▼

What is meaningfulness?

How does meaningfulness relate to retrieval?

The Value of Mnemonic Devices. Retrieval is enhanced when we elaborate on the material we are learning—when we organize it or make it meaningful during the encoding process. Now we'll look at a few specific encoding strategies, **mnemonic devices**, that we can use to aid our retrieval by helping us organize and add meaningfulness to new material.

Research by Bower and Clark (1969) shows us that we can improve the retrieval of unorganized material if we can weave it into a meaningful story. This technique is called **narrative chaining**. One group of college students was asked to learn a list of 10 nouns in order. It is not a difficult task, and subjects had little trouble with it. Then they were given another list of 10 nouns to learn, and then another—12 lists in all. The students were given no instructions other than to remember each list of words in order.

A second group of students was given the same 12 lists of 10 nouns each to learn. It was suggested to them that they make up little stories that used each of the words on the list in turn. Immediately after each list was presented, both groups were asked to recall the list of words they had just heard. There was virtually no difference in the recall scores for the two groups. Then came a surprise. *After all 12 lists had been recalled*, students

meaningfulness the extent to which information evokes associations with information already in memory

mnemonic devices strategies for improving retrieval that take advantage of existing memories in order to make new material more meaningful

narrative chaining the mnemonic device of relating words together in a story, thus organizing them in a meaningful way

were tested again on their recall for each list. The experimenters provided one word from one of the 12 lists, and the students were to recall the other nine words from that list. The difference in recall between the two groups of students in this instance was striking (see Figure 7.5). Those who used a narrative chaining technique recalled 93 percent of the words (on average), whereas those who did not use narrative chaining to organize the random list of words recalled only 13 percent of them. The message is clear: Organizing unrelated words into stories helps us remember them.

Forming *mental images,* or pictures in our minds, is another technique that improves memory. Using imagery at encoding to improve retrieval has proven to be very helpful in many different circumstances (Begg & Paivio, 1969; Marschark, et al., 1987; Paivio, 1971; 1986). Mental imagery is what helps us to retrieve words such as *horse, rainbow,* and *typewriter* more readily than words such as *treason, session,* and *effort*—even when other factors such as frequency of occurrence and meaningfulness are equated.

Assume you have to memorize the meanings of Spanish words. You could use simple rote repetition, but this technique is tedious and not very

Figure 7.5

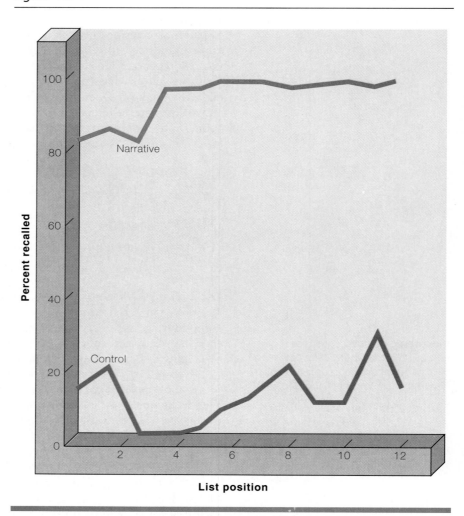

▲ *Percent correct recall for words from 12 lists learned under two conditions. In the narrative condition, subjects made up short stories to aid recall, while in the control condition, rote memorization—no mnemonic device—was used. (After Bower & Clark, 1969.)*

Figure 7.6

PATO — POT — DUCK

▲ An illustration of how the key word method can help foreign vocabulary retention. (After Atkinson, 1975.)

peg word method the mnemonic device of forming interactive visual images of materials to be learned and items previously associated with numbers

method of loci the mnemonic device that mentally places information to be retrieved at a series of familiar locations (loci)

Figure 7.7

Piano   Cigar

▲ The key word method can also be used to help remember pairs of English words. (After Wollen, Weber, & Lowry, 1972.)

efficient. Atkinson (1975) suggested that to improve memory for foreign language vocabulary, it is useful to imagine some connection visually tying the two words together. He calls this the *key word method* of study. For example, the Spanish word for "horse" is *caballo*, pronounced *cab-eye-yo*. To remember this association, you might choose *eye* as the key word and picture a horse kicking someone in the eye. If you are not prepared to be that gruesome, you might imagine a horse with a very large eye. The Spanish word for "duck" is *pato*. Here your key word might be *pot*, and you could picture a duck wearing a pot on its head (see Figure 7.6) or sitting in a pot on the stove. This may sound strange, but research data suggest that it actually works very well (Pressley et al., 1982).

The same technique works whenever you need to remember any paired information. Bower (1972) asked students to learn lists of pairs of English words. Some subjects were instructed to form a mental image that showed some interaction between the two words. One pair was *piano-cigar*. There are many ways to form an image of a piano and a cigar: The cigar could be balanced on the edge of the piano, for one. Recall for word pairs was much better for those subjects who formed mental images than it was for those who did not. It's also the case that common and interactive images are *more useful* than strange and bizarre ones (Bower, 1970; Wollen, et al., 1972). That is, to remember the *piano-cigar* pair, it is better to picture a cigar balanced on a piano than it is to picture a piano actually smoking a cigar (see Figure 7.7). To remember that it was Bower and Clark who did the experiment on narrative chaining, try to picture two story-tellers chained together, each holding a *Clark Bar* in their hands as they take a bow on a theater stage.

One of the better-known mnemonic devices that also involves imagery is called the **peg word method** (Miller, Galanter & Pribram, 1960). This strategy is most useful when we must remember items in order. Using this device is a two-step process. The first step is to associate common nouns (peg words) that rhyme with the numbers from 1 to 10 (and beyond if you're up to it). Figure 7.8 is the set of associations that Miller and his colleagues suggested. The second step is to form an interactive image of the word you're memorizing and the appropriate peg word.

Suppose that you have to remember these words in order: *book, glass, ring, nose*. Having already memorized your peg words, you make up an image associating each word on the list and its peg word, for example: (1) a *book* in the middle of a hamburger *bun*, (2) a *shoe* in a *glass*, (3) a large *ring* around the trunk of a *tree*, (4) a *nose* stuck in a door, and so on. At retrieval, you first recall the peg words in order (*bun, shoe, tree*, and *door*), and then recall the word that you've associated with each peg word. It may sound like a lot of extra work to go through, but once you've mastered your peg word scheme, the rest is remarkably easy.

The last imagery-related mnemonic device I'll mention may be the oldest. It is the **method of loci**, attributed to the Greek poet Simonides (Yates, 1966). The idea is to get in your mind a well-known location (*loci* are locations), say the floor plan of your house or apartment. Visually place the material you are trying to recall in different locations throughout your house in some sensible order. When the time comes for you to retrieve the material, mentally walk through your chosen locations, retrieving the information you have stored at each different place.

Some time ago, I was asked to give a short talk at a high school. There were several points I wanted to make, and I didn't want to use written notes. I also didn't want to appear nervous, so I decided to try the method of loci. I divided my talk into five or six major ideas, imagined my house, and walked through it in my mind. I stored my introduction at the front

Figure 7.8

THE PEG WORD MNEMONIC SCHEME

One is a Bun
Two is a Shoe
Three is a Tree
Four is a Door
Five is a Hive
Six are Sticks
Seven is Heaven
Eight is a Gate
Nine is a Line
Ten is a Hen

Proposed by Miller, Galanter, & Pribam (1950)

schema a system of organized general knowledge, stored in long-term memory, that guides the encoding and retrieval of information

door, point #1 got me to the living room, point #2 to the dining room, and so on through the house until I got to my conclusion at the back door. Even though I have been telling others about the method of loci for many years, this was the first time that I'd chosen to use it, and I was very impressed with how easy it was to remember my little speech.

Before You Go On
▼▼▼▼▼▼▼▼▼

Describe narrative chaining, mental imagery, the peg word method, and the method of loci as mnemonic devices.

The Role of Schemas. The encoding specificity hypothesis tells us that how we retrieve information is affected by how we have encoded it. One of the processes that influences how we encode and retrieve information is our use of schemas (sometimes referred to as "scripts"). A **schema** is an organized, general knowledge structure that is stored in long-term memory (Mayer, 1983). Schemas provide a framework that we can use to understand new information and also to retrieve that information later (Alba & Hasher, 1983; Lord, 1980).

Let's look at an example of research that involves the use of schemas as encoding strategies. Before you go any further, stop and read the short passage in Figure 7.9. As it stands, the paragraph doesn't make much sense, does it? All the words are sensible. Even individual sentences seem reasonable. But as a story, it seems virtually meaningless because without additional information, you have no schema available to comprehend its meaning (Bransford & Johnson, 1972). Now look at the drawing in Figure 7.14 at the very end of the chapter. This drawing provides a schema that gives meaning to the paragraph. Subjects who were shown this picture *before* they read the passage recalled more than twice as much about it than did subjects who did not see the picture at all or who were shown the picture *after* they read the paragraph. The message here is that schemas seem to help retrieval only if the same schemas were available at or before encoding.

So what is the bottom line? Whenever to-be-remembered information is consistent with prior, existing information (such as schemas) retrieval is enhanced. If to-be-remembered material is at odds with existing schema, those schemas may actually inhibit retrieval.

Before You Go On
▼▼▼▼▼▼▼▼▼

What are schemas, and how do they affect retrieval?

▶ Factor III: How We Schedule Practice

A point I have made repeatedly is that retrieval largely depends on how one goes about encoding or practicing information. Retrieval also depends on the amount of practice and how that practice is scheduled. One of the reasons why some students do not do as well on classroom exams as they would like is that they simply do not have (or make) enough time to study or practice the material covered on the exams. A related reason is that some students do not schedule wisely what time they do have.

▲ Chess experts, such as Karpov and Kasparov, pictured here, have very detailed and elaborate schemas to aid them in the retrieval of information about the positioning of the pieces during a chess match.

Figure 7.9

THE BALLOONS PASSAGE (SEE FIGURE 7.14).

If the balloons popped, the sound would not be able to carry since everything would be too far away from the correct floor. A closed window would also prevent the sound from carrying since most buildings tend to be well insulated. Since the whole operation depends on a steady flow of electricity, a break in the middle of the wire would also cause problems. Of course the fellow could shout, but the human voice is not loud enough to carry that far. An additional problem is that a string could break on the instrument. Then there could be no accompaniment to the message. It is clear that the best situation would involve less distance. Then there would be fewer potential problems. With face-to-face contact, the least number of things could go wrong.

From Bransford & Johnson, 1972.

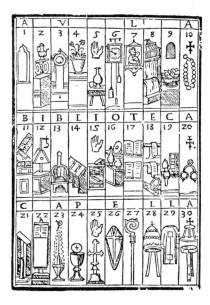

▲ *The method of loci is an ancient mnemonic device. This illustration was done by a Dominican monk in the sixteenth century. On top are the abbey and the surrounding buildings through which the speaker will mentally walk, picking up the ideas (illustrated on the bottom) that he or she needs to recall.*

overlearning the practice or rehearsal of material over and above what is needed to learn it

What you and I often do once we decide to learn something is to read, practice, and study the material until we just know it. In other words, we practice until we are satisfied that we have encoded and stored the required information in our memories, and then we quit. Another way of expressing this is to say that we often fail to engage in **overlearning**—the process of practicing or rehearsing material over and above what is needed to learn it. Consider this fictitious example, and see if you can extend this evidence to your study habits.

A subject comes to the laboratory to learn a list of syllables such as: *dax, wuj, pib, zuw,* and so on. There are 15 items on the list which has to be presented repeatedly before our subject can recall all the items correctly. Our subject is dismissed with instructions to return two weeks later for a test of his recall of the syllables. Not surprisingly, he doesn't fare very well on the retrieval task.

What would have happened to our subject's recall if we had continued to present him with the list of syllables at the time of learning, well beyond the point where he first learned them? Say the list was learned in 12 trials. We have the subject practice the list for six more presentations (50 percent overlearning—practice that is 50 percent over that required for learning). Or let's require an additional 12 trials of practice (100 percent overlearning). What if we required an additional 48 trials of practice (400 percent overlearning)?

The effects of such overlearning practice are well-documented and predictable. The recall data for this imaginary experiment might look like those presented in Figure 7.10. Note three things about these data: (1) If we measure retrieval at different times after learning, forgetting is impressive and rather sudden. (This is one of the results of the work on memory that Hermann Ebbinghaus reported back in 1885, and that many other researchers have confirmed since then.) (2) Overlearning improves retrieval, having its greatest effects with longer retention intervals. (3) There is a "diminishing returns" phenomenon present; that is, 50 percent overlearning is much more useful than no overlearning; 100 percent overlearning *is* better than 50 percent; and 400 percent is a bit better than 100 percent, but not by very much. For any task or individual, there is probably an optimum amount of overlearning. In summary, with everything else being equal, the more we practice what we learn the easier it will be to retrieve it. How one *schedules* one's practice or learning time is also important.

Some of the oldest data in psychology tell us that retrieval can be improved if practice (encoding) is spread out over time with rest intervals spaced in between. The data provided in Figure 7.11 are fairly standard. In fact, this 1946 experiment provides such reliable results, it is commonly

Figure 7.10

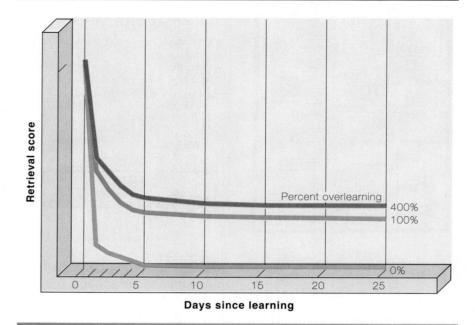

▲ *Idealized data showing the effect of overlearning on retrieval. Note the "diminishing returns" with additional overlearning. (Krueger, 1929.)*

used in psychology laboratory classes. The task is to write the letters of the alphabet, but upside down and from right to left. (If you think that sounds easy, you should give it a try.)

Subjects are given the opportunity to practice this task under four different conditions. The *massed practice* group works on the task without a break between trials. The three *distributed practice* groups receive the same amount of actual practice, but get rest intervals interspersed between each 1-minute practice trial. One group gets a 3- to 5-second break between trials, a second group receives a 30-second rest, and a third group gets a 45-second break between practice trials.

As we can see in Figure 7.11, subjects in all groups begin at the same (poor) level of performance. After 20 minutes of practice, the performance of all the groups shows improvement. By far, the massed practice (no rest) group does the poorest, and the 45-second-rest group does the best.

The conclusion to be drawn from years of research is that, almost without exception, distributed practice is superior to massed practice. There are exceptions, however. There are some tasks that could suffer from having rest intervals inserted in practice time. In general, when you must keep track of many things at the same time, you should continue practice until you have finished whatever it is you are working on. If, for example, you are working on a complex math problem, you should work it through until you find a solution, whether it's time for a break or not. And, of course, you should not break up your practice in such a way as to disrupt the meaningfulness of the material you are studying.

Quite clearly, what we're talking about here is the scheduling of study time. Discussions of study schedules make up the major part of all how-to- study books. The message is always the same: Many short (and meaningful) study periods with rest periods interspersed are more efficient than a few study periods massed together.

Figure 7.11

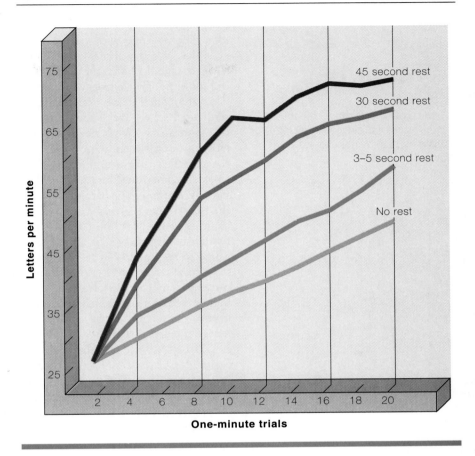

▲ *Improvement in performance as a function of distribution of practice time. The task was the printing of inverted capital letters, with twenty 1-minute trials separated by rest intervals of varying lengths. (After Kientzle, 1946.)*

Before You Go On
▼▼▼▼▼▼▼▼▼

What is overlearning, and how does it affect retrieval?

Compare and contrast massed and distributed practice, noting their effects on retrieval.

▶ Factor IV: How We Overcome Interference or Repression

So far we have discussed specific steps that can be taken at the encoding of information to enhance the retrieval of that information. In this section, we argue that there may be processes that actually work to promote forgetting. These processes will need to be overcome if retrieval is to be successful. We'll consider two inhibitory factors: the interference of other information stored in memory and the repression of anxiety-producing, unpleasant and painful memories.

Interference. The idea that interference can account for forgetting, or retrieval failure, is an old one in psychology. Early experiments showed that subjects who are active for a period of time after learning remember what they learned less well than do subjects who use the intervening time for sleep (Jenkins & Dallenbach, 1924). Figure 7.12 shows data from two experiments—one with college students who had learned a list of nonsense syllables, and the other with cockroaches that had learned to avoid an area of their cage. In both cases, subjects who engaged in normal waking activity did more poorly on tests of retrieval over different retention intervals.

When interfering activities come after the learning of material to be remembered, we are dealing with **retroactive interference**. Let's go back into the laboratory. We'll need two groups of subjects randomly assigned to either an experimental group or a control group (You can follow along with the summary diagram in Figure 7.13). The subjects in both groups are asked to learn something (anything will do; we'll say a list of nonsense syllables). Having learned their lists, the groups are then treated differently. Subjects in the experimental group are asked to learn something else, perhaps a new list of nonsense syllables. Control group subjects are asked to do nothing (which is impossible, of course, in a literal sense). These subjects might be asked to rest quietly or to play some simple game.

Now for the test. Both groups are asked to remember whatever was presented in the *first* learning task. Control group subjects will show a higher retrieval score than experimental group subjects. For the latter group, the second set of learned material interferes with the retrieval of the material learned first.

Most of us are familiar with retroactive interference from our own educational experiences. A student who studied French in high school takes a few courses in Spanish at college and now can't remember very much French. The Spanish keeps getting in the way. I have two students who are scheduled to take a psychology exam tomorrow morning at 9:00. Both are equally able and well-motivated. One student is taking only one class: mine.

retroactive interference the inhibition of retrieval of previously learned material caused by material learned later

Figure 7.12

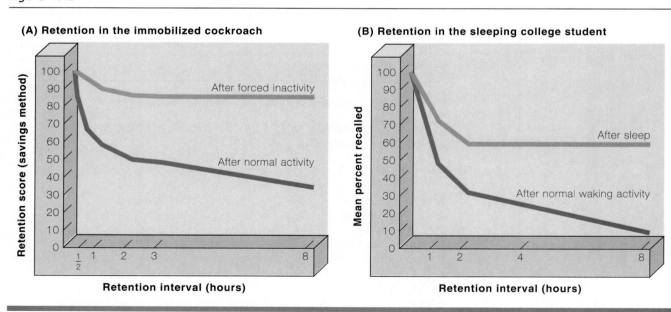

▲ These graphs illustrate how activity following learning can interfere with the retrieval of the learned material. In both cases, normal waking activiity caused more interference with retrieval than did forced inactivity (for cockroaches) or sleeping (for students). (Minami & Dallenbach, 1946.)

She studies psychology for two hours, watches TV for two hours, and goes to bed. She comes in the next morning to take the exam. The second student also studies psychology for two hours, but then reads a chapter and a half in her sociology textbook, just in case she is called on in class. After reading the sociology, she goes to bed, comes to class, and takes the psychology exam. Everything else being equal, this student will be at a disadvantage. The sociology that she studied will retroactively interfere with her retrieval of the psychology she learned previously. What is this student to do? Perhaps all she can do is set herself up for proactive interference.

Proactive interference occurs when *previously* learned material interferes with the retrieval of material learned later. First follow along in Figure 7.13(B), then we'll get back to our student and her studying problem. We have two groups of subjects, experimental and control. The experimental group again starts off by learning something—that same list of syllables, perhaps. This time the control group subjects begin by resting quietly while the experimental group goes through the learning task. Both groups learn a second list of syllables. We now test for retrieval, but this time we test for the retrieval of the more recently learned material. Once again, the control group subjects will be at an advantage. They have none of that first list in their memories to interfere with retrieval. The advantage is not as great as it was for retroactive interference. Proactive interference is seldom as detrimental as retroactive interference.

Although both retroactive and proactive interference effects are well documented, there are many factors that influence the *extent* of such interference (Underwood, 1957). Very meaningful, well-organized material is less susceptible to interference than is less meaningful material, such as nonsense syllables. It should also strike you as reasonable that *the nature of the interfering task* matters a great deal. As a general rule of thumb, the more similar the interfering material is to the material being retrieved, the greater will be the interference. Think of my student who had to study for her psychology exam *and* read a sociology text. She will experience more interference (retroactive *or* proactive) than will a student who has to study for the psychology exam and work on calculus problems. This is because there is little about calculus problems to get in the way, or interfere, with the psychology lesson. Hence, the following advice: If you're going to take more than one course at a time, those courses should be as different from each other as possible—to minimize interference effects.

proactive interference the inhibition of retrieval of recently learned material caused by material learned earlier

---

Before You Go On

▼▼▼▼▼▼▼▼

Briefly describe retroactive and proactive interference.

Repression. It was the view of Sigmund Freud that the contents of our minds (including our memories) are not always accessible. Some ideas, desires, motives, and memories are actively pushed out of our conscious awareness into our unconscious minds. This is particularly true for those memories that cause us to feel anxiety, dread, or discomfort when we think about them.

The process of forcing anxiety-producing events into our unconscious is called **repression**. It is an automatic process that happens without our awareness. We cannot purposely repress something.

Perhaps your doctor or dentist charges a fee for patients who fail to show up for scheduled appointments. Many do so because missing scheduled appointments is a common occurrence, and repression may explain

repression "motivated forgetting" in which stressful events are forced from awareness into the unconscious and can no longer be remembered directly

Figure 7.13

**DESIGNS OF EXPERIMENTS TO DEMONSTRATE
RETROACTIVE AND PROACTIVE INTERFERENCE.**

(A) Retroactive Interference

	Learn	Learn	Test
Experimental Group	Task A	Task B	Retrieval of Task A
Control Group	Task A	Nothing	Retrieval of Task A

(B) Proactive Interference

	Learn	Learn	Test
Experimental Group	Task A	Task B	Retrieval of Task B
Control Group	Nothing	Task B	Retrieval of Task B

Note: If intererence is operating, the control group will demonstrate better retrieval than will the experimental group.

why, at least in some cases. Let's say you really don't like going to the dentist; you shudder at the very thought of it. But today you can readily recall that you have a dentist's appointment scheduled for next Friday. As Friday approaches and your anxiety builds (so the theory goes), you become more and more likely to repress your appointment. On the preceding Thursday, a friend asks you to join him on a shopping trip the next day. "Let's see, Friday afternoon. No, I'm not doing anything tomorrow afternoon. I'll meet you at one o'clock." Friday evening, just after dinner, the memory of your appointment returns to you in a flash, "Oh no! I had a dental appointment this afternoon. I forgot!" How easy it is to recall the appointment that evening, secure in the knowledge that you won't even be able to call and reschedule the appointment until Monday. The pressure is off, and there's no longer any reason to repress the dreaded event.

It is very unlikely that you'll be able to convince your instructor that you forgot the difference between retroactive and proactive interference because you repressed it. To the extent that repression works at all, it deals with material that is emotionally-laden and anxiety-producing.

Before You Go On

What is repression?

▼▼▼
Thinking Critically About Memory

1. The ancient Greek metaphor of human memory being likened to a block of wax in one's head is no longer thought to be valid, even though it does present an intriguing picture. Can you think of any other metaphors for human memory that work as well or better?

2. Is there any way in which an individual can be conscious of the differences among the three major processes of memory: encoding, storage, and retrieval? That is, can you tell when one ends and the next begins?

3. How do we retrieve information from sensory memory?

4. Can you imagine how you could do an experiment to test the capacity or the duration of sensory memory for each of the senses?

5. When we hear that "So-and-so doesn't have any problems studying because he has a 'photographic memory,'" what do people mean when they use the term "photographic memory" in this context? How could we demonstrate whether such a thing exists?

6. How is short-term memory useful in the processing of spoken language? That is, could we talk to each other sensibly if we did not have short-term memories?

7. In what way does your own experience confirm the research finding that information in short-term memory is processed acoustically, or in terms of how it sounds?

8. How do all of the different types of classroom exams that you have taken compare in terms of the question providing useful retrieval cues? [Multiple-choice and fill-in-the-blank are easy. What about other types of exams?]

9. What mnemonic devices can you think of other than the ones listed in the text?

10. Is there such a thing as "test anxiety?" What might be done about it?

Figure 7.14

 A picture for the balloons passage. (From Bransford & Johnson, 1972.)

Summary

▼▼▼▼▼▼▼▼▼▼▼▼▼▼▼▼▼▼▼▼▼▼▼▼▼▼▼▼▼▼▼▼▼▼

How do we define memory? Memory is the cognitive process of actively representing information in memory (encoding), keeping it there (storage) and later bringing it out again (retrieval). *Pages 230–231*

What is sensory memory? Sensory memory gives us the ability to store large amounts of information for very brief periods of time. We cannot encode or manipulate this information, so it is stored in the form in which it was presented to the senses. The capacity of sensory memory may approximate the capacity of our senses, but its duration is very limited. Visually presented information lasts in sensory memory for but a fraction of a second; orally presented material may last for a few seconds at best. *Pages 231–232*

For how long is information stored in STM? Once entered into short-term memory, information can be held there for approximately 15–20 seconds before all of it fades or is replaced by new information. Some information will be inaccessible soon after encoding. *Pages 232–233*

What is required to get information into STM and then keep it there? Processing information into this memory requires that we attend to it. Information can enter into short-term memory either from sensory memory or from long-term memory. We can keep information in STM by reattending to it, a process called maintenance rehearsal. *Pages 232–235*

How much information can be held in STM? It is reasonable to say that the capacity of STM is limited to approximately 7±2 bits of unrelated information. *Pages 235–236*

How can chunking affect the capacity of STM? By "chunking" information together into meaningful clusters or units, more can be processed in STM, but the limit remains at about 7±2 chunks. *Pages 235–236*

How is information encoded (represented) in short-term memory? Information in our short-term memories may be encoded in several different forms, but acoustic encoding seems to be the most common. *Pages 236–237*

Are long-term memories necessarily permanent? Although LTM may hold information for a very long time, we cannot claim LTM to be a permanent memory. The problem is that there is at the moment no scientific means of determining whether information is unavailable or inaccessible. Once in long-term memory, information may be subject to distortion or replacement. *Pages 237–238*

Contrast elaborative rehearsal with maintenance rehearsal as a means of encoding information into long-term memory. Although maintenance rehearsal may sometimes be sufficient to encode or move material from STM into LTM, there seems to be little doubt that the best mechanism for placing information into LTM is elaborative rehearsal—that is, to think about the material, forming associations or images of the material and relating it to something already stored in LTM. The more one can elaborate, or the "deeper" the elaboration, the better retrieval will be. *Pages 238–240*

Name and briefly describe three possible systems or types of LTM. Information may be stored in different ways in a variety of LTM systems. One of the most basic is our procedural memory, in which we retain learned connections between stimuli and responses—in essence, how we perform simple, well-learned behaviors. Episodic memories are autobiographical; they are related to one's life experiences and events. Semantic memories store facts, knowledge and vocabularies. *Pages 238–240*

How do recall and recognition measures affect our assessment of retrieval? Our retrieval of information from memory is often a function of how we ask for retrieval. When we ask for retrieval by recall, we provide the fewest possible retrieval cues. For recognition, we provide the information to be retrieved and ask that it be identified as familiar. Retrieval by recognition is generally superior to retrieval by recall. *Pages 240–244*

What are implicit tests of retention, and what do they tell us about long-term memory? As opposed to explicit tests of retrieval, implicit tests assess the extent to which previously experienced material is helpful in subsequent tasks. For example, relearning shows us that even when once-learned material can be neither recalled nor recognized, that material will be easier to relearn than it was in the first place. Implicit tests of memory show us that even information that cannot be consciously or voluntarily retrieved from memory still can be influential. *Pages 240–244*

How does the situation in which one encodes information affect retrieval of that information? The greater the extent to which the cues or context available at encoding match the cues or context available at retrieval, the better retrieval will be. The *encoding specificity hypothesis* asserts that how we retrieve information depends on how it was encoded. Psychologists have found that even matching the individual's state of mind at encoding and at retrieval is helpful. Heightened emotionality at encod ing may also help to produce memories that are more vivid, even if they are not more accurate. *Pages 244–246*

What is meaningfulness? Meaningfulness is the extent to which material is related to, or associated with, information already stored in memory. *Pages 246–247*

How does meaningfulness relate to retrieval? In general, meaningful material (or material that is made meaningful) is easier to retrieve than meaningless material. Meaningfulness resides in the individual, not in the material to be learned, however. *Page 247*

Describe narrative chaining, mental imagery, the peg word method, and the method of loci as mnemonic devices. Mnemonic devices are strategies used to organize and add meaningfulness to material that is to be retrieved. *Narrative chaining* involves making up a story that connects meaningfully a list of otherwise unrelated items that need to be remembered. Several mnemonic devices suggest forming *visual images* of the material to be learned, which may provide an additional code for that material. The *peg word method* required first learning a word associated with each of the numbers 1 to 10 (if there are 10 items to be learned) and then forming an interactive image of these words and items that need to be retrieved in order. The *method of loci* also uses mental imagery and involves mentally placing items to be retrieved in a sequence of familiar locations (loci). *Pages 247–250*

What are schemas, and how do they affect retrieval? Schemas are organized, general knowledge systems that we have stored in long-term memory. Based on one's past experiences, schemas summarize the essential features of common events or situations. They are used as a means of guiding the organization and meaning of new information. The more complete one's schema for information, the better will be encoding and retrieval. *Pages 250*

What is overlearning, and how does it affect retrieval? Overlearning involves the rehearsal over and above that needed for immediate recall of a specific bit of information. Within limits, the more one overlearns, the greater the likelihood of accurate retrieval. *Pages 250–252*

Compare and contrast massed and distributed practice, noting their effects on retrieval. In massed practice, one's study or rehearsal occurs without intervening rest intervals. Distributed practice uses shorter segments of rehearsal, interspersed with rest intervals. In almost all cases, distributed practice leads to better retrieval than does massed practice. *Pages 251–253*

Briefly describe retroactive and proactive interference. Retroactive interference occurs when previously learned material cannot be retrieved because it is inhibited or blocked by material or information that is learned *later*. Proactive interference occurs when information cannot be retrieved because it is inhibited or blocked by material that was learned *earlier* Retroactive interference is generally more detrimental to retrieval than is proactive interference. *Pages 253–255*

What is repression? Repression occurs when anxiety-producing or traumatic events are forced into the unconscious level of the mind, from which retrieval is very difficult. Thus repression, a concept introduced by Freud, may occasionally account for forgetfulness. *Pages 255–256*

7.1 The ancient Greeks wrote that human memory was like   a) the grains of sand at the sea shore.   b) fluid that ran through the tubes of the nervous system   c) a block of wax in a person's head.   d) an octopus with many tentacles. *Page 230*

7.2 Psychologists talk about passing information through three different types of memory called: a) encoding, storage, and retrieval.   b) primary, secondary, and tertiary.   c) central, peripheral, and somatic.   d) sensory, short-term, and long-term. *Page 230*

7.3 Which of the following best describes how information is represented, or coded, in sensory memory? We can say that the code for information in sensory memory is essentially: a) physical.   b) semantic.   c) acoustic.   d) symbolic. *Page 232*

7.4 True or False?   For information to be processed into memory, the first thing that we do to or with that information is to learn it. *Page 231*

7.5 The minimal requirement for keeping information in short-term memory with maintenance rehearsal is that we   a) elaborate on it in some way.   b) make it meaningful.   c) organize it.   d) reattend to it. *Page 232*

7.6 The amount of information held in STM (i.e., its capacity) can be extended if we can _____ that information.   a) rehearse   b) attend to   c) chunk   d) elaborate. *Page 235*

7.7 The best way to encode information in long-term memory is   a) rote repetition.   b) taking extensive notes.   c) maintenance rehearsal.   d) by elaborating on it. *Page 238*

7.8 Elaboratively rehearsing information is mostly a process of organizing it and   a) making it meaningful.   b) re-attending to it.   c) retrieving it.   d) repeating it. *Page 239*

7.9 Imagine a 42-year-old man who has not ice skated since he was 12 years old. Even though it has been 30 years, he finds that he still can skate quite well. His ability to ice skate has been stored in his _____ memory.   a) physical   b) procedural   c) episodic   d) semantic. *Page 239*

7.10 The answer to which question is most likely to be found in episodic memory?   a) When and where did you learn to ride a bicycle?   b) When and where did Wundt open his laboratory?   c) What sorts of information are stored in episodic memory?   d) What is the result of dividing 134 by 12? *Page 240*

7.11 True or False?   Information in semantic memory is probably stored in chronological order, i.e., in the order in which it was experienced. *Page 240*

7.12 When psychologists talk about "retrieval failure," what assumption do they make?   a) We are dealing with short-term memory.   b) Information is available, but not accessible.   c) There must be some sort of brain damage involved.   d) The material was never stored in the first place. *Page 244*

7.13 True or False?   Retrieval measured by recall is usually superior to retrieval measured by recognition. *Page 241*

7.14 Research that involves _____ is dealing with implicit measures of memory.   a) recognition   b) free recall   c) serial recall   d) relearning. *Page 243*

7.15 Even in the worst cases of amnesia, many memories stored in _____ can be retrieved with relative ease.   a) procedural memory   b) semantic memory   c) the hippocampus   d) the cerebral cortex. *Page 244*

7.16 True or False?   We may think of explicit memory retrieval as an unconscious process. *Page 240*

7.17 Most people cannot remember all of the features on a dollar bill. Which one of the following phrases best describes the problem in such instances?   a) lack of availability   b) poorly worded questioning   c) improper encoding   d) proactiveness. *Page 244*

7.18 What does the "encoding specificity hypothesis" tell us?   a) Retrieval is enhanced to the extent that retrieval cues match encoding cues.   b) We tend to remember pleasant experiences more readily than we remember unpleasant experiences.   c) Retrieval is enhanced to the extent that we use explicit measures rather than implicit measures.   d) The effects of interference are most noticeable at encoding, not retrieval. *Page 245*

7.19 Studies of "state dependent memory" provide support for   a) recognition being superior to recall.   b) retrograde amnesia.   c) the encoding specificity hypothesis.   d) the value of studying for exams. *Page 246*

7.20 True or False?   Flashbulb memories are usually stored in procedural LTM. *Page 246*

7.21 Mnemonic devices enhance or improve retrieval because they   a) involve the continued repetition of information.   b) make material more meaningful.   c) involve the right brain as well as the left brain.   d) lengthen the storage in LTM. *Page 247*

7.22 Making up a little story that contains all of the words in a list to be recalled is a mnemonic technique called: a) the pegword method.   b) the method of loci.   c) mental imagery.   d) narrative chaining. *Page 247*

7.23 True or False?   Mnemonic devices are useful at retrieval, but are unrelated to encoding information. *Page 247*

7.24 Organized but general representations of knowledge stored in long-term memory are called a) mnemonic devices.   b) schemas.   c) episodes. d) retrieval strategies. *Page 250*

7.25 After a list of words has been presented to Bob 8 times, we have evidence that he has learned the list. If we want Bob to engage in 200% overlearning, how many additional presentations of this list would be required?   a) 0   b) 8   c) 16 d) 20. *Page 251*

7.26 Which is true most often?   a) Retroactive interference is less disrupting than proactive interference.   b) Overlearning increases the capacity and duration of STM.   c) Overwhelming anxiety explains most retrieval failures on classroom exams.   d) Distributed practice is superior to massed practice. *Page 252*

7.27 If, during the course of a semester, you have 9 classroom exams, for which exam will proactive interference be the greatest?   a) the first b) the fifth (the one in the middle)   c) the ninth d) Proactive interference will be the same for all nine exams. *Page 255*

7.28 You are in an experiment to demonstrate retroactive interference that may occur between two learning tasks, A and B, and are assigned to the experimental group. The first thing that you will be asked to do is: a) take a test on your retrieval of Task A.   b) learn Task A.   c) learn Task B.   d) rest while the control group learns Task A. *Page 254*

7.29 If someone were to forget one of the following, which case of forgetting would be most understandable in terms of repression?   a) a list of nonsense syllables learned in the psychology laboratory   b) the names of the people who were invited to their sixth birthday party   c) the details of an accident they were in as a teenager d) events stored in procedural, rather than episodic, memory. *Page 256*

Chapter 8

▼▼▼▼▼

Higher Cognitive Processes

▲ **Preview**

▲ **Problem Solving**

▲ **Language**

▲ **Intelligence**

   ▼ *Psychology in the Real World:*
     Racial and Ethnic Differences and IQ

▲ **Thinking Critically About Higher Cognitive Processes**

▲ **Summary**

▲ **Test Yourself**

▲▲▲▲▲▲

You started off in Chapter 1 by taking a short true-false test on psychology. Here's an even shorter multiple-choice test. It is part of an approximation of an IQ test. It tests some of your "higher cognitive processes." Try to do your best. Answers are furnished below.

1. T-Bone Walker was famous for playing
     a. trombone.
     b. piano.
     c. T-flute.
     d. guitar.
     e. hambone.

2. "Boogie Jugie" means the same as
     a. tired.
     b. worthless.
     c. old.
     d. well put together.

3. If you throw dice and seven is showing on the top, what is facing down?
     a. seven
     b. snake eyes
     c. boxcars
     d. Little Joe
     e. eleven

4. Black Draught is a
   a. winter's cold wind.
   b. laxative.
   c. black soldier.
   d. dark beer.

5. Hully Gully came from
   a. East Oakland.
   b. Fillmore.
   c. Watts.
   d. Harlem.
   e. Motor City.

6. An alley apple is a
   a. brick.
   b. piece of fruit.
   c. dog.
   d. horse.

7. A gas head is a person who has a
   a. fast-moving car.
   b. "stable of lace."
   c. process.

d. habit of stealing cars.

e. long jail record for arson.

8. A blood is

a. a vampire.

b. a dependent individual.

c. an injured person.

d. a person of color.

9. A handerkerchief head is a(n)

a. cool cat.

b. porter.

c. Uncle Tom.

d. hoddi.

e. preacher.

10. "Boot" refers to

a. a cotton farmer.

b. a black

c. an indian.

d a vietnamese citizen.

How do you think you did on this little test? The answers (honest) are as follows: 1–d; 2–b; 3–a; 4–b; 5–c; 6–a; 7–c; 8–d; 9–c; 10–b. This quiz combines items from two well-known tests. The odd-numbered items come from the Counterbalance General Intelligence Test authored by Adrian Dove (1968), and the even-numbered items come from the BITCH—that's the Black Intelligence Test of Cultural Homogeneity, by Robert Williams (1972).

Both of these tests make the same basic point when we consider any comparisons of individuals or groups in terms of intelligence, we must seriously consider the fairness or appropriateness of the test(s) used to assess that intelligence. Their authors argue that the above-mentioned tests are not unreasonable tests of intelligence (or at least general information) for urban ghetto blacks who grew up in the 1960s. Most white, middle-class, college students do very poorly on these tests.

▶ *Preview*

Cognitions include one's ideas, beliefs, thoughts, and images. When we know, understand, or remember something, we use cognitions to do so. Cognitive processes, which involve the formation, manipulation, and use of cognitions, are many and varied. We already have discussed several basic cognitive processes when we covered the selective and organizing nature of *perception,* the relatively permanent changes in mental processes that take place with *learning,* and the encoding, storing, and retrieving of information that is *memory.*

In this chapter, we will consider three complex cognitive processes: problem solving, language use, and intelligence. Because these tasks rely so heavily on the fundamental processes of perception, learning, and memory, we can refer to them as "higher" cognitive processes.

We'll begin with problem solving. Our daily lives are filled with all sorts of problems. Some are simple, straightforward, or trivial; others are complex and very important to us. We'll focus on problems that require the manipulation of cognitions for their solution and define the nature of problem solving.

The second cognitive process we'll examine in this chapter is the use of language. Language use involves a remarkable set of cognitive processes. Again, our first step will be to define language; then we'll review some research and theories that deal with our ability to produce and comprehend language. We'll also take a brief look at language acquisition.

Finally, we'll consider intelligence. The use of one's intelligence may be considered the most complex of cognitive processes, involving as it does perception, learning, memory, problem solving, and language. We'll examine how psychologists have characterized and measured intelligence (which will get us involved with psychological testing) and look at differences in intelligence as determined by IQ tests.

▶ Problem Solving

Sometimes our goals are obvious, our present situation is clear, and how to get from where we are to where we want to be is obvious. In these cases, we really don't have a problem, do we? Say you want to have a nice breakfast. You have butter, eggs, bacon, and bread. You also have the implements needed to prepare these foods, and you know how to use them. You know that, for you, a nice breakfast would be two eggs over easy, three strips of fried bacon, and a piece of buttered toast. With little hesitation, you can engage in the appropriate behaviors to reach your goal.

A **problem** exists when there is a discrepancy between one's present state and one's perceived goal, *and* there is no readily apparent way to get from one to the other. In situations where the path to goal attainment is not clear or obvious, you need to engage in problem-solving behaviors.

A problem situation has three major components: (1) an *initial state,* which is the situation as it is perceived to exist at the moment; (2) a *goal state,* which is the situation as the problem solver would like it to be; and (3) *routes or strategies* for getting from the initial state to the goal state.

In addition, psychologists make a distinction between well-defined and ill-defined problems. Well-defined problems are those in which both the initial state and the goal state are clearly defined. "What English word can be made from the letters *teralbay*?" We recognize this question as presenting a problem. We understand the question, have some ideas about how we might go about answering it, and surely we'll know when we have succeeded. "How do you get home from campus if you discover that your car won't start?" We know our initial state, we'll know when we have reached our goal (when we are at home), but we have to undertake a new or different way to get there.

Most of the problems that we face every day, though, are of the ill-defined variety. We don't have a clear idea of what we are starting with, nor are we able to identify a ready solution. "What should my college major be?" Many high school seniors (and some college seniors) do not even know what their options are. They have few ideas about how to find out about possible college majors. And once they have selected a major, they are not at all sure that their choice was the best one—which may be why so many college students change their majors so often.

Because ill-defined problems usually involve many variables that are difficult to define, much less control, psychologists tend to study problems that are at least reasonably well-defined.

problem a situation in which there is a discrepancy between one's current state and one's desired or goal state, with no clear way of getting from one to the other

▲ These students are faced with an ill-defined problem: "What should I choose as a college major?"

Problems come in a variety of forms, from the academic problems of physics to finding the right piece for a jigsaw puzzle. Often, the correct representation of a problem is the most difficult aspect of problem solving.

What are the three components of a problem?

Contrast well-defined and ill-defined problems. Give an example of each.

▶ **Problem Representation**

Once we realize that we're faced with a problem, the first thing we need to do is to put it in a form that allows us to think about it in terms that we can work with. We need to come up with a way to *represent* the problem in our own minds, interpreting it so that the initial state and the goal state are clear to us. We also need to note if there are restrictions on how we can go about seeking solutions. In short, we need to understand the nature of the problem. We need to make the problem meaningful, relating it to information we have available in our memories.

By examining a few of the problems of the sort that have been used in the psychology laboratory, we can see that how we choose to represent a problem can be critical. Refer to the problem in Figure 8.1. Thinking about this problem as it is presented here—in words—can be maddening. You may picture yourself walking up and down a mountain on different days, mentally visualizing a narrow path, trying to find a point on the path where you might be at precisely the same time on two different days.

As is often the case with real-life problems, this problem statement contains a good deal of irrelevant information. Problem representation often involves sorting out what matters and what doesn't. Certainly the fact that we're dealing with a monk is not relevant and neither are the temple, the dried fruit, the fact that the path happens to be narrow, or that the trip was made on two different days.

You might think about or represent this problem in terms of just one climber making the trip in one day. Or, better still, imagine that there are two climbers involved—one starting from the top of the mountain, the other starting from the bottom. Because both take the same path, surely they will meet somewhere on that mountain trail sometime during the day (See Figure 8.2). When you represent the problem this way, the solution becomes readily apparent.

Figure 8.1

THE MOUNTAIN-CLIMBING MONK PROBLEM— ANOTHER EXAMPLE OF THE IMPORTANCE OF PROBLEM REPRESENTATION.

One morning, exactly at sunrise, a Buddhist monk began to climb a tall mountain. A narrow path, no more than a foot or two wide, spiraled around the mountain to a glittering temple at the summit. The monk ascended at varying rates of speed, stopping many times along the way to rest and eat dried fruit that he carried with him. He reached the temple shortly before sunset. After several days of fasting and meditation, he began his journey back along the same path, starting at sunrise again walking at variable speeds with many pauses along the way. His average speed descending was, of course, greater than his average climbing speed. Show that there is a spot along the path that the monk will occupy on both trips at precisely the same time of day.

From Dunker, 1945.

Figure 8.2

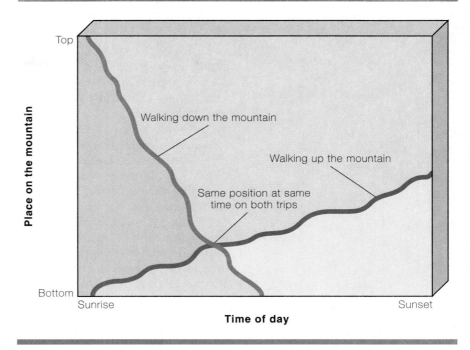

▲ *A graphic representation that makes the solution easier to see.*

So it might help to represent the mountain climbing problem visually, actually drawing out the ascending and descending pathways on paper. As it happens, visually representing the problem presented in Figure 8.3 in this way would not be wise. One can imagine someone working on this problem by drawing little train stations with trains moving toward each other, tracing the path of a bird racing back and forth between the trains. If you tried this, you discovered that it didn't help much.

Instead of visualizing this problem, think about the arithmetic and the logic involved. The stations are 50 miles apart, and the trains travel at 25 miles per hour. At that rate, how long will it take for the trains to meet? Exactly one hour. You also know that the bird flies at a rate of 100 miles per hour. If the bird flies for one hour (back and forth—or any place else for

Figure 8.3

ANOTHER PROBLEM WHOSE SOLUTION MAY DEPEND MOST ON HOW IT IS REPRESENTED IN THE MIND OF THE PROBLEM SOLVER.

Two train stations are fifty miles apart. At 2:00 P.M. one Saturday afternoon two trains start toward each other, one from each station. Just as the trains pull out of the stations, a bird springs into the air in front of the first train and flies ahead to the front of the second train. When the bird reaches the second train it turns back and flies toward the first train. The bird continues to do this, flying back and forth between the two trains until the trains meet.

If both trains travel at the rate of twenty-five miles per hour and the bird flies at one hundred miles per hour, how many miles will the bird have flown before the two trains meet?

From Posner, 1973.

that matter), how far will it fly? Right! Exactly 100 miles. As in the previous example, the solution becomes obvious as soon as the problem is stripped to its essentials and is represented in such a way that a solution is possible.

Here's one final example of the importance of problem representation (from Adams, 1974). "Imagine you have a very large sheet of paper, 1/100 of an inch thick. Imagine folding it over onto itself so that now you have two layers of paper. Fold it again so that there are four layers. It is impossible to actually fold a sheet of paper 50 times, but imagine that you could. About how thick would the paper be if it were folded 50 times?" Picturing what a piece of paper folded 50 times would look like is difficult. Some subjects guess a few inches, while others imagine that the folded paper would be several feet thick. Many have no idea at all. So representing this problem in visual terms is of little help. If one recognizes this as a problem of mathe- matics, involving exponents, then a correct solution is more likely. Actually, 50 folds would increase the paper's thickness by a factor of 2^{50}. That comes to 1,100,000,000,000,000 folds, and the resulting paper would be so high as to nearly reach from the earth to the sun!

Finding the best way to represent a problem is not a simple task. Very often, problem representation is *the* stumbling block to finding a solution (Bourne, et al., 1983). Once you realize that you are faced with a problem, your first step should be to represent it in a variety of ways. Eliminate any inessential information. Relate the problem to other problems of a similar type that you have solved before. Having done so, if the solution is still not obvious, you may have to develop some strategy to find a solution. We now turn to how one might go about generating possible solutions.

Before You Go On
▼▼▼▼▼▼▼▼▼

In the context of problem solving, what is meant by problem representation?

▶ Problem-Solving Strategies

Once you have represented the initial state of a problem and have a clear idea of what an acceptable goal might be, you still have to figure out how to get to your goal. Even after you have adequately represented a problem, how to go about solving it may not be readily apparent. You might spend a few minutes guessing wildly at a solution, but soon you'll have to settle on some strategy. In this context, a **strategy** is a systematic plan for generating possible solutions that can be tested to see if they are correct. The main advantage of cognitive strategies appears to be that they permit the problem solver to exercise some degree of control over the task at hand. They allow individuals to choose the skills and knowledge that they will bring to bear on any particular problem (Gagné, 1984). There are several possible strategies that one might choose. In this section, we'll consider two different types of strategies—algorithms and heuristics.

An **algorithm** is a problem-solving strategy that guarantees that you will arrive at a solution. It will involve systematically exploring and evaluating all possible solutions until the correct one is found. It is sometimes referred to as a *generate-test* strategy because one generates hypotheses about potential solutions and then tests each one in turn. Because of their speed of computation, most computer programs designed to solve problems use algorithmic strategies.

Simple anagram problems (letters of a word presented in a scrambled fashion) can be solved using an algorithm. "What English word has been

strategy in problem solving, a systematic plan for generating possible solutions that can be tested to see if they are correct

algorithm a problem-solving strategy in which all possible solutions are generated and tested and an acceptable solution is guaranteed

scrambled to make *uleb*?" With sufficient patience, you systematically can rearrange these four letters until you hit on a correct solution: *leub, lueb, elub, uleb, buel, beul, blue!* There it is, *blue*. With only four letters to deal with, finding a solution generally doesn't take long—there are only 24 possible arrangements of four letters (4 x 3 x 2 x 1= 24).

On the other hand, consider the anagram composed of eight letters that we mentioned earlier: *teralbay*. There are 40,320 possible combinations of these eight letters—8 x 7 x 6 x 5 x 4 x 3 x 2 x 1 = 40,320 (Reynolds & Flagg, 1983). Unless your system for moving letters around just happens to start in a good place, you could spend a lot of time before finding a combination that produces an English word. If we were dealing with a 10-letter word, there would be 3,628,800 possible combinations to check.

Imagine that you go to the supermarket to find just one item: a small jar of horseradish. You're sure the store has horseradish, but you have no idea where to find it. One plan would be to systematically go up and down every aisle of the store, checking first the top shelf, then the second, then the third, until you spied the horseradish. This strategy will work *if* the store really does carry horseradish *and if* you search carefully. There must be a better way to solve such problems. We could use some heuristic strategy.

A **heuristic** strategy is an informal, rule-of-thumb method for generating and testing problem solutions. Heuristics are more economical strategies than algorithms. When one uses a heuristic, there is no guarantee of success. On the other hand, heuristics are usually less time-consuming than algorithm strategies and lead toward goals in a logical, sensible way.

A heuristic strategy for finding horseradish in a supermarket might take you to different sections in the store in the order you believed to be most reasonable. You might start with spices, and you'd be disappointed. You might look among the fresh vegetables. Then, upon recalling that horseradish needs to be refrigerated, you go to the dairy case, and there you'd find the horseradish. You would not have wasted your time searching the cereal aisle or the frozen food section—which you might have done if you tried an algorithmic search. Another, more reasonable, heuristic would be to ask an employee where the horseradish is kept.

If you have tried the *teralbay* anagram problem, you probably used a heuristic strategy. To do so, you rely on your knowledge of English. You seriously consider only those letter combinations that you know occur frequently. You generate and test the most common combinations first. You just don't worry much about the possibility that the solution may contain a combination like *brty*. Nor do you search for a word with an aae string in it. You explore words that end in *able*, because you know these to be fairly common. But that doesn't work. What about *br* words? No, that doesn't work either. How about words with the combination *tray* in them? *Traybeal?* No. *Baletray?* No. "Oh! Now I see it: betrayal."

heuristic a problem-solving strategy in which hypotheses about problem solutions are generated and tested in a time-saving and systematic way, but that does not guarantee an acceptable solution

Before You Go On
▼▼▼▼▼▼▼▼▼

How are algorithmic and heuristic strategies used to solve problems?

▶ *Barriers to Effective Problem Solving*

By and large, it is difficult to solve problems without relying heavily on one's memory. If you forgot how fast the bird was flying, you couldn't deal with the problem in Figure 8.3. If you couldn't remember the recipe for something you wanted for supper, you would have a hard time buying the

mental set a predisposed (set) way to percieve something; an expectation

functional fixedness the phenomenon in which one is unable to see a new or use or function for an object because of an experience using the object in some other function

Figure 8.4

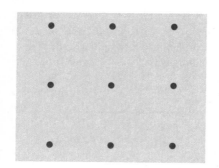

▲ The classic "nine-dot problem." The task is to connect all nine dots with just four straight lines, without removing your pen or pencil from the paper. (From Scheerer, 1963.)

correct ingredients when you went to the store. There are times, however, when previous experiences (and our memories of them) create difficulties in problem solving.

Mental Set and Functional Fixedness. In Chapter 5, pp. 163–164, we saw that perceptions can be influenced by our expectations or mental set. We often perceive what we are set to perceive. The concept of mental set is also relevant in problem solving. A **mental set** is a tendency to perceive or respond to something in a given (set) way. It is a cognitive predisposition. We may develop expectations that interfere with effective problem solving.

Figure 8.4 provides a classic example of how an inappropriate mental set can interfere with problem solving. Most subjects when first presented with this problem make an assumption (form a mental set). They assume the nine dots form a square and that their lines somehow must stay within that square. Only when this mental set is "broken" can the problem be solved. See Figure 8.11 (page 295) for one solution to Figure 8.4.

I should point out that mental sets do not necessarily hinder problem solving. A proper or appropriate mental set can be facilitating. For example, if I were to have told you to look beyond the confines of any imagined square when attempting the problem in Figure 8.4, *that* mental set—which seems strange out of context—would have made the problem easier to solve.

Functional fixedness may be thought of as a type of mental set. The process was defined by Duncker (1945) as the inability to find an appropriate new use for an object because of experience using the object in some other function. The problem solver fails to see a solution to a problem because he or she has "fixed" some "function" to an object that makes it difficult to see how it could help with the problem at hand.

A standard example is one from Maier (1931). Two strings hang from the ceiling. The problem is that they are so far apart that a subject cannot reach both of them at the same time. The goal is to do just that: to hold on to both strings at once. If there were nothing else in the room, this problem might never get solved. However, there are other objects in the room that the subject can use, including a pair of pliers (see Figure 8.5). One solution is to tie the pliers to one string and start them swinging like a pendulum. As the subject holds the other string, the string with the pliers attached can be grasped as it swings over to the subject. Because many subjects fail to see pliers as useful (functioning) for anything but turning nuts and bolts, they fail to see them as a potential pendulum weight and thus may fail to solve the problem. They have "fixed" the "function" of the pliers in their mind.

Another famous example that demonstrates functional fixedness is one reported by Duncker (1945). Subjects are given a box of tacks, a candle, and some matches. The task is to use these materials to mount the candle to the wall and light it. Obviously, one cannot just tack a candle to the wall. The solution requires breaking the mental set of functional fixedness for the box holding the tacks, seeing it as a candleholder, tacking it to the wall, and mounting the candle on it (see Figure 8.6).

Before You Go On
▼▼▼▼▼▼▼▼▼

What is a mental set, and how might a mental set hinder problem solving?

What is functional fixedness, and how might it hinder problem solving?

Figure 8.5

▲ *Maier's two-string problem. The subject is to manage to get both strings in his grasp. They are separated so that when one string is held, the other cannot be reached. See text for an explanation of the solution. (After Maier, 1931.)*

Figure 8.6

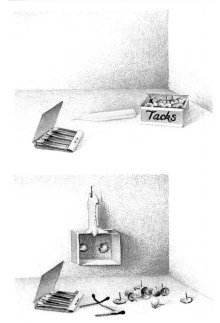

▲ *The materials provided in the candle problem, and how the problem can be solved. (After Dunker, 1945.)*

divergent thinking the creation of many ideas or potential problem solutions from one idea

convergent thinking the reduction or focusing of many different ideas into one possible problem solution

Overcoming Barriers with Creative Problem Solving. Creative solutions to problems are innovative and useful. It is very important to note that in the context of problem solving, "creative" means much more than unusual, rare, or different. Someone may generate a very original plan to solve a given problem, but unless that plan is likely to *work*, we shouldn't view it as creative (Newell, et al., 1962; Vinacke, 1974). For example, if you were to think about how to keep warm on a cold winter's night, you might come up with the idea of popping bushels of warm popcorn for everyone to sit in. The popped corn would keep everyone warm—at least for a short while. Such a solution may border on the unique or unusual, but it certainly doesn't seem very workable. Creative solutions should be put to the same test as more ordinary solutions: Do they solve the problem at hand?

Creative solutions generally involve new and different organizations of problem elements. As mentioned earlier, it is often at the stage of problem representation that creativity is most noticeable. Seeing a problem in a new light or combining elements in a new and different way may lead to creative solutions. One observation has been made many times: There is virtually no correlation between creative problem solving and what is usually referred to as "intelligence" (Barron & Harrington, 1981; Horn, 1976; Kershner & Ledger, 1985).

Creative problem solving often involves **divergent thinking**—that is, starting with one idea and generating from it a number of alternative possibilities and new ideas (Dirkes, 1978; Guilford, 1959). One simple test for divergent thinking skills requires one to generate as many uses as possible for simple objects such as a brick or a paper clip. When we engage in **convergent thinking**, we take many different ideas and try to focus and reduce them to just one possible solution (Figure 8.7). An example of convergent thinking would be trying to come up with just one or two courses of action (from dozens of possibilities that have been offered) to reduce the dropout rate of high school students. Obviously, convergent thinking has its place, but for *creative* problem solving, divergent thinking is generally more useful, because many new and different possibilities are explored. We need to remember, however, that all these new and different possibilities for a problem's solution need to be judged ultimately in terms of whether they really work.

Solving problems, creatively or otherwise, is easier for humans than for nonhumans, because humans can take advantage of a unique cognitive skill-language. We use language not only to help in problem solving, but also to communicate with others. We now turn to the higher cognitive process of language use.

Before You Go On

▼▼▼▼▼▼▼▼▼▼

What is the difference between divergent and convergent thinking?

▶ Language

Language allows us to communicate to others how we feel and how we think. Using it is a social process that reflects a marvelously complex set of cognitive processes.

▶ A Definition of Language

language a collection of arbitrary symbols that follow certain rules of combination and that have significance for the language-using community

Language is a large collection of arbitrary symbols that have significance for a language-using community and that follow certain rules of combination

Figure 8.7

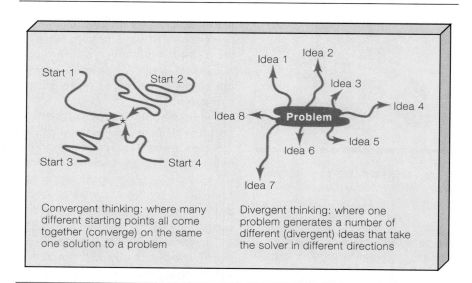

Convergent thinking: where many different starting points all come together (converge) on the same one solution to a problem

Divergent thinking: where one problem generates a number of different (divergent) ideas that take the solver in different directions

▲ *A schematic representation of the nature of convergent and divergent thinking in the context of problem solving.*

No More Oversleeping

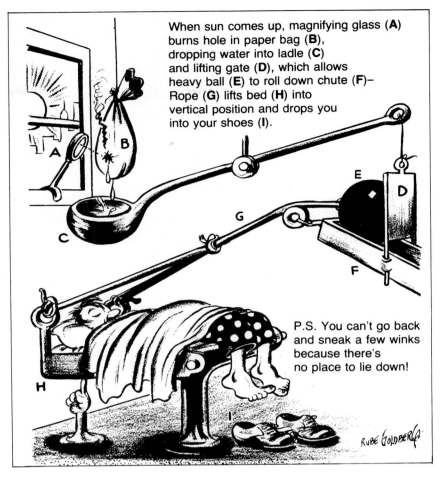

When sun comes up, magnifying glass (**A**) burns hole in paper bag (**B**), dropping water into ladle (**C**) and lifting gate (**D**), which allows heavy ball (**E**) to roll down chute (**F**)– Rope (**G**) lifts bed (**H**) into vertical position and drops you into your shoes (**I**).

P.S. You can't go back and sneak a few winks because there's no place to lie down!

RUBE GOLDBERG

▲ *Creative problem solutions must be more than different or unusual—they must provide a workable solution to the problem at hand.*

(after Morris, 1946). Let's pull apart this definition of language and examine the points that it raises.

First, language is made up of a large number of *symbols*. The symbols that comprise language are commonly referred to as words—labels that we have assigned for the mental representation of our experiences. With language, we can communicate about owls and pussycats in teacups, four-dimensional, time-warped hyperspace, and a beagle that flies his doghouse into battle against the Red Baron. Words stand for our cognitions, our concepts, and we have a great number of them.

The symbols of language are *arbitrary*. You call what you are reading a book. We have all agreed (in English) that *book* is the appropriate symbol for what you are reading. But we don't have to. We could agree to call it a *fard,* or a *relm,* if we liked. On the other hand, once a word is established by common use or tradition, it becomes part of a language and must be learned and used by each new language user.

To be part of a language, language symbols need to have *significance for a language-using community*. That is, a number of people need to agree on the language symbols and what those symbols mean. This is another way of saying that language use is a social enterprise. There is a language-using community for which the utterance, *"Kedinin üstünde halt var"* makes

▲ *Language is the vehicle for communicating our understanding of events to others.*

sense or has significance. I'm not part of that community, but many people are. To them—people who know Turkish—the statement reads roughly, "The cat is on the mat" (from Slobin, 1979, p. 4).

The final part of our definition tells us that the symbols of a language must *follow certain rules of combination.* What this means is that language is structured, or rule-governed. There are rules about how we can and cannot string symbols together in language. In English, we say "The small boy slept late." We do not say "Slept boy late small the." Well, we could say it, but no one would know for sure what we meant by it, and everyone would recognize that the utterance violates the combinatorial rules of English.

Even with this complex definition of language, there are a few points we've left out. For one, using language is a remarkably *creative, generative* process. Virtually every time we use our language, we use it in new and creative ways, a fact that emphasizes the importance of the underlying rules or structure of language. A second point: Language allows for *displacement,* the ability to communicate about the "not here and the not now." We can use language to discuss yesterday's lunch and tomorrow's class schedule. We can talk about things that are not here, never were, and never will be. Language is the only form of communication that allows us to do so.

One final observation: Language and speech are not synonymous terms. Speech is but one (common) way in which language is expressed as behavior. There are others, including writing, coding (as in Morse code), or signing (as in American Sign Language).

Before You Go On
▼▼▼▼▼▼▼▼

What are some of the defining characteristics of language?

▶ *Language Acquisition*

One of the most significant achievements of childhood is the acquisition of language. There are few cognitive skills that can compare to language in complexity and usefulness. How children acquire language has long been a

▲ *Although we say the symbols of language are arbitrary, a number of people need to agree on what the symbols are and how they will be used.*

concern of psycholinguists. The process seems nearly magical: gooing, cooing, babbling one day, then a word or two, then "Why is the sky blue, Daddy, why is the sky blue?"—and all in the span of just a few months' time.

There simply is no answer to the question, "How do humans acquire language?" Steven Pinker, director of the Center for Cognitive Science at M.I.T., calls language acquisition "the jewel in the crown of cognition—it is what everyone wants to explain" (deCuevas, 1990, p. 63). At best, we have tentative theories and hypotheses. We are only now close to adequately describing *what* happens. Describing *how* it happens will take longer.

What Happens in Language Acquisition. Infants create speech sounds spontaneously. They come into the world with a cry, and make noise with regularity forever after. At about the age of 6 months, random cries and noises are replaced by the more regular sounds of **babbling**—speech sounds, often in repetitive, rhythmic patterns, such as "da-da-da" or "lu-lu." A curiosity is that when children babble, they do so by producing virtually all the known sounds of all known languages. (Those sounds that are not part of a child's language then drop out of its repertoire.) All babies babble in the same way (Nakazima, 1962; Oller, 1981). Adults cannot distinguish the babbling of a Chinese infant from that of a Greek or an American infant. Even deaf infants produce babbling sounds that cannot be distinguished from those of hearing children (Lenneberg, Rebelsky & Nichols, 1965).

The acquisition of vocabulary follows soon after babbling begins. In all cases, comprehension comes before production. That is, children understand and respond appropriately to the meaning of utterances long before they are able to produce those utterances themselves. We usually notice the appearance of a child's first word or two at about the age of one year (parents may argue that the onset of meaningful speech comes sooner, but independent observers often fail to confirm what may be parental wishful thinking). Once it begins, word acquisition is truly remarkable. A one-year-old may produce only two or three words (remember, he or she may very well understand dozens of words, but can produce only a few). By the age of two years, word production is up to about 50. In terms of comprehension, by age 2 1/2, a child understands 200–300 words; by age 3, over 1000; by age 6, somewhere between 8000 and 14,000 words (Benedict, 1979; Brown, 1973; Carey, 1978).

Describing the development of syntactic rules, or grammar, in children has proven to be quite difficult. As linguists began to understand the rules that govern adult language, it seemed reasonable to look for these same rules in the language of children. What soon became apparent was that the grammar of adult forms of language do not emerge until long after children have begun stringing words together in utterances. Although we do not find adult structure in the language use of children, children use language in a rule-governed way. That is, young children do not just speak adult language badly; instead, their language follows its own rules.

The first use of speech as language is called **holophrastic speech.** Holophrastic speech is the use of just one word to communicate a range of intentions and meanings—dependent upon gestures, intonation, and so on. Before this stage, a child may produce a number of words, but will do so only as a naming exercise. Words are used as labels for concepts and nothing else. With holophrastic speech, individual words are used to communicate a range of possibilities. Picture a young child sitting in a highchair. Can't you just see how the one-word utterance "milk" could be used to communicate such things as "I WANT MY MILK!" or "uh-oh, I dropped my milk" or "oh yea! here's my milk" or "Yuck, not milk again."

babbling speech sounds produced in rhythmic, repetitive patterns

holophrastic speech the use of one word to communicate a number of different meanings

At about the age of 2 years, we can note the appearance of two-word utterances. When carefully analyzed, these two-word utterances are very regular—as if they were being put together according to some fairly strict rules. Given an understanding of the words *big* and *little* and many nouns, a child may say, "big ball," "big plane," "big doggie," "little stick," "little cup," and so on. What is curious is that this child will never reverse this word order. He will not say "ball big" or "doggie little" (Braine, 1976).

From the point of the two-word utterance on, language development is so rapid that it is difficult to note the stages through which the process passes. From the two-word utterance stage there is a period that is typified by "telegraphic speech," comprised of nouns, verbs, and adjectives, but hardly any "function words" such as articles or prepositions. We hear children say things such as: "Daddy go store now" or "Billy draw pictures." Then, at about age 2 1/2 years, language use expands at an explosive rate. There really is no noticeable three-word or four-word stage of development. Phrases are lengthened, noun phrases first, so that "Billy's ball" becomes "Billy's red ball" which soon becomes "Billy's red ball that Mommy got at the store." By the time children are ready to begin school—about age 5— they demonstrate the understanding and the production of virtually every type of acceptable sentence structure in their language.

Now that we have a very basic idea of *what* happens when children acquire language, we'll consider how we can account for the process.

Before You Go On
▼▼▼▼▼▼▼▼▼

What are some of the landmark events that occur during language acquisition?

Theories of Language Acquisition. How does language acquisition happen? If you took a foreign language in high school (or if you're taking one now) did it ever occur to you that there were little children somewhere in the world who were acquiring the same language that you were struggling with? They were not having any problems with it at all. Acquiring one's language is a cognitive feat at which all (normal) humans succeed.

Throughout this section I have avoided the phrase "language learning," referring instead to "language acquisition" or "language development." This was intentional because I did not want to suggest that acquiring language is simply a matter of learning. On the other hand, language is certainly not instinctive in the usual sense, or everyone would speak the same language. Some language acquisition can be accounted for by learning (in all the ways we discussed in Chapter 6), but some aspects of language acquisition defy explanation in terms of learning and suggest an inherited basis. We cannot get into all of the details of the debate over which aspects of language development are a function of learning (one's nurture) and which seem to have a biological basis (one's nature), but we can review some of the issues.

Theories of language development in terms of learning (*e.g.*, Skinner, 1957; Whitehurst, 1982) certainly have their place. No one will claim that language emerges free of the influence of learning, experience, conditioning, reinforcement, and the like. We can be most comfortable with learning approaches when we try to account for the acquisition of speech sounds and word meanings. Indeed, acquiring the sounds of a language seems to be a straightforward process, albeit slightly backward. The infant spontaneously produces phonemes from all languages, but learns, through imitation and reinforcement, which sounds need to be "saved" for use in his or her language. Those that are not appropriate for the child's language are simply not used and disappear from the child's repertoire (deVillers and deVillers, 1978).

Learning theories are not terribly strained when it comes to the acquisition of words. What we're dealing with here is the development of labels for concepts that are undoubtedly learned. There are many varieties of learning involved in word acquisition. Some of the meanings of words comes from classical conditioning (Chapter 6, p. 202). Use of some words is reinforced and the use of others is not—as predicted by operant conditioning. Some vocabulary growth results from observational learning—using words that others use. Some words develop through direct instruction. By and large, learning seems to handle the acquisition of vocabulary rather nicely. But . . . there are a few problems.

For one thing, as children begin to acquire the rules that change the meaning of a word, they do so with disturbing regularity. For no good reason that learning theory can account for, children learn to add "-ing" to words before they learn to form possessives (by adding "-'s"), which they learn before learning to form the past tense of verbs (by adding "-ed"). That is, when asked what he is doing, a child may be expected first to respond "I draw." Later will come "I drawing." Only later may we expect "That Billy's picture." Later still we will hear something like "I drawed it yesterday." In other words, there is a predictable sequence in which many word sequences seem to be acquired.

Another example that provides a problem for learning theory is called **overregularization**—the continued application of an acquired language rule (for forming plurals or past tense, for example) in a situation where it is not appropriate. A child might say, "I have two foots," or "four mans," or "I goed to the store," even after using the words "feet," "men" and "went" in similar contexts. What accounts for overregularization? Biologically oriented theories (*e.g.,* Chomsky, 1965; 1975; Lenneberg, 1967; McNeill, 1970) suggest that there must be some innate, "prewired" biological mechanism that the child uses to seek out and apply rules during acquisition. This mechanism (called a Language Acquisition Device, or LAD) becomes active and useful when we are about 1 year old, and effectively turns off by the time we are 5 or 6 years old. In this scenario, the child is so predisposed to find and use rules that she or he will do so with great consistency, even when a particular application of the rule is wrong. Actually, "two foots" is a much more reasonable construction than "two feet" even though "two foots" is not likely to be heard in standard adult speech (Anisfeld, 1984).

Reliance on some sort of LAD becomes even more sensible when we consider the acquisition rules of the sort that are reflected in the generation of sentences. (I should add that nobody has the slightest idea of what a LAD would look like or how it would work.) The basic argument for an innate predisposition for the acquisition of language rules comes largely from the orderliness of language development. The ages of the children are not always the same, but with uncanny regularity, children everywhere acquire their different languages in virtually the same pattern. Holophrastic speech, the stability of the two-word utterance, the expansion of noun phrases, and the ordered acquisition of word endings has been noted over and over as a consistent pattern—a pattern more consistent than we could ever expect from the learning histories of the children being observed (Slobin, 1979).

Another point that is often raised against the learning approach is related to the rules of grammar, or sentence construction. Most adults (by far) cannot even tell us what the rules of their language *are*. The argument then follows: How can you begin to teach something to someone else, if you

overregularization the excessive application of an acquired language rule (*e.g.,* for plurals or past tense) in a situation where it is not appropriate

▲ Some people are born with the predisposition to become extremely intelligent. This inherited potential must be encouraged and nurtured in a stimulating environment to be fully realized.

haven't got the slightest idea yourself of what it is that you're teaching? The argument is sensible. Yet, there is the logic that as adults we *do* have certain linguistic intuitions. We can tell when an utterance is correctly formed, even if we can't specify why. We can use this intuition to reinforce proper use and to correct improper use. The problem is that when we watch adults interacting with young children, we find that they are much more likely to correct the *content* of what the child says than the *form* in which it is said. For example, if a child says, "Me no like oatmeal," a parent is likely to respond with a statement such as, "Sure you do; you eat it all the time" (Brown, 1973; Brown, Cazden & Bellugi, 1969).

So when it comes to explaining language acquisition, just where are we? Well, we're a long way from any final answers, but at the moment we seem to be where we always seem to be—faced with two theoretical positions, one favoring learning (or nurture) while the other favors innate factors (or nature). Some aspects of language are learned. For most language acquisition processes, learning, imitation, and reinforcement provide unsatisfactory explanations. A conservative position, for now, is an interactionist one: Humans are born with a predisposition to acquire certain aspects of language. Which language they acquire, and which aspects, will reflect their experiences in their language-using community.

Before You Go On
▼▼▼▼▼▼▼▼▼

Briefly summarize the learning-oriented and biology-oriented theories of language acquisition.

▶ Intelligence

In a chapter on higher cognitive processes, it is sensible to consider what is, perhaps, the ultimate reflection of human cognitive processing: intelligence. Intelligence is a troublesome concept in psychology. We all know what we mean when we use the term, but we have a terrible time trying to define it concisely.

Intelligence has been defined as the sum total of everything you know, as the ability to learn or profit from experience, and as the ability to solve problems or to cope with the environment. Of course, there is nothing wrong with any of these definitions. The problem is that none seems to say it all. We have gotten into the habit of using "intelligence" as a general label for so many cognitive abilities that it defies specific definition.

Nonetheless, we need to settle on some definition to guide our study through the rest of this chapter. I propose that we accept two definitions, one academic and theoretical, the other operational and practical. For our theoretical definition, let us say that **intelligence** is "the capacity of an individual to understand the world about him [her] and his [her] resourcefulness to cope with its challenges" (Wechsler, 1975, p. 139).

This definition (and others like it) presents some ambiguities. Just what do we mean by "capacity"? What is meant by "understand the world"? What if the world never really challenges one's "resourcefulness"? Would such people be less intelligent? What at first reading may seem like a very sensible and inclusive definition of intelligence may, upon reflection, pose even more definitional problems.

intelligence the capacity to understand the world and the resourcefulness to cope with its challenges; that which an intelligence test measures

Perhaps we ought to follow our advice from Chapter 1, where we saw that using operational definitions can help overcome theoretical problems. We have to be careful here, but we may operationally define intelligence as "that which intelligence tests measure." Notice that using this definition simply sidesteps the thorny conceptual problem of coming to grips with the "true" nature of intelligence; it doesn't solve it. But it does what operational definitions are supposed to do—it gives us a definition we can work with. To use this definition, we need to understand how tests measure intelligence.

Before You Go On

▼▼▼▼▼▼▼

Provide a theoretical and an operational definition of intelligence.

▶ The Nature of Psychological Tests

There are several ways to define intelligence. We'll soon see that there are also several different ways of measuring it. Although the focus of our discussion here *is* intelligence, we must recognize that psychological tests have been devised to measure the full range of human abilities and characteristics. For that reason, we'll begin this section with a few words about psychological tests in general.

We define a **psychological test** as "an objective, standardized measure of a sample of behavior" (Anastasi,1988). A psychological test measures behavior. It measures behavior because that is all we *can* measure. We just cannot measure those mental concepts that we call feelings, aptitudes, or abilities. On the basis of our behavioral assessment, we may be willing to make inferences and assumptions about underlying internal processes.

A psychological test can measure only a *sample* of behavior. Let's say that I want to know about your tendency to be aggressive. I cannot very well ask you everything that relates to aggression in your life ("List *all* of the situations in which you have ever acted aggressively," for instance). What I have to do instead is sample (systematically identify a portion of) the behaviors in which I am interested. I then assume that responses to my sample of items can be used to predict responses to related questions that I have not asked. Even a classroom exam only asks you about a sample of the material you have learned in preparation for that exam.

There are two other definitional points to consider. If a test is to have any value, its administration must be *standardized* and its scoring must be *objective*. Here is where your experience as a test-taker may be relevant. Imagine taking a college placement test that will be used to determine which courses in English composition you will be required to take. You are given 45 minutes to answer 50 multiple-choice questions *and* write a short essay on a prescribed topic. Later, you discover that some students were given the same examination, but with instructions to "take as long as you like to finish the test." You also discover that those students could write their essay on any one of three suggested topics. You would be justified in complaining that something is wrong with the testing system. It lacks standardization.

A psychological test should be objective. Objectivity in this context refers to the evaluation of the responses that exam takers make—scoring the test, in other words. Different examiners (at least those of the same level of expertise) should be expected to give the same interpretation and evaluation

psychological test an objective, standardized measure of a sample of behavior

to a test response. If the same responses to a psychological test lead one psychologist to declare a person perfectly normal, a second to consider the person a mass of inner conflict and anxiety, while a third wonders why this person is not now in a psychiatric institution, we have a problem. Assuming that the problem is with the test and not the psychologists, the problem is one of objectivity. Although strict, literal objectivity is a goal seldom reached by psychological tests (particularly those designed to assess personality characteristics), it is a worthy goal. Note that I am *not* claiming here that a psychological test must yield exactly the same results every time it is scored. Testing situations that yield subjective impressions *can* be useful. Still, the criteria for evaluating test responses must be objective enough to yield a degree of consistency in the interpretation.

It appears that all we need for a psychological test is a series of items for subjects to respond to that are administered in a standard fashion and scored objectively. That doesn't sound dificult to do. It isn't. The world is full of "tests" that meet these criteria. Weekly papers at the supermarket, scores of magazines, newspapers, and television programs regularly include "psychological tests." As a consumer of such tests, as well as a student of psychology, you should be able to assess the value of the measuring devices that we call psychological tests.

To qualify as a good psychological test, a technique needs to have three characteristics: reliability, validity, and adequate norms. To ensure that a test has these characteristics takes time and effort (and money). It is for this reason that many of the tests found in the popular press tend not to be good tests.

In the context of psychological testing, **reliability** means the same thing it means in other contexts: consistency or dependability. Suppose someone gives you an objective, standardized measure of a sample of your behavior and, on the basis of your responses, claims that you have an IQ that is slightly below average—94, let's say. Two weeks later, you take the same test and are told that your IQ is now 127—nearly in the top 3 percent of the entire population! Something is wrong. We have not yet discussed IQ scores, but surely we recognize that one's IQ—as a measure of intelligence—does not change by 33 points within two weeks.

The type of reliability with which we are usually concerned is called **test-retest reliability**. As its name suggests, test-retest reliability involves administering a test to the same group of subjects on two different occasions. Scores on the two administrations are then correlated with each other. Correlation will tell us directly if the test in question is reliable. If the correlation coefficient is near zero, the test may be declared unreliable. The reliability of a test is indicated by a correlation coefficient (where those above +0.70 are taken as acceptable).

When people worry about the usefulness of a test, their concern is usually with that test's **validity**. Measures of validity tell us the extent to which a test actually measures what it claims to measure. It is the extent to which there is agreement between a test score and the quality that the test is believed to measure (Kaplan & Saccuzzo, 1989).

We determine a test's reliability by correlating the test with itself (at a later time). We determine a test's validity by correlating test scores with some independent measure, or *criterion*. One of the most practical types of validity is **predictive validity**. A test has predictive validity to the extent that it adequately predicts future behavior. Does this test predict which students are most likely to join clubs, sororities, or fraternities? Does this aptitude test predict who will do well in college and who will not? Does this assessment predict whether or not this patient is likely to injure himself or others in the future?

reliability consistency or dependability; in testing, consistency of test scores

test-retest reliability a check of a test's consistency determined by correlating the results of a test taken by the same subjects at two different times

validity in testing, the extent to which a test measures what it claims to measure

predictive validity the extent to which a test can be used to predict future behaviors

Determining a test's predictive validity is a matter of correlation. The test is given to a large group of subjects. Subjects are later measured on the independent criterion, and test scores are correlated with criterion scores. Now you find out if those who earn high test scores also earn good grades in college courses. (Determining the validity of a test requires that we have a good, reliable, and valid criterion to correlate the test with.)

If a psychological test is well correlated with other tests or measures of the same characteristic, the test is said to have **concurrent validity**. If you generate a new test to measure anxiety that is not at all correlated with any of the well-established techniques already available for measuring anxiety, your technique lacks concurrent validity.

We may want to know the extent to which an applicant can do a job *now* (concurrently). We can assess the concurrent validity of an employment test for auto mechanics by giving our test to currently employed mechanics. If efficient, successful mechanics do well on our test and if mechanics who are less able do poorly, we have demonstrated a degree of concurrent validity for our test.

One additional form of validity ought to be mentioned here because it is relevant for students taking classroom exams. **Content validity** is the extent to which a test adequately samples the behaviors that it claims to be testing. For example, you may be told that you are to be given an exam on all of the learning chapter. The test consists of 50 multiple-choice items. You might be more than a little upset if you were to find that 48 of the 50 items deal only with classical conditioning. You would claim that the test was not fair. In this case, it lacks content validity because the content of the test does not cover a broad range of material on learning. Content validity usually is determined by the judgment of content area experts.

Let's say that you have just filled out an objective, paper-and-pencil questionnaire designed to measure the extent to which you are extroverted. You know that the test is a reliable and valid instrument. You are told that you scored a 50 on the test. So what? What does a score of 50 mean? It doesn't mean that you answered 50 percent of the items correctly, because on this test there are no correct or incorrect answers. Does a 50 mean that you are extroverted, introverted, or neither, or both? If you don't have a basis of comparison, any one test score by itself is meaningless. You need to compare your score with the scores of other people like yourself who have already taken the test. Results of a test taken by a large group of subjects whose scores are used to make comparisons are called **norms**.

You may discover by checking the norms that a score of 50 is average and indicative of neither extreme extroversion nor extreme introversion. On the other hand, a 50 might be a very high score, indicating extroversion, or a very low score, indicating introversion. An aptitude test score of 134 sounds pretty good until you discover that the average score was 265 and that scores in the norms range from 115 to 360. If the norms tell you that the average score on the aptitude test was only 67 and that scores tend to range between 30 and 140, then your score of 134 would be very good indeed.

Writing a good psychological test, then, is not as easy as it may at first appear. Writing a series of questions and deciding on answers may be quite simple, but the rest takes considerable time and effort. Now that we have an idea of the types of considerations that need to be made when constructing a psychological test, we can examine the attempts of psychologists to measure intelligence. Given the difficulty we've had coming to any agreement on the nature of intelligence in theory, you won't be surprised to find that not all psychologists are pleased with currently available intelligence tests.

concurrent validity the extent to which the scores on a test are correlated with other assessments made at about the same time

content validity the extent to which a test provides an adequate and fair sample of the behaviors being measured

norms in the context of psychological testing results of a test taken by a large group of subjects whose scores can be used to make comparisons or give meaning to new scores

What is a psychological test?

In the context of psychological testing, what are reliability, validity, and test norms?

▶ Testing Intelligence

Now we can briefly review some of the psychological tests used to measure intelligence. As we do so, there are two ideas you will need to keep in mind. First, you'll need to remember the definition of a psychological test (as an objective, standardized measure of a sample of behavior) and the criteria for evaluating them (reliability, validity, and norms). Second, you'll have to remember that test scores provide only one measure of intelligence, and no one measure is going to provide a universally satisfactory description or assessment of a concept as complex as intelligence.

The Stanford-Binet Intelligence Scale. Alfred Binet (1857–1911) was the leading psychologist in France at the turn of the century. Of great concern in 1900 were those children in the Paris school system who seemed unable to profit from the educational experiences they were being given. Binet set out to construct a test to measure the intellectual abilities of children. Binet and his most important collaborator, Théodore Simon, wanted to identify students who should be placed in special (largely remedial) classes, where their education could proceed more efficiently than in the standard classroom.

Binet's first test appeared in 1905 and was revised and expanded in 1908. The test was an immediate success. It caught the attention of Lewis M. Terman at Stanford University, who supervised a translation and revision of the test in 1916. (This revision included changing some clearly French questions into items more suitable for American children.) Since then, the test has been referred to as the Stanford-Binet and has undergone a number of subsequent revisions. The most recent version of the Stanford-Binet was published in 1986. This edition, the fourth, made a number of significant changes in the test and in its scoring. So what is this test like?

The test now follows what its authors call a three-level hierarchical model of cognitive ability (Thorndike, et al., 1986). As did Binet's original test, the current edition yields an overall test score which reflects **g**, or general intellectual ability, which the test's authors describe as "what an individual uses when faced with a problem that he or she has not been taught to solve" (1986, p. 3). Underlying **g** are three second-level factors (Figure 8.8). *Crystallized abilities* represent those skills required for acquiring and using information about verbal and quantitative concepts to solve problems. They are influenced by schooling and comprise an academic ability factor. *Fluid-analytic abilities* are skills needed to solve problems that involve figural or nonverbal types of information. The bases of these skills are less tied to formal schooling. Essentially, they involve the ability to see things in new and different ways. The third factor at this level of the model is *short-term memory*. Items that test the ability to hold information in memory for short periods of time can be found on Binet's original test.

The third level of abilities tested on the new Stanford-Binet provides a more specific, content-oriented factor. As you can see from Figure 8.8, at this level, crystallized abilities are divided into verbal and quantitative rea-

▲ *Alfred Binet*

g on an intelligence test, a measure of one's overall, general intellectual abilities, commonly thought of as IQ

▲ *Lewis Terman*

Figure 8.8

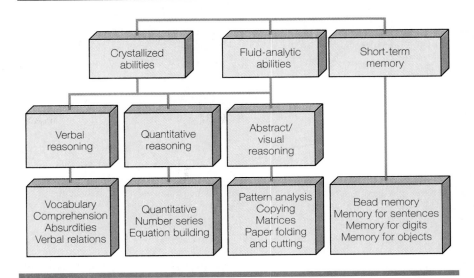

▲ *The factors tested by the Stanford-Binet, Fourth Edition, arranged in three levels, including a listing of each subtest. (After Thorndike et al., 1986.)*

soning, fluid analytic abilities are seen as abstract/visual reasoning, and there is no ability at this level that corresponds to short-term memory. At the base of the hierarchy are the 15 subtests that operationally define the structure of the actual Stanford-Binet test.

What all of this means is that the authors of the 1986 revision of the Stanford-Binet acknowledge that a person's measured intelligence should be reflected in more than just one test score. Now, not only can we determine an overall **g** score, but we also can calculate scores for each factor at each of three levels. In addition, we can calculate scores for the 15 subtests by themselves, although it is difficult to say that individual subtest scores are very meaningful. It's also unlikely that an examiner would administer all 15 of the subtests to any one subject. Figure 8.9 shows the way that **g**-scores on the Stanford-Binet are distributed in the general population.

Before we go on, let's take a minute to discuss what has happened to the concept of IQ. **IQ** is an abbreviation for the term *intelligence quotient*. As you know, a quotient is the result you get when you divide one number by another. If one divides 8 by 6, the quotient is 1.33. For the early versions of the Stanford-Binet, the examiner's job was to determine a subject's *mental age* (or *MA*), the age level at which the subject was functioning in terms of intellectual abilities. A subject with the intellectual abilities of an average 8 year old has an MA of 8. IQ was determined by dividing the subject's earned mental age by his or her actual age (called *chronological age*, or *CA*). This quotient was then multiplied by 100 to determine IQ, or IQ= MA/CA x 100. If an 8-year-old girl has a mental age of 8, that girl would be average, and her IQ would equal 100 (8/8x100= 1x100). If the 8-year-old were above average, with the intellectual abilities of an average 10-year-old, then her IQ would be 125 (that's 10/8x100, or 1.25x100). If she were below average, say with the mental abilities of an average 6 year old, then her IQ would be 75. Because it is a term that is engrained in our vocabulary, *we will continue to use "IQ" as a measure of general intelligence,* even though we now report test results as standard scores and no longer compute MAs or calculate quotients.

▲ *Pictured here are some of the materials that make up the revised Stanford-Binet test. The fourth edition represents the most significant changes made to the test and its scoring.*

Figure 8.9

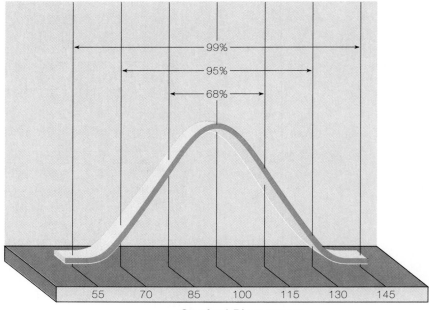

99%
95%
68%

| 55 | 70 | 85 | 100 | 115 | 130 | 145 |

Stanford-Binet scores

▲ *An idealized curve that shows the distribution of scores on the Stanford-Binet Intelligence Scale if the test were taken by a very large sample of the general population. The numbers at the top of the curve indicate the percentage of the population expected to score within the indicated range of scores, 68 percent score between 85 and 115; 95 percent between 70 and 130; and 99 percent score between 55 and 145.*

Before You Go On
▼▼▼▼▼▼▼▼▼▼

Briefly describe the Stanford-Binet Intelligence Scale.

The Wechsler Tests of Intelligence. David Wechsler published his first general intelligence test in 1939. Unlike the Stanford-Binet that existed at that time, it was designed for use with adult populations and to reduce the heavy reliance on verbal skills that characterized Binet's tests. With a major revision in 1955, the test became known as the *Wechsler Adult Intelligence Scale (WAIS).* The latest revision (the WAIS-R) was published in 1981. The WAIS-R is appropriate for subjects between 16 and 74 years of age and is reported to be the most commonly used of all psychological tests (Lubin, et al., 1984).

A natural extension of the WAIS was the *Wechsler Intelligence Scale for Children (WISC),* originally published 11 years after the WAIS. After a major revision in 1974, it became known as the WISC-R. With up-dated norms, and a number of new items (designed to minimize bias against any ethnic group or gender), the WISC-III appeared in late 1991. The WISC-III is appropriate for testing children between the ages of 6 and 16 (there is some overlap with the WAIS-R). A third test in the Wechsler series is for younger children between the ages of 4 and 6 1/2. It is called the *Wechsler*

Preschool and Primary Scale of Intelligence (WPPSI.) It was first published in 1967. It, too, was revised recently—in 1989—and is now the WPPSI-R. There are some subtle differences among the three Wechsler tests, but each is based on the same general logic. Therefore, we'll consider only one, the WAIS-R, in detail.

The WAIS-R is made up of 11 subtests. The subtests of the WAIS-R are arranged by the type of ability being tested. The subtests are organized into two categories. Six subtests define *verbal scale,* and five subtests constitute a *performance scale.* Figure 8.10 lists the different subtests of the WAIS-R and describes some of the sorts of items found on each. With each of the Wechsler tests, we can compute three scores: a verbal score, a performance score, and a total (or full-scale) score. As with the Stanford-Binet, the total score can be interpreted as an approximation of **g**, or general intellectual ability.

To administer the WAIS-R, you present each of the 11 subtests. The items within each subtest are arranged in order of difficulty. You start with relatively easy items—those you are confident your subject will respond to correctly—and then you progress to more difficult ones. You stop when your subject fails a specified number of items. You alternate between the verbal and nonverbal subtests. The whole process may take up to an hour and a half.

Each item on each subtest is scored. (Some of the performance items have strict time limits that affect scoring.) You now have 11 scores earned by your subject. As is now the case with the fourth edition of the Stanford-Binet, each subtest score is compared to the score provided with the test's norms. How your subject's score compares to the score earned by subjects in the norm group determines your subject's *standard score* for each of the Wechsler subtests. In addition to one overall **g** score, the Wechsler tests provide verbal and performance scores, which provide information about a person's particular strengths and weaknesses.

For many years, there has been controversy about the use and quality of individually administered intelligence tests, such as the Wechsler tests and the Stanford-Binet. The extent to which the tests may be culturally biased, thus favoring one group of subjects over another, whether they truly measure intelligence and/or just academic success, and whether test results can

g on an intelligence test, a measure of one's overall, general intellectual abilities, commonly thought of as IQ

▲ *The Wechsler tests provide verbal and performance scores that are compared to scores earned by subjects of the same age in the norm group. The Wechsler Intelligence Scale for Children (WISC-R) is a general intelligence test for children between the ages of 6 and 17.*

Figure 8.10

THE SUBTESTS OF THE WECHSLER ADULT INTELLIGENCE SCALE-REVISED (WAIS-R)

Verbal scale

Information	(29 items) Questions designed to tap one's general knowledge about a variety of topics dealing with one's culture; for example, "Who wrote *Huckleberry Finn?*" or "How many nickels in a quarter?"
Digit span	(7 series) Subject is read a series of three to nine digits and is asked to repeat them; then a different series is to be repeated in reverse order.
Comprehension	(16 items) A test of judgment, common sense, and practical knowledge; for example, "Why is it good to have prisons?"
Similarities	(14 pairs) Subject must indicate the way(s) in which two things are alike; for example, "In what way are an apple and a potato alike?"
Vocabulary	(35 words) Subject must provide an acceptable definition for a series of words.
Arithmetic	(14 problems) Math problems must be solved without the use of paper and pencil; for example, "How far will a bird travel in 90 minutes if it flies at the rate of 10 miles per hour?"

Performance scale

Picture completion	(20 pictures) Subject must identify or name the missing part or object in a drawing; for example, a truck with only three wheels.
Picture arrangement	(10 series) A series of cartoonlike pictures must be arranged in an order so that they tell a story.
Block design	(9 items) Using blocks whose sides are either all red, all white, or diagonally red and white, subject must copy a designed picture or pattern shown on a card.
Object assembly	(4 objects) Free-form jigsaw puzzles must be put together to form familiar objects.
Digit symbol	In a key, each of nine digits is paired with a simple symbol. Given a random series of digits, the subject must provide the paired symbol within a time limit.

be used for political purposes, perhaps as a basis for discrimination are just a few of the questions that keep finding their way into the popular press. A survey of over 600 experts in psychological testing indicates considerable agreement about the basic value of intelligence (or IQ) tests (Snyderman & Rothman, 1987). Although experts are willing to allow that the tests may be slightly biased on racial and socioeconomic grounds, they "believe that such tests adequately measure more important elements of intelligence" (p. 143).

Before You Go On
▼▼▼▼▼▼▼▼▼

What are the major features of the Wechsler intelligence scales?

Group Tests of Intelligence. Individually administered tests such as the Wechsler tests and the Stanford-Binet have advantages. Perhaps most important is that the examiner has the opportunity to interact meaningfully with the subject taking the test. The examiner can use the testing session to develop opinions and impressions about the examinee and can observe at first hand how the subject goes about responding to test items.

The major disadvantage of the individually administered tests is that they are time-consuming and expensive. There are, of course, alternatives. Group IQ tests are generally paper-and-pencil tests that can be administered to many individuals at one time.

When World War I began, Binet's test already had gained wide approval, and the notion of using psychological methods to measure personal abilities had been generally accepted. There was good reason to know the intellectual abilities of the thousands of recruits who were entering the armed services, but obviously all these men could not be tested individually. A committee of psychologists was charged with the task of creating a group intelligence test. The result, published in 1917, was the *Army Alpha Test,* a paper-and-pencil test that made rough discriminations among examinees on the basis of intelligence. In the same year, the same committee published the *Army Beta Test.* The Beta was designed for illiterates who could not read the Army Alpha. It was largely a performance test. The instructions were given orally or were acted out to the examinees.

The military continues to be a major publisher and consumer of group intelligence tests. World War II provided the opportunity for a major revision of the Army Alpha and Beta. The revision was so complete that the result was a new test, the *Army General Classification Test (AGCT).* The AGCT was a paper-and-pencil test that was published in four alternate forms. Like today's individual IQ tests, it was scored using standard scores, with the average being equal to 100. The AGCT also provided subscores for verbal ability, arithmetic computation, arithmetic reasoning, and spatial relations. The AGCT has now been replaced by the *Armed Forces Qualification Test (AFQT),* and anyone who goes through the process of military induction will have first-hand experience with this test.

In addition to the military, the other large-scale consumer of group IQ tests is the educational establishment. There are literally dozens of group-administered tests designed to provide an assessment of overall intellectual functioning. Let's note just a few of the more commonly used tests.

There has been a long history of group IQ tests associated with Arthur Otis, one of Terman's students at Stanford. The one used most often is the *Otis-Lennon School Ability Test (OLSAT),* designed for children in kindergarten through high school. It yields an IQ score approximation. Its main advantage is the huge sample of subjects who comprise its norm group.

When psychological tests are used to make predictions about future behaviors, we call them *aptitude tests.* However, the fact is that many of the aptitude tests used in the context of education are essentially tests of general intellectual ability. In their construction and administration, they are much like any general intelligence test. The difference is in the use to which the score is put: predicting future academic success. The two most commonly used college entrance tests are the *SAT (Scholastic Aptitude Test),* which yields verbal and mathematics subscores as well as an overall score, and the *ACT (American College Testing Program).* In the fall of 1990, the College Entrance Examination Board, which publishes the SAT, announced a major revision of the test (to be called the SAT-I, and to be introduced in the spring of 1994). The new SAT will include math items that are not in the usual multiple-choice format, and the verbal section will put more emphasis on reading comprehension. At the same time, a new, optional SAT-II will be made available. The SAT-II will include a written essay section, language proficiency tests for native speakers of Japanese and Chinese, and tests for non-native English speakers. The College

Entrance Examination Board also publishes the *PSAT (Preliminary Scholastic Aptitude Test)*, which is becoming increasingly popular. It is designed for high school juniors who take the test to qualify for certain scholarships or as practice for the SAT.

As their college careers come to a close, students may once again face the task of taking a standardized aptitude test if they wish to go to a graduate or professional school. Each type of professional school—medical school, law school, and so on—has its own type of exam, and the more general *Graduate Record Exam (GRE)* is like an advanced form of the SAT. These tests, too, are essentially paper-and-pencil IQ tests, but they are used for prediction purposes.

Before You Go On
▼▼▼▼▼▼▼▼

What are the advantages of group intelligence tests?

How are paper-and-pencil IQ tests and educational aptitude tests alike?

▶ The Mentally Gifted

When we look at the IQ scores earned by large random samples of individuals, we find that the IQ scores are distributed in a predictable pattern. The most frequently occurring score is the average IQ score, 100. Most other earned scores are very close to this average. In fact, about 95 percent of all IQ scores fall between scores of 70 and 130 (See Fig. 8.9, p. 284). In this section, we consider those people whose IQ scores place them in the upper extreme. Then we'll look at the lower extreme.

There are several ways in which a person can be gifted. The United States Office of Education (1972) defines giftedness as a demonstrated achievement or aptitude for excellence in any one of six areas:

1. *Psychomotor ability.* This is one of the most overlooked areas in which some individuals clearly can excel. We are dealing here with people of outstanding abilities in behaviors or skills that require agility, strength, speed, quickness, coordination, and the like.

2. *Visual and performing arts.* Some people, even as children, demonstrate an unusual talent for art, music, drama, and writing.

3. *Leadership ability.* Leadership skills are valued in most societies, and there seem to be individuals who are particularly gifted in this area. This often is true even with very young children. Youngsters with good leadership skills tend to be intellectually bright, but they are not necessarily the smartest of the group.

4. *Creative or productive thinking.* This aspect of giftedness has received considerable attention over the past 25 years. Here we are talking about individuals who *may* be intellectually or academically above average, but not necessarily so. Indeed, there is ample evidence that scores on measures of creativity are typically *un*related to measures of general intelligence (*e.g.,* Horne, 1976; Kershner & Ledger, 1985). Among other things, people with this type of giftedness are able to generate unique and different, but still useful, solutions to problems. I also should mention that persons who demonstrate exceptional creative talents in one area (art, math, or

language, for instance) usually show no particular creativity in other areas (*e.g.,* Amabile, 1985; Weisberg, 1986).

5. *Specific academic aptitude.* In this case, we are talking about people who have a special ability in a particular subject or two. Someone who is a whiz in math, history, or laboratory science, without necessarily being outstanding in other academic areas, would fit this category.

6. *Intellectually gifted.* Inclusion in this group is based on scores earned on a general intelligence test, usually a Wechsler test or the Stanford-Binet intelligence scale. It is most likely that when people use the term *mentally gifted,* they are referring to someone who fits this category—people of exceptionally high IQ. (IQ scores of 130 or above usually qualify for inclusion in this category. Some prefer to reserve the label for those with IQs above 135. In either case, we are dealing with a very small portion of the population—fewer than three percent.)

How can we describe intellectually gifted individuals? The truth is, there have been few large-scale attempts to understand the nature of mental giftedness or to understand the cognitive processing of people at the upper end of the IQ distribution (Horowitz and O'Brien, 1985; Reiss, 1989). Indeed, a good deal of what we know about the mentally gifted comes from a classic study begun by Lewis Terman in the early 1920s. (This is the same Terman who revised Binet's IQ test.) Terman supervised the testing of more than a quarter of a million children throughout California. His research group at Stanford University focused on those childen who earned the highest scores—about 1500 in all, each with an IQ above 135.

Lewis Terman died in 1956, but the study of those mentally giften individuals, who were between the ages of 8 and 12 in 1922, continues. Ever since their inclusion in the original study, and at regular intervals ever since, they have been retested, interviewed, and polled by psychologists still at Stanford (Goleman, 1980; Oden, 1968; Sears & Barbee, 1977).

The Terman study has drawbacks—choosing a narrow definition of giftedness in terms of IQ alone is an obvious one. Failing to control for factors such as socioeconomic level or parents' education level is another. There also is evidence that researchers may have excluded children who showed signs of psychological disorders or problems, whether their IQ scores were high or not. Nonetheless, the study is an impressive one for having been continued for 60 years, if nothing else. What can this long-term analysis tell us about people with very high IQs?

Most of Terman's results fly in the face of the common stereotype of the bright child as being skinny, anxious, clumsy, of poor health, and almost certainly wearing thick glasses (Sears & Barbee, 1977). The data just do not support that stereotype. In fact, if there is any overall conclusion to be drawn from the Terman-Stanford study, it is that gifted children experience advantages in virtually everything. They are taller, faster, stronger, better coordinated, have better eyesight, fewer emotional problems, and tend to stay married longer than average. These findings have been confirmed by others with different samples of subjects (Holden, 1980). Many obvious things are also true of Terman's sample of children, now oldsters. They got much more education, found better, higher-paying jobs, and had brighter children than did people of average intelligence. By now, we know better than to overgeneralize. Every one of Terman's children (sometimes referred to as "Termites") did not grow up to be rich and famous and live happily ever after. Many did, but not all. The study's conclusions, like so many others, are valid only "in general, on the average."

Racial and Ethnic Differences and IQ

That there are significant differences between the IQ test scores of black and white Americans is not a new discovery. It was one of the conclusions drawn from the testing program for Army recruits during the First World War. Since then, many studies have reconfirmed the fact that whites score approximately 15 points higher on tests of general intelligence (IQ) than do blacks. Blacks even seem to earn lower scores on performance tests and on intelligence tests that supposedly minimize the influence of one's culture (called "culture fair" tests) (Jensen, 1980). There also is consistent data that tell us that Japanese children (between the ages of 6 and 16) score significantly higher on IQ tests—about 11 points *on the average*—than do American children of the same age (*e.g.,* Lynn, 1982; 1987). The superiority of Japanese children on mathematics tests is even greater (Stevenson, Lee & Stigler, 1986). Asian American students recently have been scoring considerably higher on the SAT than have other students, again, particularly in mathematics (e.g. average math scores on the SAT of 525 compared to 476) (College Board, 1989; Hsia, 1988; Lynn, 1991; Sue & Okazaki, 1990). The nagging question, of course, is *why?* Why do these differences appear with such consistency?

The proposed answers have been controversial and return us to three possibilities we've touched on before in other contexts: (1) The *tests are biased* and unfair. IQ tests simply may reflect the experiences of white Americans to a greater extent than they reflect the lives and experiences of blacks or Hispanics. Whether or not such biases occur by intention is not relevant. (2) Differences in IQ scores can be attributed to *environmental and motivational factors,* such as economic and/or educational opportunities, and the perceived importance of doing well on standardized tests. (3) There are *genetic factors* involved that place some groups at a disadvantage. Now, test bias may account for some of the observed differences in IQ scores, but let's assume for the moment that our available techniques for assessing general intelligence are as valid as possible. What then? Let's first concentrate on black-white differences in IQ.

In the 1950s and 1960s, psychologists were confident that the bulk (if not all) of the difference between the IQ scores of whites and blacks could be explained in environmental terms. There weren't many studies to support the position, but the logic was compelling and was consistent with prevailing attitudes. Blacks were at a disadvantage on standard tests of intelligence because they were often denied access to enriching educational opportunities.

In 1969, Arthur Jensen shocked the scientific community with a long, thoughtful article in the *Harvard Educational Review*. Jensen argued that there was insufficient evidence to warrant the conclusion that the environment could produce such a large racial difference in IQ scores. The alternative was obvious: The differences were attributable to genetic factors. Many took Jensen's claim to mean that blacks are genetically inferior to whites. However, Jensen claims that his argument was meant only as a hypothesis, intended to provoke scientific efforts to explore such a possibility (Jensen, 1981).

Perhaps you can imagine the furor created by Jensen's1969 article. Researchers took up the challenge and tried to find specific and convincing evidence that the environment *is* the cause of lower black IQ scores. After reviewing the body of literature that has grown from these efforts, Brian Mackenzie (1984) wrote: "What is finally clear from such research, therefore, is that environmental factors have not been identified that are sufficient to account for all or even most of the 15-point mean difference in IQ between blacks and whites in the United States. Jensen's conclusion that half to two- thirds of the gap remains unaccounted for by any proposed combination of environmental influences is still unrefuted" (p. 1217).

Now what does *that* mean? Does that mean that racial differences in IQ *are* caused by genetic factors? *Are* blacks genetically less able than whites? Of course not; at the very least, there isn't sufficient evidence to support such a conclusion (Mackintosh, 1986). To understand why we've not yet resolved this issue requires that we understand three points: (1) Just because there is evidence that genetic factors affect differences in intelligence *within* races, we cannot automatically use that data as evidence of genetic factors affecting differences in intelligence *between* races. (2) It is improper to assume that the failure to identify any specific environmental causes of racial differences in IQ is sufficient reason to drop the environmental factors argument. (3) Just because we have not identified the specific environmental factors that cause racial differences in IQ doesn't mean that we must accept genetic explanations. Similar arguments have been proposed by psychologists trying to understand the superiority of Asian American students on standard tests of academic achievement. Some argue for at least a degree of innate superiority (*e.g.,* Lynn, 1977; 1991), while others point to socioeconomic, cultural, and motivational factors (*e.g.,* Stevenson, Lee & Stigler, 1986; Sue & Okasaki, 1990; 1991).

So where do we stand on the issue of racial-ethnic differences in IQ? We stand in a position of considerable uncertainty. There is research data to underscore the contributions of both genetic and environmental influences on what we call intelligence. Whether any of these data can be used to settle the issue of racial differences in IQ scores is debatable. We would do well to keep in mind the following position, as stated here by Angoff: "the debate over whether intelligence is largely genetically or largely environmentally determined is actually irrelevant in the context of group differences. The real issue is whether intelligence can be changed, an issue that does not at all go hand in hand with the issue of heritability." (1988, p. 713).

▶ *The Mentally Retarded*

Our understanding of mental retardation has changed considerably over the past 25 years. We have seen changes in treatment and care, and great strides in prevention. There even have been substantial changes in how psychology defines mental retardation (Baumeister, 1987; Landesman & Ramey, 1989).

Issues of Definition. Intelligence as measured by IQ tests is often used to confirm suspected cases of **mental retardation.** As is the case for the mentally gifted, however, there is more to retardation than IQ alone. The definition provided by the American Association of Mental Deficiency (AAMD) cites three factors to consider: "subaverage general intellectual functioning which originated during the developmental period and is associated with impairment in adaptive behavior" (Grossman, 1973).

The IQ cutoff for mental retardation is usually taken to be 70, with the following sub-categories (Zigler & Hodapp, 1991):

> IQ 70–85: *borderline or slow*
> IQ 55–69: *mildly mentally retarded*
> IQ 40–54: *moderately mentally retarded*
> IQ 25–39: *severely mentally retarded*
> IQ less than 25: *profoundly mentally retarded*

As you review this list, you need to keep two things in mind. First, these IQ test scores are suggested limits. Given what we know about IQ tests and their reliability, it would be ridiculous to claim after one administration of a test that a person with an IQ of 69 was mentally retarded, while someone else with an IQ of 71 was not. Second, a diagnosis of mental retardation is not (should not be) made on the basis of IQ score alone.

To fit the definition of mental retardation, the cause or the symptoms of the below-average intellectual functioning must show up during the usual period of intellectual development (up to age 18). In many circles, the term "developmentally delayed" is coming to replace the narrower term "mentally retarded." Diagnosis may come only after the administration of an IQ test, but initial suspicions generally come from perceived delays in an individual's normal developmental or adjustive patterns of behavior.

By making "impairment in adaptive behavior" a part of their definition of mental retardation, the AAMD acknowledges that there is more to getting along in this world than the intellectual and academic sorts of skills that IQ tests emphasize. Being mentally retarded does not necessarily mean being totally helpless, particularly for those who fall in the moderate levels of retardation. Of major consideration is (or ought to be) an individual's ability to adapt to the environment. In this regard, such skills as the ability to dress oneself, to follow directions, to make change, to find one's way home from a distance, and so on become relevant (Coulter & Morrow, 1978).

Even without a simple, one-dimensional definition, it is clear that the population of retarded citizens is a large one. It is difficult to obtain exact

mental retardation a condition indicated by an IQ below 70 that began during the developmental period and is associated with impairment in adaptive functioning

figures, because many individuals who might fit the criteria and be classified as mildly retarded have never been diagnosed as such. Even so, standard estimates indicate that approximately 3 percent of the population at any one time falls within the IQ range for retardation. Two other relevant estimates are that approximately 900,000 children with mental retardation between the ages of 3 and 21 years are being served in the public schools (Schroeder, et al., 1987) and that nearly 200,000 mentally retarded individuals are to be found in community residential facilities, state and county mental hospitals, and nursing homes (Landesman & Butterfield, 1987). Let's now turn to a brief discussion of the causes, treatment, and prevention of mental retardation.

Before You Go On
▼▼▼▼▼▼▼▼▼

Summarize the adolescent's search for identity as described by Erikson.

Causes, Treatment, and Prevention. We don't really know what causes average intelligence. We have virtually no idea what causes someone to be mentally gifted. We cannot begin to explain the causes of all types of mental retardation, but at least we have some good ideas. We believe that there are hundreds of possible causes; the list of known, or highly suspected causes exceeds 200 (Grossman, 1983). The more we learn about the sources of mental retardation, the better able we will be to treat it or to prevent it.

Approximately one-quarter of all cases of mental retardation reflect some problem that developed before, during, or just after birth. Between 15 and 20 percent of those persons referred to as mentally retarded were born prematurely—at least 3 weeks before the due date or at a weight below 5 pounds, 8 ounces.

We now appreciate how the health of the mother during pregnancy can affect the health of her child. All sorts of prenatal conditions are thought to cause developmental delays, including hypertension, exposure to X-rays, lowered oxygen intake, rubella (German measles), maternal syphilis, and the mother's use of drugs—from narcotics to aspirin, alcohol, and nicotine. To greater or lesser degree, each of these has been linked to retardation. In addition, some cases stem from difficulties or injuries during the birth process itself.

As we've seen, the extent to which normal levels of intelligence are inherited is open to debate. Some types of mental retardation, however, are clearly genetic in origin. One of the clearest examples of such a case is the intellectual retardation accompanying **Down's syndrome**, first described in 1866. We don't know why it happens, but occasionally a fetus develops with 47 chromosomes instead of the usual 46, or 23 pairs. (We know that Down's syndrome becomes more likely as the age of either parent increases.) The signs of Down's syndrome are well known: small round skull, flattened face, large tongue, short broad nose, broad hands, short stubby fingers, and so on. Throughout childhood, behavioral development is noticeably delayed. Down's syndrome children may fall into any of the levels of retardation listed above. Many are educable and lead lives of considerable independence, although it is generally true that even as adults, many will require supervision at least some of the time.

Fragile X syndrome is a variety of mental retardation with a genetic basis that was discovered more recently—in the late 1960s (Bregman, et al., 1987). Although it does occur in females, it is found primarily in males.

Down's syndrome a condition of many symptoms, including mental retardation, caused by an extra (forty-seventh) chromosome

Males with the disorder characteristically have long faces, big ears, and, as adults, large testes (Zigler & Hodapp, 1991). Individuals with this form of mental retardation have difficulty processing sequences of events, or events in a series, which means that they have many problems with language skills. One curiosity is that whereas males with Down's syndrome show a gradual but steady decrease in IQ scores with age, males with Fragile X syndrome show more noticeable declines during puberty.

About one-half to three-quarters of the cases of mental retardation do not have known organic or biological causes (Zigler & Hodapp, 1986).

To some degree, our ability to treat mental retardation depends on our ability to specify its causes. Special education programs have helped, but not all have been equally successful (Zigler & Hodapp, 1991). Preparing teachers and mental health professionals to be sensitive to the wide range of behaviors and feelings that mentally retarded persons are capable of has helped. Impressive changes can be made in raising the IQs of some mildly retarded and a few moderately retarded children (Landesman & Ramey, 1989). For severely and profoundly retarded persons, the outlook is not bright—at least not in terms of raising IQ points (Spitz, 1986), although we always need to remind ourselves that quality of life is not necessarily a function of IQ. The emphasis in recent years has been to focus less on intellectual growth in general and more on those specific skills and abilities—social as well as intellectual—that *can* be improved.

There is greater hope in the area of prevention. As we continue to appreciate the influences of the prenatal environment on the development of cognitive abilities, we can educate mothers (and fathers) about how their behaviors can affect their child even before it is born. We have already noted that intellectual retardation is one of the symptoms associated with fetal alcohol syndrome (Chapter 3, p. 84). Educating pregnant women to avoid alcohol consumption is a clear step to preventing one source of retardation. Another example of how mental retardation can be prevented concerns **phenylketonuria,** or **PKU.** This disorder is genetic in origin, and 50 years ago it was discovered to be a cause of mental retardation. PKU results when a child inherits genes that fail to produce an enzyme that normally breaks down chemicals found in many foods. Although a newborn with PKU usually appears quite normal, a simple blood test has been developed that can detect the disorder soon after birth. Upon detection, a prescribed diet (which must be maintained for about four years) can reduce or eliminate the disorder. Unfortunately, most cases (about 70 percent) of mental retardation cannot be detected at birth, which means that preventive or therapeutic intervention also has to wait until the child is older (Scott & Carran, 1987).

phenylketonuria (PKU) a genetically caused disorder that produces mental retardation and that is now detectable and preventable

Before You Go On
▼▼▼▼▼▼▼▼▼

List some of the possible causes of mental retardation.

▼▼▼
Thinking Critically About Higher Cognitive Processes

1. Given the definition that we used in this chapter, how many specific tasks can you characterize as "higher cognitive processes?"

2. What problems did you encounter yesterday? Which were ill-defined and which were well-defined?

3. Imagine a group of scientists trying to build and program an enormous computer to think as a human. How would we know if the scientists were successful? That is, how could you test a computer to see if it thinks as people think?

4. Over the years, there has been considerable controversy over the issue of whether any other organism beside a human can demonstrate real language communication. The basic issue is: How would you demonstrate that a chimp, an ape, or a dolphin for that matter, possessed the ability to use language?

5. If it is true that most language users acquire the rules of their language before they are 6 years old, what do we really teach when we offer classes in English grammar?

6. Why do some students have a much easier time than others learning a second or a third "foreign" language?

7. What is wrong and what is right about the heavy reliance we put on intelligence testing in American culture? What might be some alternatives? If IQ does not equal intelligence, then what is it?

8. What are the short-and long-term advantages and disadvantages of "mainstreaming," of placing children with intellectual disadvantages in regular classrooms?

Figure 8.11

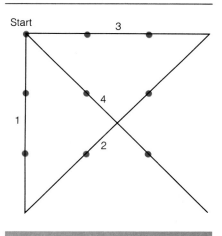

▲ *A solution to the "nine-dot problem."*

Summary

▼▼▼▼▼▼▼▼▼▼▼▼▼▼▼▼▼▼▼▼▼▼▼▼▼▼▼▼▼▼▼▼▼▼▼▼▼

What are the three components of a problem? A problem has three components: an initial state—the situation as it exists at the moment; a goal state—the situation as the problem solver would like it to be; and routes or strategies for getting from the initial state to the goal state. *Page 265*

Contrast well-defined and ill-defined problems. Give an example of each. Whether a problem is ill-defined or well-defined is a matter of the extent to which the elements of the initial state and the goals state are clearly delineated and understood by the problem solver. An example of a well-defined problem might be that which you face when a familiar route home from campus is blocked. An example of an ill-defined problem might be that which you face when you are required to write a term paper on a topic of your choice. *Page 265*

In the context of problem solving, what is meant by problem representation? Problem representation involves the mental activity of thinking about the nature of a problem and putting it in a form we can deal with effectively. In essence, representation means reducing a problem into familiar terms. *Page 266*

How are algorithmic and heuristic strategies used to solve problems? Algorithms and heuristics are types of strategies, or systematic plans, we can use for seeking problem solutions. Algorithms involve a systematic search of all possible solutions until the goal is reached; with algorithms, a solution is guaranteed to be found, if there is one. A heuristic strategy—of which there are many—is a more informal, rule-of-thumb approach that involves generating and testing hypotheses that *may* lead to a problem solution in a sensible, organized way. *Pages 268–269*

What is a mental set, and how might a mental set hinder problem solving? A mental set is a tendency or a predisposition to perceive or to respond in a particular way. Mental sets generally develop from past experience and involve the continued use of strategies that may have been successful in the past, but may no longer be relevant. *Page 270*

What is functional fixedness, and how might it hinder problem solving? Functional fixedness is a type of mental set in which an object is seen as serving only a few fixed functions. Because we may not see a familiar object as being able to serve new and different functions, fixedness can interfere with effective problem solving. *Page 270*

What is the difference between divergent and convergent thinking? Divergent thinking is a useful technique in which a large number of alternative problem solu-

tions are generated and tested later for usefulness. Convergent thinking involves taking a large number of ideas or possibilities for problem solution and reducing them to one or a few. *Pages 271–272*

What are some of the defining characteristics of language? Language use is a complex and creative cognitive process used for communication. A language is made up of a large number of arbitrary symbols (usually words) that stand for or label our conceptualization of objects and events, which have meaning for users of the language, and which are combined in accordance with rules. The use of language is a generative process that, among other things, allows us to communicate about the not-here and the not-now. *Pages 273–274*

What are some of the landmark events that occur during language acquisition? Although infants cry and babble, the first truly linguistic utterances are called holophrastic speech. This occurs when one word is used to communicate a range of feelings, intentions, and meanings. A two-word stage of development shows the presence of structure in word-ordering—a grammar that is not a simple reflection of adult language. From the two-word utterance on, language development is extremely rapid. By the time a child is 5 years old he or she will know thousands of words (will understand more than he or she will produce) and will combine many of those words in virtually every acceptable sentence structure allowed by the language. *Pages 275–276*

Briefly summarize the learning-oriented and biology-oriented theories of langauge acquisition. Neither learning-experiential nor instinctual-biological theories can totally account for language acquisition. Learning history has an impact on language development, particularly in the acquisition of words and word meanings. At the same time, learning theory is challenged by the cross-cultural regularities that seem to occur in language acquisition—by the fact that all children of all languages seem to develop their language in the same general, patterned way. The complex process just seems too rapid and too regular not to have some strong biological basis. *Pages 276–278*

Provide a theoretical and an operational definition of intelligence. In theory we may define intelligence as the capacity of an individual to understand the world about him or her and the resourcefulness to cope with its challenges. An operational definition of intelligence would be "that which intelligence tests measure." *Page 278*

What is a psychological test? A psychological test is an *objective* (not open to multiple interpretation), *standardized* (administered and scored in the same way for everyone) *measure of a sample* (we cannot measure all we are interested in) of *behavior* (because behavior is all we can measure). *Page 279*

In the context of psychological testing, what are reliability, validity, and norms? Reliability means consistency or dependability. We measure the reliability of a psychological test by administering it to the same group of subjects on two different occasions and calculating the correlation between scores from the two administrations. Although correlations are not expected to be perfect, they should be in excess of 0.70 for a reliable test. Validity is the extent to which a test measures what it claims to measure. For validity to be demonstrated, a set of test scores should be correlated with some independent criterion. Test norms are the average scores of large numbers of subjects, similar to those for whom the test has been designed. It is against the standard of these scores that an individual's test score can be compared. *Pages 280–281*

Briefly describe the Stanford-Binet Intelligence Scale. The Stanford-Binet is the oldest of the tests of general intelligence (commonly called IQ tests). Its most recent (1986) revision provides an overall score as well as subscores for several abilities that are assumed to underlie general intelligence. The test is comprised of 15 subtests, each assessing a specific cognitive task, where items are arranged in order of difficulty. Scores on the test, standardized by age, reflect the subject's performance as compared to others of the same age level. *Pages 282–284*

What are the major features of the Wechsler intelligence scales? The Wechsler scales are individually administered tests of general intelligence. There are three of them, each recently revised, and each appropriate for a different age group ranging from ages 4 to 74 overall. Each test is made up of several subtests of different content. The subtests are grouped as either verbal or performance. Hence, three scores can be determined: and overall score (usually taken as IQ), a score on verbal subtests, and a score on performance subtests. Scores on all the Wechsler tests are standard scores that compare one's abilities to those of others the same age. *Pages 284–286*

What are the advantages of group intelligence tests? Group intelligence tests may not provide as much information or be as valid as individually administered IQ tests, but they are much less expensive and quite reasonable to use as screening devices. *Pages 286–288*

How are paper-and-pencil IQ tests and educational aptitude tests alike? Many educational aptitude tests are essentially paper-and-pencil tests of general intelligence. The only difference is that they are used specifically to make predictions about success in narrowly defined academic areas. *Pages 287–288*

List six ways in which individuals can be considered to be gifted. Giftedness can refer to a number of things, including (1) overall intellectual ability as measured by IQ tests (usually taken to be an IQ over 130 points), (2) talent in the visual and performing arts, (3) psychomotor skills, (4) leadership, (5) creativity, and (6) abilities in specific academic areas. *Pages 288–289*

Summarize the basic findings of the Terman-Stanford study of the intellectually gifted. Most simply, individuals who were tested to have very high IQs were also found to do well in almost everything else measured by the researchers. *Page 289*

How might we best define mental retardation? Mental retardation should be thought of as reflecting subaverage intellectual functioning (usually indicated by IQ test scores below 70), originating during the developmental period (within 18 years), and associated with impairment in adaptive behavior (as well as academic behaviors). *Pages 292–293*

List some of the possible causes of mental retardation. In addition to genetic causes, most of the known causes of mental retardation (and there may be over 200) revolve around the health and care of the mother and the fetus during pregnancy, where drugs, lack of oxygen, poor nutrition, and the like have been implicated in mental retardation. In other words, many of the biologically-based causes of mental retardation seem to be preventable. *Pages 293–294*

8.1 More than anything else, what makes a problem "well defined" as opposed to "ill defined?" a) knowing with certainty when a solution is found b) the extent to which we realize that we are faced with a problem c) the adequacy of problem representation d) the choice of an adequate strategy for problem solving. *Page 265*

8.2 Which provides the best example of a well-defined problem? a) How can Israeli- Palestinian differences be peacefully resolved? b) Which country in North America has the longest coastline? c) What would be required to establish a psychology laboratory in a new college? d) What is the best way to organize a surprise birthday party for a co-worker? *Page 265*

8.3 When we say that problem solving begins with problem representation, we are suggesting that one needs to a) put the problem in numerical or mathematical form. b) examine all possible solutions before one begins. c) decide if the problem has a solution. d) make the problem meaningful. *Page 266*

8.4 Problem representation typically is easiest when: a) the problem deals with familiar information. b) the problem is well-defined. c) there is only one way in which a solution can be found. d) the problem is ill-defined. *Page 268*

8.5 As more and more solutions and routes to problem solution become available, the more sensible it is to use a) a comprehensive, systematic search of all possibilities. b) a heuristic strategy. c) fewer and fewer hypotheses. d) an algorithmic approach. *Page 268*

8.6 The major advantage of a heuristic rather than an algorithmic strategy for problem solving is that heuristics a) guarantee that eventually you'll reach your goal. b) are systematic. c) tend to save time and effort. d) produce solutions that can be tested and confirmed. *Page 269*

8.7 True or False? Computers cannot use algorithms to solve problems effectively—only people can. *Page 268*

8.8 Which statement concerning mental sets and problem solving is FALSE? a) Mental sets influence how we represent problems. b) Mental sets always interfere with problem solving. c) Mental sets generally evolve from past experiences. d) Mental sets are mental predispositions. *Page 270*

8.9 Functional fixedness is essentially a type of a) problem representation. b) heuristic strategy. c) creativity. d) mental set. *Page 270*

8.10 The ultimate test of a creative solution to a problem is whether a) anyone else has ever thought of it before. b) it is artistic, balanced, or beautiful. c) it works to solve the problem at hand. d) it is convergent or divergent. *Page 271*

8.11 True or False? Divergent thinking involves generating as many potential solutions as possible, while convergent thinking involves reducing the number of possibilities in problem solving. *Page 271*

8.12 Which of these is LEAST descriptive of language? Language is a) rule-governed. b) correct or incorrect. c) creative or generative. d) both cognitive and social. *Page 273*

8.13 Which term is most general and includes the other three? a) communication b) language c) speech d) word. *Page 273*

8.14 When we say that language allows us to communicate about things that are not present, neither here nor now, we are saying that language demonstrates: a) displacement. b) a behavior that follows rules. c) a cognitive process. d) arbitrariness. *Page 274*

8.15 True or False? Children do not show an appreciation of language as a form of communication until they are producing 3-or 4-word utterances. *Page 275*

8.16 A child says, "I got two hands, and I got two foots," providing us with an example of a) displacement. b) holophrastic speech. c) the emergence of a two-word grammar. d) overregularization. *Page 277*

8.17 Which of the following provides an operational definition of intelligence? Intelligence is a) the sum of those cognitive abilities that allow us to adapt to the environment. b) that which is measured by an IQ test. c) the accumulation of information over a lifetime. d) the ultimate problem-solving skill. *Page 278*

8.18 When we talk about a psychological test being objective, what is our major concern? a) that test performance be evaluated fairly b) that subjects understand what they are to do c) that it is not possible to measure everything d) that each question have only one correct answer. *Page 279*

8.19 Dr. Harvey has written a test. She gives the test to one of her classes, and then gives the same test to the same class two weeks later. Dr. Harvey's concern is with: a) assessing the reliability of her test.   b) collecting scores for a norm group.   c) the predictive validity of her test.   d) establishing the test's objectivity. *Page 280*

8.20 True or False?   Psychological tests provide measures of samples of behaviors. *Page 279*

8.21 True or False?   A test can be valid without being reliable. *Page 280*

8.22 When Binet and Simon wrote their test of intelligence, their major concern or intent was to   a) study the long-term consequences of being judged mentally gifted as a child.   b) determine how much of one's intelligence is inherited and how much is due to the influence of the environment.   c) identify those children who needed to be placed in remedial or special education classes.   d) discover if intelligence is one unitary **g** factor, or several specific, **b** factors. *Page 282*

8.23 The current version of the Stanford Binet provides estimates of intellectual skills at several different levels. Which of these is the highest level?   a) short-term memory   b) **g**   c) crystallized abilities   d) vocabulary. *Page 282*

8.24 Using the classic approach to IQ as an intelligence quotient, if 10-year-old Sally demonstrates intellectual functioning typical of an average 8-year-old, Sally's IQ is: a) 70.   b) 80.   c) 100.   d) 125. *Page 283*

8.25 True or False?   The current revision of the Stanford-Binet test yields just one score—a measure of general intelligence, **g**. *Page 283*

8.26 When David Wechsler first introduced his tests, what did he introduce to IQ testing?   a) individually administered tests   b) tests that were more valid for children than for adults   c) nonverbal items on which one's performance was scored   d) the number of items correct minus the number of items that are incorrect. *Page 284*

8.27 Which of the following is probably the most reliable and most valid as a test of general intellectual ability?   a) the army General Classification Test (AGCT)   b) the Otis-Lennon School Ability Test (OLSAT)   c) the Scholastic Aptitude Test (SAT)   d) the Wechsler Adult Intelligence Scale (WAIS-R). *Page 287*

8.28 Down's syndrome: a) can be treated by changes in diet if diagnosed at birth.   b) children are invariably either severely or profoundly retarded intellectually.   c) develops as a result of a chromosomal abnormality.   d) is usually caused by alcohol or drug use during pregnancy. *Page 293*

8.29 True or False? We stand a better chance of preventing mental retardation than we do of treating it effectively. *Page 294*

Chapter 9 ▼▼▼▼▼ *Motivation and Emotion*

▲▲▲▲▲▲

You had a great time. You and your friends spent the day backpacking in the mountains. The signs of spring are everywhere to be found, and you enjoyed each minute spent searching for them. The day was so perfect that you decided to hike all the way around Lake Willoweemoc. That hike was long and tiring, so getting back to camp for dinner was welcomed by all.

After a full day in the fresh mountain air, no one was terribly choosy about what to have for dinner. The amount of food seemed more critical than its quality or elegance. Large, heaping piles of beef stew and baked beans were enjoyed by everyone. You even found room for dessert, a toasted marshmallow and a piece of chocolate squeezed between two graham crackers. As hungry as you had been, there is no doubt that you ate too much.

As your friends settle around the campfire, darkness just beginning to overtake the campsite, you excuse yourself. You need to "walk off" some of that dinner, so you decide to take a stroll down a narrow trail that leads away from the campsite.

As you wander down the trail, you feel totally relaxed, at peace with the world. Your mind reflects on the pleasantness of the day, noting the smell of the wildflowers, and wondering what tomorrow will bring. When you are about 200 yards from the campsite, you think you hear a strange sound in the woods, off to your left. Looking back, you notice that you can barely see the campfire's glow through the trees and underbrush, even though their leaves are not yet fully formed. Well, maybe you'd better not venture too much farther, perhaps just over that ridge, and then you'd better. . . Suddenly, without warning, from behind a dense thicket, a large, growling black bear appears. It takes one look at you, bares its teeth and lets out a mighty roar. *What will you do now?*

In this situation, and in many similar but less dramatic ones, we can be sure of one thing: Your reaction will involve motivational and emotional states. You will be motivated to do something. You will be emotional, and in quite predictable ways. We'll return to this meeting-a-bear-in-the-woods story throughout this chapter as we explore what psychologists know about motivation and emotion.

▶ Preview

You certainly don't need a psychologist to convince you that motivation and emotion are important concepts in your everyday life. In fact, we've already seen how motivation affects important cognitive processes. Motivation influences our ability to learn, affects our memory, and even has an impact on so basic a process as perception. By the same token, most of us like to think of ourselves as reasonable, rational, intellectual, and logical. We like to talk about our cognitive abilities—perceiving, learning, remembering, and problem solving. But if we were honest with each other, we would admit that our emotions often concern us most. We enjoy reflecting on pleasant emotions and seek ways to minimize unpleasant emotions.

There are two observations about motivational and emotional states that allow us to combine our treatment of them in this one chapter: Both involve *arousal*—becoming excited, activated, prepared to *do* something, and both involve underlying physiological reactions that often are quite similar. In fact, motivation and emotionality are usually so much related that it is a bit artificial to separate our treatment of them, but for the sake of clarity, this is just what we will do in this chapter.

We'll start with motivation and get our discussion under way by considering some of the ways that psychologists have approached the study of motivation, defining important terms along the way. Having defined the relevant terminology, we will then summarize some of what we know about two different sorts of motivating forces: those related to survival and rooted in biology (which we'll call *physiologically-based drives*), and those more clearly learned and/or social in nature (which we'll call *psychologically-based motives*).

Then we can turn to the study of emotions. In a parallel fashion, we will start by considering how psychologists have conceptualized emotional states; then we'll touch on two areas of research that have proven particularly fruitful: physiological aspects of emotionality, and how inner emotional states are expressed in behavior.

▶ Approaches to Motivation

arousal one's level of activation or excitement; indicative of a motivational state

Motivation consists of two subprocesses. First, it involves **arousal**—one's overall level of activation or excitement. Motivation is the force that initiates or activates one's behaviors, that gets an organism going, energized to *do* something. Second, motivation provides *direction* or focus to one's behaviors. In addition to simply being aroused and active, a motivated behavior is viewed as goal-directed or in some way purposeful. Hence our definition: **Motivation** is the process that arouses, directs, and maintains behavior.

motivation the process of arousing, maintaining, and directing behavior

From its earliest days in the 1800s, psychology has tried to find a systematic theory that could summarize what different motivational states have in common. Psychologists have long struggled to develop one general scheme that could be used to account for *why* organisms do what they do. In this section, we'll review some of these theories. As you might anticipate, no one approach to motivation will answer all our questions. Although each of the approaches summarized below may have its drawbacks, we should focus on how each makes a contribution to our understanding of behavior and mental processes.

▶ Approaches Based on Instincts

instincts unlearned, complex patterns of behavior that occur in the presence of particular stimuli

In the early days of psychology, behaviors often were explained in terms of **instincts,** defined as unlearned, complex patterns of behavior that occur in

▲ That salmon — such as these sock-eyes — swim upstream at mating season, can be explained by instinct: Unlearned, complex patterns of behavior that occur in the presence of certain stimuli

need a lack or shortage of some biological essential resulting from deprivation

drive a state of tension resulting from a need that arouses and directs an organism's behavior

the presence of certain stimuli. Why do birds build nests? A nest-building instinct. When conditions are right, birds build nests. Why do salmon swim upstream to mate? Instinct. Swimming upstream at mating season is part of what it means to be a salmon. These behaviors can be modified somewhat by the organisms' experiences, but the basic driving force behind them is unlearned or instinctive.

That may explain some of the behavior of birds and salmon, but what about people? William James (1890) reasoned that humans, being more complex organisms, had to have many more instincts than did the "lower" animals. No one expressed the instinctual explanation of human behaviors more forcefully than William McDougall (1908). He suggested that human behaviors were motivated by 11 basic instincts: repulsion, curiosity, flight, parental, reproduction, gregariousness, acquisitiveness, construction, self-assertion, self-abasement, and pugnacity. Soon McDougall extended his list to include 18 instincts. As new and different behaviors required explanation, new and different instincts were devised to explain them.

As lists of human instincts got longer and longer, the problem with this approach became obvious. Particularly for humans, *explaining* behavior patterns by alluding to instinct simply renamed or relabeled them and didn't explain anything at all. But, we need to remember that psychologists who argued for instincts did draw attention to an idea that is still with us—that we may engage in behaviors for reasons that are basically physiological, and more inherited than learned.

▶ **Approaches Based on Needs and Drives**

An approach that provided an alternative to explaining behavior in terms of instinct was one that attempted to explain the whys of behavior in terms of needs and drives. This approach, dominant in the 1940s and 1950s, is best associated with the psychologist Clark Hull (*e.g.*, Hull, 1943).

In Hull's system, a **need** is a shortage or lack of some biological essential required for survival. Needs may arise from deprivation. When an organism is kept from food, it develops a need for food. If deprived of water, a need develops. A need then gives rise to a drive. A **drive** is a state of tension, arousal, or activation. When an organism is in a *drive state,* it is motivated. It is aroused and directed to do something to satisfy the drive by reducing or eliminating the underlying need. Needs produce tensions (drives) that the organism seeks to reduce; hence, this approach is referred to in terms of drive reduction.

This approach *is* less circular than an appeal to instincts. For example, having gone without food for some time, a need develops. The need for food gives rise to a hunger drive. Then what? Then learning and experience come into play. Instincts are directly tied to a specific pattern of behavior, but needs and drives are not. They can be used to explain why we do what we do, while clearly allowing for the influence of experience and the environment. Doing without food gives rise to a need, which in turn gives rise to a drive, but how that drive is expressed in behavior is influenced by one's experience and learning history.

One problem with a drive-reduction approach centers on the biological nature of needs. To claim that drives arise only from needs that result from biological deprivations seems unduly restrictive. Surely not all of the drives that activate a person's behavior are based on biological needs. We often engage in behaviors to satisfy *learned* drives. Drives based on one's learning experiences are called *secondary drives,* as opposed to *primary drives,* which are based on unlearned, physiological needs. In fact, most of the drives that arouse and direct our behavior have little to do with our physiology.

▲ *Activities ranging from mountain climbing to exploring around the house, suggest that people often try to reduce primary (biological) or secondary (learned) drives in order to satisfy certain needs.*

You may feel that you need a new car this year. I may convince myself that I need a new set of golf clubs, and we'll both work very hard to save the money to buy what we need. Although we may say that we are driven to work for money, it's difficult to imagine how your car or my golf clubs could be satisfying a biological need. A good bit of advertising is directed at trying to convince us that we "need" many products and services that will have very little impact on our survival.

So what does all this mean? People often do behave in order to reduce drives and, thereby satisfy needs. How either primary or secondary drives are to be satisfied will reflect the learning history of the organism. So the concept of drive reduction is a useful one and is still with us in psychology, but it cannot be accepted as a complete explanation for motivated behaviors.

Abraham Maslow is a name we associate with the humanistic movement in psychology. Humanistic psychologists have emphasized the person and his or her psychological growth. Maslow proposed that human behavior responds to needs, but not all needs are physiological. It was Maslow's belief that the needs that motivate human action are limited in number and arranged in a hierarchy (Maslow, 1943; 1970). Figure 9.1 summarizes this hierarchy of needs in pictorial form.

Maslow's is essentially a stage theory. It proposes that what motivates us first are *physiological needs*. These include the basic needs that are related to survival—food, water, shelter, and so on. Until these needs are met, there is little reason to suspect that a person will be concerned with anything else. Once physiological needs have been met, a person is still motivated, but now by *safety needs*—the need to feel secure, protected from dangers that might arise in the future. We are now motivated to see to it that the cupboard has food for later, that we won't freeze this winter, and that there's enough money saved to protect against sudden calamity. Notice here the hierarchical nature of this scheme. We're not going to worry about what we'll be eating tomorrow if there's not enough to eat today; but if today's needs *are* taken care of, we can then focus on the future. Once our safety needs are met, our concern shifts to needs for *love and belongingness*—the need for someone else to care about us, to love us. After these needs are satisfied, then our concern is for *esteem*. Our aim is to be

Figure 9.1

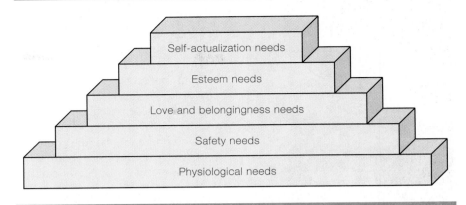

▲ *Maslow's hierarchy of needs.*

recognized for who we are, what we do, our achievements, our efforts. These needs are social in nature; they imply that our behaviors are motivated by our awareness of others and our concern for their approval. And the list goes on. One moves higher in the hierarchy only if lower needs are met. Ultimately, we may get to the highest level of needs in Maslow's hierarchy: *self-actualization needs.* These are the most difficult to satisfy. We self-actualize when we try to become the best that we can be, taking the fullest advantage of our potential as human beings. We are self-actualizing when we strive to be as creative or productive as possible.

In many ways, Maslow's arrangement of needs in a hierarchical fashion conforms to common sense. We hardly can expect people to be motivated to grow and achieve "success" when they are worried about their very survival on a day-to-day basis. Even when a person's needs for safety, belonging, and esteem are reasonably met, they don't just stop, unmotivated to do anything else. It should be clear to you, as it was to Maslow, that many people never make it to the self-actualization stage of this hierarchy of needs.

As a comprehensive theory of human motivation, Maslow's hierarchy has some serious difficulties. Perhaps the biggest stumbling block is the idea that one can assign ranks to needs and put them in order—regardless of what that order may be. It is quite clear that some persons are motivated in ways that violate the stage approach of this theory. Some individuals will, for example, freely give up satisfying basic survival needs for the sake of "higher" principles (as in hunger strikes). For the sake of love, people may very well abandon their own needs for safety and security. There is little empirical, research support for Maslow's approach to ranking needs in a hierarchy. It remains the case, however, that because of its intuitive appeal, Maslow's theory of human motivation has found favor both within and outside of psychology.

▶ *Approaches Based on Incentives*

One alternative to a drive-reduction approach to motivation focuses not on the inner state of the individual, but on the *end state,* or goal of behavior. From this point of view, external stimuli serve as motivating agents, or **incentives** for our behavior. Incentives are external events that act to *pull* our behavior, as opposed to drives, which are internal events (somehow "in the person") that *push* our behavior. Incentive theory frees us from relying on biological concepts to explain the "whys" of one's behaviors.

▲ *By participating in organized competitions, such as the International Games for the Disabled, individuals strive to be the best that they can be, responding to what Maslow calls a need to self-actualize.*

incentives external stimuli that an organism may be motivated to approach or avoid

▲ Having children help with household chores may involve motivating them to do so. In such cases, the child must learn to appreciate the incentive value of the task at hand.

When a mountain climber says that she climbs a mountain "because it is there," the climber is indicating a type of motivation through incentive. After a very large meal, we may order a piece of cheesecake, not because we *need* it in any physiological sense, but because it's there on the dessert cart and *looks* so good (and because previous experience tells us that it is likely to taste very good).

Some parents want to know how to motivate their child to clean up his or her room. We can interpret this case in terms of establishing goals or incentives. What those parents *really* want to know is how they can get their child to value and work for a clean room. What they want is a clean room, and they would like to have the child clean it. If they want the child "to be motivated" to clean his or her room, the child needs to learn the value or incentive of having a clean room. You can imagine the child's response: "Why should I?" "Because I told you to" is the almost reflexive response. *How* to teach a child that a clean room is a thing to be valued is, in fact, another story, probably involving other incentives that the child does value. For now, let's simply acknowledge that establishing a clean room as a valued goal is the major task at hand. Clearly, having a clean room is not an innate, inborn need. The parents have learned to value clean rooms, and there is hope that their child also can learn to be similarly motivated.

If this discussion of incentives sounds something like our treatment of operant conditioning, you're right. The basic tenet of operant conditioning is that one's behaviors are controlled by their consequences. We are motivated to do whatever leads to reinforcement (positive incentives), and not to do whatever leads to punishment or failure of reinforcement (negative incentives).

Before You Go On
▼▼▼▼▼▼▼▼▼

How have the concepts of instinct, drive, and incentive been used to explain motivated behaviors?

▶ Approaches Based on Balance or Equilibrium

A concept that has proven to be useful in discussions of motivated behavior is that of balance, or equilibrium. The basic idea is that we are motivated or driven to maintain a state of balance. What is it that we are motivated to keep in balance? We may be motivated to maintain equilibrium among: (1) physiological processes, or (2) our overall level of excitement, or (3) our thoughts or cognitions.

Homeostasis. One of the first references to the need for equilibrium is found in the work of Walter Cannon (1932). Cannon was concerned with internal physiological reactions, and the term he used to describe a state of balance among those reactions was **homeostasis**. Each of our physiological processes has a balanced, **set point**, which can be interpreted as the normal or most suitable level of activity. When anything happens to upset our homeostasis, we become motivated to do whatever we can to return to our set point. If we drift slightly out of balance, our own physiological mechanisms act to return us to homeostasis without our intention or awareness. When these involuntary processes are unsuccessful, then we take action to maintain equilibrium.

For example, everyone has a normal, set level of body temperature, blood pressure, basal metabolism (the rate at which energy is consumed in

homeostasis a state of balance or equilibrium among internal, physiological conditions

set point a normal, optimum level (or value) of equilibrium or balance among physiological or psychological reactions

normal bodily functions), heart rate, and so on. When any of these deviate from their set point, we become motivated to do something that will return us to balance. Cannon's concept of homeostasis was devised to explain physiological processes. As we shall soon see, however, the basic ideas of balance and optimum level of operation have been applied to psychological processes as well.

Arousal. Arousal is defined in terms of overall level of activation or excitement. A person's level of arousal may change from day to day and throughout the same day. After a good night's sleep, a cup of coffee, and a morning shower, your level of arousal may be quite high. (Your arousal also may be high as your instructor moves through your class handing out exams.) Late at night, after a busy day at school, your level of arousal may be low. Your arousal is at its lowest when you are in the deepest stages of sleep.

Arousal theories of motivation (*e.g.,* Berlyne, 1960; 1971; Duffy, 1962; Hebb, 1955) claim that there is an optimal level (or set point) of arousal that organisms are motivated to maintain. Drive reduction approaches, remember, argue that we are motivated to reduce tension or arousal by satisfying needs. Arousal theories argue that sometimes we may seek out arousing, tension-producing activities, motivated to maintain our optimal arousal level. If we find ourselves bored and in a rut, the idea of going to an action-adventure movie may seem like a good one. On the other hand, if we've had a very busy and hectic day, just staying at home doing nothing may sound appealing. This approach is, of course, much like Cannon's idea of homeostasis, but it refers to psychological as well as physiological processes.

The implication is that for any activity or situation, there is a "best," most efficient level of arousal. To do well on an exam, for example, requires that a student have a certain level of arousal. If a student is tired, bored, or just doesn't care about the exam, we can expect a poor performance. If, on the other hand, a student is *so* worried, nervous, and anxious that he or she can barely function, we can also predict a poor score. The relationship between arousal and the efficiency of performance is depicted in Figure 9.2.

Figure 9.2

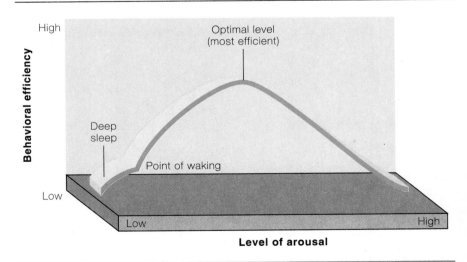

▲ *For each task we attempt there is an optimal level of arousal. What that level is will depend on the task. In other words, it is possible to be too aroused (motivated), just as it is possible to be under aroused. (After Hebb, 1955.)*

▲ For many of us, jumping out of an airplane would be overly arousing to say the least. For "sensation seekers," sky diving may provide a near-optimum level of arousal.

An interesting twist on the theory of arousal is the observation that, for unknown reasons, optimum levels of arousal may vary considerably from person to person. Some people seem to need and seek high levels of arousal and excitement in their lives. They are what Marvin Zuckerman (1978; 1980) calls "sensation seekers." They enjoy skydiving or mountain climbing and may actually look forward to the challenge of driving in heavy city traffic. Zuckerman predicted that sensation seekers would have a disturbance in the hormonal system related to arousal levels. Such a disturbance—also linked to pathological gambling—has been discovered (Roy, DeJong & Linnoila, 1989).

Cognitive Dissonance. There is also a theory that we are motivated to maintain a balance among our ideas or beliefs (our cognitions) as well as our physiological processes and our levels of arousal. This approach claims that we are motivated to preserve what Leon Festinger (1957) calls a *state of consonance* among our cognitions.

Suppose you believe yourself to be a good student. You study hard for an exam in biology. You think that you're prepared. You judge the exam to be a fairly easy one. But when you get your exam paper back, you discover that you failed the test! Now that's hard to accept. You believe you're a good student. You believe that you studied adequately. You believe the test wasn't difficult. But you also know that you failed the test. Here are a number of cognitions that don't fit together—they are not consonant, not balanced. You are experiencing *cognitive dissonance,* a state of tension or discomfort that exists when we hold inconsistent, dissonant cognitions. When this occurs, Festinger argues, we are motivated to bring about a change in our system of cognitions. You may come to believe that you're not such a good student after all. You may come to believe that your exam was graded unfairly. Or you may come to believe that you are a poor judge of an exam's difficulty. This theory doesn't predict specifically *what* will happen, but it does predict that cognitive dissonance produces motivation to return to a balanced state of cognitive consonance.

These days, almost all smokers experience cognitive dissonance. They *know* that smoking is a very dangerous habit, and yet they continue to smoke. Smokers often reduce dissonance by convincing themselves that although smoking is bad for one's health in general, it really isn't bad for them, at least when compared to perceived "benefits." We'll return to Festinger and cognitive dissonance again when we discuss attitude change (in Chapter 14).

▶ An Interim Summary

Let's go back now to our meeting-a-bear-in-the-woods story with which I opened this chapter. Granted that the example is somewhat far-fetched, and that we'll have to oversimplify a bit, but can we apply these approaches to explain your behavior in this circumstance? Let us say that upon seeing the bear, you throw your arms straight up in the air, scream at the top of your lungs, and race back to camp as fast as you can. Your friends, still sitting around the campfire, can see and hear you coming. How might they explain your behavior?

(1) "Clearly, it's a matter of instinct. Humans have a powerful and very useful instinct for avoiding large animals in the wild. In this situation, running away is an unlearned, natural, instinctive reaction." (2) "No, I think that the fear that arose upon seeing the bear created a tension—a drive—that needed to be relieved. There were several options available, but in your need to reduce your fear, you chose to run away." (3) "Why do you folks

keep relying on all this internal instinct-need-drive nonsense? Previous learning experience, even if it was second-hand, or vicarious, taught you that bears in the wild are incentives to be avoided. They are negative goals. You ran back here simply to reach the goal of safety with friends." (4) "I see your reaction as an attempt to maintain a state of equilibrium or balance. Seeing that bear was an emotional experience that increased many physiological functions. Your running away was just one way to try to return those physiological conditions to their normal, homeostatic level." (5) "Why get so complicated with different physiological functions? Why not just say that your overall arousal level was much higher than normal, higher than you wanted it to be, so you ran away from the bear simply in need of lowering arousal levels?" (6) "The same argument can be made for cognitions—and cognitive dissonance reduction. You know that you like being safe and pain-free. You believe that bears in the wild can be very hurtful and there's one in front of you. These two ideas conflict. You will do something. In your case, you chose to run away. If you believed that a bear in the woods will be afraid of you and of no potential harm, then there wouldn't be any dissonance, and you wouldn't have run."

▲ When our body temperature is above or below its normal level, we are motivated to return the temperature to its normal 98.6°. Feeling cold may motivate you to put on more clothes before starting the long trek to the bus stop. Feeling hot may motivate you to douse yourself with water after running a long race.

Before You Go On

How can the concept of balance or equilibrium be used to help us understand motivated behaviors?

In what way is cognitive dissonance theory based on equilibrium?

▶ Physiologically-Based Drives

Now that we have reviewed some theoretical approaches to the motives that activate and direct our behaviors, we can turn our attention to a few specific examples. As you can imagine, this discussion could be organized in several ways. We'll use a simple system that refers to just two types of motivators: those that have a biological basis, which we will call *physiologically-based*, and those that are more clearly learned or social in nature, which we'll call *psychologically-based*.

There are two points to keep in mind throughout this discussion. For one thing, we will follow convention and use the term *drive* for activators and directors of behavior that have a known biological or physiological basis (*e.g.*, a hunger drive) and the term *motive* for those that do not (*e.g.*, a power motive). Second, note that even drives rooted in an organism's physiology are often influenced by psychological processes. Hunger, for example, is clearly a physiologically-based drive, but what we eat, when we eat, and how much we eat often are influenced by psychological and social factors.

▶ Temperature Regulation

Most of us seldom give our own body temperature much thought. We all have a fuzzy notion that 98.6°F is a normal, homeostatic body temperature. That body temperature has anything to do with motivation becomes sensible only in the context of homeostasis. When anything happens to change our body temperature from its homeostatic set point, we become motivated. We become motivated to return our body temperature to its normal 98.6°.

Let's say that you are outside on a very cold day, and you are improperly dressed for the low temperature and high wind. Your body temperature drops. Automatically, your body responds to do what it can to elevate your temperature back to normal: Blood vessels in the hands and feet constrict, forcing blood back to the center of the body to conserve heat (and as a result, your lips turn blue); you start to shiver, the involuntary movements of your muscles creating small amounts of heat energy. These are exactly the sorts of reactions that Cannon had in mind when he wrote about homeostasis.

As another example, imagine that you are walking across a desert, at noon on a day in August. Your temperature begins to rise. Automatically, blood is forced toward the body's surface and your face becomes flushed. You perspire, and as the moisture on the surface of the skin evaporates, the skin is cooled, and so is your blood, now near the surface—all in an attempt to return your body's temperature to its homeostatic level.

There are two centers that act together as a thermostat and instigate these attempts at temperature regulation. Both are located in the **hypothalamus** deep inside the brain (see Figure 9.3). One is particularly sensitive to elevated body temperatures, the other to lowered temperatures.

If automatic reactions are not successful, you may be motivated to take some voluntary action on your own. You may have to get inside, out of the cold or heat. You may need to turn on a furnace or air conditioner. In fact, you may *anticipate* the lowering or raising of your body temperature and act accordingly—by putting on your coat before going out on a blustery day, for example. Over and above what your body can do automatically, you may have to engage in voluntary behaviors in order to maintain homeostasis.

hypothalamus a small structure near the limbic system in the center of the brain, associated with feeding, drinking, temperature regulation, sex, and aggression

Figure 9.3

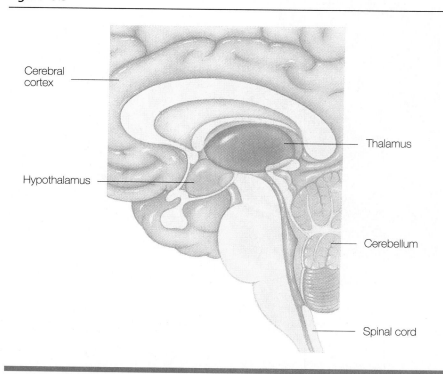

Cerebral cortex

Thalamus

Hypothalamus

Cerebellum

Spinal cord

▲ *The brain, showing the location of the hypothalamus.*

▲ Drinking behaviors may be motivated by any one of several internal or external cues, but basically, they are a response to our need for water.

Before You Go On
▼▼▼▼▼▼▼▼

Given the concept of homeostasis, how might temperature regulation be thought of as a physiologically-based drive?

▶ The Thirst Drive and Drinking Behavior

We need water for survival. If we don't drink, we die. As the need for water increases, it gives rise to a thirst drive. The intriguing issue is not so much that we need to drink, but how do we *know* that we're thirsty. What actually causes us to seek liquid and drink it?

For a very long time, it was thought that we drink simply to relieve the discomfort caused by the dryness of our mouths and throats. No doubt, the unpleasantness of a dry mouth and throat *can* cause us to drink. But there is more to drinking behavior than this.

Animals with no salivary glands, whose mouths and throats are always dry, drink no more than normal animals (more frequently, yes, but no more). Normal bodily processes (urination, exhaling, perspiration, and so on) cause us to lose about 2 1/2 liters of water a day (Levinthal, 1983). That water needs to be replaced, but what motivates us to do so?

About two-thirds of the fluid in our bodies is contained *within* our body's cells (intercellular), the rest in the spaces *between* cells (extracellular). There seem to be two separate mechanisms sensitive to losses of fluid. Intercellular loss of fluid is monitored by the hypothalamus, where one small center acts to "turn on" the thirst drive when fluid levels are low, and another center "turns off" thirst when fluid levels are adequate. Thirst that stems from extracellular fluid loss is monitored (in a complex chain of events) by the kidneys, which stimulate the production of a hormone that leads to a thirst drive.

Sometimes, our drinking is motivated by a physiological drive that arises from our physiological need for water. Sometimes, however, our drinking behavior may be influenced by external factors, or incentives. The implication here, as I mentioned earlier, is that we become motivated to drink in response to external stimulation, not in response to internal needs. A frosty glass of iced tea may look too good to refuse. The aroma of freshly brewed coffee may stimulate us to have a second (unneeded) cup. We may drink a cold beer or a soda simply because it tastes good, whether we *need* the fluid they contain or not.

Notice also that once our thirst drive has been aroused, *what* we drink may be strongly influenced by our previous learning experiences. Some people prefer Coke, some prefer Pepsi, while others would choose a different brand. Some people don't like cola drinks at all. Choices and preferences for what we drink are shaped by availability (people in Canada do not regularly drink coconut milk) and by past experience. Even with so obvious a physiological drive as thirst, and so obvious a physiological need as our need for water, we see that psychological factors can be very relevant.

Before You Go On
▼▼▼▼▼▼▼▼

List some of the internal and external factors that influence drinking behavior.

▶ The Hunger Drive and Eating Behavior

Our need for food is as obvious as our need for water. If we don't eat, we die. Again, the interesting question is what gives rise to the hunger drive? As it happens, there are many factors that motivate a person to eat. Some of them are physiological in nature. Some are more psychological, reflecting learning experiences. Some involve social pressures.

People and animals with no stomachs still feel hungry periodically and eat amounts of food similar to those eaten by people with their stomachs intact. Cues from our stomachs, then, don't seem to be very important in producing a hunger drive. The two structures most involved in the hunger drive are the hypothalamus (again) and the liver, which is involved in the production and breakdown of fat.

Theories of hunger that focus on the hypothalamus have been referred to as *dual-center* theories, because they suggest that there are *two* regions in the hypothalamus that regulate food intake. One is an "eat center" that gives rise to feelings of hunger, while the other is a "no eat center" that lets us know when we've had enough.

There are two places (called *nuclei*) in the hypothalamus that have predictable effects on eating behavior when they are electrically stimulated or when they are destroyed. Removing the "eat center," for example, leads to starvation, while lesioning the "no eat center" leads to extreme overeating—called *hyperphagia* (Friedman & Stricker, 1976; Keesey & Powley, 1975).

The hypothalamus may be involved in the hunger drive, but normal eating patterns are not caused by electrical stimulation or lesioning. What activates the brain's hunger-regulating centers in a normal organism? To the extent that the hypothalamus may act as a major (not the only) control device for eating behaviors and the maintenance of body weight, we still have to ask what it is within the body that the hypothalamus reacts to. There seem to be many cues that are monitored at the same time. Here, we are still at the level of hypothesis and conjecture, not fact (Martin, White & Hulsey, 1991).

One long-accepted view was that the body responds to levels of blood sugar (glucose) in our blood. When glucose metabolism is low—which it is when we haven't eaten for a while—we are stimulated to eat. When blood sugar levels are adequate, we are stimulated to stop eating. It may be that our liver is the organ that most closely monitors such blood chemistry for us.

Another position holds that we respond to levels of fat stored in our bodies. When fat stores are adequately filled, we feel no hunger. When fat supplies are depleted, a hunger drive arises. Once again, the liver is thought to be involved in the cycle of storing and depleting fat supplies.

Yet another view that emphasizes the role of internal, physiological cues relies heavily on the concept of homeostasis. The essence of this position is that a person's overall *body weight,* is regulated (Nisbett, 1972), just as blood pressure or temperature. "Being so regulated, weight is normally maintained at a particular level or set-point, not only by the control of food intake, as is often assumed, but also by complementary adjustments in energy utilization and expenditure" (Keesey & Powley, 1986). The implication is that as body weight decreases significantly, either through dieting, exercise, or both, the organism becomes motivated to return to the set-point level. The result may be to abandon the diet, cut down on exercise, or both. What is yet to be determined are the mechanisms involved in establishing the set points of body weight and energy utilization to begin with. There is some evidence that these are influenced by both genetic factors (Nisbett, 1972) and feeding behaviors during infancy (Knittle, 1975).

for achievement and approval. There is evidence that patients with eating disorders show relatively high rates of depression. But the depression may be a response to an eating disorder rather than a cause (Garner, et al., 1990).

Psychologists have looked at parenting and family style as contributors to eating disorders. Anorexia nervosa patients *do* tend to come from very rigid, rule-governed, over-protecting families. And bulimic patients often experienced inordinate blame and rejection in childhood (Bruch, 1980; Yates, 1990). You know by now not to overinterpret general findings like these; there are many exceptions.

Researchers have considered physiological processes as potential causes of eating disorders. One significant line of scientific detective work stems from the often-confirmed observation that bulimic patients do not "feel full" after they eat—even after they binge (Mitchell, Pyle & Eckert, 1981; Walsh, et al., 1989). This may be due to the fact that the hormone *cholecystokinin* (or CCK) is produced in very low levels in bulimic patients. This is significant because CCK is a hormone normally produced in the small intestine that may signal that one is full and need eat no more. When drug treatment elevates CCK levels in bulimic patients, they often (not always) show fewer symptoms of the disorder.

I'm afraid that evidence on the treatment of eating disorders is sketchy, unclear, and very tentative. In part this reflects the fact that we do not know for sure what causes the disorders. The prognosis (prediction of the future course of a disorder) for anorexia nervosa is particularly poor. Nearly 50 percent of those who *are* released from treatment relapse within one year (Yates, 1990). Approximately 5 percent of patients with anorexia actually die from excessive weight loss (Hsu, 1986). At first, treatment will be medical in response to nourishment needs. Hospitalization may be required. Virtually all forms of psychotherapy have been tried, but with little consistent success. No one form of therapy seems significantly more effective than any other. The best predictor of the success of psychotherapy is the extent to which the family of the patient gets involved—confirming the idea that parental and family pressures may be part of the cause of eating disorders.

The outlook for bulimia is usually much better. If nothing else, bulimic patients are seldom malnourished, and thus do not require hospitalization. The prognosis is much better with family-oriented therapy programs rather than with individual treatment. With bulimic patients there has been some good (but generally short-lived) success with antidepressant medications (Geracioti & Liddle, 1988; Pope, et al., 1985; Pope & Hudson, 1986).

satisfaction. If we don't drink, we die; if we don't regulate our temperature, we die; if we don't eat, we die. If we don't have sex—well, we don't die. The survival of the *species* requires that an adequate number of its members respond to a sex drive, but an individual can get along without doing so.

Second, most physiologically-based drives, such as hunger and thirst, provide mechanisms that ultimately replenish and/or maintain the body's energy. When satisfied, the sex drive depletes bodily energy. In fact, the sex drive actually motivates the organism to seek tension, as opposed to drives that seek to reduce tension to return to homeostasis.

▲ The sex drive in humans may have an internal, physiological basis, but its expression in behavior is influenced by many nonphysiological factors, such as cultural, societal, and religious pressures, past experiences, personal preferences, and opportunity.

A third point is that the sex drive is not present at birth, but requires a certain level of maturation (puberty) before it is apparent. The other drives are present, and even most critical, early in life.

A fourth unique quality of the sex drive is the extent to which internal and external influences differ depending on the species involved. The role of internal physiological states is much greater in "lower" species than it is in primates and humans. For humans, sex hormones may be necessary, but they are seldom sufficient to maintain sexual response; and for an experienced human, they may not even be necessary.

Internal and External Cues for the Sex Drive. For rats, matters of sex are very simple and straightforward. If adequate supplies of testosterone (the male sex hormone) are present, and if there is the opportunity, a male rat will respond to the hormone-induced sex drive and will engage in sexual behaviors. If adequate supplies of estrogen and progesterone (the female sex hormones) are present, and if the opportunity is available, the female rat also will engage in appropriate sexual behaviors. For rats at least, learning or experience seem to have little to do with sexual behaviors—they are tied closely to physiology, to hormonal levels. There is little difference between the mating behaviors of sexually experienced rats, rats that have mated once or twice, and virgin rats. If the sex hormones of a female rat are removed (by surgically removing the ovaries), there will be a complete and immediate loss of sexual receptivity. If these sex hormones are replaced by injection, sexual behaviors quickly return to normal (Davidson, et al., 1968). Removing the sex hormone from male rats produces a slightly different story. Sexual behaviors diminish and may disappear, but they take longer to do so. Again, injections of testosterone return the male rat to normal sexual functioning.

Removal of the sex hormones from male dogs or cats ("higher" species than rats) also produces a reduction in sexual behaviors, but more gradually. An experienced male primate ("higher" still) may persist in sexual behaviors for the rest of his life, even after his sex hormones have been removed. (The same also seems true of human males, although the data here are sketchy.)

So what we find is that the sex drive in "lower" species is tied to its physiological, hormonal base. As the complexity of the organism increases, from rats, to dogs, to primates, to humans, the role of internal cues becomes less certain and less noticeable.

No one would get far arguing that sex is not an important human drive. However, it is easy to lose sight of the fact that it is a *biological* drive. In societies like ours, where so much learning is involved, one easily could come to believe that sex drives are learned through experience and practice alone. Hormones may provide humans with an arousing force to do something, but *what* to do, and *how* to do it, and *when* to do it seem to require training and practice. Sex manuals of a "how to" nature sell well, and sex therapy has become a standard practice for many psychologists trying to help people cope with the pressures that external factors put on their "natural" sexual motivation.

In addition to the internal forces produced by the hormones, sex drives can be stimulated by a wide range of stimuli. Some people engage in sexual behaviors simply to reproduce; others do so for the physical pleasure they experience; others because they feel it demonstrates a romantic "love"; yet others want to display their femininity or masculinity. Sex drives in humans are seldom satisfied with "just anybody." Social (external) and cognitive constraints often are placed on one's choice of a sexual partner. Virtually any of the senses—touch, smell (particularly important in lower mammals and primates), sight, and sound—can stimulate sexual arousal, and there are considerable individual differences in terms of what will be effective.

Before You Go On
▼▼▼▼▼▼▼▼

In what ways is the sex drive a unique physiologically-based drive?

Homosexuality. The complexities of human sexual responsiveness and behaviors are no more apparent than when we consider *homosexuals.* These persons are sexually attracted to and aroused by members of their own sex, as opposed to heterosexuals, who seek outlets for their sexual drives among members of the opposite sex. Psychologists argue that homosexuality should be referred to as an orientation and *not* as a matter of preference. Like handedness, for example, it is not chosen voluntarily.

Psychologists agree that homosexuality and heterosexuality are not mutually exclusive categories, but rather end points of a dimension of sexual orientations and that many combinations are possible. Alfred Kinsey and his colleagues (1948; 1953) first brought the prevalence of homosexuality to the attention of the general public. Kinsey devised a seven-point scale (0 to 6) of sexual orientation with those who are exclusively heterosexual at one end point and persons who are exclusively homosexual at the other extreme (see Figure 9.4). Kinsey found that about half of the males who responded to his surveys fell somewhere *between* these two end points. Even though homosexuality is now more openly discussed than it was in the 1940s and 1950s (more "out of the closet"), it is still difficult to get accurate estimates of the numbers of persons who are exclusively or predominantly homosexual. Conservative estimates suggest that about 2 percent of North American males are exclusively homosexual, and that 8 to 10 percent have had more than just an occasional homosexual encounter. Comparable data indicate that female homosexuality is about half as prevalent as male homosexuality.

In most ways, there is little difference between homosexuals and heterosexuals, including the pattern of their sexual responsiveness. Most

Figure 9.4

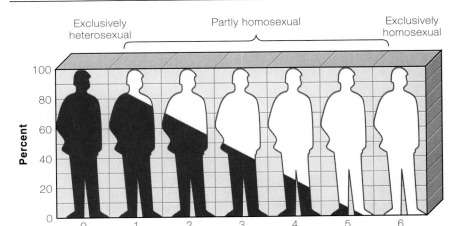

▲ *Kinsey's seven-point scale of sexual orientation.*

▲ *Though homosexuals are able to be more open about their sexual orientation, homosexuality is still a controversial issue.*

homosexuals have experienced heterosexual sex. They simply find same-sex relationships more satisfying. In fact, homosexual couples are often more at ease and comfortable with their sexual relationship than most heterosexual couples (Masters & Johnson, 1979). Contrary to popular opinion, most homosexuals are indistinguishable from heterosexuals in their appearance and mannerisms.

As yet, we have no generally accepted theory of the causes of homosexuality. What we do know is that the matter is not simple and probably involves some interaction of genetic, hormonal, and environmental factors (Money, 1987). There are now a number of hypotheses along each of these lines.

One hypothesis with research support suggests that *prenatal* hormonal imbalances may affect one's sexual orientation in adulthood (Money, 1987). The hypothesis claims that embryos (genetically male or female) exposed to above average levels of female hormones will develop into adults attracted to persons having masculine characteristics, the reverse also being true (Ellis & Ames, 1987).

In August 1991, Dr. Simon LeVay of the Salk Institute in San Diego, California published an article on his research that became headline news (LeVay, 1991). LeVay had performed a post mortem examination of the brains of 19 homosexual men, 16 heterosexual men, and 6 heterosexual women. He found that there is a small area in the hypothalamus (technically, a group of cells called INAH-3) that was significantly smaller in homosexual men than in heterosexual men. In fact, in homosexual men this area was precisely the same size as he found in the hypothalamus of women. Here was the best evidence yet of a physical, biological correlate of homosexuality. Notice that LeVay has not claimed that he located a *cause* of homosexuality. His observations lead us only to an association or a correlation, from which cause-and-effect conclusions would be unwarranted. But as one brain scientist (Dennis Landis of Case Western Reserve University) said about LeVay's work, "It would begin to suggest why male homosexuality is present in most human populations, despite cultural constraints. It suggests it's a biological phenomenon" (Barinaga, 1991).

Some psychologists remain unwilling to disregard hypotheses that emphasize the importance of environmental influences. It is clear, however, that sexual orientation cannot be attributed to any one simple early childhood experience. A reasonable position at the moment would be to hypothesize that genetic and hormonal predispositions may interact with subtle environmental influences in complex ways to form one's adult sexual orientation.

Before You Go On

▼▼▼▼▼▼▼▼▼

What is homosexuality?

What causes homosexuality?

sexually transmitted diseases (STDs) contagious diseases that are usually transmitted through sexual contact

Sexually Transmitted Diseases. **Sexually Transmitted Diseases** (STDs) are contagious diseases that are usually passed on through sexual contact. In this section, we'll briefly describe a few of the most common STDs. Even though STDs present medical problems, I've chosen to include them here for two reasons: (1) Sexually transmitted diseases, or the fear of them, often have a profound influence on sexual behaviors, and (2) people with STDs often suffer as many psychological consequences as medical ones. We'll focus on AIDS because it *is* deadly, but will cover some much more common STDs first.

chlamydia a very common STD; a bacterial infection of the genital area

gonorrhea an STD caused by a bacterial infection of moist tissues in the genital area

syphilis an STD caused by a bacterial infection, which may pass through four stages, ultimately resulting in death

genital herpes (Herpes type II) the most common STD; a skin infection in the form of a rash or blisters in the genital area

acquired immune deficiency syndrome (AIDS) a deadly disease caused by a virus (HIV) that destroys the body's natural immune system, and which can be transmitted by sexual behaviors

Chlamydia is one of the most common of the STDs in North America. It is caused by a bacterial infection and is usually diagnosed in persons younger than 35 years old. Its incidence is soaring. Approximately 4 million Americans are stricken, and about 100,000 women a year become sterile because of the infection. Symptoms include burning urination in men and women. Left untreated in women, chlamydia can lead to pelvic inflammatory disease (PID), which can cause infertility. Once diagnosed, treatment with an antibiotic usually is effective within one week.

Gonorrhea is also a disease of the young and the sexually active. Of the more than 1.8 million cases that will be diagnosed this year, most will be men between the ages of 20 and 24. It, too, is a bacterial infection that affects the moist tissue areas around the genitals. The bacteria that produce the symptoms of gonorrhea can live for only a few seconds outside of the human body, so the likelihood of contracting the disease from toilet seats, eating utensils, or drinking fountains is very slim. Fortunately, treatment for gonorrhea—penicillin, or tetracycline for those allergic to penicillin—is simple and usually successful.

Syphilis is an STD with a long and ignoble history. It too is a disease caused by a bacterium. If left untreated, syphilis may run its course through four known stages, from a relatively simple and painless sore, all the way to the infection of nonsexual organs, which may lead even to death. As many as 25 percent of those with syphilis ultimately may die as a result. Just ten years ago, it was believed that syphilis was becoming a disease of the past. Then, in the fall of 1990, the Centers for Disease Control (CDC) reported that since 1985, the number of syphilis cases has skyrocketed—rates are up 60 percent (132 percent among blacks) to levels not seen since 1949. Nearly 85,000 new cases can be expected this year. Treatment is quite simple, once diagnosis has been confirmed. Penicillin (or tetracycline) is used, and the prognosis is related to length of infection—the sooner treatment begins, the better.

Genital herpes is a virus-caused disease that affects the genital area, producing small sores and blisters. It is one of the most common STDs. Some estimates place incidence as high as 40 million Americans, with 500,000 new cases diagnosed each year. Genital herpes has no cure, although some medications can reduce the painful symptoms. A person with genital herpes is most infectious when the sores and blisters are active. There may be long periods during which the infected person remains symptom-free, only to have the reddening and sores recur.

No STD has attracted so much public attention as **acquired immune deficiency syndrome,** or **AIDS.** AIDS was unknown in the United States before 1981. Just ten years later, over 161,000 cases of the disease and more than 100,000 deaths in the United States had been reported by the Centers for Disease Control (CDC). Of the 100,000 deaths, 31,000 were in 1990 alone. In January of 1992 the CDC reported the grim statistics that the number of persons with AIDS had passed 200,000, with 133,232 deaths (the 300,000 landmark was expected by 1994) . More than 11,000 heterosexual AIDS cases were reported with expectations that that number will double by 1995. Recently, AIDS has risen to be the fifth most common killer of women. Just what is AIDS?

AIDS is caused by a virus called the *human immunodeficiency virus,* or HIV. The HIV almost always enters the body through sexual contact or the use of contaminated needles in intravenous (IV) drug use. Concentrations of the virus are highest in the blood and semen. Once infected, a person may experience few symptoms other than those associated with a common cold. Then the person enters what is called a "carrier state." He or she is infected with the virus and may pass it on to others, but remains free of noticeable

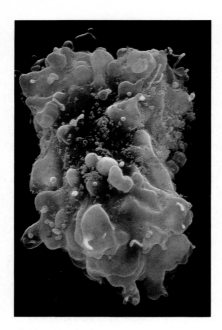

▲ Here, under the microscope, the AIDS virus (blue) attacks a helper T cell. © Boehringer Ingelheim International GmbH. Photo: Lennart Nilsson.

symptoms. What is not clear is just how many persons infected with the HIV will develop the full-blown symptoms of AIDS. Of those with a diagnosis of AIDS (not just the HIV), virtually all will die within four years.

The HIV directly attacks the body's immune system, the system that naturally fights off infections. With a weakened or nonfunctioning immune system, a person with AIDS does not have the resources to defend against other infections that normally would not be life-threatening. In other words, patients don't die from AIDS directly, but from other diseases or infections (often cancer or pneumonia) that the body cannot defend itself against.

AIDS cannot be transmitted by casual contact—there has to be an interchange of bodily fluids, blood or semen. Early in the 1980s, it was believed that AIDS was a disease found only in homosexual males and intravenous drug users. This is clearly not the case. Intercourse, anal intercourse in particular, often leads to the transmission of the HIV, and whether or not both sex partners are male seems to matter little.

Whereas other STDs may cause discomfort and/or pain, AIDS will be fatal. There is no vaccine to prevent it. There is no cure for AIDS, and it is unlikely that one will be discovered soon. At present, the only reasonable way to protect against AIDS is through the monitoring of behavior. Totally abstaining from sexual activity, not sharing needles with IV drug users, and donating your own blood prior to surgery would minimize personal risk.

On the assumption that many adolescents and adults will not abstain from sex altogether, many experts counsel "safe" sex. There is disagreement on just what safe sex *is*. In general, the advice seems sensible. The fewer sexual contacts one has, the less the probability of encountering someone infected with AIDS. The more selective one is in choosing a partner, the less the risk. The use of condoms significantly reduces (but does not eliminate) the likelihood of infection. Engaging in sex behaviors in which there is no exchange of bodily fluids at all (such as mutual masturbation, for example) also constitutes safe sex (Masters, et al., 1987).

AIDS is a physical disease. A biological organism (a virus) attacks a physiological system (the immune system), which increases the possibility of further infection, which ultimately can result in death. But AIDS is a physical disease with unprecedented psychological complications. In fact, patients who have been diagnosed as carrying the HIV virus, but who have not yet developed AIDS, tend to be more depressed and disturbed than those who have developed the full-blown and fatal symptoms of the disease (Chuang, et al., 1989). AIDS researcher Tom Coates put it this way, "AIDS, as I see it, is primarily a psychological problem. What we're dealing with is a disease that gets in the way of people relating in intimate ways. And it becomes a psychological problem to figure out how we, as people who know something about motivation and know something about behavior, can help people not do something that's natural" (quoted in Landers, 1987, p. 28). Because AIDS is such a frightening disease, AIDS patients often are shunned—by loved ones and even by health care professionals. Because AIDS began in the homosexual community (and is still largely concentrated there), homosexuals fear that they will become the focus of even greater discrimination than they have suffered in the past. The fear, alienation, and stress experienced by AIDS patients (and often their friends and family) are in many ways as painful as the disease itself and require psychological treatment (Knapp & Vandecreek, 1989).

Before You Go On
▼▼▼▼▼▼▼▼▼

Name and briefly describe five sexually transmitted diseases.

▶ Psychologically-Based Motivation

From time to time, you may be able to analyze your own behavior in terms of physiologically-based needs and drives. That you had breakfast this morning soon after you got up might have reflected your response to a hunger drive. That you got dressed might have been your attempt to do what you could to control your body temperature, which may have influenced your choice of clothes. Perhaps some sexual motivation affected what you chose to wear.

Many of our behaviors seem to be aroused and directed (motivated) by forces that are less clearly biological in origin. In this section, we'll review some of the motivators that reflect learned or social influences on behavior. Remember that we are going to refer to these psychologically-based drives as *motives*. Although there are potentially a large number of such motives, we'll review three that have proven useful for "explaining" human behavior: achievement, power, and affiliation motivation.

▶ Achievement Motivation

need to achieve (nAch) the learned need to meet or exceed some standard of excellence in performance

Thematic Apperception Test (TAT) a projective personality test requiring a subject to tell a series of short stories about a set of ambiguous pictures

The hypothesis that people are motivated to varying degrees by a need to achieve was introduced to psychology in 1938 by Henry Murray. The **need to achieve** (nAch) is defined as the acquired need to meet or exceed some standard of excellence in one's behaviors. Measuring nAch and determining its sources and implications have been the major work of David McClelland and his associates (*e.g.*, McClelland, et al., 1953; McClelland, 1975; 1985).

Although there are short, paper-and-pencil tests for the same purpose, achievement motivation usually is assessed by means of the **Thematic Apperception Test**, or (**TAT**). This test is a *projective test*. Subjects are asked to tell short stories about a series of ambiguous pictures depicting people in various settings (see Figure 9.5). Subjects' stories are interpreted and scored according to objective criteria that note references to attempting difficult tasks, succeeding, being rewarded for one's efforts, setting short-term and long-term goals, and so on. Because there are no right or wrong

Figure 9.5

▲ *A picture like one of those found in the TAT. What is going on here? What led up to this situation? What is going to happen next? Because the answers to these questions are not immediately obvious , a subject may project some of his or her own feelings, beliefs, and motives into a response to these questions.*

responses to the TAT pictures, judgments are made about the references to achievement that a subject "projects" into the picture.

One of the first things that McClelland and his coworkers found was that there were consistent differences in measured levels of nAch among the male subjects they tested. One of the most reliable findings concerning people with high needs for achievement involves the nature of tasks they choose to attempt. When given a choice, they generally try tasks in which success is not guaranteed (otherwise, there is no challenge), but in which there is a reasonable chance of success. Both young children (McClelland, 1958) and college students (Atkinson & Litwin, 1960) high in nAch were observed playing a ring-toss game, where the object was to score points by tossing a small ring over a peg from a distance. The farther away from the peg one stood, the more points could be earned with success. High nAch subjects in both studies chose to stand at a moderate distance from the peg. They didn't stand so close as to guarantee success, but they didn't choose to stand so far away that they would almost certainly fail. Subjects with low nAch scores tended to go to either extreme—very close, where they earned few points for their successes, or so far away they rarely succeeded.

McClelland would argue that you are reading this text at this moment because you are motivated by a need to achieve. You want to get a good grade in this course, and you have decided that to do so, you need to study the text material. Some students read assignments not because they are motivated by a need to achieve, but because they are motivated by a fear of failure (Atkinson & Feather, 1966). In such a case, the incentive that is relevant is a negative one (avoid an F), which is a different matter than working toward a positive incentive (earn an A). Individuals motivated by a fear of failure tend to take very few risks. They either choose to attempt tasks that they are bound to do well or to attempt tasks that are virtually impossible (if the task is impossible, they can't blame themselves for their failures). There *are* explanations for why people choose tasks of the difficulty they do that do not rely on the notions of achievement or failure. One (*e.g.,* Dweck, 1986) suggests that persons choose tasks of moderate difficulty when they are motivated to learn from their experience, and improve themselves, while people choose easy tasks when they are motivated to "show off" and demonstrate superior performance.

It seems that the need to achieve is learned, usually in childhood. Children who show high levels of achievement motivation are generally those who have been encouraged in a positive way to excel. High nAch children are encouraged to work things out for themselves, independently, perhaps with parental support and encouragement ("Here, Leslie, you see if you can do this" as opposed to, "Here, let me do it. You'll never get it right!"). McClelland is convinced that achievement motivation can be taught and acquired by almost anyone, of any age, and he has developed training programs designed to increase achievement motivation levels (*e.g.,* McClelland & Winter, 1969).

Before You Go On
▼▼▼▼▼▼▼▼▼

What is achievement motivation, and how is it usually measured?

▶ Power Motivation

Some people are motivated not only to excel, but also to be in control—to be in charge of the situation and of others. In such cases, we may speak of a **need for power** (McClelland, 1982; Winter & Stewart, 1978). Power needs generally are measured in the same way as achievement needs, through the

need for power the learned need to be in control of events or persons, usually at another's expense

▲ *Some people are strongly influenced by a need for power; to be in control of the fate of others, to be "in charge."*

need for affiliation the need to be with others and to form relationships and associations

interpretations of stories generated with the Thematic Apperception Test. Notice that a high need for power is, in itself, neither good nor bad. What matters is the end to which one's power is put.

People with high power needs like to be admired. They prefer to be in situations where they can control the fate of others, usually by manipulating access to information. They present an attitude of, "If you want to get this job done, you'll have to come to me to find out how to do it." People with low power needs tend to avoid situations in which others would have to depend on them. They tend to be rather submissive in interpersonal relationships. Even though the situation is changing ever so slowly, men in Western cultures are more commonly to be found in positions of power than are women (Darley & Fazio, 1980; Falbo & Peplau, 1980; Mulac, Incontro & James, 1985). At the same time, there seem to be *no* reliable differences between men and women in measured needs for power (Winter, 1988).

▶ *Affiliation Motivation*

Another psychologically-based motivator that has been helpful in explaining some behaviors is the **need for affiliation.** This motive involves a need to be with others, to work with others toward some end, and to form friendships and associations.

One interesting implication of having a high need for affiliation is that it is often at odds with a need for power. If you are simultaneously motivated to be in control *and* to be with others in a truly supportive way, conflicts may arise. It is more difficult to exercise power over people whose friendship you value than it is to exercise control over people whose friendship is of little concern to you. It remains the case, however, that there *are* circumstances in which we find persons who are high on both power and affiliation needs. These are often politicians who certainly enjoy the exercise of power, but who also value being public figures and being surrounded by aides and advisors (*e.g.,* Winter, 1987). It is also the case that affiliation and achievement motives are somewhat independent. Achievement and success can be earned either with others (high affiliation) or on one's own (low affiliation).

Although we might be quite confident that achievement and power motives are learned, we are less confident about the sources of affiliation motivation. There is a reasonable argument that the need to affiliate and be with others is at least partly biologically based. We are basically social animals for whom complete social isolation is quite difficult (particularly when we are young). On the other hand, it is clear that the extent to which we come to value relationships can be attributed to our learning experiences.

▲ *Some people are strongly influenced by a need for affiliation; to be with others, socializing, perhaps working together for common goals.*

Before You Go On
▼▼▼▼▼▼▼▼▼

Define the needs for power and affiliation.

▶ **The Nature of Emotions**

Psychology has investigated emotion since its earliest days. Psychologists have learned a lot about emotional reactions, but answers to some critical questions have remained elusive. We wish psychology could tell us just what emotions are and where they come from. We want to know what we can do to increase the pleasant emotions and avoid the unpleasant ones. It is in regard to our emotional reactions that we most want simple, easy, and direct answers.

▶ *Defining Emotion*

For the moment, try to recall the last time you experienced an emotional reaction of some significance—perhaps the fear of going to the dentist, the joy of receiving an A on a classroom exam, the sadness at the death of a friend, or the anger at being unable to register for a class you really wanted to take. A careful analysis suggests that there are four components to your emotional reaction, whatever it may be. (1) You will experience a *subjective feeling*, or *affect*, which you may label fear, joy, sadness, or anger. (2) You will have a *cognitive* reaction; you'll recognize, or "know," what has just happened to you. (3) You will have an internal, *physiological* reaction. This reaction will be largely visceral, involving your glands, hormones, and internal organs. (4) And you will (probably) engage in an overt, observable, *behavioral* reaction. You may tremble as you approach the dentist's office. You may run down the hallway, a broad smile on your face, waving your exam paper over your head. You may cry at the news of your friend's death. You may shake your fist and yell at the registrar when you cannot enroll in the class of your choice.

Notice that when we add a behavioral component to emotion, we most clearly can see how emotion and motivation are related. Emotions are often viewed as being motivational in nature (Greenberg & Safran, 1989; Lang, 1985). As we saw earlier, to be motivated is to be aroused and directed to action. Emotional experiences often arouse and direct our behavior.

There has been considerable debate within psychology concerning the definition of emotion. The major issues have been: What are the basic components of an emotional reaction? In what way or ways are those components related? Different answers to these questions have given rise to what are called *theories of emotion*, which we'll review next. For now, we need a working definition of emotion. We'll take a classic view and define an **emotion** as an experience that includes a subjective feeling, a cognitive interpretation, a physiological reaction, and a behavioral expression.

emotion a reaction involving subjective feeling, physiological response, cognitive interpretation, and behavioral expression

▲ *Emotions have four components: subjective interpretations, bodily reactions, and behavioral response. Viewing the Vietnam Veterans War Memorial in Washington D.C. is an emotional experience that causes sadness for many visitors. Graduation brings on a variety of emotions; while being a sad time of leaving friends and favorite school activities, it is also one of the most joyful times.*

▶ Theories of Emotion

Psychologists have long sought an acceptable theoretical model of emotion. Theories of emotion are attempts to explain how we become emotional, and how the various components of an emotional state interact. In this section, we'll briefly review some of the theories that have impact on the way we think about emotion.

The James-Lange Approach. In the late 1890s, William James in the United States and Carl Lange in Denmark both arrived at essentially the same view of emotion. Common sense suggested that one perceives an emotion-producing stimulus, experiences an appropriate emotion, and then behaves accordingly. You see a low grade on a term paper, you become angry, and then slam your fist against the desk. Your behavior occurs because you are in an emotional state.

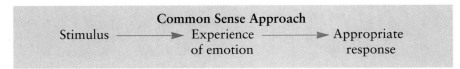

Common Sense Approach

Stimulus ⟶ Experience of emotion ⟶ Appropriate response

James and Lange suggested a different chain of events. According to their theory, you felt angry *because* you slammed your fist on the desk. You saw the low grade, banged the desk—*then* you felt angry because you noticed what you had done. If you had realized that you were laughing and smiling, you would have interpreted your emotional reaction as joy or happiness.

The James-Lange theory claims that we experience an emotion as we do because of our awareness of the physiological and bodily responses we make to a stimulus situation. As James said (1890), we are sad because we cry, afraid because we tremble, and happy because we smile; not the other way around. If nothing else, the James-Lange theory was the first serious statement about the relationships among the different components of an emotional reaction.

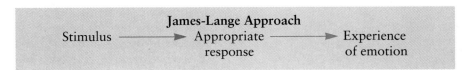

James-Lange Approach

Stimulus ⟶ Appropriate response ⟶ Experience of emotion

Cannon-Bard Approach. One of the toughest critics of the James-Lange approach was Walter Cannon (1927). It seemed to Cannon that the internal, visceral changes that we were supposed to be responding to were very slow in coming. Often stimulated by hormonal changes, they would be too slow to give rise to emotional feelings quickly enough. Cannon also knew that physiological reactions such as those that occur in emotion do not necessarily produce the true experience of an emotional state (aerobic exercise, for example, can produce physiological reactions very much like those that occur when we are emotional). Cannon proposed a theory of his own, which was later expanded upon by Philip Bard (1934), and has come to be called the Cannon-Bard theory.

▲ *Walter Cannon recognized that the physiological reactions that occur when we are emotional can also occur in nonemotional situations. For example, aerobic exercise produces many physiological reactions that are similar to those found in emotional states.*

Cannon and Bard proposed that a lower brain center, the thalamus, receives emotion-producing stimulation and immediately sends messages to the cerebral cortex for interpretation AND to yet lower brain centers to initiate a physiological reaction. (We now might feel more comfortable replacing the role of the thalamus with that of the limbic system, but the idea is the same in either case.)

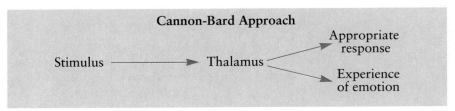

Cannon-Bard Approach

Stimulus ⟶ Thalamus ⟨ Appropriate response / Experience of emotion

For this theory, the perception of an emotion-producing stimulus goes first to a lower brain center, and then simultaneously to the cortex for interpretation and to the sympathetic division of the autonomic nervous system for expression. Cannon's focusing on the thalamus may have been misplaced, but it did direct attention to lower brain centers, and it did suggest that higher brain centers also are involved early in an emotional reaction.

The Schachter-Singer Approach. The model offered by Stanley Schachter and Jerome Singer (1962) was more cognitive in its orientation. This theory claimed that how we feel at any point in time reflects several interacting factors. First, there is a stimulus in the environment. Then there is a sense of heightened arousal, followed by our cognitive appraisal of the situation. The critical thing is how we use cognitions to *interpret* the situation. Without this cognitive appraisal, there would be too much ambiguity for us to know just how we feel.

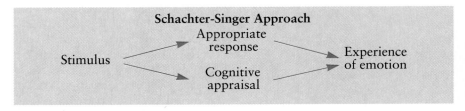

Schachter-Singer Approach

Stimulus ⟨ Appropriate response / Cognitive appraisal ⟩ ⟶ Experience of emotion

The Opponent-Process Approach. A different sort of theoretical approach to emotionality is called the *opponent-process theory* (Solomon & Corbit, 1974; Solomon, 1980). This approach provides us with a reminder of the similarity between emotional states and motivational states. The claim here is that emotions tend to occur in pairs that are basically opposite in their nature: fear-relief, pleasure-pain, depression-elation, for example.

When one member of the pair is stimulated (say, fear caused by a strange sound in the night) the other—relief—is suppressed. If the stimulus that causes the emotional reaction remains (the strange sound is still there), the level of the first reaction weakens somewhat and the second starts to take effect (eventually there is some relief in knowing that nothing terrible has happened—yet).

If the emotion-arousing stimulus is no longer present (the strange sound just stops), the initial emotional reaction (fear) drops to zero and the opponent emotion (relief) becomes the experienced emotional reaction. The now-experienced relief has been there all along, but because the sound was there also, the fear overrode it. Now, no strange sound = no fear = a sense of relief—the opponent process.

One good, but unusual, example of this process involves skydiving. On a skydiver's first attempt, fear predominates, followed by a sense of relief only after being earthbound for some time. On subsequent jumps, the initial fear is not as great when leaping from the plane—but the sense of relief (or accomplishment, or joy) is not as great either (Epstein, 1967; Solomon & Corbit, 1974).

I'm sure that you won't be surprised to learn that none of the approaches we've reviewed here has proven to be completely satisfactory. Psychologists continue to propose models or theories to account for the nature of an emotional reaction (*e.g.,* Berkowitz, 1990; Buck, 1985; Frijda, 1988; Greenberg & Safron, 1989; Lazarus, 1991a; 1991b; Ortony, Clore & Collins, 1988; Ortony & Turner, 1990; Weiner, 1985).

Richard Lazarus (1991a; 1991b) is in the process of proposing a new theory about the nature of emotion, in which he stresses the motivational role of emotionality. He further claims that emotion is a result of specific relationships between people and their environments. Some relationships are perceived as (potentially) harmful to one's well-being and yield negative emotions, such as anger, anxiety, fear, shame, or guilt. On the other hand, some such relations are (potentially) beneficial and give rise to positive emotions, such as joy, pride, gratitude, and love.

Before You Go On
▼▼▼▼▼▼▼▼

What are the major issues involved in theories of emotion?

▶ *Physiological Aspects of Emotion*

Let's return now to our opening story about meeting a bear while walking in the woods. One question we raised was, "What will you do now?" To say that your reaction would be an emotional one seems an understatement. You will experience affect (fear if not panic). You will have a cognitive reaction (realizing that you've just encountered a bear). You will engage in some overt behavior (racing back to the campfire). In addition, a significant part of your reaction in this situation (or one like it) will be internal, physiological, and "gut-level." Reacting to a bear is not something that most people would do in a purely cognitive, intellectual sort of way. When we are emotional, we respond with our insides; our viscera respond.

Biological reactions to emotional situations take place at different levels. Of primary interest is the autonomic nervous system. As you will recall, the *autonomic nervous system, or ANS,* is made up of two parts that serve many of the same organs, but that have quite the opposite effect on those organs. The *parasympathetic division* is actively involved in maintaining a relaxed, calm, and unemotional state. As you strolled down the path into the woods, the parasympathetic division of your ANS actively directed your digestive processes to do the best they could with the meal you'd just eaten. Blood was diverted from the extremities to the stomach and intestines. Saliva flowed freely. With your stomach full, and with blood diverted to it, you tended to feel somewhat sleepy as your brain responded to the lower levels of blood supply. Your breathing was slow, deep, and steady, as was your heart rate. Again, all of these activities were under the control of the parasympathetic division of your autonomic nervous system.

Suddenly, there's that bear! Now the *sympathetic division* of your ANS takes over. Automatically, many physiological changes take place—changes that are usually quite adaptive. (1) The pupils of your eyes dilate, letting in as much of what light is available—you need to see what's going on. (2) Your heart rate and blood pressure are elevated—energy needs to be mobilized as fast as possible. (3) Blood is diverted away from the digestive tract to the limbs and brain, and digestion stops; you've got a bear to deal with, so dinner can wait until later. Let's get the blood out there to the arms and legs where it can do some good (with what is called the "fight or flight" response). (4) Respiration increases, becoming deeper and more rapid—you'll need all the oxygen you can get. (5) Moisture is brought to the surface of the skin in the form of perspiration—as it evaporates, the body is cooled, thus conserving energy. (6) Blood sugar levels increase, making more energy available. (7) You may lose control of your bladder and bowels—messy, perhaps, but there are more important things to worry about now. (8) Blood will clot more readily than usual—for obvious, but hopefully unnecessary reasons.

The sympathetic system makes some of these changes rather directly (*e.g.*, stopping salivation and stimulating the cardiac muscle). The others are made indirectly through the release of hormones into the bloodstream.

Because part of the physiological component of emotion *is* hormonal, under the control of the endocrine system, it *does* take a few seconds for the hormones to have their effect. As a result, we may sense a delayed reaction in an emotional response. If you were, in fact, confronted by a bear in the woods, you probably would not have the presence of mind to notice, but the physiological reactions of sweaty palms, gasping breaths, and "butterflies in your stomach" take a few seconds to develop.

When we become emotional, our sympathetic nervous system does not spring into action on its own. Autonomic nervous system activity is closely related to, and coordinated by, central nervous system activity.

The two brain structures most intimately involved in emotionality are the *limbic system* and the *hypothalamus*, that small structure in the middle of the brain that is so involved with physiological drives. The limbic system is a "lower" center in the brain made up of several small structures (the amygdala may be the most important for emotionality). These centers are "lower" in the sense of being below the cerebral cortex and in the sense of being present (and important) in the brains of "lower" animals, such as rats and cats.

The limbic system (Chapter 2, p. 64) is most involved in emotional responses that call for either defensive or attacking responses—emotions stimulated by threat. Electrical stimulation or destruction of portions of the limbic system reliably produces predictable changes in emotional reactions.

The hypothalamus has a role to play in emotionality, being involved in many motivational states. Strong emotional reactions can be produced by hypothalamic stimulation—including reactions that lead to attacking and killing any nearby prey (Flynn, et al., 1970). Just how the limbic system and hypothalamus are coordinated in the normal experience and expression of emotion is not yet fully understood.

The role of the cerebral cortex in emotionality is also poorly understood. Its role seems to be largely inhibitory. That is, the limbic system and hypothalamus seem to act as (primary) sources for extreme and rather poorly directed emotional reactions. The cortex interprets impulses from these lower centers along with other information available to it and then modifies and directs the emotional reaction accordingly.

The clearest involvement of the cerebral cortex in emotionality is in the *cognitive* aspect of an emotional response. It is the cerebral cortex that is involved in the interpretation and memory of emotional events. When you get back to the campfire, having just been frightened by a bear, you will use your cortex to tell all the emotional details of your story. There is evidence that emotional reactions tend to be processed more in the right hemisphere of the human brain than in the left (Sperry, 1982; Tucker, 1981).

To review, along with the autonomic nervous system, two lower brain centers, the limbic system and the hypothalamus, appear to be centers of emotional reaction. These centers are coordinated and often inhibited by higher centers in the cerebral cortex, which, among other things, provides the cognitive interpretation of emotional responses.

Another aspect of emotional reactions that has long intrigued psychologists is how emotional states are expressed or communicated to others. Charles Darwin first popularized the idea that facial expressions provide a meaningful indicator of emotional state. Now, more than 100 years later, psychologists are discovering new evidence that Darwin was correct.

Figure 9.6

▲ *Animals have many complex and instinctual patterns of behavior that communicate emotion. To display aggression and threat, mandrills bare their teeth and grimace, while Australian frilled lizards unfurl flaps of skin on their necks in order to appear larger than they really are.*

Before You Go On

Summarize the activities of the sympathetic division of the autonomic nervous sytem during emotional states.

What brain centers are involved in emotionality?

▶ Outward Expressions of Emotion

It is extremely useful for one organism to be able to let another know how it is feeling. As one wild animal approaches another, the second had better have a good idea about the emotional state of the first. Is it angry? Does it come in peace? Is it just curious, or is it looking for dinner? Is it sad, looking for comfort, or is it sexually aroused, looking for a mating partner? Being unable to make such determinations—quickly—can be disastrous.

Charles Darwin (1872) was among the first to recognize how important it is to display one's emotions accurately to others. Nonhuman animals have many ritualistic, instinctive patterns of behavior to communicate interest in courtship, aggressiveness, submission, and other emotional states (see Figure 9.6).

Humans also can express their emotional state in a variety of ways, including verbal report. If I am happy, sad, angry, or jealous, I can try to *tell* you how I feel. In fact, the human ability to communicate with language often puts us at a great advantage. Even without verbal language, there is a school of thought that suggests that the human animal, like the nonhuman, uses a *body language* to communicate emotional condition (*e.g.,* Birdwhistell, 1952; Fast, 1970). Someone sitting quietly, slumped slightly forward with head down, may be viewed as feeling sad, even from a distance. We similarly may interpret postural cues and gestures as being associated with fear, anger, happiness, and so on. But such expressions often result from learning and may be modified by cultural influences.

Darwin recognized facial expression as a common cue to emotion in animals, especially mammals. Might facial expression provide a key? Might there be facial expressions of emotional states that are universal among the human species, as there appear to be among nonhumans (Andrews, 1963)? A growing body of evidence suggests that facial expressions of emotional state may be an innate response, only slightly sensitive to cultural influence (Adelmann & Zajonc, 1989; Buck, 1980; Gellhorn, 1964; Tomkins, 1962).

Paul Ekman has conducted several studies to see if there is a reliable relationship between emotional state and facial expression that can be found across cultures (Ekman, et al., 1987). In one study, Ekman and his associates (1973) showed college students six pictures of people's faces. In each picture, a different emotion was being displayed: happiness, disgust, surprise, anger, sadness, and fear. When students from the United States, Argentina, Japan,

Brazil, and Chile were asked to name the emotion being felt by the people in the photos, their agreement was remarkable (see Figure 9.7).

A problem with this study is that all the subjects did have many shared experiences, even though they were from different cultures. As college students they may have seen the same movies, watched the same TV shows, and so on. So even though Ekman's subjects came from different countries, their agreement as raters could be explained in terms of the similarities of their experiences, rather than some innate tendency to express emotions through facial expression.

A counter to this criticism is found in another project by Ekman (1972). Natives of a remote New Guinea tribe were asked to make faces showing different emotional reactions (*e.g.*, "A friend has come and you are happy"). No one in our culture (or any other) would have much difficulty deciding what emotion the subjects (who were videotaped) were trying to display (see Figure 9.8).

A follow-up study (Ekman, et al., 1983) has shown that simply moving one's facial muscles into the positions that are associated with emotional expression actually can cause distinctive physiological changes associated with an emotional state (see also Adelman & Zajonc, 1989; Laird, 1984; Matsumoto, 1987). As bizarre as that sounds, the idea is that if you raise your eyebrows, open your eyes widely, and raise the corners of your mouth, you will produce an internal physiological change very much like that which occurs when you are happy, and you will smile as a result!

Before You Go On

▼▼▼▼▼▼▼▼▼▼

What is the relationship, if any, between facial expression and emotion?

Figure 9.7

PHOTOS WITH THESE TYPES OF FACIAL EXPRESSIONS WERE SHOWN TO SUBJECTS FROM THE UNITED STATES, BRAZIL, CHILE, ARGENTINA, AND JAPAN.

The subjects were asked to identify the emotion being displayed. The percentage of subjects who identified the photographs with the emotions listed is indicated.

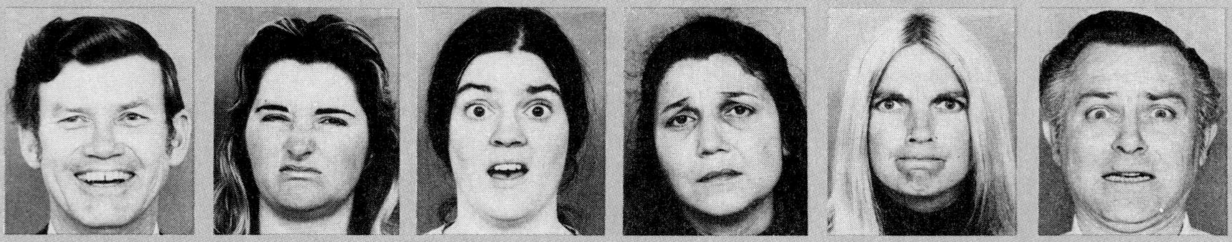

	Happiness	Disgust	Surprise	Sadness	Anger	Fear
United States (N = 99)	97%	92%	95%	84%	67%	85%
Brazil (N = 40)	95%	97%	87%	59%	90%	67%
Chile (N = 119)	95%	92%	93%	88%	94%	68%
Argentina (N = 168)	98%	92%	95%	78%	90%	54%
Japan (N = 29)	100%	90%	100%	62%	90%	66%

Figure 9.8

 Paul Ekman went to New Guinea to study the relationship between facial expressions and emotional state. The man at the far left was told that he was happy because a friend was coming. The man in the second picture was told his child had died. The man in the third picture was told that he was angry and about to fight. And the man in the last photograph was told he had just seen a dead pig that had been lying in one place for a long time. People from any culture would have no trouble identifying their facial expressions as indicating happiness, grief, anger, and disgust, respectively.

Thinking Critically About Motivation and Emotion

1. This chapter used a somewhat dramatic example of meeting a bear in the woods to discuss approaches to motivation and to discuss physiological reactions to emotion-producing stimuli. Can you recast the same discussions with more likely examples, for instance a big exam coming up tomorrow, or being fired from a job for no apparent reason?

2. Have you determined in your own mind the difference (and it *is* subtle) between an instinctive behavior and a reflexive behavior?

3. What am I really trying to do when I try to "motivate" students in my classes to do as well as they can?

4. What motivated you to take this class in psychology? How do you feel about it now?

5. Can you examine your own life in terms of how it fits Maslow's hierarchy of needs?

6. How is it that music and art can influence our emotions? How much of that influence is innate; how much is learned?

7. Examine your own experience. Why do you eat what you eat when you eat?

8. To what extent do you believe that homosexuality or heterosexuality are a matter of choice freely made or orientations rooted in biology?

9. As it happens, knowledge of sexually transmitted diseases is NOT significantly changing sexual behaviors among young, sexually active persons. Why not?

10. Do you think that the sorts of things that motivate women are the same as or different from the sorts of things that motivate men? How?

11. If you were asked to list the basic, primary human emotions, which would we find on your list?

Summary

▼▼▼▼▼▼▼▼▼▼▼▼▼▼▼▼▼▼▼▼▼▼▼▼▼▼▼▼▼▼▼

How have the concepts of instinct, drive, and incentive been used to explain motivated behaviors? In trying to explain why organisms do what they do, three concepts have proven useful. *Instincts* are complex patterns of behavior that occur in the presence of certain stimuli. Instinct approaches take the position that some complex behavior patterns are unlearned or innate. The concept of instinct has not proven to be very satisfactory to account for most human behaviors. *Needs* are shortages of some biological necessity. Deprivation may lead to a need, which gives rise to a drive, which arouses and directs behavior. The relationship between deprivation, need, drive, and behavior is often not very straightforward; many drives are more learned than biological. Maslow has proposed that human needs can be placed in a hierarchy, beginning with basic survival needs and ending with a need to self-actualize. Focusing on *incentives* explains behaviors in terms of goals and outcomes rather than on internal forces of any kind. We say that incentives "pull" behaviors, while drives "push" behaviors. In this sense, we become motivated to reach a desired end state. These three approaches are not mutually exclusive, and each may be used to explain some types of motivated behavior. *Pages 302–306*

How can the concept of balance or equilibrium be used to help us understand motivated behaviors? Organisms are motivated to reach and maintain a state of balance—a set point level of activity. In *homeostasis* we have a general drive to maintain a state of equilibrium among internal physiological processes such as blood pressure, metabolism, and heart rate. Other psychologists argue for a general drive to maintain a balanced state of *arousal*, with different optimal levels of arousal being best suited for different tasks or situations. *Pages 306–309*

In what way is cognitive dissonance theory based on equilibrium? Festinger claims that we are motivated to maintain balance among cognitive states, thereby reducing *cognitive dissonance*. *Page 308*

Given the concept of homeostasis, how might temperature regulation be thought of as a physiologically-based drive? Temperature regulation can be viewed as a physiological drive because we clearly have a need (thus are driven) to maintain our body temperatures within homeostatic levels. Doing so may involve voluntary as well as involuntary responding. *Pages 309–310*

List some of the internal and external factors that influence drinking behavior. We are motivated to drink for a number of reasons: to relieve dryness in our mouths and throats; to maintain a homeostatic level

(monitored by the hypothalamus) of fluid within our bodies; and also in response to external cues (stimulus values), such as taste, aroma, or appearance. What we drink is often influenced by our learning experiences. *Page 311*

List the internal and external factors that influence eating. Internal factors include cues mediated by the hypothalamus, which may be responding to stored fat levels, blood sugar levels, or some other indication that our normal, homeostatic balance has been disrupted. Associated with this view is the position that body weight is maintained at a given set point by both intake and exercise levels. There is evidence that body size may be determined largely by genetic factors. External factors may include the stimulus properties of foods, as well as habit patterns and social pressure. *Pages 312–313*

In what ways is the sex drive a unique physiologically-based drive? There are four ways in which the sex drive is an atypical physiological drive. (1) Individual survival does not require its satisfaction. (2) The drive involves seeking or creating tension, not relieving tension. (3) It is not fully present at birth, but matures later. (4) The extent to which it is affected by learned or external influences varies from species to species. *Pages 314–317*

What is homosexuality? Homosexuals are individuals who are attracted to and sexually aroused by members of their own sex. There is thought to be a continuum, or gradual dimension, that extends from exclusive homosexuality on the one extreme to exclusive heterosexuality on the other. Kinsey found that more than half the males in his sample fell somewhere between these two endpoints. *Pages 317–318*

What causes homosexuality? We do not know what causes homosexuality, but strongly suspect that three factors interact in complex ways: genetic predispositions, prenatal hormonal influences, and perhaps early childhood experiences. *Pages 317–318*

Name and briefly describe five sexually transmitted diseases. Sexually transmitted diseases (STDs) are very common. Among the most troublesome are: (1) *Chlamydia,* a bacterial infection of the genital area that results in painful urination and fluid discharge, is the most common of the STDs in North America. Left untreated in women, chlamydia may lead to pelvic inflammatory disease (PID) and infertility. (2) *Gonorrhea,* a bacterial infection of the moist tissues around the genitals, is transmitted only by sexual activity. Its symptoms increase in severity when the disease is left untreated.

Penicillin is an effective treatment. (3) *Syphilis,* a bacterial infection, may progress through four stages as symptoms increase in severity. Left untreated, it may result in death. Penicillin, again, is an effective treatment. (4) *Genital herpes,* a viral infection that affects the skin in the genital area, is a very common STD and has no cure. A person with herpes may go for prolonged periods without any symptoms. (5) *Acquired immune deficiency syndrome (AIDS)* is perhaps the most frightening of all the STDs. It is a viral (HIV) infection that can be transmitted only through the exchange of bodily fluids, as in sexual activity. Once infected, a person may remain symptom-free (but capable of infecting others) in a "carrier state" until the full-blown symptoms of AIDS develop. Virtually all persons with AIDS will die within four years. There is, at the moment, no effective vaccine or treatment. *Pages 318–320*

What is achievement motivation, and how is it usually measured? Achievement motivation (nAch) is defined as one's need to attempt and succeed at tasks in such a way as to meet or exceed some standard of excellence. Achievement needs are usually assessed through the interpretation of stories generated in response to the Thematic Apperception Test, or TAT, in which one looks for themes of striving and achievement. *Pages 321–322*

Define the needs for power and affiliation. The need for power is defined as the need to be in charge, to be in control of the situation and of others, often at the expense of others. Affiliation needs involve being motivated to be with others, to form friendships and interpersonal relationships. *Pages 322–323*

What are the four components that define an emotional experience? There are four possible components of an emotional reaction: the experience of a subjective feeling, or *affective* component; a *cognitive* appraisal or interpretation; an internal, visceral *physiological* reaction; and an overt *behavioral* response. *Page 324*

What are the major issues involved in theories of emotion? Theories of emotion are attempts to specify in a systematic way the components of an emotional experience and show how those components are related. *Pages 325–327*

Summarize the activities of the sympathetic division of the autonomic nervous system during emotional states. Among the many changes that take place when we become emotional are those produced by the sympathetic division of the ANS. Occurring to varying degrees dependent on the situation are such reactions as: dilation of the pupils, increased heart rate and blood pressure, cessation of the digestive process, deeper and more rapid breathing, increased perspiration, and elevation of blood sugar levels. *Pages 327–329*

What brain centers are involved in emotionality? The cerebral cortex is involved in the cognitive interpretation of emotional events and also acts as an inhibitory mechanism, exerting some degree of control over the activity of lower brain centers for emotionality (largely the hypothalamus and the limbic system). Basically, the brain coordinates physiological aspects of emotionality. *Pages 327–329*

What is the relationship, if any, between facial expression and emotion? Facial expressions indicate the internal, emotional state of an individual. What leads us to believe that facial expression of emotion is unlearned is that there is such universal reliability in the interpretation of facial expressions, even across widely different cultures. *Pages 329–330*

9.1 Which of these is LEAST involved in motivational states? a) the arousal of behavior b) the memory of behavior c) the directing of behavior d) the maintenance of behavior. *Page 302*

9.2 The major difference between what your text calls "drives" and what your text calls "motives" is whether or not the motivator: a) involves the ANS or the CNS. b) is physiologically or psychologically based. c) is intrinsic or extrinsic. d) is essentially positive or essentially negative. *Page 302*

9.3 What is the major problem with using the concept of instinct to explain human behaviors? a) There are just too many human instincts to keep track of. b) There are too few human behaviors that have a biological basis. c) Referring to instincts may describe or name behaviors, but doesn't explain them. d) Too many human instincts have opposites, such as needs to socialize and needs to be alone. *Page 303*

9.4 Which of these does NOT go with the others? a) acquired drives b) learned drives c) primary drives d) conditioned drives. *Page 304*

9.5 In Hull's theory (as an example), what gives rise to a drive? a) a need b) a motive c) a behavior d) a goal or incentive. *Page 303*

9.6 Of these needs from Maslow's hierarchy, which is likely to be satisfied LAST, after the others? a) physiological needs b) esteem needs c) needs for love and belongingness d) safety needs. *Page 305*

9.7 Approaches to motivation that focus on stimuli or events outside the organism are approaches that focus on a) incentives. b) drives. c) arousal. d) needs. *Page 305*

9.8 Which term or concept is most like Cannon's concept of homeostasis? a) drive b) sensation-seeking c) fulfillment d) balance. *Page 306*

9.9 Which approach to motivation would be most appreciated by those psychologists who value the concepts of operant conditioning? Approaches based on: a) instincts b) drives c) incentives d) balance or equilibrium. *Page 306*

9.10 We are motivated to change the way we think about things when we experience: a) homeostasis. b) a mental set point. c) cognitive dissonance. d) arousal. *Page 308*

9.11 True or False? Arousal theory tells us that one's performance on a task will continue to improve so long as one's level of arousal continues to increase. *Page 307*

9.12 More than anything else, what "informs us" that our body temperatures have become too high or too low? a) our cerebral cortex b) our skin c) our hypothalamus d) our autonomic nervous system. *Page 310*

9.13 Most of the water in our bodies is contained a) in our bloodstream. b) within the cells of our body. c) in sweat glands. d) in spaces between the cells of our body. *Page 311*

9.14 Which of these is LEAST directly involved in motivating us to eat or not eat? a) the physical appearance of food b) our hypothalamus c) how empty our stomachs are d) reactions of our liver. *Pages 312–313*

9.15 True or False? Although our hypothalamus may inform us that we are thirsty or hungry, learning and experience inform us about what to drink or eat. *Page 312*

9.16 How much you weigh is determined by: a) how much you eat b) genetic factors c) early childhood experiences d) all of these. *Page 313*

9.17 In what way is the sex drive in humans most different from the sex drive in rats? a) It does not appear until after puberty. b) Its satisfaction does not determine the survival of the individual. c) It is strongly influenced by learning and experience. d) Its physiological basis is largely hormonal. *Page 316*

9.18 With regard to homosexuality, which observation is most TRUE? a) Sexual preference is a matter of choice freely made. b) Adult male homosexuals have excess female hormones in their systems. c) Homosexuality is a dimension, a matter of degree, not either/or. d) Most homosexuals (male or female) have never tried heterosexual sex. *Page 317*

9.19 At the moment, which of these is taken as the most reasonable hypothesis for the development of homosexuality? a) genetic differences in the X and Y chromosomes b) lack of a father-figure in single-parent homes c) unsatisfying or frustrating sexual encounters in adolescence d) hormonal imbalances that occur during prenatal development. *Page 318*

9.20 Of these, a person is LEAST likely to be diagnosed as having: a) chlamydia. b) gonorrhea. c) syphilis. d) AIDS. *Page 319*

9.21 The essential cause of AIDS is   a) a virus.   b) bad habits.   c) bacterial infection.   d) a genetic deficiency. *Page 319*

9.22 True or False?   Once AIDS develops, death is certain. *Page 320*

9.23 If given a choice, a person with a high need to achieve (nAch) probably would choose a job in which he or she: a) could succeed with little effort.   b) would be in a position to control the fate of others.   c) would be working with as many people as possible.   d) could do well, but only with effort and hard work. *Page 322*

9.24 The James-Lange approach to emotion suggests that the SECOND event in the chain of events we call an emotional reaction is   a) the subjective, felt aspect of emotion, the affect.   b) a noticeable bodily reaction or reactions.   c) a cognitive appraisal of the whole situation.

d) the perception of an emotion-producing stimulus. *Page 325*

9.25 Which of these is central to the approach to emotion proposed by Schachter and Singer?   a) physiological arousal   b) the thalamus   c) common sense   d) a cognitive appraisal. *Page 326*

9.26 Which change is LEAST likely during an emotional reaction?   a) Heart rate decreases.   b) Digestion stops.   c) Blood flow is diverted to the limbs.   d) Pupils dilate. *Page 327–328*

9.27 Which structure of the brain is most involved in emotion?   a) the thalamus   b) the limbic system   c) the brain stem   d) the cerebellum. *Page 328*

9.28 Which expression of emotional state is uniquely human?   a) verbal descriptions   b) facial expressions   c) body language   d) posture and gestures. *Page 329*

Personality: Theories and Assessment

▲▲▲▲▲▲▲

I have been teaching introductory psychology for more than 25 years. During that time, I have been observing the personality characteristics of thousands of students. By now, I feel that I understand the basic personalities of most introductory psychology students quite well. Here, in no particular order, are some of my observations. To test the accuracy of these observations, simply go through the list and indicate the extent to which each of these statements applies to you. If you think that the statement is a true, accurate appraisal, mark it with a 1. If you think that it is true of you only sometimes, give it a 2. If you think that the statement does not apply to you at all, give it a 3.

_____ You have a rather strong need for other people to like you and for them to admire you.

_____ You have a tendency to be critical of yourself.

_____ You feel somewhat uncomfortable when called on in class, even if you know the answer to the instructor's question.

_____ While you have some personality weaknesses, you generally are able to compensate for them.

_____ Disciplined and controlled on the outside, you tend to be worrisome and insecure inside.

_____ You prefer a certain amount of change and variety, and become dissatisfied when hemmed in by restrictions and limitations.

_____ You have found it unwise to be too frank in revealing yourself to others.

_____ At times you are extroverted, easy-going, and sociable, while at other times you are introverted, wary, and reserved.

_____ Some of your aspirations tend to be pretty unrealistic.

_____ You occasionally have difficulty relating what you are reading in your psychology class to your own experiences.

_____ Your sexual adjustments have presented some problems for you.

_____ At times you have serious doubts as to whether you have made the right decision or done the right thing.

Now that you have provided a score (1, or 2, or 3) for each item, add them up so we can see how well I have been able to assess your personality. A low score would mean that I did pretty well—a score of 12 would indicate that I was accurate with each observation. How did I do?

When I do this exercise in class, I find that nearly 90 percent of my students get a score of 18 or less. That's pretty good, isn't it? But, wait a minute. How could I possibly have any real insight about the personality of students in my class, most of whom I hardly know at all. How could I manage to describe _your_ personality, when we have never even met? Something is surely wrong here.

This little "personality test" is a version of a classic demonstration that dates back at least to 1956 and an Instructor's Manual that accompanied an introductory psychology textbook (Munn, 1956). Ten of these twelve items come from the "General Personality Test" (or "GPT") described in an article by Ulrich, Stachnick, and Stainton in 1963. This exercise serves as a reminder that the nature of personality and personality assessment need to be approached with care. Please note that I really do not claim to have any special wisdom or insight about the personalities of introductory psychology students—or anyone else, for that matter. The truth is that the statements listed above are so general that they are virtually meaningless, while at the same time, they can apply to nearly everyone. Did you also notice that they are very similar to the sorts of statements one commonly finds in daily horoscopes?

Most of us think that we understand ourselves fairly well. We believe that we have a good sense of who we are, how we tend to think and feel, and what we are likely to do in most situations. To a somewhat lesser extent, we also feel that we understand a few other people we know well, such as very close friends and family members. We've come to believe that knowing someone's personality is required if we are to truly understand that person. We also have come to appreciate that knowing someone's personality is not easily done—that what constitutes someone's personality are internal and private experiences, often difficult to determine from the outside.

Psychology has valued the concept of personality throughout its history. Over the years, many theories have emerged that have sought to describe the nature of personality. In this chapter, we'll examine some of them. We care about these theories because each in its own way has contributed to our contemporary understanding of personality. Before we consider individual theories, let's see what we mean by *theory* and what we mean by *personality* in this context.

theory an organized collection of ultimately testable ideas used to explain a particular subject matter

A **theory** is a series of assumptions; assumptions about people and their personalities. The ideas or assumptions that constitute a theory must be reasonably and logically related to each other. Further, the assumptions of a theory should lead to specific, testable hypotheses. So, a theory is an organized collection of ultimately testable ideas used to explain a particular subject matter.

Now then, what is personality? Few terms in psychology have been as difficult to define; in many ways, each of the approaches we will study in this chapter generates its own definition. What we are looking at with *personality* are the *a*ffects, *b*ehaviors, and *c*ognitions of people that can characterize them in a number of situations over time. (Here, again, is our ABC from Chapter 1.) Personality also includes those dimensions we can use to judge people to be different from one another. So we are looking for ways to describe how individuals remain the same over time and circumstances, and which allow us to describe differences that we know exist among people (Baumeister, 1987). Psychologist David Buss put it this way, "The field of personality psychology is centrally concerned with the traits that characterize our species as well as the major ways in which individuals characteristically differ" (1984, p. 1143).

▶ *The Psychoanalytic Approach*

psychoanalytic approach the approach to personality associated with Freud and his followers that relies on instincts and the unconscious as explanatory concepts

We begin our discussion of personality by considering the **psychoanalytic approach.** This approach is associated with Sigmund Freud and his students. We begin with Freud because he was one of the first to present a truly unified theory of personality.

Freud's theory of personality has been one of the most influential and, at the same time, most controversial in all of science. Although there are many facets to Freud's theory (and those of his students), two basic points characterize the psychoanalytic approach: (1) reliance on innate, inborn drives as explanatory concepts for human behavior, and (2) acceptance of the power and influence of unconscious forces to mold and shape our behavior.

▶ *Freud's Approach*

Freud's ideas about the nature of personality arose largely from observations of his patients, his reading of the works of many philosophers, and intense self-examination. The context of his private practice provided Freud with experiences from which he proposed a theory of personality and developed a technique of therapy, both of which are referred to as *psychoanalysis*. Freud's approach to psychotherapy is discussed in Chapter 13. For now, let's review some of Freud's basic ideas about the structure and dynamics of human personality.

Levels of Consciousness. Freud thought that only a small portion of one's mental life was readily available to a person's awareness at any one time. Ideas, memories, feelings, and motives of which we are actively aware at the moment are said to be *conscious*.

Aspects of mind that are not conscious, but that easily can be brought to awareness, are stored or housed at a *preconscious* level. For example, right now you may not be thinking about what you had for dinner last night or what you might have for dinner tonight. But with little effort, the matter of tonight's or last night's dinner can be brought into conscious awareness.

Cognitions, feelings, and motives that are not available at the conscious or preconscious level are said to be in the *unconscious*. At this level we keep many ideas, memories, and/or desires of which we are not aware and cannot easily become aware. This is a strange notion—that there are thoughts, desires, and feelings stored away in our minds of which we are completely unaware. Nonetheless, the unconscious mind does influence us. Unconscious content passing through the preconscious may show itself in slips of the tongue, humor and, of course, dreams. There was no doubt in Freud's mind, at least, that unconscious forces could be used to explain behavior that otherwise seemed irrational and beyond description.

As we shall see, a good deal of Freudian psychoanalysis as a technique of psychotherapy is aimed at helping a patient learn about the contents of the unconscious level of the mind. A husband, for instance, who constantly forgets his wedding anniversary and occasionally can't remember his wife's name when he tries to introduce her may be experiencing some unconscious conflict or doubts about being married in the first place. (There *are*, of course, other possibilities.)

Before You Go On
▼▼▼▼▼▼▼▼▼

What are the three levels of consciousness proposed by Freud?

---

life instincts (eros) inborn impulses, proposed by Freud, that compel one toward survival; these include hunger, thirst, and sex

death instincts (thanatos) inborn impulses, proposed by Freud, that compel one toward destruction; they include aggression

Basic Instincts. According to Freudian theory, behaviors, thoughts, and feelings are governed largely by innate biological drives, or *instincts*. These are inborn impulses or forces that rule our personalities. There may be many separate drives or instincts, but they can be grouped into two categories.

On the one hand are **life instincts** (eros), or impulses for survival; in particular, those that motivate sex, hunger, and thirst. Each has its own energy that compels us into action (drives us). Freud called the energy through which the sexual instincts operate *libido*. Opposed to the life instincts are **death instincts** (thanatos). These are largely impulses of destruction. Directed inward, they lead to feelings of depression or suicide; directed outward, they result in aggression toward other people or their property. In large measure, life (according to Freud) is an attempt to resolve conflicts between these two natural but diametrically opposed instincts.

The Structure of Personality. Freud proposed that the human personality is composed of three separate, though interacting, structures or subsystems: the id, ego, and superego. Each subsystem has its own job to do and its own principles.

id the instinctive aspect of personality that seeks immediate gratification of impulses; it operates on the pleasure principle

The **id** is the totally inborn or inherited portion of personality. The id resides in the unconscious level of the mind, and it is through the id that one's basic instincts develop. The driving force of the id is libido, or sexual energy, although it may be more fair to Freud to say "sensual" rather than "sexual."

pleasure principle the impulse of the id to seek immediate gratification to reduce tensions

The id seeks satisfaction for instinctual impulses, regardless of the consequences. It operates on what Freud labeled the **pleasure principle**, indicating that the major function of the id is to find satisfaction for basic pleasurable impulses. Although the other divisions of personality develop later, our id remains with us as the basic energy source in our lives.

ego the aspect of personality that encompasses the sense of "self"; in contact with the real world; operates on the reality principle

The **ego** is that aspect of the personality that develops through one's experience with reality. In many ways, it is our self, the rational, reasoning part of our personality. The ego operates on the **reality principle.** One of the ego's main jobs is to try to find satisfaction for the id, but in ways that are reasonable and rational. The ego may have to delay gratification of some libidinal impulse or may need to find an acceptable outlet for some need.

reality principle the force that governs the ego, arbitrating between the demands of the id, the superego, and the real world

superego the aspect of personality that refers to ethical or moral considerations; operates on the idealistic principle

The last of the structures to develop is the **superego**, which we can liken to one's sense of morality or conscience. It reflects our internalization of society's rules. The superego operates on what might be called an **idealistic principle.** One problem we have with our superegos is that they—like the id—have no contact with reality, and therefore place unrealistic demands on the individual. The superego demands that we do what it deems to be right and proper, no matter what the circumstances. Failure to do so may lead to guilt and shame. Again, it falls to the ego to try to maintain a realistic balance between the conscience of the superego and the libido of the id.

idealistic principle the force that governs the superego; opposed to the id, it seeks adherence to standards of ethics and morality

Now this isn't as complicated as it may sound. Let's suppose a bank teller discovers an extra $20 in her cash drawer at the end of the day. She certainly could use an extra $20. "Go ahead. Nobody will miss it. The bank can afford a few dollars here and there. Think of the fun you can have with an extra $20," is the basic message from her id. "You shouldn't even think about taking that money. Shame on you! It's not yours. It belongs to someone else and should be returned," the superego protests. "The odds are that you'll get caught if you take this money. If you *are* caught, you may lose your job, then you'll have to find another one," reasons her ego. The interaction of the three components of one's personality is not always this straightforward, but perhaps this example illustrates the general idea.

Before You Go On

▼▼▼▼▼▼▼▼▼

According to Freud, what are the three structures of personality, and by what principle does each operate?

Defense Mechanisms. When the ego cannot find acceptable ways to satisfy the drives of the id, or when it cannot deal with the demands of the superego, conflict and anxiety result. Then, ways must be found to combat the resulting anxiety. It was for this purpose that Freud proposed the existence of **defense mechanisms**—*unconsciously* applied techniques that protect

defense mechanisms unconsciously applied techniques that protect the self (ego) from feelings of anxiety

repression "motivated forgetting" in which stressful events are forced from awareness into the unconscious and can no longer be remembered directly

denial refusing to acknowledge the presence of stressors

rationalization generating excuses to explain one's behaviors rather than facing the real (anxiety-producing) reasons for those behaviors

fantasy an escape from stress through imagination and/or daydreaming

projection seeing in others those very characteristics and motives that cause stress in one's self

regression a return to earlier, childish patterns of previously reinforcing behaviors as an escape from stress

the self (ego) against strong feelings of anxiety. What follows is a list of some of the more common ego defense mechanisms, with an example of each.

Repression is the most basic of all the defense mechanisms. We first encountered repression in the memory chapter (p. 253). It is sometimes referred to as *motivated forgetting*, which gives you a good idea of what is involved. Repression is a matter of (conveniently) forgetting about some anxiety-producing event or desire. Paul had a teacher he did not get along with at all. After spending the entire semester trying his best to do whatever was asked, Paul failed the course. The following summer, while out walking with his girlfriend, Paul encountered this teacher. When he tried to introduce him to his girlfriend, Paul could not remember the teacher's name. He had repressed it. Surely, forgetting about everything and everyone that ever caused us anxiety is not a very adaptive response. But pushing some anxiety-producing memories into the depths of the unconscious mind can protect us from dwelling on unpleasantness.

Denial is a mechanism of defense in which a person simply refuses to acknowledge the realities of an anxiety-producing situation. When a physician first tells a patient that he or she has a terminal illness, a common reaction is denial; the patient refuses to believe or accept that the diagnosis is accurate.

Rationalization amounts to making up excuses for one's behaviors rather than facing the (anxiety-producing) real reasons for them. The real reason Kevin failed his psychology midterm is that he didn't study for it and had missed several classes. Kevin hates to admit, even to himself, that he could have been so stupid as to flunk this big exam because of his own actions or inactions. He rationalizes: "It really wasn't my fault. I had a terrible instructor. The test was grossly unfair. We used a lousy textbook. And I've been fighting this flu all semester."

Fantasy provides an escape from anxiety through imagination or daydreaming. It is one of the more common defense mechanisms among college students. Particularly after a week of exams and term paper deadlines, isn't it pleasant to sit back in a comfortable chair and fantasize about graduating from college with honors? Remember that to engage in fantasy from time to time is normal and an acceptable reaction to anxiety and stress. On the other hand, there are potential dangers here. One needs to be able to keep separate activities that are real from those that occur in fantasies. And surely you recognize that fantasy in itself will not solve the problems or resolve the conflicts that caused the anxiety in the first place. Daydreaming about academic success may help one feel better for a while, but it is not likely to make anyone a better student.

Projection is a matter of seeing in others those very motives or traits that would make one anxious if seen in oneself. Under enormous pressure to do well on an exam, Mark decides to cheat. But at exam time, his conscience (superego) won't let him. Because of projection, Mark may think that he sees cheating going on all around him. Projection is a mechanism that often is used in conjunction with aggression or hostility. When people feel uncomfortable with their own levels of hostility, they often project their aggressiveness onto others, coming to believe that others are "out to do me harm," and "I'm only protecting myself."

To employ the defense of **regression** is to return to earlier, more primitive, even childish levels of behavior that were once productive. Oddly enough, we often find regression occurring in children. Imagine a 4-year-old who until very recently was an only child. Now Mommy has returned from the hospital with a new baby sister. The 4-year-old is no longer the "center of the universe," as his new sister gets parental attention. He reverts to earlier behaviors and starts wetting the bed, screaming for a bottle of his own, and crawling on all fours. He's regressing.

displacement directing one's motives at some substitute person or object rather than expressing it directly

The defense mechanism of **displacement** usually is discussed in the context of aggression. It is a matter of directing one's motives or behaviors at some substitute person or object rather than expressing it directly—which would be anxiety-producing. Dorothy expects to get promoted at work, but someone else gets the new job she wanted. She's upset and angry at her boss, but feels (perhaps correctly) that blowing her top at her boss will do more harm than good, so she displaces her hostility toward her husband, children and/or the family cat.

This list of defense mechanisms is not an exhaustive one. These are among the most common, and should give you an idea of what Freud had in mind. There are a couple of points about defense mechanisms that deserve special mention. (1) Using defense mechanisms is a normal reaction. You shouldn't be alarmed if you find that some of these mechanisms sound like reactions you have used. In moderation, they help us cope with the anxieties and conflicts of everyday life. (2) Although they are normal, and even common, they can become maladaptive. So long as these mechanisms are successful in alleviating the unpleasant feelings of anxiety, we may no longer feel a need to search for the true sources of our anxiety and thus will be less likely to resolve the conflicts that produced the anxiety in the first place. We'll have more to say about this point in our next chapter when we discuss effective and ineffective strategies for dealing with stress.

Before You Go On
▼▼▼▼▼▼▼▼▼

List and define seven defense mechanisms.

The Development of Personality. Freud obviously put a lot of stock in the biological bases of personality, relying as he did on concepts such as drive and instinct. This same orientation flavored his view of personality development. According to Freud, personality develops naturally, in a series of overlapping stages. The events that occur in early stages have the potential to produce profound effects on later development.

One of Freud's most controversial assumptions about human behavior was that even infants and young children were under the influence of the sexual strivings of the id and its libidinal energy. The outlet for the sexual impulses (again, *sensual* may be a better term in today's usage) of young children is not the reproductive sex act. But Freud thought that much of the pleasure derived by children is essentially sexual in nature; hence we refer to Freud's stages of development as *psychosexual.* Freud claimed that there are five such stages:

1. *Oral stage* (birth to 1 year). Pleasure and satisfaction come from oral activities: feeding, sucking, and making noises. The mouth continues to be a source of pleasure for many people long into adulthood as demonstrated by overeating, fingernail biting, smoking, or talkativeness.

2. *Anal stage* (age 1 to 3 years). Sometime in their second year, children develop the ability to control bowel and bladder habits. At this time, the anus become the focus of pleasure. Satisfaction is gained through bowel control. Aggressiveness (the id again) can be displayed (particularly against parents) by either having bowel movements at inappropriate times or by refusing "to go" when placed on the potty chair. Here we clearly can see the thoughtful, reasoning ego emerging and exercising some control. After all,

the parents can't *make* their child do what they want it to do. The child is in control, and that control can lead to great satisfaction.

3. *Phallic stage* (age 3 to 5 years). Here there is an awareness of one's sexuality. The genitals replace the mouth and anus as the source of pleasure, and masturbation or fondling of the genitals may become a common practice. It is during this stage of development that children tend to form close (sexually-based) attachments to the parent of the opposite sex, and feelings of jealousy and/or fear of the same-sex parent may arise. This pattern of reaction is called the *Oedipus complex* in boys and the *Electra complex* in girls. It is in the phallic stage that the superego begins to develop.

4. *Latency stage* (age 6 years until puberty). At this stage in life, sexual development gets put on hold. Now the ego is developing very rapidly. There is much to be learned about the world and how it operates. Sexual development can wait. Sexuality is suppressed. Friends tend to be of the same sex. You have no doubt heard the protestations of a 9-year-old boy, "Oh yuck; kiss a girl? Never! Yuck!" And you counsel, "Just wait; soon girls won't seem so 'yucky.'"

5. *Genital stage* (from puberty on). With puberty, there is a renewal of the sexual impulse, a reawakening of desire, and an interest in matters sexual, sensual, and erotic.

Before You Go On

Briefly review Freud's five psychosexual stages of development.

▶ The Psychoanalytic Approach after Freud

Sigmund Freud was a persuasive communicator. In person, he was a powerful speaker. In his writings, he was without peer. His ideas were challenging and new, and they attracted many students. Freud founded a Psychoanalytic Society in Vienna. He had many friends and colleagues who shared his ideas, but some of his colleagues did not entirely agree with his theory. Among other things, they were bothered by the strong emphasis on biological drives and libido, and what they perceived as a lack of concern for social influences. Some of these psychoanalysts left Freud and proposed theories of their own; they became known as **neo-Freudians.** Because they had their own ideas, they had to part from Freud; he would not tolerate disagreement with his theory. One had to accept all of psychoanalysis—including psychoanalysis as a treatment for mental disorders—or leave Freud's inner circle.

Remembering that a theory consists of a set of logically interrelated, testable assumptions, it is obvious that we cannot do justice to someone's theory of personality in a short paragraph or two. What we can do, perhaps, is sketch the basic idea behind the theories of a few neo-Freudians.

Alfred Adler (1870–1937). As the psychoanalytic movement was first taking shape, Adler was one of Freud's closest friends. However, Adler left Freud and, in 1911, founded his own version of a psychoanalytic approach to personality. Two things seemed to offend Adler: the negativity of Freud's views (*e.g.*, the death instinct) and the idea of sexual libido as the prime impulse in life.

Adler proposed that we are a product of the social influences on our personality. We are motivated not so much by drives and instincts, but by goals and incentives. The future and the hope for what it holds for us can be

neo-Freudians personality theorists (including Adler, Jung, and Horney) who kept many basic psychoanalytic principles, but differed from a strict Freudian view, adding new concepts of their own

▲ *Alfred Adler*

▲ Carl Jung

▲ Karen Horney

more important than the past. For Adler, our major goal is the achievement of success or superiority. This goal is fashioned in childhood when, because we are weak and vulnerable, we develop an *inferiority complex.* Though we may seem inferior as children, with the help of social influences and our own creativity, we can overcome and succeed.

Carl Jung (1875–1961). Another student and colleague of Freud, Carl Jung, was chosen by Freud to be his successor. But disagreements developed, mostly about the role of sexuality and the nature of the unconscious—two central themes in psychoanalysis. Jung was more mystical in his approach to personality and, like Adler, was certainly more positive about the ability to control one's own destiny. He believed that our major goal in life was to unify all aspects of our personality, conscious and unconscious, introverted (inwardly directed) and extroverted (outwardly directed). Libido was energy for Jung, but not sexual energy; it was energy for personal growth and development.

Jung accepted the idea of an unconscious mind, but expanded upon it, claiming that there are two types of unconscious: the *personal unconscious,* which is very much like Freud's view of the unconscious, and the *collective unconscious,* which contains very basic ideas and notions that go beyond an individual's own personal experiences. These ideas and notions are common to all of humanity and are inherited from all past generations. The contents of our collective unconscious include what Jung called *archetypes*—universal forms and patterns of thought. These are very basic "ideas" that transcend generations, and transcend history. They include themes that repeatedly show up in myths: motherhood, opposites, good, evil, masculinity, femininity, and the circle as a symbol representing travel from a beginning back to where one started, or the complete, whole self.

Karen Horney (1885–1952). Trained as a psychoanalyst in Germany, Horney came to the United States in 1934. She held onto some Freudian concepts, but changed most of them significantly. Horney believed that the idea of levels of consciousness made sense, as did anxiety and repression. But she theorized that the prime impulses that motivate behavior are not biological and inborn or sexual and aggressive. A major concept for Horney was *basic anxiety,* which grows out of childhood when the child feels alone

▲ Being "left out" and ignored can foster feelings of inferiority.

and isolated in a hostile environment. If proper parental nurturance is forthcoming, basic anxiety can be overcome. If parents are overly punishing, inconsistent, or indifferent, children may develop *basic hostility* and feel hostile and aggressive toward their parents. Young children cannot express hostility toward their parents openly, so the hostility gets repressed (into the unconscious) building even more anxiety.

Horney placed great emphasis on early childhood experiences, but from a perspective of social interaction and personal growth. She claimed that there are three distinct ways in which people tend to interact with each other. In some cases, people *move away from* others, seeking self-sufficiency and independence. The idea here is something like "If I am on my own and uninvolved, you won't be able to hurt me." On the other hand, some may *move toward* others, tending to be compliant and dependent. This style of interaction protects against anxiety in the sense of "If I always do what you want me to do, you won't be upset with me." Horney's third interpersonal style involves *moving against* others, where the effort is to be in control, to gain power and dominate: "If I am in control, you'll have to do what I want you to." Now the ideal, of course, is to maintain a balance among these three styles of interpersonal relationships, but Horney argued that many people tend to have one of these three predominate in their dealings with others.

Horney also disagreed with Freud's position regarding the biological necessity of differences between men and women. Freud's theories have been taken to task a number of times for their male chauvinist bias (*e.g.*, Fisher & Greenberg, 1977). Horney was one of the first to do so.

Before You Go On
▼▼▼▼▼▼▼▼

Briefly summarize the contributions of Adler, Jung, and Horney to the psychoanalytic approach to personality.

▶ The Behavioral/Learning Approach

Many American psychologists in the early twentieth century did not think much of the psychoanalytic approach, regardless of its form or who happened to propose it. American psychology was oriented toward the laboratory and theories of learning. Explaining personality in terms of learning seemed to be a reasonable course of action (you might want to review these approaches as they were first presented back in Chapter 6).

John B. Watson (1878–1958) and his followers in behaviorism argued that psychology should turn away from the study of consciousness and the mind because they are unverifiable and ultimately unscientific. Behaviorists argued that psychologists should study observable behavior. Yet here were the psychoanalysts arguing that *un*conscious and *pre*conscious forces are determiners of behavior. "Nonsense," the behaviorist would say. "We don't even know what we mean by consciousness, and you want to talk about levels of unconscious influence!"

Watson and his followers emphasized the role of the environment in shaping one's behaviors. Behaviorists could not accept the Freudian notion of inborn traits or impulses, whether called id or libido or anything else. What mattered was *learning*, not a personality theory. A theory of learning would include all the details about so-called personality that one would ever need.

▲ *The behaviorists believe that who we are is determined by our early learning experiences. For example, concern for the well-being of others would be attributed to our childhood experiences, rather than to any innate tendencies.*

Who we are has been determined by our learning experiences, and early experiences count heavily—on that Watson and Freud might have agreed. Even our fears are conditioned (remember Watson's Little Albert study). So convinced was Watson that instincts and innate impulses had little to do with the development of behavior that he wrote: "Give me a dozen healthy infants, well-formed, and my own specified world to bring them up in and I'll guarantee to take any one at random and train him to become any type of specialist I might select—doctor, lawyer, artist, merchant, chief, and yes, even beggarman and thief, regardless of his talents, penchants, tendencies, abilities, vocations, and race of his ancestors" (Watson, 1925).

In this context, I should again mention B. F. Skinner (1904–1990), even though he claimed to have proposed no particular theory of learning, much less of personality. Skinner's behaviorism refused to refer to any sort of internal variables to explain behavior—which is just what personality theories try to do. Look only at observable stimuli, observable responses, and for relationships among them; we cannot go meddling about in the mind of the organism, Skinnerians argue.

Behavior is shaped by its consequences. Some behaviors result in reinforcement and tend to be repeated; some behaviors do not, and tend not to be repeated. Consistency in behavior simply reflects the consistency of one's reinforcement history. The real question is, how shall external conditions be manipulated to produce the consequences we want?

John Dollard (1900–1980) and Neal Miller (b. 1909), as behaviorists and learning theorists, tried to see if they could use the basic principles of learning theory to explain personality and how it developed. What matters for personality, Dollard and Miller argued, was the system of habits one developed in response to cues in the environment. Behavior was motivated by primary drives, upon whose satisfaction survival depended, and on learned drives, which developed through experience. Motivated by drives, habits that are reinforced are those that tend to be repeated and eventually become part of the stable collection of habits that make up one's personality. Repression into the unconscious, for example, is a matter of learned forgetfulness—forgetting about some anxiety-producing experience is reinforcing and, thus, tends to be repeated. It was Miller (1944) who proposed

▲ *Neal Miller*

that conflict can be explained in terms of tendencies (habits) to approach or avoid goals and has little to do with the id, ego, and superego or with unconscious impulses.

Albert Bandura (b. 1925) is one learning theorist who is quite willing to consider the internal, cognitive processes of the learner. Bandura claims that many aspects of our behavior, and our personality, *are* learned, but they often are learned through observation and social influence. For Bandura, learning involves more than the formation of connections between stimuli and responses or between responses and resulting reinforcers; it involves a cognitive representation and rearrangement of those representations. In simpler terms, this approach argues that you may very well learn to behave honestly, for example, through the observation of others. If you view your parents as being honest and see their behaviors being reinforced (vicarious reinforcement), you may acquire similar responses.

Before You Go On
▼▼▼▼▼▼▼▼▼▼

Specify a contribution to the concept of personality contributed by Watson, Skinner, Dollard and Miller, and Bandura.

▶ The Humanistic/Phenomenological Approach

To some degree, the humanistic/phenomenological approach to personality contrasts with both the psychoanalytic and behavioral approaches. For one thing, it claims that people can shape their own destiny, chart and follow their own course of action, and that biological, instinctive, or environmental influences can be overcome or minimized. The humanistic view may be thought of as more optimistic than either the Freudian view (with its death instincts and innate impulses) or the view of learning theories (with its emphasis on control exerted by forces of the environment). It also tends to focus much more on the here-and-now than on early childhood experiences as important molders of personality. This point of view tends to emphasize the wholeness or completeness of personality, rather than focusing on its structural parts. What matters most is *how people view themselves and others*, which is essentially what **phenomenological** means. (I trust that you recognize this concept from our discussion of important themes in Chapter 1.)

Carl Rogers's (1902–1986) approach to personality is referred to as a person-centered or self theory. Like Freud, Rogers developed his views of human nature through the observation of clients in a clinical setting. Rogers believed that the most powerful human drive is to become fully functioning.

To be *fully functioning* implies that the person has become all that he or she can be, and it means more than that. When we are children, some of what we do brings reward, but some of what we do does not. How we are regarded by those we care about is often conditional on how we behave. We tend to receive only conditional positive regard. *If* we do what is expected or desired, *then* we get rewarded. As a result, we try to act in ways that bring rewards and avoid punishment, in ways that satisfy others rather than ourselves. Our feelings of self and self-worth are thus dependent on the actions of others who either reward us, don't reward us, or punish us.

So long as we act only to please others, we are not fully functioning. To be fully functioning involves an openness to one's own feelings and desires, an accurate awareness of one's inner self, and a positive self-regard. Helping

phenomenological relating to an approach that emphasizes one's perception and awareness of events as being more important than the events themselves

▲ To illustrate his theory of self-actualization, Maslow cites Thomas Jefferson and Eleanor Roosevelt as individuals who reached their fullest potentials, or became self-actualized.

children to become fully functioning requires that we offer them more of what Rogers calls unconditional positive regard and that we separate the child's behaviors from the child's self. What that means is that we may punish a child for doing a bad thing, but never for being a bad child (e.g., "I love you very much, but what you have done is wrong and, therefore, you will be punished"; or more simply, "You're a good girl, but you've done a bad thing."). Helping people to achieve positive self-regard is one of the major goals of person-centered therapy.

Notice that what matters here is often not so much what *is*, but what is *felt* or *perceived*. One's true self (whatever that may be) is less important than one's *image* of one's self. How the world is experienced is what matters—a clearly phenomenological point of view. You may be an excellent piano player (better, perhaps, than 98 percent of all of us). But if you feel that you are a bad piano player, that perception or self-regard is what most matters.

Abraham Maslow's (1908–1970) basic criticism of the psychology he had studied was that it was altogether too pessimistic and negative. The individual was seen as being battered about by either a hostile environment or by depraved instincts, many of which propelled the person on a course of self-destruction.

There must be more to living than this, thought Maslow. Someone should attend to the positive side of human nature. Maslow felt that people's needs are not base, but are positive or, at worst, neutral (Maslow, 1954). Our major goal in life is to realize and put into practice those needs—to *self-actualize*. (Perhaps you'll recall that Maslow's views were presented in Chapter 9 in the context of our discussion of motivation.)

Let's look, Maslow argued, at the very best among us. Let's focus our attention on the characteristics of those who have realized their fullest potential and have become self-actualized (see Figure 10.1). In his search for such individuals, Maslow couldn't find many. Most were historical figures, such as Thomas Jefferson and Eleanor Roosevelt.

Figure 10.1

SOME OF THE CHARACTERISTICS OR ATTRIBUTES OF SELF-ACTUALIZERS.

1. They tend to be realistic in their orientation.
2. They accept themselves, others, and the world for what they are, not for what they should be.
3. They have a great deal of spontaneity.
4. They tend to be problem-centered rather than self-centered.
5. They have a need for privacy and a sense of detachment.
6. They are autonomous, independent, and self-sufficient.
7. Their appreciation of others (and of things of the world) is fresh, free, and not stereotyped.
8. Many have spiritual or mystical (although not necessarily religious) experiences.
9. They can identify with humankind as a whole and share a concern for humanity.
10. They have a number of interpersonal relationships, some of them very deep and profound.
11. They tend to have democratic views in the sense that all are created equal and should be treated equally.
12. They have a sense of humor that tends more to the philosophical than the hostile.
13. They tend to be creative in their approach.
14. They are hard working.
15. They resist pressures to conform to society.

After Maslow, 1954

▶ The Trait Approach

Trait theories of personality have a markedly different flavor from any of the approaches we have looked at so far. Trait theories are more concerned with the adequate *description* of personality than with the *explanation* of personality. Arnold Buss put the agenda of trait theorists this way: "Trait psychologists typically seek to reveal the psychological dimensions along which people differ and ways in which traits cluster within individuals" (1989, p. 1379). We may define a **trait** as "any distinguishable, relatively enduring way in which one individual differs from others" (Guilford, 1959, p. 5). This definition points out the meaninglessness of our opening "test," doesn't it?

Notice that traits are descriptive *dimensions*. That is, any trait (such as friendliness) is not a simple either/or proposition. Friendliness falls along a continuum, ranging from extremely unfriendly to extremely friendly, with many possibilities in between. To be useful, personality traits need to be measurable, and our measurements should yield numerical scores so that we can assess the extent to which people differ on those traits (Hogan & Nicholson, 1988; Kagan, 1988).

The issue for psychologists who have taken this approach has been to determine which traits are the important ones. Which dimensions best characterize a person and how is she or he different from everyone else? How can personality traits be organized? The answers to these and similar questions have given rise to several trait theories. We'll summarize three, and then look at a contemporary trait theory.

▶ Three Classic Examples

For Gordon Allport (1897–1967), personality traits exist within a person and can be used to explain the consistency in that person's behavior. In different situations, for example, a personality trait of friendliness might produce a range of different specific responses, but those responses would be, in their essence, very much alike.

Allport's theory proposes two types of personality traits: *common traits* and *personal traits*. Common traits are aspects of personality shared by almost everyone (to greater or lesser degrees perhaps, but shared with everyone else). Aggressiveness is an example of a common trait, and so is intelligence. These are traits that we can use to make comparisons among people. Personal traits, on the other hand, are unique to a person. How one displays a sense of humor (sharp wit, cutting sarcasm, dirty jokes, philosophical puns, long stories, and so on) is thought of as being a unique disposition.

Allport went on to claim that personal traits are of three different subtypes. Allport wrote of cardinal, central, and secondary personal traits. A *cardinal trait* is one that is so overwhelming that it influences virtually everything that the person does. The personalities of very few of us are ruled by cardinal traits. Even Allport could imagine only a few examples (Don Quixote, the Marquis de Sade, and Don Juan among them). No, what predominates in influencing your behaviors and mine are not likely to be cardinal traits, but *central traits,* or dispositions. These traits usually can be described in just

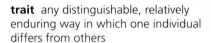

trait any distinguishable, relatively enduring way in which one individual differs from others

▲ *Gordon Allport*

one word, and they are the 5–10 traits that best characterize someone (*e.g.*, honest, friendly, outgoing, fair, kind, and so on). Finally, each of us is occasionally influenced by *secondary traits*. These are characteristics (dispositions) that seldom govern many of our reactions and may be applied only in specific circumstances. For example, someone may be very calm and easygoing, even when threatened (reflecting central traits), but when threatened in his or her own home (by intruders, let's say) can be very aggressive and not calm at all.

Raymond Cattell's (b. 1905) approach to personality is an empirical one, relying on psychological tests, questionnaires, and surveys. Talking about personality traits without talking about how they are measured makes little sense to Cattell. Cattell used a statistical technique called *factor analysis*. Factor analysis is a correlational procedure that identifies groups of highly interrelated variables that may be assumed to measure the same underlying factor (here, a personality trait). The logic is that if you know that someone is outgoing, you really don't need to test them to see if they are sociable or extroverted—such information would be redundant.

Cattell argued that there are two types of personality traits. *Surface traits* are the clusters of behaviors that go together, like those that make up curiosity, trustworthiness, or kindliness. These traits are easily observed and can be found in a number of different settings. More important than surface traits are the fewer number of underlying traits from which surface traits develop. These he called *source traits*. It is one's pattern of source traits that determines which surface traits will get expressed in behavior. Source traits are not as easily measured as surface traits because they are not directly observable. Cattell's source traits are listed in Figure 10.2.

The theory of Hans Eysenck (b. 1916) claims that personality can be divided into just two main *types,* and each is defined by a dimension. One is the *extroversion-introversion* dimension. People who rate high on measures of extroversion seek stimulation; they are active and sociable. Introverts, on the other hand, are reserved, cautious, and withdrawn. (Few people are pure extroverts or introverts—most of us fall somewhere in between.)

Eysenck's other major dimension is one of *stability-instability* (often called *neuroticism)*. People high on stability tend to be calm and easygoing;

Figure 10.2

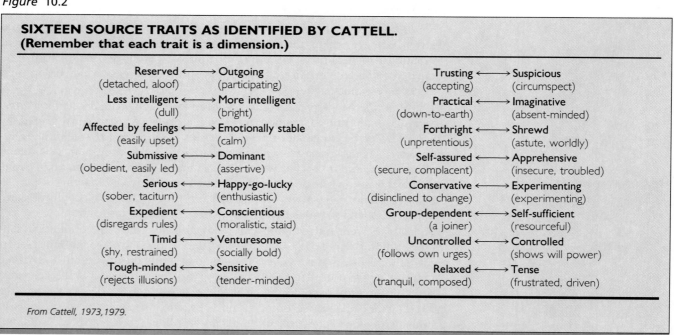

SIXTEEN SOURCE TRAITS AS IDENTIFIED BY CATTELL.
(Remember that each trait is a dimension.)

Reserved ⟷ Outgoing	Trusting ⟷ Suspicious
(detached, aloof) (participating)	(accepting) (circumspect)
Less intelligent ⟷ More intelligent	Practical ⟷ Imaginative
(dull) (bright)	(down-to-earth) (absent-minded)
Affected by feelings ⟷ Emotionally stable	Forthright ⟷ Shrewd
(easily upset) (calm)	(unpretentious) (astute, worldly)
Submissive ⟷ Dominant	Self-assured ⟷ Apprehensive
(obedient, easily led) (assertive)	(secure, complacent) (insecure, troubled)
Serious ⟷ Happy-go-lucky	Conservative ⟷ Experimenting
(sober, taciturn) (enthusiastic)	(disinclined to change) (experimenting)
Expedient ⟷ Conscientious	Group-dependent ⟷ Self-sufficient
(disregards rules) (moralistic, staid)	(a joiner) (resourceful)
Timid ⟷ Venturesome	Uncontrolled ⟷ Controlled
(shy, restrained) (socially bold)	(follows own urges) (shows will power)
Tough-minded ⟷ Sensitive	Relaxed ⟷ Tense
(rejects illusions) (tender-minded)	(tranquil, composed) (frustrated, driven)

From Cattell, 1973, 1979.

Figure 10.3

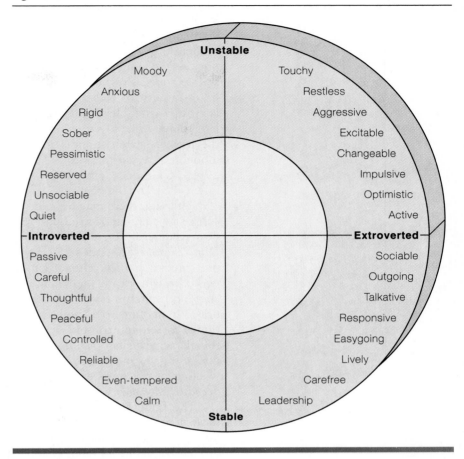

▲ *The interaction of Eysenck's extroversion-introversion and stability-instability dimensions and the traits they produce. (From Eysenck, 1973.)*

people at the other extreme tend to be moody, anxious, and temperamental. The interaction of these two types or dimensions gives rise to several different, specific traits (see Figure 10.3). For example, if someone were extroverted and unstable, we might find them to be impulsive, while someone who is introverted and unstable might be reserved.

Eysenck later proposed a third major personality type, a *psychoticism* dimension, which interacts with the first two (1976). This dimension is a measure of the degree to which a person takes a realistic view of life or is in some way out of touch with reality. Although the specific traits that develop through the interaction of these three personality types may be molded by learning and experience, Eysenck claims that one's position on his three main dimensions is largely inherited or instinctive.

Before You Go On
▼▼▼▼▼▼▼▼▼▼▼

What is a personality trait?

What are the major traits that influence personality, according to Allport, Cattell, and Eysenck?

▶ A Contemporary Perspective: The Big Five

We've taken only a brief look at three theories that have tried to identify distinguishable, relatively enduring personality traits, and we've seen a number of points of view. Allport named common traits and personal dispositions; Cattell found many surface traits and a smaller number of source traits; Eysenck talked about extroversion-introversion and stability-instability, as well as psychoticism. Who is correct? Which set of traits is most reasonable? It may surprise you to learn that personality theorists lately have come to something of a consensus concerning which traits have the most research support to qualify as descriptors of personality. This model is referred to as the "Five-Factor Model" (Carson, 1989; Digman, 1990; McCrae & Costa, 1986, 1987). Which dimensions of personality are now called The Big Five?

Although there may be some consensus that five major dimensions will suffice to characterize the nature of human personality, disagreement on how to describe these five remain. The following is from Digman (1990). *Dimension I* is Eysenck's "Extroversion/Introversion" dimension just as we presented it earlier. *Dimension II* is "Agreeableness" or "Friendliness" with altruism, caring, and emotional support at one end; hostility, indifference, and spitefulness on the other. *Dimension III* is called "Conscientiousness." It amounts to a "will to achieve" (or simply "Will"). It includes such things as self-control and dependability. It is well correlated with educational achievement. *Dimension IV* is Eysenck's "Stability/Instability" dimension. In many ways, this is a dimension of one's emotionality, and whether or not one's emotional reactions are stable or in some way disordered. *Dimension V* is simply "Intellect," "Intelligence," or "Openness."

The finding that personality traits can be reduced to just five, with these names (or names like these) is quite remarkable. What we have to do now remember is that each of these five traits represents a full dimension of possible habits and individual responses that a person may bring to bear in any given situation. There is still much work to be done. These five traits have been gleaned from nearly fifty years of research. They have emerged repeatedly, regardless of the subject pool of individuals being assessed, and "The Big Five have appeared now in at least five languages, leading one to suspect that something quite fundamental is involved here" (Digman, 1990, p. 443).

Before You Go On
▼▼▼▼▼▼▼▼▼

What are the Big Five personality dimensions?

▶ Evaluating the Four Approaches to Personality

Given that we have reviewed only a few of the major ideas from a sample of personality theories, can we make any judgments about which approach is the best? Are any of these theories better than the others? These appear to be reasonable, natural questions to ask, but I suspect that you can anticipate the nature of our answers. There are supporters and critics of each of the approaches we've summarized in this topic. So long as we recognize that our evaluations are somewhat superficial, we still may profit from reflecting on the strengths and weaknesses of each approach.

There is little doubt that the psychoanalytic approach, particularly as modified by the neo-Freudians, is the most comprehensive and complex of the theories we've reviewed. Psychologists have been debating the relative merits of Freud's contributions for decades. On the plus side, Freud (and the other psychoanalytically-oriented theorists) must be credited for focusing our attention on the importance of the childhood years and for suggesting that some (even biologically determined) impulses may affect our behaviors even though they are beyond our immediate awareness. Although Freud may have overstated the matter, drawing our attention to the impact of sexuality and sexual impulses as influences on personality is also a significant contribution. On the other hand, many psychologists have been critical of psychoanalytic theory. We already have seen how the neo-Freudians tended to minimize innate biological drives and take a more social approach to personality development than did Freud. One of the major criticisms of the psychoanalytic approach is that so many of its insights and propositions are untestable. Freud thought of himself as a scientist, but he tested none of his ideas about human nature experimentally. Some concepts seem to be beyond testing. What, after all, *is* libidinal energy? How can it be measured? How would we recognize it if we saw it? Concepts such as id, ego, and superego may sound sensible, but how can we prove or disprove their existence? It also seems that a heavy reliance on instincts, especially instincts with sexual and aggressive overtones, as explanatory concepts goes beyond where most psychologists are willing to venture.

With regard to the behavioral/learning approach to personality, many psychologists argue that Watson, Dollard, Miller, and Skinner "dehumanize" personality, and that even the social learning theory of Bandura tends to be too deterministic. That is, virtually everything a person may do, think, or feel is in some way determined by his or her environment through learning or conditioning. This leaves nothing for the person, for personality, to contribute. Behavioral/learning approaches to personality often are not theories at all—at least not very comprehensive ones. They tend to avoid mention of biologically determined characteristics. To their credit, they demand that terms be carefully defined and that conclusions be verified experimentally.

Like the others, the humanistic/phenomenological approach has a number of strengths. For one, it reminds us of the wholeness of personality and of the danger in analyzing something so complex into artificial segments. That the approach, stressing as it does personal growth and development, is positive and upbeat in its flavor serves to inform us that at least such views are possible. And as we shall see in our discussion of psychotherapy (Chapter 13), the humanistic/phenomenological approach has had a major impact on many therapists and counselors. The basic problem with this approach is not unlike the basic problem with Freud's theory. It may make sense, but how does one go about testing any of the observations and statements of the approach? Many of the key terms are defined in very general, fuzzy ways. What really is self-image? How do we really know when someone is "growing?" How can one test the effects of unconditional positive regard? In many ways, what we have here is a blueprint, a vision for the nature of personality and not a scientific theory.

As I've already mentioned, trait approaches to personality are quite different from the others, even in their basic intent. They have a few obvious advantages. They provide us not only with descriptive terms, but also with means of measuring the important dimensions of personality. They also give us a sense of how measured traits are related to one

By Your Shape Shall I Know You

Wouldn't it be convenient if there were some simple way to make judgments about the personalities of others based simply on the observation of physical characteristics? The basic idea behind *constitutional theories* is that there is a correlation between physical appearance (one's constitution) and significant psychological characteristics (one's personality). Several such theories have been proposed, but none has gained as much attention as that of William H. Sheldon (1940; 1942; 1944; 1954).

Sheldon claimed that people could be classified in terms of their body type. He used a three-part classification system. People who were soft, flabby, rounded, and unmuscled he called *endomorphs*. Those who were hard, tough, rectangular of build, and well-muscled are *mesomorphs*. People who are extremely thin, fragile, and delicately boned are called *ectomorphs*. Although people can be found who characterize each of these to an extreme, Sheldon allowed for degrees of each of these body types. That is, people who are basically well-built and athletic in appearance but have (perhaps, with age) developed a softness of muscle tone, or a pot belly, would be classified as mesomorphs with a tendency toward endomorphy. Sheldon's scheme for classifying body types yields a numerical score and is quite remarkable, in that there is usually a high level of agreement among raters on an individual's body-type score.

Sheldon further proposed that personality, or temperament, could be measured using a three-dimensional rating scheme. His three dimensions of personality included *viscerotonia*, including such things as love of physical comfort, love of eating, complacency, and evenness of emotional flow), *somatotonia*, (including love of physical exercise, love of chance and risk, and competitive aggressiveness), and *cerebratonia* (including very fast reactions, love of privacy, mental overintensity, and poor sleep habits). In fact, each of these three temperamental types was defined by 20 separate rating scales and yielded a numerical score. Now all that remained was for Sheldon to demonstrate a relationship between body type and temperament. That he did, and with outstanding success.

Over a five-year period, Sheldon interviewed, tested and rated 200 men. He found extremely high correlations between body type and personality. Endomorphs tended to be visceratonic; mesomorphs were somatotonic, and ectomorphs were clearly cerebratonic (see Figure 1.4). Sheldon's reported correlations were all around +.80, a degree of correlation seldom equaled in personality research.

There were two major flaws in Sheldon's efforts. First, many of his temperament scales *insured* that there would be a correlation. It's hardly surprising to find that people who love to eat and relax should turn out to be overweight and flabby, or that people who love to exercise and

another. On the other hand, as theories, they offer little more than description. To say that someone acted in a certain way "because he is introverted" does not go far to *explain* that action. It functions merely as a label. And—even with the so-called Big Five traits—there continues to be disagreement about how to characterize the most basic traits that describe personality.

love physical adventure should turn out to be athletic and well-muscled. Second, the measurements of body type and temperament type were both made by the same person—Sheldon. Sheldon thus placed himself in an excellent position to be accused of experimenter bias (see Chapter 1). When judgments of constitution and personality are made by independent raters, correlations are still positive, but drop to less impressive levels (Stagner and Burke, 1982).

We need not simply dismiss Sheldon's approach to personality. There *is* some truth behind the notion that there is a relationship between physical characteristics and personality or temperament. It's just not as compelling as we might like it to be. As one example of research influenced by Sheldon's findings we have the studies by Glueck and Glueck (1950; 1956) that compared the somatotypes of delinquent and nondelinquent boys. They found that delinquent boys tended to be mesomorphs or (to a lesser degree) ectomorphs, but hardly ever mesomorphs. It is also the case that our physical stature may set limits on what we can and cannot do or may limit the range of our possible reactions. And our personalities may have direct effects on our physical appearance through overindulgence, vanity, or neglect. But as much as such stereotypes still exist, fat people are not necessarily jolly, and people who have a "lean and hungry look" do not necessarily think too much, nor are they necessarily dangerous (Shakespeare, *Julius Caesar,* Act I, Scene ii).

Figure 10.4

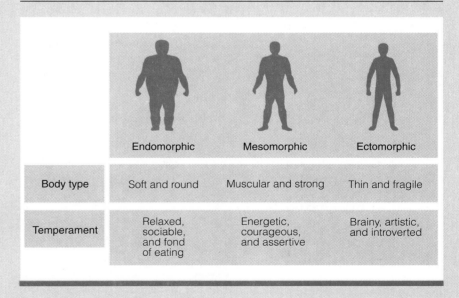

	Endomorphic	Mesomorphic	Ectomorphic
Body type	Soft and round	Muscular and strong	Thin and fragile
Temperament	Relaxed, sociable, and fond of eating	Energetic, courageous, and assertive	Brainy, artistic, and introverted

So as we might have predicted, when we try to evaluate the different theories or approaches to personality, there are no *overall* real winners or losers. Each approach has its shortcomings, but each adds something to our appreciation of the complex concept of human personality.

Now, let's turn our attention to the techniques that psychologists use to measure or assess personality.

▶ Personality Assessment

As we know, personality is a difficult concept to define. Common to most definitions is the idea that there are characteristics of an individual that remain fairly consistent over time and over many (if not all) situations. It is further reasoned that if we know which traits are typical of a person, we can use that knowledge to make predictions about his or her behaviors or mental processes. The key, then, is to find characteristics of a person that can be reliably and validly measured.

If we find those characteristics, what then? Why do psychologists engage in personality assessment in the first place? There are three goals that lie behind the measurement of personality. One goal is to adequately diagnose a person's problem. One of the first questions that a psychologist in a clinical setting may ask is, "What is wrong with this person?" In fact, the first question is often, "*Is* there anything wrong with this person?" (Burisch, 1984).

A second use for personality assessment is in theory building, where there are a number of interrelated questions: Which personality traits can be measured? How may traits be organized within the person? Which measured traits are most important for describing a person's personality? For trait theorists, this is obviously *the* purpose for constructing personality tests.

The third goal involves the question of whether a measured personality characteristic can be used to predict some other behavior. This concern

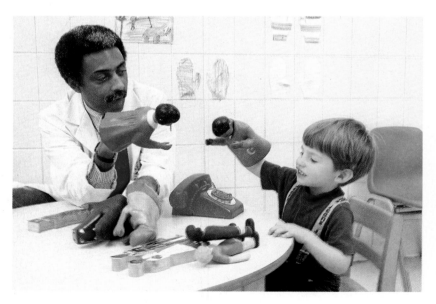

▲ *Behavioral observation involves drawing conclusions about an individual's personality on the basis of his or her behaviors. Role-playing is one technique psychologists use to gain insights about a child's behavior.*

also is a practical one—particularly in vocational placement. For example, if we know that Joe is dominant and extroverted, what does that knowledge tell us about his leadership potential? What characteristics are associated with success as a sales clerk? What personality traits best describe a successful astronaut, police officer, or secretary?

In brief, personality assessment has three goals: diagnosis, theory building, and/or behavioral prediction. These goals may interact. A clinical diagnosis made in the context of some theoretical approach is often used to predict possible outcomes, such as which therapy is most appropriate for a given diagnosis.

▶ Behavioral Observations

As you and I develop our own impressions of the personalities of our friends and acquaintances, we do so largely by relying on **behavioral observation.** As its name suggests, this approach involves drawing conclusions about an individual's personality on the basis of observations of his or her behaviors. We judge Dan to be bright because he was the only one who knew the answer to a question in class. We feel that Maria is submissive because she always seems to do whatever her husband demands.

As helpful as our observations may be, there may be problems with the casual, unstructured observations that you and I normally make. Because we have only observed a small range of behaviors in a small range of settings, we may be overgeneralizing when we assume that those same behaviors will show up in new, different situations. Dan may never again know the answer to a question in class. Maria may give in to her husband only because she knows that we are there. That is, the behaviors we happen to observe may not be typical or characteristic at all.

behavioral observation the personality assessment technique of drawing conclusions about one's personality based on observations of one's behaviors

Figure 10.5

	Poor				Superior
Dependability	Requires prodding and supervision	Needs occasional prodding	Steady; responsible worker	Needs little supervision; uses own judgment	Self-starter; needs no supervision
Personal relations	Rude; causes trouble	Inconsiderate; unkind	Relations with others usually good	Helpful; kind; polite	Well liked; good social skills
Poise	Nervous; ill at ease	Easily upset; tense	Average poise and self-assurance	Self-assured	Composed; handles crises well

▲ *A graphic rating scale such as this might be used by an employer in evaluating employees or potential employees. It could also be used by psychologists studying behavior.*

Nonetheless, behavioral observations can be an excellent source of information, particularly when the observations being made are purposeful, careful, and structured—as opposed to the casual observations that you and I usually make. Behavioral observations are commonly a part of any clinical assessment. The clinical psychologist may note any number of behaviors of a client as being potentially significant—style of dress, manner of speaking, gestures, postures, and so on.

Let's consider an example. A small child is reportedly having trouble at school, behaving aggressively and being generally disruptive. One thing a psychologist may do is visit the school and observe the child's behaviors in the natural setting of the classroom. It may be that the child does behave aggressively and engage in fighting behavior, but only when the teacher is in the room. Otherwise, the child is quite pleasant. It may be that the child's aggressive behaviors reflect a ploy to get the teacher's attention.

Some observational techniques are supplemented with some sort of *rating scale* (see Figure 10.5). Rating scales provide many advantages over casual observation. For one thing, they focus the attention of the observer on a set of specified behaviors to be observed. Rating scales also yield a more objective measure of a sample of behavior. Using rating scales, one can have behaviors observed by a number of raters. If different raters are involved in the observation of the same behaviors (say, children at play in a nursery), you can check on the reliability of the observations. That is, if all five of your observers agree that Timothy engaged in "hitting behavior" five times per hour, on the average, the consistency (or reliability) of that assessment adds to its usefulness.

Before You Go On

▼▼▼▼▼▼▼▼▼

What are the basic goals of personality assessment?

How are behavioral observations used to assess personality?

▶ Interviews

We can learn some things about people by watching them. We also can gain insight about some aspects of their personality simply by asking them about themselves. In fact, the **interview** "remains the most important instrument of clinical assessment" (Korchin & Schuldberg, 1981). It also is "one of the oldest and most widely used, although not always the most accurate, of the methods of personality assessment" (Aiken, 1984, p. 296).

The basic data of the interview are what people say about themselves, rather than what they do. The interview is not, strictly speaking, a measurement technique, because the results of interviews usually are impressionistic and not easily quantifiable (although some interview techniques are clearly more structured and objective than others). The interview is more a technique of discovering generalities than specifics.

A major advantage of the interview is its flexibility. The interviewer can decide to drop a certain line of questioning if it is producing no useful information, and to pursue some other area of interest. Unfortunately, there is little evidence that unstructured interviews have very much reliability or

interview the personality assessment technique involving a conversational interchange between the interviewer and subject to gain information about the subject

▲ *Although the data derived from casual interviews is seldom very reliable, psychologists can gain useful insights about someone's personality by using formal, structured interviews.*

validity. In discussing interviews used to assess personality characteristics of job applicants, Tenopyr (1981) calls the validity of interviews "dismal." She says that the employment interview, "despite various innovations over the years, has never been consistently shown to improve selection" (p. 1123).

As is the case for observational techniques, there is variation in the degree to which interviews may be unstructured or structured. In the latter type of interview, there are a specific set of questions to be asked in a prescribed order. The structured interview is more like a psychological test to the extent that it is objective, standardized, and asks about a particular sample of behavior.

Before You Go On
▼▼▼▼▼▼▼▼▼

Cite one advantage and one disadvantage of the interview as a technique of personality assessment.

▶ *Paper-and-pencil Tests*

Minnesota Multiphasic Personality Inventory (MMPI) a paper-and-pencil inventory of 567 true-false questions used to assess a number of personality dimensions, some of which may indicate the presence of a psychological disorder

Observational and interview techniques barely qualify as psychological tests. They are seldom as standardized or as objective as we would like them to be. As we saw at the very beginning of this chapter, paper-and-pencil tests of personality can also be sorely lacking in validity. (You might want to review our discussion of psychological tests in Chapter 8.) In this section, we'll focus on one of the most often used paper-and-pencil personality tests, the **Minnesota Multiphasic Personality Inventory**, or **MMPI** for short. The test is referred to as "multiphasic" because it measures a number of different personality dimensions with the same set of items.

The MMPI was designed to help in the diagnosis of persons with mental disturbances and hence is not a personality test in the sense of identifying personality traits. The test is the most researched test in all of psychology, and remains one of the most commonly used (Lubin, et al., 1984). In August, 1989, a revision of the MMPI (called the MMPI-2) was made available. The revision made two major changes, and a number of lesser ones. Antiquated and offensive items (having to do with religion or sexual practices) were replaced. The norm group for the MMPI-2 is much larger (2600 subjects) than for the MMPI (about 700 subjects). The intent of the authors of the MMPI-2 was to update and improve, but *not change*, the basic design or the meaning of test scores. The extent to which the revision succeeded remains to be seen (*e.g.*, Adler, 1990). Many psychologists had grown very comfortable with the original MMPI and some were against changing such a well-researched test.

The MMPI-2 is composed of 567 true-false questions that ask about feelings, attitudes, physical symptoms, and past experiences. Because of the way in which it was constructed, the MMPI is called a *criterion-referenced* test, which means that items on the test are referenced to one of the criterion groups—either normals or patients with a particular diagnosis. Some items appear very sensible. "I feel like people are plotting against me," seems like the sort of item that someone with paranoia would call "true," while normals would tend to respond "false." Many items, however, are not so obvious. "I like to visit zoos," is not an MMPI-2 item, but it might have been if subjects of one diagnostic group responded to the item differently from the way other subjects did. What the item looks like is irrelevant. The only thing that matters is if subjects of different groups respond differently to the item.

The MMPI-2's "validity scales" are made up of items from among the 567 that assess the extent to which the subject is attending to the task at hand, or is trying to present herself or himself in a particularly favorable light, instead of responding truthfully to the items. For example, responding "true" to several statements such as "I always smile at everyone" would lead an examiner to believe to doubt the validity of the subject's responses.

Although the MMPI is the most commonly used personality inventory, it certainly is not the only paper-and-pencil personality test. There are dozens of such tests. *The California Personality Inventory, CPI*, was written using only normal subjects, not people who were diagnosed as having some psychological problem or disorder. The CPI assesses 18 personality traits, including self-acceptance, dominance, responsibility, and sociability. Because it is designed to measure a number of different traits, it can also be referred to as a multiphasic test.

Some multiphasic tests have been designed in conjunction with a particular personality theory. For example, Cattell's trait theory approach investigates a number of potential personality traits. These traits are measured with Cattell's *16 PF Questionnaire* (PF stands for "personality factors"). Analyses of responses on this test results in a personality profile. That profile can then be compared with one gathered from a large norm group.

Finally, I should mention that there are many personality inventories or questionnaires that are designed to measure just one trait and, thus, are not multiphasic. One example is the *Taylor Manifest Anxiety Scale*. Taylor began with a very large pool of items—many of them from the MMPI—and asked psychologists to choose items that they thought would best measure anxiety. The 50 items most commonly chosen make up this test, which has gained wide acceptance as an indicator of anxiety.

Before You Go On
▼▼▼▼▼▼▼▼▼

What does multiphasic mean?

How was the MMPI constructed?

What can paper-and-pencil tests tell us about personality?

▶ Projective Techniques

projective technique a personality assessment technique requiring a subject to respond to ambiguous stimuli, thus projecting his or her self into the responses

A **projective technique** involves asking a subject to respond to ambiguous stimuli. The stimuli involved can be any number of things, as we shall see, and there are clearly no right or wrong answers. The procedure is reasonably unstructured and open-ended. The basic idea is that because there is, in fact, so little content in the stimulus presented, the subject will *project* some of his or her own self into the response. In many ways, projective techniques are more of an aid to interviewing than they are psychological tests (Korchin & Schuldberg, 1981).

Some projective techniques are very simple. The word association technique, introduced by Galton in 1879 and used in psychoanalysis, is a sort of projective technique. "I will say a word, and I want you to say the first thing that pops into your head. Do not think about your response; just say the first thing that comes to mind." There certainly are no right answers in this type of procedure. The idea is that the psychologist can gain some insight, perhaps into the problems of a patient, by using this technique.

A similar technique is the *unfinished sentences* or *sentence completion* test. For example, a sentence is begun, "My greatest fear is: . . . " The subject is asked to complete the sentence. Although there are a number of published tests available (*e.g.*, the *Rotter Incomplete Sentences Blank*), many clinicians prefer to make up their own forms. There are no right or wrong responses, and interpreting responses is rather subjective, but a skilled examiner can use these procedures to gain insights about a subject's personality.

Rorschach inkblot test a projective technique in which the subject is asked to say what he or she sees in a series of inkblots

Of all the projective techniques, none is as famous as the **Rorschach inkblot test.** This technique was introduced in 1921 by Hermann Rorschach, who believed that people with different personalities respond differently to inkblot patterns (see Figure 10.6). There are 10 cards in the test, five are black on white, two are red and gray, and three are multicolored. Subjects are asked to tell what they see in the cards or what the inkblot represents.

Scoring of Rorschach test responses has become quite controversial. Standard scoring procedures require attending to a number of factors: what the subject says (content), where the subject focuses attention (location), mention of detail versus global features, reacting to color or open spaces, and how many different responses there are per card. Many psychologists have questioned the efficiency of the Rorschach as a diagnostic instrument. Much of what it can tell an examiner may be gained directly. For example, Rorschach responses that include many references to death, sadness, and dying are probably indicative of a depressed subject. One has to wonder if inkblots are really needed to discover such depression. As a psychological

Figure 10.6

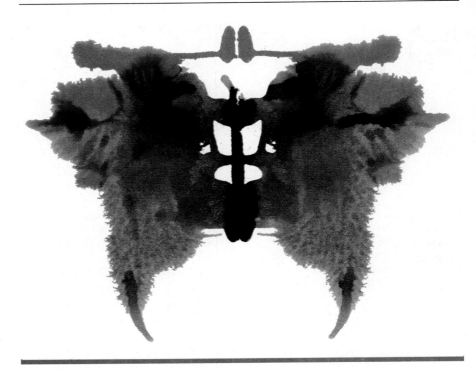

▲ *A sample Rorschach-like inkblot. The subject is asked what the inkblot represents or what he or she sees in the inkblot.*

test, the Rorschach seems neither very reliable nor valid, yet it remains a very popular instrument. It is used primarily as an aid to assessment and the development of subjective impressions.

A projective device we've discussed before (in Chapter 9, in the context of achievement motivation), is the **Thematic Apperception Test**, or **TAT**, devised by Henry Murray in 1938. This test is made up of a series of ambiguous pictures about which a subject is asked to tell a story. The subject is asked to describe what is going on, what led up to this situation, and what the outcome is likely to be.

The test is designed to provide a mechanism to discover the subjects' hidden needs, desires, and emotions, which will be projected into their stories. The test is called a *thematic* test because scoring depends largely on the interpretation of the themes of the stories that are told. Although some formal scoring schemes are available, scoring and interpretation are usually quite subjective and impressionistic. It is likely that the TAT remains popular for the same reason as the Rorschach: Psychologists are used to it, comfortable with the insights it provides, and willing to accept any source of additional information they can use to make a reasonable assessment or diagnosis.

Thematic Apperception Test (TAT)
a projective personality test requiring a subject to tell a series of short stories about a set of ambiguous pictures

Before You Go On
▼▼▼▼▼▼▼▼

What is the essence of a projective technique, the Rorschach and TAT in particular?

▼▼▼
Thinking Critically About Personality: Theories and Assessment

1. No matter what its proposals, hypotheses, or predictions, to what extent is it reasonable to assume that a theory of personality *can* emerge from the study and treatment of persons with psychological disorders?

2. Humankind is a unique species. For one thing, it is among the very few that regularly kill its own kind on purpose (in murder or war, for example). How can a personality theory take this aspect of human nature into account? (Freud was one of the few to try.)

3. Is it even possible to employ defense mechanisms consciously, or "on purpose?"

4. Freud proposed his theory of personality near the turn of the century. Now, nearly 100 years later, what might Freud think of his own theory's relevance in today's world?

5. Watson and Skinner never proposed a personality theory as such. How do you suppose either of them would have accounted for mental illness or psychological disorders?

6. Can you generate examples of how each of the "Big Five" dimensions of personality show up in behavior? Can you judge where you fall on each of the five proposed dimensions?

7. What are the major problems with the so-called "personality tests" that we commonly find in magazines and newspapers? For that matter, what (if anything) is "wrong" with the little personality test with which we began this chapter?

8. How can one determine the reliability of a test that measures anxiety if we know that anxiety is a characteristic that is itself very unreliable (i.e., sometimes we are more or less anxious than at other times)?

9. If you were to take the logic of projective techniques seriously, what could you conclude about someone who viewed all of the inkblots in the Rorschach series and said for each card, "It just looks like an inkblot to me."

Summary

▼▼▼▼▼▼▼▼▼▼▼▼▼▼▼▼▼▼▼▼▼▼▼▼▼▼▼

What are the three levels of consciousness proposed by Freud? Freud claimed that at any one time, we were only fully aware or *conscious* of a few things. With a little effort, some ideas or memories can be accessed from our *preconscious,* while others—those in our *unconscious* mind—can only be accessed with great effort. *Page 339*

According to Freud, what are the three structures of personality, and by what principle does each operate? The three structures of personality according to Freud are the inborn, instinctive *id,* operating on the *pleasure principle* and seeking immediate gratification, the *ego,* or sense of self, which operates on the *reality principle,* mediating needs in the context of the real world, and the *superego,* or sense of morality or conscience, which operates on the *idealistic principle,* attempting to direct one to do what is right and proper. *Page 340*

List and define seven defense mechanisms. When aspects of the personality (id, ego, and superego) are in conflict, anxiety may result. To fend off feelings of anxiety, the ego may unconsciously employ one of the many defense mechanisms. *Repression* is motivated forgetting—forcing into the unconscious those ideas, beliefs, or desires that cause us anxiety. *Denial* involves the simple refusal to acknowledge the realities of an anxiety-producing situation. *Rationalization* is the process of making up acceptable excuses for our anxiety-producing behaviors rather than facing their real causes. *Fantasy* is a matter of escaping from anxiety and reality through daydreaming or imagination. *Projection* involves seeing in others those very characteristics that would cause us anxiety if we were to acknowledge them in ourselves. *Regression* amounts to acting in a primitive, childish way—taking on old behaviors that at one time were reinforcing. *Displacement,* usually of aggression, is a matter of directing one's motives or behaviors at some "safe" substitute person or object. *Pages 340–342*

Briefly review Freud's five psychosexual stages of development. Freud believed that one's personality developed through five stages, each with a different sexual/sensual focus: the oral stage (birth to 1 year), the anal stage (age 1–3), the phallic stage (age 3–5), the latency stage (age 6–puberty), and the genital stage (from puberty on). *Pages 342–343*

Briefly summarize the contributions of Adler, Jung, and Horney to the psychoanalytic approach to personality. Adler, Jung, and Horney each parted with Freud on theoretical grounds, while remaining basically psychoanalytic in their orientation. For Adler, social influ-

ences and inferiority complexes mattered much more than Freud's innate drives. Jung was less biological, more positive, and expanded on Freud's view of the unconscious mind, adding the idea of the collective unconscious. Horney also rejected the stress on instinctual impulses and discussed instead the notion of basic anxiety and how one reacts to it as the sculptor of one's personality. *Pages 344–345*

Specify a contribution to the concept of personality contributed by Watson, Skinner, Dollard and Miller, and Bandura. Many psychologists have argued that personality can be approached using basic learning principles and observable behaviors—without reference to "internal" dispositions. Watson first emphasized focusing on behavior and abandoning mental concepts. Dollard and Miller tried to explain personality in terms of learning theory and habit development. Skinner emphasized the notion of the consequences of one's behaviors as molding what one does. Bandura stressed the role of observation and social learning in the formation of personality. *Pages 345–347*

Briefly summarize the humanistic-phenomenological approach to personality as epitomized by Rogers and Maslow. The theories of Rogers and Maslow are alike in several ways, emphasizing the integrity of the self and the power of personal growth and development. Both deny the negativity and biological bias of psychoanalytic theory and the environmental determinism of behaviorism. *Pages 347–348*

What is a personality trait? A personality trait is a characteristic and distinctive way in which one person may differ from others. *Page 349*

What are the major traits that influence personality according to Allport, Cattell, and Eysenck? According to Allport, there are two kinds of traits, *common traits* and *personal traits*—the former found to varying degrees in virtually everyone, the latter specific to some individuals. Cattell also feels that there are two kinds of traits: *surface traits* which are readily observable, and *source traits,* from which surface traits develop. Eysenck believes that personality can be described as an intersection of three major dimensions: *extroversion-introversion, stability-instability,* and *psychoticism.* *Pages 349–351*

What are the Big Five personality dimensions? Recent research in personality trait theory suggests that from all the traits that have been proposed over the years, five emerge most regularly, although there is yet no total agreement on how to name these dimensions. One theorist calls them (1) "extroversion-introversion,"

(2) "agreeableness" or "friendliness," (3) "Will" or "conscientiousness," (4) "stability-instability," and (5) "intelligence." *Page 352*

What are some of the strengths and weaknesses of each of the four approaches to personality that we have discussed? The psychoanalytic approach is the most comprehensive and may be credited with focusing our attention on the importance of early childhood experiences, biological drives, and sexuality. Unfortunately, many of its insights and ideas are scientifically untestable. Behavioral-learning approaches profit from their strict definitions and experimental basis, but lack comprehensiveness. They put what many feel is too much emphasis on the environment as the determiner of one's behaviors. The humanistic-phenomenological approach is quite positive, emphasizing personal growth and development, but many of its concepts are poorly defined and many of its predictions difficult to test. Trait approaches are not really theories, but are descriptions, and as such, they explain little about personality. Although there may be a growing consensus, there is less than perfect agreement on which traits are most important, where they come from, or how they are related. *Pages 352–355*

What are the basic goals of personality assessment? Personality assessment (including testing) is used to make a clinical diagnosis about the presence or nature of a psychological disorder, help build theories of personality based on which traits are important and how they are interrelated, and predict what someone may do in the future. *Pages 356–357*

How are behavioral observations used to assess personality? Conclusions about an individual's personality can be inferred from the observation of that individual's behaviors. Behaviors should be observed in a large number of settings. Observations should be as objective as possible, and may involve the use of behavioral rating scales to check on observer reliability. *Pages 357–358*

Cite one advantage and one disadvantage of the interview as a technique of personality assessment. The major advantage of the interview is its flexibility, allowing the interviewer to pursue avenues of interest and to abandon lines of questioning that are not informative. Unfortunately, there is little research support for the position that interviewing is a valid technique for many of the purposes to which it is put. The more structured the interview, the more valid (generally) the interview. *Pages 358–359*

What does multiphasic mean? In the context of psychological testing, multiphasic instruments attempt to measure a number of different characteristics or traits with the same set of items. *Page 360*

How was the MMPI constructed? The MMPI was designed (in the early 1940s and revised as the MMPI-2 in 1989) as an aid to psychological diagnosis. The test includes items that discriminate between subjects of different diagnostic categories (including "normal"). The test also includes items to assess the extent to which the subject is doing a thorough and honest job of answering the 567 true-false questions of the test. *Page 360*

What can paper-and-pencil tests tell us about personality? Paper-and-pencil tests can serve as useful screening devices to indicate which traits or patterns of traits are likely to be found within an individual. *Pages 359–361*

What is the essence of a projective technique, the Rorschach and TAT in particular? With a projective technique, the assumption is that in responding to an ambiguous stimulus (describing what is indicated in a series of inkblots for the Rorschach, or telling short stories about a set of pictures for the TAT), a subject will *project* conscious and unconscious aspects of his or her self into his or her responses. *Pages 361–362*

10.1 Ideas, thoughts, or memories of which we are not immediately aware, but which we can think about with reasonably little effort are said by Freudians to be stored in our _____ level of awareness. a) immediate b) unconscious c) preconscious d) subconscious. *Page 339*

10.2 Freud would tend to "explain" war and mankind's inhumanity to man in terms of a) thanatos. b) libido. c) wish-fulfillment. d) eros. *Page 339*

10.3 Which aspect of one's personality—according to Freudian theory—operates on a "reality principle"? a) the id b) the ego c) the superego d) each of these operates on a reality principle. *Page 340*

10.4 The aspect or structure of personality that is responsible for feelings of guilt and/or blame is the a) id. b) superego. c) libido. d) ego. *Page 340*

10.5 Seeing in others those motives that would make us anxious if we were to see them in ourselves involves the use of the defense mechanism of a) denial b) suppression c) projection d) displacement. *Page 341*

10.6 Otis doesn't get invited to a party that he really hoped to attend. He soon convinces himself that he "really didn't want to go to that dumb party in the first place." It sounds like Otis is engaging in: a) repression. b) fantasy. c) projection. d) rationalization. *Page 341*

10.7 The stage of Freudian psychosexual development in which sexuality is suppressed or "put on hold" is called the _____ period. a) anal b) latency c) genital d) phallic. *Page 343*

10.8 The neo-Freudians left Freud and devised their own personality theories because they objected to—more than anything else—Freud's heavy emphasis on a) instincts and biological concepts. b) the importance of early childhood. c) parent-child social interactions. d) the notion of levels of consciousness. *Page 344*

10.9 The notion of "moving away" or "moving toward" or "moving against" others is best associated with: a) Freud b) Jung c) Adler d) Horney. *Page 345*

10.10 With which personality theorist do we best associate the concept of "inferiority complex?" a) Charles Spearman b) Carl Jung c) Alfred Adler d) Karen Horney. *Page 344*

10.11 More so than other theorists, psychologists such as Watson, Dollard, Miller, and Skinner tended to talk about personality in terms of a) conscious choices made by people with difficult decisions to make. b) how a person's behaviors could be explained by referring to external, environmental factors. c) personality traits that remained reasonably stable once they were formed. d) cognitive representations of the environment that guide one's behaviors. *Page 345*

10.12 To say that a personality theory takes a phenomenological approach is to say that it tends to emphasize a) instinctive, biological mechanisms. b) how people see themselves and their environments. c) unconscious, unknowable influences. d) learning and conditioning. *Page 347*

10.13 Which term, from Carl Roger's approach to personality, is most similar to Maslow's concept of self-actualization? a) archetype b) unconditioned positive regard c) self-fulfilling prophesy d) to be fully functioning. *Page 348*

10.14 True or False? Unlike Freud, Carl Rogers never engaged in psychotherapy of any sort. *Page 347*

10.15 Personality traits most commonly have been *defined* a) in terms of how personality is related to survival. b) by how someone scores on a personality test. c) to explain individual differences among people. d) in the context of life-span development. *Page 349*

10.16 Factor analysis is largely a _____ technique a) correlational b) experimental c) common sense d) subjective. *Page 350*

10.17 Perhaps the greatest advantage of the trait theories of personality is that they a) give us operational definitions of the terms they use. b) emphasize the importance of early childhood experiences. c) tend to be social or interpersonal in nature. d) are directly related to concepts from the learning laboratory. *Page 349*

10.18 In the context of personality theory, what makes The Big Five so remarkable? a) Five major theorists have agreed on what personality is. b) We can show when one's personality is important and when the situation is important. c) There seems to be a consensus on how to describe personality. d) There are actually five levels of consciousness, not just the three that Freud described. *Page 352*

10.19 True or False? Most trait theories, including the so-called Big Five, do not include intelligence as a personality trait. *Page 352*

10.20 When assessing personality, interviews are most useful when they are a) spontaneous and free-flowing b) highly structured c) as unlike psychological tests as possible d) conducted by someone who knows the individual being interviewed. *Page 359*

10.21 To say that a test such as the MMPI-2 is "criterion referenced" implies that a) questions do not have right or wrong answers. b) people from different groups respond to items differently. c) the test has been designed to predict who is likely to suffer mental illness in the future. d) test scores have been factor analyzed. *Page 360*

10.22 As opposed to intellectual assessment, personality assessment a) seldom uses psychological tests. b) attempts to measure you at your best. c) is used to predict behavior. d) measures one's usual, or typical behaviors. *Page 356*

10.23 True or False? Both the Rorschach and the TAT are projective tests. *Pages 361–362*

Stress and Health

▲▲▲▲▲▲▲ _____

—It's Friday afternoon and you have a chance to get away for the weekend with friends. Unfortunately, you have two big exams scheduled for Monday and need the weekend to study.

—I put 50¢ in the vending machine, expecting to get a cup of coffee. The paper cup comes down the chute upside-down, and my coffee runs down the drain.

—Cindy and Jerry have known each other since grade school. They dated throughout high school and college. Next week, family and friends will join in the celebration of their wedding.

—The Dean has to make a decision. If she chooses Plan A, the faculty may be outraged. If she opts for Plan B, the student body may stage protest demonstrations. If she does nothing, she may lose her job.

—Doug wants to make the basketball team, but the coach informs him that, in spite of his best efforts, he's just too short to make the team.

—Marion has learned that the lump she discovered in her breast last week is, in fact, a small but operable cancerous tumor.

—Joanne has enough change with her to buy one single-dip ice cream cone. When she walked into the store she wanted cherry-vanilla. Now that she sees that the flavor-of-the-month is "Fresh Peach," she can't make up her mind which flavor she wants.

—After 11 years on the road as a salesman, Mike is being promoted to District Sales Manager—an office job with a substantial raise in pay.

—For the first time in his life, Jim is standing on the high diving board. He wants to dive (or jump) to impress his friends, but now that he's up there, he realizes just how high that diving board really is. There's no way he'll climb back down the ladder.

—Three-year-old Mindy keeps asking her mother for a cookie. Mother steadfastly refuses because it's almost dinner time. Mindy returns to her room and promptly pulls an arm off her favorite doll.

—You are late for class, driving down a two-lane road, when someone pulls out in front of you and then drives along 10 miles an hour below the speed limit.

—Christmas vacation is coming.

—It's raining.

Life is filled with stress, frustration, and conflict. This list provides only a very small sample of different types of stress, frustration, and conflict that we often encounter on a daily basis. We'll return to these examples later in the chapter. In this chapter we'll see where stress comes from, and how we may respond to it. We'll explore the relationships between psychological stress and the state of our physical health.

▶ Preview

In this chapter, we'll discuss stress and the role of psychological factors as they affect our physical health or well-being. This discussion flows very naturally from the issues we've raised in the last two chapters. Chapter 9 dealt with motivation and emotion. We'll now see that stress is very much like an emotion—it involves both physiological reactions and unpleasant feelings, or affect. Stress is also like a motivator—people who experience stress are motivated to do something to deal with its sources. Chapter 10 dealt with human personality. Stress is so common, so pervasive, that we may argue that knowing how someone handles the stress in their life can tell us a great deal about the kind of person they are.

Our exploration of stress will be divided into two major sections. First, we'll consider several common stressors, or sources of stress. Then, we'll examine the complex patterns of responses we make when we are under stress. It will be clear by the end of this discussion that psychologists care about stress for the same reason that most people do: Stress is central to our life experience.

An issue of considerable interest in psychology is the extent to which stress produces negative consequences for one's physical health. Exploring this issue will provide us with an opportunity to look at a rapidly growing field of psychology called health psychology. In general, health psychologists are trying to understand the relationships among psychological variables and physical health. There are several related issues we could examine here. We'll choose two: (1) Is there a relationship between our behaviors, thoughts, and feelings and our state of physical health? (2) What role can psychologists play in improving our physical health?

▶ Stressors: The Causes of Stress

As we have so often in previous chapters, let's begin with some definitions. First, just what *is* stress? In truth, psychologists have struggled with the conceptualization of stress for nearly 60 years—and the issue is far from settled (Hobfoll, 1989). We will define **stress** as a complex set of reactions made by an individual under pressure to adapt. In other words, stress is a response made to a perceived threat to one's well-being. There are physiological reactions and unpleasant feelings (distress/discomfort) associated with stress.

There are many circumstances or events that can produce stress in our lives. The sources or stimuli for stress are called **stressors**. In this section, we will consider three types of stressors: frustration, conflict, and life events. In each case, we'll provide examples, some of which you may view as being quite trivial. I've chosen to include such examples as a reminder that stress is not necessarily a response to some overwhelming, catastrophic event, such as the death of a loved one. An important theme throughout this discussion is that stress is unavoidable. We all have experienced stress in our lives, albeit to varying degrees. Once we've seen where stress may come from, we'll consider different techniques and mechanisms that people use to cope with it.

▶ Frustration-induced Stress

Let us begin with an assumption: *All behavior is goal-directed.* In a way, this means that all behavior is motivated. In all of our behaviors, we are pushed or pulled toward positive goals and away from negative goals.

stress a complex pattern of reactions to real or perceived threats to one's sense of well-being that motivates adjustment

stressors real or perceived threats to one's sense of well-being; sources of stress

▲ We experience frustration when our progress toward a goal is blocked or thwarted. Being caught in a traffic jam is an example of environmental frustration.

frustration a stressor, the blocking or thwarting of goal-directed behavior

Figure 11.1

▲ A depiction of frustration. A person's goal-directed behavior is being blocked or thwarted.

Note that there are some assumptions that we are *not* making here. We are not willing to assume, for example, that you can always tell what goals are directing your behavior. In a real sense, you may not know. I may ask you why you did something: "What was the goal for that behavior?" Your honest answer may be, "I really don't know." But just because you're not able to tell me about the goals that direct your behaviors does not mean that our basic assumption that there *is* a goal or reason is wrong.

Another reality about goals and behavior is that it is often difficult to infer one from the other. That is, people may engage in exactly the same behaviors but for very different reasons—to reach different goals. Many students have registered for a course in introductory psychology this term. Why? In order to reach what goal? There may be as many goals as there are students in your class. It also is true that many people share the same goal, but engage in a variety of different behaviors in order to reach it. A goal for many people is "acquiring lots of money." To reach this end, some work very hard, some enroll in college classes, some rob gas stations, while some try to "marry money," and so on.

A second assumption we make is this: *Organisms don't always reach all of their goals.* Have you always gotten everything you've ever wanted? Have you always been able to avoid unpleasantness, pain, or sorrow? Do you know anyone who has?

Sometimes we are totally prohibited from ever reaching a particular goal. At other times our progress may be slower or more difficult than we would like. In either case, we are being frustrated. **Frustration**, then, is the blocking of goal-directed behavior, which may be total and permanent or partial and temporary (see Figure 11.1).

Seen in this way, the stress that results from frustration is a normal, commonplace reaction. Frustration is a stressor, and the stress it produces is a fact of life. The stress that results from frustration does not imply weakness, pathology, or illness. What matters is how individuals react to the stressors in their lives. Before we consider reactions to frustration, let's look at some of the varieties of frustration.

To someone who feels the stress that results from frustration, the actual source of that stress may be of little consequence. However, in order to respond adaptively to frustration-induced stress, it is helpful to be able to recognize the source of the blocking—the particular stressor—that is keeping us from our goals. There are two types of frustration: environmental and personal.

Environmental frustration implies that the blocking or thwarting of goal-directed behavior is being done by something or by somebody in the environment. (We should talk about the *source* or origin of frustration, not *fault* or *blame*, which are evaluative terms. All we are trying to do here is describe, not judge.)

Remember the example of my losing 50¢ in a coffee vending machine? This is a simple type of environmental frustration. I want a cup of coffee. My goal-directed behavior leads me to slip two quarters into the coin slot. Something in my environment—a piece of faulty machinery—interferes and keeps me from reaching my goal. You want to be outside at a picnic, but it's raining. As a result, you may experience stress because your goal-directed behavior is being thwarted by your environment.

Remember three-year-old Mindy? She wants a cookie, but her mother says, "No, it's almost suppertime." Mindy also is being frustrated by her environment, but in a slightly different way. She wants a cookie, and her mother is blocking that motivated behavior. This type of environmental frustration, in which the source of the blocking is another person, is usually called "social frustration."

Occasionally we are frustrated not because someone or something in our environment is blocking progress toward our goals, but because of some more internal or personal reason. This is *personal frustration*. Doug fails to make the basketball team simply because he is too short. Someone wanting to be a concert pianist may be frustrated in her attempts to do so because she happens to have short, stubby fingers and can only reach half an octave on the piano keyboard. She may learn to be a good pianist, but she probably won't make it in the world of classical piano. Her frustration and resulting stress is not the fault of people who write piano music or build piano keyboards. Her failure to play some piano music is certainly not her fault, but if she persists in this goal-directed behavior, she will be frustrated, and the source of her frustration will be more personal than environmental. Some of us are learning that getting older can be stressful. We are frustrated when we have difficulty doing things that at one time we were able to do easily. The stress we experience is frustration-induced, and the type of frustration is personal.

Before You Go On

▼▼▼▼▼▼▼▼▼

What is meant by frustration-induced stress?

Define environmental and personal frustration, citing an example of each.

▶ *Conflict-induced Stress*

Sometimes we are unable to satisfy a particular drive or motive because it is in **conflict** with other motives that are influencing us at the same time. Thus, stress may result not from frustration caused by the blocking of our goal-directed behaviors, but from conflicts within our own motivational system.

With motivational conflicts, there is the implication of a decision or a choice that has to be made. Sometimes the decision is easy to make, and the resulting stress will be slight; sometimes decision making is very difficult, and the resulting stress will be greater. When discussing conflict, it is useful to talk about positive goals or incentives we wish to approach and negative goals or incentives we wish to avoid. Let's look at some stress-inducing motivational conflicts.

(1) Approach-approach Conflicts. Conflicts are necessarily unpleasant and produce stress; they will be so even when the goals involved are positive and sought after. In an approach-approach conflict, an organism is caught between two (or more) alternatives, both of them are potentially reinforcing (see Figure 11.2). If the subject chooses alternative A, he or she will reach a desired goal. If B is chosen, a different desirable goal will be attained. What makes this a conflict is that *both* alternatives are not available. It has to be one or the other. A choice has to be made.

Once an approach-approach conflict is resolved, the subject ends up with some desired goal no matter which alternative is chosen. In the opening example, Joanne in the ice cream shop trying to decide which flavor to buy is in an approach-approach conflict. Typical of conflict, we'll probably see some vacillation in Joanne's behavior, some swaying back and forth between alternatives. But we can assume that this conflict will be resolved with a choice, and Joanne will at least walk out of the store with an ice

conflict a stressor in which some goals can be satisfied only at the expense of other goals

Figure 11.2

▲ *A diagram of an approach-approach conflict. Here, the subject is faced with two (or more) positive, attractive goals and must chose from among them.*

Figure 11.3

▲ An avoidance-avoidance conflict. Here, the subject is faced with two (or more) negative, unattractive goals, and one must be chosen. This is a no-win situation.

cream cone of some flavor she likes. Her life might have been easier (less stressful) if the store provided just one flavor in the first place and she didn't have to make such choices, but she'll contemplate that possibility with an ice cream cone in hand.

Sometimes the choices that we are called upon to make are much more serious than those involving ice cream cones. What will be your college major? On the one hand, you'd like to go to medical school and be a surgeon (a positive goal). On the other hand, you'd like to cultivate your aptitude for music and study composition and conducting at a school of music (also a positive incentive). At the moment, you cannot do both. The courses that you would take as a pre-med student are quite different from those you'd take if you were to follow music as a career path. Both avenues are constructive, desirable alternatives; but now, at registration, you have to make a choice, one that may have long-lasting repercussions. The nature and consequences of such a conflict qualifies it as a stressor.

(2) Avoidance-avoidance Conflicts. Perhaps the most stressful of all conflicts are the avoidance-avoidance conflicts (Figure 11.3). In this type of conflict, a person is faced with a number of alternatives, and each of them is negative or in some way punishing. No matter which way one turns, he or she is going to "get burned." Here's where the example of the college Dean comes in. No matter what course of action she chooses, someone is going to be unhappy—yet she has to choose. To be in an avoidance-avoidance conflict is, in a way, to be boxed in so that no matter what you do, the result will be punishing.

This sort of conflict is not at all unusual in the workplace. Imagine that you are a supervisor in charge of a reasonably large department. Word comes down from management that you must cut your operating budget by 20 percent by next month. There *are* ways that you can reduce expenses—limit travel, cut down on supplies, reduce pay, eliminate a few positions—but each involves an action you'd rather not take. The result is stress, and the stressor is an avoidance-avoidance conflict.

(3) Approach-avoidance Conflicts. With approach-avoidance conflicts, a subject is in the position of considering only one goal, or one possibility (Figure 11.4). What makes this situation a conflict is that the person would very much like to reach that goal, but, at the same time, would very much like not to. It's a matter of "Yes, I'd love to. . . .Well, as a matter of fact, I'd rather not. . . . Well, maybe I would. . . . No, I wouldn't . . . yes . . . no." Consider the possibility of entering into a relationship with someone you think of as special. On the one hand, such a relationship might turn out to be wonderful and rewarding. On the other hand, initiating such a relationship might put you in the position of being hurt and rejected. Typical of conflict in general, what we see in these conflicts is vacillation, swinging back and forth between options—motivated to approach and at the same time motivated to avoid. My opening example of Jim on the high diving board was meant to suggest this type of conflict.

Figure 11.4

▲ A simple approach-avoidance conflict. Here, the subject is faced with but one goal. What puts the subject in conflict is that the goal has both positive and negative features.

It's easy to see how we might set up such a conflict situation for a rat. In fact, Brown (1948) and Miller (1959) have demonstrated all of these conflicts using rats rather than humans. For an approach-avoidance conflict, we'd place a nice, attractive pile of food at the end of a runway. We also would arrange to shock the runway floor around the food. A hungry rat on that runway would be in a true approach-avoidance conflict. It would want to get to the end of the runway to get the food, but it also would want to avoid that same end to avoid getting shocked. What will the rat do in this situation? It will run back and forth, toward the food and away from the shock, eventually settling down somewhere in the middle of the runway. As it gets hungrier (and the food becomes more positive), it

Stressors: The Causes of Stress ▲ **373**

Figure 11.5

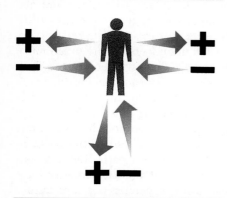

▲ A multiple approach-avoidance conflict. Here, the subject is faced with a number of alternative goals, each of which has positive and negative characteristics, and a choice must be made.

will again move toward the food, get shocked and retreat. Back and forth it goes again, this time settling down in the runway somewhat closer to the food than when it stopped before.

You and I usually try not to get into approach-avoidance conflicts in the first place. We generally try to arrange things to "keep our options open," so that we are not faced with just one option.

(4) Multiple Approach-avoidance Conflicts. The type of conflict most commonly found among adult humans is the multiple approach-avoidance conflict (see Figure 11.5). As its name implies, this type of conflict arises when an individual is faced with a number of alternatives, each one of which is in some way positive and in some way negative at the same time.

Perhaps you and some friends are out shopping on a Saturday morning. You suddenly discover that it's getting late and you're all hungry. Where will you go to lunch? You may have a multiple approach-avoidance conflict here. "We could go to Bob's Diner, where the food is cheap and the service is fast, but the food is terrible. Or we could go to Cafe Olé, where the food is better, but service is a little slower, and the food is more expensive. Or we could go to The Grill, where the service is elegant and the food superb, but the price is very high." Granted this is not an earth-shaking dilemma, but in each case there is a plus and a minus to be considered in making the choice. The more difficult the choice, and the more important or valued the goal, the greater the induced stress.

Life is filled with such conflicts, and some of them can be severe and very stressful. They may very well encompass questions of the "What shall I do with the rest of my life?" sort. "Should I stay at home with the children (+ and –), or should I have a career (+ and –)?" "Should I attend University X`(+ and –), or should I go to College Y (+ and –)?" "Should I get married or stay single, or is there another way (again, + and – in each case)?" "Should I work for Company A (+ and –), or should I work for Company B (+ and –)?" Quite clearly, lists like this could go on and on. You might want to reflect on the conflicts you have faced during the past few weeks. You should be able to categorize each of them into one of the four types we have listed here.

Before You Go On

▼▼▼▼▼▼▼▼

Name and describe four types of motivational conflict.

▶ Life-induced Stress

It is clear that frustration and conflict are potent sources of stress in our lives and are often unavoidable consequences of being a motivated organism. Psychologists have attempted also to deal with sources of stress that do not fit neatly into our descriptions of either frustration or conflict. One useful approach has been to look at certain events and changes in life as potential sources of stress.

In 1967, Holmes and Rahe published their first version of the *Social Readjustment Rating Scale,* or *SRRS* (see also Holmes & Holmes, 1970). The basic idea behind this scale is that stress results whenever life situations change. The scale provides subjects with a list of life events that might be potentially stressful. The original list of such events was drawn from the reports of patients suffering from moderate to high levels of stress in their lives. Marriage was arbitrarily assigned a value of 50 stress points (called

▲ *Many of our life experiences are stressors—some more so than others.*

life change units). With "marriage" = 50 as their guide, the subjects rated a number of other more-or-less typical life changes in terms of the amount of stress they might provide. "Death of a spouse" got the highest rating (100 units), followed by "divorce" (with 73 units). "Pregnancy" (40 units, or rating points), "trouble with the boss" (23 units), "changing to a new school" (20 units), and "minor violations of the law" (11 units) are some of the other stress-inducing life change events on the scale. In a rather direct way, the SRRS gives us a way to measure the stress in our lives.

There is a positive correlation between scores on the SRRS and the incidence of physical illness and disease (Rahe & Arthur, 1978). People with scores between 200 and 299 have a 50-50 chance of developing symptoms of physical illness within the next two years. *Eighty* percent of those with scores above 300 develop physical symptoms within the same time period. The logic is that stress predisposes one to physical illness, particularly cardiovascular disorders. But we must remember what we said in Chapter 1 about correlations: They do not tell us about cause and effect. After all, some of the SRRS items themselves are related to physical illness or are in some way health-related. It may not be much of a surprise, then, to find scores on this scale correlated to levels of physical illness. (We'll return to this discussion of the relationships between stress and physical health later in this chapter.)

Richard Lazarus (1981) argues that we ought to focus more attention on causes of stress that are less dramatic than big life changes as the death of a family member or marriage. What often matters most are life's little hassles—the traffic that goes too slowly, the toothpaste tube that splits, ants at a picnic, the cost of a pizza compared to what it was just a few years ago, and so on. Part of Lazarus's argument is that big crises or major life change events often are too large to have a direct impact on us. What may cause us to feel stressed are the ways in which these big events produce little changes in our lives (hassles). Being retired may mean a lack of access to friendly conversation at coffee break time. A spouse who starts to work may make life a little more difficult; the other spouse may have to cook dinner for the first time. Thus, stress results not so much from the event itself, but from the minor hassles it creates.

Notice that to be stressful, events in our lives do not have to be in themselves negative. Many events that we look forward to, that we judge to be changes for the better can bring with them many of the hassles associated with stress. We listed two such examples at the beginning of the chapter. Everybody is happy about Cindy and Jerry getting married, no doubt a pleasant, positive life event. But at the same time—as anyone who has ever gone through the process will attest—weddings can be stressors. If they invite Aunt Sarah, does that mean that they have to invite Aunt Louise? Cindy and Jerry are planning an outdoor reception. What if it rains? What if the caterer misjudged the number of eggrolls that people will eat? Mike has been a salesman for 11 years. He is used to the freedom of setting his own hours. What will the promotion to District Sales Manager mean in terms of his daily routine?

Another view of stress in our daily lives (Hobfoll, 1988; 1989) claims that stressors are perceived threats to our "resources." Resources are those objects, personal characteristics, conditions, or energies that we value; that we work to keep and save. The basic supposition is that people strive to retain, protect, and build resources. When environmental events (stressors) threaten status, position in the community, economic stability, loved ones, home, or possessions (examples of resources), the result is stress. An interesting aspect of this position is that we may expect to experience stress even when our present resources are not being threatened. Stress also can result from our inability to acquire and save new resources.

▶ Reacting to Stressors

So far we have defined stress and reviewed a number of potential stressors —frustration, conflict, and life events that involve making changes. Now we need to consider what someone might do when he or she experiences stress. We often hear about people trying to "cope with the stress in their lives." Consistent with the terminology we're using in this topic, it would be more correct to speak of "coping with, or dealing with, the *stressors* in one's life." Remember, stress is a reaction to stressors (frustration, conflict or life events). Stress may motivate us, but it motivates us to do something about the perceived threats to our well-being that are stressors.

Before we go any further, there is an important point that we must note. As with so many other things, there are large individual differences in response to stressors. What constitutes a stressor, and what someone may do when he or she experiences stress, vary considerably from person to person. Some people fall apart at weddings; others don't find them stressful at all. For some people, even simple choices are difficult to make; for others, choices are not enough—they seek challenges. Indeed, some people seem so generally resistant to the negative aspects of stress that they have been labeled as having *"hardy personalities."* These hardy types typically have an optimistic outlook on life, feel in control of their own destinies, and see stressful situations as opportunities for personal growth (*e.g.,* Kobasa, 1979; 1982; Maddi & Kobasa, 1984). The variability in stress levels that we see among different people usually can be found within any one person at different times. You know this from your own experience. On one day, being caught in slow-moving traffic may drive you up the wall. In the very same situation a few days later, you find that you couldn't care less. So we need to remember that reactions to stressors vary from time to time and from person to person.

Having said all that, I need to make another general point about dealing with stressful situations: Some responses are more effective or adaptive than others. Adaptive or effective responses are strategies that deal with stressors in a way that will ultimately reduce the experience of stress. To think that one can *avoid* stress altogether is probably unrealistic. A certain amount of stress in our lives is natural and to be expected. Stress often follows as a natural consequence of being alive and motivated in the real world. What may be unfortunate and distressing is that we occasionally develop poor, ineffective strategies for dealing with the stress we experience. Ineffective or maladaptive responses to stressors are reactions that in the long run will be unsuccessful in reducing stress. Let's start with a discussion of how one might react to stress adaptively.

▶ Coping with Stressors Effectively

One of the most effective ways of dealing with stress is to make relatively permanent changes in behavior as a result of the experience of stress. You'll recall that we defined learning as a relatively permanent change in behavior that occurs as the result of practice or experience. This response makes particularly good sense for frustration-induced stress. Here, our

Figure 11.6

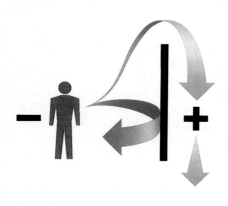

▲ *Reacting to frustration with learning. If progress toward a positive goal (or away from a negative goal) is blocked, one can learn a new route to reach the same goal, or one can learn to modify the goal so that it can be attained.*

▲ If we were never challenged, if we never set difficult goals, if we never faced stressful situations, we would miss out on many opportunities for personal growth and learning.

path to a goal is being blocked or thwarted. An adaptive way to handle such a situation is to find a new way to reach our goal or to learn to modify our goal.

In fact, much of our everyday learning is motivated by frustration-induced stress. We have learned many new responses as a means of coping with frustration. Let's look at a few imaginary examples. Having been frustrated once (or twice) by locking yourself out of your house or car, you have learned to hide a second set of keys somewhere where you can easily find them. Having been denied promotion because you didn't have a college degree, you are learning about general psychology on the way toward earning such a degree. Having been caught at home in a blizzard with no cookies in the house, you learned to bake them yourself. Having discovered that you're too short to make the basketball team, you learned to play tennis. As a child, you may have learned to get what you wanted from your parents by smiling and asking politely. In each of these cases, what prompted or motivated the learning of new responses or the establishing of new goals was stress resulting from frustration.

Learning motivated by stress also may have taught you the value of escape and avoidance. You know how to avoid getting into many motivational conflicts. You try to plan things to keep your options open, so as not to get into avoidance-avoidance or approach-avoidance conflicts in the first place. You may have learned that the only sensible thing to do once you are in such a conflict is to escape or to make major changes in what is motivating you. This is one way in which stress can be seen as a positive force in our lives. If we were never challenged, if we never set difficult goals, if we never faced stressful situations, we would miss out on many opportunities for personal growth and learning. The stress we experience might be unpleasant at the time, but it may produce positive consequences.

To say that we should respond to stressful situations by learning new, more effective behaviors is sensible enough, but are there any specific measures we can take to help alleviate the unpleasantness of stress in our lives? Yes, there are many. A few of the more useful strategies for dealing with life's stressors are described briefly in the Psychology in the Real World section (see pp. 380–381).

Now let's consider some other reactions that stress may produce that are not so adaptive.

Before You Go On

▼▼▼▼▼▼▼▼▼

What are some adaptive ways of dealing with stress?

▶ Dealing with Stressors Ineffectively

Logic tells us that if one experiences stress and does *not* do any of the things we've just mentioned, then that person is not dealing effectively with the stressors of life. Not to change is to *fixate*, to keep accepting the same stress from the same stressor over and over. Fixation is seldom an adequate reaction to stress. Don't get me wrong here. "If at first you don't succeed, try, try, again." Why, of course, this is sound advice. But, again, and again, and again? At some point one must be able to give up a particular course of action to try something else. In addition to not changing one's behavior, there are two other relatively common reactions to stressors that are maladaptive: aggression and anxiety.

▲ Acts of aggression are usually unhelpful but are common reactions to frustration.

frustration-aggression hypotheses the view (now discredited) that all aggression stems from frustration

It is clear that there are many causes of aggression and that one thing that motivates aggressive behavior is stress, particularly the stress that results from frustration. At one time, it was proposed that frustration was *the* only cause of aggression, the so-called **frustration-aggression hypothesis** (Dollard, et al., 1939). This point of view claimed that frustration could produce a number of reactions, including aggression, but that aggression always is caused by frustration. We are now aware that there *are* other sources of aggression (some view it as innate or instinctive, while others see it as a response learned through reinforcement or modeling); however, it is true that frustration remains a prime candidate as the cause of a great deal of aggression. It doesn't do much good in the long run, but a flash of aggressive behavior often follows stress (Berkowitz, 1978; 1982; 1989; 1990).

There you are in the parking lot, trying to get home from class, and your car won't start. Over and over you crank the ignition. Frustrated, you swing open your door, get out, kick the front left fender, throw up the hood, and glower at the engine. Having released a bit of tension, you might feel better for a few seconds, but being angry and kicking at the car (or yelling at someone who offers to assist) won't help you solve your problem.

Another debilitating consequence of stress is *anxiety*—a general feeling of tension, apprehension, and dread, which involves predictable physiological changes. Anxiety is a very difficult concept to define precisely, but everyone "knows" what you're talking about when you refer to anxiety. It is a reaction that we all have experienced. Often, it is a reaction that follows or accompanies stress. In many ways we can think of anxiety as an unpleasant emotional component of the stress response. As much as anything else, we want to rid ourselves of stress in order to minimize our anxiety.

Sometimes, the amount of stress and anxiety in one's life becomes more than one can cope with effectively. Then, feelings of anxiety start to interfere with natural, normal adaptation to the environment and to other people. Feelings of anxiety may become the primary focus of one's attention. More anxiety follows, and more distress, and more discomfort, and more pain. For many people—perhaps tens of millions of people in the U. S. and Canada—the anxiety that results from the stress in their lives is so discomforting and so maladaptive that we may say that they are suffering from an anxiety-based psychological disorder. In our next chapter we begin our discussion of psychological disorders (sometimes called "mental illness") and we'll start with the anxiety-based disorders. Please try to keep in mind when you get to that discussion just how commonplace stress and anxiety are.

Before You Go On
▼▼▼▼▼▼▼▼

What are some maladaptive reactions to stressors?

What is the frustration-aggression hypothesis?

▶ Stress as a Physiological Reaction: Selye's GAS

No matter how we ultimately cope with stress, there is little doubt that stressors produce a series of physiological reactions. In this way, stress is much like any other reaction to emotion-producing stimuli in our environments. When we are under stress, a demand is made on the physiological systems of the body, and that demand can be interpreted as a real and often persistent challenge to a person's well-being.

Figure 11.7

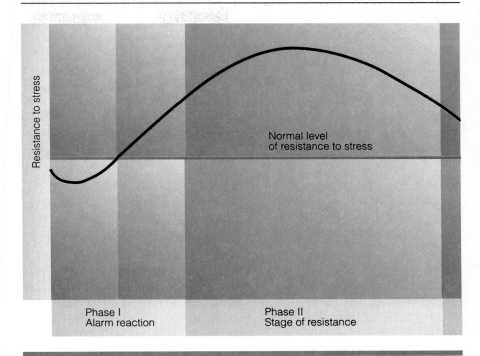

Phase I
Alarm reaction

Phase II
Stage of resistance

▲ *The general adaptation syndrome (GAS), shown in the diagram above, graphically illustrates the individual's general response to stress. In the first phase (alarm reaction), the organism shows an initial lowered resistance to stress or shock. If the stress persists, the organism shows a defensive reaction or resistance (resistance phase) in an attempt to adapt to stress. Following extensive exposure to stress, the energy necessary for adaptation may be exhausted, resulting in the final stage of the GAS— (collapse phase).*

general adaptation syndrome (GAS) a pattern of physiological reactions to stress, producing alarm to resistance and exhaustion

The most widely accepted description of the physiological reactions to stressors is described in Hans Selye's **general adaptation syndrome,** or **GAS.** According to Selye (1956; 1974) the pattern of reaction to stressors occurs in three stages: alarm, resistance, and exhaustion (see Figure 11.7).

The first response to the perception of a stressful situation is *alarm.* A perceived threat produces rapid and noticeable changes in the sympathetic division of the autonomic nervous system. Consistent with changes that take place when we are emotional, the sympathetic system directly or indirectly causes an increase in blood pressure and heart rate, pupillary dilation, a cessation of digestion, and a rerouting of the blood supply to the extremities of the body. The adrenal glands secrete norepinephrine into the bloodstream and mobilize the body's resources, providing increased levels of blood sugar. All of these reactions are similar to those we experience in any emotional situation. (Perhaps you recall from Chapter 9 [p. 327] our discussion of the reactions that are likely if one were to run across a wild bear in the woods.)

This strong, even dramatic, reaction cannot last very long. We usually can maintain high levels of sympathetic activity for no more than several minutes, a few hours at the most.

Let's start an illustrative example. Imagine Pam, in the midst of a very important semester. Pam is strongly motivated to do well in all her courses. It is just past midterms and she gets word from home that her father has had

Psychology in the Real World

Eight Strategies for Coping with Stress

We've seen that it is unrealistic to think that we can totally avoid all of the stressors that we might encounter in our daily lives. But that does not mean that there is nothing that we can do to combat the negative fallout of stress. Indeed, there are several specific steps that we can take. Here we'll review eight such strategies.

1. Identify the stressor. Remember that stress is a reaction to any one of several different types of stressors. If you are experiencing stress in your life, where is it coming from? Are you having difficulty resolving a motivational conflict? Just what positive and/or negative goals are involved? Is your goal-directed behavior being blocked or thwarted? Just what is the source of your frustration? What recent changes or events in your life are particularly problematic or upsetting? Any successful strategy for coping with stress will require some change—and effort—on your part. The first thing to do is to see to it that your effort is well directed.

2. Remove or negate the stressor. Once a stressor has been identified, the next logical question is, "Can anything be done about it?" Do we *have* to stay in this situation, or can we bring about a change? If, for example, a particular interpersonal relationship has become a constant, nagging source of stress, might this be the time to consider breaking off the relationship? If the stress you experience at work has become overwhelming, might this be a good time to consider a change of jobs? The issue here is one of taking control, of trying to turn a challenge into an opportunity. Even those people faced with a terminal illness fare much better if they take control; find out everything there is to know about their illness; seek second and third opinions; make the most of whatever time they have left, and so on (Folkman, 1984).

3. Reappraise the situation. At the very least, we should try to assess whether the stressors in our lives are real or (even partially) imagined threats to our well-being. Making this sort of determination is part of what is called a *cognitive reappraisal* of one's situation (*e.g.,* Schulz & Decker, 1985). In the context of stress management, cognitive reappraisal means a rethinking of a situation to put it in the best possible light. Is that coworker *really* trying to do you out of a promotion? Do you *really* care if you get invited to that party? *Must* you earn an A on the next test in order to pass the course? Are things *really* as bad as they may seem? Meichenbaum (1977) argues that we can deal with a lot of stress simply by talking to ourselves, replacing negative statements (such as, "Oh, I'm in trouble now. I'm sure to be called on and I'll embarrass myself in front of the whole class") with coping statements (such as, "I'll just do the best I can. I'm as prepared as anyone in here, and in a little while this will all be over"). This cognitive approach does take a bit of practice, but it can be very effective.

4. Inoculate against future stressors. This strategy involves truly accepting and internalizing much of what we have been saying about the universality of stress and stressors. It's a matter of convincing yourself that stress has occurred before, will occur again, and that this too will pass. It's a matter of anticipation and preparation. We know, for example, that surgery patients recover faster and with fewer post-surgical complications if they are fully informed *before their surgery* of what they can expect, how they are likely to feel, and (importantly) what they can do to aid in their own recovery (*e.g.,* MacDonald & Kuiper, 1983).

a massive heart attack. She leaves school, drives straight home—a 16-hour drive—and rushes to the hospital. Her father never has been seriously ill before; now he's in coronary intensive care. The shock and disbelief are nearly overwhelming during Pam's alarm stage reaction.

In *resistance,* the second stage of the general adaptation syndrome, the stressor remains present, and resistance to the stressor remains above normal levels. Pam's father begins to show some signs of recovery, but will be in intensive care for at least another week and will be hospitalized well beyond that. There's little Pam can do to help her father, but she feels that she can't

5. Engage in physical exercise. There is a growing body of evidence that physical exercise is a useful agent in the battle against stress (Crews & Landers, 1987; McCann & Holmes, 1984; Wheeler & Frank, 1988). It is sometimes difficult to say if physical exercise combats stress directly, or if it does so indirectly by improving physical health, stamina, self-esteem, and self-confidence. And of course, one must be careful. Deciding that tomorrow you'll start running five miles each day, rain or shine, may be a decision that in itself will create more stress than it will reduce. One needs to choose an exercise program that is enjoyable, that is not overly strenuous, and that helps one feel better about oneself.

6. Learn techniques of relaxation. Dealing with stress successfully may also entail learning how to relax. Learning effective relaxation techniques may not be as easy as it sounds, and may take some time and effort. The logic is simple: Feeling stressed and being relaxed are incompatible responses. If you can learn to become totally relaxed, the experience of stress will be diminished (*e.g.*, Lehrer & Woolfolk, 1984). Hypnosis may help. Meditation may help (see our discussion of these issues in Chapter 5). A variety of operant conditioning called **biofeedback** can provide relief from the tension associated with stress (Kamiya, et al., 1977; Kimmel, 1967; Yates, 1980). Biofeedback is "the process of providing information to an individual about his [or her] bodily processes in some form which he [or she] might be able to use to modify those processes" (Hill, 1985, p. 201). One's heart rate, let us say, is constantly monitored, and the rate is fed back to the subject, perhaps in the form of an audible tone. As heart rate increases, the pitch of the tone becomes higher and higher. With a lowering heart rate, the pitch becomes lower and lower. Once the learner knows (through the feedback) what his or her heart rate (or blood pressure, or muscle tension, etc.) is doing, a certain degree of control over that response is possible. The reinforcement involved here usually is just the newly gained knowledge that a desired change is being made. As a result of being reinforced, these stress-fighting responses increase in their rate or frequency (Kaplan, 1991; Kimmel, 1974; Miller, 1978; Thackwray-Emmerson, 1989).

7. Take your time with important decisions. Stress often accompanies the process of making tough decisions. You're frustrated. Some goal-directed behavior is being blocked. Now you have to decide if you'll pursue some other course of action. Which course of action? Or would it be wiser simply to change your goal? Remember we virtually define motivational conflict in terms of difficult decisions. Do you want to do this (+ and –), or do you want to do that (+ and –)? All we are implying with this strategy is that we sometimes make matter worse by rushing to make a decision "just to have it over with." Occasionally we are faced with deadlines by which final decisions must be made. But in many cases, we add to already stressful situations by racing to conclusions before we have all the facts, before we have explored all of the costs and benefits associated with the alternatives we are contemplating (*e.g.*, Hogan, 1989). For example, if really can't make up your mind about a new car you're thinking about buying, why not spend the time and the money now to rent one for a day or two to see if you'll be happy with it in the long run?

8. Seek social support. Finally, I should mention the advantage of social support for persons who are experiencing stress. Stress is a common phenomenon. Perhaps no one else knows precisely how you feel, or has experienced exactly the situation in which you find yourself, but all of us have known stress, and we are all aware of the kinds of situations that give rise to it, and how upsetting it can be. Social support, from friends and relatives if possible, from others such as physicians, clergypersons, therapists, or counselors if need be, can be very helpful (Coyne & Downey, 1991; Gottlieb, 1981; Hobfoll, 1986; Janis, 1983; Leiberman, 1983; Rook, 1987). If at all possible, one should not face stress alone.

leave to go back to school right now. Every day that she stays home, she gets farther behind in her classes.

Pam's bodily resources were mobilized in the alarm stage of the GAS. Now she's discovered that there is no means of lessening or escaping the source of her stress. The drain on her body's resources continues. If other stressors appear, Pam will be less able to deal with them effectively. She will become vulnerable to physical illness and infection to a greater degree than she would be without the constant stress she is experiencing. Her internal, sympathetic response *seems* to return to near normal, but Pam's physiological systems continue to try to resist and mobilize bodily reserves. High blood pressure, ulcers, skin rashes, or respiratory difficulties may develop. In the resistance stage of the GAS a person is more susceptible to a range of physical problems from the common cold to cancer. Pam may appear to be in control, but the reality of her father's condition and the approach of her final exams continue to eat away at her, intruding on her awareness.

If Pam cannot discover some useful way to deal with the stress she is experiencing, her physical reaction to the still-present stressor may be *exhaustion*. In this stage, her bodily resources become nearly depleted. She is running out of energy and out of time. If effective means of coping with her father's condition and her college course work are not found, Pam may break down—psychologically and/or physically. Although the resistance stage may last several months, eventually one's resources become expended. In extreme cases, the exhaustion stage of the general adaptation syndrome may result in death.

For Selye, then, stress is the three-stage mobilization of the body's resources to combat real or perceived threats (stressors) to our well-being. We have limited supplies of such resources. Repeated exposure to stressors tends to have cumulative effects. Dire consequences can result when a person is faced simultaneously or successively with a number of stressful situations.

Selye's vision of stress as a physiological response provides us with a good bridge between our discussion of stress and a consideration of a variety of psychological variables as they affect the condition of one's physical health. This takes us to a relatively new field of psychology called health psychology.

Before You Go On
▼▼▼▼▼▼▼▼▼▼

Name and describe the three stages of the general adaptation syndrome.

▶ Psychology and Physical Health

Health psychology is a field of applied psychology that is just over twenty years old, although the issues involved have been of general concern for a very long time. Health Psychology became a division of the American Psychological Association in 1978 and has approximately 3,000 members (Taylor, 1990). By definition, **health psychology** is the study of psychological or behavioral factors that affect physical health and illness. Involving psychologists in the medical realm of physical health and well-being is based on at least four assumptions:

1. Certain behaviors increase the risk of certain chronic diseases.

2. Changes in behaviors can reduce the risk of certain diseases.

3. Changing behaviors is often easier and safer than treating many diseases.

4. Behavioral interventions are comparatively cost-effective (Kaplan, 1984).

In this section, we'll look at the role of psychologists in the understanding, treatment, and prevention of physical disease.

health psychology the field of applied psychology that studies psychological factors affecting physical health and illness

Is there a relationship between aspects of personality and a person's state of physical health? Can psychological evaluations of an individual be used to predict physical as well as psychological disorders? Is there such a thing as a "disease-prone personality?" Our response is very tentative, and the data are not all supportive, but for the moment we can say, "Yes, there does seem to be a positive correlation between some personality characteristics and physical health."

One analysis of 101 previously published research articles looked for relationships between personality and physical disease (coronary heart disease, asthma, ulcers, arthritis, headaches). The strongest associations were those that predicted coronary heart disease from personality variables, although depression, anxiety, and anger/hostility were each associated with some degree with all of the physical components studied (Friedman & Booth-Kewley, 1987). On the basis of their analysis, the authors argued that there is sufficient (albeit inconclusive) data that links some personality variables to some physical diseases to "argue for a key role for psychological research on the prevention and treatment of disease" (p. 539).

type A behavior pattern (TABP) a collection of behaviors (competitive, achievement-oriented, impatient, easily aroused, often hostile or angry) often associated with coronary heart disease

When we talk about relating personality variables to physical diseases, what commonly comes to mind is the **Type A behavior pattern (TABP)** and its relationship to coronary heart disease. As it originally was defined, TABP refers to a competitive, achievement-oriented, impatient individual who generally is working at many tasks at the same time, is easily aroused, and generally is hostile or angry (Friedman & Rosenman, 1959; Rosenman, et al., 1964). Coronary heart disease (CHD) is a general label given to a number of physical symptoms, including chest pains and heart attacks, caused by a build-up of substances (*e.g.*, cholesterol) that block the supply of blood to the heart.

For nearly 20 years—from the early 1960s to the early 1980s—study after study seemed to show a clear, positive relationship between coronary heart disease and behaviors typical of the Type A personality (Jenkins, 1976; Rosenman, et al., 1975; Wood, 1986). A review panel of the National Institutes of Health declared the Type A behavior pattern an independent risk factor for heart disease (NIH Panel, 1981). It all seemed quite clear. Find people who have the Type A behavior pattern, intervene to change their behaviors, and just watch how coronary heart disease rates decline. By now you know to be suspicious when complex problems seem to have such simple solutions.

▲ *People who exhibit the Type A behavior pattern are usually impatient, easily angered, and highly competitive. While many studies support the idea that there is a link between Type A behavior and coronary heart disease, the Type A behavior pattern remains difficult to diagnose.*

Beginning in the early 1980s, data began to surface that failed to show a clear relationship between TABP and CHD (Fishman, 1987; Krantz & Glass, 1984; Matthews, 1982; 1988; Shekelle, et al., 1985; Wright, 1988). Perhaps people with Type A personalities were no more at risk for heart disease than anyone else. Perhaps studies that failed to find a relationship between TABP and CHD were seriously flawed. In fact, both of these alternative hypotheses have some evidence to support them. For one thing, the Type A behavioral pattern is, by its nature, complex and difficult to diagnose. It seems likely that simple paper-and-pencil inventories—of the sort that have been used in many studies—fail to identify correctly a large number of people with the TABP.

It also may be that the TABP, as it is presently defined, is simply too global a pattern of behaviors (Dembroski & Costa, 1987). Perhaps there is a subset of behaviors within the constellation of Type A behaviors that *does* predict coronary disease. This is a hypothesis now under investigation by psychologist Logan Wright, a self-confessed Type A personality, who was required to undergo bypass surgery to relieve blockage of a coronary artery. As Wright put it, "… if certain so-called active ingredients, or sub-components of the TABP are what is really responsible for coronary-prone risk, one would expect to find them to correlate more highly with CHD than does the global Type A pattern itself" (1988, p. 3).

What are Wright's candidates for the most likely active ingredients of the Type A personality?

1. Time urgency—concern over wasting small bits of time; shifting lanes while in traffic to gain a car length

2. Chronic activation—the tendency to stay alert, aroused and ready nearly all the time; being "fired up" for everything, no matter how silly or mundane

3. Multiphasia—the tendency to have a number of projects all going at once; having many irons in the fire; doing homework and eating while watching TV.

There is evidence that suggests that these components may be predictors of coronary heart disease. But the evidence is not conclusive. More work needs to be done. We need more research on adequate diagnosis for Type A behavior patterns. We also need more research on the mechanisms that underlie whatever relationships there may be between TABP and CHD. And we need research on how to bring about psychological changes in people that would reduce the likelihood of their contracting any physical disease. In many ways, the so-called "active ingredients" of the Type A personality are precisely the characteristics that many people in our society learn to value and to imitate in their quest to "get ahead." But, as Wright says, "Although much Type A functioning may be productive, one *must* still learn to glide" (1988, p. 12). How can psychologists best intervene to help people glide? How can psychologists help people change behaviors that impact on their health? It is to matters of intervention that we now turn.

Before You Go On

▼▼▼▼▼▼▼▼

Briefly summarize the relationship between the Type A behavioral pattern and coronary heart disease.

▶ Psychological Interventions and Physical Health

At the very least, it is possible that some personality characteristics have an impact on the state of one's physical health. The specific traits involved and the nature of that impact are the subject of debate and research. There is no debate and no doubt, however, that certain behaviors put people at risk for certain physical ailments. Today, the leading causes of death in this country are cardiovascular disorders and cancers. These diseases are caused and maintained by the interaction of a number of factors, including biological, social, environmental, and behavioral influences. Among the latter, such variables as cigarette smoking, nutrition, obesity, and stress have been identified as important risk factors (Krantz, et al., 1985). What this means is that for millions of people, factors we may collectively call "lifestyle" are

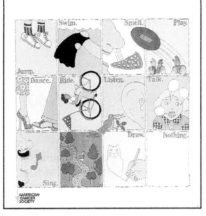

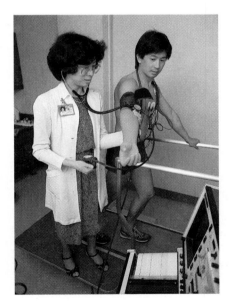

▲ Anti-smoking ads such as this one from the American Cancer Society are aimed directly at young people. Studies reveal that quitting on one's own is much more effective in the long-run than specialized programs.

▲ Health psychologists continue to search for relationships between psychological variables and coronary heart disease.

deadly. (A deadly lifestyle may involve behaviors that lead to death quite directly, such as failure to wear safety belts, or knowingly engaging in other unsafe behaviors at work or play. Recall that we covered the relationship between psychological factors and AIDS in Chapter 9.)

One role of the health psychologist is to bring about changes in potentially dangerous behaviors (Kirscht, 1983; Matarazzo, 1980; Miller, 1983). In fact, "7 of the 10 leading causes of death in the United States are in large part behaviorally determined. We believe these unhealthy behaviors can be significantly reduced with help from psychologists" (Heffernan & Albee, 1985, p. 202).

Interventions designed to prevent health problems have been applied to a wide range of behaviors, including smoking, misuse of alcohol, nutrition, physical fitness and exercise, stress, high blood pressure, family planning, immunization, and sexual activity (Jeffery, 1989; McGinnis, 1985; Rodin & Salovey, 1989). Psychologists also use behavioral techniques to promote healthy and safe behaviors such as the wearing of car safety belts (Geller, et al., 1987).

Although efforts to effect attitudinal and behavioral change have been moving forward on all these fronts, few have received as much attention as efforts to discourage young people from smoking. Part of the reason for the special efforts in this area is that smoking is so deadly, accounting for about one-third of all cancer deaths (Doll & Peto, 1981). Another way to put it is to say that there would be nearly 100,000 *fewer* deaths in any one year if no one smoked (Jeffery, 1989). In the 1990s, concern has extended to include the impact of "secondhand smoke," as we see emerging evidence that children of parents who smoke are significantly at risk for lung cancer even if they, as adults, have never smoked. Yet another reason for concern among health psychologists is that the success rates of programs to persuade smokers to quit have been less than encouraging: Nearly 80 percent of "quitters" relapse within a year (Cohen, et al., 1989; Glasgow & Lichtenstein, 1987; Leventhal & Cleary, 1980). In fact, most smokers who quit permanently do so without any special program of intervention. Approaches that use role models and peers to teach skills for resisting the pressure to begin smoking have been quite successful (*e.g.*, Murray et al., 1984).

Health psychologists also intervene to help in the actual treatment of physical illness and disease (Meichenbaum & Turk, 1987; Rodin & Salovey, 1989). As an example of this sort of work, consider efforts to help patients comply with physicians' orders. Even the best medical advice will be useless if it is not followed. One estimate (Ley, 1977) suggests that as many as 50 percent of patients fail to follow doctors' orders with regard to taking prescribed medicines. This will be particularly true when the illness produces no immediate discomfort or apparent risk (Rodin & Salovey, 1989). There are many reasons why patients fail to comply with doctors' orders, including lack of communication between patient and doctor, the financial burden imposed by expensive medications, the extent of disruption of daily routine required to follow the regimen of daily medication, and the lack of a clear vision of the advantage of doing so.

Psychologists can assist in improving patient/physician communication concerning medication and can assist patients in monitoring their daily medications. For example, many diabetics find it difficult to maintain their daily treatment regimens. A number of strategies have proven useful for this purpose including:

1. **specific assignments** that unambiguously define what is to be done

2. **skill training** to develop new behaviors relevant to treatment

3. cueing specific behaviors with salient stimuli

4. tailoring the regimen to meet the schedule and particular needs of the patient

5. contracts between patient, therapist, and significant others for prescribed behavior change

6. shaping successive approximations of the desired treatment regimen

7. self-monitoring behaviors relevant to treatment

8. reinforcement of new behaviors (Surwit, et al., 1983, p. 260).

Health psychology professionals, then, are involved in a wide range of activities. Some investigate the relationships between psychological variables and the incidence of disease; some try to use psychological methods to ease the symptoms of physical illness; some seek ways to help people change their attitudes and behaviors in order to prevent health problems; some assist patients in complying with prescribed treatment plans; and others fill a more traditional role, dealing directly with the emotional distress that often accompanies the awareness that one has a serious or life-threatening disorder.

Before You Go On
▼▼▼▼▼▼▼▼▼

What are some of the ways health psychologists intervene to promote physical health?

▼▼▼
Thinking Critically About Stress and Health

1. This is the second time that I've mentioned that psychologists assume that all behaviors are motivated or goal-directed (the last time was in Chapter 9, of course). Can you think of any behaviors for which this statement might not be true?

2. Is stress an emotion? Why or why not?

3. What is the relationship, if any, between a society's degree of "technology" or "civilization" and the likelihood of encountering environmental frustration? Do you suppose that frustration, stress, or anxiety were as common at the turn of the 20th century as it is in the United States at the turn of the 21st century?

4. Describe how each of the types of motivational conflicts could be demonstrated with rats. How relevant (or similar) are the behaviors of rats in these situations to the behaviors of people in similar situations?

5. How is it possible to reflect on all of the stressors in life and remain optimistic?

6. Recall the discussion of Freud's defense mechanisms in the last chapter. Just where do these fit in to our discussion of stressors, stress, and reactions to them?

7. Do you see any general sex differences in the manner in which people you know tend to deal with the stressors in their lives?

8. Freud "explained" war in terms of a death instinct (to oversimplify a bit). How can the frustration-aggression hypothesis and our discussion of stress be used to "explain" war?

9. Can you think of any situation in your experience where a stressor caused you to go through the three stages of the general adaptation syndrome?

Summary

▼▼▼▼▼▼▼▼▼▼▼▼▼▼▼▼▼▼▼▼▼▼▼▼▼▼

What is meant by frustration-induced stress? Stress is a reaction to stressors in our lives, i.e., reactions to real or perceived threats to one's sense of well-being. One source of stress is frustration—the blocking or thwarting of goal-directed behaviors. When something or someone in our environment blocks our goal-directed behaviors, we say that we experience environmental frustration. When our goal-directed behaviors are thwarted by our own short-comings, the frustration is referred to as personal frustration. The amount of stress that we experience depends on both the importance of the goal we are seeking and the completeness or totality of the blocking or thwarting. *Page 371*

Name and describe four types of motivational conflict. Motivational conflicts are stressors. They are situations in which we find that we cannot achieve all of our goals because our own motives and goals are in conflict. In an *approach-approach* motivational conflict, one is faced with two (or more) attractive goals and must choose from among them. In an *avoidance-avoidance* conflict, a choice must be made among unpleasant, potentially punishing alternatives. In an *approach-avoidance* conflict, there is but one goal under consideration; in some ways that goal is attractive, while in others it is not—it both attracts and repels at the same time. Perhaps the most common conflict for humans is the *multiple approach-avoidance* conflict in which one faces a number of alternatives, each with its strengths and weaknesses. *Pages 372–373*

In what ways might simply being alive in the world produce stress? Many psychologists argue that life events, particularly changes in one's life situation, often act as stressors. The Social Readjustment Rating Scale (SRRS), for example, is an attempt to measure the severity of stress in one's life by having a person note recent life change events. Some events are rated as more stress-inducing than others. High scores on the SRRS have been correlated with increased incidence of physical illness. Some psychologists argue that little "hassles" in life are often more stress-producing than large, catastrophic events. Another view holds that we experience stress whenever life events lead us to perceive that our psychological and/or physical resources are being threatened. *Pages 374–375*

What are some adaptive ways of dealing with stress? The only way to deal with stress effectively in the long run is to bring about a relatively permanent change in the situation or in one's self. That is, one must learn to change one's goal-directed behaviors or learn to modify one's goals. To think that one can deal with stress by avoiding stressors is simply unrealistic. In many cases, stress (frustration-induced stress in particular) provides experiences that motivate new learning. This observation underscores the point that stressors need not be evaluated as negative experiences. That is, some events that we might rate as positive and productive may still lead to stress. Specific strategies for dealing with the negative felt aspects of stress (its affective component) include cognitive reappraisal (rethinking a situation in a more positive way), developing relaxation techniques (including biofeedback), physical exercise, and seeking social support. *Pages 376–377*

What are some maladaptive reactions to stressors? Unfortunately, many of our reactions to stressors are maladaptive or unhealthy, both in a physical and psychological sense. They are maladaptive because they really do nothing to remove the ultimate source of our stress. Maladaptive reactions to the experience of stress include fixation (in which one tries the same unsuccessful behaviors over and over), aggression (which may release tension momentarily but will not remove the stressor itself), and anxiety. *Pages 377–378*

What is the frustration-aggression hypothesis? The frustration-aggression hypothesis holds that frustration may produce several reactions, but that aggression is always caused by frustration. This view is now seen as overly simplistic, but there is no doubt that much aggression does, in fact, stem from frustration. *Pages 378*

Name and describe the three stages of the general adaptation syndrome. According to Hans Selye, a prolonged stress reaction progresses through three stages, collectively referred to as the general adaptation syndrome. At first there is the mobilization of the sympathetic nervous system of the ANS in the *alarm* stage as the body prepares to cope with the stress. If the stressor is not removed, the body then goes through a stage of *resistance,* when resources continue to be mobilized, but when new stressors will be difficult to deal with, and physical illness becomes more and more likely. If the stressor remains, one may finally enter a stage of *exhaustion,* where the body's resources become depleted, adaptation breaks down, and death or serious illness may result. *Pages 379–382*

Briefly summarize the relationship between the Type A behavioral pattern and coronary heart disease. Many health psychologists believe that there is a relationship between personality variables and physical health, i.e., that some psychological traits put one at risk for disease.

Beginning in the late 1950s, evidence accumulated that seemed to show a strong positive relationship between the Type A behavioral pattern, or TABP, (typified by a person who is competitive, achievement-oriented, impatient, easily aroused, often angry or hostile, and who tends to have many projects all going at once) and coronary heart disease (blockage of major arteries). More recent evidence suggests that perhaps only some of the characteristics of TABP (time urgency, chronic activation, and multiphasia) are predictors of coronary heart disease. *Page 383*

What are some of the ways health psychologists intervene to promote physical health? Reacting to the observation that approximately 70 percent of the lead-ing causes of death in the United States are in large part determined by lifestyle behaviors that put an individual at risk, many health psychologists try to bring about changes in self-destructive behaviors such as smoking, the abuse of alcohol, overeating, and not exercising. Health psychologists also assist in the actual treatment of physical disease, for example, by helping patients to understand and to comply with physicians' orders. Health psychologists are also actively involved in efforts to deal directly with the emotional distress that accompanies the awareness that one has a serious or life-threatening physical disease. *Pages 384–386*

11.1 A real or perceived threat to one's sense of well-being defines   a) stress.   b) anxiety.   c) a psychological disorder.   d) a stressor. *Page 370*

11.2 The concept of frustration is based on which basic assumption?   a) People are basically good and well-meaning.   b) Motivation and emotion both involve physiological reactions.   c) All behavior is motivated, or goal-directed.   d) Stress results from negative experiences. *Page 371*

11.3 Which of these is the best example of frustration?   a) You get a flat tire on the way to an important meeting.   b) You can't decide which courses to take next semester.   c) Your best friend is going to get married.   d) You win a lottery and now everybody wants to be your best friend. *Page 371*

11.4 Which of these provides the clearest example of personal frustration?   a) Bob is unable to qualify for the city golf tournament.   b) Yolanda has the stereo stolen from her new car.   c) Tim gets a letter telling him that the I.R.S. will be auditing his 1991 tax returns.   d) The power goes out, erasing a term paper that Louise was writing on her computer. *Page 372*

11.5 As adults, which conflict situation are we LEAST likely to encounter?   a) approach-approach   b) avoidance-avoidance   c) approach-avoidance   d) multiple approach-avoidance. *Page 372*

11.6 Scott is going to get a new car, but can't decide if he wants a red one or a white one. Scott may be experiencing a(n) _____ conflict.   a) approach-approach   b) avoidance-avoidance   c) approach-avoidance   d) multiple approach-avoidance. *Pages 372–373*

11.7 True or False?   Motivational conflicts are stressful only some of the time. *Pages 372–373*

11.8 Which one word best describes the essential nature of motivational conflicts?   a) blocking   b) fatigue   c) choice   d) disappointment. *Page 374*

11.9 It is the position of Richard Lazarus that the real stressors we face in life are   a) necessarily negative, unpleasant events that we try to avoid.   b) those of which we are typically unaware.   c) the little hassles of life, not big catastrophes.   d) can be rated on a scale from 1 to 100. *Page 375*

11.10 Josh used to be able to play 36 holes of golf in a day with little apparent effort. Now, given his age and general physical condition, he finds it too tiring to play that much, a situation he finds stressful. We would best describe Josh's stress as induced by   a) environmental frustration.   b) personal frustration.   c) motivational conflict.   d) a perceived threat to resources. *Page 375*

11.11 True or False?   To be alive in the world is to experience stress in some form or another. *Page 375*

11.12 Of these, which is the most effective or adaptive reaction to stress?   a) learning   b) frustration   c) aggression   d) simply giving up. *Pages 376–377*

11.13 True or False?   Stress is so unpleasant and so negative a reaction that we can say that the only way to be truly happy in life is to avoid stress altogether. *Pages 376–377*

11.14 Of these mechanisms for coping with stress and stressors, which is the most inefficient or ineffective?   a) engaging in cognitive reappraisal   b) gathering social support   c) fixating   d) relaxation training. *Page 378*

11.15 True or False?   The "frustration-aggression hypothesis" claims that all aggression results from frustration. *Page 378*

11.16 Which of the following was NOT listed by Selye as one of the stages of the general adaptation syndrome?   a) depletion   b) resistance   c) exhaustion   d) alarm. *Pages 379–382*

11.17 The focus of the general adaptation syndrome is largely   a) evolutionary.   b) cognitive.   c) social.   d) physiological. *Page 379*

11.18 True or False?   If someone were to reach the exhaustion stage of the GAS, that means that they would die. *Pages 381–382*

11.19 True or False?   When faced with difficult, stress-inducing decisions, the best thing to do is to simply decide quickly and get the decision over with. *Page 381*

11.20 Whereas clinical psychology is concerned with psychological disorders, the field of health psychology is concerned with   a) persons who do not have and have never had psychological disorders.   b) personality disorders.   c) physical health and well-being.   d) only psychological disorders that have physical symptoms. *Page 382*

11.21 The most positive correlation between personality variables and physical health are for associations that predict   a) stomach problems, such

as ulcers.   b) skin rashes and disorders.
c) coronary heart disease.   d) many varieties
of cancer. *Page 383*

11.22 Which characteristic or description is NOT
included in the Type A behavior pattern or
TABP?   a) high cholesterol levels   b) lack of
patience   c) achievement orientation   d) general hostility. *Page 383*

11.23 Logan Wright suggests that there are three
"active ingredients" of the Type A behavioral
pattern. Which of the following is NOT one of
these three?   a) time urgency   b) perfectionistic   c) chronic activation   d) multiphasia.
Page 384

11.24 What one behavior change would have the
greatest impact on physical health in the United
States?   a) stopping smoking   b) eating less
saturated fat   c) drinking less caffeine
d) using condoms. *Pages 384–385*

11.25 Psychologists estimate that _____ of the 10 leading causes of death in the United States are in
large part behaviorally determined.   a) 1
b) 3   c) 5   d) 7. *Page 385*

11.26 With regard to cigarette smoking, which statement is FALSE?   a) There would be 100,000
fewer deaths in the U. S. if no one smoked.
b) Secondhand smoke is unrelated to lung
cancer.   c) About 80% of those who quit
smoking start up again within a year.   d) We're
better at getting people not to start smoking than
we are at getting smokers to stop. *Page 385*

11.27 True or False?   As many as 50 percent of
patients fail to follow their doctor's orders with
regard to taking prescribed medications.
Page 385

Chapter 12

Abnormal Psychology: The Psychological Disorders

Before you sits George, a 20-year-old male. His appearance is that of someone who has dressed hurriedly; hair disheveled, shirt partially buttoned. Throughout the interview, George either looks down at the table or off into space, seemingly not focusing on anything.

Psychologist: Good morning, George. How do you feel today?

George: [with a sing-song tone] Better than yesterday, but not as good as tomorrow.

Psych: You think you'll feel better tomorrow?

Geo: Oh yeah. Gotta. Can't feel worse. Know what day this is?

Psych: No, what day is this?

Geo: It's my birthday. [In fact, it is not.] Gonna have a big party.

Psych: So today's your birthday? How old are you today?

Geo: 95

Psych: Really. You're 95 years old today? That's really old.

Geo: Yes, but not many people know that [speaking now very rapidly and with no feeling or intonation in his voice]. Last year I was 94; now I'm 95. I was born in 1652 and know that Columbus sailed the ocean blue. I told him to go even though he didn't want to. He didn't think it was safe, but I knew that he wouldn't fall off. [long pause] You gonna be at my party?

Psych: Who's having this party for you, George?

Geo: Everybody here at school; even some of the teachers, too. Those who know I'm not crazy. Those who know about the voices.

Psych: What voices, George?

Geo: [no response]

Psych: Tell me about the voices, George. What voices do some people know about?

Geo: The voices that talk only to me. They tell me what to think when I can't figure it out.

Psych: Can't figure what out?

Geo: Everything, man. God, you're stupid. Are you one of the dumb teachers here? Sometimes I don't like this school. You're dumb, man.

Psych: I'd like to know more about those voices that talk to you.

Geo: They're telling me not to talk to you any more.

Psych: Are they telling you that right now?

Geo: I can't talk to you any more. That would be a crime and I'm not a bad person.

Psych: Of course you're not a bad person. But I would like to talk to you some more.

Geo: [For the next 6 minutes, George says nothing and simply stares at the table. Occasionally he seems to chuckle softly to himself. He is then returned to his room.]

This is George's third day in the inpatient ward at a community mental health center. His parents brought him to the center when he unexpectedly returned home from college, went into his old room and refused to come out because "voices" were telling him not to. When he was brought to the center he claimed that he had come home because "his voices told him to." It took considerable coaxing to get him from his room. A check with college officials revealed that George had not attended classes for the past 3 weeks. George is obviously a severely disturbed young man. As we shall see, he is showing many of the symptoms of a devastating disorder that afflicts approximately one percent of the population worldwide, including more than 2 million Americans: schizophrenia.

▶ Preview

In this chapter we begin a discussion of psychological disorders, or mental illness. If we can say nothing else about psychological disorders, we can acknowledge that they are unpleasant, distressful, painful, and often even devastating in their effects. We can also acknowledge that psychological disorders have an impact on us all. We'll talk about the statistics on the prevalence of specific disorders as we encounter them. For now we need only note that overall, the best available estimates tell us that as you read this sentence, at least 40 million men, women, and children in the United States are suffering from a psychological disorder (*e.g.,* National Institute of Mental Health, 1984; Offord, et al., 1987). Another commonly made claim is that at any point in time, "one in five Americans has mental illness" (*e.g.,* Anderson, et al., 1987; Baker & Richardson, 1989). In many respects, statistics such as these are both astounding and frightening; they are also impersonal. It is difficult to conceptualize what it really means to say that tens of millions of persons are suffering from a mental disorder. What we can say is that it is unlikely that any of us can be exempt from personally experiencing, or having someone close to us experience the pain and suffering of mental illness.

We'll begin with matters of definition. We've begun many chapters in this way, but when it comes to defining who may be mentally ill and who may not be, we need to exercise particular care. Once we have a general idea of what it means to use the term "abnormal" in a psychological context, we'll review what is known about several of the more common (and some of the more bizarre) of the psychological disorders.

Simply to describe all of the identifiable psychological disorders is well beyond the scope of our needs. The intent of this chapter is to give you an idea of what some of the psychological disorders are like. There is little justification for covering the disorders in the sequence I have here except that it does make sense to begin with the anxiety-based disorders because this discussion follows naturally from our discussion of stress in the last chapter, and to end our discussion with schizophrenia, perhaps the most debilitating of all the psychological disorders.

▶ Definition and Classification

We all have a basic idea of what is meant by such terms as *abnormal, mental illness,* and *psychological disorder,* but it is difficult to formulate a very precise definition of these terms. In this section, we'll do two things: We'll generate a working definition of *abnormal* from a psychological perspective, and we'll consider some of the implications of classifying and labeling psychological disorders.

abnormal statistically uncommon, maladaptive cognitions, affect, and/or behaviors that are at odds with social expectations and that result in distress or discomfort

▲ What is considered abnormal or deviant in one society may be quite normal in another. Cultures vary in many respects, including styles of dress. This Arab woman's layered clothing (top) is a sharp contrast to the way these Bororo tribesmen of West Africa are dressed (bottom).

▶ *Defining Abnormality*

The concept of abnormal as it is used in psychology is a complex one. We'll use this definition: **Abnormal** means possessing statistically uncommon, maladaptive cognitions, affect, and/or behaviors that are at odds with social expectations and that result in distress and discomfort. That's a lengthy definition, but to be complete, our definition should include each of these crucial points.

One way to think about abnormality is to take a *statistical* approach. Literally, abnormal means "not of the norm" or "not average." Thus, behaviors or mental processes that are rare should be considered abnormal, and in a literal sense, of course, they are. The problem is that this approach would identify the behaviors of Michael Jordan, Albert Schweitzer, Frank Lloyd Wright, Mother Theresa, and Madonna as abnormal. Statistically, they *are* rare or abnormal; there are few others who do what these people do (or did); yet, as far as we know, none of these people has (or had) a psychological disorder. Psychological disorders are not average or the norm in any statistical sense, but that in itself is not enough.

The reactions of people who suffer from a psychological disorder are *maladaptive*. This is a critical part of our definition. Thoughts, feelings, and behaviors are such that the individual does not function as well as he or she could without the disorder. To be different or to be strange does not mean in itself that someone has a psychological disorder. There must be some degree of impairment, some interference with growth and functioning.

Another observation reflected in our definition is that abnormality may show itself at a number of different levels. A person with a psychological disorder may experience abnormal *affect*, engage in abnormal *behaviors*, have abnormal *cognitions*, or any combination of these. Once again we see our ABCs from Chapter 1.

A definition of psychological abnormality has to acknowledge social or cultural expectations. What may be clearly abnormal and disordered in one culture may be viewed as quite normal or commonplace in another. In some cultures, loud crying and wailing at the funeral of a total stranger is thought to be strange or deviant; in others, it is common and expected. To claim that you have been communicating directly with dead ancestors would be taken as a sign of severe disturbance in some cultures; in others, it would be treated as a great gift. Even in your own culture, behaviors that are appropriate or at least tolerated in one situation, say a party, may be judged to be quite inappropriate in another context, such as a religious service.

One other issue needs to be addressed: Psychological disorders involve *distress* or *discomfort*. People whom we consider abnormal are suffering, or are the source of suffering in others. Psychological disorders involve emotional distress, and individuals with psychological disorders are often the source of distress and discomfort to others—friends and family who care and worry about them.

So, although it is a complex one, I hope that you can see that there is a reason for each of the points in our definition of abnormal—behaviors or mental processes that are statistically uncommon, at odds with social expectations, and result in distress or discomfort.

Now that we see what abnormal means in the context of psychology, let us be sure that we understand a few things that it does not mean.

1. Abnormal and normal are not two distinct categories. They may be thought of as endpoints on some dimension that we can use to describe people, but there is a large gray area between the two where distinctions get fuzzy.

2. Abnormal does not mean dangerous. True, some people diagnosed as having a mental disorder *may* do great violence to themselves or to others, but most people with psychological disorders are not dangerous.

▲ In 1979, Ted Bundy, pictured here, was convicted of the murder of two sorority girls in Tallahasse, FL. He confessed to the murder of 16 other women, and he was suspected of killing many others across the country. He was electrocuted on January 24, 1989. His is a fascinating case that illustrates the difficulty of understanding why patterns of behavior develop or what we can do about them even if we can give those behaviors a name.

diagnosis the act of recognizing a disorder on the basis of the presence of particular symptoms

▲ Emil Kraepelin

3. Abnormal does not mean bad. People who are diagnosed to have psychological disorders are not necessarily bad people, or weak people, in any evaluative sense. They may do bad things, and bad things may have happened to them, but it is not in psychology's tradition to make moral judgments about good and bad.

Before You Go On

▼▼▼▼▼▼▼

How do we define psychological abnormality?

▶ Classifying Abnormal Reactions

One way of dealing with the broad topic of psychological abnormality is to consider each individual psychological disorder separately, in terms of how that disorder is diagnosed, where **diagnosis** is the act of recognizing a disorder on the basis of particular symptoms. Once we've described individual disorders, it also would help if we could organize them in a systematic way.

Systems of classification are common in science and not at all new to psychology. In 1883, Emil Kraepelin published the first significant classification scheme for mental disturbances. It was based on the premise that each disorder had identifying symptoms and a specific biological cause.

In 1952, the American Psychiatric Association published a scheme for classifying mental disorders. The book was the *Diagnostic and Statistical Manual of Mental Disorders* and became known as the *DSM*. In 1987, a revised version of the third edition, the *DSM-III-R* was published. The *DSM-IV* is in preparation, to be available in the mid-1990s. The *DSM-III-R* is the system of classification most widely used in all mental health fields. Figure 12.1 presents a partial listing of the disorders listed in the *DSM-III-R* and shows some of the subtypes for each major category of disorder.

There are many advantages to having a classification scheme for psychological disorders. The major advantage, of course, is ease of communication. If I mean one thing when I use the term *phobia* and you mean something quite different, we cannot hold a very reasonable conversation about your patient's phobia. If we both agreed on the *DSM-III-R*'s definition, we would at least be using the term in the same way. A related advantage is that a reliable way of classifying disorders allows psychologists to think in terms of how best to prescribe appropriate treatment or therapy. I can't leave the impression that there is only one appropriate treatment for each of the categories in the *DSM-III-R*. As we'll see in the next chapter on treatment and therapy, that is far from the case, but it makes sense that we be able to classify disorders before we treat them.

Classification can cause difficulties, however. First, applying labels to people may be convenient, but it is often dehumanizing. It is occasionally difficult to remember that Sally Jane is a complex and complicated human being with a range of feelings, thoughts, and behaviors, not just a "paranoid schizophrenic." In response to this concern, the *DSM-III-R* refers only to disordered behaviors and patterns of behaviors, not to disordered people. That is, it refers to paranoid reactions, not to people who are paranoid; to persons with anxiety, not anxious persons.

A second problem inherent in classification and labeling is that it is so easy to fall into the habit of believing that labels *explain,* when clearly they don't. Reliably diagnosing and labeling a pattern of behaviors does not explain those behaviors. It does not tell us why such a pattern of behaviors developed or what we can or should do about them now.

▲ Gladys Burr is a tragic example of the dangers of labeling. In 1936 Burr's mother committed her to an institution because of "personality problems." She was 29 years old at the time and was declared mentally retarded. During the years 1946 to 1961, IQ tests given to her revealed that she was of normal intelligence. Despite these findings, supported by several doctors, she remained institutionalized until 1978. She was then released and awarded financial compensation after 42 years of unnecessary commitment.

Figure 12.1

A SAMPLE OF THE DSM-III-R CLASSIFICATION OF PSYCHOLOGICAL DISORDERS

Type of disorder	Subtype (examples)
Disorders usually first evident in infancy, childhood, or adolescence	a. mental retardation b. attention deficit with hyperactivity c. separation anxiety d. eating disorders e. gender identity disorder
Organic mental disorders	a. Alzheimer's disease b. substance induced disorders c. organic hallucinations
Psychoactive substance use disorders	a. alcohol abuse and dependence b. drug abuse and dependence c. nicotine dependence
Schizophrenic disorders	a. schizophrenia (one of five varieties)
Delusional disorders	a. paranoia (one of six varieties)
Mood disorders	a. depression b. bipolar disorders
Anxiety disorders	a. phobias b. panic disorder c. obsessive-compulsive disorder
Somatoform disorders	a. conversion disorder (hysterical neurosis) b. hypochondriasis
Dissociative disorders	a. psychogenic amnesia b. fugue c. multiple personality
Sexual disorders	a. paraphilias b. sexual dysfunctions
Impulse control disorders	a. pathological gambling b. pyromania c. kleptomania
Personality disorders	a. schizoid b. histrionic c. paranoid d. narcissistic e. compulsive f. antisocial g. passive-aggressive

Third, labels often create unfortunate and lasting stigmas of negative attitudes about people (*e.g.,* Piner & Kahle, 1984). To learn that someone is labeled as "psychologically disordered" often carries with it a wide range of negative reactions, and the labels may stick long after the disorder has been treated and the symptoms are gone.

One final consequence of diagnostic labeling is that the brunt of the issue tends to fall on the individual. It is the individual who has psychological disorders; not the group, the family, or the society of which the person is a part. Classification schemes tend to focus on the person and not on the larger context in which individuals live (Gorenstein, 1984; Szasz, 1960; 1982). This issue is complex and has been debated for many years. An example of the difficulty is as follows: Mary Beth, a third-grader, is referred to the school psychologist because she is very withdrawn, often seems to be on the verge of tears, will not talk about her home life, and is doing poorly in her academic work. Without going into the particulars of how to diagnose Mary Beth's problem, doesn't it seem misguided to focus all of our attention on Mary Beth (disregarding her family or the demands of the

▲ In 1991, Jeffrey Dahmer was accused of mutilating, sexually assaulting, and murdering several boys and young men. Whether Dahmer was or is sane or insane is more of a legal issue than a psychological one.

insanity a legal term for diminshed capacity and inability to tell right from wrong

school) as we try to identify *her problems*? Is it acceptable to diagnose and label the individual without attending to the larger social networks of which that person is a part?

So far I have used terms such as *mental illness, behavior disorder,* and *psychological disorder* interchangeably. I shall continue to do so because the differences between such terms are of no real consequence. There is a term, however, with which we need to exercise particular care, and that is *insanity.*

Insanity is not a psychological term. It is a legal term. It relates to problems with psychological functioning, but in a rather restricted sense. Definitions of **insanity** vary from state to state, but to be judged as insane usually requires evidence that a person did not know or fully understand the consequences of his or her actions at a given time, could not discern the difference between right and wrong, and was unable to exercise control over his or her actions.

A related issue has to do with whether a person is in enough control of his or her mental and intellectual functions to understand courtroom procedures and aid in his or her own defense. If one is not, one may be ruled "not competent" to stand trial for his or her actions, whatever his or her actions may have been.

Having discussed the problems of defining abnormality and classifying psychological disorders, we now turn our attention to specific disorders.

Before You Go On
▼▼▼▼▼▼▼▼

What is the DSM-III-R?

What are some of its advantages and disadvantages?

▶ *Anxiety Disorders*

anxiety a general feeling of apprehension or dread accompanied by predictable physiological changes

Although anxiety is a term that is difficult to define precisely, we can be confident that everyone has experienced anxiety and recognizes it as being unpleasant. **Anxiety** usually is defined as a feeling of apprehension or dread accompanied by physiological changes—increased muscle tension, shallow rapid breathing, cessation of digestion, increased perspiration, and drying of the mouth. Thus, anxiety involves two levels of reaction: subjective feelings (*e.g.*, dread/fear) and physiological responses (*e.g.*, rapid breathing).

As a group, anxiety disorders are the most common of all the psychological disorders. The National Institute of Mental Health reports high rates: within any 6-month period, from 7 to 15 percent of the population can be diagnosed with "one or more of the several anxiety diagnoses" (Freedman, 1984). These may be underestimates—rates in excess of 20 percent of the population, or nearly 50 million people in the U.S. alone may be more accurate (Reich, 1986; Weissman, 1988). Anxiety disorders are two to three times more common in women than in men (Roth & Argyle, 1988). In any case, percentages of this sort do not convey the magnitude of the problem. We need to remember that we're talking about real people here—people like you and me.

In this section, we'll consider five subtypes of anxiety disorder: phobic disorder, panic disorder, generalized anxiety disorder, obsessive-compulsive disorder, and posttraumatic stress disorder. Keep in mind the one thing that all of these disorders have in common: experienced anxiety, usually coupled with avoidant behaviors, which are attempts to resist or avoid the stimulus situation that produces the anxiety reaction.

▶ *Phobic Disorder*

The essential feature of a **phobic disorder** (or **phobia**) is a persistent fear of an object, activity, or situation that consistently leads a person to avoid that object, activity, or situation. Implied in this definition is the notion that the fear is intense enough to be disruptive or debilitating. The definition also implies that there is no real or significant threat involved in the stimulus that gives rise to a phobia, that is, the fear is unreasonable, exaggerated, or inappropriate.

There are many things in this world that are life-threatening and downright frightening. If, for example, you were driving down a rather steep hill and suddenly realized that the brakes on your car were not working, you would be likely to feel an intense reaction of anxiety. Such a reaction would not be phobic, because it is not irrational.

Similarly, there are few of us who enjoy the company of large numbers of bees. Just because we don't like bees and would rather they weren't around does not qualify us as having a phobic disorder. What is missing here is the *intensity* of the response. People who have a phobic reaction to bees (called mellissaphobia) often will refuse to leave the house in the summer for fear of encountering a bee, and become genuinely upset and anxious at the buzzing sound of any insect, fearing it to be a bee. People with this disorder may be uncomfortable simply reading a paragraph such as this one about bees.

There are many different types of phobias. Most are named after the object or activity that is feared. Figure 12.2 lists some of the most common phobic reactions. Most phobias involve a fear of animals—although these phobias are not the ones for which people most commonly seek treatment (Costello, 1982). In many such cases, the person with a phobic disorder simply avoids the source of fear and as a result never seeks treatment. But when a fear cannot be avoided, and it begins to affect one's day-to-day adjustment, treatment is often necessary. Fortunately, the **prognosis** (the prediction of the course of a disorder) is good for phobic disorders. In other words, therapy for persons with a phobia is likely to be successful. You might want to review our earlier discussion of phobias (in Chapter 6) where we examined possible causes and treatments for simple phobias.

phobic disorder an intense, irrational fear that leads a person to avoid the feared object, activity, or situation

prognosis the prediction of the future course of an illness or disorder

Figure 12.2

A SAMPLE OF PHOBIC REACTIONS

Phobia	Is a fear of
Acrophobia	High places
Agoraphobia	Open places
Algophobia	Pain
Astraphobia	Lightning and thunder
Autophobia	One's self
Claustrophobia	Small, closed places
Hematophobia	Blood
Monophobia	Being alone
Mysophobia	Dirt or contamination
Nyctophobia	The dark
Pathophobia	Illness or disease
Pyrophobia	Fire
Thanatophobia	Death and dying
Xenophobia	The unknown
Zoophobia	Animals

agoraphobia a phobic fear of open places, of being alone, or being in public places from which escape might be difficult

panic disorder a disorder in which anxiety attacks suddenly and unpredictably incapacitate; there may be periods free from anxiety

▲ A job as a construction worker, laboring high above a city, would be out of the question for an individual afflicted with acrophobia, the fear of high places. Following the idea of avoidance, a person with agoraphobia, the fear of open places, would never participate in a crowd-filled activity, such as Earth Day in Central Park, April 22, 1990.

One of the most commonly *treated* varieties of phobia is **agoraphobia,** which means "fear of open places." The fear of agoraphobia is not reserved for those occasions in which one stands in the middle of a large open field, however. The diagnosis is for people who have an exaggerated fear of being alone or of venturing forth into the world where they may be trapped in an unpleasant or embarrassing situation. People with agoraphobia tend to avoid crowds, streets, stores, and the like. They establish for themselves a safe home base and may, in extreme cases, refuse to leave it altogether.

Before You Go On
▼▼▼▼▼▼▼▼

What are the essential characteristics of a phobic disorder?

▶ Panic Disorder

In phobic reactions, there is always a specific stimulus that brings about an intense fear response, and we find people taking steps to avoid the stimulus or object of their phobias. For a person suffering from **panic disorder,** the major symptom is recurrent, unpredictable unprovoked attacks of sudden, intense anxiety, or a panic attack (*DSM-III-R,* 1987, p. 236). These attacks may last for a few seconds or for hours. The subjective experience is quite similar to the fear of a phobic reaction, except that there is no particular stimulus to bring it on. The panic attack is unexpected. It just happens. And because it just happens, without warning, a complication of this disorder is that the person soon begins to fear the next attack and the loss of control that it will bring.

At some point in their lives, about 1.5 percent of the adult population experiences panic disorder. (That 1.5% doesn't sound very significant until we realize that that is nearly 4 million people!) The age of onset for panic disorder is commonly the mid-twenties (Markowitz, et al., 1989). Initial panic attack episodes often are associated with stress, particularly the stress that results from the loss of an important relationship (Ballenger, 1989). For a person to be diagnosed with panic disorder, panic attacks must have occurred at a rate of at least four within a four-week period and be accompanied by a number of physiological symptoms (*e.g.,* chest pain, trouble breathing, dizziness, hot and cold flashes, sweating, or trembling). As it happens, most people who are diagnosed as having a panic disorder are also agoraphobic. The reverse is also true: Most cases of agoraphobia are seen as complications of a panic disorder.

Another complication of panic disorder is that it can be accompanied by intermittent feelings of depression (Noyes, et al., 1990). This may be why the rate of suicide and suicide attempts is so high for persons with this diagnosis (20 percent), which is higher than for persons diagnosed with depression alone (15 percent) (Johnson, Weissman & Klerman, 1990; Weissman, et al., 1989).

Before You Go On
▼▼▼▼▼▼▼▼

What is a panic disorder?

We will save our discussion of the treatment of the psychological disorders until the next chapter. Nonetheless, let me note again that one treatment method for schizophrenia involves the use of medication to ease its symptoms. Largely because of the introduction of these so-called antipsychotic medications, the outlook for patients with schizophrenia is not nearly as dismal as it was just 25 years ago. The estimate is that nearly one-third of all persons diagnosed as schizophrenic will recover (be symptom-free for at least five years). About one-third will be at least partially recovered and may assume, at least to some degree, the normal responsibilities of adaptive living in society. Nearly one-third of patients diagnosed as having schizophrenia will never recover to the point where they will be freed from daily supervision or institutionalization (Bloom, et al., 1985). This so-called "rule of thirds" has been around for a over a decade and is still reasonably accurate, but as new and more effective medications are introduced, we can expect that in the very near future the breakdown will be a bit more positive.

Before You Go On
▼▼▼▼▼▼▼

Describe some of the factors that have been implicated as possible causes of schizophrenic symptoms.

▼▼▼

Thinking Critically About Abnormal Psychology: The Psychological Disorders

1. Given that the differences between normality and abnormality are often difficult to determine precisely, under what circumstances is it justifiable to declare that some has a psychological disorder?

2. Why is it that someone who might be willing to tell us about his or her physical illnesses (*e.g.,* all the gory details of a recent surgery), will probably be unwilling to openly share experiences about any personal experiences with mental illness?

3. Did you notice that throughout all of Chapter 12 there was no mention of anyone having a "nervous breakdown?" This is because, technically, there is no psychological diagnosis of nervous breakdown, even though the term is used frequently outside of psychology. What do you think would be the appropriate diagnosis (or diagnoses) for someone said to have had a nervous breakdown?

4. Phobias are characterized by an intense, irrational fear. What is the difference, if any, between "fear" and "anxiety?"

5. What is the source of most of the anxiety that is associated with the anxiety disorders? (Hint: Think back to our last chapter.)

6. Women are diagnosed as suffering from major depression much more commonly than are men. This could be because the disorder simply occurs more frequently in women. If this is the case, why does it? What other reasons might there be for the diagnosis being more common for women than for men?

7. What does the fact that schizophrenia occurs at about the same rate worldwide suggest about its cause or its source?

Summary

▼▼▼▼▼▼▼▼▼▼▼▼▼▼▼▼▼▼▼▼▼▼▼▼▼▼▼▼▼▼▼▼

How do we define psychological abnormality? In the context of psychological disorders, we take abnormal to mean statistically uncommon maladaptive behaviors, cognitions, and/or affect that are at odds with social expectations and that result in distress or discomfort. *Pages 395–396*

What is the DSM-III-R? What are some of its advantages and disadvantages? The *DSM-III-R* is the revised third edition of the *Diagnostic and Statistical Manual of Mental Disorders,* the "standard" classification system for psychological disorders as determined by a committee of psychologists and psychiatrists. The major advantage of the system is that it provides one standard label and symptoms for each disorder, which all mental health professionals can use; it is an aid to communication. It has its limitations, however. Labels tend to dehumanize. They put the brunt of a disorder on the person, not the group to which the individual belongs. Also, classification systems and labels only describe; they do not explain. *Pages 396–398*

What are the essential characteristics of a phobic disorder? By definition, a phobic disorder is typified by an intense, persistent fear of some object, activity, or situation that is in no real sense a threat to the individual's well-being; in brief, an intense, irrational fear. *Pages 399–400*

What is a panic disorder? The defining symptom of a panic disorder is a sudden, often unpredictable attack of extreme anxiety, called a panic attack. These attacks may last for seconds or hours. Unlike phobic reactions, there is no particular stimulus to prompt the attack. *Page 400*

Describe generalized anxiety disorder, and contrast it with panic disorder. Panic disorders and generalized anxiety disorders are alike in that their major defining characteristic is a high level of anxiety that cannot be attributed to any particular source. The major difference between the two is that for the generalized anxiety disorder, the felt anxiety is chronic, persistent, and diffuse. In the panic disorder, there may be periods during which the person is totally free from feelings of anxiety; the anxiety occurs in acute, debilitating attacks. *Page 401*

In the context of psychological disorders, what is an obsession, and what is a compulsion? Obsessions and compulsions are the main presenting complaint in obsessive-compulsive disorder. An obsession is an idea or thought that constantly intrudes on awareness. A compulsion, on the other hand, is a repeated and stereotyped act that intrudes on one's behavior. *Pages 401–402*

Describe the symptoms of posttraumatic stress disorder. Posttraumatic stress disorder, or PTSD, is an anxiety disorder in which the symptoms of high levels of anxiety, recurrent and disruptive dreams and recollections of a highly traumatic event (e.g., rape, combat, or natural disaster) occur well after the danger of the event has passed. *Page 403*

Describe hypochondriasis and conversion disorder. These are two of the somatoform disorders—psychological disorders reflected by a physical or bodily symptom or complaint. In each case, however, there is no known biological cause for the complaint. In hypochondriasis, a person lives in fear and dread of contracting some serious illness or disease, when there is no medical evidence to justify such a fear. In conversion disorder, there is an actual loss or alteration in physical functioning—often dramatic —not under voluntary control, which suggests a physical disorder, but with no physical basis for the loss or alteration. *Pages 404–405*

What is the defining symptom of the dissociative disorders? Dissociative disorders are marked by a retreat or escape (dissociation) from some aspect of one's personality. It may be a matter of an inability to remember some life event (psychogenic amnesia), sometimes accompanied by unexplained travel (fugue state). In some rare cases, certain aspects of one's personality become so dissociated that we may say that the person suffers from multiple personality disorder, where two or more personalities are found within the same person. *Pages 405–407*

What are the defining characteristics of the personality disorders? Personality disorders are enduring patterns of perceiving, relating to, and thinking about the environment and oneself that are inflexible and maladaptive. These are essentially life-long patterns of maladjustment and are classified as belonging to one of three clusters, or groups. Group 1 includes PDs involving odd or eccentric reactions, such as the paranoid or schizoid personality disorders. Group 2 includes disorders of dramatic, emotional, or erratic reactions, such as the antisocial or histrionic personality disorders. Group 3 includes disorders involving fear or anxiety, such as the passive-aggressive personality disorder. *Pages 407–410*

How are the mood disorders defined?
What do we know about their prevalence and their causes? Although many psychological disorders involve disturbances of affect, in the mood disorders, a disturbance in mood or feeling is the prime, perhaps

the only, major symptom. Most commonly we find the disorder to be one of depression alone; less commonly we find depression and mania occuring in cycles (in bipolar mood disorder). In any case, whether the major symptom is depression, mania, or a combination, there is no apparent reason for the mood. Depression is a common disorder, affecting as many as 20 percent of all women and 10 percent of men at some times in their lives. The disorder seems to have a strong hereditary basis. Neurotransmitters (biogenic amines) such as serotonin and dopamine have been implicated in depression. Psychological explanations tend to focus on the learned ineffectiveness of reinforcers, and cognitive factors such as poor self-image, as models for explaining the causes of depression. *Pages 410–413*

What are the major symptoms of schizophrenia?
Schizophrenia is a label applied to several disorders that all involve varying degrees of cognitive impairment (delusions, hallucinations, disturbances of thought, and the like), social isolation, and disturbances of affect and behavior. *Pages 413–416*

What characterizes the following varieties of schizophrenia: process vs. reactive, positive vs. negative, catatonic, disorganized, paranoid, undifferentiated, and residual? *Process* schizophrenia is the term used when symptoms develop slowly and gradually. We call cases in which the symptoms arise suddenly *reactive* schizophrenia. The latter often has a better prognosis than the former. We talk about *positive* symptoms of schizophrenia when a patient has hallucinations, delusions, or bizarre behaviors. *Negative* symptoms refer to losses: social withdrawal, loss of appropriate affect, apathy, and/or loss of attention. *Catatonic* schizophrenia is characterized by catatonia (states of physical impassivity) and/or extreme excitement. *Disorganized* schizophrenia is marked by a more severe disintegration of personality, with emotional distortions, inappropriate laughter, and bizarre behaviors, while *paranoid* schizophrenia is characterized by delusions, usually absurd and disorganized. *Undifferentiated* schizophrenia involves a wide variety of symptoms, none of which dominate, and *residual* schizophrenia indicates a mild form of the disorder that follows a schizophrenic episode. *Pages 416–417*

Describe some of the factors that have been implicated as possible causes of schizophrenic symptoms.
Although we certainly do not know the causes of schizophrenia, three lines of investigation have produced helpful leads. (1) There seems to be little doubt of a genetic predisposition for the disorder. Although schizophrenia is not directly inherited, it does tend to run in families. (2) Research on biochemical correlates of schizophrenia have localized the neurotransmitter dopamine as being involved in the production of schizophrenic symptoms, although dopamine's role in the disorder is now being questioned. (3) It also seems reasonable to hypothesize that early childhood experiences, particularly those involving parent-child interactions and communications, also may predispose one to the disease. Probably the most reasonable position at the moment is that for some persons, environmental events, such as extreme stressors, trigger biochemical and structural changes in the brain that result in the symptoms of schizophrenia. *Pages 417–421*

12.1 As you read this item, which provides the best estimate of the percentage of Americans who are suffering from a psychological disorder? a) 10 percent b) 20 percent c) 40 percent d) There is no way to make such an estimate. *Page 394*

12.2 Which of these is NOT included in our definition of psychological abnormality? a) maladaptive b) bizarre or strange c) distress or discomfort d) affect, behavior, and/or cognition. *Pages 394–395*

12.3 Which of the following is TRUE concerning people with psychological disorders? a) They tend to be more dangerous than others. b) They usually realize that they have some sort of problem. c) They are distinctly different from people who are normal. d) They are people who have poor self-control or will power. *Pages 395–396*

12.4 Classification schemes and labels for psychological disorders, such as those found in the *DSM-III-R*, have some potential problems. Which of these is NOT one of those problems? a) Labels tend to dehumanize real human suffering. b) There is no logical or sensible rationale behind such schemes. c) They usually focus on the individual and the groups to which the individual belongs. d) Schemes and labels may define and describe, but they do not explain. *Pages 396–398*

12.5 True or False? Insanity is a term that comes from the legal profession, not from psychology or psychiatry. *Page 398*

12.6 Everything else being equal, which disorder has the best prognosis? a) schizophrenia b) multiple personality c) phobic disorder d) antisocial personality disorder. *Pages 396–398*

12.7 True or False? The most common phobia is a fear of the dark. *Pages 399–400*

12.8 What two words or terms best differentiate between panic disorder and generalized anxiety disorder? a) acute and chronic b) stimulus and response c) rational and irrational d) distress and discomfort. *Pages 400–401*

12.9 Constantly checking to confirm that the front door is really locked may be a sign of: a) a fugue state. b) a phobia. c) a conversion disorder. d) an obsessive-compulsive disorder. *Pages 401–402*

12.10 By definition, what do the somoatoform disorders have in common? a) either hallucinations or delusions b) bodily symptoms or complaints c) exaggerated fears and anxieties d) feelings of profound depression. *Pages 404–405*

12.11 True or False? Persons with hypochondriasis typically show symptoms of blindness, deafness, or paralysis. *Pages 404–405*

12.12 Multiple personality disorder a) is significantly less common than it was 50 years ago. b) is one of the most common of the schizophrenic disorders. c) is classified as a dissociative disorder. d) is characterized by a sense of "la belle indifférence." *Pages 406–407*

12.13 True or False? Fugue states are typically accompanied by amnesia. *Page 406*

12.14 Which is characterized in terms of being overly dramatic, with intensely expressed behaviors? a) histrionic personality disorder b) avoidant personality disorder c) antisocial personality disorder d) paranoid personality disorder. *Pages 407–410*

12.15 Tracy reports feeling anxious, nervous, and "on edge" all day long. She is tired, but cannot sleep well, and sometimes feels like crying for no apparent reason. If Tracy has a disorder, the best diagnosis is that Tracy is experiencing a(n) _____ disorder. a) psychogenic fugue b) obsessive-compulsive c) generalized anxiety d) panic. *Pages 400–406*

12.16 True or False? The personality disorders are classified as anxiety-based disorders. *Pages 407–410*

12.17 The collection of disorders called mood disrders has as its major symptom a) disorganized thinking and confusion. b) the experience of strange, unexplainable behaviors. c) disturbances of affect. d) cognitive disorientation. *Page 410*

12.18 By far, the most common form of mood disorder is a) depression. b) bipolar. c) paranoia. d) mania. *Pages 410–413*

12.19 Concerning the mood disorders, each of the following is true EXCEPT a) Depression is more common in women than in men. b) It is more common to find depression alone than mania alone. c) Depression generally occurs in a series of episodes. d) The symptoms of mania rarely reoccur or relapse. *Pages 410–413*

12.20 Of these factors, which seems to be the LEAST involved as a cause of depression? a) early

childhood experiences   b) genetic predispositions
c) neurotransmitters   d) biogenic amines.
Pages 410–413

12.21 True or False?   By definition, patients cannot be
depressed and anxious at the same time.
Pages 400–413

12.22 In what way can we refer to schizophrenia as the
text does—as the "ultimate" psychological disorder?   a) It is the most prevalent or common
disorder.   b) It impairs affect, behavior, and
cognitions.   c) It is a disorder from which virtually no one recovers.   d) It produces symptoms that are wild and bizarre. *Pages 413–416*

12.23 Which of these symptoms is NOT associated
with schizophrenia?   a) high levels of felt anxiety   b) social withdrawal or retreat from others
c) flattened or inappropriate affect   d) disturbed cognitions, including delusions.
Pages 413–416

12.24 True or False?   Schizophrenia means split
mind—literally splitting the mind into two (or
more) different and distinct personalities.
Page 416

12.25 When the symptoms of the disorder develop
gradually, even over a period of years, we are
seeing an example of _____ schizophrenia.
a) positive   b) process   c) undifferentiated
d) negative. *Page 416*

12.26 Each of these is a symptom of schizophrenia.
Which is a positive symptom?   a) social withdrawal   b) poor attention   c) hallucinations
d) gradual onset. *Page 416*

12.27 For which statement concerning the causes of
schizophrenia may we feel most certain?
a) Excessive levels of dopamine cause
schizophrenia.   b) Schizophrenia results from
child abuse.   c) Schizophrenia runs in families.
d) Parents of schizophrenics are cold and aloof.
Pages 418–421

12.28 True or False?   About one-third of those diagnosed as having schizophrenia recover from the
disorder and remain symptom free for at least
five years. *Page 421*

Chapter 13

Treatment and Therapy for Psychological Disorders

▲▲▲▲▲▲▲

Philippe Pinel (1745–1826) was a French physician who, in the midst of the French Revolution (on April 25, 1793), was named Director of the Bicêtre in Paris, a hospital-asylum for mentally ill men. Two years later, he also was placed in charge of the Salpertière, a similar institution for women.

We know of Pinel today largely because of an act of compassion and courage. On September 2, 1793, he ordered the chains and shackles removed from about 50 inmates of his hospital. To do so required special permission from the French government, because the patients were chained according to the law at the time. Pinel's humane gesture produced surprising effects: The conditions of the patients, in most cases, improved markedly.

As we begin our discussion of treatment and therapy for psychological disorders, let us consider just what faced Pinel as he took over the management of what was at the time one of the "better" of the asylums for the mentally disturbed. The following descriptions are Pinel's (from Shipley, 1961).

▲ On my entrance to my duties of that hospital, everything presented to me the appearance of chaos and confusion. Some of my unfortunate patients labored under the horrors of a most gloomy and desponding melancholy. Others were furious, and subject to the influence of a perpetual delirium. . . Symptoms so different, and all comprehended under the general title of insanity. . .

* * *

▲ The halls and the passages of the hospital were much confined, so arranged as to render the cold of winter and the heat of summer equally intolerable and injurious. The chambers were exceedingly small and inconvenient. Baths we had none, though I made repeated applications for them; nor had we extensive liberties for walking, gardening or other exercises. So destitute of accommodations, we found it impossible to class our patients according to the varieties and degrees of their respective maladies.

* * *

▲ A working man. . . was transferred to Bicètre. The idea of his death haunted him night and day, and he unceasingly repeated that he was ready to submit to his impending fate. Constant employment at his trade, which was that of a tailor, appeared to me the most probable means of diverting the current of his morbid thoughts. I applied to the board for a small salary for him, in consideration of his repairing the clothes of the other patients in the asylum. This measure appeared to engage his interest to a very high degree. He undertook the employment with great eagerness, and worked without interruption for two months. A favorable change appeared to be taking place. He made no complaints nor any allusions to his supposed condemnation.

* * *

▲ A young gentleman, twenty-two years of age, of a robust constitution was deprived of part of his property by the revolution. He gave way to melancholy, began to look forward to futurity with extreme despondency, and lost his sleep. He was, at length, seized by violent maniacal fury. . . . With his hands and feet tied he was suddenly immersed in the cold bath. Notwithstanding the violence with which he resisted this treatment, it was practiced upon him for some time. . . . Upon my first interview with him he appeared exceedingly enraged. . . . The bath was never mentioned to him. He was treated with mildness and put on a diluent regimen [a bland diet], with the liberty of walking at all hours in the pleasant garden. The amusement which he derived from this liberty, exercise and familiar conversation, in which from time to time I would engage him, gradually induced a state of calmness, and toward the end of a month he was not remarkable either for haughtiness or diffidence. In about three months his delirium had completely left him. . . . Upon his departure he returned into the country, where for the past two years he has been occupied partly by literary pursuits, and partly by those of agriculture. No symptom of delirium has since appeared.

▶ Preview

In Chapter 12, we discussed psychological disorders, and noted that such disorders are, unfortunately, far from rare. Tens of millions of Americans are afflicted with psychological problems—from minor difficulties in adjusting to stress, to those disorders that involve excessive anxiety, to the devastating disorders of schizophrenia. Put in a different way, nearly one-quarter of all the days that Americans spend in the hospital can be accounted for by mental disorders (Kiesler & Sibulkin, 1987). In this chapter, we turn our attention to what can be done to help people suffering from psychological disorders.

The basic premise that persons with psychological disorders should be treated humanely is remarkably recent in our history. Accepting the position that we should actively intervene to improve the quality of life of persons suffering from mental disorders is even more recent. We can claim that the systematic, humane treatment of persons with psychological problems is a twentieth-century phenomenon.

To begin, we'll take a very brief look at the history of treatment for psychological disorders. This history provides us with some insight as to why, even today, so many people have such strong negative attitudes about people with psychological disorders.

We'll quickly review a list of the types of professionals who provide treatment or therapy for psychological disorders, then we'll consider methods of treatment that generally fall outside the realm of psychology: treatments that are medical or physical in nature. We'll consider psychosurgery and shock therapies but will concentrate on the use of drugs to control and treat the symptoms of mental illness.

Most of this chapter will be devoted to varieties of **psychotherapy**. All varieties of psychotherapy are techniques "designed to influence the patient's behavior by psychological means, that is, they seek to persuade the patient to think, feel, or act differently" (Strupp, 1986, p. 128). Just 30 years ago, only 13 percent of the population sought psychotherapy at any time in their lives (Meredith, 1986). Now we find that almost 30 percent

psychotherapy the treatment of mental disorders through psychological means, effecting change in cognitions, affect, and/or behavior

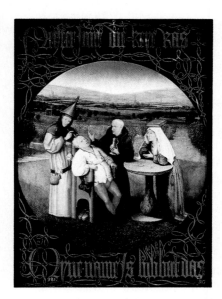

▲ This painting by Hieronymus Bosch depicts one of the measures used on the mentally ill in the Middle Ages. Here, people believing that stones were the cause of this patient's insanity, attempt to remove them by boring a hole in his head.

will have some experience in psychotherapy at some point. In 1987 alone, "15 million of us [made] roughly 120 million visits to mental health professionals—nearly twice as many visits as to internists" (Hunt, 1987, p. 28). We'll discuss five types of therapy: psychoanalytic (or Freudian) techniques, humanistic techniques, behavioral techniques, cognitive techniques, and group techniques. Having reviewed some of the major methods, we will try to evaluate psychotherapy as a whole. Does it work? Under what circumstances?

▶ A Historical Perspective

The history of the treatment of psychological disorders is not a pleasant one. By today's standards, therapy—in the sense of active, humane intervention to improve the condition of persons in psychological distress—does not even seem like an appropriate term to describe the way in which most disordered persons were dealt with in the past.

Mental illness is not new. Among the earliest written records from the Babylonians, Egyptians, and ancient Hebrews we can find descriptions of what we now recognize as psychological disorders (Murray, 1983).

The ancient Greeks and Romans believed that people who were manic, depressed, irrational, intellectually retarded, or who had hallucinations and delusions had in some way offended the gods. Severely disturbed patients were seen as being physically possessed by evil spirits. These cases were more difficult, often impossible to cure. The goal of the ancients was to exorcise the evil spirits and demons inhabiting the minds and souls of the mentally deranged. Many unfortunate people died as a direct result of their treatment, or were killed outright when treatment failed. Treatment was left to the priests who were, after all, thought to be skilled in the ways and means of spirit manipulation.

There were those in ancient times who had a more reasonable view of psychological disorders. Among them was Hippocrates (460–377 B.C.), who believed that mental disorders had physical causes, not spiritual ones. He identified epilepsy as being a disorder of the brain, for example. Some of his views were incorrect (*e.g.,* that hysteria is a disorder of the uterus), but at least he tried (without success) to demystify mental illness.

During the Middle Ages (A.D. 1000–1500) the oppression and persecution of the mentally disordered were at their peak. During this period, the prevailing view continued to be that psychologically disordered people were "bad people," under the spell of the devil and evil spirits. They had brought on their own grief, and there was no hope for them, except that they save their immortal souls and confess their evil ways.

For hundreds of years, well into the eighteenth century, the attitude toward the mentally ill continued to be that they were in league with the devil or that they were being punished by God for sinful thoughts and deeds. They were witches who could not be cured except through confession. When confessions were not forthcoming, the prescribed treatment was torture. If torture failed to evoke a confession, death was the only recourse; often it was death by being burned at the stake.

We also must keep in mind that it was not until very recently (the late 1800s) that a real distinction was made between persons who suffered from a psychological disorder and persons who were intellectually retarded.

When the insane were not tortured or immediately put to death, they were institutionalized in asylums. The first insane asylum was St. Mary of Bethlehem Hospital in London, which housed "fools" and "lunatics" in 1547. The institution became known as Bedlam (a cockney pronunciation of Bethlehem). It was a terrible place. Inmates were tortured, poorly fed, or

▲ The first insane asylum became known as Bedlam. Even today we use the word bedlam to describe a condition or scene of wild uproar and confusion which is conveyed in this painting. In the eighteenth century, it was considered entertaining to view the lunatics, as the two ladies of fashion shown here are doing.

starved to death. To remove the "bad blood" from their systems (thought to be a cause of their symptoms), patients were regularly led to bleeding chambers, where a small incision was made in a vein in the calf of their legs so that their blood would ooze into leather buckets. There was no professional staff at Bedlam. The keepers, as they were called, could make extra money by putting their charges on view for the general public. Viewing the lunatics of Bedlam became an established entertainment for the nobility. Inmates who were able were sent into the streets to beg, wearing a sign that identified them as "fools of Bedlam." Notice that even today we use the word *bedlam* to describe a condition or scene of wild uproar and confusion.

It would be comforting to think that Bedlam was an exception. It was not. In the eighteenth and nineteenth centuries (and well into this century) institutions like Bedlam were commonplace. Recall the words of Pinel with which we opened this chapter. Pinel's unchaining of the insane and his personal belief in humane treatment for the mentally ill can be viewed as the beginning of a very gradual enlightenment about mental illness, even though Pinel's success did not lead to broad, sweeping reforms.

Thus history tells us that until recently, the prevailing understanding of the psychologically disturbed was that they were bad people, possessed by demons and devils, unable to control their behaviors and thoughts and unable to be cured; and the only recourse was to separate them from everyone else—to "put them away." Since the early 1900s, progress in providing help for the mentally ill has been both slow and unsteady. World War I and the Depression reduced the funds available to support state institutions for mental patients. Within the past 50 years, conditions have improved immeasurably, but there is still a long way to go.

Before You Go On

▼▼▼▼▼▼▼▼▼

Briefly trace the history of the treatment of persons with psychological disorders.

▶ Who Provides Treatment and Therapy?

Many professionals are equipped to provide treatment or therapy for psychological disorders. Let's begin by providing a list of the most common types of mental health providers, as they are sometimes called. Please keep in mind that this is a list of generalities; descriptions will not hold true for everyone within a given category. Remember also that because of their experience and/or training, some professionals develop specialties within their fields. That is, some therapists specialize in the disorders of children and adolescents; some work primarily with adults; some prefer to work with families; some devote their efforts to people with substance and alcohol abuse problems. Finally, it is important to understand that a psychotherapist can and will use several of the techniques of therapy outlined in this chapter. In other words, few therapists take one approach to treatment exclusively. As many as 40 percent of therapists in the United States claim to have no particularly dominant approach to their psychotherapy (Norcross, 1986). The following types of professionals may be described as psychotherapists:

1. The *clinical psychologist* usually has earned a Ph.D. in psychology from a program that provides practical, applied experience, as well as an

Psychoanalysts, like the one pictured above, are trained and certified in the methods of Freudian psychoanalysis. A number of professionals, including social workers and licensed counselors are involved in family and group therapy. The picture on the left shows a counselor working with family members of AIDS victims.

emphasis on research. The Ph.D. clinician spends a year on internship, usually at a mental health center or psychiatric hospital. The clinical psychologist has extensive training in psychological testing (in general, *psychodiagnostics*). Some clinical psychologists have a Psy.D. (pronounced sigh-dee, which is a Doctor of Psychology, rather than the more common Doctor of Philosophy degree). Psy.D. programs generally take as long to complete as Ph.D. programs, but emphasize more practical, clinical work and less research.

2. Psychiatry is a specialty area in medicine. In addition to the course work required for an M.D., the *psychiatrist* spends an internship (usually one year) and a residency (usually 3 years) in a mental hospital, specializing in the care of psychologically disturbed patients. At least at the moment, the psychiatrist is the only kind of psychotherapist permitted to use the biomedical treatments (surgery, electroconvulsive shock, and prescribing of drugs) we will be discussing. [There is a campaign underway to get some medical privileges for Ph.D psychologists.]

3. The *counseling psychologist* usually has a Ph.D. in psychology. The focus of study (and the required one-year internship), however, is generally on patients with less severe psychological problems. Rather than spending an internship in a psychiatric hospital, a counseling psychologist would more likely spend time at a university counseling center.

4. A *licensed professional counselor* has a degree in counselor education and will have met state requirements for a license to do psychotherapy. Counselors can be found in school settings, but also work in mental health settings, specializing in family counseling and drug abuse.

5. *Psychoanalyst* is a special label given either to a clinical psychologist or a psychiatrist who also has received intensive training and certification in the methods of Freudian psychoanalysis.

6. The terminal degree for *clinical social workers* is generally the master's degree, although P.h.Ds in social work are becoming more common. Social workers can and do engage in a variety of psychotherapies, but their traditional role has been involvement in family and group therapy.

Psychotherapy may be offered by other professionals and paraprofessionals. Some practice therapy or counseling with a master's degree in

Deinstitutionalization

The first institution for the mentally ill was St. Mary of Bethlehem Hospital, or Bedlam, so designated in 1547. Despite many well-intentioned efforts to promote mental health, not much changed for nearly 400 years. By the middle of the 20th century, large state-supported institutions had become the commonplace residences of the mentally retarded and mentally ill. As the institutions were overcrowded and unmanageable, individual therapy and personal care for patients were all but unknown. Privacy was unheard of, food inedible, filth and squalor prevailed—not in all institutions, of course, but in most.

Within the last 35 years, there has been a revolutionary shift in mental health care. For a number of seemingly sound and sensible reasons, many patients have been *deinstitutionalized*. They have been released from the large mental institutions to return to family and community. The drop in institutional patient population has been dramatic. Compared to 1955, the number of patients in state and county mental hospitals has fallen nearly 75 percent. What has brought about this great change, and has it been a change for the better or the worse? There are several reasons for deinstitutionalization, and we've already alluded to some of them. Let's consider three.

1. *A concern for the rights of the patient arose.* The overcrowded and virtually inhumane conditions that existed in many institutions simply became more than society was willing to bear. The courts entered the picture, ordering that either patients receive adequate and proper treatment or be released.

2. *Symptoms now can be managed through chemical means.* We've already touched on this matter. In the mid-1950s, the introduction of effective drugs that at least suppressed or masked psychotic symptoms made it all the more reasonable that patients no longer displaying unusual or bizarre behaviors could be released from institutional care.

3. *Community mental health centers were to be established.* In 1963, Congress passed the Community Mental Health Act. This law included a provision for the establishment of a large number of mental health centers to be located in local communities (rather than centralized in one or two state institutions). The plan was for there

psychology (although because of licensing or certification laws in many states, they may not advertise themselves as psychologists). *Occupational therapists* usually have a master's degree (less frequently, a bachelor's degree) in occupational therapy, which includes many psychology classes and internship training in aiding the psychologically and physically handicapped. *Psychiatric nurses* often work in mental hospitals and clinics. In addition to their R.N. degrees, psychiatric nurses have special training in the care of mentally ill patients. *Pastoral counseling* is a specialty of many with a religious background and a masters degree in either psychology or educational counseling. The *mental health technician* usually has an associate's degree in mental health technology (MHT). MHT graduates seldom are allowed to provide unsupervised psychotherapy, although they may be involved in the delivery of many mental health services.

to be one easily accessible mental health center for every 50,000 people in the country. These centers would accommodate people on an outpatient basis and were to provide many other services, including short-term inpatient care, as well as consultation, education, and prevention programs.

Has the system of deinstitutionalization worked? On this question, the house is divided. There are those who applaud the change (Braun, et al., 1981) and argue that, within limits, "continued optimism about community care seems warranted" (Shadish, 1984). On the other hand, many see deinstitutionalization as trading one set of problems for a host of others. Many of the patients released from mental hospitals are, quite literally, "dumped" back into their home communities where resources to assist them often are minimal. For example, there is seldom adequate housing for those who have been released. (Frequently, negative attitudes seem to be involved, as in, "We don't want housing for those people in *our* neighborhood.") Many released patients become street people, particularly in large cities. Recent estimates from the National Institute of Mental Health place the percentage of homeless with psychological disorders at 30 to 35 percent. Many require the support of the welfare system. And no matter how capable a community mental health center may be (assuming there *is* one nearby), if patients do not seek its support, it will do them little good. Inadequate funding for community mental health centers has become a chronic condition. As we have noted, most of the antipsychotic medication that patients require does not have lasting effects. When patients stop taking their medication (perhaps because of expense or side effects), symptoms return, and they will likely need to return once again to the institution. In fact, since deinstitutionalization has become a matter of policy, admissions to mental hospitals have actually increased, although the average length of stay has decreased (Kiesler, 1982). Those who work in community mental health centers often refer to this phenomenon as the "revolving door" of deinstitutionalization.

It appears that the trend to reduce the population of patients in mental institutions is likely to continue. Effective community programs and more resources are needed to assist those released from these institutions to ensure that discharge is appropriate for them and for the community to which they return.

Before You Go On

▼▼▼▼▼▼▼▼▼▼

Who may offer psychotherapy?

What is the major difference between psychologists and psychiatrists?

▶ Biomedical Treatments of Psychological Disorders

As we have just noted, treatments that are medical in nature are not used by psychologists. Currently, performing surgery, administering shock treatments, or prescribing drugs requires a medical degree. Psychologists often are involved in biomedical treatments, however. Psychologists may recommend medical treatment and refer a client to the care of a physician or psychiatrist.

Here we'll review three biomedical interventions: psychosurgery, which was quite common just 50 years ago, but is now quite rare; shock treatment, which is far from uncommon; and drug therapy, which is the newest and one of the most promising developments in the treatment of mental illness.

▶ *Psychosurgery*

psychosurgery a surgical procedure designed to affect one's psychological or behavioral reactions

lobotomy a psychosurgical technique in which the prefrontal lobes of the cerebral cortex are severed from lower brain centers

Psychosurgery is the name we give to surgical procedures (usually directed at the brain) designed to affect psychological reactions. Most psychosurgical techniques in use today can be considered somewhat experimental. They are aimed at making rather minimal lesions in the brain (to treat chronic pain, epilepsy, or depression, for example). Small surgical lesions in the limbic system have been found to be effective in reducing or eliminating violent behaviors. Surgical techniques also have been used (though infrequently) to reduce extreme anxiety and the symptoms of obsessive-compulsive disorder. Of all the varieties of psychosurgery, none has ever been used as commonly as a procedure called a prefrontal **lobotomy** (Valenstein, 1980; 1986), which severs the major neural connections between the prefrontal lobes (the area at the very front of the cerebral cortex) and lower brain centers.

Lobotomy was first performed in 1935 by a Portuguese psychiatrist, Egas Moniz. For developing the procedure, Moniz was awarded the Nobel Prize in 1949. (The next year, in an ironic twist of fate, Moniz was shot by one of his lobotomized patients. He was rendered paraplegic and was confined to a wheelchair for the rest of his life.) The logic behind a lobotomy was that the frontal lobes influence the basic emotional centers of the brain, and that psychotic patients had difficulty in coordinating these lower brain centers. It was reasoned that if they were separated surgically, the more depressed, agitated, or violent patients could be brought under control.

Treating severely disturbed, depressed, and schizophrenic patients had always been difficult. Perhaps we shouldn't be surprised that this relatively simple surgical technique was accepted so widely and uncritically at first. The procedure often was done under local anesthetic in the doctor's office. It took only ten minutes. An instrument that looks very much like an ice pick was inserted through the eye socket, on the nasal side, and was pushed up into the brain. A few simple movements of the instrument and the job was done—the lobes were severed. Within hours, the patient was ready to return to his or her room.

It always was appreciated that the procedure was an irreversible one. What took longer to realize was that it often carried with it terrible side effects. Between 1 and 4 percent of patients receiving lobotomies died (Carson, et al., 1988). Many of those who survived suffered seizures, memory loss, an inability to plan ahead, a general listlessness and loss of affect. Many behaved childishly and were difficult to manage within institutions. By the late 1950s, lobotomies had become rare. Contrary to common belief, it is not an illegal procedure, although the conditions under which it might even be considered are very restrictive. Prefrontal lobotomies are not done anymore for the simple reason that they are no longer needed. There are other means, with fewer side-effects, that can produce similar beneficial results more safely and reliably.

▶ Electroconvulsive Therapy

electroconvulsive therapy (ECT) a treatment, usually for the symptoms of severe depression, in which an electric current passed through a patient's head causes a seizure and loss of consciousness

As gruesome as the procedures of psychosurgery may seem, many people find the very notion of **electroconvulsive therapy (ECT)**, or shock treatments, even more difficult to appreciate. This technique, first introduced in 1937, involves passing an electric current (of between 70 and 150 volts) across a patient's head for a fraction of a second. The patient has been given a fast-acting general anesthetic and is unconscious when the shock is delivered. As soon as the anesthetic is administered, the patient also receives a muscle relaxant to minimize muscular contractions, which were quite common—and dangerous—in the early days of ECT. The electric shock induces a reaction in the brain that is similar to an epileptic (grand mal) seizure. The procedure takes about five minutes. One of the side effects of ECT is a memory loss for events just preceding the shock and for the shock itself.

At first, the treatment was used to help calm agitated schizophrenics, but it soon became clear that its most beneficial results were for patients suffering from deep depression. It often alleviates depression and, in some cases, has beneficial effects on other psychotic symptoms as well. In fact, the patients that seem best suited to the ECT procedure are those for whom depression is a major symptom, but for whom other psychotic symptoms (*e.g.,* hallucinations or delusions) are present also (Joyce & Paykel, 1989).

Virtually all patients (97 percent) receiving ECT give their consent to the procedure, and negative side effects are quite rare. The most commonly reported side effect is memory loss and general mental confusion. In nearly all cases, these effects disappear in a few days or weeks. On the other hand, the poor reputation that ECT has among the general population and even among some psychologists and psychiatrists did not develop without some foundation. There *are* horror stories of the negative side effects that can follow abuse of the procedure. (At first, the seizures of the shock treatment were induced by drugs, not electricity. It was from these treatments that we have the stories of convulsions so massive as to result in broken bones.) It is now recommended that no more than a dozen treatments be given, and that they be administered over an extended period of time. Some patients in the past have received hundreds of ECT treatments. In such cases, there may have been brain damage and permanent memory loss.

We do not fully understand why ECT produces the benefits that it does. Most research efforts today are focusing on the action of neurotransmitters in the brain for possible explanations. Even though we do not understand how ECT works, and even though it is a treatment that must be used with extreme care, ECT is still very much in practice today. Although the numbers declined during the late 1970s, nearly 100,000 patients receive shock treatments each year, and numbers again are on the rise (Thompson & Blaine, 1987).

The introduction of psychoactive medications has reduced the need to use ECT. But psychiatrists realize that drug treatment is not always successful, and even when it is, it often takes 6 to 8 weeks for the drugs to produce beneficial results. Researchers also have found that in many cases ECT is a

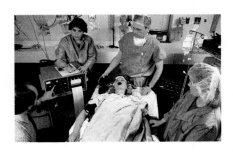

▲ *A patient is prepared to receive electro-convulsive therapy (ECT). This technique involves passing an electric current (of between 20 and 150 volts) across a patient's head for a fraction of a second.*

more effective treatment than are antidepressant medications (*e.g*, Small, et al., 1988). Some researchers have argued that administering a shock to just one side of the brain, called a *unilateral ECT*, is a safer, equally effective procedure with even fewer side effects. More success has been found by creating seizures in the right hemisphere of the cerebral cortex (thought to be more associated with emotional reactions) than in the left (Squire & Slater, 1978).

Before You Go On
▼ ▼ ▼ ▼ ▼ ▼ ▼ ▼

What is ECT?

Why is it still being used?

▶ *Drug Therapy*

psychoactive drug a chemical that affects psychological processes and consciousness

Chemicals that alter a person's cognitions, affect, or behavior are referred to collectively as **psychoactive drugs**. As we've seen, there are many of them, and most are used to produce an altered state of consciousness or awareness. Using chemicals to improve the condition of the mentally disordered has been a much more recent development and has been hailed as one of the most significant scientific achievements of the last half of the twentieth century (Snyder, 1984).

antipsychotic drugs chemicals, such as chlorpromazine, that are effective in reducing psychotic symptoms

Antipsychotic Drugs. As their name suggests, **antipsychotic drugs** have the effect of alleviating or eliminating the major symptoms of psychoses—those severe disorders, such as schizophrenia, that involve gross impairment in functioning and a loss of contact with reality. The real breakthrough in the use of antipsychotic drugs came with the introduction of *chlorpromazine*. In 1950, a French neurosurgeon, Henri Laborit, was looking for a drug to calm his patients just before surgery. Laborit wanted to help his patients relax because he knew that if they did, his patients' postsurgical recovery would be improved. A drug company gave Laborit chlorpromazine to try. It worked better than anyone had expected, producing relaxation and calm in his patients. Laborit convinced some of his colleagues to try the drug on their more agitated patients, who had mental disorders. The experiments met with great success, and by the late 1950s the drug was widely used both in North America and in Europe. By 1956 more than half a dozen antipsychotic medications were available in the United States. From 1976 to 1985 the use of antipsychotic medications remained quite stable, overall, with between 19 and 21 million prescriptions being written each year during the period (Wysowski & Baum, 1989).

Chlorpromazine is just one of many drugs being used with success to treat psychotic symptoms. Most antipsychotic drugs are of the same general type, and most work in essentially the same way—by blocking receptor sites for the neurotransmitter dopamine (see pp. 55–56). Antipsychotic drugs are most effective in treating the positive symptoms of psychosis—delusions, hallucinations, and bizarre behaviors (see p. 410). A recently introduced medication, *clozapine* (trade name Clozaril) may be an exception, because it seems to be effective in reducing negative symptoms as well as positive ones (see p. 417). Unfortunately, clozapine carries with it the risk of some very serious side effects, some of which can be fatal. As a result, the use of this drug is very carefully monitored.

Although most antipsychotic drugs are prescribed for patients with schizophrenia, an exception is *lithium* salts, which are effective in treating some patients with bipolar mood disorders. The drug occasionally alleviates depression, but seems much more useful in controlling the manic cycle of bipolar disorders. There are those for whom the drug has no effect, and its prolonged use can lead to convulsions, kidney failure, and other serious reactions.

The effects of the antipsychotic drugs are remarkable and impressive, and they have revolutionized the care of psychotic patients. Nonetheless, they are not the ultimate solution for disorders such as schizophrenia and the other psychoses. For one thing, there are patients for whom the drugs have no effect or have harmful effects. With high dosages or prolonged use, a variety of side effects emerge that are very unpleasant at best, including dry mouth and throat, sore muscles and joints, heavy sedation, sexual impotence, and muscle tremors. Sometimes side effects are even more significant, including seizures and cardiovascular damage. Although the most effective of the antipsychotic drugs do control symptoms, the question is: Are they in any sense curing the disorder? Symptom-free patients, who often are released from institutional care to the outside world, soon stop using their medication only to find that their psychotic symptoms return.

Before You Go On
▼▼▼▼▼▼▼▼

What are antipsychotic drugs, and what are their effects?

antidepressant drugs chemicals, such as MAO inhibitors and tricyclics, that reduce and/or eliminate the symptoms of depression

Antidepressant Drugs. **Antidepressants** elevate the mood of persons who are feeling depressed. They are of two types: *MAO inhibitors* (MAO is a chemical in the brain that reduces levels of two neurotransmitters; MAO inhibitors thus increase levels of these neurotransmitters), and *tricyclics*. An antidepressant drug that has no measurable effect on one person may produce severe unpleasant side effects in another person and yet may have remarkably beneficial effects for a third person.

Antidepressant drugs would be of little use for anyone who was a bit depressed about receiving a low grade on a history exam. These medications generally require weeks to have their maximum effect and need to be taken on a long-term basis to prevent a recurrence of the depression. They can elevate the mood of many truly depressed individuals, but they have virtually no effect on people who are not depressed. That is, they do not make people who already feel good feel even better.

Of the two classes of antidepressants, the tricyclic types (trade names Elavil or Tofranil, for example) are more commonly used. As you might have guessed, the tricyclic drugs can produce unfortunate side effects, including intellectual confusion, increased perspiration, and weight gain. A major problem with the MAO inhibitor drugs is that they require adherence to a strict diet and carefully monitored dosages to have their best effect. They also produce a wide range of serious side effects, such as dizziness, sexual impotence, elevated blood pressure, and liver damage.

A relatively new antidepressant, *fluoxetine* (trade name Prozac) was introduced in December 1987. It is currently the single most prescribed antidepressant (about 650,000 new or renewed prescriptions are written each month). It is chemically unrelated to either the tricyclics or the MAO inhibitors, although it, too, affects a brain neurotransmitter (serotonin).

Often a very effective medication, its major advantage is that it seems to produce fewer negative side effects. Nonetheless, occasionally these side effects (*e.g.*, skin rashes, agitation, and weight loss) are so unpleasant that patients stop using it. Before it was openly marketed, fifteen percent of the patients receiving Prozac on a trial basis discontinued treatment because of adverse side effects. Since it has been available for a relatively short time, long-term effects of its use are as yet unknown.

Unlike antipsychotic drugs, there is evidence that when antidepressant drugs *are* effective, they may actually bring about long-term cures rather than symptom suppression. In other words, the changes in mood caused by the drugs may outlast use of the drug itself. The hope and plan, in fact, is to gradually reduce the dosage of the drug over time. For persons with mood disorders who do not respond to the medications presently available, other varieties are being tested, and for such patients, electroconvulsive therapy may be indicated.

Before You Go On

▼▼▼▼▼▼▼▼▼

What are the antidepressant drugs, and what are they meant to do?

antianxiety drugs chemicals, such as chlorpromazine, that are effective in reducing psychotic symptoms

Antianxiety Drugs. **Antianxiety drugs** (or tranquilizers) help reduce the felt aspect of anxiety. They are the most commonly prescribed of all drugs. Some antianxiety drugs, the *meprobamates* (trade names Miltown or Equanil, for example), are basically muscle relaxants. When muscle tension is reduced, the patient often reports feeling calm and at ease.

The other major variety of antianxiety drug is the group of chemicals called *benzodiazepines* (trade names Librium and Valium, for example). These drugs act directly on the central nervous system. The impact of these drugs is obvious and significant. They help anxious people feel less anxious. At first, the only side effects appear to be a slight drowsiness, blurred vision, and a slight impairment of coordination. Unfortunately, the tranquilizing effects of the drugs are not long lasting. Patients can fall into a pattern of relying on the drugs to alleviate even the slightest of fears and worries. Soon a dependency and addiction can develop from which withdrawal can be difficult. In fact, a danger of the antianxiety medications is the very fact that they *are* so effective. So long as one can avoid the unpleasant feelings of anxiety simply by taking a pill, there is little to motivate that person to seek and deal with the actual cause of anxiety.

Before You Go On

▼▼▼▼▼▼▼▼▼

What are the common antianxiety drugs, and what are the dangers inherent in their use?

psychoanalysis the form of psychotherapy associated with Freud, aimed at helping the patient gain insight into unconscious conflicts

▶ Psychoanalytic Techniques

Having covered biomedical treatments, we begin our review of psychotherapy with **psychoanalysis.** Psychoanalysis began with Sigmund Freud around

▲ To help his patients relax, Freud had them lie on this couch while he sat out of view.

the end of the nineteenth century. As a technique of therapy, it did not really evolve from Freudian personality theory (Chapter 10). If anything, the reverse is true—Freud's theories about human nature came, in large part, from his experiences with his patients.

Psychoanalysis is based on a number of assumptions, most of them having to do with the nature of conflict and the unconscious mind. For Freud, one's life is often a struggle to resolve conflicts between naturally opposing forces: instincts for life and instincts for death. The biological, sexual, and aggressive strivings of the id are often in conflict with the superego, which is associated with overcautiousness and guilt. The strivings of the id also may be in conflict with the rational, reality-based ego, which is often called upon to mediate between the id and the superego. Conflicts that are not resolved are repressed; that is, they are forced out of awareness into the unconscious levels of the mind. Conflicts and anxiety-producing traumas of childhood can be expected to produce symptoms of psychological disturbance later on in life.

According to Freud, the best way to rid oneself of anxiety is to enter the unconscious, identify the nature of repressed, anxiety-producing conflicts, bring them out into the open, and resolve them as best as possible. The first step is to gain insight into the nature of one's problems; only then can problem solving begin. Thus, the major goals of Freudian psychoanalysis are insight and resolution of repressed conflict.

Sigmund Freud died in 1939, but his approach to psychotherapy did not die with him. It has been modified, but it remains true to the basic thrust of Freudian psychoanalysis. Before we consider how it has changed, let's look at Freudian analysis as Freud practiced it.

▶ Freudian Psychoanalysis

Psychoanalysis with Sigmund Freud was a time-consuming (up to five days per week for six to ten years), often tedious process of self-examination and introspection. The task for the patient was to talk openly and honestly about all aspects of his or her life, from early childhood memories to the dreams of the present. The task of the therapist/analyst was to interpret what was being expressed by the patient, always on the lookout for clues to possible repressed conflict. Once identified, the patient and analyst together could try to resolve the conflicts that brought the patient to analysis in the first place. Several procedures and processes were used to search for repressed conflicts. We'll consider some of the most important ones.

In 1881, Freud graduated from the University of Vienna Medical School. From the start, he was interested in the treatment of what were then called nervous disorders. He went to France to study the technique of hypnosis, which many were claiming to be a worthwhile treatment for mental disorders. Freud wasn't totally convinced, but when he returned to Vienna, he and a colleague, Josef Breuer, tried hypnosis as a treatment for neurotic disorders, conversion reaction in particular. They became convinced that hypnosis itself was of little benefit. What mattered, they believed, was to have the patient talk—about anything and everything. In fact, Freud and Breuer's method became known as the "talking cure."

Soon, the method of **free association** became a central procedure of psychoanalysis. Patients were told to say out loud whatever came into their minds. Sometimes the analyst would provide a stimulus word to get going a chain of freely flowing associations. To free associate the way Freud would have wanted is not an easy task. Patients often required many sessions to learn the technique. Patients were not to edit their associations. They were to say *whatever* they thought of, and that is not always an easy thing to do.

free association the procedure in psychoanalysis in which the patient is to express whatever comes to mind without editing responses

Many people are uncomfortable (at least initially) sharing their private, innermost thoughts and desires with anyone, much less a stranger. Here is where the "Freudian couch" came in. To help his patients relax, Freud would have them lie down, be comfortable, and avoid eye contact with him. The job of the analyst through all this was to try to interpret the apparently free-flowing and random verbal responses, always looking for expressions of unconscious desires and conflicts.

During the course of psychoanalysis, the analyst listens very carefully to what the patient is saying. The analyst also carefully listens for what the patient is *not* saying. Freud believed that **resistance**—the unwillingness or inability to freely discuss some aspect of one's life—was a significant process in analysis. Resistance can show itself in many ways, from simply avoiding the mention of some topic, to joking about matters as being inconsequential, to disrupting a session when a particular topic came up for discussion, to missing appointments altogether.

Let's say, for example, that over the last six months in psychoanalysis a patient has talked freely about a wide variety of subjects, including early childhood memories and all the members of her family—all, that is, except for her brother. She has talked about all sorts of very private experiences, some of them sexual, some of them pleasant, some unpleasant. But after six months of talking, she has not had anything to say about her older brother. The analyst, noting this possible resistance, suggests that during the next visit, he would like to hear more about this older brother. Then, for the first time since analysis began, the patient misses her appointment. She comes to the following appointment, but she's 10 minutes late. The analyst may now suspect that there is some problem with the relationship between the patient and her older brother, a problem that may have begun in childhood, and has been repressed ever since. Of course, *there may be no problem here at all,* but for analysis to be successful, resistances need to be broken down and investigated.

We should not be surprised to learn that analyzing a patient's dreams is an important part of psychoanalysis. Freud referred to dreams as the "royal road" to the unconscious level of the mind. Freud often trained his patients to recall and record their dreams in great detail. Then he would have them share the content of their dreams with him. He analyzed dreams at two levels; *manifest content*—the dream as recalled and reported by the patient; and *latent content*—the dream as a symbolic representation of the contents of the unconscious. Symbolism hidden in the latent content of reported dreams has been one of the most controversial of Freud's beliefs. The basic idea was that true motives and feelings might be camouflaged in a dream. For example, someone who reports a dream about suffocating under a huge pile of pillows *may* be expressing negative feelings about parental overprotectiveness. Someone who dreams of driving into an endless tunnel and becoming lost there *may* be expressing fears or concerns of a sexual nature. The job for the analyst, Freud argued, was to interpret dreams in terms of whatever insights and information they could provide about the true nature of the patient's unconscious mind.

Another controversial aspect of Freudian psychoanalysis is his concept of transference. **Transference** occurs when the patient unconsciously comes to view and feel about the analyst in much the same way he or she feels about some other important person in his or her life, usually a parent. As therapy continues over a long period of time, the relationship between analyst and patient does become a complex and often emotional one. If feelings that were once directed toward someone else of significance are now directed toward the analyst, they are more accessible, more easily observed by the analyst, and more readily interpreted and dealt with. Therapists have

resistance in psychoanalysis, the inability or unwillingness to freely discuss some aspect of one's life

transference in psychoanalysis, the situation in which the patient comes to feel about the analyst in the same way he or she once felt about some other important person

to guard against doing the same thing themselves—letting their own feelings and past experiences interfere with their neutral and objective interactions with their patients. Failing to do so is called *countertransference.*

▶ Post-Freudian Psychoanalysis

Early in the twentieth century, Freudian psychoanalysis was the only form of psychotherapy. In the 1940s and 1950s, it was *the* psychotherapy of choice. "Psychoanalytic theory was the dominant force in psychiatry in the postwar period and was embraced by a large number of clinical psychologists. To a certain extent, and for all practical purposes, there was no rival orientation" (Garfield, 1981, p. 176). Recently, psychoanalysis has become a much less common form of therapy, and strict, Freudian-style psychoanalysis is rare indeed. Let's see how the Freudian notion of therapy has been changed, but first we should note what hasn't changed.

To still qualify as a psychoanalytic approach, the basic aim of therapy must be the uncovering of deep-seated, unconscious conflict (usually) caused by early childhood experiences. This broad statement is about all that unites psychoanalytic approaches to therapy today.

Probably the most significant change since Freud's time is the concern for shortening the length of analysis (*e.g.*, Strupp & Binder, 1984). Today we talk about time-limited and short-form psychoanalysis. Today's analyst will also take a more active role than did Freud. The couch as a requirement is usually gone; the comfort of the patient is what matters, and some patients feel more comfortable pacing or sitting than they do lying on a couch.

Another shift in emphasis is that modern psychoanalysts, although not insensitive to the effects of early childhood experiences, tend to spend more time exploring the present, the here and now. For example, a patient comes for analysis complaining of feeling depressed and angry to the point where the analyst believes there is a real and present danger that the patient might cause self-harm, or even commit suicide. The thrust of therapy is going to be in the here and now, dealing with the patient's current anger and depression until the analyst is convinced that the patient's anger is under control.

Before You Go On
▼▼▼▼▼▼▼▼

Describe the essential nature of Freudian psychoanalysis and some of its major features.

How is psychoanalysis different today from when it was practiced by Freud?

▶ Humanistic Techniques

There are many different brands of humanistic psychotherapy. What they have in common is a concern for self-examination, personal growth, and development. The goal of these therapies is not to uncover any deep-seated conflicts, but to foster psychological growth, to help the person take fullest advantage of life's opportunities. Based on the premise that we all can take charge of ourselves and our futures, grow and change, therapy is devised to assist us with that process.

client-centered therapy the humanistic psychotherapy associated with Rogers, aimed at helping the client grow and change from within

empathic able to understand and share the essence of another's feelings, or to view from another's perspective

▲ Fritz Perls

Client-centered therapy, sometimes called Rogerian therapy after its founder, Carl Rogers, is the therapy that best typifies the humanistic approach. As its name suggests, the client is the center of the therapeutic interaction. (Rogers never used the term "patient," and before his death in 1987 began using the term person-centered rather than client-centered to describe his approach to therapy.) For Rogers, therapy provides a special opportunity for a person to engage in self-discovery and take full advantage of all opportunities to grow personally. Another way to say the same thing is to suggest that a goal of client-centered therapy is to help the individual self-actualize. Self-actualization is a concept we discussed in Chapter 10 when considering humanistic approaches to personality (see pp. 347–348).

What are the characteristics of client-centered therapy? Again, there are many variants, but the following ideas generally characterize a client- centered approach. The focus is on the present, not one's past or childhood. The focus is on one's feelings or affect, not beliefs or cognitions; that is, you are more likely to hear, "How do you feel about that?" than "What do you think about that?" The therapist will attempt to reflect or mirror, not interpret, how a client is feeling (using statements such as, "You seem angry about that" or "Does that make you feel sad?"). I should point out that assessing the true nature of a client's feelings is not necessarily easy to do. To do so accurately requires that the therapist be an active listener and **empathic,** or able to understand and share the essence of another's feelings.

Throughout each session, the therapist will express what is called *unconditional positive regard.* This is the expression of being accepting and noncritical without condition. "I won't be critical. If that's the way you feel, that's the way you feel. Whatever you have to say in here is okay with me." This contrasts considerably with the situations in which one usually gains acceptance and/or positive regard. In most cases, positive regard is conditional. "*If* you do so-and-so, *then* I will think highly of you." That is, positive regard is typically conditional upon some action or behavior of the person. Not so in client-centered therapy. The exchange between client and therapist presented in Figure 13.1 is rather typical.

A friend of mine, a Rogerian psychotherapist, was once elated about how well a session with an undergraduate student had gone. When I asked him why he thought it had gone so well, he said that when the student came to his office and sat down, he asked her how she was feeling and what she'd like to talk about. She said that she didn't want to talk about anything. So my friend said, "If you don't want to talk, that's okay. If you change your mind, I'm right here, and I'm willing to listen." For the next 50 minutes, the two of them sat there, neither doing or saying anything. At the end of their hour, the therapist said, "Well, our time's up. I'll see you next week." The student replied, "Right, see you then." It was my friend's point of view that the value of this (rather quiet) session was that his client had learned something. She had learned that if she did not want to talk about anything, she didn't have to. That acceptance may then lead her to the realization that if she *did* want to talk about anything (no matter what), that would be okay too.

Gestalt therapy is associated with Fritz Perls (1893–1970) and shares many of the same goals as Rogers's client-centered approach (Perls, 1967; 1971; Perls, Hefferline & Goodman, 1951). You'll remember that we've used the term *gestalt* several times before (mostly in Chapters 1 and 4), and that it means (roughly) "whole" or "totality." Thus, the goal of gestalt therapy is largely to assist the individual integrate his or her thoughts, feelings, and actions; to assist in increasing the person's self-awareness, self-acceptance and growth. The therapy is aimed at helping the person become aware of his or her whole self—including conflicts and problems, and to begin working on ways to deal with those problems and conflicts.

Figure 13.1

A THERAPEUTIC DIALOG

Barbara is an 18-year-old freshman at City Community College. Still living at home with her parents and two younger brothers, she is having difficulty coping with demands on her time. She has a full-time job at a restaurant and is trying to manage four classes at college. The pressures of home, school, and work seem to be making Barbara uncharacteristically anxious and depressed. She is falling behind in her school work, performing poorly on her job, and is finding life at home nearly unbearable. On the recommendation of her psychology instructor, Barbara has been seeing a counselor at the Student Services Center. She has had six visits there.

Psychotherapist: Good morning, Barbara, how do you feel today?

Barbara: [snapping back quickly] Good lord, can't you ever say anything but "how do you feel today?" I feel fine, just fine.

Therapist: You sound angry.

Barbara: [in a sarcastically mocking tone] "You sound angry."

Therapist: [silence]

Barbara: Well I'm not angry, so there.

Therapist: Um, hmm.

Barbara: Well, maybe a little angry.

Therapist: So you feel "a little angry?"

Barbara: Yeah, so I'm angry. So big deal! So what of it? Is there something wrong with being angry?

Therapist: Of course not.

Barbara: You'd be angry too.

Therapist: Oh?

Barbara: My old man threatened to throw me out of the house last night.

Therapist: He threatened you?

Barbara: He said that if I didn't get my act together and shape up, he'd send me packing. God knows where I'd go, but if he pulls that crap on me one more time, I'll show him. I will leave.

Therapist: Would you like to leave?

Barbara: Yes! No! No, I don't really want to leave. It's just that nobody cares about me around there. They don't know how hard it is to work and go to school and everything, ya know?

Therapist: [nods]

Barbara: They never went to college. What do they know? They don't know what it's like.

Therapist: You feel that your parents can't appreciate your problems?

Barbara: Damn right! What do they know? They never tried to work and go to school at the same time.

Therapist: They don't know what it's like.

Barbara: Right! Of course I suppose it's not all their fault. They've never been in this situation. I suppose I could try to explain it to them.

Therapist: You mean that it would be helpful to share with them how you feel about this, about how hard it is for you, and maybe they'd understand?

Barbara: Yeah. I guess that's a pretty good idea. I think I'll do that. At least I'll try. I don't want to just whine and complain and be bitchy all the time. Maybe I can get them to understand what it's like. Boy that sure would help—just to have somebody besides you understand and maybe be on my side once in awhile instead of on my case all the time. That's a real good idea.

This dialogue is no doubt idealized. Things seldom go quite this smoothly this quickly, but it does reflect several principles of Rogerian, client-centered therapy.

What makes Perls's therapy significantly different from Rogers's is that it is a very directive approach in which the therapist is actively involved, challenging the client. Whereas a client-centered technique is accepting, a gestalt technique is questioning. If a patient were to say, "But I never really feel very anxious," the therapist would immediately challenge that assertion, "Oh come on, Heather, be serious. Do you really want us to believe that you *never* feel very anxious? Being anxious from time to time is a part of being alive! Deal with it. Admit to it." Indeed, what we have here is a matter of "getting in touch with one's feelings," acknowledging them as valid, and moving to get on with one's life. Although the focus of gestalt therapy is the individual, sessions are often convened in small group settings. Patients may be given role-playing exercises in which they have to play several parts. They may be asked to act out how they feel about a given situation and then act out how they wish they could respond in that situation.

Before You Go On
▼▼▼▼▼▼▼▼▼

What are the essential characteristics of humanistically oriented psychotherapy?

▶ Behavioral Techniques

behavior therapy techniques of psychotherapy founded on principles of learning established in the psychological laboratory

In a literal sense, there is no one **behavior therapy**. Behavior therapy is a collection of many specific techniques. What unites these techniques is that they are "methods of psychotherapeutic change founded on principles of learning established in the psychological laboratory" (Wolpe, 1981, p. 159). There are many different principles of learning, and many disorders to which such methods and principles can be applied. The basic idea is that we learn to interact with the environment and with other people. Sometimes, one's learning experiences lead to the acquisition of inappropriate or maladjusted responses. Therapy, then, should be aimed at helping people to learn more appropriate, better adjusted responses. We have already discussed two varieties of behavior therapy in our learning chapter (see pp. 208–209 and 213). In this section, we will list some of the more prominent applications that have become part of behavior therapy.

systematic desensitization the application of classical conditioning procedures to alleviate anxiety in which anxiety-producing stimuli are paired with a state of relaxation

Systematic desensitization, the application of classical conditioning procedures to alleviate feelings of anxiety, is one of the first applications of learning principles to have met with success, and it has experienced lasting acceptance. It was formally introduced by Joseph Wolpe in the late 1950s (Wolpe, 1958; 1982), although others had used similar procedures earlier. The therapy is designed to alleviate extreme anxieties, particularly of the sort we find in phobic disorders. You'll recall from our discussion back in Chapter 6 that systematic desensitization is basically a matter of first teaching a patient to relax totally and then to remain relaxed as he or she thinks about or is exposed to a range of stimuli that produce anxiety at ever increasing levels. If the patient can remain calm and relaxed, that response can be conditioned to replace the anxious or fearful response that previously was associated with a particular stimulus.

flooding a technique of behavior therapy in which an aversive stimulus, such as a shock, is paired with an undesired behavior

Flooding is another behavioral procedure aimed at eliminating fears or anxieties associated with specific stimuli. Flooding is usually an *in vivo*, or real-life, procedure in which the subject, accompanied by the therapist, is placed in his or her most fear-arousing situation and is prohibited from escaping. For example, someone afraid of heights may be taken to the top of a tall building or to a very high bridge. Someone afraid of water might be taken out on a large lake or to a nearby swimming pool. There, with the therapist close at hand providing encouragement and support, the individual comes face to face with his or her fear, survives the situation (although

▲ *Joseph Wolpe is shown here conducting systematic desensitization therapy to reduce a client's anxiety. The client, in a relaxed state, is told to imagine the weakest anxiety on her list. If she feels anxious, she is instructed to stop and relax again.*

aversion therapy a technique of behavior therapy in which an aversive stimulus, such as a shock, is paired with an undesired behavior

contingency management bringing about changes in one's behaviors by controlling rewards and punishments

contingency contracting establishing a token economy of secondary reinforcers to reward appropriate behaviors

the session may be terrifying for some), and thus comes to learn that the fear is irrational. Although flooding may sound a bit bizarre and is not for everyone (some therapists have difficulty dealing with such focused anxiety), it is often effective and requires less time than does systematic desensitization.

You should recognize **aversion therapy** as another example of learning applied to solving psychological problems. In aversion therapy, a stimulus that may be harmful, but that produces a pleasant response is paired with an aversive, painful stimulus until the original stimulus is avoided. Every time you put a cigarette in your mouth, I deliver a painful shock to your lip. Every time you take a drink of alcohol, you get violently sick to your stomach. Every time a child molester is shown a picture of a young child, he receives a shock.

None of these situations sounds like the sort of thing that anyone would agree to voluntarily. Many people do, however. They volunteer for such treatments for two reasons: (1) aversion therapy is very effective at suppressing a specific behavior, at least for a while, and (2) it is seen as the lesser of two evils—shocks and nausea-producing drugs are not fun, but subjects see the continuation of their inappropriate behaviors as even more dangerous in the long run.

It is probably aversion therapy more than any other technique that has given behavior therapy a bad reputation among the general public, which often equates behavior therapy with cruel and unusual punishment and mind control. There are a couple of things that we need to recognize. One is that aversion therapy—in any form—is not commonly practiced. A second reality is that, at best, it tends to suppress behaviors for a relatively short time. During that time, other techniques may be used in an attempt to bring about a more lasting change in behavior. That is, the techniques of aversion therapy seldom are effective when used alone; they should be used in conjunction with some other form of therapy.

Contingency management and contingency contracting borrow heavily from the learning principles of operant conditioning. The basic idea, of course, is to have an individual come to appreciate the consequences of his or her behaviors. Appropriate behaviors lead to rewards and opportunities to do valued things; inappropriate behaviors do not lead to reinforcement and provide fewer opportunities to engage in valued activities.

In many cases, these basic procedures work very well. Their ultimate effectiveness often is a case of the extent to which the therapist has control over the situation. If the therapist can control rewards and punishments, in a setting called **contingency management,** he or she stands a good chance of modifying a client's behaviors. The therapist modifies behavior by managing contingencies. *If* a patient (say, a severely disturbed, hospitalized person with schizophrenia) engages in appropriate behavior (leaving her room to go to dinner), *then* she will get something she really wants (say, an after-dinner cigarette).

Contingency contracting amounts to establishing a token economy of secondary reinforcers (see Chapter 6, p. 213). What that means is that the patient is first taught that some token—which may be a checker, a poker chip, or a mark on a pad—can be saved. When enough tokens are saved, they can be cashed in for something of value to the patient. With contracting, the value of a token for a specific behavior is spelled out ahead of time. That is, the therapist and patient enter into a "contract" that indicates exactly how certain appropriate behaviors will be reinforced. Because control over the environment is most complete in such circumstances, this technique is particularly effective in institutions and with young children.

▲ *Bandura uses modeling to help people overcome phobias. By watching other people handle snakes without fear, people can overcome their fears and handle the snakes themselves.*

modeling the acquisition of new responses through the imitation of another who responds appropriately

Realizing that all learning cannot be explained in terms of classical or operant conditioning, you should not be surprised that some types of behavior therapy use learning principles other than those from simple conditioning. **Modeling,** a term introduced by Albert Bandura, involves the acquisition of a new, appropriate response through the imitation of a model. As we saw in Chapter 6, modeling can be an effective means of learning.

In a therapy situation, modeling often amounts to having (or allowing) patients watch someone else perform a certain appropriate behavior, perhaps earning a reward for it (called vicarious reinforcement, you'll recall). Some phobias, particularly those in children, can be overcome through modeling. A child who is afraid of dogs, for example, may profit from watching another child (which would be more effective than using an adult) playing with a dog. Assertiveness training involves helping individuals stand up for their rights and come to the realization that *their* feelings and opinions matter and should be expressed. Such training involves many processes (including direct instruction, group discussion, role-playing, and contingency management) and often relies on modeling to help someone learn appropriate ways to express how they feel and what they think in social situations.

Before You Go On
▼▼▼▼▼▼▼▼▼

Briefly describe some of the techniques used in behavior therapy, including systematic desensitization, flooding, aversion therapy, contingency management and contracting, and modeling.

▶ Cognitive Techniques

Psychotherapists who use *cognitive techniques* do not deny the importance of a person's behaviors (these therapies are often called *cognitive-behavioral*). Rather, they believe that what matters most in the therapeutic session is the client's set of thoughts, perceptions, attitudes, and beliefs about himself or herself and the environment. The principle here is that to change how one feels and acts, therapy should first change how one thinks. As we have seen with other approaches to psychotherapy, there is not just one type of cognitive-behavioral therapy; there are many. A recent survey identified

▲ *Albert Ellis*

rational-emotive therapy (RET) a form of cognitive therapy, associated with Ellis, aimed at changing the subject's irrational beliefs or maladaptive cognitions

nearly two dozen distinct varieties (Dobson, 1988). We'll examine two of these: rational-emotive therapy and cognitive restructuring therapy.

Rational-emotive therapy (RET) is associated with Albert Ellis (1970; 1973; 1991). Its basic premise is that psychological problems arise when a person tries to interpret (a cognitive activity) what happens in the world on the basis of irrational beliefs. "Rational-emotive therapy (RET) hypothesizes that people largely disturb themselves by thinking in a self-defeating, illogical, and unrealistic manner—especially by escalating their natural preferences and desires into absolutistic, dogmatic musts and commands on themselves, others, and their environmental conditions" (Ellis, 1987, p. 364). In other words, disturbed behaviors and feelings arise from maladaptive cognitions, which in most cases are unrealistic beliefs about oneself and one's environment.

When compared to client-centered techniques, RET is quite directive. In fact, Ellis takes exception with techniques of psychotherapy that are designed to help a person *feel* better without providing useful strategies by which the person can *get* better (Ellis, 1991). In RET, the therapist takes an active role in interpreting the rationality of a client's system of beliefs and encourages active change. Therapists often act as role models and make homework assignments for clients that help them bring their expectations and perceptions in line with reality.

To give a very simplified example, refer back to the dialogue between Barbara and her client-centered therapist in Figure 13.1. A cognitive therapist might see a number of irrational beliefs operating in this scene, including two that Ellis (1970) claims are very common ones: (1) a person should always be loved for everything they do, and (2) it's better to avoid problems than to face them. These, claims Ellis, are exactly the sort of cognitions that create psychological difficulties (others are listed in Figure 13.2). Rather than waiting for self-discovery, which might never come, a rational-emotive therapist would point out to Barbara that the fact that her parents never went to college and don't understand what it is like to work and go to

Figure 13.2

SOME OF THE IRRATIONAL BELIEFS THAT LEAD TO MALADJUSTMENT AND DISORDER. THE MORE RATIONAL ALTERNATIVE TO THESE BELIEFS SHOULD BE OBVIOUS.

1. One should be loved by everyone for everything one does.
2. Because I strongly desire to perform important tasks competently and successfully, I absolutely must perform them well at all times.
3. Because I strongly desire to be approved of by people I find significant, I absolutely must always have their approval.
4. Certain acts are wicked and people who perform them should be severely punished no matter what.
5. It is horrible when things are not the way we want them to be.
6. It is better to avoid life's problems, if possible, than to face them.
7. One needs something stronger or more powerful than oneself to rely on.
8. One must have perfect and certain self-control.
9. Because I very strongly desire people to treat me considerably and fairly, they must absolutely do so.
10. Because something once affected one's life, it will always affect it.

From Ellis, 1970. 1987

cognitive restructuring therapy a form of cognitive therapy, associated with Beck, in which patients are led to overcome negative self-images and pessimistic views of the future

school at the same time is *their* problem, not hers. Rather than agonizing over the fact that her parents don't seem to appreciate her efforts, she needs to set them straight (pleasantly, of course, which might constitute a homework assignment for Barbara) or move out (there are a number of other possibilities, of course).

Similar to rational-emotive therapy is **cognitive restructuring therapy**, associated with Aaron Beck (1976). Although the basic ideas and goals are similar, restructuring therapy is much less confrontational.

Beck's assumption is that considerable psychological distress stems from a few simple but misguided beliefs (cognitions, again). According to Beck, people with psychological disorders share certain characteristics. For example:

1. They tend to have very negative self-images. They do not value themselves or what they do.

2. They tend to take a very negative view of life experiences.

3. They overgeneralize. For example, having failed one test, a person comes to believe that there is no way he or she can do college work and withdraws from school and looks for work, even though he or she believes there's little chance that anyone would offer a job to someone who is such a failure and a college dropout.

4. They actually seek out experiences that reinforce their negative expectations. The student in the above example may apply for a job as a law clerk or as a stockbroker. Lacking even minimal experience, he or she will not be offered either job and, thus, will confirm his or her own worthlessness.

5. They tend to hold a rather dismal outlook for the future.

6. They tend to avoid seeing the bright side of any experience.

In cognitive restructuring therapy, the patient is given opportunities to test or demonstrate her or his beliefs. The patient and therapist make up a list of hypotheses based on the patient's assumptions and beliefs and then actually go out and test these hypotheses. Obviously, the therapist tries to exercise enough control over the situation so that the experiments do not confirm the patient's beliefs about himself or herself, but will lead instead to positive outcomes. (For example, given the hypothesis, "Nobody cares about me," the therapist need only find one person who does care to refute it.) This approach, of leading a person to the self-discovery that negative attitudes directed toward oneself are inappropriate, has proven very successful in the treatment of depression, although it has been extended to cover a wide range of psychological disorders (Beck, 1985).

Before You Go On
▼▼▼▼▼▼▼▼▼

Briefly summarize the logic behind rational-emotive therapy and cognitive restructuring therapy.

▶ Group Approaches

Many patients profit from some variety of *group therapy*. Group therapy is a label applied to a variety of situations in which several people are involved in a therapeutic setting at the same time. If nothing else, group therapy provides an economic advantage over individual psychotherapy—a therapist can interact with a number of people at once.

In standard forms of group therapy, clients are brought together at the same time (under the guidance of a therapist) to share their experiences and feelings. Most groups are quite informal, and no particular form of psychotherapy is dominant. In other words, meeting with people in groups is something that a psychotherapist with any sort of training or background might do from time to time.

There are a number of possible benefits from this procedure, including an awareness that "I'm not the only one with problems." The sense of support that one can get from someone else with problems occasionally may be greater than that afforded by a therapist —a sort of "she really knows from her own experience the hell that I'm going through" logic. And there is truth in the idea that helping someone else with a problem is in itself a therapeutic process. Yet another advantage of group therapy is that a person may learn new and more effective ways of "presenting" herself or himself to others.

A group approach that has become quite popular is **family therapy**, which focuses on the roles, interdependence, and communication skills of family members. Family therapy is often implemented after one member of a family enters psychotherapy. After discussing the person's problems for a while, other members of the family are invited to join in therapy sessions. There is evidence that getting the family unit involved in therapy benefits patients with a wide range of disorders, from alcoholism and agoraphobia to depression and schizophrenia (Goldfried, Greenberg & Marmar, 1990).

Two related assumptions underlie a family therapy approach. One is that each individual family member is a part of a *system* (the family unit), and his or her feelings, thoughts, and behaviors necessarily impact on other family members (*e.g.,* Minuchin & Fishman, 1981). Bringing about a change (even a therapeutic change) in one member of the family system without involving the other members of the system will not last for long without the support of the others. This is particularly true when the initial problem appears to be with a child or adolescent. I say appears to be because other family members may have at least contributed to the troublesome symptoms of the child's or adolescent's behavior. A therapist is going to have a very difficult time bringing about significant and lasting change in a child whose parents refuse to become involved in therapy.

A second assumption that is often relevant in family therapy sessions is that difficulties arise from improper methods of family *communication* (*e.g.,* Satir, 1967). Quite often, individuals develop false beliefs about the feelings and/or needs of family members. The goal of therapy in such situations is to meet with the family in a group setting to foster and encourage open expressions of feelings and desires. It may be very helpful for an adolescent to learn that her parents are upset and anxious about work-related stress and financial affairs. The adolescent has assumed all along that her parents yelled at her and each other because of something *she* was doing (remember how egocentric adolescents can be). And the parents didn't want to share their concerns over money with the adolescent for fear that it would upset her.

Evaluating group therapy techniques is particularly difficult, and few good outcome studies are available. In general, there seems to be support for the sorts of group approaches we have outlined here, and there is some indication that family therapy is a better approach for many problems than is individual treatment (Gurman, et al., 1986).

family therapy a variety of group therapy focusing on the roles, interdependence, and communication skills of family members

▲ Family therapy may be used as an alternative to individual therapy or as a continuation of it. By meeting together, families are given an opportunity to express their feelings and resolve their problems under a therapist's guidance.

▶ *Evaluating Psychotherapy*

Evaluating psychotherapy has proven to be a difficult task. Is psychotherapy effective? Compared to what? Is any type of psychotherapy better than any other? These are obviously important questions, but the best we can do, I'm afraid, is offer partial, tentative answers. Yes, psychotherapy is effective. Compared to what? Compared to doing nothing. "By about 1980 a consensus of sorts was reached that psychotherapy, as a generic treatment process, was demonstrably more effective than no treatment" (VandenBos, 1986, p. 111; also Gelso & Fassinger, 1990; Goldfried, Greenberg & Marmar, 1990), and more treatment appears to be better than less treatment (Howard, et al., 1986) (see Figure 13.3). Research also

Figure 13.3

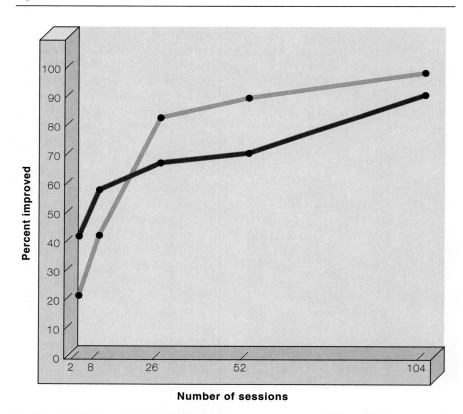

Number of sessions

▲ *The relationship between the number of sessions of psychotherapy and the percentage of patients improved. Objective ratings made by professionals are indicated by the blue line, subjective ratings of well-being made by the patients themselves are indicated by the orange line. In other words, most improvement in psychotherapy is made early on, but improvement continues as therapy continues.*

confirms the logical assertion that the sooner one begins therapy, the better the prognosis (*e.g.*, Kupfer, Frank & Perel, 1989). There is evidence that some therapists are more effective than others, regardless of what type of therapy is practiced (Beutler, Crago & Arizmendi, 1986; Lafferty, Beutler & Crago, 1989).

Here I should mention just a few of the problems involved in doing research on the effectiveness of psychotherapy. First, we have little good quality data on how people might have responded without treatment. In other words, we often do not have a good baseline for comparison. We know that sometimes there is a spontaneous remission of symptoms. Sometimes people get better without the formal intervention of a therapist. But saying that people get better on their own is not literally accurate. There are many factors that can contribute to the improvement of one's mental health, even for one not officially in psychotherapy (Erwin, 1980). You can imagine several such factors—in an experiment we call them extraneous variables. Perhaps the source of one's stress is removed; a nagging parent moves out of state; an aggravating boss gets transferred. Perhaps an interpersonal relationship is begun that provides needed support.

Second, we can't seem to agree on what we mean by recovery. For some, it is simply the absence of observable symptoms for a specified period of time. For others, however, the goal of therapy is something different—the self-report of "feeling better," personal growth, a relatively permanent change in behavior, a restructuring of cognitions, or insight into deep-seated motivational conflicts.

Figure 13.4

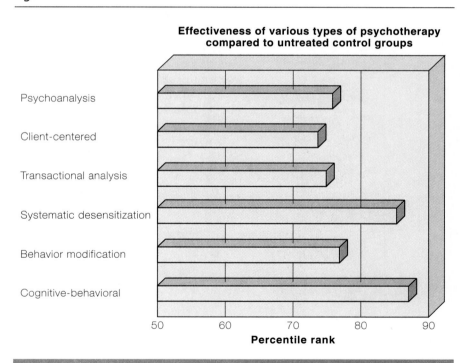

A summary of the results of 475 studies that assessed the effectiveness of psychotherapy. These data reflect the percentage of clients treated with various forms of therapy who scored higher, or more favorably, on a number of outcome measures compared to similar clients who were not treated. That is, the average subject of behavior modification scored higher on outcome measures than did 75 percent of subjects not treated.

Finally, even when we can agree on criteria for recovery, there is often concern about how to measure or assess therapy outcomes. It hardly seems realistic to expect unbiased responses from therapists *or* their patients if we were to ask them to report if therapy had been a helpful experience.

These are three of the most commonly cited problems with studies designed to evaluate the outcome of psychotherapy. Even so, a number of valuable studies have been done. Most have focused on just one technique at a time, and in most cases the results have been very positive (Erwin, 1980; Eysenck, 1952; Greenberg & Safran, 1987; Kazden, et al., 1987; Marziali, 1984; Miller & Berman, 1983; Wolpe, 1981). Several studies also have indicated that even when the the primary treatment option is medical (say, an antidepressant drug), psychotherapy and medication together provide the best prognosis (*e.g,* Frank, et al., 1990; Free & Oei, 1989; Klerman, 1990).

Research by Smith, Glass, and Miller (1980) showed positive results for psychotherapy, and has become a commonly cited study of its effectiveness. Smith and her colleagues found that a variety of techniques produce results that are significantly better than what might be expected through spontaneous remission. As Figure 13.4 shows, an average patient in psychotherapy scored better on a number of outcome variables than did 75 percent of control subjects who received no treatment. The researchers did not go out and collect new data for their report; they reviewed and statistically analyzed 475 published studies on the effectiveness of psychotherapy.

What about comparing psychotherapy methods? Here the answer is also quite clear: *In general,* there are no differences. There is virtually no evidence that any one type of therapy is significantly better than any other (Stiles, et al., 1986). This conclusion is based on a broad generality. There *is* evidence that some types of therapy may be better suited for some types of psychological problems than are other treatments. Behavioral methods, such as systematic desensitization, are useful for phobic disorders, whereas cognitive therapies seem best suited to patients with depression (although even this differentiation may be questionable (Mervis, 1986)).

Which therapy is best suited for which particular disorder is one of the questions to which we do not have a definitive answer, and is one of the most active areas of research in psychotherapy today (Deffenbacher, 1988; Goldfried, Greenberg & Marmar, 1990).

Before You Go On

▼▼▼▼▼▼▼▼

Is there any evidence that psychotherapy is effective?

Is any one type of psychotherapy better than the others?

▼▼▼

Thinking Critically About Treatment and Therapy for Psychological Disorders

1. In this chapter we have reviewed several techniques for dealing with psychological disorders. How do these processes get started? That is, how does a person "get into" therapy in the first place?

2. If you felt that you had problems and could profit from some form of therapy, how would you go about getting in contact with a therapist?

3. Without going into detail, I slipped in the notion that regardless of one's approach to therapy, some therapists seem to be more effective than others. What sorts of characteristics do you think would be found among effective therapists?

4. Think about what is meant by the concept of "asylum." In what way did insane asylums ever grant asylum to the insane?

5. What ethical considerations are involved in asking a person with a severe psychological disorder (perhaps depression or schizophrenia) to give his or her informed consent to a procedure like ECT or psychosurgery?

6. Is it reasonable for a patient or client to ask a therapist what approach to psychotherapy he or she uses? What do you suspect the answer to such a question to be?

7. Assume that you are asked to treat a child with a psychological disorder. Why do I make the claim that it is crucially important to get the child's parents involved in the therapy?

8. Although treating people with psychological disorders is often very effective, what steps can be taken to try to prevent or reduce the prevalence of psychological disorders in the first place?

9. Psychotherapists often claim that it is inadvisable, even dangerous, for persons without formal training in psychology and therapy (like you and me) to engage in "amateur psychotherapy." Why do they make this claim?

Summary

▼▼▼▼▼▼▼▼▼▼▼▼▼▼▼▼▼▼▼▼▼▼▼▼▼▼▼▼▼▼▼▼▼▼▼▼▼▼▼

Briefly trace the history of the treatment of persons with psychological disorders. In ancient times, and throughout the Middle Ages, the prevailing view of the mentally ill was that they were possessed by evil spirits. As a result, treatment was often harsh, involving torture and placement in dungeonlike asylums. Throughout history there have been attempts to provide humane treatment, but it really wasn't until the twentieth century that the treatment of the mentally ill could be classified as humane or therapeutic. *Pages 429–430*

Who may offer psychotherapy? What is the major difference between psychologists and psychiatrists? Many different types of mental health professionals provide psychotherapy, including clinical psychologists, Ph.D.s or Psy.D.s in psychology who have had a one-year clinical internship; psychiatrists, M.D.s who have had an internship and residency in a mental hospital; counseling psychologists, Ph.D.s in psychology specializing in less severe disorders; licensed counselors, who often have degrees in education; psychoanalysts, who specialize in Freudian therapy; clinical social workers, who usually have a master's degree; and others, including pastoral counselors and mental health technicians. *Pages 430–433*

What is a prefrontal lobotomy? Why was it ever used, and why is it not used today? A prefrontal lobotomy is a psychosurgical technique that severs connections between the prefrontal lobes and lower brain centers. It was a common treatment in the 1940s and 1950s because it was often successful in alleviating the worst of psychotic symptoms. It is no longer used because more effective, safer, and reversible treatments are now available. *Page 434*

What is ECT? Why is it still being used? ECT stands for electroconvulsive therapy. In this procedure, a brain seizure is produced by passing an electric current across a patient's head. Although there may be a few negative side effects, ECT is often used as an effective means of reducing or eliminating severe depression. *Page 435*

What are antipsychotic drugs, and what are their effects? Antipsychotic drugs reduce the severity of psychotic symptoms such as hallucinations, delusions, disordered thought, and the like. They function by altering the action of neurotransmitters in the brain. Unfortunately, the symptoms of psychotic disorders often return when the drugs are discontinued. *Page 436*

What are the antidepressant drugs, and what are they meant to do? Unlike the antipsychotic drugs, antidepressants often have long-term beneficial effects (allevi-

ating feelings of depression) even after the patient stops taking them. They often take weeks to have their effects, do not work for everyone, and often have harmful or unpleasant side effects. *Pages 437–438*

What are the common antianxiety drugs, and what are the dangers inherent in their use? The most common antianxiety drugs (or tranquilizers), including meprobamates and benzodiazepines, are effective in reducing felt aspects of anxiety. Some patients who use the drugs develop an addiction. These drugs suppress symptoms; they do not cure the underlying causes of the anxiety the patient is experiencing. *Page 438*

Describe the essential nature of Freudian psychoanalysis, defining some of its major features. How is psychoanalysis different today from when it was practiced by Freud? Psychoanalysis aims to uncover repressed conflicts (perhaps developed in early childhood) so that they can be resolved. The process involves: (1) free association, in which the patient is to say whatever comes to mind; (2) resistance, in which patients seem unable or unwilling to discuss some aspect of their lives; (3) dream interpretation, in which latent and manifest content are analyzed for insights about the patient's unconscious; and (4) transference, in which feelings that were once directed toward someone significant are now directed toward the analyst. Today's psychoanalysis is likely to be shorter, spend less emphasis on early childhood, and be more directive than when it was practiced by Freud. *Pages 438–441*

What are the essential characteristics of humanistically oriented psychotherapy? Client-centered therapy (associated with Carl Rogers) is based on the belief that people can control their lives and solve their own problems if they can be helped to understand the true nature of their feelings. It promotes self-discovery and personal growth. Gestalt therapy (associated with Fritz Perls) is also aimed at achieving insight, getting in touch with honest feelings, personal growth and experiencing "wholeness." It is more directive than client-centered therapy. *Pages 441–444*

Briefly describe some of the techniques used in behavior therapy, including systematic desensitization, flooding, aversion therapy, contingency management and contracting, and modeling. Systematic desensitization is well suited for the treatment of phobic disorders. The subject is taught how to relax. An anxiety hierarchy is constructed, listing stimuli in order of their capacity to elicit anxiety. Desensitization is accomplished by presenting more anxiety-producing stimuli while the subject remains relaxed. *Flooding* is a more dramatic form of behavior therapy in which the subject is confronted with the object of his or her fear while accompanied by the therapist. *Aversion therapy* pairs an unwanted behavior with a strongly negative stimulus, such as a shock or a nausea-producing drug. *Contingency management* amounts to exercising control over the rewards that a subject receives for appropriate behaviors. *Contracting* usually involves a token economy system in which a subject agrees to engage in certain appropriate behaviors in order to earn specified rewards. *Modeling* implies that persons can acquire appropriate behaviors by imitating the behaviors of models. *Pages 444–446*

Briefly summarize the logic behind rational-emotive therapy and cognitive restructuring therapy. Cognitive therapies are designed to alter the ways in which one thinks about oneself and the environment. Rational-emotive therapy (RET) operates from the premise that people often form irrational assumptions about themselves and the world. Cognitive restructuring is somewhat less directive, but is also based on the premise that some people have formed negative self-images and negative views about the future that are not founded in reality. *Pages 446–448*

What are some advantages of group therapy? Describe two assumptions underlying family therapy. The advantages of group approaches include: (1) One's basic problem may be largely interpersonal and understood best in an interpersonal situation. (2) There is value in realizing that one is not the only person with a problem. (3) There is value in providing support for someone else. (4) The dynamics of communication can be analyzed and changed in a group setting. Family therapy is based on the assumptions that: (1) family members are part of a system in which one member affects all others, and that (2) many problems arise from faulty styles of communication within the family. *Pages 448–449*

Is there any evidence that psychotherapy is effective? Is any one type of psychotherapy better than the others? It is safe to take the tentative position that, in general, psychotherapy is effective. Some therapies may be better suited to some persons and to some disorders than other therapies, but there is no evidence that any one technique is generally better than any other. *Pages 450–452*

13.1 We can claim that the treatment of persons with psychological disorders in humane, systematic ways was generally accepted: a) during the Greek and Roman empires. b) early in the Middle Ages (about 1200 A.D.). c) late in the seventeenth century. d) at the beginning of the twentieth century. *Pages 429–430*

13.2 Throughout history, the treatment of the mentally ill has been guided mostly by a) those politicians in power wanting to remain in power b) whatever religion happened to dominate the period. c) the profit motive—the desire to profit from the grief of others. d) the contemporary understanding of what caused the disordered symptoms. *Pages 429–430*

13.3 True or False? Hippocrates believed that what we now call hallucinations and delusions arose when an individual had offended the Greek gods. *Page 429*

13.4 Which of these psychotherapists can prescribe drugs or medication for psychological problems? a) psychiatric nurses b) clinical psychologists c) psychiatrists d) Any of these can prescribe medications. *Pages 430–432*

13.5 A prefrontal lobotomy a) severs connections between the cerebral cortex and lower brain centers. b) lesions or removes the corpus callosum, thus separating the two hemispheres of the brain. c) destroys the amygdala of the limbic system. d) involves gradually removing more and more brain tissue until symptoms disappear. *Page 434*

13.6 Prefrontal lobotomies a) were very dangerous; nearly one-quarter of patients died as a result. b) were discovered by accident when a psychotic patient was shot in the head and his symptoms disappeared. c) are now outlawed in the United States. d) were done on tens of thousands of persons in the 1940s and 1950s. *Page 434*

13.7 True or False? "Psychosurgery" means "lobotomy." *Page 434*

13.8 Why does electroconvulsive therapy produce the effects that it does? a) Levels of the neurotransmitter dopamine are increased. b) Pleasure centers of the brain are stimulated. c) Unpleasant, depressing memories are destroyed. d) No one really knows why it works. *Page 435*

13.9 ECT is most commonly used to treat a) schizophrenia. b) persons with aggressive or violent tendencies. c) depression. d) many (but not all) anxiety disorders. *Page 435*

13.10 True or False? ECT produces a seizure in the brain very much like an epileptic seizure. *Page 435*

3.11 The general name for chemicals that affect one's psychological functioning is a) hallucinogenic. b) psychoactive. c) narcotic. d) analgesic. *Page 436*

13.12 The first anti-psychotic drug used effectively was: a) chlorpromazine. b) valium. c) lithium salts. d) Prozac. *Page 436*

13.13 True or False? Anti-psychotic medications suppress symptoms, but rarely can they be said to cure a disorder. *Page 436*

13.14 True or False? The main advantage of antidepressant medications over ECT is that, when the medications work, they work more quickly than does ECT. *Pages 436–437*

13.15 Anti-anxiety drugs a) have long-lasting effects. b) are classified as either tricyclics or MAO inhibitors. c) cure the symptoms of hallucinations and delusions. d) ease or alleviate the feelings of anxiety. *Page 438*

13.16 Freudian psychoanalysis is based on many assumptions, including each of the following EXCEPT a) The patient genuinely may be unable to tell the analyst why he or she is experiencing anxiety. b) Early childhood experiences can have an impact on how one feels as an adult c) Once the analyst gets the patient to *act* better, he or she will also feel better and think better. d) The true nature of the patient's problems may be revealed in the content of his or her dreams. *Pages 438–440*

13.17 In Freudian psychoanalysis, the process of coming to feel about the analyst as one used to feel about an important or significant other person is a process called a) transference. b) free association. c) latent analysis. d) resistance. *Pages 439–440*

13.18 One thing that psychoanalysts after Freud still hold to as a basic assumption is that a) there is no good reason for anxiety to feel so unpleasant b) hypnosis can be a useful way of establishing transference. c) anxiety stems from some sort of repressed conflict. d) analysis is to be a time-consuming process, usually lasting for years. *Page 441*

13.19 True or False? As opposed to latent content, the manifest content of a dream is the content as expressed and reported by the patient. *Page 440*

13.20 What do client-centered therapy and psychoanalysis have in common? a) the assumption of an active role by the therapist to interpret and evaluate what the client has to say b) an assumption that, at least at the beginning of therapy, the client may not understand the source of his/her distress c) the assumption that the focus of therapy should be on what the person feels, not what the person thinks d) the assumption that earlier, childhood experiences are more significant than how one feels currently. *Page 442*

13.21 To be an active listener and to be able to share and understand the feelings of another is to a) offer unconditional positive regard. b) be existential. c) self-actualize. d) be empathic. *Page 442*

13.22 Most of the techniques used in behavior therapies come from a) suggestions made by previous patients. b) Freud's theories. c) the learning laboratory. d) research in education. *Page 442*

13.23 Which of these is least appropriate (or least likely) for treating phobic disorders: a) flooding b) aversion therapy c) systematic desensitization d) implosive therapy. *Pages 444–446*

13.24 Which behavioral therapy technique derives most directly from the work of Albert Bandura: a) aversion therapy b) contingency contracting c) gestalt therapy d) modeling. *Page 446*

13.25 True or False? By definition, contingency management is essentially the opposite of unconditional positive regard. *Page 445*

13.26 A basic premise of cognitive therapies is that people a) don't realize how they feel. b) develop irrational beliefs about themselves and the world. c) do strange things in order to be reinforced by attention. d) act out childhood fantasies when they become adults. *Pages 446–448*

13.27 One type of disorder for which cognitive therapy seems particularly well suited is a) schizophrenia. b) personality disorders. c) depression. d) phobias. *Pages 446–448*

13.28 True or False? All psychotherapies are equally effective for any particular psychological disorder. *Pages 450–452*

▲ **Preview**

▲ **The Social-Psychological Perspective Attitudes**

  ▼ *Psychology in the Real World:*
   Television and Violent Behavior

▲ **Social Perception**

▲ **Social Influence**

▲ **Thinking Critically about Social Psychology**

▲ **Summary**

▲ **Test Yourself**

▲▲▲▲▲▲

In the late 1960s, a third-grade teacher in a small elementary school in Riceville, Iowa wanted to provide her students with a first-hand experience of prejudice. Jane Elliott announced to her students that she had discovered that blue-eyed children were superior in all regards to children with brown eyes. Clearly, brown-eyed children were second-class citizens. Brown-eyed children were to sit in the back of the classroom. They had to stand at the back of the lunch line. They were not allowed second help-ings of food. They were not to use the drinking fountain. The superior blue-eyed chil-dren were given special privileges, including extra recess time. To make their status more visible, brown-eyed children were to wear paper collars that identified their lowly status even from a distance.

It wasn't long before the students in Ms. Elliott's third-grade class became active participants in her demonstration. The classroom behaviors of the brown-eyed chil-dren deteriorated; they performed below their usual levels on several academic tasks. The blue-eyed children did better than usual. Children with blue eyes voluntarily avoided contact with their inferior classmates. Fights and arguments broke out. The behavior of the blue-eyed children became aggressive, contemptuous, and occasion-ally vicious—and all in one day!

The next school day, Ms. Elliott informed the class that she had made a terrible mistake. She had gotten the evidence reversed. It was blue-eyed children who were inferior; the best people were those with brown eyes! With displays of great enthusi-asm and joy, the brown-eyed children tore off their offensive collars and helped fit the blue-eyed children with paper collars that identified *them* as inadequate and infe-rior. Even after their experience of the previous day, the behaviors of the children were exactly the same, only the roles were reversed. Those who just the day before were the objects of prejudice now sat in the front of the class, performed well on

classroom tests, rushed to be first at lunch time, and treated their blue-eyed classmates very badly.

On the third day, Jane Elliott shared her original intent with her pupils and told them that none of what she had said the last two days was, in fact, true.

The effects of this classroom demonstration were short-lived. The children soon returned to their normal classroom routine. The artificially induced prejudice disappeared almost as quickly as it had been created. This exercise was not a carefully controlled experiment, and given our concerns about the ethics of such manipulations, it is unlikely to be replicated. Nonetheless, the experience was a meaningful one for those Iowa third-graders and a significant one for us, too. It tells us much about the irrationality of prejudice—particularly prejudice based solely on physical characteristics (Elliott, 1977; Leonard, 1970; Peters, 1971). We will have occasion to return to this demonstration several times within this chapter.

▶ Preview

social psychology the scientific study of how others influence the thoughts, feelings, and behaviors of the individual

In a sense, **social psychology** deals with us as we live: in a social world, interacting with, influencing, and being influenced by others. As we have seen many times, other areas of psychology often are interested in reactions that are social in nature also. In this chapter we consider the individual in the real, social world.

To provide the proper context, we begin with a discussion of the perspective from which social psychologists study behavior and mental processes; then we'll move on to consider the nature, the formation, and the changing of attitudes. We'll review what is referred to as "social cognition." Cognitions, you'll recall, are our thoughts, beliefs, perceptions, and the like. When we talk about social cognitions, we are referring to such issues as interpersonal attraction and how we explain—at least in our own minds—the behaviors of others, a process called attribution.

We will then move on to deal with matters of social influence. The major topics here are conformity and obedience, but a related issue is the matter of the circumstances under which an individual will come to the aid of another in distress, a topic which in social psychology is often referred to as "bystander intervention." We'll end the chapter with a discussion of two issues that also are related to the influence of group membership: Does the presence of others enhance or inhibit the behavior of the individual? Do people tend to make better judgments when in a group or when they are alone? In terms of practical, day-to-day application, there may be no more relevant chapter than this one.

▶ The Social-Psychological Perspective

Since we are social organisms, each of us is familiar in our own way with many of the concerns of social psychology. Getting along with other people is considered to be an asset, and those who are able to do so easily may be demonstrating an appreciation of social psychology in the sense of being skilled in predicting the behaviors of others.

To claim that we are familiar with the concerns of social psychology has certain implications. On the one hand, it means that social psychology tends to be perceived as interesting and relevant because it deals with everyday situations that affect us all. On the other hand, it means that often we are willing to accept common sense and personal experience as the basis for many of our assumptions about social behavior. Although common sense occasionally may be valid, it is not an acceptable basis for a science of social behavior. Social psychology relies on scientific methods, even if the results of applying these methods are contrary to intuition. As we'll see in this chapter, some of the most influential discoveries in social psychology have been unexpected and counterintuitive. Like many other areas of psychology, social psychology recently has taken on a *cognitive* flavor. That is, social psychologists are attempting more and more to understand social behavior by examining the underlying mental structures and processes that are reflected in such behavior.

To provide an example of a psychological approach to social behaviors, let's review Jane Elliott's classroom demonstration of prejudice as a social psychologist might. On the first day, children with blue eyes developed some unfavorable ideas, or cognitions, about brown-eyed classmates. Pupils with brown eyes were thought of as inferior, lazy, and irresponsible. These ideas developed without any real test. With no actual evidence or data to back them up, blue-eyed children were willing to think of all brown-eyed children as inferior. They were willing to ignore their previous experiences

▲ The results of the experiment third-grade teacher Jane Elliot conducted with her students were visible in the children's drawings, as well as their behavior in class and their performance on tests. When children were in the "superior" group for a day, their drawings conveyed confidence and happiness such as the top one. When the same children were in the less-favored group their drawings reflected feelings of inferiority and anger, such as the drawing on the bottom by the same student.

stereotype a generalized mental (cognitive) representation of someone that minimizes individual differences and is based on limited experience

with their classmates. They formed a **stereotype**—a generalized set of cognitions about members of a group that is based on limited experience and does not allow for individual differences.

This example of a stereotype has negative implications because it is based on erroneous information, but stereotypes are not necessarily bad. When they are based on accurate information they are useful tools that help us simplify and deal more efficiently with a complex world (Jussim, et al., 1987). All of us have formed many stereotypes. Some of our stereotypes are based on accurate, reliable appraisals; some are based on false information.

Notice also that once the pupils in Jane Elliott's class developed the idea of superiority and inferiority on the basis of eye color, their behaviors changed accordingly. The students had rather strong notions about how one deals with or reacts to classmates who are "inferior." They are to sit at the back of the class, they are to stand at the end of lunch lines, and they are not to be spoken to in a friendly manner, *because* they are inferior.

norms rules or expectations that guide our behavior in certain social situations by prescribing how we ought to behave

We all develop a complex set of rules or expectations about behavior that guides and directs our social actions. In other words, we have come to know what we are supposed to do in different social situations. Perhaps you recall our discussion of discrimination learning in Chapter 6, where we found that we often learn to make discriminations about which behaviors are acceptable in a given social situation and which behaviors are unacceptable. Shared expectations about how the members of a group *ought to behave* are called social **norms** (Levine & Moreland, 1990). Clearly, norms have a cognitive basis if we are to use them consistently. Like stereotypes, they are cognitions that we use to help simplify our social world. Note how uncomfortable you feel when you find yourself in a new and different situation—perhaps a foreign country, or a strange religious ceremony, or a country club, or a ghetto. Our feelings of discomfort reflect the fact that we do not know what is expected of us; we don't know the rules of behavior; we have not learned the appropriate norms. Now that we have a sense of what we mean by social cognition, let's explore some areas of social psychology in which this concept has been useful.

Before You Go On

▼▼▼▼▼▼▼▼▼

What are stereotypes and norms, and in what way are they cognitive?

▶ Attitudes

attitude a relatively stable and general evaluative disposition directed toward some object, consisting of feelings, behaviors, and beliefs

Since the 1920s, the nature of attitudes has been a central concern to social psychologists (McGuire, 1985). We'll define **attitude** as a relatively stable and general evaluative disposition directed toward some object; it consists of beliefs, feelings, and behaviors.

The concept of *evaluative* in this (rather traditional) definition refers to an aspect of attitudes that includes feelings as being for or against, pro or con, positive or negative. By *disposition* we mean a tendency or a preparedness to respond to the object of the attitude (actual responding is not necessary). Also notice that by definition, attitudes have objects. We have attitudes *toward* or *about* something. We don't just have attitudes, good or bad, in general. I realize that the word *attitude* can be used differently in common speech. We hear that someone has a "bad attitude," or just "an attitude" in general, as in "Boy, does *he* have an attitude!" In psychology, an attitude—as a technical term—requires an object.

▲ Attitudes consist of beliefs, feelings, and behaviors. Thus, if we believe that our water supply is being damaged by unauthorized dumping of waste, we may show our feelings and beliefs by participating in a demonstration.

Anything can be the object of an attitude, whether it be a person, an object, or an idea (Petty & Cacioppo, 1986). You may have attitudes about this course, the car you drive, your father, the President, or the corner fast food restaurant where you occasionally eat lunch. Some of our attitudes are more important than others, of course, but the fact that we have attitudes toward so many things is precisely the reason why the study of attitudes is so central in social psychology.

▶ The Nature of Attitudes

Although many different definitions of attitude have been proposed over the years, most of them suggest that an attitude consists of three components (Chaiken & Stangor, 1987). When we use the term *attitude* in our everyday conversation, we most likely are referring to the *affective component*, which consists of our feelings about or our evaluation of the attitudinal object. The *behavioral component* consists of our response tendencies toward the object of our attitude. This component includes our actual behaviors and/or our intentions to act should the opportunity arise. The *cognitive component* includes our beliefs or thoughts about the attitudinal object. By now, these three components of affect, behavior, and cognition, or ABC, ought to be quite familiar to you.

All three components are required to fit our definition (Breckler, 1984). If you believe that brown-eyed children are lazy, you have a belief, not an attitude. If you hate brown-eyed children, you have an emotional reaction, not an attitude. If you make fun of brown-eyed children, you are engaging in behavior, but you do not necessarily have an attitude toward them. Strictly speaking, to say that you have attitude toward brown-eyed children would require evidence of all three components.

In many cases, the cognitive, affective, and behavioral components of our attitudes are consistent. We think that classical music is relaxing and like to listen to it, so we buy classical music recordings. You believe that a knowledge of psychology will be an asset in your career, you are enjoying your psychology class, and you plan to take more psychology classes in the future. However, there are occasions when our behaviors are not consistent with or do not reflect our true beliefs and feelings (Ajzen & Fishbein, 1980).

Because actual behaviors may not reflect true feelings or beliefs, some psychologists (*e.g.,* Fazio, 1989; Fishbein & Ajzen, 1975) exclude the behavioral component from their definition; they reserve the term *attitude* to refer to a fundamental liking or disliking for the attitudinal object. Other psychologists argue that attitude is two-dimensional, involving both affect and cognition, but not behavior (Bagozzi & Burnkrant, 1979; Zajonc & Markus, 1982).

This discussion may sound very theoretical, but you have had personal experience with the basic issue involved here. Fishbein and Ajzen maintain that attitudes (how you feel about something) *may* lead to actual behaviors, but in many social situations they do not. The situation may "overpower" the affective and cognitive components of our attitudes. For example, we may have strong, unfavorable beliefs and negative feelings about someone, yet when we encounter that person at a social gathering, we smile, extend our hand, and say something pleasant. You realize that this is another way of saying that the components of an attitude may lack consistency—and it is the behavioral component that is most often inconsistent with the other two.

Figure 14.1

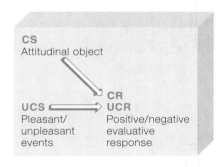

▲ *The classical conditioning of attitudes.*

▲ *Advertisers often bring sexual connotations to everyday products, illustrating classical conditioning.*

Before You Go On

▼▼▼▼▼▼▼▼▼

What is an attitude and what are its three components?

▶ Attitude Formation

As it happens, we have formed many attitudes about a wide range of objects and events. Let us now briefly consider where they came from. Most experts agree that attitudes are learned and that simple conditioning processes go a long way toward explaining attitude formation.

Some attitudes are no doubt acquired through the simple associative process of *classical conditioning*. As shown in Figure 14.1, pleasant events (unconditioned stimuli) may be paired with an attitudinal object (conditioned stimulus). As a result of this pairing or association, the attitudinal object comes to elicit the same good feeling (a positive evaluative response) that originally was produced by the unconditioned stimulus. The good feeling, originally an unconditioned response elicited by some pleasant event, now becomes a conditioned response elicited by the attitudinal object. Of course, negative attitudes can be acquired in the same way.

Some advertising attempts to work in this way by taking an originally neutral object (the product) and trying to create positive associations to it. For instance, a soft drink advertisement may depict young, attractive people having a great time playing volleyball, dancing, or enjoying a concert while drinking a particular soft drink. The intent is that you and I will associate the product with good times and having fun. That sports figures often wear brand name logos and trademarks on their uniforms also may suggest that manufacturers want us to learn to associate their product with the skills of the athlete we're watching.

Attitudes also can be formed as a result of the direct reinforcement of behaviors consistent with some attitudinal position, that is, through operant conditioning. Several studies have shown that verbal reinforcement (saying "good," "fine," or "right") when subjects agree with attitude statements leads those subjects to develop attitudes consistent with the position expressed (Insko, 1965). The blue-eyed children in Ms. Elliott's third-grade class no doubt received much reinforcement and social support from their peers for acting in negative and derogatory ways toward their "inferior" brown-eyed classmates. And it is no small matter that simply having others (perhaps of different race or ethnic origin) to view as inferior may be in itself somewhat reinforcing. People can feel much better about themselves if they come to believe that they are somehow above, or better than, others.

As we discussed in Chapter 6, people often tend to imitate behaviors that they have seen reinforced in others (called vicarious reinforcement). To the extent that we perceive that others are gaining reinforcers for having and expressing some attitude, we are likely to adopt that attitude ourselves.

Advertising that relies on testimonials from satisfied customers is appealing to a sort of observational learning (see Figure 14.2). The potential consumer is shown someone who has used a product with success (has received reinforcement), and the advertiser hopes that this exposure will lead the potential buyer to develop a favorable evaluation of the product. Obviously, the advertiser is going to show us only people who are happy with their product or service. We seldom stop to think about how many people may have used the product or service and are unhappy with it.

Figure 14.2

▲ *Observational learning is demonstrated in advertising that uses satisfied customers to promote the product or service.*

Before You Go On
▼▼▼▼▼▼▼▼▼

Briefly describe three ways in which attitudes might be acquired.

▶ Attitude Change and Persuasion

Much of the research on attitudes has been concerned with the very practical questions of when and how attitudes change. This research has dealt largely with conscious, planned attempts to change attitudes, a process called **persuasion**. In this section, we'll examine a few factors involved in attitude change, beginning with one of those unexpected and counterintuitive findings to which we referred earlier.

Cognitive Dissonance Theory. Common sense would seem to suggest that one's attitudes will mold one's behaviors, and that attitude change will lead to behavior change. In 1957, Leon Festinger proposed the reverse: that one's attitudes can be shaped by one's behavior. Festinger's proposal referred to **cognitive dissonance**. Cognitions are beliefs, thoughts, perceptions, and the like. Dissonance means discord, discomfort, or distress that is due to things being out of balance or not fitting

persuasion the process of intentionally attempting to change an attitude

cognitive dissonance a motivating discomfort or tension caused by a lack of balance or consonance among one's cognitions

together well. When cognitions are dissonant, one possibility is that attitudes will change in order to reduce the unpleasantness of that dissonance. (The concept of cognitive dissonance was first introduced back in Chapter 9 on motivation.)

One of the best examples of how this might work is found in one of the original demonstrations of the phenomenon (Festinger & Carlsmith, 1959). Participants in the research were asked to perform an extremely boring task that required them to rotate row after row of small wooden knobs. After a lengthy knob-turning session, the experimenter explained that the research really had to do with the effects of motivation on such a task. The subject was told that the person sitting in the waiting area just outside the laboratory was to be the next subject in the project. This next subject was to be led to believe that the task was fun, interesting, and educational. Explaining that his assistant, who usually told these "lies" to the waiting subject, was absent, the experimenter asked the subject to do this selling job for him and offered to pay the subject for his or her help. Subjects invariably agreed and actually worked very hard at trying to convince the next subject (who wasn't a real subject, but was in on the experiment) that the project was enjoyable and a lot of fun. Weeks later, at the end of the semester, all subjects filled out a questionnaire that asked about their reactions to the knob-turning experiment in which they had participated.

The only experimental manipulation was a simple one: Some of the subjects were paid $20 for trying to convince the waiting "subject" that the clearly boring task was fun and interesting, while others were paid only $1. In all other respects, all subjects had the same experience in the laboratory.

At the end of the semester, which subjects do you suppose expressed more positive attitudes about the project in which they had participated: the ones paid $20 or those paid $1? Doesn't it seem logical that those paid $20 would remember the task as fun and enjoyable and indicate a willingness to participate in other similar projects? Festinger and Carlsmith predicted just the opposite. They reasoned that subjects paid only $1 would feel that their behavior had not been sufficiently justified. They had told a lie and had been given only a trivial amount of money for doing so. These subjects would experience a great deal of tension or discomfort about this inconsistency—cognitive dissonance would have been created. "I lied for a lousy dollar." One way to resolve their dissonance would be to modify their attitude about the project so that it fit better with their behavior, or was more consonant. The prediction was that these subjects would convince themselves that they had not lied at all; the experiment *had* been fun and interesting.

The subjects paid $20, on the other hand, had plenty of justification for their action (in 1959 $20 was a lot of money for a college student living in a dormitory). Sure, they had lied, but they had "good reason" to do so. These subjects would experience little cognitive dissonance and should not be expected to change their attitude about the experiment. "Yeah, I lied, but I got paid 20 bucks to do so." The results are presented in Figure 14.3. Seldom do we find differences in an experiment as clear-cut as these.

The results of this experiment (and by now numerous others) suggest that one good way to change people's attitudes is to get them to change their behaviors first. Not only that, but there is a clear advantage in offering as *little* incentive as possible to bring about that change in behavior. Simply buying someone off to change his or her behavior may get you compliance, but it will not produce the sort of cognitive dissonance required to bring about lasting attitude change.

Figure 14.3

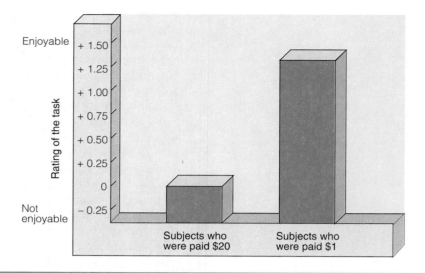

▲ *After being paid either $1 or $20 to "lie" about a boring task, subjects were later asked to rate the task in terms of enjoyment and interest. As can be seen in this figure, those paid $1 (with cognitive dissonance) gave the task much higher ratings. (After Festinger & Carlsmith, 1959.)*

You should be able to generate many examples of cognitive dissonance influencing attitude change. A student who supports a military intervention in a Middle East conflict is invited by a good friend to attend a "peace rally." Accepting the invitation might produce dissonance: "I favor military involvement, but there I was at a peace rally." These two cognitions are dissonant. What will happen next? We can't say, but we can predict that something is likely to change in order to reduce dissonance; perhaps it will be the student's initial attitude. Consider the number of students who have changed their attitude about a course, or a discipline, because they were required to take a course in that discipline. I know that as a chemistry major at the time, my (rather negative) attitudes about psychology and psychology classes changed because of the dissonance created when I was required to take a (very enjoyable) class in introductory psychology.

Before You Go On
▼▼▼▼▼▼▼▼▼▼

What is cognitive dissonance, and how does it operate?

▲ *Cognitive dissonance is occurring when you find yourself test-driving and considering a new car that you have previously been against.*

The Source of Persuasive Communication. Research tells us that, in general, a highly credible (believable) source will be more persuasive than will a less credible source (Petty & Cacioppo, 1986). There are probably several factors involved in source credibility, but two that seem especially important are perceived expertise and trustworthiness.

Several studies (Aronson, et al., 1963; Hovland & Weiss, 1951) indicate that the greater the perceived expertise of the communicator, the greater the amount of persuasion that occurs. People who are convinced that they are listening to an expert are more likely to be persuaded than they

▲ We are more likely to be persuaded by communicators we perceive as having expertise and trustworthiness. Often cited as an example is Jessie Jackson, who as a communicator, conveys a high degree of credibility for many people. Here Spike Lee is directing Jackson in an anti-drug campaign.

would be if they thought that the speaker knew little about the subject matter—even if the message were exactly the same! For example, I am much more likely to be persuaded by Michael Jackson if he were trying to change my attitudes about a stereo system than I would be if he were trying to sell me a certain brand of toaster oven or aftershave. Celebrities *are* used to promote or sell products even without any apparent expertise, on the basis of the following logic: First, you'll recognize them and attend to what they say, and second, their credibility and expertise in some other area, which has brought about their celebrity or fame, will transfer to the product they are selling.

A second factor likely to enhance a communicator's credibility is a high degree of trustworthiness (Cooper & Croyle, 1984). Studies by Walster and Festinger (1962) demonstrated that more attitude change resulted when subjects overheard a persuasive communication than when they believed that the communication was directed at them. Trustworthiness and credibility apparently were enhanced by the perceived lack of intent to persuade ("Why should they lie? They don't even know we can hear them?"). Haas (1981) maintains that persuasive information will be examined (cognitively) in an attempt to assess its validity or truth value. People are less likely to question and argue with information they get from a source they rate as credible; they simply expect it to be accurate.

Before You Go On

▼▼▼▼▼▼▼▼

What communicator characteristics are known to have an impact on attitude change?

Television and Violent Behavior

One type of social behavior in which psychologists have been interested for a long time is aggression. Aggression refers to behaviors that are intended to harm or hurt another. *Violence* is a form of aggression in which one purposively inflicts physical injury or pain on another. (The implication, of course, is that aggression may lead to psychological as well as to physical harm.) The research literature on the forces that influence violent behaviors is extensive. Here, we'll focus only on the extent to which violent behaviors may be influenced by television programming.

The basic question is a simple one: Does television viewing have an impact on the violent behaviors of viewers? By now, you know that such simple questions seldom have simple answers, but in this case, we do seem to have a simple and direct answer: Yes, watching violence on television does have an effect on violent behaviors, particularly for children.

There is no doubt that television viewing is a popular pastime among children. In fact, "the average child born today will by the age of 15 have spent more time watching television than going to school" (Liebert, 1986, p. 43). Is watching television related to increased violence? "In the simplest terms, only three possibilities exist in this equation. (1) Television has no significant relationship to aggressive behavior. (2) Television reduces aggressive behavior. (3) Television increases aggressive behavior. Almost all the studies reviewed in the past decade support the third possibility. No studies of any consequence support the second possibility" (Rubenstein, 1983).

Televised violence seems to have an effect (mostly, but not exclusively on children) in two ways: direct imitation and desensitization. The imitation aspect follows nicely from the work of Bandura (*e.g.*, Bandura, 1973), which we reported back in Chapter 6. Many studies have shown that aggressive and violent behaviors increase almost proportionally with viewing violence on TV (*e.g.*, Comstock, 1980; Eron, 1982; Freedman, 1984; Hearold, 1986; Huesmann & Malamuth, 1986; Huston, Watkins & Kunkel, 1989; Turner, Hesse & Peterson-Lewis, 1986). What may be equally disturbing is evidence that even if one does not engage directly in violent behaviors after watching violence on TV, one's *tolerance*, or insensitivity increases. This is, in a sense, a sort of perceptual adaptation. At first, scenes of great physical violence may be very upsetting and objectionable, but after repeated exposures, one adapts and becomes more accepting (Geen & Thomas, 1986; Linz, et al., 1984; Singer & Singer, 1981).

Is there anything we can do (perhaps as parents) to lessen the effects of violence on television? Here are three practical suggestions (from Liebert, 1986): (1) Restrict overall TV viewing time. [This is clear and obvious, but often difficult to manage.] (2) Selectively encourage some programming and discourage others. [It's generally quite easy to predict which shows are most likely to contain high doses of violence—cartoons and crime shows among them.] (3) Watch TV with children, taking advantage of every opportunity to discuss the long-term ramifications of violence and your own disapproval of such behaviors. Remember Bandura's work showing that children are more likely to imitate those who are rewarded for their behaviors than they are to imitate those whose behaviors lead to punishment or disapproval.

▶ Social Perception

When psychologists talk about "social perception," they refer to factors that influence how one comes to see, interpret, judge, or perceive, other people. There are two issues to consider. The first concerns a process called *attribution* and the second deals with *interpersonal attraction*.

▶ Attribution Theory

attribution the cognitions we generate when we attempt to explain the sources of behavior

A facet of the cognitive orientation that we find in social psychology is the study of **attribution theory**. Social psychologists working on attribution theory are interested in understanding the cognitions we use in trying to explain the sources of behavior, both our own and that of others. The question is, "Do we tend to attribute behaviors we observe to internal or external sources—to personal dispositions or to environmental situations?" You may recognize this question as related to issues we raised in the chapter on personality, when we discussed the extent to which behaviors reflect internal, personality factors or external, environmental factors.

internal attribution an explanation of behavior in terms of something (a trait) within the person; a dispositional attribution

Internal attributions explain the source of behavior in terms of some characteristic of a person, often a personality trait or disposition, and for this reason internal attributions are sometimes called *dispositional attributions*. **External attributions**, on the other hand, explain the sources of behavior in terms of the situation or social context outside the individual; they are referred to as *situational attributions*.

external attribution an explanation of behavior in terms of something outside the person; a situational attribution

The evidence indicates that people tend to rely on different types of information when making judgments about the sources of behavior. Imagine, for example, that your best friend shows his temper only when he is with his girlfriend. That information is useful because of its *distinctiveness* (his bad temper only shows up when he's with his girlfriend). As a result, you may take it as a signal of a troubled relationship.

Imagine that you've just received an A on a test in your history class. In this case, you could (and probably would) use information about how well everyone else did on the test before you decide about your own superiority; this kind of information is concerned with *consensus*. If you find that everyone else also received an A, your explanation of your behavior (and theirs) might be different from a situation in which you discover that yours is the only A in the class. Before you got too grandiose about your accomplishment, you might wait for some sign of *consistency* over time lest this one exam be just a fluke. Using information about distinctiveness, consensus, and consistency is the basis of one major theory about attributions we make about behavior (*e.g.*, Kelley, 1967; 1973; Kelley & Michela, 1980). Figure 14.4 shows a few of the ways in which these types of information may lead one to attribute behavior to internal or external sources.

fundamental attribution error the tendency to overuse internal attributions when explaining behavior

An active area of research in social psychology deals with errors we tend to make in our social thinking. One well-documented example of bias in the attribution process is called the **fundamental attribution error** (Jones, 1979; Ross, 1977). This bias reflects the tendency to favor internal, personal attributions for behavior rather than external, situational ones. We see a man pick up a wallet that has been dropped on the pavement and race half a block to return it to its true owner. We say to ourselves, "Now there's an honest man." (And we'll probably predict that the person will act honestly in a variety of different situations.) The truth is, however, that the fellow returned the wallet only because he knew that we (and many others) saw him pick it up in the first place. It may be that if no one else were around, the wallet would not have been returned. The fundamental attribution error then, is the tendency to disregard, or overly discount situational

Figure 14.4

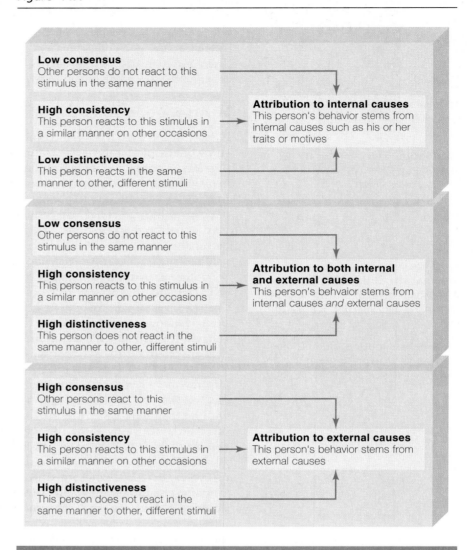

▲ *Attributing behavior: some important considerations and possible outcomes. From SOCIAL PSYCHOLOGY: UNDERSTANDING HUMAN INTERACTION, fourth edition by Robert A. Baron and Donn Byrne, page 59. Copyright © 1984, 1981, 1977, 1974 by Allyn and Bacon, Inc. Reprinted by permission.*

factors in favor of internal, dispositional factors when we make inferences about the causes of behaviors. I should also mention that there is some evidence that biases such as the fundamental attribution error may be more common in Western cultures. Subjects from India, for example, particularly adults, make many fewer dispositional attributions than do American subjects (Miller, 1984). They are much more likely than Americans to explain behavior in terms of the nature of the situation than in terms of personality characteristics.

As you might imagine, there are other biases that may lead us to make incorrect attributions about ourselves or others. One is called the **just world hypothesis,** in which people take on the belief that we live in a just world where good things happen to good people and bad things happen to bad people (Lerner, 1965; 1980). It's a sort of "everybody ultimately gets what

just world hypothesis the belief that the world is just and that people get what they deserve

self-serving bias the tendency to attribute our successes to our own effort and ability and our failures to external, situational factors

actor-observer bias the overuse of internal attributions to explain the behaviors of others and external attributions to explain our own behaviors

they deserve" sort of mentality. We see this bias (I might say fallacy) when we hear people claim that victims of rape often "ask for it by the way they dress and act." In fact, victims of rape sometimes even engage in self-blame in an attempt to explain why in the world *they* were singled out for what was in fact a crime in which they were the true victim (Janoff-Bulman, 1979).

Another bias that affects our attributions is called the **self-serving bias** (Miller & Ross, 1975; Harvey & Weary, 1984). It occurs when we attribute positive or successful outcomes to personal, internal sources and failures or negative outcomes to situational, external sources. We tend to think that when we do something well it is because we're talented and work hard, whereas when we do poorly it's the fault of someone or something else. "Boy, didn't I do a great job of painting that room" versus "The room looks so shoddy because the paint was cheap and the brush was old" would be an example. (Perhaps you'll recall from our discussion of depression in Chapter 12 that some cognitive theorists argue that at least some depression can be explained as a sort of reverse of the self-serving bias. That is, some people get in the habit of blaming themselves for failures and negative outcomes regardless of where the real blame resides; or regardless of whether there *is* any blame.)

Yet another attribution error is the so-called **actor-observer bias** (Jones & Nisbett, 1971; Monson & Snyder, 1977). What we find here is a basic discrepancy between the way we explain our behavior (as actor) and the way we explain someone else's (as observer). What usually happens is that we use external attributions when we talk about why we do things. The basis of our explanation has to do with something about the situation or the environment. "I took that class because the instructor is entertaining." "I date Bill because he's so caring and considerate." "I went there because the rates were lower." When we explain someone else's behaviors, we tend to use internal attributions and refer to characteristics of the person whose behaviors we have been observing. "He took that class because he's so lazy." "I know that she's dating him only because she wants to be seen with an athlete." "He went there because he wanted to show off." That we explain our behaviors in ways that are different from the ways in which we account for the behaviors of others should not be surprising. For one thing, we have much more information about ourselves and our own past experiences than we do about anyone else. In fact, the more information we have about someone else, the less likely we are to use internal attributions to explain their behaviors. Also, in any situation, the actor gets quite a different view of what is happening than does the observer. In other words, the actor and the observer attempt to attribute the cause of behavior on the basis of different information.

Before You Go On
▼▼▼▼▼▼▼▼

What are the two basic types of attribution?

Explain the ways in which attributions can be distorted or biased.

▶ *Interpersonal Attraction*

Interpersonal attraction can be seen as a favorable, powerful attitude toward another person. It reflects the extent to which a person has formed positive feelings and beliefs about another person and is prepared to act on those affects and cognitions.

Theories of Interpersonal Attraction. Social psychologists have put forth several models or theories to explain the bases of interpersonal attraction. Probably the simplest theory is the *reinforcement model* which claims that we are attracted to people we associate with rewards (Clore & Byrne, 1974; Lott & Lott, 1974). We learn to like people and are attracted to them through conditioning, by associating them with rewards or reinforcers that are present when they are. It follows that we tend not to be attracted to those we associate with punishment. An implication of this model is that you will like your instructor more, and seek him or her out for other classes in the future, if you get (or earn) a high grade in his or her class than you would if you get a low grade.

Another theory of interpersonal attraction is not quite so direct. It is called the *social exchange model* (Kelley & Thibault, 1978; Thibault & Kelley, 1959). According to this model, what matters most is a comparison of the costs as well as the benefits of establishing or maintaining a relationship. For example, Leslie may judge that John is physically attractive, but that entering into an intimate relationship with him is not worth the grief that she would get from friends and family, who believe that John is shiftless and lazy. On the other hand, if Leslie has just gone through a series of failed relationships with other men who were not physically attractive, she might take a chance on John, judging (in her frustration) that he was "worth it." What this theory takes into account are a number of comparative judgments that people make in social situations. Being attracted to someone else is not just a matter of, "Is this a good thing?" It's more a matter of, "Is the reward that I might get from this relationship worth the cost, given the alternatives that exist at the moment?"

A third theoretical approach to interpersonal attraction is called the *equity model,* and it is more an extension of social exchange theory than a departure from it (Greenberg & Cohen, 1982; Walster, et al., 1978). Social exchange theory added the notion of cost to that of reward. Equity theory adds the appraisal of rewards and costs of *both* members of a relationship. That is, you may feel that a certain relationship is worth the effort you've been putting into it, but if your partner in that relationship does not feel likewise, the relationship is in danger. What matters, then, is that both (or all) members of a relationship feel that they are getting a fair deal (equity). Notice two things about this model: (1) Both members of a relationship do not have to share rewards *equally.* What matters is that the ratio of costs to rewards be equitable for both members. (2) If one person were to feel that he or she was getting more from a relationship than was deserved (on the basis of costs and compared to the other's rewards), the relationship would not be equitable and would be in danger. The best relationships are those in which all members receive an equal ratio of rewards to costs.

A more recent approach to understanding interpersonal relationships is based more on feelings and affect than cognitions. This model is referred to as *attachment theory* (Hazen & Shaver, 1987; Feeney & Noller, 1990). It suggests that interpersonal relationships can be classified into one of three types depending on the attitudes that one has about them (descriptions from Shaver, Hazen & Bradshaw, 1988, p. 80):

> *Secure: "I find it relatively easy to get close to others and am comfortable depending on them and having them depend on me. I don't often worry about being abandoned or about someone getting too close to me."*

> *Avoidant: "I am somewhat uncomfortable being close to others; I find it difficult to trust them completely, difficult to allow myself to depend on them. I am nervous when anyone gets too close, and*

often, love partners want me to be more intimate than I feel comfortable being."

Anxious/ambivalent: *"I find that others are reluctant to get as close as I would like. I often worry that my partner doesn't really love me or won't stay with me. I want to merge completely with another person, and this desire sometimes scares people away."*

One of the things that makes attachment theory particularly appealing is the evidence that suggests that one's "style" of forming attachments with others is remarkably stable throughout the life span. It may be that the kind of interpersonal relationships we form as adults are influenced by the kind of attachments we developed as very young children.

Finally, before we go on, I should point out that few people enter into relationships having carefully considered all the factors that these models imply. That is, assessments of reinforcement, or exchange, or equity value are seldom made at a conscious level; nor do we purposively seek out relationships that mirror those we had in childhood.

Before You Go On
▼▼▼▼▼▼▼▼

Briefly summarize four theoretical models that account for interpersonal attractions.

Factors Affecting Interpersonal Attraction. Having reviewed four models of interpersonal attraction, now let's examine some empirical evidence related to attraction. What determines whom you will be attracted to? What factors tend to provide the rewards, or the reward/cost ratios, that serve as the basis for strong relationships?

Reciprocity, our first factor, is perhaps the most obvious. Not surprisingly, we tend to value and like people who like and value us (Backman & Secord, 1959; Curtis & Miller, 1986). Remember that we've already noted, in our discussion of operant conditioning, that the attention of others often can be a powerful reinforcer. This is particularly true if the attention is positive, supportive, and/or affectionate. Research indicates that the value of someone else caring for us is particularly powerful when that someone initially seemed to have neutral or negative attitudes toward us (Aronson & Linder, 1965). That is, we are most attracted to people who like us now, but who once didn't. If someone we meet for the first time expresses nothing but positive feelings and attitudes toward us, we are likely to attribute their reaction internally to the way the person is—rather shallow and the sort who likes everybody. But if someone at first were to express neutral, or even slightly negative, feelings toward us and then were to become more and more positive, we might have a different, more positive view of their ability to judge others.

Our second principle, *proximity,* claims that physical closeness tends to produce attraction. Sociologists, as well as your own experience, will tell you that people tend to establish friendships (and romances) with others with whom they have grown up, worked, or gone to school. Similarly, social-psychological studies consistently have found that residents of apartments or dormitories tend to become friends with other residents living closest to them (Festinger, et al., 1950). Being around others gives us the opportunity to discover just who can provide those rewards we seek in friendship.

▲ *Proximity leads to liking, which is why teenagers who go to the same school are likely to form friendships.*

mere exposure phenomenon the tendency to increase our liking of people and things the more we see of them

There may be another social-psychological phenomenon at work here: the **mere exposure phenomenon.** Research pioneered by Robert Zajonc (1968) has shown with a variety of stimuli that liking tends to increase with repeated exposure. Examples of this phenomenon are abundant in everyday life. Have you ever bought a record album that you've not heard before, assuming that you will like it because you have liked other albums made by this performer? The first time you listen to your new album, however, your reaction may be lukewarm at best, and you may be disappointed. Not wanting to feel that you've wasted your money, you play the album a few more times over the next several days. What often happens is that you soon realize that you like this album after all. The mere exposure effect has occurred, and this commonly happens in our formation of attitudes about other people as well. (Doesn't this sound like our earlier discussion of cognitive dissonance? We can't imagine having repeated contacts with someone we don't like—that would be dissonant—so we find that we like them after all.) Familiarity is apt to breed attraction, not contempt. I also have to add that although there seems to be ample evidence that the mere exposure phenomenon is real, there is still disagreement about *why* familiarity and repeated interactions breed attraction (*e.g.*, Birnbaum & Mellers, 1979; Kunst-Wilson & Zajonc, 1980).

Physical attractiveness is a factor related to interpersonal attraction. Most people are aware of the role of appearance in interpersonal communication and may spend many hours each week doing whatever they can to improve the way they look. The power of physical attractiveness in the context of dating has been demonstrated in a classic experiment directed by Elaine Walster (Walster, et al., 1966). University of Minnesota freshmen completed several psychological tests as part of an orientation program. The students were then randomly matched for dates to an orientation dance during which they took a break and evaluated their assigned partners. This study allowed researchers the possibility of uncovering intricate, complex, and subtle facts about interpersonal attraction, such as which personality traits might tend to mesh in such a way as to produce attraction. As it turned out, none of these complex factors, so carefully controlled for, was important. The effect of physical attractiveness was so powerful that it wiped out all other effects. For both men and women, the more physically attractive their date, the more they liked the person, and the more they wanted to go out again with that individual. Numerous studies of physical attractiveness followed. Some of these studies simply gave subjects a chance to pick a date from a group of several potential partners (usually using descriptions and pictures). Almost invariably, subjects selected the most attractive person available as their date (Reis, et al., 1980).

matching phenomenon the tendency to select partners whose level of physical attractiveness matches our own

It may have occurred to you that in real life, we seldom have the opportunity to request a date without at least the possibility of being turned down. When experimental studies built in the possibility of rejection, an interesting effect emerged: Subjects stopped picking the most attractive candidate and started selecting partners whose level of attractiveness was more similar to their own. This is called the **matching phenomenon,** and it is an effect that has been verified repeatedly (Walster & Walster, 1969).

The positive effects of physical attractiveness can be found in many social situations. Studies suggest that attractive persons are assumed to have other desirable characteristics as well (*e.g.*, Dion, et al., 1972; Hatfield & Sprecher, 1986; Vaughn & Langlois, 1983). Attractive persons—both men and women—are judged to be more intelligent, to have happier marriages, to be more successful in their careers and social lives, and so on. This overgeneralizing is referred to as the *physical attractiveness stereotype.*

Our fourth factor is *similarity.* There is a large body of research on similarity and attraction, but the findings are quite consistent, so we can summarize them briefly. Much of this research has been done by Donn Byrne

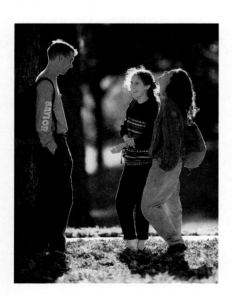

▲ *Physical attractiveness is a powerful influence in interpersonal relationships. Numerous studies have found that physical attractiveness is at least at first, the single most important factor in selecting friends and dates.*

▲ The more similar another person is to you, the more you will tend to be like that person. Our friends tend to be people who share our attitudes and who like to do the things we like to do.

and his colleagues (*e.g.,* Byrne, 1971). It indicates that there is a strong positive relationship between attraction and the proportion of attitudes held in common. Simply put, the more similar another person is to you, the more you will tend to like that person (Buss, 1985; Davis, 1985; Rubin, 1973). We also tend to be repelled, or put off by persons we believe to be dissimilar to us (Rosenbaum, 1986).

That similarity enhances interpersonal attraction makes sense in light of the reinforcement theory of attraction we described earlier. Among other things, agreement with our attitudinal positions is reinforcing; it confirms that we were right all along. In Ms. Elliott's third-grade class, brown-eyed pupils made friends with other brown-eyed pupils, if only for a short time, and regardless of whether they thought of themselves as favored or unfavored. Similarity is probably the glue that—over the long haul—holds together romances and friendships.

Before You Go On

▼▼▼▼▼▼▼▼▼

What are four determinants of interpersonal attraction?

▶ Social Influence

So far we've reviewed some of the ways in which our social nature has an impact on our cognitions—our perceptions and beliefs—about ourselves and others. Now it is time to consider more direct influences of the social world and how social forces influence our everyday behaviors.

▶ Conformity

conformity the changing of one's behavior, under perceived pressure, so that it is consistent with the behavior of others

One of the most direct forms of social influence occurs whenever we modify our behavior, under perceived pressure to do so, so that it is consistent with the behavior of others, a process referred to as **conformity**. Although we usually think of conformity in a negative way, to conform is a natural and often desirable process. Conformity helps to make social behaviors efficient and, at least to some degree, predictable.

When he began his research, Solomon Asch believed that people are not very susceptible to social pressure when the social situation is clearcut and unambiguous. Asch hypothesized that subjects would behave independently of group pressure when there was little question that their own judgments were accurate, and he developed an interesting technique for testing his hypothesis (Asch, 1951; 1956).

A subject in Asch's procedure would join a group seated around a table. In his original study, the group consisted of seven people. Unknown to the subject, six individuals were confederates of the experimenter; that is, they were "in on" the experiment. The subjects were led to believe that the study dealt with the ability to make perceptual judgments. The participants had to do nothing more than to decide which of three lines was the same length as a standard line (see Figure 14.5). The experimenter showed each set of lines to the group and then collected responses, one by one, from each member of the group. There were 18 sets of lines to judge, and the real subject was always the last one to respond.

It is important to note that each of the 18 judgments the subjects made involved unambiguous stimuli. The correct answer was always obvious. However, on 12 of the 18 trials, the confederates gave a unanimous, but *incorrect* answer. Now what would the subjects do? How would they

Figure 14.5

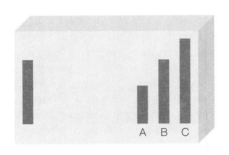

▲ The type of stimuli used in Asch's conformity experiment. Subjects are to say which of the three lines on the right (A, B, or C) equal the line on the left. Associates of the experimenter will occasionally make incorrect choices.

▲ *After consistently disagreeing with the other subjects in Asch's study, the one dissenter begins to doubt his judgment and looks again at the card, even though the correct answer is obvious.*

resolve this conflict? Their own perceptual experience was telling them what the correct answer was, but the group was saying something else. Should they trust the judgments of the others, or should they trust their own ability?

The results of his initial study surprised Asch, because they did not confirm his original hypothesis. Across all of the critical trials (when the confederates gave "wrong" answers), conformity occurred 37 percent of the time. That is, subjects responded with an incorrect answer that agreed with the majority on more than one-third of the critical trials. Moreover, three-quarters of Asch's subjects conformed to the group pressure at least once.

In subsequent studies, Asch tried several variations of his procedure. In one experiment, he varied the size of the unanimous, incorrect majority. As you might now expect, the level of conformity increased as the size of the majority increased, leveling off at about three or four people (Asch, 1956; Knowles, 1983). Subjects gave an erroneous judgment only 4 percent of the time if only one incorrect judgment preceded their own. In another study, Asch found that subjects gave an erroneous judgment only 10 percent of the time when there was just one dissenter among the six confederates who voiced an accurate judgment before the subjects gave theirs. In short, when the real subjects had any social support for what their eyes had told them, they tended to trust their own judgment. Recent experiments have shown that the minority opinion (say, one dissenter in an Asch-type procedure) can have particularly significant effects on conformity if that minority position is maintained consistently (*e.g.*, Moscovici, et al., 1969; 1985; Nemeth, 1986).

Conformity involves yielding to the perceived pressure of a group. In most circumstances, it is assumed that group members are peers, or at least similar to the conformer. When one yields to the pressure of a perceived authority, the result is obedience. It is to obedience that we turn next.

Before You Go On

▼▼▼▼▼▼▼▼

Briefly describe the methodology and the basic findings of the Asch conformity studies.

▲ Extreme, unquestioning obedience to authority can have negative consequences. Consider concentration camp commander Franz Hoessler, whose blind obedience to Hitler's decrees led to the brutal murder of millions of innocent people.

Figure 14.6

▲ A shock generator apparatus of the sort the teacher would use to punish the learner in Stanley Milgram's research on obedience. In the photo on the bottom, the subject is given a sample shock.

▶ Obedience to Authority

Although the subjects in Asch's studies took the procedure seriously, the consequences of either conforming or maintaining independence were rather trivial. At worst, Asch's subjects might have experienced some discomfort as a result of voicing their independent judgments. There were no external rewards or punishments for their behavior, and there was no one telling them how to respond. Stanley Milgram (1933–1984), a social psychologist at Yale University, went beyond Asch's procedure. Milgram's experiments pressured subjects to comply with the demand of an authority figure—a demand that was both unreasonable and troubling (Milgram, 1963; 1965; 1974).

The original impetus for Milgram's research was his interest in the obedience to Nazi authority displayed by many German military personnel during World War II. Milgram wondered whether mass executions and other forms of cruelty perpetrated by the Nazis might reflect something about the German character. The original goal of his research was to determine if people of different nationalities differ in the degree to which they will obey a request to inflict pain on another person. Milgram's research was designed to serve as a basis for making such comparisons.

All of the studies carried out in this series involved the same basic procedure. Subjects arrived at the laboratory to discover that they would be participating with another person (again, a confederate of the experimenter). The experimenter explained that the research dealt with the effects of punishment on learning, and that one subject would serve as a teacher while the other would act as learner. The two roles were assigned by a rigged drawing in which the actual subject was always assigned the role of teacher, while the confederate was always the learner. The subject watched as the learner was taken into the next room and wired to electrodes that would be used for delivering punishment in the form of electric shocks.

The teacher then received his instructions. First, he was to read to the learner a list of four pairs of words. Then the teacher would read the first word of one of the pairs, and the learner was to supply the second word. The teacher sat in front of a rather imposing electric "shock generator" (see Figure 14.6) that had 30 switches, each with its voltage level labeled. From left to right, the switches increased by increments of 15 volts, ranging from 15 volts to 450 volts. Labels were also printed under the switches on the generator. These ranged from "Slight" to "Moderate" to "Extreme Intensity" to "Danger: Severe Shock." The label at the 450-volt end simply read "XXX."

As the task proceeded, the learner periodically made errors according to a prearranged schedule. The teacher had been instructed to deliver an electric shock for each incorrect answer. With each error, the teacher was to move up the scale of shocks on the generator, giving the learner a more potent shock with each new mistake. (The learner, remember, was part of the act, and no one was receiving any shocks.)

Whenever the teacher hesitated or questioned if he should continue, the experimenter was ready with one of several verbal prods, such as "Please continue," or "The experiment requires that you continue." If the subject protested, the experimenter would become more assertive and offer one of the alternative prods: "You have no choice; you must go on," he might say. The degree of obedience—the behavior of interest to Milgram—was determined by the level of shock at which the teacher refused to go further.

Milgram was astonished by the results of his study, and the results continue to amaze students of psychology more than 25 years later. Twenty-six of Milgram's 40 subjects—65 percent—obeyed the experimenter and went all the way to the highest shock value and closed all the switches. In fact, *no subject* stopped prior to the 300-volt level, the point at which the learner pounded on the wall in protest. One later variation of this study added vocal responses from the learner, who delivered an increasingly stronger series of demands to be let out of the experiment. The level of obedience in this study still was unbelievably high, as 25 of 40 subjects, or 62.5 percent, continued to administer shocks to the 450-volt level.

It is important to note that all of the subjects (teachers) experienced genuine and extreme stress in this situation. Some fidgeted, some trembled, many perspired profusely. Several subjects giggled nervously. In short, the people caught up in this unusual situation showed obvious signs of conflict and anxiety. Nevertheless, they continued to obey the orders of the authoritative experimenter even though they had good reason to believe that they might well be harming the learner.

Milgram's first study was performed with male subjects ranging in age from 20 to 50. A later replication with adult women produced precisely the same results: 65 percent obeyed fully. Other variations of the basic procedure, however, uncovered that several factors could reduce the amount of obedience. Putting the learner and teacher in the same room, or having the experimenter deliver his orders over the telephone, for example, reduced obedience markedly. Another variation produced an interesting parallel to one of the Asch studies we discussed: When the shocks were delivered by a team consisting of the subject and two disobedient confederates, full-scale obedience dropped to only 10 percent.

When one first hears about these rather distressing results, there is a tendency for many people to think that Milgram's obedient subjects were cold, callous, unfeeling, or downright cruel and sadistic people (Safer, 1980). Nothing could be further from the truth. As I mentioned, the participants in this research were truly troubled by what was happening. If you thought that Milgram's subjects must be strange or different, perhaps you were a victim of what we identified as an *attribution error*. That is, you were willing to attribute the subjects' behavior to (internal) personality characteristics instead of recognizing the powerful situational forces at work.

Attributing negative personality characteristics to the "teachers" is particularly understandable in light of the unexpected nature of the results. A number of psychologists in commenting on this research have suggested, in fact, that the most significant aspect of Milgram's findings is that they *are* so surprising to us. As part of his research, Milgram asked people (including a group of psychiatrists and a group of ministers) to predict what they would do under these circumstances, and he also asked them to predict how far others would go before refusing the authority. Needless to say, respondents in both cases predicted very little obedience, expecting practically no one to proceed all the way to the final switch on the shock generator.

In reading about Milgram's research, it should have occurred to you that putting subjects in such a stressful experience might be considered morally and ethically objectionable. Milgram himself was quite concerned with the welfare of his subjects. He took great care to debrief them fully after each session had been completed. He told them that they had not really administered any shocks and explained why deception had been necessary.

Milgram reported that the people in his studies were not upset over having been deceived and that their principal reaction was one of relief when they learned that no electric shock had in fact been used. Milgram also indicated that a follow-up study performed a year later with some of the same subjects showed that no long-term adverse effects had been created by his procedure.

Despite these precautions, Milgram was severely criticized for placing people in such an extremely stressful situation. Indeed, one of the effects of his research was to establish in the scientific community a higher level of awareness of the need to protect the well-being of human research subjects.

It is probably safe to say that because of the nature of Milgram's experience, no one would be allowed to perform such experiments today.

Before You Go On
▼▼▼▼▼▼▼▼

Briefly describe Stanley Milgram's experimental demonstrations of obedience.

▶ Bystander Intervention

In March of 1964, a New York City cocktail waitress named Kitty Genovese was brutally murdered in front of her apartment building as she returned from work at approximately 3:30 A.M. Although murders may have become somewhat commonplace in our large urban centers, there were some unusual and particularly disturbing circumstances surrounding this incident:

> ▲ For more than half an hour, thirty-eight respectable law-abiding citizens in Queens watched a killer stalk and stab a woman in three separate attacks in Kew Gardens.
> Twice the sound of their voices and the sudden glow of their bedroom lights interrupted him and frightened him off. Each time he returned, sought her out and stabbed her again. Not one person telephoned the police during the assault; one witness called after the woman was dead (New York Times, March 27, 1964).

This tragic event stimulated public concern and sparked a good deal of commentary in the media. People wondered how the witnesses could have shown such a lack of concern for a neighbor. Alienation and apathy were terms often used in describing what had happened. One positive outcome of this unfortunate incident was that a program of research was begun that helped to establish a basic understanding of the social factors that can influence people to intervene or not to intervene in such a situation.

Bibb Latané and John Darley, two social psychologists who at the time were at universities in New York City, were not satisfied that terms such as *bystander apathy* or *alienation* adequately explained what happened in the Genovese case. They were not willing to attribute people's failure to help to internal, dispositional, or personality characteristics. They were convinced that situational factors make such events possible.

Latané and Darley (1970) pointed out that there are several logical reasons why people should *not* be expected to offer help in an emergency. Emergencies tend to happen quickly and without advance warning. Except for medical technicians, firefighters, and a few other select groups, people generally are not prepared to deal with emergencies when they do arise. In fact, one good predictor of who will intervene in an emergency turns out to be previous experience with similar emergency situations (Huston, et al., 1981). By their nature, emergencies are not commonplace occurrences for most of us. It also goes without saying that the risk of physical injury, as was clearly present in the Genovese case, is an understandable deterrent to helping. Finally, people may fail to help because they want to avoid the legal consequences that might follow. They simply do not want to get involved.

Latané and Darley (1968) suggest that a series of cognitive events must occur before a bystander can intervene in an emergency (Figure 14.7). First, the bystander must *notice* what is going on. A person who is window shopping and thus fails to see someone collapse on the opposite side of the street cannot

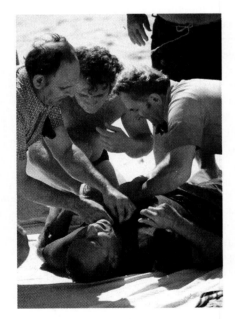

▲ Researchers have found that there are many reasons why people should not be expected to get involved in an emergency, including risk of physical injury and legal consequences. Nevertheless, some bystanders will choose to intervene as was the case with the heart attack victim pictured here.

Figure 14.7

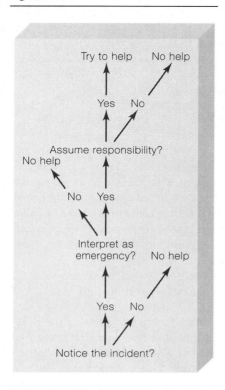

▲ *Some of the decisions and outcomes involved as a bystander considers intervening. (After Latané & Darley, 1968.)*

audience inhibition reluctance to intervene and offer assistance in front of others

pluralistic ignorance a condition in which the inaction of others leads each individual in a group to interpret a situation as a nonemergency, thus leading to general inactivity

be expected to rush over and offer assistance. If the bystander does notice something happen, he or she still must *interpret* the situation as an emergency; perhaps the person who has collapsed is simply drunk or tired and not really having a stroke or a heart attack. The third step involves the decision that it is the bystander's (and not someone else's) *responsibility* to do something.

Even if the bystander has noticed something occurring, has interpreted the situation as one calling for quick action, and has assumed responsibility for helping, he or she still faces the decision of what form of assistance to offer. Should he or she attempt to administer first aid? Should he or she try to find the nearest telephone? Or should he or she simply start shouting for help? As a final step in the process, the person ultimately must decide how to implement his or her decision to act. What is the appropriate first aid under these circumstances? Just where can a phone be found? We can see that intervening on behalf of someone else in a social situation involves a series of cognitive choices.

A negative outcome at any of these cognitive steps of decision making will lead a bystander to decide not to offer assistance. When one considers the cognitive chain of events necessary for actually helping, along with the many potential costs associated with intervention, it becomes apparent that the deck is stacked against the victim in an emergency. As Latané and Darley have suggested, perhaps we should be surprised when bystanders *do* offer to help (Cunningham, 1984; Shotland, 1985). There may be many psychological processes that account for what is called the *social inhibition of helping,* or *bystander effect.* Let's review three such processes (Latané & Darley, 1970; Latané & Nida, 1981).

Audience inhibition refers to the tendency to be hesitant to do things in front of others, especially when the others happen to be strangers. We tend to be concerned about how others will evaluate us. In public, no one wants to do anything that appears to be silly, incompetent, or improper. The bystander who intervenes risks embarrassment if he or she blunders. That risk increases as the number of people present increases.

Emergencies tend to be ambiguous: Is the raggedly dressed man who has collapsed on the street ill or drunk? Is the commotion in a neighboring apartment an assault or a family quarrel that's just a little out of hand? When social reality is unclear, we turn to others for clues. While a person is in the process of getting information from others, he or she probably will try to remain calm and collected, behaving as if there is no emergency. Everyone else, of course, is doing exactly the same thing, showing no outward sign of concern. The result is that each person is led by the others to think that the situation is really not an emergency after all, a psychological state called **pluralistic ignorance** (Miller & McFarland, 1987). Pluralistic ignorance amounts to the belief on the part of the individual that only he or she is confused and doesn't know what to do in an emergency, while everyone else is standing around doing nothing for some good reason. The group becomes paralyzed, and the phenomenon can be interpreted as a type of conformity—conformity to the inaction of others.

This process was demonstrated clearly in a classic experiment by Latané and Darley (1968; 1970). Columbia University students reported to a campus building to participate in an interview. They were sent to a waiting room and were asked to complete some preliminary forms. While they did so, white smoke began to billow through a vent in the wall. After six minutes (the point at which the procedure was terminated if the "emergency" had not been reported), there was enough smoke in the room to cause difficulty in breathing and prevent seeing across the room.

When subjects were alone in the waiting room, 75 percent of them emerged to report the smoke. However, when two passive confederates were in the room with the subject, only 10 percent responded. Those people who reported the smoke did so quickly. Those from the groups who failed to do so generated all sorts of explanations for the smoke: steam, vapors from the air conditioner, smog introduced to simulate an urban environment, and even "truth gas." In short, the subjects who remained unresponsive had been led by the inaction of their peers to conclude just about anything other than the obvious—that something was wrong.

In the Kitty Genovese murder, it was terribly clear that an emergency was in progress; there was very little ambiguity about what was happening. Furthermore, the 38 witnesses were not in a face-to-face group that would allow social influence processes such as pluralistic ignorance to operate. Latané and Darley suggested that a third important process is necessary to complete their explanation of bystander behavior.

diffusion of responsibility the tendency to allow others to share in the obligation to intervene

A single bystander in an emergency situation must bear the full responsibility for offering assistance, but the witness who is part of a group shares that responsibility with other onlookers. The greater the number of other people present, the smaller is each individual's perceived obligation to intervene, a process referred to as **diffusion of responsibility.**

Latané and Darley devised a clever demonstration of this phenomenon. In this study, college students arrived at a laboratory to take part in a group discussion of some of the personal problems they experienced as college students in an urban environment. To reduce the embarrassment of talking about such matters in public, each group member was isolated in his or her own cubicle and could communicate with the others through an intercom system. Actually there were no other group members, only tape-recorded voices. Thus, there was only one subject in each group, and the perceived size of the group could be easily manipulated to see whether diffusion of responsibility would occur.

The first person to speak mentioned that he was prone to seizures when under pressure, such as when studying for an exam. The others, including the actual subject, then took turns talking for about 10 minutes about their problems. A second round of discussion then began with the seizure-prone student who, shortly after he started talking, began to suffer a seizure.

Just as in the Genovese incident, it was obvious that something was wrong. As the "victim" began stammering, choking, and pleading for help, the typical subject became quite nervous—some trembled, some had sweaty palms. This study had another feature in common with the Genovese episode: Subjects could not be sure if any other bystanders had taken any action. (In fact, remember, there were no others.)

As expected, the likelihood of helping decreased as the perceived size of the group increased. Eighty-five percent of those in two-person groups (just the subject and victim) left the cubicle to report the emergency. When the subject thought that he or she was in a three-person group, 62 percent responded. Only 31 percent of the participants who believed that they were in a six-person group took any step to intervene. The responsibility for reporting the seizure was clearly divided (diffused) among those thought to be present.

Incidentally, diffusion of responsibility does come in forms that are less serious in their implications. Those of you with a few siblings can probably recall times at home when the telephone has rung five or six times before anyone has made a move to answer it, even though the entire family was there at the time. And some of you probably have been at parties where the doorbell went unanswered while everyone thought that "someone else will get it."

The situational determinants of helping behaviors continued to be a popular research topic for social psychologists throughout the 1970s. Many of these studies included a manipulation of the size of the group witnessing the event that created the need for help in the first place. Latané and Nida

(1981) reviewed about 50 studies involving nearly 100 different helping-or-not-helping situations. Although these experiments involved a wide range of settings, procedures, and participants, the social inhibition of helping (the bystander effect) occurred in *almost every instance*. The researchers concluded that there is very little doubt that a person is more likely to help when he or she is alone rather than in a group. In other words, the bystander effect is a remarkably consistent phenomenon, perhaps as predictable as any phenomenon in social psychology.

Before You Go On

▼▼▼▼▼▼▼▼▼

What effect does the presence of others have on a person's willingness to help in an emergency?

How do audience inhibition, pluralistic ignorance, and diffusion of responsibility account for the lack of bystander intervention?

▶ Social Loafing

social loafing the tendency for a person to work less hard when part of a group in which everyone's efforts are pooled

Latané, Williams, and Harkins (1979) have identified a phenomenon they call **social loafing,** which refers to the tendency to work less (decrease one's individual effort) as the size of the group in which one is working becomes larger. Their initial studies required subjects to shout or clap as loudly as possible, either in groups or alone. If individuals were led to believe that their performance could not be identified, they invested less and less effort in the task as group size increased. Other studies (*e.g.*, Petty, et al., 1977; Weldon & Gargano, 1988) have used more cognitive tasks, such as evaluating poetry. The results tend to be consistent: When people can hide in the crowd, their effort (and hence their productivity) declines. Although social loafing is a widespread phenomenon, it does not *always* follow from working in a group situation. Social loafing can be virtually eliminated if group members believe that their effort is special and required for the group's success, or if group members believe that their performance can be identified or evaluated individually (Harkins, 1987; Harkins & Petty, 1982; Williams, et al., 1981; Williams, et al., 1989). This is not unlike the behavior of a student in a very large lecture class, virtually assured that he won't be called on, as opposed to his behavior in a small discussion class. Indeed, there are situations in which the social influence of group participation facilitates behavior.

▶ Social Facilitation

social facilitation improved performance due to the presence of others

Many years ago, a psychologist by the name of Norman Triplett observed that bicycle riders competing against other cyclists outperformed those racing against a clock. He then performed what is considered to be the first laboratory experiment in social psychology (Triplett, 1898). Triplett had children wind a fishing reel as rapidly as possible. They engaged in this task either alone or with another child alongside doing the same thing. Just as he had noticed in his records of bicycle races, Triplett found that the children worked faster when another child was present. We now know that such an effect sometimes occurs not only with coactors (others engaged in the same task), but also if a person performs in front of an audience. When the presence of others improves an individual's performance on some task, we have evidence of what is called **social facilitation.**

Numerous studies on social facilitation were performed early in the twentieth century, but with a puzzling inconsistency in their results. Sometimes social facilitation was obvious, but occasionally, just the opposite

▲ *Because of social facilitation, we perform better when we are in the presence of others. Bicycle racers ride faster when racing against other riders than when racing against the clock.*

social interference impaired performance due to the presence of others

effect would occur. Sometimes people actually performed more poorly in the presence of others than they did alone, an effect social psychologists called **social interference.** These inconsistencies were so bewildering that most psychologists eventually gave up investigating social facilitation.

In 1965, Robert Zajonc resurrected the topic of social facilitation by providing a plausible interpretation for the lack of consistency in social facilitation effects. In his examination of the research, Zajonc noticed that social facilitation occurred whenever the behavior under study was simple, routine, or very well learned (such as bicycle riding or winding a fishing reel). Social interference, on the other hand, tended to occur whenever the behavior involved was complex or not well practiced. Zajonc suggested that the presence of others creates increased *arousal,* which in turn energizes the dominant (most likely) response. When the dominant response is correct, as with a simple, well-practiced task, facilitation occurs. When the dominant response is incorrect, as with a complex task or one with which we have had little practice, the result is interference.

You may have experienced this effect yourself if you have ever tried to acquire a skill at a sport that is totally new to you. Whereas skilled athletes tend to perform better in front of audiences, the novice tends to do better when alone. (There is evidence that, however, skilled athletes don't always perform better in front of audiences, sometimes "choking" in front of home crowds during important games (Baumeister, 1985).) You may have experienced—as a novice, that is—the frustration of finding it difficult even to hit a golf ball or tennis ball when there are others standing nearby watching you.

As an overall conclusion, we may safely assume that social loafing and social interference are more common phenomena than is social facilitation. Although there are occasions in which coworkers or an audience may enhance individual performance, the presence of others is more likely to inhibit it.

Before You Go On
▼▼▼▼▼▼▼▼▼

What can we conclude concerning the effects of social influence on the quality of an individual's performance?

▲ *Many of the decisions we face daily are the sort that are best made in groups, whether committees, boards, or family groups.*

group polarization the tendency for members of a group to give more extreme judgments following a discussion than they gave initially

groupthink a style of thinking of cohesive groups concerned with maintaining agreement to the extent that independent ideas are discouraged

▶ *Decision Making in Groups*

Many of the decisions that we face in our daily lives are the sort that must be made in groups. Committees, boards, family groups, and group projects for a class are only a few of many possible examples. There is logic in the belief that group efforts to solve problems should be superior to the efforts of individuals. One could reason that problem solving ought to be more effective in a group because individuals can pool resources. Having more people available should necessarily mean having more talent and knowledge available. It also seems logical that the cohesiveness of the group should contribute to a more productive effort (and for some groups and for some problems, this is exactly the case). But by now we know better than to assume that simply because a conclusion is logical that it is necessarily true. Consider two curious phenomena that can occur in the process of group decision making.

When he was an MIT graduate student in industrial management, James Stoner gave subjects in his research a series of dilemmas to grapple with (Stoner, 1961). The result of each decision was to be a statement of how much risk a fictitious character in the dilemma should take. To his surprise, Stoner found that the decisions rendered by groups generally were much riskier than those that the individual group members had made prior to the group decision. Stoner called this move away from conservative solutions a *risky shift*. For example, if several doctors were asked individually, each might express the opinion that a patient's present problem (whatever it was) could be handled with medication and a change in diet. If these very same doctors were to get together to discuss the patient's situation, they might very well end up concluding that what was called for here was a new and potentially dangerous (risky) surgical procedure.

Several hundred studies later, we now know that this effect can occur in the opposite direction as well (Levine & Moreland, 1990; Moscovici, et al., 1985). In other words, the risky shift is simply a specific case of a more general **group polarization** phenomenon. The process of group discussion usually leads to an enhancement of the beliefs and attitudes of the group members that existed before the discussion began. The group process tends to push members further in the direction in which they leaned initially. One explanation for group polarization suggests that open discussion gives group members a chance to hear persuasive arguments they have not previously considered, leading to a strengthening of their original attitudes (Isenberg, 1986). Another possibility is that after comparing attitudinal positions with one another, some group members feel pressure to catch up with other group members who have more extreme attitudes (Hinsz & Davis, 1984).

Irving Janis (1972; 1983) has described a related phenomenon of social influence that he calls **groupthink**—an excessive concern for reaching a consensus in group decision making to the extent that critical evaluations of input are withheld. Janis maintains that this style of thinking emerges when group members are so interested in maintaining harmony within the group that differences of opinion are suppressed. Groupthink is especially likely to occur in cohesive groups. Alternative courses of action are not considered realistically and the frequent result is a poor decision. Janis has analyzed several key historical events—including the Pearl Harbor and the Bay of Pigs invasions and the escalation of the Vietnam War—in terms of the operation of groupthink. Janis argues that each of these situations involved a cohesive decision-making group that was relatively isolated from outside judgments, a directive leader who pressured others to conform to his position, and an illusion of unanimity.

Before you conclude that decision making in a group or social situation always leads to negative consequences, let me point out that there are circumstances in which groups *are* more efficient than individuals working alone. As I implied above, groups are useful when problems are complex and require skills and abilities that are more likely to be found in a number of different individuals working together. Group decision making also can serve to identify errors that individuals might not identify.

Before You Go On
▼▼▼▼▼▼▼▼▼

How does social influence affect decision making in groups?

▼▼▼

Thinking Critically About Social Psychology

1. We often hear the claim that humans are social animals. What would be the long-term consequences of social isolation? How do you suppose that you would react to being literally stranded alone on a remote island? How can social isolation be used in brainwashing?

2. Are there some periods in human history in which we might expect to find more or less conformity, both in society and in the laboratory? Can you cite examples?

3. If we violate those expectations about our behaviors that are codified in our laws, we may be arrested and punished. What are the typical consequences of violating those expectations that comprise society's norms?

4. See if you can identify some of the stereotypes that you have formed. To what extent do you believe them to be accurate summaries of others?

5. Many early social psychological and sociological studies tell us that, in general again, the political and social attitudes of students become more liberal as they pass through college. Why do you think this is so? Do you think that this is so for you?

6. Imagine that you want to change a friend's attitude about abortion (in either direction). How would you do so?

7. Why is the fundamental attribution error so common, particularly in Western cultures?

8. Can you explain your interpersonal attraction to any of your friends in terms of the theories presented in this chapter?

9. Which statement is true: "Out of sight, out of mind" or "Absence makes the heart grow fonder"?

10. Now that you know all about the results of his project, how do you think that *you* would have reacted if you were one of Milgram's "teachers?"

11. To what extent can you observe "bystander apathy" occurring on your campus? When there is a Student Government election, what percentage of the student body votes?

12. What sorts of problems are likely to get better quality solutions from groups than from individuals?

Summary

▼▼▼▼▼▼▼▼▼▼▼▼▼▼▼▼▼▼▼▼▼▼▼▼▼▼▼▼▼

What are stereotypes and norms, and in what way are they cognitive? Both stereotypes and norms are sets of ideas or beliefs (i.e., cognitions) that we form about our social world. Stereotypes are generalized mental representations that we have of other people and are often based on very little information. Norms are learned expectations or rules that guide and influence our behaviors in social situations. *Pages 460–461*

What is an attitude and what are its three components? An attitude is an evaluative disposition (positive or negative) directed toward some object. An attitude consists of feelings (affects), behaviors, and beliefs (cognitions). Although the affective and cognitive components of attitudes are often consistent with each other, behavior—influenced by so many variables—may be inconsistent with the other two major components. *Page 461*

Briefly describe three ways in which attitudes might be acquired. Attitudes may be acquired through classical conditioning: After positive or negative experiences are associated with an attitudinal object, the object by itself comes to produce a positive or negative evaluation. Attitudinal behaviors also may be directly reinforced (operant conditioning) or they may be reinforced vicariously (observational learning). *Pages 461–464*

What is cognitive dissonance, and how does it operate? Cognitive dissonance is an unpleasant state of tension between or among cognitions that may occur when we behave in a fashion inconsistent with our attitudes. Because we are motivated to reduce dissonance, we may do so by changing our attitudes so that they become consistent with the way we behave. *Pages 464–465*

What communicator characteristics are known to have an impact on attitude change? Concern with communicator characteristics and other situational variables reflects a focus on peripheral routes to attitude change. Those communicators perceived as being expert or trustworthy are seen as credible sources of information and hence are more persuasive. *Pages 464–467*

What are the two basic types of attribution? Explain the ways in which attributions can be distorted or biased. Attributions are cognitions we use to explain the sources of the behaviors we see in our social worlds: The two basic types of attribution are internal and external. An internal attribution identifies the source of behavior as within the person and is sometimes called a dispositional attribution. An external attribution finds the source of behavior to be outside the person and is sometimes called a situational attribution.

The *fundamental attribution error* leads us to overuse internal, or personal attributions when explaining behaviors. Those persons who hold to the *just world hypothesis* are likely to believe that good things happen only to good people and bad things happen only to bad people who in some way deserve their misfortune. The *self-serving bias* has us tend to attribute successes to our own efforts and actions and our failures to other, external factors. The *actor-observer* bias refers to the tendency to use external attributions to explain our own behaviors (as actor), while using internal attributions to explain the behaviors of others (as observer). *Page 469*

Briefly summarize four theoretical models that account for interpersonal attractions. The *reinforcement model* claims simply that we tend to be attracted to those persons we associate with rewards or reinforcers. The *social exchange model* adds the notion of cost to the equation, claiming that what matters in interpersonal relationships is the ratio of the benefits received to the costs invested in that relationship. The *equity model* suggests that both or all members of a relationship assess a benefit/cost ratio and the best, most stable relationships are those in which the ratio is nearly the same (equitable) for both or all parties, no matter what the value of the benefits for any one member of the relationship. *Attachment theory* tells us that there are only a few relationship styles, and that people are consistent over their lifetime in the style they use when relating to others. *Pages 469–471*

What are four determinants of interpersonal attraction? The principle of *reciprocity* states that we tend to like people who like us back. This is the most straightforward example of interpersonal attraction being based on a system of rewards. *Proximity* promotes attraction by means of the mere exposure phenomenon: Being near another person on a frequent basis gives us the opportunity to see what that other person has to offer. We also tend to be attracted to people whom we judge to be *physically attractive*. Finally, the principle of *similarity* suggests that we tend to be attracted to others whom we believe are similar to ourselves. *Pages 471–473*

Briefly describe the methodology and the basic findings of the Asch conformity studies. In the Asch studies, people made simple judgments about unambiguous perceptual stimuli—the length of lines. On some trials, confederates gave clearly incorrect judgments before the actual subject had a chance to respond. Although there were situations in which yielding to the perceived group pressure could be lessened, many of Asch's subjects followed suit and conformed. *Pages 475–476*

Briefly describe Stanley Milgram's experimental demonstrations of obedience. Subjects in Milgram's experiments were led to believe that they were administering more and more potent shocks to another subject in a learning task. Whenever they hesitated to deliver the shocks, an authority figure, the experimenter, prodded them to continue. All subjects obeyed to some degree, and nearly two-thirds delivered what they thought was the most intense shock, even over the protests of the learner. Those who obeyed in Milgram's experiments were neither cruel nor inhumane. Rather, the experimenter created a powerful social situation that made it very difficult to refuse the authority figure's orders. *Pages 477–479*

What effect does the presence of others have on a person's willingness to help in an emergency? How do audience inhibition, pluralistic ignorance, and diffusion of responsibility account for the lack of bystander intervention? Research data tell us that the likelihood that someone will intervene on the behalf of another in an emergency situation is lessened as a function of how many others (bystanders) are present at the time. A number of factors have been proposed to account for this phenomenon. *Audience inhibition* is the term used to describe the hesitancy to intervene in front of others, perhaps for fear of embarrassing oneself. *Pluralistic ignorance* occurs when other bystanders lead one to think (by their inactivity) that nothing is really wrong in an ambiguous emergency situation. *Diffusion of responsibility* causes a member of a group to feel less obligated to intervene (less responsible) than if he or she were alone. Each of these processes tends to discourage helping and is more likely to operate as the number of persons present increases. *Pages 479–482*

What can we conclude concerning the effects of social influence on the quality of an individual's performance? The data suggest that as group size increases, social loafing increases. That is, one is less likely to invest full effort and energy in the task at hand as a member of a group than he or she would if working alone. It is also the case that the quality of one's performance also tends to suffer when one works in a group, a phenomenon called social interference. On the other hand, when tasks are simple or well rehearsed, performance may be enhanced, a process called social facilitation. *Pages 482–483*

How does social influence affect decision making in groups? There are some advantages to problem solving in a group setting. With proper leadership and communication, the combined expertise present in a group may provide better solutions and provide a better check on errors than we might find if individuals worked independently. On the other hand, *group polarization,* the tendency of group discussion to solidify and enhance preexisting attitudes, and *groupthink,* the unwillingness to promote an unpopular view in front of others in a group, operate to detract from group decision making. *Pages 484–485*

14.1 When the children in Ms. Elliott's class developed a set of cognitions about their classmates that did not allow for individual differences, they had developed a(n)   a) stereotype.   b) social norm.   c) prejudice.   d) attitude. *Page 460*

14.2 True or False?   Stereotypes have little value in social interactions because they misrepresent reality. *Pages 460–461*

14.3 Most psychologists believe that attitudes are made up of different components or aspects. The one aspect that seems most central to attitude is a) some attitudinal object.   b) a belief or cognition.   c) a tendency to behave in a certain way.   d) an evaluative (+ or –) feeling. *Pages 461–462*

14.4 True or False?   Attitudes have three components: personal, social, and environmental. *Page 462*

14.5 When an advertiser tries to change your attitude about a product, in which component of your attitude is the advertiser most interested? a) cognitive   b) evaluative   c) affective d) behavioral. *Page 463*

14.6 If I can get you to do something that is contrary to an attitude you currently hold, you may change your attitude. If I am successful, I have changed your attitude using: a) cognitive dissonance. b) classical conditioning.   c) coercive persuasion. d) cognitive response theory. *Pages 464–466*

14.7 A communicator is trying to persuade others to change their attitudes. Which characteristic of the communicator is LEAST important in predicting whether the communication will be successful?   a) credibility   b) celebrity c) expertise   d) trustworthiness. *Pages 466–467*

14.8 Attributions typically are made in terms of each of the following EXCEPT   a) internal vs. external factors.   b) dispositional vs. situational factors.   c) learned vs. inherited factors. d) intrinsic vs. extrinsic factors. *Page 469*

14.9 When we tend to overemphasize personal reasons in our explanations of another's behaviors and overlook the forces of the situation or the environment, we are   a) making a fundamental attribution error.   b) demonstrating our belief in the just world hypothesis.   c) employing a self-serving bias in our judgment.   d) failing to take into account the actor-observer bias. *Pages 469–471*

14.10 Basically, attributions deal with   a) different techniques for changing the attitudes of others. b) how we tend to explain the behaviors of ourselves and others in social situations.   c) factors and processes that lead to interpersonal attraction. d) forming expectations about how we should act in a variety of social situations. *Pages 469–471*

14.11 True or False?   Most people attribute their own successes to dispositional factors and their own failures to situational factors. *Pages 469–471*

14.12 With regard to interpersonal attraction, attachment theory suggests that   a) Every one relates to others in essentially the same way.   b) How one forms relationships as a child predicts how one will form relationships as an adult. c) Women tend to form interpersonal attachments that are different from those of men. d) How one forms attachments depends more on the situation than it does on the persons involved. *Pages 472–473*

14.13 With regard to interpersonal attraction, which is FALSE?   a) The "mere exposure phenomenon" tells us that familiarity breeds contempt.   b) We tend to like and value those who like and value us. c) Physical attractiveness is positively correlated with attraction.   d) People tend to be attracted to those who have similar attitudes. *Pages 473–475*

14.14 Which of these is likely to have the LEAST impact on interpersonal attraction?   a) physical closeness   b) physical attractiveness   c) attitudinal similarity   d) perceived sexuality. *Pages 473–475*

14.15 True or False?   Even if someone likes us now, if they did not like us originally, we probably will not value them as a friend. *Pages 473–475*

14.16 When Solomon Asch studied conformity, he found each of the following EXCEPT that a) even subjects' perceptual judgments could be influenced by group pressure.   b) most of his subjects (more than 75%) conformed at least once.   c) the least amount of social support was sufficient to help a subject resist group pressure.   d) most of the subjects continued to conform even after they learned that others in the group were confederates of the experimenter. *Pages 475–476*

14.17 True or False?   Up to a point, the more people who express the same judgment, the more likely will an individual yield or conform to that judgment. *Pages 475–476*

14.18 The major difference between conformity and obedience is   a) peer pressure.   b) the presence of an authority figure.   c) the nature of the task involved.   d) the subject's perception of social influence. *Pages 475–479*

14.19 Which conclusion from Milgram's research on obedience is justified?   a) Persons of some nationalities are more likely to obey than are others.   b) When told to harm others, few subjects felt guilty about it.   c) The perception of authority is a strong force in conformity. d) Women are more likely to obey than are men. *Pages 477–479*

14.20 True or False?   Even Milgram was surprised by the results of his experiment. *Pages 477–478*

14.21 Which of the following is NOT taken to be a necessary step in considering whether or not to intervene in an emergency?   a) One must notice or perceive the emergency.   b) One must interpret the situation as an emergency.   c) One must know or care about the victim.   d) One must decide to take responsibility to do something. *Pages 479–482*

14.22 Which of these best characterizes pluralistic ignorance?   a) the feeling that one doesn't know what to do in an emergency   b) the perception that there is a good reason why others are not acting   c) the decision that there is nothing that could be done to help   d) the belief that intervention will cause more harm than good. *Page 480*

14.23 The concept of "diffusion of responsibility" tells us that if you were in need of assistance, you most likely would receive such assistance if: a) there were only a few people around at the time   b) the persons who see you are women not men   c) you happen to be in a small town, not a large city   d) there happens to be a large crowd present. *Page 481*

14.24 Based on his observation of bicycle riders in competition, Norman Triplett performed one of the first experiments in social psychology on the phenomenon he called   a) bystander apathy. b) cognitive dissonance.   c) audience inhibition.   d) social facilitation. *Page 482*

14.25 Zajonc and others suggest that the presence of others is likely to improve the quality of one's performance if   a) the task is easy and/or well-learned.   b) those others act in a supportive, approving fashion.   c) the task is difficult or complex.   d) those others act in a hostile, disapproving fashion. *Page 483*

14.26 True or False?   Social interference and social loafing are more common phenomena than is social facilitation. *Pages 482–483*

14.27 In the context of group decision making, "polarization" refers to the observation that   a) groups are consistently better at making decisions than are individuals.   b) being in a group is likely to enhance and solidify initially held attitudes. c) the more groups discuss an issue, the riskier their decision will be.   d) throughout the discussion, one person will emerge as actual group leader. *Pages 484–485*

14.28 Janis's concept of "groupthink" tells us that a) groups strive to reach consensus, right or wrong.   b) people are more likely to express divergent opinions in a group than when they are alone.   c) members of a group prefer that other members do most of the work.   d) group decisions tend to be conservative and unoriginal. *Page 484*

Chapter 15

Psychology Applied: I/O, Environmental, and Sports Psychology

▲ **Preview**

▲ **Industrial-Organizational Psychology**

  ▼ *Psychology in the Real World:*
  The Hawthorne Studies

▲ **Psychology and the Environment**

▲ **Psychology and Sports**

▲ **Thinking Critically about Psychology Applied**

▲ **Summary**

▲ **Test Yourself**

▲▲▲▲▲▲

Greg Farwell has just been named Plant Manager for Acme Flange Fabrication, Inc., a small manufacturing company in the midwest that is facing several problems. Pressures from foreign imports and a reduced demand for the high quality flanges that AFF produces have reduced profits severely.

Greg sees the need for increased productivity as an opportunity to introduce some changes at AFF. He wants to implement some of the technological advances that have revolutionized flange manufacturing. But more than that, he realizes that to return Acme Flange to its once highly respected status in the industry, management will have to take a new look at leadership styles and means to motivate a group of talented but discouraged rank-and-file workers.

Installing new equipment and restructuring the organization will mean retraining at almost all levels of the company. In some cases, training will be directed at the acquisition of new skills; in others, it will mean bringing about changes in attitudes and communication styles. To complicate matters further, contract negotiations with the local labor union begin in two weeks. Farwell wants to be sure that what he is proposing can be implemented while maintaining—perhaps enhancing—job satisfaction among AFF employees. He knows, for example, that he is going to have to address many of his female employees' concerns about such issues as day care, flexible time schedules, and pregnancy leave.

It is clear to Greg that he needs to hire a new assistant plant manager to help him put all these changes into practice. The last assistant manager resisted change in any form. He proved to be inefficient, and one of the first things that Farwell had to do when he came to the job was fire him. He does not want to make a mistake hiring his new assistant manager.

Two other realities are in the mind of the new plant manager—visits from government agencies. OSHA will be by soon to check the operation for potential safety

violations, and right before contract negotiations. Even more troublesome is an anticipated visit from the Environmental Protection Agency—there's concern about waste
water from the plant polluting nearby streams and well water.

Although Greg Farwell is plant manager of a manufacturing firm, many of the tasks
he has before him are psychological in nature. Farwell's challenges have more to do
with affect, behaviors, and cognitions than with steel and flanges. The challenges facing Greg Farwell reflect many of the concerns of industrial/organizational (I/O) psychology. We'll see what psychology has to say about these issues in this chapter.

▶ Preview

We have noted repeatedly that psychology has many practical applications in everyday life. Indeed, this is one of the themes introduced back in Chapter 1. The principles of psychology can be brought to bear on many of the problems we face from day to day. In this chapter, we will focus on three areas where psychology is applied regularly.

We begin with a brief examination of industrial/organizational (I/O) psychology. Industrial/organizational psychologists specialize in the study of affect, behavior, and cognition in work settings. Often, professionals in this field are concerned with using evidence from psychology to improve the effectiveness and efficiency of business or industrial organizations. That does not mean that I/O psychologists are "company people," only concerned with the best interests of management. I/O psychologists care about the workplace in general, and that includes a consideration of workers' needs as well as management's needs.

We'll focus on just two of the I/O psychologist's concerns. First we'll discuss how best to fit the right person to a given job. This will entail a consideration of how we can select, train, and motivate someone to do a job well. Then we'll examine how best to fit a job to a person, which will mean looking at such matters as job satisfaction, quality of work life, and worker safety. Each of the issues raised in this discussion is relevant and meaningful to anyone who has ever entered the world of work.

We'll finish this chapter with a brief look at two other subfields of applied psychology. First, we'll sample some of the work of psychologists who are concerned about interactions between the physical environment and one's psychological state of well-being. We'll examine the notions of space and territory, using life in a big city as an example. We'll review some of the evidence concerning the psychological reactions to environmental pollutants such as noise, temperature, and toxins. We'll see how psychologists can help people change their behaviors so as to have a positive impact on the environment. Finally, we'll look at a few ways in which psychologists apply their knowledge in the world of sports and athletics.

▶ Industrial-Organizational Psychology

It is generally to everyone's advantage to have the best available person assigned to any particular job. Employers benefit from having workers who are well qualified and motivated to do their work. Employees benefit from being assigned tasks that they enjoy and that are within the scope of their abilities. When I was a college student, a summer job required that I fill in for another employee one day and drive a large truck loaded with milk from a dairy in upstate New York to various locations in New York City. That I ever got that milk delivered had more to do with good luck and youthful enthusiasm than anything else. It took me twice as long as the regular driver to make the deliveries, and, to say the least, I did not enjoy spending most of a summer's day lost in New York City with a truck filled with milk. I clearly was not the best worker for the task.

▶ Fitting the Person to the Job

What is involved in getting the best person to do a job? The relevant issues from the perspective of I/O psychology are personnel selection, training, and motivation. That is, one way to get a person to do good work is to *select* and hire a person who already has the ability and the motivation to do that work. On the other hand, we may choose to *train* people to do good work. We also may have to face the task of *motivating* people with ability to do good work. These are the processes we examine in this section. However, before we can begin selecting, training, or motivating someone for a job, we need to understand the nature of the job itself.

▶ *Defining "Good Work"—The Job Analysis*

Assume that you are an industrial-organizational psychologist hired to help a company select a manager for one of its retail stores in a local shopping mall. You could not begin to tell the company what sort of person it was looking for until you had a full description of the job this manager was to do. In general terms, you would have to know the duties and responsibilities of a store manager. Then, you could translate that job description into a set of measurable characteristics that a successful store manager should possess. In other words, you would begin by doing a **job analysis,** "the systematic study of the tasks, duties, and responsibilities of a job and the knowledge, skills, and abilities needed to perform it" (Riggio, 1990, p. 59).

Typically, writing a job analysis is a two-step process. The first step involves compiling a complete description of what a person in that job is to do. There are many sources of information that one could use to generate this description. Most companies have job descriptions for their employees, but these usually are stated in general terms, such as "supervise workers in the store; maintain acceptable levels of sales; prepare payrolls; monitor inventory; schedule work periods," and the like.

To be useful, a job analysis must be specific and describe the actual *behaviors* engaged in by someone in a given position. Does a store manager have to know how to operate the cash register and inventory control devices? Does the manager deal with the sales staff on a one-to-one basis or in groups? Are interactions with employees informal, or are there regularly scheduled formal meetings that need to be organized? To what extent is the store manager responsible for employee training and development? Will he or she be involved in labor negotiations? Clearly, this list of questions can be a long one. The underlying concern at this level is "On a daily basis, just what does a store manager *do*?"

Once duties and responsibilities have been specified, the second step requires that these be translated into terms of measurable personal characteristics. That is, one determines the **performance criteria** required to do a job well. Now the goal is to list the characteristics that a person in the position should have in order to do that job as well as possible.

There are several areas that might be explored at this point. Smith (1976), for example, distinguishes between what she calls "hard" (objective) criteria and "soft" (subjective) criteria. The former come from available data—salary, number of units sold, number of days absent, and the like. Soft criteria require some degree of judgment—sense of humor, creativity, congeniality, and so forth. Let's use an academic example. Suppose your psychology department wants to give an award to its "outstanding senior." Some of the criteria that determine which student is worthy of the award may be objective—senior class standing, grade-point average, a minimum number of courses, and so on. Other criteria may be subjective. The department may want to give this award to a student only if she or he is well-known to many members of the faculty, has impressive communication skills, or has been active in the Psychology Club. These criteria require the judgment of those making the award. Indeed, most job analyses involve consideration of both hard, objective and soft, subjective criteria.

job analysis a complete and specific description of a job including the qualities required to do it well

performance criteria specific behaviors or characteristics that a person should have in order to do a job as well as possible

Remember that the basic task is to find the best available person to do a job as well as possible. If we are not fully aware of the demands of a job and have not translated those demands into specific performance criteria, we'll have difficulty determining if we have found the right person. In other words, we need to build in procedures by which our selection (or training or motivation) program can be evaluated (Dunnette & Borman, 1979). Once a job analysis is ready—once we know what an applicant is expected to do on the job *and* we have translated those tasks into measurable criteria—we are ready to begin designing an assessment procedure.

Before You Go On

▼▼▼▼▼▼▼▼

What is involved in doing a job analysis?

▶ Selecting People Who Can Do Good Work

Personnel selection not only involves devising procedures to help one decide which of many applicants to hire, but it also involves decisions relating to retention, promotion, and termination (Guion & Gibson, 1988). As you can imagine, a wide variety of techniques and sources of information is available to the employer for screening and evaluating applicants for any position. If the job analysis has been done properly, the I/O psychologist has a complete list of those duties and characteristics in which the employer is interested. The task now is to find the person who has those characteristics.

Some useful information can be gleaned from a well-constructed *job application form*. An application form can serve three functions. (1) It can be used as a rough screening device. Some applicants may be denied simply because they do not meet some basic requirement for the job, such as a minimal educational level or specified job experience. (2) It can supplement and/or provide cues for interviewing. Bits of data from application forms can be pursued later during in-depth interviews. (3) It provides biographical data (called *biodata*), including educational and work history, that may be useful in making direct predictions about a candidate's potential for success. Some I/O psychologists list biographical information of the sort that can be uncovered on job application forms as the best source of data for predicting success on the job (Baley, 1985; Drakely, Herriot & Jones, 1988; Muchinsky, 1987; Reilly & Chao, 1982).

An integral part of many selection procedures is the *employment interview*. We've already commented (Chapter 10, pp. 358–359) on the dangers of relying too heavily on information gained through interviews. Unstructured interviews in particular are subject to error. Nonetheless, the interview is the most widely used of employee selection procedures (Arvey & Campion, 1982; Thayer, 1983), even though most results of validity studies are "dismal" and that "despite various innovations over the years, [the interview] has never been consistently shown to improve selection" (Tenopyr, 1981, p. 1123). Interviews involve the interaction of two people—the interviewer and the person being interviewed. As a result, the biases of the interviewer, conscious or unconscious, may influence the results of an interview (Cash & Kilcullen, 1985).

There is evidence of considerable individual differences in interviewer skill. Some interviewers consistently obtain more valid information than do others (*e.g.*, Thayer, 1983; Zedeck, et al., 1983). Training interviewers to be sensitive to bias can improve the validity of the technique, but such training

▲ *The interview remains an integral part of the employees selection process, though studies reveal that biases on the part of the interviewer may influence the results.*

is expensive. According to Cronbach, "In employment practice, interviews have several functions and will continue to be used. The best general advice is to make sure that interviewer judgments are not given excessive weight in selection" (1984, p. 406).

Within the last few years, the outlook for the use of the interview has become a bit more positive and optimistic. In large measure, this is because of the increased use of the structured interview. Structured interviews use a carefully prescribed set of questions that is asked of all applicants in the same order. Structured interviews may take away some of the interviewer's latitude and freedom to explore different issues, but they are demonstrably more valid than are unstructured interviews (Arvey, et al., 1987; Schmitt & Robertson, 1990; Wiesner & Cronshaw, 1988).

Personnel selection often involves administering and interpreting *psychological tests* (see Chapter 8). Many tests are designed to assess only one specific characteristic (*e.g.*, finger dexterity, which a job analysis may indicate to be very relevant for an assembly-line worker in an electronics plant). Other tests are more general, assessing several different skills and abilities in one session. Tests of intelligence and/or personality traits may be called for, particularly when evaluating candidates for managerial or supervisory positions. There are literally hundreds of paper-and-pencil tests designed to measure traits from typing skills, to critical thinking skills, to mechanical aptitude, to leadership style, to motivation for sales work. Some popular tests of general traits have been modified to focus more sharply on work-related applications (Gough, 1985). In general, the data suggest that the most useful of all psychological tests are those that assess some sort of cognitive function, such as ability or achievement tests (Guion & Gibson, 1988).

A very important issue when psychological tests are used for personnel decisions is the demonstrated validity of such tests. You'll recall from our discussion of testing (Chapter 8, pp. 280–281) that there are different types of validity. What is particularly crucial in employee testing is that a test used for selection be related to performance on the job.

training a systematic and intentional process of altering the behaviors of employees to increase organizational effectiveness

▲ *Retraining employees to learn new skills and procedures will help keep worker motivation high and will also help industries stay abreast of new technologies.*

Before You Go On
▼▼▼▼▼▼▼▼

What are some of the sources of information that can be used in making personnel decisions?

▶ Training People to Do Good Work

The training of employees is one of the major concerns of business, industry, and government. The cost of employee training runs into billions of dollars every year. Training or retraining employees will become even more critical in the years ahead as the number of people entering the workforce decreases (Offermann & Gowing, 1990).

In the context of industrial/organizational psychology, **training** means "a systematic intentional process of altering behavior of organizational members in a direction which contributes to organizational effectiveness" (Hinrichs, 1976). This definition implies that training is meant to increase the skills or abilities of employees to do their job. Training also implies a systematic intervention, as opposed to hit-or-miss instruction.

New York University psychologists Raymond Katzell and Richard Guzzo (1983) reviewed more than 200 research studies dealing with approaches to improving productivity and concluded that, "Training and instruction activities represent the most frequently reported approach to productivity improvement during 1971–1981" (p. 469). Training programs have been found to be successful in a wide range of settings, with various types of personnel, as indicated by several productivity criteria, including quantity and quality of work, cost reduction, turnover, accident reduction, and absenteeism (Katzell & Guzzo, 1983).

Developing a successful training program is a complex, multifaceted enterprise. What are the steps involved in the design and implementation of a training program? Our discussion is based on the system proposed by Goldstein (1980; 1986) and is summarized in Figure 15.1.

Assessing Training Needs. Training programs are designed to address a need within the organization. So one of the first things you will have to do is a complete assessment of instructional needs. In many ways, this assessment is like a job analysis in personnel selection. There are many questions that must be raised and answered at this critical stage. Just what is the problem that training is supposed to solve? Is production down? Is there a new product that salespeople need to know about? Is the accident rate getting too high? The first stage of assessing instructional needs will be to state the general goals of your training program. At this point, a very difficult question is whether or not a training program is the best solution for a given problem. Often, the most crucial decision to be made about training is if it is really needed (Latham, 1988).

The second step requires translating general goals into actual training objectives. At this stage, general statements will no longer suffice. Now you need *specific* statements of what the training program should do. Precisely what do you want trainees to know (or be able to do) at the end of the training session that they do not know (or cannot do) now? Your training program probably will be evaluated in terms of these specific objectives.

Figure 15.1

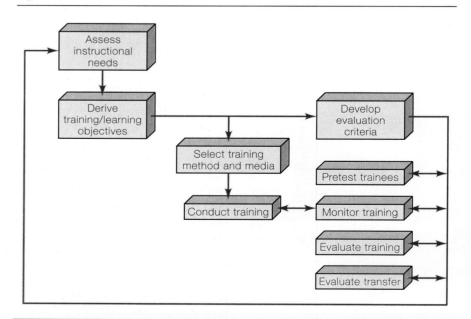

▲ *A flowchart of the steps involved in planning and conducting a training program. (After Goldstein, 1986.)*

With your objectives in mind, but before you begin actual training, you will want to specify criteria by which your training can be evaluated when it is over. For your program evaluation to be effective, you must specify now, before training begins, how you will evaluate outcomes (Latham, 1988). There are many factors you might want to consider. Did the trainees develop the skills and acquire the information you intended them to? How did the trainees feel about the program? Did the program have an impact on the organizational needs that prompted the training in the first place? You might want to consider designing a pretest procedure to assess your trainees in terms of present skills or information levels. Pretesting may provide you with a means of showing the impact of your program.

In this context I also should mention that training outcomes need to be evaluated repeatedly. Evaluating training programs is commonly an on-going process. What are the immediate effects of training, if any? Is the training still having the desired impact a month later? Is the training responsible for year-end increases in profits? Evaluating a training program should not be thought of as a one-shot intervention.

Training Techniques. After you've determined the criteria for assessing outcomes, you have to decide how you will go about the actual training. Given what you know about your needs and objectives and what you know about your employees, what will be the most efficient type of training mechanism you can use to reach your specified goals?

There are many methods that might be used. In some cases, bringing workers together for classroom instruction works well. On the other hand, there are situations in which assembling large numbers of workers would be unrealistic. Automobile manufacturers, for example, can hardly be expected to have all car salespeople report to the home office for instruction on improvements in the new models of cars they will be selling. Occasionally, training has to go to the worker—as printed material, audio cassettes, videotaped programs, or live presentations by a trainer—rather than having the worker go to the training.

As designer of a training program, you will have many decisions to make about the methods you will use. Should you use live instructors, or should information be presented in the form of media: print, audiotapes, videotapes, videodisks, and the like? Should the training be formalized and time-limited, or can trainees be allowed to work alone, at their own pace? Will there need to be hands-on experience? Will training be in groups or will it be individually oriented? Will on-the-job training be efficient or disruptive? Can the job be simply simulated for the purposes of training? As you can see, your options are many, and some are clearly more effective than others for certain kinds of training. Too many trainers get into the habit of using only one or two techniques for a variety of different needs and objectives. For example, televised instruction may be very useful to point out a few new features of an automobile to a salesperson, but quite ineffective as a means of describing a new health insurance program. By and large, presenting information is less effective than demonstrating it, and involving one's audience as participants is the most effective method (*e.g.,* Thornton & Cleveland, 1990).

Having decided on a training technique, you are ready to begin. If you have worked through the procedures outlined so far, you'll find that actually conducting the training is much easier than if you hadn't the time to do so. I should add, of course, that you will have to monitor the effectiveness of the training program as it runs its course (review Figure 15.1). Even the best of plans may need to be adjusted during actual training.

Measuring Training Effectiveness. When you have administered the training program, you're ready to consider (again) what may be the most difficult part of training and development. You must evaluate the success of your intervention. Now you need some measure of the extent to which your training affects the actual job in the workplace and meets the organizational needs that prompted the training in the first place.

There are many difficulties involved in the evaluation of training programs, and we need not review them all here. We will only make these three observations:

1. Training programs can be evaluated at different levels. You may ask participants to rate *how they feel about* or evaluate the program. You may assess the extent to which the training has produced *behavioral changes.* You may try to measure *how much has been learned,* perhaps with a formal testing before and after training. (Do you recognize our ABC here?) Or you may go right to the bottom line and ask about *increases in productivity or profit* (Kirkpatrick, 1976).

2. Training programs that do not include ways of evaluating short-term *and* long-term effectiveness generally will be of little value. Sadly, few training programs are well evaluated. Many are taken simply on faith or face value because of their logical appeal (*e.g.*, Schultz & Schultz, 1990).

3. The greater the effort put into the assessment of organizational needs, job analysis, performance criteria, and the establishment of training objectives at the beginning of a training project, the easier it will be to evaluate the program when it is over.

Before You Go On
▼▼▼▼▼▼▼▼▼

List some of the factors that need to be considered in the design, implementation, and evaluation of a training program.

▶ Motivating People to Do Good Work

Let's review for a moment. Our concern in this section is "fitting the person to the job"—finding someone to do good work. The first step in that process involves carefully delineating just what is meant by a good job. To this end, one does a job analysis and lists specific performance criteria for the job. An employer then can go through the process of selection to locate the best person—someone who already has all the skills to do the job well. Another possibility is to train a present employee to do good (or better) work. There remains an important consideration: the motivation to do good work. Being able to do a job well and wanting to do a job well are two different matters. Notice, too, that issues of training and motivation generally are continuous, ongoing concerns. People change, and jobs change. Seldom will one training program or one attempt to motivate employees be sufficient in the long term.

As you can imagine, I/O psychologists have long been interested in how to motivate employees. When we talk about work motivation, we're referring to three interrelated processes: *arousing* (getting the worker to do a task), *directing* (getting the worker to do what we want done), and *sustaining* (keeping the worker at the task). As you can also imagine, there is no one simple answer to questions about what motivates workers to do a particular job well and stick with it. We'll briefly review a few popular approaches.

▲ *Motivation to do quality work can reach creative proportions as in this television assembly plant. Here, signs of encouragement were posted by workers themselves.*

expectancy theory the view that workers make logical choices to do what they believe will result in their attaining outcomes of highest value

Values and Expectations. The expectancy theory of work motivation has been around for many years and has been modified by many theorists, but it is best associated with Victor Vroom (1964). It is cognitive in its orientation. **Expectancy theory** claims that workers behave rationally and logically, making work-related decisions based on their beliefs, judgments, and expectations.

Vroom's theory is quite complex, but what it amounts to is that we are motivated to work if (1) we expect to be rewarded on the basis of the level of our performance, and (2) we value the rewards that are being offered. We also must believe that rewards are attainable, that we actually can do the work to a level of performance that will earn those rewards.

There are clear implications here for employers who want to motivate their employees to do good work. For one thing, they should see to it that the outcomes that follow good work are truly valued by the workers. For example, in one company, doing good work is rewarded by recognition with a plaque and a free trip awarded at the annual company dinner. (The company dinner is viewed by management as a reward for a profitable year.) What if most of the workforce found company dinners to be a huge bore, plaques to be an embarrassment, and free trips a nuisance (arranging for transportation, babysitters, and so on)? What if the employees would much rather have a cash bonus? That is, what if the employees actually believed that there was little or no value in what the company defined as rewards?

Another implication of expectancy theory is that it is important that workers understand the relationship between their behaviors and outcomes (*e.g.*, Ilgen & Klein, 1989). Simply put, workers need to know what to expect will happen if they behave in a certain way. Which behaviors lead to positive outcomes, and which lead to negative outcomes? Why should an employee work hard, put in overtime, and take work home on the weekend if he or she has little reason to believe that such behaviors will lead to real rewards? Indeed, one reality is that fewer than one-third of workers believe that their compensation is based on their work performance (Plawin & Suied, 1988).

equity theory the view that workers are motivated to match their inputs and outcomes with those of fellow workers in similiar positions

Fair Rewards. Another approach to motivation that has received support is called **equity theory**, and it is associated with J. Stacy Adams (1965). Equity theory is also cognitive in nature, claiming that what matters most to workers is their perception of the extent to which they are being treated fairly compared to fellow workers in similar work situations.

In Adams's view, workers make many social comparisons (or cognitive judgments). They judge how much they are getting from the organization compared to what they are putting into it. That is, the worker judges the extent to which effort, skill, education, experience (inputs) are rewarded by salary, fringe benefits, praise, awards, and the like (outcomes). Then, this ratio of inputs and outcomes is compared with a ratio earned by some other, similarly placed employee. If the relationship is seen as being about the same, or equitable, the worker will not be motivated to change. If, however, there is a perceived inequity when compared to the inputs and outcomes of a fellow worker, then changes can be predicted. The worker may increase or decrease inputs (work longer or shorter hours; take fewer or more breaks) or try to effect a change in outcomes. What matters most here is not the real value of what a worker gains for his or her efforts. What matters is the *perception of equity*—what he or she perceives in comparison to others. (Recall our theme from Chapter 1: Things are not always as they seem?) A worker will be much more willing to maintain effort (input) and take a cut in pay (outcome) if that worker believes that everyone else is taking a similar cut in pay (Locke, 1976; Middlemist & Peterson, 1976; Mowday, 1983).

Goal-setting. Attention to establishing goals has been the centerpiece of several approaches to worker motivation, particularly that of Edwin Locke (1968; Locke & Latham, 1984). This approach also has a cognitive basis, assuming that workers are best motivated to perform a task for which goals are clearly and specifically delineated. For goal-setting to have a positive influence on a worker's behavior, two things are necessary. First, the employee must be clearly *aware* of just what he or she is working for. Second, the employee must *accept* that goal as worth the effort.

The mechanisms of goal-setting for motivating workers have received much research interest. Here are some general conclusions. (1) Difficult, but achievable goals tend to increase productivity more than easy goals. The issue here seems to hinge on the acceptance of goals as being worthwhile. Goals that are too easy to reach may not require any change in performance. At the same time, goals that are perceived as being *too* difficult and beyond the abilities of workers are not likely to be very useful (Erez & Zidon, 1984). (2) Specific goals are better than general ones. Simply telling workers to "do better" or "do your best" provides little information about what behaviors are expected. (3) Feedback that informs workers of their progress toward established goals is important in maintaining motivated behaviors. Feedback delivered soon after an appropriate response is made is more effective than delayed feedback (*e.g.*, Geller, et al., 1985; Geller, et al., 1987). (4) Although it may seem reasonable to predict that goals set by employers and employees working together are more effective than goals established by employers alone, the evidence suggests that this is not necessarily the case. What matters most is that the employee simply be aware of specific goals and accept those goals as reasonable (Locke, et al., 1981).

As you can imagine, there are other approaches to work motivation. Some refer directly to motivational concepts we introduced back in Chapter 9 when we discussed motivation in general. That is, some approaches stress the importance of workers' needs (as in Maslow's theory about a hierarchy from basic physiological needs to needs to self-actualize). Some approaches stress the importance of behavior change through operant conditioning and attention to the consequences of behavior (an approach called "organizational behavior management" when applied in work environments).

Here's a brief summary of our discussion. Workers will be motivated to do a good job if:

1. Clear and specific goals are established and accepted.

2. The goals that employers set match workers' expectations and needs.

3. Workers clearly see the relationship between their work performance and accepted outcomes.

4. Workers judge the outcomes that follow from their efforts as being in line with those earned by fellow workers making similar efforts.

5. Workers are given feedback about the nature of their work (Katzell & Thompson, 1990).

Now let's shift our emphasis slightly from a concern about finding and fitting the person to the job to the issue of fitting the job to the person. In large measure, our interest here is with what we call job satisfaction. What can be done to make jobs more satisfying? What is the result of doing so?

Before You Go On
▼▼▼▼▼▼▼▼▼

Briefly summarize some of the factors that affect the motivation of workers to do a good job.

▶ Fitting the Job to the Person

To this point, we have considered what an employer can do to find the best person for a given task. Now we'll change our perspective a bit and focus on some of the issues that are relevant to the person on the job. The major issue here relates to job satisfaction. We'll define the concept, and then we'll see if job satisfaction is correlated with job performance measures.

job satisfaction an attitude; a collection of positive feelings about one's job or job experiences

Job satisfaction refers to the attitude that one holds toward one's work—"a pleasurable or positive emotional state resulting from the appraisal of one's job or job experiences" (Locke, 1976). Although we often talk about job satisfaction in general terms (what Riggio (1990) calls a "global approach"), it's clear that an employee's satisfaction can vary considerably for different aspects of the job (a "facet approach"). As you know from your own work experience, you can be reasonably happy with your physical working conditions, very unhappy with base salary, pleased with your fringe benefits, satisfied with the level of challenge provided by the job, very dissatisfied with relationships with coworkers, and so on. In fact, there may be as many facets of job satisfaction and/or dissatisfaction as there are aspects to the job.

A great deal of research has studied possible relationships between job satisfaction and personal characteristics of workers. We can summarize some of that research briefly. (1) There is a positive correlation between overall satisfaction and age. Younger workers tend to be most dissatisfied with their jobs (Rhodes, 1983). (2) Data on sex differences in job satisfaction tend to be inconsistent. By and large, however, sex differences are quite small (Sauser & York, 1978) and virtually nonexistent when pay, tenure, and education are controlled (Hulin & Smith, 1964). (3) Racial differences in job satisfaction consistently have been shown to be small, with whites

▲ *Although it seems logical that job satisfaction should be a predicator of productivity, the relationship between quality of work life and job productivity is tenuous at best.*

having slightly more positive attitudes about their jobs than do nonwhites (Weaver, 1980). (4) Satisfaction is positively related to the perceived level or status of one's job, where those positions of lowest rank tend to be filled by least-satisfied workers (King, et al., 1982). Of course, the real issue for I/O psychologists is to determine *why* these differences in job satisfaction occur (or why they do not). All we've listed here are results of correlational studies, and we need to keep in mind that correlational studies tell us nothing about cause and effect.

quality of work life (QWL) a group of factors concerning one's work that influence one's attitude toward one's job

Recently, I/O psychologists have become interested in a somewhat broader concept than job satisfaction called **quality of work life**, or **QWL**. QWL is a difficult concept to define concisely, but may be taken to include such factors as (1) a sense of respect from supervisors; (2) employment security (the future of the job); (3) income adequacy and equity (present and future); (4) a sense of self-esteem, challenge, and independence; (5) opportunities for social interaction; (6) a sense of making a real contribution; (7) a relationship between life on the job and life off the job; and (8) active participation in decision making (Davis & Cherns, 1975; Levine, et al., 1984; Stein, 1983). The major concern of I/O psychology in this area has been to develop strategies for improving the quality of work life within an organization (Beer & Walton, 1987; Lawler, 1982; Tuttle, 1983). A related question is whether there is any support for the hypothesis that increased worker satisfaction leads to increased productivity and increased profitability.

It may seem reasonable to assert that "a happy worker is a productive worker"—that increased satisfaction necessarily will be reflected in increased worker productivity. For the last 50 years, many executives have assumed without question a cause and effect relation between satisfaction and productivity. In many ways, satisfaction and productivity *may* be positively correlated, but such a relationship is not a simple one and is at best a weak one (Iaffaldano & Muchinsky, 1985). Research on job satisfaction often refutes the claim that better performance *necessarily* results from increased worker satisfaction (Howell & Dipboye, 1982). Over and over, we find contradictory evidence, which, among other things, reflects the difficulties involved in agreeing on good operational definitions for both quality of work life and worker productivity (Hartman, et al., 1986). The only conclusion we can draw about these two variables is that in some instances they may be correlated. Cause-and-effect statements are out of the question.

The lack of a strong, consistent relationship between satisfaction and productivity may not be that difficult to explain. Some workers may hate their present jobs but work very hard at them so that they can be promoted to some other position that they believe they will prefer. Some workers may be very satisfied with their present positions simply because expectations for productivity are low—if demands for productivity increase, satisfaction may decrease, at least in this situation. *Increasing productivity may have the effect of increasing satisfaction*, rather than vice versa. A motivated employee, who wants to do her best at her job, will be pleased to enter a training program to improve her on-the-job efficiency. Doing the job well leads to pride and an overall increase in satisfaction for this worker; for another, the same training program may be viewed as a ploy on management's part to make life miserable.

I shouldn't give the impression that job satisfaction is not consistently or meaningfully related to *any* work behavior. There is evidence that job satisfaction measures can be used to aid the prediction of which workers are likely to be absent from work or are likely to quit (what Saal and Knight (1988) call "withdrawal behaviors"). As it happens, job satisfaction is not the best predictor of absenteeism (marital status, age, and size of one's work group are better (Watson, 1981)), but the correlations are at least reasonably consistent (Porter & Steers, 1973). The relationship between dissatisfaction with one's job and turnover seems to be stronger, although even this relationship may not be direct. That is, dissatisfaction may be an important contributing factor, but it is only one of several variables that can be used to explain why one leaves a job. (Many times people are forced to quit for reasons that have nothing to do with their job or their employer—illness and family concerns, for example.) Nonetheless, the logic that those who are most unhappy with their work are the ones most likely to leave it does have research support (Mobley, 1977; Muchinsky & Tuttle, 1979).

Before You Go On
▼▼▼▼▼▼▼▼

Briefly summarize the relationship between job satisfaction and job productivity.

▶ Psychology and the Environment

environmental psychology the field of applied psychology that studies the effect of the general environment on organisms within it

Environmental psychology is the subfield of psychology that studies how the general environment (as opposed to specific stimuli) affects the behavior and mental processes of organisms living in it. Environmental psychologists are also concerned with how people, in turn, affect their environments. This field tends to be interdisciplinary (Saegert & Winkel, 1990). Environmental psychologists work with urban planners, economists, clinical psychologists, sociologists, architects, landscape designers, builders, and others.

The range of interest areas within environmental psychology is quite large. Some psychologists are interested in such matters as how color and lighting affect workers' productivity, students' learning, or nursing home patients' mental and physical health. Some match psychological or behavioral reactions to poisons or toxins in our environments. Some are interested in the design and construction of physical space that maximizes the functions for which that space is constructed. Some seek efficient ways of changing personal behaviors in order to influence the natural environment in positive ways, through anti-littering campaigns, for example. Others focus on the impact of crowding, territoriality, or adjustment to the demands of city living. Of course, many of these issues are interrelated.

Consistent with a theme I introduced back in Chapter 1, environmental psychologists recognize that what often influences behavior most is one's *perception* of the environment. A room with ten persons in it can appear to be terribly small and crowded if it is perceived as an office. The same room can seem large and uncrowded if the room is perceived as a waiting area. In fact, two rooms of exactly the same area, one square the other rectangular, will not be perceived as being the same size; the square room will appear smaller than the rectangular room (Sadalla & Oxley, 1984). Let's begin our introduction to environmental psychology by considering the perception of space and distance.

Before You Go On
▼▼▼▼▼▼▼▼

Define environmental psychology, and list some of the issues that environmental psychologists study.

▲▲▲▲▲▲▲▲▲▲▲▲▲▲▲

The Hawthorne Studies

One of the first experimental interventions in an industrial setting was begun in 1924 at the Hawthorne Plant of the Chicago Western Electric Company in Cicero, Illinois. Among other things, the plant assembled electric relays used in the manufacture of telephones. The studies begun here lasted for more than a decade and are referred to as "the Hawthorne studies." The results of these experiments were controversial when they were first described, and they still are.

It all started innocently enough. The initial issue was whether or not the lighting in the factory had a measurable effect on productivity. What the researchers found was that as they varied illumination, production tended to increase. What was surprising was that productivity went up whether the illumination levels were increased or decreased, and in one study, production went up just when the workers *thought* that illumination was being changed when in fact it was not changed at all. How curious! A noticeable effect was being produced on worker output, but there was no clear relationship between the output and the manipulations of the experimenters.

In another series of experiments, output also appeared to increase steadily regardless of the specific manipulations of the independent variable. Five women were separated from other workers and put in a special room where several factors were studied. One factor that was chanegd was the style of supervision these workers received. Several physical changes were also introduced, including rest breaks, free lunch periods, and shorter working hours. When these benefits were introduced, production increased, and when they were eliminated, production also appeared to increase. As we shall see, the key word here is *appeared*.

Two psychologists, Elton Mayo (1933) and Fritz Roethlisberger (Roethlisberger & Dickson, 1939), analyzed the findings of the Hawthorne experiments and came to some rather sweeping generalizations about the nature of the workplace, relations between management and the worker, and the relationship between job satisfaction and productivity. One of their conclusions has become so entrenched in psychology, it has been given a label: **the Hawthorne effect**. The Hawthorne effect is "the tendency of human beings to be influenced by special attention from others" (Stagner,

▶ *Space and Territory*

Imagine that you are seated in the library, studying at a large table. There is no one else at your table. Then another student enters and sits right next to you. Although there are seven other chairs available, this student opts to sit in the one just to your left. Or imagine that you are buying a used car. While you are examining one of the cars on the lot, a salesperson approaches, stands right in front of you (not more than eight inches away) and begins to tell you about the features of the car you are looking at. Or imagine that in your psychology class you always sit in the same seat. The semester is about over, and you have gotten to know some of the people who sit near you. Then, the next time you go to class, you find that there is someone else in "your" seat. Or imagine that you are a homeowner. You've

1982). The straightforward translation of this principle is that workers (or anyone else) will change (or improve) their behavior (their productivity) if they are led to believe that someone cares about what they are doing.

Mayo and Roethlisberger explained the improved performance of the workers largely in terms of humane treatment and enlightened management practices that involved workers in decision making and that tended to the personal and social needs of employees. For example, the output of the five assemblers increased because of changes in supervisory style and because they were treated differently—given their own special room and work hours—regardless of what that difference was. At least that was the argument at the time. It is commonly claimed that what we now call the *human relations movement* in industry began with this interpretation of the data from the Hawthorne plant experiments.

Three important points need to be made concerning the Hawthorne studies and their interpretation. First, early analyses significantly overstated the actual effects of some of the experimental interventions. For example, weekly productivity *did* increase when workers were switched from a schedule that included breaks and a free lunch to a schedule of solid work time, *but* hourly production actually declined. Total output increased only because the workers spent more hours of each day working, even though they worked at a slower pace. Second, very little mention was made in the early reports of significant flaws in experimental design and the lack of naivete of the subject/workers who were often told ahead of time what the experiments were trying to do (Parsons, 1974). Finally, resistance on the part of workers to some of the changes instituted at the Hawthorne plant were downplayed in early analyses. In fact, two of the original five workers in the special room were dismissed from the experiment for "gross insubordination and low output" and were replaced with two other more willing workers (Bramel & Friend, 1981, p. 871).

Even with these flaws, the Hawthorne studies are of lasting importance. Though the Hawthorne effect was overstated in early reports, it has been observed reliably in a wide range of situations. The fact that managers and psychologists today are showing renewed concern for the quality of work life can be traced to the Hawthorne studies.

In brief, the experiments done at the Hawthorne plant often were basically flawed and misinterpreted (or overinterpreted), but they were landmark efforts of industrial psychology's early days. They led the way for the many other experimental manipulations that followed.

spent years getting your backyard to look just the way you want it to. Then neighborhood children discover that going through your rose garden makes a great shortcut for them on their way to school.

In each of these scenarios—and in hundreds of others we might easily imagine—you probably would feel a sense of discomfort from the invasion of your space or territory. The study of the effects of invading personal space and territory has been an active research area for environmental psychologists.

Personal space is mobile. It goes with you wherever you go. It is an imaginary "bubble" of space that surrounds you and into which others may enter by invitation only. The extent of your personal space depends on the situation, as well as a number of other factors, including your age (Aiello & Aiello, 1974), gender (Evans & Howard, 1973), and who the "intruder"

personal space the mobile "bubble" of space around you reserved for intimate relationships into which others may enter only by invitation

▲ *Personal distance is reserved for day-to-day interactions with acquaintances and friends as illustrated in the far-left picture. Social distance, as in the middle photo, involves a space of 4 to 12 feet between the people and is appropriate for people who do not know each other well. Public distance is used in formal situations, such as a lecture, performance on stage, or address to business associates as in the far-right picture.*

happens to be. You'll be much more likely to allow an invasion of your personal space by someone you know well, by someone your own age, or by an attractive member of the opposite sex (Hayduk, 1983). The anthropologist Edward Hall (1966) claimed that the extent of one's personal space is also determined in part by one's culture. Westerners, for example, are said to require a larger personal space than either Arabs or Japanese. This cultural stereotype may be somewhat overgeneralized. The evidence supporting cultural differences in personal space is not that compelling (Hayduk, 1983).

Hall (1966) claimed that personal space can be subdivided into four different distances, each relevant for different types of social interaction.

1. *Intimate distance* is defined as being between actual contact and about 18 inches. This space is reserved for very special, intimate communications: displays of affection by lovers, offerings of comfort, and the like. This space usually is reserved only for people whom you know very well and care about, and you will feel uncomfortable if anyone else is in it.

2. *Personal distance* is reserved for day-to-day interactions with acquaintances and friends. It extends from about 18 inches to approximately 4 feet, or just beyond arm's length. This space can be seen clearly in social gatherings, where small clusters of persons gather to share in conversation. Actual physical contact in this sort of situation is unusual and unwelcomed. We typically keep our bubble of personal space adjusted to this size.

3. Hall refers to the distance of 4 to 12 feet as *social distance*. This distance is appropriate for social interactions with persons we do not know well. It commonly includes some sort of physical barrier, such as a desk or table, between us and others around us. Within this space, communication can continue, but there is an implied lack of intimacy. This is the distance used when conducting business or at formal meetings.

4. Finally, there is *public distance,* in which personal contact is kept to a minimum, although communication remains possible. This distance is defined as between 12 and 25 feet. Formal lectures in large classrooms, performances from a stage, and after-dinner talks presented from behind the head table are examples. Because of the distances involved, communication in these settings tends to flow in only one direction.

We will tend to feel pressured, stressed, or discomforted whenever these distances are violated. When that perfect stranger sits right next to you in the library, he or she is violating your personal space. The salesman with his

territoriality the setting off and marking of a piece of territory (a location) as one's own

nose almost touching yours is violating your intimate space. When a lecturer leaves the podium and begins to wander through the audience, we feel strange because our public space is being invaded.

Territoriality is also related to an individual's use of space in the environment. It involves the setting off and marking of a piece of territory (a geographical location) as one's own. It is the tendency to declare that "this space is mine, and someone else can enter here only with permission."

Territoriality was first studied extensively in nonhumans (*e.g.*, Lorenz, 1969). Many species of animals have been observed to establish, mark, and defend geographical areas that they use either for hunting or for mating and rearing their young. These territories are often defended vigorously—most commonly with ritualistic posturing and threats of aggression, but only occasionally with actual combat.

It seems clear that people, too, establish territories as their own, not to be entered without invitation. Reviewing the evidence for territoriality in humans, Altman (1975) noted that like personal space, our territories vary in their value to us. Some are *primary territories*, defined by us as ours and no one else's. "This is my room, and you'd better stay out of it." We often invest heavily in our primary territories. We decorate our homes, yards, dormitory rooms, or apartments, to put our mark on our space. By controlling our primary territory, we maintain a sense of privacy and identity.

Altman claims that we are sensitive to two other types of territory: secondary and public. *Secondary territories* are more flexible and less well-defined than primary territories. They are areas we set aside for social gatherings, not so much for personal privacy. Teenage gang members who stake out a portion of a city park as being "their turf" may have established a secondary territory. It is where they meet and interact with their peers. They make it clear (often in threatening ways) that outsiders are unwelcome. Members of the faculty may claim a room in a college building for a faculty lounge and may be quite unnerved to discover students using it, even if they are using it to study. Secondary territories are not "owned" by those who use them and tend not to be used for expressing personal identity. That is, there may be a sign on the door that says "Faculty Lounge," but the area *can* be used for other functions, and occasional intrusions may be tolerated.

Public territories are those we usually occupy for only a short time. They are not ours in any literal sense, and we will not feel much distress if they are violated. While waiting for your plane, you sit in a seat in the airport terminal and place your luggage at your feet. You get up for a minute to buy a

▲ *Primary territory, shown at left, is space defined and marked as one's own, such as a child's room at home. Public territory, center, is space we occupy for only a short time, such as on public transportation. Secondary territory, right, is set aside for social gatherings such as the "turf" of an inner city gang.*

newspaper, and when you return, you discover that someone has taken your seat. In such a situation, you may be momentarily annoyed, but you will probably just find another seat—rather than starting a major confrontation.

Personal space and territories in the environment that we claim as our own serve many functions. They provide a sense of structure and continuity in what otherwise may seem to be a complex and ever-changing environment. They help us claim some sense of identity. They help us set ourselves apart from others. They regulate and reinforce needs for privacy. When space and territory are violated, we can predict negative outcomes: anxiety, distress, and sometimes even aggressive attempts of reclamation.

Before You Go On
▼▼▼▼▼▼▼▼▼

Define the concepts of personal space and territoriality.

▶ *Life in the City—An Example*

In 1962, John B. Calhoun published a paper on the overcrowding of rats. The data were impressive and intriguing. Calhoun raised colonies of rats in a number of different environments. In some environments, population density was allowed (encouraged) to increase to the point where the overcrowding began to affect the behavior of the rats within the colony. Male rats became aggressive, newborn rats were often cannibalized or ignored and left to die; female rats became unreceptive to sexual advances from male rats; and when mating did occur, litter size decreased; all this apparently in response to the pressures of colony overpopulation. As you might imagine, it didn't take long for psychologists to look for parallels between Calhoun's rat studies and life in modern cities. Indeed, early research found several correlations between population density and negative behavioral consequences, such as mental illness, crime, stress, and delinquency (Altman, 1975; Freedman, 1975).

As psychologists began to look more closely at the lives of people in urban environments, it became clear that the translation of the data from Calhoun's rats to residents of metropolitan centers wasn't all that straightforward. The first thing we need to do is distinguish between two easily confused terms (Stokols, 1972). The first is **population density**, which refers to the number of persons (or animals) per unit of area. Density is an objective, descriptive measure. **Crowding**, on the other hand, is really a psychological concept. It is a *subjective feeling* of discomfort or distress produced by a *perceived* lack of space. Crowding may be independent of the number of persons involved. You might feel crowded and very uncomfortable if you had to sit in the back seat of a small car with just two other people, but not at all crowded when you get to the football stadium and are jammed together with 60,000 others to watch a game (Freedman, 1975).

Crowding is a negative condition that leads to discomfort and stress. As such, it tends to produce a number of negative consequences. But it is not correct to conclude that living in a densely populated city *necessarily* produces negative consequences. Other potential stressors, such as noise, pollution, and the threat of crime, that we commonly associate with city life may be more than offset by better medical care, better sanitation, and better systems for handling emergencies (Creekmore, 1985). One's perception of control also matters. Someone who believes that he or she could leave the city whenever he or she so chooses will have more positive attitudes about living in that city than will someone who feels trapped there.

population density a quantitive measure of the number of persons (or animals) per unit of area

crowding the subjective feeling of discomfort caused by a sense of lack of space

Indeed, there is increasing evidence to support the claim that living in the city can be healthier, in a number of physical and psychological ways, than living in the country (Creekmore, 1985; Krupat, 1985; Milgram, 1970, 1977). Many of the advantages of city living will be unavailable to residents of smaller communities. Few cities with populations of less than 50,000 can support large symphony orchestras, opera companies, museums, or art galleries—or fully-staffed emergency rooms or trauma centers such as are found in larger, urban areas. Nor can they afford stadiums and arenas for professional sports (Barker, 1968). The challenge for psychologists is to help urban planners and architects design living spaces in areas of high population density that minimize the subjective experience of crowding, that maintain privacy, and that allow for expressions of individual territoriality.

Before You Go On
▼▼▼▼▼▼▼▼

What is the difference between population density and crowding?

What are some of the positive and negative aspects of city living?

▶ Noise, Temperature, and Environmental Toxins

In this section, we'll review some of the evidence that suggests that three types of environmental variables can have a profound effect on behavior. We'll consider noise, temperature, and environmental toxins (poisons) and how they affect human performance.

noise any intrusive, unwanted, or excessive experience of sound

Noise is defined as any intrusive, unwanted, or excessive experience of sound. Almost any environment provides some level of background noise, and noise *per se* need not be disruptive or stressful. In fact, the complete absence of sound can induce stress. Noise becomes most stressful when it is loud, high-pitched, and unpredictable (Glass & Singer, 1972). Continued exposure to high-intensity sound can produce lasting deafness (Scharf, 1978; Taylor, et al., 1965), although prolonged exposure to high levels of noise seem to produce few other serious physical problems (Matlin, 1983). However, there is ample evidence that prolonged exposure to noise increases levels of stress, anxiety, and aggressive behaviors (Bell, et al., 1978).

Noise levels have predictable effects on the performance of cognitive tasks. Cohen and his associates (1980; 1986), for example, have shown that children who attended schools near the busy Los Angeles airport tended to have higher blood pressure and were more easily distracted from their work than children who attended schools in quieter neighborhoods. In fact, there is evidence that persistently high levels of noise can have a negative impact on all sorts of everyday behaviors (*e.g.,* Smith & Stansfield, 1986). On the other hand, absolute levels of ground noise may not be the major determinant of disruption (Glass & Singer, 1972). What matters more in the disruption of performance is the *predictability* of the noise and the degree of one's control over that noise. The results of one experiment that demonstrated this phenomenon are presented in Figure 15.2 (Glass, et al., 1969).

Subjects were given the task of trying to solve problems that, in fact, had no solution. Subjects worked on these puzzles under three levels of background noise. In one condition, there was no noise; in a second, a relatively soft (68 decibel) noise was presented; in the third, a loud (110 decibel) noise was introduced. In the conditions using background noise, the predictability of the noise was also manipulated. That is, in one condition, the onset of the noise was regular and predictable; in the other, the noise was introduced on a

Figure 15.2

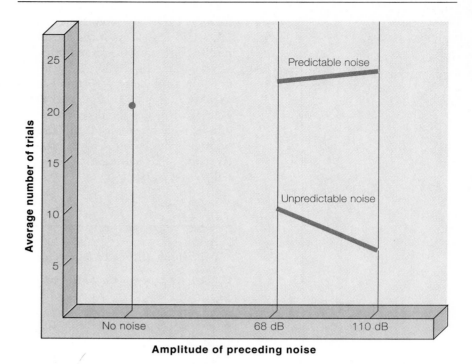

Amplitude of preceding noise

▲ *The effects of the predictability of noise as a distractor during a cognitive task. When stimulus noise occurred unpredictably, subjects spent fewer trials attempting to solve insolvable puzzles. (After Glass, Singer & Friedman, 1969.)*

random schedule. The introduction of predictable noise did not significantly alter the subjects' persistence in working on the problems. Unpredictable noise, however, significantly reduced the number of trials that the subjects were willing to invest in the problem task. Glass and Singer (1972) also report that when subjects are able to control the occurrence of noise, their problem solving was unaffected. When noise was uncontrollable, performance levels dropped—and often remained poor even after the noise had been removed.

It is clear that extremes of temperature can have adverse effects on behavior. Probably any task can be accomplished most effectively within a range of moderate environmental temperatures (Baron, 1977). It is no doubt important, for example, to try to keep the temperature of a workplace within reasonable limits. If temperatures become excessively hot or cold, performance will deteriorate, although the specific effects of temperature on performance depend in large measure on the type of task being performed.

Environmental psychologists have also been concerned with the effects that extremely high temperatures have on social interactions and on aggression, in particular. There is a common perception that riots and other more common displays of violent behaviors are more frequent during the long, hot days of summer. This observation is largely supported by research evidence (Anderson, 1989; Anderson & Anderson, 1984; Rotton & Frey, 1985). Anderson, for example, reported a series of studies (1987; 1989) that show that violent crimes are more prevalent in hotter quarters of the year and in hotter years, although nonviolent crimes were less affected. Anderson also found that differences in crime rates are better predicted by temperature than by social, demographic (age, race, education), or economic variables. Baron and Ransberger (1978) point out that riots are most likely to occur when the

▲ Environmental neurotoxin pollution can pose a serious threat not only to people's health, but also to their entire way of life. Imagine this tranquil setting as the site of illegal chemical dumping, and you can imagine the quality of life for the people who live here would be changed.

neurotoxins chemicals (poisons) that affect psychological processes through the nervous system

outside temperature is only moderately high, between about 75° and 90° Fahrenheit. When temperatures get much above 90°, energy (even for aggression) becomes rapidly depleted, and rioting is less likely.

As societies become heavily invested in technological advancement, an accompanying side effect is an increased level of environmental toxins or pollutants. Psychologists concerned with issues of the quality of life are becoming increasingly involved in issues related to the quality of the natural environment (Daniel, 1990; Fischhoff, 1990; Kaplan, 1987; Stokols, 1990).

Of the nearly 100,000 chemicals in use in this country's industries, more than 600 have been declared dangerous in large doses by the federal government (Anderson, 1982). Many of the chemicals that poison the natural environment are called **neurotoxins** because they have toxic effects on the human nervous system. Even in small doses, they can cause detectable behavioral and emotional changes in individuals.

Environmental psychologists are involved in research on neurotoxins at a number of different levels. Education is a high priority—workers and consumers need to know about the short- and long-term effects of contact with chemical toxins and how to deal with them. Because many of the effects of pollutants are psychological in nature, and particularly because these chemicals may affect the behaviors of young children (and the unborn), it is becoming more common to find psychologists involved in the diagnosis of reactions to toxins (Fein, et al., 1983). Exposure to neurotoxins often may be more readily diagnosed through behavioral and/or psychological means than through medical diagnosis.

Just to give you an idea of the extent of the effects that neurotoxins may have on behavior, refer to Figure 15.3, in which you'll find some of the more common neurotoxins and the effects they are likely to have through prolonged exposure.

Before You Go On
▼▼▼▼▼▼▼▼▼

What are some of the effects that noise, extreme temperature, and neurotoxins have on behavior?

▶ Changing Behaviors That Impact on the Environment

In 1962, Rachel Carson published *Silent Spring.* That powerful and poignant bestseller helped to raise public consciousness about environmental issues as no book had done before. It spoke eloquently about the fragility of our natural environment, the limits of earth's resources, and the relationships among the inhabitants of the planet. In particular, it made clear the dangers inherent

Figure 15.3

WORKERS AT RISK FROM NEUROTOXINS.

Neurotoxins used in industry that most commonly affect people, the symptoms associated with them, and the numbers of workers chronically exposed according to government estimates. Chemicals in capital letters pose the greatest risk.

Substance	Industry	Year of First Report of Neurotoxicity	Effect	Number of Workers Potentially at Risk
TOLUENE	Paints, explosives	1961	Tremors; vertigo; lack of coordination; bizarre behavior; emotional instability	4.8 million
TRICHLOROETHYLENE	Degreasing, dry cleaning	1915	Loss of facial sensation; impaired memory and concentration; tremors	3.6 million
METHYLENE CLORIDE	Solvent—multiple uses	1967	Delusions; hallucinations	2.2 million
CARBON TETRACHLORIDE	Dry cleaning	1909	Visual-field constriction	2 million
Cadmium	Metalworking	1930	Loss or impairment of sense of smell	1.4 million
Thalium	Glass making	1862	Nerve damage in lower limbs; damage to optic nerves and eye	853,000
N-HEXANE	Gluing, shoemaking	1960	Nerve damage in lower limbs	764,000
LEAD, INORGANIC	Smelters	Before Christ	Disorientation; blindness; nerve damage to hands and feet	649,000
STYRENE	Plastics, manufacturing	1963	Short-term memory loss; nerve damage in hands and feet	329,000
METHYL BROMIDE	Fumigation	1899	Nerve damage in hands and feet	105,000

Data from the National Institute for Occupational Safety and Health, Figure "Workers at Risk from Neurotoxins" by Alan Anderson. Reprinted with permission from *PSYCHOLOGY TODAY MAGAZINE.* Copyright © 1982 by Sussex Publishers, Inc.

applied behavior analysis (ABA) an approach, based on operant conditioning, that attempts to find solutions to human environmental problems in the real world

in the continued use of the pesticide DDT. After *Silent Spring* was published, the word *environmentalist* took on new meaning and significance. A movement had begun; a broad-based coalition of people from all walks of life became concerned with the quality of the environment and the limitations of our natural resources. The agenda of the environmentalist is to conserve those resources that are still available and when possible to restore the environment to its clean, natural state. DDT application is now banned in this country, although it is still being manufactured here and exported to other countries. In the late spring of 1988, a few chemical companies suspended the production of products that contained chlorofluorocarbons (or CFCs), used in refrigeration and in the manufacture of styrofoam products, because of undeniable evidence that these chemicals, once in the atmosphere, were destroying the earth's protective ozone layer.

Psychologists have long been active in helping to establish programs aimed at changing behaviors in such a way as to benefit the environment. In this context, finding solutions to real-world problems is one of the major goals of **applied behavior analysis** (**ABA**). The specific techniques of applied behavior analysis derive from the work of B. F. Skinner and the procedures of operant conditioning. In simple terms, ABA attempts to operationally define a target behavior that one wishes to modify (*e.g.*, the conservation of energy or water or the reduction of roadside litter), find the antecedent environmental conditions that set the occasion for (or signal) the behavior, and determine the consequences that can increase, decrease, or maintain the targeted behavior (Geller & Nimmer, 1985; Geller, 1986). Many programs of this sort have been implemented successfully to affect on a number of environmentally sensitive issues, such as natural gas energy conservation (Shippee & Gregory, 1982), home-based energy conservation (Winett, et al., 1985), home weatherization projects (Pavlovich & Greene, 1984), gasoline conservation (Hake & Foxx, 1978), and paper recycling (Witmer & Geller, 1976).

Let's look at an example: motivating waste management behavior (Geller, 1985; Geller & Lehman, 1986). We recognize that solid waste management *is* a major problem—millions of tons of solid waste are disposed of daily, often in ways that directly threaten the quality of the environment. The first step is to develop a precise definition of target behaviors. Just what behaviors do we want to change? Do we want to increase the use of trash receptacles? to have litter removed from roadsides? to increase the use of solid waste recycling?

Once we have decided which behavior is to be modified, our attention shifts to antecedent strategies (prompting procedures). We have to let the people know just what it is that we want done. This is an educational part of the program. Prompts may be general ("Please dispose of litter properly") or specific ("Leave your old newspapers here"). Prompts may also communicate possible consequences of one's actions ("Fine for Littering: $50" or "Bring your own container and receive a 5% discount"). Securing a behavioral commitment to a waste management program has proven to be an effective means of prompting or priming participation. For example, people who sign pledges, or engage in a discussion of the benefits of waste management are more likely to follow through.

As we have learned through the study of operant conditioning in the laboratory, behaviors will change and be maintained to the extent that they produce certain consequences. An important point for the success of large-scale programs designed to modify behavior that impacts on the environment is that consequences be tied to a person's *response*, not to some potentially *long-term outcome*. For example, scouts who volunteer to remove trash from the area surrounding a highway should be immediately given a tangible reward for each bag of litter they collect, rather than given an award (or even a reward) at a civic ceremony held once a year. Positive consequences for desired actions (thanking someone for picking up loose trash) are generally more effective than negative consequences (fining someone for leaving a soda can on a beach). Intervention programs that are successful and have a positive impact on the environment should be designed so that they can be maintained by an agency or institution within the community.

We've come a long way since the publication of *Silent Spring*. There is still a very long way to go. Scattered and uncoordinated attempts to recycle solid waste materials or preserve wildlife habitat or control the pollution of industrial emissions only begin to take us in the right direction. At least there is some hope that the 1990s *can* be the decade of the environment and that significant improvements can be made. If such is to be the case, applied psychologists will have much work to do.

Before You Go On
▼▼▼▼▼▼▼▼▼

How can environmental psychologists help to have a positive impact on the environment?

▶ *Psychology and Sports*

Sports psychology is yet another new and exciting area of applied psychology. Although it has had a long history in Europe, sports psychology has become an organized field in the United States only within the last 15 to 20 years. *Sports psychology* is "the application of psychological principles to

▲ Psychologists try to help athletes give their peak performance. Mental practice, or "imagery", can enhance the benefits of physical practice.

sport and physical activity at all levels of skill development" (Browne and Mahoney, 1984, p. 605). Although there are many applications of psychology to sports and athletes, we'll review just two: analyzing the psychological characteristics of athletes and maximizing athletic performance.

Psychology's history is filled with research on the assessment of individual differences. Wouldn't it be useful to be able to predict who might become a world-class athlete on the basis of psychological testing? It is certainly the case that there are physiological differences between athletes and nonathletes—amount and type of muscle, height, weight, lung capacity, and so on. Are there any differences between athletes and nonathletes on personality measures?

Generally, research in this area has been less than satisfactory, and results often simply tend to confirm the obvious. Although differences tend to be small, athletes do tend to score higher than nonathletes on measures of assertion, dominance, aggression, and need for achievement; they score lower on such traits as anxiety, depression, and fatigue (Browne & Mahoney, 1984; Cox, 1990; Morgan, 1980). This is particularly true when the athletes are at a high skill level. Athletes in some sports, such as football and hockey, are more tolerant of pain than are athletes in other sports, such as golf and bowling (e.g., Ryan & Kovacic, 1966). Tolerance of pain, however, may be more of an outcome (or result) of their activity for some athletes than a determinant of success. And this last point raises a problem that has plagued research on the athlete's personality; How shall we define "athlete?" Given the differences among hockey players, long-distance runners, golfers, billiards players, cowboys, rock climbers, fencers, bowlers, and gymnasts, it would be a bit surprising if we could cite any research that finds significant differences between athletes and nonathletes. In fact, when general trends are sought, they often are not found (e.g., Fisher, 1977).

Of practical importance to coaches and athletes (and psychologists) is maximizing the performance of the athlete in competition. One area of interest focuses on manipulating the arousal level of the athlete. Clearly, the athlete in competition needs to be fully aroused and motivated to perform—"psyched up." We also know that too much arousal can interfere with athletic performance. (If this argument sounds familiar, it's because we addressed it in general terms back in Chapter 9.) Psychologists can help athletes be sensitive to maintaining high levels of arousal while still keeping appropriate levels of concentration on the task at hand (e.g., Harris, 1973; Landers, 1982).

In a similar vein, sport psychologists now claim that the so-called home field advantage (Varca, 1980) often may be exaggerated, particularly in important games (Baumeister, 1985; Baumeister & Steinhilber, 1984). The argument is that the frenzied, yelling, screaming hometown fans may raise arousal levels of the home team *beyond* the point of maximum efficiency. The negative effect of fans reactions seems more potent when teams are on offense than when they are playing defense, and is clearly more potent in end-of-season playoff and championship games.

One psychologist who researches sports and athletes, Michael Mahoney, commenting on Olympic athletes, has said, "At this level of competition, the difference between two athletes is 20 percent physical and 80 percent mental" (quoted in Kiester, 1984a, pp. 20–21). To the extent that this view is accurate, psychologists have tried to help athletes to do their best—to give what is called *peak performance*. Mental practice or "imagery" combined, of course, with physical practice has proven to be quite beneficial (e.g., Smith, 1987). In addition to manipulating acceptable levels of arousal, mental practice is useful in

1. mentally rehearsing a particular behavioral pattern (Think about and mentally picture that golf swing and the flight of the ball before you step up to the tee)

2. reducing negative thoughts that may interfere with performance (Forget about an earlier error and focus on positive experiences, perhaps past victories)

3. rehearsing one's role in a team sport (Mentally practice what you are supposed to do and when you are supposed to do it in different game situations)

4. setting realistic goals (Don't get tense worrying about a competitor in this race, simply try to better your last performance) (Creekmore, 1984; Fenker & Lambiotte, 1987; Kiester, 1984a; 1984b; Ogilvie & Howe, 1984; Scott & Pelliccioni, 1982; Smith, 1987; Suinn, 1980)

Obviously, using mental imagery is not the only way in which athletes can improve their performance. It's just one technique with which sports psychologists can help.

Before You Go On
▼▼▼▼▼▼▼▼

What are some of the ways in which psychologists may become involved in sports and athletics?

▼▼▼
Thinking Critically About Psychology Applied

1. In Chapter 1, I stated as a general principle that "psychology has practical application in the real world." This is clearly true in this chapter. Can you now go back through the chapters in the text and cite an example where psychological principles from each have had an impact on *your* life?

2. Imagine that you are an employer trying to hire someone who, among other things, will be responsible for handling large amounts of money. Do you think that you should have the right to access information about the criminal records of applicants? What information about applicants (if any) do you think that you should not have access to?

3. Consider your most recent job. Could you write a complete job analysis for that position? What would it include?

4. Consider jobs that you have had. What motivated you to do your best at those jobs? What could have been done to motivate you to work harder? Can you describe any of these factors in terms of the theories of work motivation summarized in this chapter?

5. List examples from your own experience of occasions when your personal space or territoriality has been invaded. How did you feel about such invasions?

6. Upon graduation you are offered a position with a large company that gives you a choice of location in which to work. You could work either in a large metropolitan area or a small farm community. What are the advantages and disadvantages that you see associated with each location?

7. One slogan of the environmentalists' movement is to "Think globally and act locally." What are the psychological implications of such a challenge?

8. Many professional sports teams now employ full-time psychologists. What are some of their duties and responsibilities?

Summary

▼▼▼▼▼▼▼▼▼▼▼▼▼▼▼▼▼▼▼▼▼▼▼▼▼▼▼▼▼▼▼▼▼▼▼▼▼▼▼

What is involved in doing a job analysis? Doing a proper job analysis involves two stages: (1) constructing a complete and specific description of the activities performed by someone in a given position, i.e., a listing of those characteristics required to do the job, and (2) developing a means of evaluating the performance of a person in that job (performance criteria). This information is gathered through an inspection of official documents, interviews, questionnaires, and the direct observation of job activities. *Page 493*

What are some of the sources of information that can be used in making personnel decisions? Once a job analysis has been completed, personnel selection involves using assessment tools to measure the relevant characteristics of applicants. Many tools are available, including application forms, structured and unstructured interviews, and psychological tests. Of these, unstructured interviews seem to be of the least value. *Page 494*

List some of the factors that need to be considered in the design, implementation, and evaluation of a training program. Several factors need to be considered in the design and implementation of an employee training program, including an assessment of the organization's instructional needs (what training, if any, is required?), the development of specific training objectives, the means by which training will be evaluated, and the selection of appropriate methods and media for the actual training. Once training has begun, it should be monitored constantly to see if objectives are being met. After training has been completed, the program itself should be evaluated in the short and long term, as should the transfer of information and skills from training to actual on-the-job performance. *Pages 495–498*

Briefly summarize some of the factors that affect the motivation of workers to do a good job. Even workers with ability may not do a good job unless they are motivated to do so. There are many theories to describe what motivates workers. We looked at three. Vroom's *expectancy theory* says that workers develop expectations about the relationship between their work behaviors and the likelihood of certain outcomes. They also assign values to different outcomes. They will be most highly motivated to behave in ways that earn valued rewards. Adams' *equity theory* says that what matters most is the perception of fairness or equal reward for equal effort when one's work behaviors are gauged against those of a comparable other. Locke's *goal-setting* approach says that what matters most is that

workers be clearly aware of just what they are working for and that they accept that goal as worth the effort. *Pages 498–501*

What is meant by job satisfaction and quality of work life? Job satisfaction and quality of work life are complex concepts, usually inferred from interview and questionnaire data. In the broadest sense, job satisfaction is an attitude, a measure of an employee's evaluation of his or her position in an organization. Quality of work life (QWL) involves many factors, such as feelings about employment conditions, job security, compensation, autonomy, opportunities for social interaction, self-esteem, and participation in the decision-making process. *Pages 501–503*

Briefly summarize the relationship between job satisfaction and job productivity. Although job satisfaction and productivity may be related, there is little evidence to suggest that the relationship is a strong one and no evidence to suggest that one causes the other. Interventions designed to increase job satisfaction sometimes have a positive impact on productivity, but interventions designed to improve production may also increase job satisfaction. Job satisfaction seems more closely related to employee turnover and somewhat related to absenteeism. *Pages 501–503*

Define environmental psychology, and list some of the issues that environmental psychologists study. Environmental psychology is the study of how the environment affects the behavior and mental processes of its inhabitants, and vice versa. Environmental psychologists study a number of different issues, including personal space, crowding, privacy, interior design, territoriality, environmental pollutants and neurotoxins, and the effects of weather and noise. *Page 503*

Define the concepts of personal space and territoriality. Personal space is the imaginary bubble of area around a person into which others enter only by invitation or in specified situations. It is mobile and goes with the person. There may be different types of personal space—acceptable distances—defined for different situations. Territoriality, on the other hand, is one's claim to certain areas (territories) in the environment. Territories may be defended against intrusion and are often used as statements of self-expression. Intrusion into one's personal space or territory leads to tension, stress, and even aggression. *Pages 504–508*

What is the difference between population density and crowding? What are some of the positive and negative aspects of city living? Population density is simply a quantitative measure of the number of units (people, for example) occupying a given geographic area. Crowding, on the other hand, involves a psychological reaction of distress that occurs when people feel that their space or privacy has been invaded. City living increases the probability of living with crowding, noise, and other pollutants, but these stressors may be offset by the advantages of a wide range of opportunities not found outside large population centers, such as modern health care, police protection, and access to the arts. *Pages 508–509*

What are some of the effects that noise, extreme temperature, and neurotoxins have on behavior? Noise, extreme temperatures, and neurotoxins may all be viewed as environmental pollutants and potentially stressful, even when not directly harmful to physical and psychological well-being. Noise is more stressful if it is unexpected, unpredictable, or uncontrollable. High temperatures may lead to aggressive, violent reactions, but extremely high (and low) temperatures tend to decrease all levels of behavior. Many chemicals commonly found in the environment have negative consequences for behavior and mental activities; those that directly affect the nervous system are called neurotoxins. *Pages 509–511*

How can environmental psychologists help to have a positive impact on the environment? Environmentalists work to conserve natural resources and to restore the environment to its natural and unspoiled state. Environmental psychologists can help in this effort by designing large-scale intervention programs. Such programs target specific behaviors, identify antecedent conditions that prompt those behaviors, and attempt to control consequences of relevant target behaviors to increase the rate of appropriate responses. *Pages 511–513*

What are some of the ways in which psychologists may become involved in sports and athletics? Psychologists have become involved in sports and athletics in a number of different ways, including trying to discover how athletes are different from nonathletes, attempting to improve an athlete's peak performance, studying the effects of audience reactions on athletic performance, and investigating the effects of participation on the athlete. *Pages 513–515*

15.1 Which of these is BEST associated with industrial/organizational psychology?   a) experimental psychology   b) applied psychology   c) clinical psychology   d) developmental psychology. *Page 492*

15.2 Typically, an employee selection program begins with   a) a listing of required or desired characteristics provided by management. b) an inventory of available tests and assessment techniques. c) an appraisal of skills of current employees. d) a complete job analysis. *Page 493*

15.3 In a job analysis, when Smith differentiates between "hard" and "soft" criteria, she is really differentiating between   a) physical labor and mental labor careers.   b) objective data and subjective judgments.   c) blue-collar and white-collar positions.   d) criteria that require professional, psychological measurement and criteria that can be assessed by almost anyone. *Page 493*

15.4 As opposed to "hard" criteria, preparing "soft" criteria in a job analysis involves: a) objective data   b) behaviors, but not affect or cognitions   c) subjective judgments   d) results from psychological tests. *Page 493*

15.5 Of the following techniques for gathering information about prospective employees, which tends to provide the LEAST useful information? a) psychological tests of specific skills b) unstructured interviews   c) application forms   d) tests of general intelligence. *Pages 494–495*

15.6 True or False?   Application forms provide a good source of biodata. *Page 494*

15.7 True or False?   Structured interviews are more valid than unstructured interviews. *Pages 494–495*

15.8 In devising a training program for employees, what is the first question that an I/O psychologist should ask?   a) Who is going to receive this training?   b) What techniques will be used to get the information across to the trainees? c) How will the outcome of this training be evaluated?   d) Is this training really necessary? *Page 496*

15.9 The evaluation of a training program should be done: a) as soon as training begins   b) as soon as training is completed   c) at points in time well after training is completed   d) at each of these stages. *Page 498*

15.10 In general, most training programs are evaluated in terms of   a) job analyses.   b) training

objectives.   c) employee's needs.   d) trainee satisfaction. *Page 496*

15.11 Although there are exceptions, which approach to employee training is generally the most effective?   a) one that involves hands-on experience   b) one that uses classroom instruction by an expert   c) one that uses as many media as possible   d) one that invovles repeated demonstrations *Pages 497–498*

15.12 Expectancy theory is mostly _____ in its orientation.   a) affective   b) cognitive   c) evaluative   d) behavioral. *Page 499*

15.13 Equity theory claims that what matters most to employees is the extent to which they   a) are making more money than employees in similar positions.   b) understand the goals they are trying to reach.   c) perceive that they are being treated fairly compared to others.   d) expect to be rewarded for what they value. *Page 500*

15.14 True or False?   Seting goals for employees is significantly more effective when those goals are set by the employees themselves. *Page 500*

15.15 True or False?   Vroom's 1964 expectancy theory is mostly cognitive in orientation. *Page 499*

15.16 Which of the following is best correlated with most measures of job satisfaction?   a) the race of employees   b) overall productivity   c) whether workers are male or female   d) the age of employees. *Page 501*

15.17 Quality of work life, or QWL, is best correlated with   a) overall productivity.   b) absenteeism.   c) job satisfaction.   d) employee turnover. *Page 502*

15.18 Environmental psychologists have defined many types of space or territories. Of these, the one with the smallest area is called _____ space.   a) intimate   b) personal   c) social   d) public. *Page 505*

15.19 The Hawthorne Effect is the: a) tendency of persons to be influenced by special attention from others   b) relationship between quality of work life and worker productivity   c) belief that all aggression stems from frustration   d) tendency to overrate the abilities of persons we see as being most like ourselves. *Page 504*

15.20 True or False?   Primary territories are those spaces we think of as ours and no one else's. *Page 507*

15.21 The difference between population density and overcrowding is mostly a difference in   a) one's previous experience.   b) the types of organisms involved.   c) feelings of distress or discomfort. d) the number of organisms per unit of area. *Page 508*

15.22 Which of the following is NOT likely to be a stressor associated with life in a big city? a) airborne toxins.   b) available resources. c) noise pollution.   d) crime rates. *Page 509*

15.23 What aspect of noise can make it particularly stressful to one attempting a cognitive task? a) its predictability   b) its tone or pitch c) its loudness   d) its melody. *Pages 509–510*

15.24 Chemicals in the environment that poison the nervous system are called: a) psychoactive drugs   b) neurotoxins   c) hallucinogenic chemicals   d) neurotransmitters. *Page 511*

15.25 At which of these temperatures are riots most likely to occur?   a) 36°F   b) 66°F   c) 86°F d) 106°F. *Pages 510–511*

15.26 True or False?   By definition, neurotoxins are chemicals that harm the environment but that need not have any discernible behavioral or emotional effects on people. *Page 511*

15.27 True or False?   Most of the procedures of applied behavioral analysis are based on operant conditioning and the laboratory work of B. F. Skinner. *Page 512*

15.28 When is frenzied, excessive fan support most likely to have a negative or adverse effect on the home team's performance?   a) early in the season when the team is on defense   b) early in the season when the team is on offense   c) in a championship game when the team is on defense d) in a championship game when the team is on offense. *Page 514*

15.29 True or False?   Mental imagery or mental practice can help an athlete reach his or her peak performance. *Page 514*

Statistical Appendix

▶ Introduction and an Example

When we do research in psychology, or apply it, our task often involves measuring some mental process or aspect of behavior. The result of our measurement is a set of numbers, which we now have to deal with. That's where statistics come in.

▲ Before we go on, I would like to insert a word of caution. In this appendix, we are going to be working with numbers and a few simple formulas. Please don't let the numbers make you anxious. Some students find dealing with numbers difficult and think that statistics are not relevant for psychology students. Keep in mind that statistics are tools, necessary ones, to help us understand our subject matter. You don't need to be mathematically sophisticated to appreciate statistics. What *is* required is a positive attitude and a few arithmetic skills, such as addition, subtraction, multiplication, and division. If you haven't had much math background, just go slowly and think about the issues involved.

When we measure something, we assign it a numerical value, and statistics help us to analyze and understand measurements once we have made them. So that we'll have some numbers to work with, let's consider the following problem.

You and your best friend are both enrolled in the same introductory psychology class this semester. You have just taken your first exam, a 50-item multiple-choice test. Your instructor provided two forms of that first exam, form A and form B. They both covered the same material, of course, but the questions were different on the two forms. By chance, you took form A of the test, and your friend took form B. You had studied together, and you thought that you both knew the material equally well. But your score on the test was eight points lower than your friend's. You suspect that perhaps the two forms of your first test were not equally difficult. You believe that your test (form A) was more difficult than your friend's (form B). You ask your instructor for all the grades on the test for both forms. Because of confidentiality, he cannot provide you with names, but does supply you with all the grades from the exam.

There are 100 students in your class who took the first exam. Fifty saw form A and 50 saw form B. When you get the scores from your instructor, you find that they are arranged as follows:

FORM A:						FORM B:				
98	86	100	60	94		82	100	90	80	60
72	80	78	66	86		72	86	82	88	80
92	62	86	96	62		82	76	84	74	84
82	86	78	88	84		86	74	78	78	78
64	86	68	76	80		78	74	84	80	80
86	96	76	72	80		90	84	68	78	86
80	82	82	64	78		80	80	80	84	80
68	74	98	98	84		76	76	80	82	82
66	64	70	90	86		86	74	70	78	76
96	92	82	68	92		82	82	80	76	80

What a mess. Just looking at all these numbers doesn't tell you much at all. Arranged as they are, it's difficult to see if either form of the exam yielded higher or lower scores. To answer your original question (was there a difference in performance on the two forms of the exam?), you're going to have to manipulate these numbers somehow. As we'll see throughout this appendix, statistics are tools that we use to help us make sense out of data we have collected. They will be helpful in analyzing these data. Statistical manipulations are more useful (even necessary) when we have collected many more than 100 numbers.

▶ Organizing Data

Let's assume that we have collected the measurements (data) in which we are interested. Now the task before us is to draw conclusions based on those data. The first thing we need to do is to assemble our data in a sensible way so that we can quickly and easily get some idea of what they mean. At the very least, we should put our data into the form of a frequency distribution.

▶ Frequency Distributions

Once we have collected a large number of numbers, we seek to organize and summarize them to make them useful and meaningful. One of the easiest

Figure A.1

FREQUENCY DISTRIBUTIONS FOR OUR SAMPLE DATA OF TWO FORMS (A AND B) OF A CLASSROOM EXAM.

Scores, or measurements, are listed in order in the left column, and the frequency with which each occurs is indicated with either a hash mark (/) or a number.

Score	Form A Frequency		Form B Frequency	
100	/	1	/	1
98	/ /	2		0
96	/ / /	3		0
94	/	1		0
92	/ / /	3		0
90	/	1	/ /	2
88	/	1	/	1
86	/ / / / / / /	7	/ / / /	4
84	/ /	2	/ / / / /	5
82	/ / / /	4	/ / / / / / /	7
80	/ / / /	4	/ / / / / / / / / / /	11
78	/ / /	3	/ / / / / /	6
76	/ /	2	/ / / / /	5
74	/	1	/ / / /	4
72	/ /	2	/	1
70	/	1	/	1
68	/ / /	3	/	1
66	/ /	2		0
64	/ / / /	4		0
62	/ /	2		0
60	/	1	/	1
		$N = 50$		$N = 50$

frequency distribution an ordered listing of all *x*-values, indicating the frequency with which each occurs

things to do with our numbers is to arrange them in a **frequency distribution**. As its name suggests, a frequency distribution lists, in order, all of the numbers or scores that we have collected and indicates the frequency with which each occurs.

Figure A.1 shows two types of frequency distributions for the scores earned on form A and form B of the exam we introduced as our working example. One type of frequency distribution indicates the frequency of each score with a hash mark (/), while the other type simply indicates the frequency of each score with a number. In this figure, I've placed the two frequency distributions side by side. You can easily see, just by inspection of these distributions, that there is a difference between the scores earned on form A and form B of our imaginary exam.

▶ Graphic Representations

It is often helpful to go one step beyond the simple frequency distribution and draw a graph of our data. A number of different graphs have been used throughout this text. Graphs of frequencies of scores are among the most common types of graphs in psychology. For such a graph, our scores (in general referred to as *X-scores*) are plotted on the horizontal (*x*) axis of the graph, and frequencies (*f*) are plotted on the vertical (*y*) axis of our graph.

histogram a bar graph; a graphical representation of a frequency distribution

Figure A.2 shows one way to graph frequencies. This sort of bar graph is called a **histogram**. The frequency of each X-score is indicated by the height of the bar above that score. When we have few X-scores, and when frequencies are not too large, histograms provide clear depictions of our data. The differences between form A and form B of the classroom exam are more clearly seen in the two histograms of Figure A.2 than in a simple frequency distribution.

Figure A.3 shows the same data in a line graph. The advantage of this sort of graph is obvious: We can easily show both distributions of test scores on the same axes. As is the case with histograms, scores are plotted on the *x*-axis and frequencies are indicated on the *y*-axis. With line graphs, it is important to provide a key indicating which line represents each group of scores.

Figure A.2

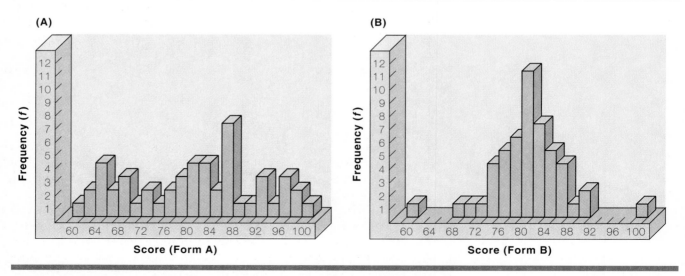

▲ *Histograms showing the frequency with which scores were earned on form A and form B of the classroom exam.*

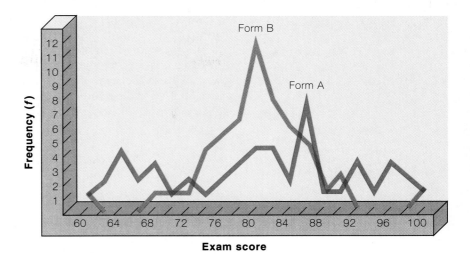

▲ *A line graph showing the frequency of scores earned on classroom exams for both form A and form B.*

▶ Descriptive Statistics

Let's continue working with our opening problem. We began with two sets of 50 numbers, scores earned on form A and form B of a classroom exam. Our basic question was whether these two forms of the same test were really equally difficult. To get started, we put the scores into frequency distributions and then constructed graphs that represented our data. That helped, but there is much more that we can do.

When describing collections or distributions of data, our two major concerns are usually with measures of central tendency and variability. Measures of **central tendency** are statistics that tell us where our scores tend to center. In general terms, measures of central tendency are called *averages*. If we want to know if performance on form A was better or worse *on the average* than performance on form B, we would have to compute a measure of central tendency for both distributions of scores. Measures of **variability** are statistics that tell us about the extent of dispersion, or the spread of scores within a distribution. Are scores clustered closely around the average, or are they more variable, deviating considerably from the average? First we'll deal with central tendency.

▶ Measures of Central Tendency

There are three statistics used to represent the central tendency of a distribution of numbers. The most commonly used is the mean. The median and mode are also measures of central tendency, but they are used less frequently.

The Mean. When we think about computing the average of a set of scores we are usually thinking about computing the **mean**. The mean of a set of scores is their total divided by the number of scores in the set. For example, if Max is 6 feet tall and Ruth is 4 feet tall, their mean height is 5 feet. Four inches of snow yesterday and 2 inches today yields a mean snowfall of 3 inches for the two days (4" + 2" = 6" ÷ 2 = 3").

central tendency a measure of the middle, or average, score in a set of data

variability the extent of spread or dispersion in a set or distribution of scores

mean a measure of central tendency computed by dividing the sum of all scores by the number of observation; sometimes called the *average*

Descriptive Statistics ▲ **523**

So, to compute the mean scores for form A of our example we add up all the scores and divide by 50 because there are 50 scores in the set. We'd do the very same thing for the scores earned on form B—add them up and divide by 50.

The mean of a set of numbers is symbolized by $\overline{X}$, read *X bar*. The uppercase Greek letter sigma, Σ, stands for "take the sum of whatever follows." We use the symbol X to represent an individual score from a set of scores and N for the number of scores in the set. So the formula for computing a mean looks like this:

$$\overline{X} = \frac{\Sigma X}{N}$$

This is just a fancy shorthand way of expressing what you already know: To find the mean of a set of scores ($\overline{X}$), add the scores (X) together and then divide by the number of scores (N). When we do this for form A and form B of our classroom exam example, we find that the mean for both sets of scores is 80. That is, $\Sigma X = 4000$ and $N = 50$ in each case, so $\Sigma X \div N = 80$ for both forms of the exam. In terms of average score (as indicated by the mean), there is clearly no difference between the two forms of the test.

The Median. Although the mean is generally the central-tendency measure of choice, there are occasions when it may not be appropriate. These occasions occur when a distribution includes a few extreme scores. For a simple example, the mean of the numbers, 2, 3, 3, 5, 7 is 4 ($\Sigma X = 20$; $N = 5$; so $X = 4$). Even on inspection, 4 looks right; it is a value near the middle or center of the set. Now consider the numbers 2, 3, 3, 5, 37. What is their mean? The sum of these 5 numbers is 50, so their mean equals 10. Here it seems by inspection that the extreme score of 37 is adding too much weight to our measure of central tendency. For a real-life example, imagine computing the average income of a small working-class community that happened to include two millionaires. The *mean* income of this community would be unduly influenced by just two persons with unusually high incomes.

In such cases, we might prefer to use the **median** as our measure of central tendency. The median is the value of a set of numbers that divides it exactly in half. There are as many scores above the median as below it. Perhaps you recognize that the median is the same as the fiftieth percentage of a distribution—50 percent of the scores are higher; 50 percent are lower.

Don't fall for this trick: "What is the median of these test scores: 42, 58, 37, 62, 55?" There is a tendency to want to say "37" because it is in the middle of the list with two scores to the left and two scores to the right. But "37" certainly isn't at the center of these scores; it's the lowest of the five! Before you choose the median, the scores must first be placed in order: 37, 42, 55, 58, 62. *Now* the score in the middle, 55, is the median score, the one that divides the set in half. Whenever we have an even number of scores, there will be no one number in the middle, will there? What is the median of these numbers: 3, 6, 8, 10, 14, 18? What we do here is calculate the mean of the two numbers in the middle (here 8 and 10). So, the median of these six numbers is 9. When we have a large number of scores to deal with, the computation of the median becomes slightly more complicated. We can't always just put our scores in order and identify the median by inspection. But in such cases, the logic is the same, and we have formulas that tell what steps to take to calculate the median. For the two distributions of our example, the median for form A of the exam is 80; for form B it is 79.

median the score above which and below which half the scores in an ordered set fall

mode the most frequently occurring
x-value(s) in a set

The Mode. No doubt the easiest measure of central tendency to calculate is the **mode**. The mode is simply the most frequently occurring value in a set or distribution of scores. If you have already constructed a frequency distribution, finding the mode is particularly easy. Just locate the *X*-value with the greatest frequency and you've found the mode. For many psychological characteristics measured for very large numbers of subjects, the mode *does* tend to fall near the center of the distribution of scores. For our example problem, the mode of scores earned on form A is 86 and on form B the mode is 80.

As it happens, the mode is seldom used as a measure of central tendency. For one thing, computing the mode disregards all of the other values in the distribution. For another, there is no guarantee that the most frequently occurring number will be at (or even near) the middle. Notice also that it is quite possible for a collection of numbers to have two modes (be "bimodal") or three modes, or more.

▶ *Variability*

If we know how two sets of scores differ "on the average," we know a lot. We know, for instance, that there is no apparent difference in central tendency for the two sets of scores we have been using as an example. There is, however, a second descriptive characteristic of distributions of numbers that may be of interest: their spread, dispersion, or variability.

It is quite possible to have two sets of scores that have identical means but that, at the same time, are clearly different from each other. This sort of difference can be seen in Figure A.3 and is even more clearly obvious in Figure A.4. In this figure, we can see that most of the scores of distribution A are clustered around the mean of the distribution. The scores of distribution B are much more spread out, or variable, even though the mean of this set of scores equals the mean of distribution A.

Figure A.4

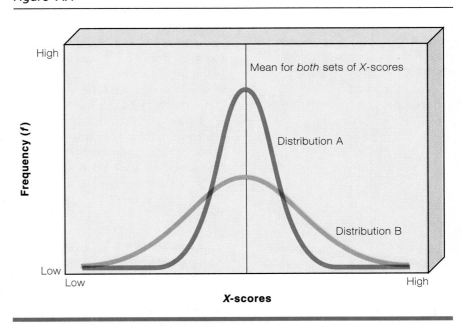

 Two distributions of X-scores (A and B) that have identical means, but clearly different variability.

Imagine for a moment that the two graphs in Figure A.4 represent grades earned by two very large classes. Further imagine that the mean grade for each class is a C. If this is the case, then these graphs tell us that almost everyone in class A received a C, a C+, or a C–. Some may have received a B– or a D+, but most grades were near the average C. In class B, on the other hand, there were obviously many more As, Bs, Ds, and Fs than were earned by the other class, even though the mean grade for the two classes was a C. So knowing about a distribution's variability is to have some useful information. How shall we represent variability statistically?

One way to measure the spread of scores in a distribution is to use a statistic called the **range**. Range is one of the easiest statistics to calculate. It is found by subtracting the lowest score from the highest. Unfortunately, range (as a measure of variability) simply disregards all the other scores between the highest and lowest. Even when most scores are bunched tightly around the mean, if there are just a couple of extreme scores, the range will be large. The range would be an inappropriate measure of variability for our example. Scores on both form A and form B of the classroom exam range from a high score of 100 to a low score of 60. Thus, the range for both sets of scores is 40 points. An inspection of our Figure A.3, however, indicates that scores on form A are generally more variable than scores on form B.

A measure of variability that does take into account all of the scores of a distribution is **standard deviation**. Standard deviation is usually abbreviated **SD**. It is a kind of average of the extent to which all the scores in a distribution are different from (deviate from) their mean. Let's go through the procedures that reflect this definition of standard deviation.

The first thing that we need is the mean of our distribution ($\overline{X}$). Then we find the difference between each score (X, remember) and the mean ($\overline{X}$). This is a simple process of subtraction, yielding a collection of ($X - \overline{X}$) scores. Because means are, by definition, in the middle of distributions, some X-scores will be above the mean (so $X - \overline{X}$ will be a positive number), and some X-scores will be below the mean (so $X - \overline{X}$ will be a negative number). If we then simply add up all of our deviations, $\Sigma(X - \overline{X})$, we will always have a sum of zero. What we do to deal with this complication is simply square each deviation score, so that we have a set of ($X - \overline{X}$)^2 scores. Any real number, even a negative one, that is squared, or multiplied by itself, will yield a positive number. *Now* we add together our squared deviations, $\Sigma(X - \overline{X})^2$. We then find an average by dividing this total by N, the number of scores we are dealing with. In formula form, what we have so far is: $\Sigma(X - \overline{X})^2/N$. This statistic is called **variance**.

In our calculations, we introduced a squaring operation just to get rid of negative numbers. We now reverse that operation by taking the square root of our result (variance). What we end up with then is our formula for standard deviation, and it looks like this:

$$SD = \sqrt{\frac{\Sigma(X - \overline{X})^2}{N}}$$

You may never be called upon to compute a standard deviation using this formula. For one thing, even simple hand-held calculators often come with a button that yields a standard deviation value once you've punched in all the X-scores. For another, there are simpler computational formulas that provide the same result in fewer, easier steps. But you should appreciate what standard deviations do. They tell us the extent to which scores in a distribution deviate, or are spread from the distribution's mean. We use them often in psychology.

range the difference between the highest and lowest scores in a distribution

standard deviation the average difference between the scores in a distribution and their mean

variance the square of the standard deviation

THE COMPUTATION OF THE STANDARD DEVIATION FOR A SMALL DISTRIBUTION OF X-SCORES.

X-scores	$X - \overline{X}$	$(X - \overline{X})^2$
12	6.5	42.25
10	4.5	20.25
7	1.5	2.25
6	.5	.25
5	−.5	.25
5	−.5	.25
4	−1.5	2.25
4	−1.5	2.25
1	−4.5	20.25
1	−4.5	20.25
		110.50 $= \Sigma(X - \overline{X})^2$

$$\Sigma X = 55$$
$$N = 10$$
$$\overline{X} = \Sigma X \div N = 5.5$$

$$SD = \sqrt{\frac{\Sigma(X - \overline{X})^2}{N}} = \sqrt{\frac{110.50}{10}} = \sqrt{11.05} = \underline{3.32}$$

To reinforce our discussion, Figure A.5 depicts the computation of a standard deviation for some simple data. When the procedure is applied to our example data we find that the standard deviation for form A of the exam is 11.29; for form B, SD = 6.18. This result conforms to our observation that the scores on form A of the test are more variable than those earned on form B.

▶ Inferential Statistics

We've already seen that statistics can be used to summarize and describe some of the essential characteristics of large collections of data. They also can be used to guide our decision making concerning the data we have collected. That is, statistics can allow us to make inferences about our data. **Inferential statistics** tell us about the *significance* of the results of our experimental or correlational studies. In general, they tell us the likelihood that the data we have collected might have occurred by chance. Let's use another example, again dealing with means.

For this example, let's say that our concern is with the effects of background music on studying. You want to do an experiment to determine if background music affects study skills. To keep matters simple, let's assume that you have two groups of volunteer subjects. Each group is to try to learn 50 words in a five-minute study session. One group will practice in silence (your control group); the other will have classical music playing in the background (the experimental group). We'll call the first group, group S and the second, group C. Let's say there are 40 subjects in each group, or N = 40. After each group studies their word lists for five minutes, you test to see how many words have been learned. Then you construct a frequency distribution of your data and compute the means and standard deviations for each set of data. What you discover is that group S has a mean number of words learned equal to 26.0 and group C's mean is 28.5. Now what? There's no doubt that 28.5 is larger than 26.0, but the difference is not very large. Is the difference large enough for you to claim that the background music had an effect? We need to backtrack just a little.

inferential statistics statistical tests of the significance of the results from experimental or correlational studies

Imagine that we had two groups of subjects in a similar experiment, but that both groups received exactly the same treatment. That is, both groups performed the same task under the same conditions. Some dependent variable is measured for both groups (perhaps the number of words that were learned in a five-minute study session). Even though both groups were treated exactly the same, would we expect the mean scores for the two groups to be *exactly* equal? Wouldn't we expect *some* chance variation in scores between the two groups? If we did this same experiment again tomorrow, or next week, would we expect (again) to get exactly the same mean scores, even though experimental conditions remain the same? No. We generally anticipate that simply because of chance factors alone there will be some difference between the scores earned by two different groups of subjects—even if they are doing the same thing under the same conditions. So if mean scores for our two groups turn out to be somewhat different, we aren't surprised; we can attribute the difference to chance. But what if the groups are treated differently? What if the differences in measured responses are large? Can these differences also be attributed to chance? Or do they reflect real, significant differences between the two groups? This is where inferential statistics come in.

Inferential statistics allow us to make probability statements. They help us to determine the likelihood that observed differences in our descriptive statistics (such as means) are differences due to chance and random factors or reflect some true difference between the groups we have measured. Differences that are not likely to have occurred by chance are called **statistically significant differences**. If the difference between two calculated means is found to be statistically significant, that difference may or may not be *important* or *meaningful*, but we can claim that the difference is not likely to be due to chance.

One way to think about statistical significance is in terms of replication. If, for example, two means are found to be significantly different, it is likely that if the measurements were taken over and over again, the same difference in the same direction would show up most of the time. Inferential statistics can be used to judge the statistical significance of any statistic. They can be used to tell us about the probability with which means, medians, standard deviations, proportions, or correlation coefficients are truly different or else are different by chance alone.

Significance is usually stated as a proportion. We talk about means being different at the "0.05 level," for instance. What this means is that the likelihood of our finding a mean difference as large as we did by chance alone is less than 5 in 100. The "0.01 level of significance" is even more conservative. It implies that the difference we have observed would have occurred by chance—if in fact no real differences exist—less than 1 time in 100.

Let's return now to the example with which we are working in this section and add a small insight. We have reported that the results of an experiment provide us with two mean scores: 26.0 for the group that studied in silence and 28.5 for subjects who studied with classical music in the background. Our interest now is in determining the extent to which these means are statistically different or due to chance factors. As we have implied, there is a statistical test of significance that can be applied to our data to this very question. The statistical test is called a *t-test*.

There are three factors that influence a test of significance such as the one that would be applied to our data for this example. One, of course, is the size of the mean difference itself. *Everything else being equal,* the larger the measured difference, the more likely that the difference reflects a real difference and not chance factors. A second factor is the size of the sample,

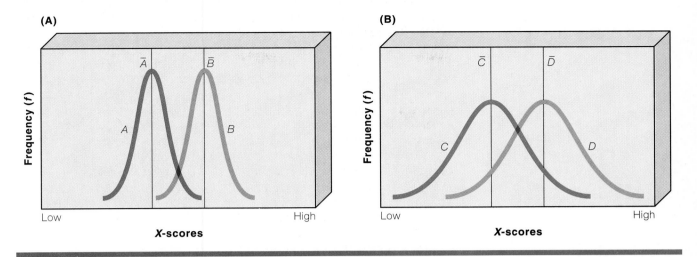

(A)

Frequency (*f*)

$\bar{A}$ $\bar{B}$

A   *B*

Low   High

***X*-scores**

(B)

Frequency (*f*)

$\bar{C}$ $\bar{D}$

C   *D*

Low   High

***X*-scores**

▲ *The possible outcomes of two experiments. In both cases, the mean differences $(\bar{A} - \bar{A})$ $(\bar{D} - \bar{C})$ are the same, and the Ns are also the same for each distribution. But because the variabilities in (A) are smaller, the difference between A and B is more likely to be significant than is the difference between C and D.*

or the number of measurements being tested. *Everything else being equal,* differences based on large numbers of observations are more likely to be significant than the same differences based on fewer observations. The third factor that influences a measure of statistical significance is the variability of the data.

To see why variability (usually standard deviation) matters in determining the significance of difference between means, refer to Figure A.6. On the left side of Figure A.6 we see two distributions of *X*-scores that have different means ($\bar{A}$ and $\bar{B}$). The right side of the figure shows two other distributions that have the very same mean difference ($\bar{C} - \bar{D}$). Because the variability (standard deviations) of distributions *A* and *B* are small, it is more likely that their means reflect significant differences than is the case for distributions *C* and *D*—even though the actual mean difference is the same in either case. In fact, the formula for the *t*-test of the significance of the difference between two means includes: (1) the mean difference itself, (2) the size of the groups involved, and (3) the standard deviations of the scores from each group.

▶ *Some Normal Curve Statistics*

As we have seen in our discussion of personality assessment and intelligence, many of the measurements we make in psychology fall into a similar pattern. Particularly when measurements are made on large numbers of subjects, we commonly find that they fall into a distribution we call the **normal curve** (see Figure A.7). The normal curve is a frequency distribution that is symmetrical and bell-shaped. As you can see, scores that are normally distributed tend to bunch around the mean and become infrequent at the extreme values of *X* (whatever the *X*-scores may be). Because this normal distribution of scores does occur so often, we tend to know a lot about the nature of this curve.

normal curve a commonly found symmetrical, bell-shaped frequency distribution

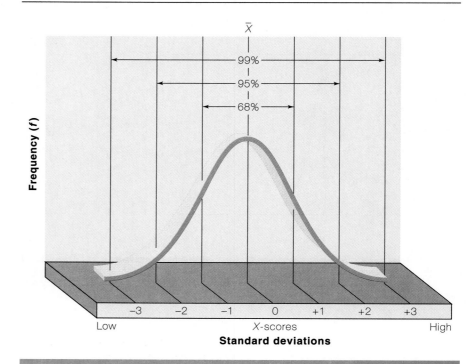

▲ *A theoretical normal curve of IQ scores. Here we can see, with mean = 100 and SD = 15, that 84 percent of the population has an IQ of 115 or less (50% to the mean and 34% from the mean to 1 SD above the mean). Thus, only 16 percent have IQs above 115.*

The normal curve is simply a graphical representation of a collection of numbers. Thus, we can compute the mean and the standard deviation of the scores that make up the distribution. Because the normal distribution is symmetrical, the mean always falls precisely in the middle of the distribution and is coincident with the median and the mode. *That is, there are just as many scores above the mean as there are below it.* We also know how many scores, or what proportion of scores, fall within standard deviation units around the mean. For example, we know that 68 percent of all scores fall between 1 standard deviation below the mean and 1 standard deviation above the mean (see Figure A.7). It is also true that 95 percent of the cases fall between ±2 standard deviations around the mean. Almost all the cases (about 99 percent) in a normal distribution fall between –3 and +3 standard deviations around the mean. What good is this sort of information? Let's look at an example problem.

When many people are measured, IQ scores tend to fall in distributions that we may consider to be normal distributions. Figure A.8 depicts a theoretical IQ distribution where, by definition, the mean equals 100 and the standard deviation is equal to 15 IQ points. We might want to know, for instance, what percentage of the population has an IQ score above 100. Well, that's an easy one. Because the mean equals 100, and because the mean divides the distribution exactly in half, 50 percent of the cases fall above 100 and 50 percent of the cases fall below an IQ of 100, so the answer is 50 percent.

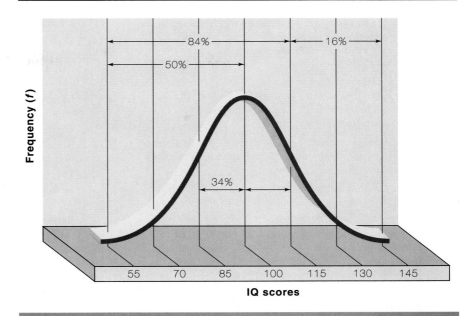

▲ *The percentage of cases in a normal distribution falling between ± 1 SD around the mean (68%). ± 2 SD (95%), and ± 3 SD (99%). Note that the curve is symmetrical and the mean divides it exactly in half, and that virtually all scores fall between 3 standard deviations below the mean and 3 standard deviations above the mean.*

What percentage of the population has an IQ score above 115? This takes a little more effort, and following along with Figure A.8 might help. We might work backward. If we know the percentage of cases in the shaded portion of the curve (up to IQ = 115), then the difference between that percentage and 100 will be the percentage who have IQs above 115. We can't determine the shaded percentage by inspection, but we can do so in a few easy steps. Up to the mean fall one-half, or 50 percent, of the cases (this we've already established). Now what about that segment between 100 and 115? What we do know (check on Figure A.7 again) is that 68 percent of the cases fall between –1 standard deviation and +1 standard deviation. In a normal distribution, the mean divides this segment exactly in half, so that between the mean and 1 standard deviation above the mean are included 34 percent of the cases. (Note that IQ =115 *is* 1 SD above the mean.) So now we have 50 percent to the mean of 100, and 34 percent from the mean to 115. We add the two together and determine that 84 percent of the cases fall *below* an IQ of 115, so 16 percent must fall above it. Using the same logic, we can convert any score to a percentage or proportion, if we are dealing with a normal curve. To do so for scores that do not fall precisely on standard deviation units above or below the mean involves a slight complication, but the general method is the same as we have indicated here. What percentage of the population (from Figures A.7 and A.8) have IQ scores above 130? The answer is 2.5 percent. Can you see where that comes from?

Chapter 1

1.1 All you need to do here is recognize the definition of the term "hypothesis." Hypotheses are part of doing science, case histories, and experiments, but the answer here is *c*. *Page 15*

1.2 Science cannot lead us to decide which issues to pursue, nor can it tell us which hypothesis is *the* correct one, but it can tell us which hypotheses to reject as unfounded. *Page 15*

1.3 This statement is false. There are many ways of gaining insight about human nature. As it happens, psychology values scientific methods. *Page 14*

1.4 Psychologists study all of these things, but the only alternative that is general enough not to exclude a part of psychology's subject matter is *c*. *Page 15*

1.5 This item assesses whether you know that "affect" refers to one's emotions, feelings, and moods. Alternatives *a*, *b*, and *c* are relevant to psychology's subject matter; affect deals only with *d*. *Page 15*

1.6 Someone may tell us about a dream that they had, but there is no way that we—or anyone else—can verify the contents of a dream. *Page 16*

1.7 Alternatives *c* and *d* tell us about psychology's subject matter, but when psychology began, the focus was on applying scientific methods to old philosophical questions about the nature of the mind; hence the best answer is *b*. *Page 16*

1.8 Neither of these men made scientific contributions that warrant mention, and neither had much to say about the spinal cord. What both did, as philosophers, was seek explanations of human activity in human terms, which is what alternative *b* claims. *Page 17*

1.9 Describing perceptual experiences in the most basic and fundamental terms is the essence of the method of introspection. *Page 18*

1.10 In fact, neither Locke nor Wundt would have known anything about Darwin's theories, which were published after each had made his mark on psychology. Although Wundt relied on scientific methods, they were not the methods of the philosopher Locke. What they had in common was their interest in the structure and contents of the human mind. *Page 20*

1.11 No, the first psychology laboratory was Wundt's. Freud, as it happens, never had a laboratory. *Page 19*

1.12 Psychology became known as the science of behavior when John Watson chaired the Psychology Department at Johns Hopkins University, right after World War I. Wundt, Titchener, and James were more interested in the mind and consciousness than in behavior. *Page 22*

1.13 This is a bit sneaky. Freud did much of his significant writing in this time period and we do call his approach "psychoanalytic," but it arose from his practice of therapy, not a laboratory or experiments, so as it stands, this statement is false. *Page 21*

1.14 Although no psychologist would violently disagree with such a statement, it is most likely to have been made by a humanistic psychologist. *Page 23*

1.15 Alternatives *a*, *b*, and *d* are all true. Naturalistic observation need not be reserved for organisms in social situations. *Page 26*

1.16 Each of these questions is one in which psychologists might be interested; however, naturalistic observation will only be useful in trying to answer the question about children during recess. *Page 26*

1.17 Most of Freud's work was based on his in-depth study of many of his patients, using the case history method. *Page 28*

1.18 Almost certainly. Indeed, the advantage of surveys is that they can reach many subjects easily. *Page 27*

1.19 This is a rather "standard" item. Alternative *d* is wrong because correlation coefficients cannot exceed −1.00 or +1.00. Useful prediction depends on the strength of a relationship, whether it is positive or negative, so a −.71 is more useful than a +.56 (−.71 is closer to the extreme of −1.00 than +.56 is to +1.00). *Page 29*

1.20 The first three pairs are clearly positively related. At least it is my experience that the less light there is in a restaurant, the more expensive the food, or as the light goes down, the price goes up, which is a negative correlation. *Page 29*

1.21 Remember: usefulness depends on the size of the number, not its sign (whether it is positive or negative). *Page 30*

1.22 Doing an experiment involves manipulating independent variables and measuring dependent variables, but the quality of that experiment hinges on the extent to which extraneous variables have been controlled or eliminated. *Page 33*

1.23 The independent variable is the one you manipulate; here the amount or dosage of the drug. Alternative *a* might be your dependent variable, and alternatives *c* and *d* are possible extraneous variables. *Page 32*

1.24 This statement is about as good a summary statement of the nature of an experiment that I can come up with. It is true. *Page 32*

1.25 Baseline designs use subjects as their own controls, where each subject gets both the experimental treatment and the control condition. None of the statements in alternatives *b*, *c*, or *d* is correct. *Page 35*

1.26 In virtually all research settings this statement is true. *Page 36*

Chapter 2

2.1 The new cell created at conception receives 23 chromosomes from each parent, for a total of 23 pairs. *Page 49*

2.2 Someone with blue eyes must have two recessive genes for blue eyes, one from each parent. Either parent may have blue or brown eyes, which makes alternatives *a*, *b*, and *d* incorrect. *Page 49*

2.3 Reflecting the interactionist's position, alternative *c* is probably the most reasonable statement we can make at present. *Page 50*

2.4 A neuron will have only one cell body and only one nucleus. As it happens, some neurons do have two axons, but the structures most likely to occur in large numbers are dendrites. *Page 51*

2.5 Myelin serves each of the functions named in alternatives *a*, *b*, and *d*. Be careful to note the NOT in this item. *Page 52*

2.6 Unlike many other cells, neurons are not replaced when they die, but their function(s) can be taken over by other neurons, particularly in younger organisms. *Page 52*

2.7 Indeed, one of the functions of myelin is to speed impulses along. *Page 52*

2.8 As logical as the statement may sound, it is simply not true. We are born with more neurons than we'll ever have again. *Page 52*

2.9 At rest, a neuron is in a position to fire, with many more negative ions inside the cell and positive ions outside the cell, which makes alternative *b* correct. *Page 53*

2.10 Nothing physically moves down a neuron when it fires. Physical movement is that of ions going in and out through the neural membrane. What moves down the neuron is where this ion movement takes place. *Page 53*

2.11 Watch out here! An important term in the stem is "in terms of their action," which means we're looking for what they do, which is either to excite or inhibit neural impulse transmission. *Page 56*

2.12 Within a neuron impulse transmission is electrochemical, but at the synapse, it is basically a chemical process, involving neurotransmitters. *Page 54*

2.13 It is important to know how the various nervous systems are interrelated, and to know the major functions of each. While the parasympathetic division is active when we are relaxed, the sympathetic is involved in emotionality. Note the spelling of alternative *c*—there is no such system as an automatic nervous system. *Page 58*

2.14 The white matter looks white because of the myelin that surrounds the axons of fibers going up and down the spinal cord, to and from the brain. *Page 60*

2.15 This is a straightforward terminology item. For the spinal reflex, we have: *in* on sensory neurons, *within* on interneurons, and *out* on motor neurons. *Page 61*

2.16 This is basically the same question in true-false form as item 2.27 was in multiple-choice form. This sequence of events is true. By now do you get the idea that this is an important concept? *Page 61*

2.17 Although it is difficult to say just where it begins, the first structure to be encountered would be the medulla. *Page 62*

2.18 The medulla contains centers that control several important reflexes, including those that control respiration, or breathing. *Page 62*

2.19 Cross laterality occurs in the medulla and in the pons. Because these two structures taken together comprise what we call the brain stem, this is the best answer. *Page 62*

2.20 The pons provides a sensory and motor bridge between the brain and the lower body. Not only would you be paralyzed, but you would also be without feeling for your body below your neck. *Page 62*

2.21 Quite the contrary. Lower brain centers develop first, and the cerebral cortex is the last to fully develop. In fact, we may argue that one's cerebral cortex continues to develop throughout most of one's lifetime. *Page 61*

2.22 Yes, speech and language centers are located in the left hemisphere of the cerebral cortex, but notice that this is not one of your choices. The issue in this item has to do with muscular coordination, which is a function of the cerebellum. *Page 63*

2.23 The reticular activating system, as its name implies, controls one's level of arousal. All that would happen in this scenario is that the cat would awaken. *Page 64*

2.24 Don't get distracted by the story of Phineas Gage and the iron bar that got blasted through his head. The basic issue here is that the limbic system is the seat of most primitive emotionality and when connections between it and the cerebral cortex are cut, control of emotionality is more difficult. *Page 64*

2.25 The hypothalamus is not only involved in the thirst drive, but it is also implicated in the hunger drive, temperature regulation drive, sex drive, and others. *Page 65*

2.26 This item describes very succinctly the function of the thalamus. *Page 65*

2.27 This does get a bit technical, but you should know the major features of cerebral localization, vision, hearing, movement, etc., and you should know that the body senses are processed at the front of the parietal lobe. *Page 67*

2.28 Notice what I did here—I inserted an item that is "out of order." This "goes back" to the spinal cord. You must be ready to deal with test items one at a time, not necessarily in the order in which they are presented in the text. Like all neurons within the CNS, these are called interneurons. *Pages 59–60*

2.29 Again, you should know the localization of major functions in the cerebral cortex, including the fact that vision is processed in the occipital lobe. *Page 67*

2.30 Don't panic just because this item is wordy. Remember the basics of the split brain procedure and remember that speech is a left hemisphere process, and that information from the left hand would be processed in the right hemisphere. Given these few details, alternative *c* is the only correct one. *Pages 70–71*

2.31 No, as a matter of fact, it is often difficult to tell that someone has had the procedure, except when certain behavioral functions are tested. Split-brain subjects can and do lead relatively normal lives. *Page 70*

Chapter 3

3.1 A zygote is formed by just two cells, one from each parent. *Page 81*

3.2 Be careful here. The periods of the zygote, embryo, and fetus are all part of what is called the prenatal period, which makes the prenatal period the longest. Within the prenatal period, the fetal period is the longest. *Page 82*

3.3 To be viable is to be able to survive in the world without (heroic or extreme) medical intervention. *Pages 82–83*

3.4 Alcohol abuse is certainly the most devastating factor (of these listed), leading to birth defects, but even moderate alcohol use is generally to be discouraged. *Page 83*

3.5 There are many signs and symptoms associated with the fetal alcohol syndrome (retarded physical growth, poor coordination, poor muscle tone, etc.). By definition, one of those is intellectual retardation. *Page 84*

3.6 The newborn, or neonate, engages in a full range of behaviors, many of them useful, few of them learned, but most of which can be described as reflexive. *Page 85*

3.7 Sure they do. Without its reflexes, a neonate probably would not survive at all. As it happens, some reflexes seem to be without specific purpose, but as it is worded, this statement is false. *Page 85*

3.8 Not only is the last statement the best of these choices, but the first three make claims that are essentially the opposite of a true claim. *Page 86*

3.9 We need to get at this one by inference and elimination. Because we know that the sense of depth, motion and sound discrimination are so well developed even at birth, we can conclude that the sense of balance is the poorest of these. *Page 87*

3.10 There is really nothing wrong with alternatives *a*, *b*, or *d*, except that they have very little to do with the question at hand, which makes the third alternative the best one. *Page 88*

3.11 The stages are determined in terms of how the child goes about forming or modifying schemas on the basis of his or her interaction with the environment. *Page 90*

3.12 Melonie is probably in Piaget's stage of concrete operations, which would be reasonable for a 9-year-old. *Page 92*

3.13 Yes, this is one of the most common criticisms of Piaget's theory. *Page 93*

3.14 Erikson's stages of development are equally relevant for girls and boys and were based on observation. What makes his stages different is that they extend through adolescence into adulthood, whereas Piaget's do not. *Page 95*

3.15 This one is fairly picky and requires that you know what occurs in each of Erikson's stages of development. Self-esteem and self-worth are most central during the resolution of the crisis of autonomy versus shame and doubt. *Page 95*

3.16 Kohlberg's is referred to as a theory of moral development. *Page 96*

3.17 Most of Kohlberg's theory of moral development was based on the study of males. Carol Gilligan suggests that females may have a different system of morality than do males. *Page 97*

3.18 Although some (including G. Stanley Hall and Anna Freud) would claim that alternative *b* is correct, current thinking would make alternative *c* your best choice. *Page 98*

3.19 To some of us this observation may seem to be true, but it is not. It reflects more of an incorrect stereotype than reality. *Page 98*

3.20 Menarche is the defining characteristic for puberty in girls, so *d* is correct. *Page 100*

3.21 Alternatives *a* and *b* are clearly false. Alternative *d* is also false, but newly controversial. Alternative *c* is most clearly true. *Page 102*

3.22 It's a matter of degree, of course, but this statement is, in fact, false. *Page 103*

3.23 I hate to ask picky questions about details and numbers, but the fact is that teenage pregnancies probably exceed one million each year, a detail I find awesome. *Page 106*

3.24 Alternatives *a*, *c*, and *d* are all reasonable and commonly offered explanations for the high rate of teenage pregnancy. *Pages 106–107*

3.25 Although they appear to be contradictory, independence and interdependence characterize early adulthood. *Page 107*

3.26 Here again, this item hinges on your knowledge of Erikson's stages. Early adulthood is associated with conflicts between intimacy and isolation. *Page 108*

3.27 This true statement is lifted virtually verbatim from the text. *Page 109*

3.28 We often hear this used as an "excuse" for some pretty silly behaviors by middle-aged adults, but there is little hard evidence for a general stage or period of development that we can characterize as a midlife crisis. *Page 110*

3.29 Alternative *c* is the only one even close to being true. *Page 112*

Chapter 4

4.1 The first alternative gives about as simple a statement of psychophysics as I can manage. *Page 122*

4.2 By definition, stimuli that are found to be below one's absolute threshold will be detected less than 50 percent of the time. *Page 123*

4.3 The complete statement that signal detection is essentially a decision making process is almost a direct quote from the text. *Page 125*

4.4 You might get this one simply by elimination. The first alternative is downright silly. The second and third alternatives say virtually the same thing, which makes alternative *d* the correct choice. *Page 126*

4.5 Not in actuality—only in theory. If it is above threshold, all we can say is that it will be detected more than 50 percent of the time. *Page 126*

4.6 Here's another analogy item, and a simple one at that. What is the issue here? Wavelength determines hue; wave amplitude determines what? Brightness. *Page 127*

4.7 You ought to be able to imagine what each of the lights described in the first three alternatives would look like. What makes the last alternative the correct choice is that white light is of the lowest possible saturation and thus one cannot have a white light of high saturation. *Page 129*

4.8 The cells that convert the physical energy of light into neural impulses are the rods and cones of the retina. *Page 132*

4.9 Indeed, what the iris does is to move to change the size of the pupil in response to the amount of light presented to the eye. *Page 130*

4.10 Sightedness has to do with whether or not images are clearly focused on the retina. There are any number of problems that can cause this to happen (poorly shaped lens, or cornea, or eyeball for that matter) but none have to do with the retina itself. *Page 131*

4.11 Because of the location of our rods, and because they function best "in the dark" or in low levels of illumination, we would want to focus the object on the periphery of the retina. *Page 134*

4.12 The dark adaptation curve has a "break" in it because at about the seven-minute mark, the cones no longer become more sensitive, while the rods continue to adapt, which makes the first statement the correct choice. *Page 135*

4.13 In fact, our rods are colorblind. Don't let the fact that this statement starts off with a correct assertion (rods operate best at low levels of illumination) confuse you. *Page 134*

4.14 This item is quite false in that there are about 20 times as many rods as cones in the human retina. *Page 134*

4.15 The major issue here is remembering that although red, blue, and yellow are the primary colors for paint, the primaries for light are red, green, and blue. *Page 136*

4.16 The stimulus for audition is sound, of course, and alternative *b* gives a reasonable definition or description of sound. *Page 139*

4.17 Amplitude determines loudness, mixture determines timbre, and—as this item asks—frequency determines pitch. *Page 139*

4.18 Another analogy. Wave amplitude of sound determines loudness. *Page 141*

4.19 This is simply by definition white noise. *Page 141*

4.20 This wordy statement contains a lot of information, but it is a fairly good description of what hearing is. *Page 140*

4.21 This one ought to sound familiar. It's the correct repeat of the definition of the decibel scale. *Page 139*

4.22 Sound waves are first collected by those flaps on the side of our head called pinnas (or pinnae); they are then passed on to the eardrum. *Page 141*

4.23 Located within the cochlea, the actual receptor cells for sound are hair cells. *Page 142*

4.24 I think that it is important for college students to know the actual ("technical") names for the various senses. Smell is olfaction. Taste is gustation. *Page 143*

4.25 This one is so silly you almost have to think about it for a minute. Of course impulses for the sense of smell go to the brain, and rather directly at that. *Page 144*

4.26 You probably got this correct. Pheromones are natural chemicals that are used to attract members of the opposite sex or mark off territory. *Page 144*

4.27 Our experience of hot can be the result of simultaneously stimulating both warm and cold receptors. There seem to be no specific receptors for "hot" alone. *Page 145*

4.28 Again, this is a matter of definition. Vestibular senses tell us about position relative to gravity; cutaneous senses about touch and pressure; and kinesthetic senses tell us about the movement of muscles and joints. There is no such thing as a "gravitational" sense. *Page 149*

4.29 The gate-control theory is a theory meant to describe the most important features involved in our experience of pain. *Page 150*

4.30 Here's one of those key words in true-false questions: *only*. Yes, pain receptors are found in the skin, but not only in the skin, as you'll realize after just a minute's reflection on all the non-skin parts of your body in which you have experienced pain. *Page 150*

Chapter 5

5.1 I hope I didn't catch you on this one, which actually goes back to Chapter 1. John Watson, remember, began behaviorism which denied the usefulness of consciousness in scientific psychology. *Page 160*

5.2 As we just said, James claimed that our consciousness is selective, continuous, personal, and changing, not stable. *Pages 160–161*

5.3 Although perception may involve our motivations, learning, and sensory input, it is best classified as a cognitive process. *Page 161*

5.4 Intensity, size, and motion are best considered to be dimensions on which stimuli may contrast with other stimuli, making contrast the most general of these factors. *Page 162*

5.5 Yes, perception *is* a basic, fundamental cognitive process, but it is still very much dependent on such "higher level" processes as one's memory of past experience and motivational state. *Page 161*

5.6 My name would attract my attention and not yours because of my past experience with that name, a personal factor. *Page 162*

5.7 To say that some stimuli are attended to because of an expectation to perceive them is to say that one has developed a mental set. *Page 163*

5.8 Speech sounds within a word are perceived and organized together because they are close together, separated by small spaces, which reflects the Gestalt factor of proximity—which means "nearness" or "togetherness." *Page 166*

5.9 Subjective contours provide compelling examples of closure. *Page 167*

5.10 This is true by definition. If you're in doubt, go back and check the definition. *Page 167*

5.11 Alternatives *a* and *b* are really quite absurd. Alternative *c* is a correct statement, but is unrelated to three-dimensionality. That makes *d* the best choice. *Page 169*

5.12 Retinal disparity—where disparity means differentness—requires that we have two retinas that receive different images of the same object. *Page 169*

5.13 This is a straightforward definition of interposition. *Page 170*

5.14 This one is almost tricky. The name is deceiving. In fact, motion parallax has little to do with our perception of motion. It is a cue to depth and distance. *Page 171*

5.15 When stationary lights are turned on and off in sequence, we experience the phi phenomenon, an illusion of motion where there isn't any. *Page 174*

5.16 Alternative *a* defines hallucinations, not illusions. Alternatives *b* and *c* are both incorrect statements (in fact, the opposite is true), while alternative *d* provides a reasonable definition of visual illusions. *Page 175*

5.17 Altered states of consciousness need not be bizarre or strange and include sleeping. They are simply changes in the way we perceive ourselves and the environment. *Page 176*

5.18 Although the first three statements (*a-c*) MAY be true, only the fourth is most generally true. Remember, in multiple-choice items, the task is to find the *best* alternative. *Page 177*

5.19 Self-report is probably the most unreliable source. The best way to know if someone is sleeping is by examination of EEG recordings. *Page 176*

5.20 EEG records tells us nothing about muscle activity, have virtually no alpha waves during REM sleep, and do not show theta waves. They appear almost like waking states. *Page 179*

5.21 During REM sleep one is likely to become paralyzed, not because of muscle tension, but because of total relaxation, called "atonia." Alternatives *b* and *c* are possible; *d* is the opposite of what actually happens. *Page 180*

5.22 All four statements sound reasonable (as they should in a good multiple-choice item) but here, only the alternative *c* is actually true. *Page 182*

5.23 Hypnosis can do little to help us learn and remember information we have not yet encountered, but can help reduce anxiety and thus enable us to remember details of anxiety-producing events that we might not be able to recall otherwise. *Page 183*

5.24 Alternative *b*, *c*, and *d* may be true of some drugs, but collectively mind-altering agents are referred to as psychoactive. *Page 183*

5.25 This one requires some thought. By definition, we find that drug abuse in some way interferes with normal functioning to the extent that it is maladaptive, getting in the way of one's proper adaptation to the environment and to others. *Page 184*

5.26 Here we have a trivia, detail item. Caffeine is the most common stimulant. *Page 184*

5.27 Nonsense. Of course all these drugs can and often do affect the way one feels and behaves as well as how one thinks. *Page 183*

5.28 Sorry. No matter the dosage in which it is taken, alcohol is a depressant drug. *Page 186*

Chapter 6

6.1 Alternative *a* is simply not true. Alternatives *b* and *c* *may* be true, but not related to the word "demonstrated," which makes *d* correct. *Page 196*

6.2 By definition, learning implies no value judgment. Alternatives *a*, *c*, and *d* are all part of the definition. *Page 197*

6.3 The first thing that will happen when that bell is sounded is that the dog will orient reflexively, to it. *Page 198*

6.4 This statement is false for two reasons: Pavlov won his Nobel Prize in 1904 not 1902 (but that's picky), and there is no such thing as a Nobel Prize for psychology. *Page 198*

6.5 Yes, this is exactly what it means to say that the response is *un*conditioned. *Page 198*

6.6 This one is straightforward, but you must have your stimuli and responses sorted out. Responding to the bell is a conditioned response. *Page 198*

6.7 The shock and the bell are both stimuli, so all alternatives including these are wrong. Withdrawal is both the CR and the UCR. *Page 199*

6.8 By definition, the strength of the CR will diminish, which is a demonstration of extinction. *Page 200*

6.9 This one, too, is by definition. Discrimination training is usually used to offset the effects of the opposite process of generalization. *Page 201*

6.10 Classical conditioning affects emotional responses, such as relief at class's end. *Page 202*

6.11 Although they may have wanted to, Watson and Rayner never got the chance to see if Little Albert's fear would extinguish. *Page 203*

6.12 Pavlov did not recognize this reality, but we now know that a stimulus will serve as an effective CS only if it signals or predicts the occurrence of a UCS that follows it. *Page 206*

6.13 I doubt that many psychologists would agree with the statements made in alternatives *a*, *b*, and *d*, which makes the third choice correct. *Page 207*

6.14 The relatively permanent change in behavior that occurs as the result of operant conditioning is a change in the rate or probability of a response. *Page 207*

6.15 Actually, Thorndike stated the law of effect. *Page 208*

6.16 This is a wordy item, but the most likely thing to happen is that the rat's rate of response will decrease, which is extinction. *Page 210*

6.17 If Mickey never does what you want him to do, there will be nothing for you to reinforce, so in this situation you'll have to try shaping his behaviors. *Page 210*

6.18 This statement is true by definition; "shaping" and "successive approximations" are nearly synonymous terms. *Page 210*

6.19 Positive reinforcers are given to organisms after an appropriate response, while negative reinforcement involves taking away something (something that is usually aversive or painful). *Page 212*

6.20 Because the root canal procedure takes away the pain of the toothache, the end result is very reinforcing (how reinforcing depends on how painful the toothache was). The reinforcement here is negative reinforcement. *Page 212*

6.21 I'd call this statement false because it is not necessarily so. Token economies involve secondary reinforcers, which may be (usually are) positive. *Page 213*

6.22 Responses learned under a continuous reinforcement schedule will extinguish more quickly than those learned under any other schedule. *Page 214*

6.23 Actually, the first three statements are quite false. The only thing that we can say for sure is that punishment decreases response rates. *Page 216*

6.24 Remember that the intention of the person doing the reinforcing is quite irrelevant, which makes this statement true. *Page 216*

6.25 Because we reinforce some stimuli and not others, we say that discrimination training is a matter of differential reinforcement. *Page 218*

6.26 Cognitive approaches emphasize the development of cognitions (cleverly enough), which means that they focus on changes inside the organism that may or may not be evidenced in behavior. *Page 219*

6.27 Latent means hidden from view, or not presently observable; hence the second alternative is the best choice. *Page 220*

6.28 I hope you didn't fall for this one. Remember, Tolman demonstrated cognitive maps in rats. As it happens, it is very easy to find human examples, but the point is that the phenomenon is not restricted to humans. Page 220

6.29 Vicarious reinforcement and vicarious punishment deal with the consequences of observing someone else being reinforced or punished and are, therefore, social concepts. *Page 221*

Chapter 7

7.1 The Greeks (including Plato) used the analogy of memory being like a block of wax in one's head upon which experience made an imprint. *Page 230*

7.2 The key to this item is that we're talking about "levels or compartments," otherwise, alternative *a* looks very good. The best alternative is the last one. *Page 230*

7.3 Information appears to be stored in sensory memory in the same way in which it is presented—technically, it is not encoded in any way. Thus, we say that the code is physical in nature. *Page 232*

7.4 No. Actually, before we learn it we must first sense the information, then attend to and perceive it. Page 231

7.5 Again, be careful. The word "minimal" is very important here. Any one of these three alternatives will do the job, but the minimum necessary is simply paying attention to it again. *Page 232*

7.6 The best term here (and there are arguments that could be made for some of the others) is the technical term "chunk," largely because the others are more related to duration than to capacity. *Page 235*

7.7 The best way is to work with it, using elaborative rehearsal. *Page 238*

7.8 We say that elaborative rehearsal gets information *into* LTM, so "retrieving it" won't do. And alternatives *b* and *d* say the same thing and are related to STM, so the answer involves making the material meaningful. *Page 239*

7.9 These procedures are most likely in procedural memory. *Page 239*

7.10 Mostly because it is personal and autobiographical, the answer to the question about learning to ride a bicycle is probably in episodic memory. (Note that actually remembering what it takes to ride the bike would be in procedural memory.) *Page 240*

7.11 Information in semantic memory is no doubt well organized, and one of the ways in which it may be organized is chronologically. Having said that, I am still going to claim that the answer here is "False" because there are better, more common ways of organizing information in semantic memory and because chronological organization better fits episodic memory. *Page 240*

7.12 When we talk about retrieval failure, we're probably going to assume that the information that cannot be remembered is in memory, but cannot be gotten out for some reason, which is essentially what the second alternative is saying. *Page 244*

7.13 No, in fact quite the opposite is true. *Page 241*

7.14 The process of relearning is an implicit way of demonstrating the presence of information in memory that cannot be consciously retrieved. *Page 243*

7.15 Even in the worst cases of memory loss, skills stored in procedural memory (talking, feeding, etc.) seem to be preserved. *Page 244*

7.16 Probably. At least assessing memory through implicit means does not involve voluntary, conscious attempts to recall or recognize. *Page 240*

7.17 The simple thing to say is that we cannot remember these features because we have never tried to, which is a way of saying that the information was not properly encoded. *Page 244*

7.18 The first sentence here is a good, concise statement of the encoding specificity hypothesis. Note that although alternatives *b* and *d* are essentially true statements, they are not related to this question. *Page 245*

7.19 State-dependent memory studies have to do with the subject's "state of mind" at encoding and at retrieval and verify what we suspect concerning the encoding specificity hypothesis. *Page 246*

7.20 This is terribly unlikely—so much so, I'd call it false. What we call flashbulb memories are usually stored in episodic memory. *Page 246*

7.21 More than anything else they may do, mnemonic devices enhance meaningfulness. *Page 247*

7.22 This item provides a pretty good description of what is involved in narrative chaining. *Page 247*

7.23 Yes, mnemonic devices impact on retrieval, but they do so by having their real impact on encoding, putting information into memory in a more meaningful way. *Page 247*

7.24 This item provides a good definition for what schemas are. *Page 250*

7.25 If Bob does no more trials, overlearning = 0%; 8 trials = 100%, 16 trials = 200%, and 20 trials = 250% overlearning. *Page 251*

7.26 Alternative *a* is virtually never true; alternative *b* incorrectly talks about STM instead of LTM; alternative *c* sounds good, but is untrue; while alternative *d* is almost always true. *Page 252*

7.27 The very last test will always suffer the most proactive interference—interference from material learned earlier. *Page 254*

7.28 You may want to go back and examine the design for both retroactive and proactive interference. The correct choice here is that, as an experimental subject, you would begin by learning Task A. *Page 254*

7.29 On the (reasonable) assumption that only the recall of an accident would be likely to elicit much anxiety, I'd say that *c* is the best choice. *Page 256*

Chapter 8

8.1 With a well-defined problem, the goal state is clear, so we know when we are there, and we know it with some certainty. We can say, "There, this problem is solved." *Page 265*

8.2 Given our answer to the last question, the only acceptable choice here is alternative *b*. *Page 265*

8.3 Once we realize that we have a problem, the first—and most difficult—step is to put that problem into terms that are meaningful to us. *Page 266*

8.4 Given the answer to the last item, it follows that if a problem already exists in a form with which we are familiar, representation will be relatively easy. *Page 268*

8.5 Heuristics (in general) allow us to reduce the number of choices we may pursue in problem solving. The more possibilities there are, the more important it is to develop a heuristic strategy. *Page 268*

8.6 Heuristics may lead us down the wrong path now and then, but the ultimate advantage of heuristic strategies is that they save time. *Page 269*

8.7 In fact, computers can solve problems with heuristic strategies, but they are best and fastest at using algorithmic strategies—checking out all the alternatives. *Page 268*

8.8 Alternatives *a*, *c*, and *d* are all quite true. The proper mental set may actually facilitate problem solving, which makes *b* false. *Page 270*

8.9 By definition, functional fixedness is a variety of mental set. *Page 270*

8.10 No matter how original, no matter how convergent or divergent, no matter how artistic or beautiful, the ultimate test of a creative solution is whether or not it actually works to solve the problem. *Page 271*

8.11 Not only is this statement true, but it also provides a pretty good definition of both convergent and divergent thinking. *Page 271*

8.12 Language IS rule-governed; it IS creative or generative, and it IS both social and cognitive. I'm not sure I know what it means to say that language is either correct or incorrect. *Page 273*

8.13 Speech is a form of language, and language is a form of communication, which makes communication the most general term. *Page 273*

8.14 Although language is an arbitrary cognitive process that follows rules, communicating about the not-here and not-now reflects displacement. *Page 274*

8.15 This is quite false; they've shown that appreciation for some time before. *Page 275*

8.16 This child probably has already indicated knowledge of the word "feet," but is here demonstrating overregularization. *Page 277*

8.17 Each of these defines intelligence, and reasonably so at that, but only the second alternative is an operational definition, specifying the operations used to measure intelligence. *Page 278*

8.18 Objectivity in the context of psychological testing usually has to do with performance—how test responses are evaluated or scored. *Page 279*

8.19 Not only is she interested in reliability, she is interested in split-half reliability. *Page 280*

8.20 This one is deceptively simple. The statement is true. *Page 279*

8.21 Think about this one. To calculate reliability, we correlate a test with itself at a later date. To calculate validity, we correlate a test with some other criterion. Doesn't it make sense that a test is bound to correlate better with itself than it will with anything else, making this statement false? *Page 280*

8.22 Their basic job was to identify children in the French school system who needed a different style of education because of some intellectual deficit. *Page 282*

8.23 This one is almost a giveaway. Alternatives *a*, *c*, and *d* are each included under the most general level of a **g**-factor. *Page 282*

8.24 What we're looking for here is MA divided by CA, times 100, or 8 divided by 10, times 100, which is 80. *Page 283*

8.25 No, what makes this revision different from previous ones is that it can provide several specific scores in addition to the one general IQ score. *Page 283*

8.26 One of Wechsler's major complaints about IQ tests was that they were so heavily verbal and vocabulary oriented. He included many performance items on his tests, and allowed for the calculation of a performance IQ. *Page 284*

8.27 Our best tests of general intelligence are the individually-administered tests. Of this group, only the Wechsler test qualifies. *Page 287*

8.28 Down's syndrome appears when a zygote picks up an extra chromosome, yielding 47 chromosomes rather than the normal 23 pairs. *Page 293*

8.29 We do. *Page 294*

Chapter 9

9.1 We say that motivation arouses, directs, and maintains behavior. Memory is surely involved in motivation—it's involved in virtually everything—but it's less critical than the other three. *Page 302*

9.2 The difference is quite arbitrary, but standard: *drive* is used for physiologically-based motivators of behavior and motive is used for psychologically-based motivators. *Page 302*

9.3 There is value in the concept of instinct, of course, but with regard to human behaviors, instinct tends to rename and describe rather than explain. *Page 303*

9.4 To say *acquires*, or *learned*, or *conditioned* is to say the same thing, so "primary" is the odd term of these four. *Page 304*

9.5 In virtually anyone's system, including Hull's, a need gives rise to a drive. *Page 303*

9.6 I do think that it's important to know Maslow's hierarchy. If you think about it, the order is very sensible. Of those listed, the highest in the hierarchy are esteem needs. *Page 305*

9.7 Drives, arousal, and needs all refer to conditions or states within the organism, while incentives are thought of as "out there" in the environment. *Page 305*

9.8 The answer here is incentive which, in most ways, is the same as the concept of reinforcement in operant conditioning. *Page 305*

9.9 By definition, homeostasis is a state of balance. *Page 306*

9.10 I argue that cognitive dissonance is very much like the concept of homeostasis; whenever our thoughts (cognitions) are out of balance (dissonant), we will be motivated to change the way we think about things. *Page 308*

9.11 Well, at first, maybe, but what makes this statement false is that if arousal continues to rise, eventually it will be so high as to be debilitating. *Page 307*

9.12 Although all of these may be involved to some extent, the fact that sometimes we feel too hot or too cold is mostly a function of the hypothalamus. *Page 310*

9.13 Most of the water in our bodies is contained within the structure of individual cells. *Page 311*

9.14 Clearly it has some impact, but of these choices, the stomach is the least important. *Pages 312–313*

9.15 If the truth of this statement is not obvious, you need to think about it a bit longer. *Page 312*

9.16 This one is almost a give-away. All of these factors, and more, contribute to one's body weight. *Page 313*

9.17 Alternatives *a*, *b*, and *d* are true of the sex drive for both humans and rats. The sex drive and sexual behaviors in rats do not seem to be affected by learning or experience. *Page 316*

9.18 Only the third alternative is true; the others are very false indeed. *Page 317*

9.19 The total picture is far from clear. We're quite sure that none of the observations made in the first three alternatives are even relevant, and are becoming convinced that the fourth alternative is the best statement we can make at the moment. *Page 318*

9.20 AIDS is very worrisome, of course, and deadly, but it is the least common (by far) of the STDs listed here. *Page 319*

9.21 AIDS is ultimately caused by a viral infection, the HIV. *Page 319*

9.22 This may be the saddest item on any test, simply because it is true. *Page 320*

9.23 The best alternative here is the last one—not the first, where there would be too little challenge to really experience a sense of achievement. *Page 322*

9.24 You should at least be aware of the James-Lange theory because it is such a classic, and so counterintuitive. The best answer here is the second statement. *Page 325*

9.25 More than anything else, the Schachter-Singer approach to emotion emphasizes a cognitive approach, a cognitive appraisal of the situation, so the correct altternative is d. *Page 326*

9.26 Heart rate increases, it doesn't decrease—in fact, think in terms of "what would happen if *you* were to meet a bear in the woods." *Pages 327–328*

9.27 As we've seen, the brain tends to work together, with all its aspects involved in everything, including emotionality, but—having said that—it is the limbic system that is most involved in emotions. *Page 328*

9.28 This item has to do with the difference between humans and other organisms. Only humans can talk (verbalize) about how they feel. *Page 329*

Chapter 10

10.1 The key here is "reasonably little effort." This indicates that the information is stored at a preconscious level. *Page 339*

10.2 In fact, Freud had quite a bit to say about war and unpleasantness that he saw about him. He suggested that humans must have some sort of drive for destruction, which he called "thanatos" to match their drive for life and survival, which he called "eros." *Page 339*

10.3 It is the ego that operates under what is called the reality principle. *Page 340*

10.4 It is our superego that informs us of moral issues and keeps us in touch with "right and wrong." Page 340

10.5 Although this may SOUND like displacement, this item provides a good definition for the defense mechanism called projection. *Page 341*

10.6 It sounds to me like Otis is rationalizing. *Page 341*

10.7 It is during the Freudian stage of latency that one's sexuality is essentially put on hold. *Page 343*

10.8 There were many grounds on which people broke away from Freud. Of these, the first statement summarizes a problem that many of them had. *Page 344*

10.9 These concepts are best associated with Karen Horney. *Page 345*

10.10 This may appear to be a picky, detailed item, but it seems to me that you ought to be able to form at least one good association with each of the theorists in this chapter (and note that Spearman is not even in this chapter). The best association here is Adler. *Page 344*

10.11 The psychologists listed here would say that forces outside the organism—in the environment, not in the person—should be used to explain behaviors. *Page 345*

10.12 Phenomenology has to do with perception. Here the issue is the perception of one's self and the perception of others. Here again we have the point that what is perceived is what matters. *Page 347*

10.13 To be fully functioning is to strive, at least, to reach what Maslow called self-actualization—in a cliché phrase: To be the best that one can be. *Page 348*

10.14 Rogers' form of psychotherapy was quite different, of course, but Rogers developed a very popular form of psychotherapy. *Page 347*

10.15 Personality traits are dimensions of description and have most often been determined or identified by factor analyzing test scores of many subjects to see which characteristics are intercorrelated. *Page 349*

10.16 Doing a factor analysis is largely a matter of computing several correlations, looking for traits that cluster together to form a "factor." *Page 350*

10.17 By definition, personality trait theories are going to tell us how to measure the trait that is being described, perhaps even providing the test that operationally defines each trait. This is a major advantage. *Page 349*

10.18 The Big Five are five personality traits (or clusters of traits, perhaps). What makes these five remarkable is the extent of consensus about their universality. *Page 352*

10.19 Virtually all personality theories, including The Big Five, include intelligence (or something very much like it) as an important aspect of one's personality. *Page 352*

10.20 Actually, most interviews are quite unreliable unless they are conducted by trained interviewers who use highly structured interviews. *Page 359*

10.21 What makes the MMPI-2, for example, a criterion-referenced test is that each item tends to be answered differently by people from different (criterion) groups. *Page 360*

10.22 On an intelligence test I want you to try to do your best, to put your best foot forward, while on a personality assessment technique, I want you to act normally and give me your most characteristic responses. *Page 356*

10.23 They are both commonly used projective techniques. *Pages 361–362*

Chapter 11

11.1 This is a good definition of a stressor—not stress, please note. *Page 370*

11.2 By definition, frustration is the blocking or thwarting of goal-directed behaviors, the assumption being that all behavior is goal-directed. *Page 371*

11.3 The first alternative is a good example of frustration—environmental frustration at that. *Page 371*

11.4 I think that we can assume that Bob's inability to qualify for the tournament is a reflection of his own poor golf game, which makes this an example of personal frustration. *Page 372*

11.5 I suppose that we could argue about this one because I do not have any quality data to support my contention

that as adults, we tend to "keep our options open," and thus less frequently get trapped in simple approach-avoidance conflicts. *Page 372*

11.6 I think that most of us will agree that we're not going to feel too sorry for Scott, momentarily stuck with an approach-approach conflict. *Pages 372–373*

11.7 It is true that some motivational conflicts cause much less stress than do others, but by definition, conflicts are stressors and are stressful all of the time (i.e., if there's no stress, there's no conflict). *Pages 372–373*

11.8 The basic issue with motivational conflicts is the difficulty of choices or decisions that have to be made. *Page 374*

11.9 Lazarus is one who would have us focus our attention on the small, nagging hassles of life as the real sources of our stress. *Page 375*

11.10 This is a long one (and somewhat self-disclosing), but what we have here is someone who is experiencing frustration because of some personal reason, hence, personal frustration. *Page 375*

11.11 This sounds awfully depressing, but needn't be—even though it is essentially true. *Page 375*

11.12 Learning—bringing about a relatively permanent change—is an adaptive response to the stressors in our lives. *Pages 376–377*

11.13 Here's an attitude destined to get one in trouble. A person is setting himself or herself up for considerable grief if he or she believes that it is possible to avoid stress altogether. *Pages 376–377*

11.14 Each of these may—in some circumstances—be a bit helpful, but fixating, just doing the same thing over and over again, obviously doesn't work and is inefficient. *Page 378*

11.15 Yes, it does. It's wrong, but that's what it claims. *Page 378*

11.16 Although Selye talks about stress depleting one's bodily resources, "depletion" as such was not one of his three stages. *Pages 379–382*

11.17 For Selye, the only sensible way to define stress was as a physiological reaction to the stressors of one's life. *Page 379*

11.18 If we could say that stress was the cause of one's death, then death probably would have occurred in the exhaustion stage, but to say that reaching this stage necessarily results in death is not true. *Pages 381–382*

11.19 Not only is this false, we might argue that the opposite is true. *Page 381*

11.20 By definition, health psychologists are involved in the management and prevention of physical illness and disease—whether psychological disorders are involved or not. *Page 382*

11.21 Perhaps because it is so deadly, there is a lot of concern about coronary heart disease (CHD), and it is one set of physical disorders that is reasonably well correlated with personality variables. *Page 383*

11.22 High cholesterol is a physical measure, not a psychological one as required to be part of TABP. *Page 383*

11.23 Type A personality is often (incorrectly) associated with someone who strives for perfection in all he or she does, but this is NOT one of the active ingredients of the pattern. *Page 384*

11.24 Surely, each of these would be helpful, but none would be as significant as to get everyone to stop smoking. *Pages 384–385*

11.25 Here we have some trivial statistics again, but these are so impressive! The best answer is that nearly three-quarters (about 70%) of the top causes of death in the United States are determined largely by behavioral causes. *Page 385*

11.26 The statement about secondhand smoke, we know now, is absolutely false. *Page 385*

11.27 This statement is (sadly) true. *Page 385*

Chapter 12

12.1 Granted, it's only an estimate, and granted it is probably a bit too conservative, but of these choices, the best would be to say that approximately twenty percent of the population has a psychological disorder. *Page 394*

12.2 Yes, some of the reactions of persons with psychological disorders may be thought of as strange and bizarre, but these terms are not in the definition of abnormality. *Pages 394–395*

12.3 One of the sad realities of mental disorders is that in virtually every case the person with a disorder is (or at one time was) aware of the fact that something is not right. The other alternatives are clearly false. *Pages 395–396*

12.4 There are several problems with schemes of labeling and classifying disorders, but each of those schemes is certainly based on some logical and sensible rationale for doing so. *Pages 396–398*

12.5 Insanity is a term that has been around for a very long time in many different contexts. As it is used today, however, it is a legal term, not a psychological one. *Page 398*

12.6 By definition, all disorders are unpleasant and distressing, but in most cases, phobias are easily treated and have a positive prognosis. *Pages 396–398*

12.7 The most common phobias include some irrational fear of some sort of animal. The most commonly *treated* phobia is agoraphobia. *Pages 399–400*

12.8 The anxiety in panic disorder is acute—of short duration, but intense. The anxiety of generalized anxiety disorder is chronic—of long duration. *Pages 400–401*

12.9 This would be a definitional symptom of obsessive-compulsive disorder. *Pages 401–402*

12.10 Soma means "body," hence, somatoform disorders involve some sort of bodily symptom or complaint. *Pages 404–405*

12.11 No, these symptoms are better associated with conversion disorder, although it is true that hypochondriasis involves bodily complaints. *Pages 404–405*

12.12 Multiple personality disorder is an anxiety-based dissociative disorder, and alternatives *a*, *b*, and *d* are clearly false statements. *Page 406*

12.13 Fugue states usually are associated with amnesia, generally psychogenic amnesia. *Page 406*

12.14 This one is a bit picky, but I think it would be useful to have at least one good solid association for each of the personality disorders. These symptoms are typical of the histrionic personality. *Pages 407–410*

12.15 This example provides a good description of the symptoms of generalized anxiety disorder. *Pages 400–406*

12.16 No, they're not. They're classified as personality disorders, an altogether different category. *Pages 409–410*

12.17 This item goes back to Chapter 1 where we first identified affect as dealing with mood and emotion. *Page 410*

12.18 This one isn't even close, and the answer is depression. Do note that paranoia isn't even a mood disorder. *Pages 410–413*

12.19 As is the case for depression, episodes of mania tend to reoccur and relapse. That is, we seldom find an isolated case of mania. *Pages 410–413*

12.20 There is likely a genetic predisposition for depression, and depression (somehow) involves the collection of neurotransmitters called biogenic amines. *Pages 410–413*

12.21 Sure they can. *Pages 410–413*

12.22 Actually, alternatives *a*, *c*, and *d* aren't even true! What makes schizophrenia so disruptive is that it tends to have its impact on all levels of psychological functioning: affect, behavior, and cognition. *Pages 413–416*

12.23 There may be some anxiety associated with schizophrenia, but the other listed symptoms virtually define the disorder. *Pages 413–416*

12.24 Schizophrenia does mean "splitting of the mind," but not into separate personalities. The split referred to is a split from reality as the rest of us experience it. *Page 416*

12.25 The gradual development of symptoms defines the variety of schizophrenia we call process schizophrenia. *Page 416*

12.26 A negative symptom is a deficit—something missing that used to be there. A positive symptom is something new, such as delusions or hallucinations, added to the person's response repertoire. *Page 416*

12.27 That schizophrenia runs in families is an assertion with which most psychologists would agree. *Pages 418–421*

12.28 This is the so-called "rule of thirds," which is only a rule of thumb, but is still reasonably accurate. About one-third recover, about one-third never show any significant improvement, and about one-third show improvement for a short while, only to have their symptoms return. *Page 421*

Chapter 13

13.1 Although there certainly were those through history who took a humane approach to the mentally ill, a general acceptance of such treatment is really a 20th century phenomenon. *Pages 429–430*

13.2 How one goes about treating psychological disorders is driven—more than anything else—by how one understands the nature and causes of those disorders, which makes the last statement the best of these choices. *Pages 429–430*

13.3 Hippocrates believed quite the opposite. His beliefs did not have much of a lasting impact, but he believed psychological disorders had a physical or biological cause. *Page 429*

13.4 The time is approaching when clinical psychologists may have the "right" to prescribe medication, under certain circumstances—but even then the best choice to answer this question is psychiatrists, who have an M.D. *Pages 430–432*

13.5 Regardless of the specific procedure involved, all lobotomies severed connections between the controlling cerebral cortex and lower brain centers. *Page 434*

13.6 None of the first three statements is true. It is true, however, that tens of thousands of these operations were performed in the mid-20th century. *Page 434*

13.7 Lobotomy is a type of psychosurgery, but it is not correct to equate the two as synonyms. There are other types of psychosurgery than lobotomies. *Page 434*

13.8 We do have some fairly reasonable hypotheses, but the truth is we still don't know why ECT has the beneficial effects that it does. *Page 435*

13.9 ECT has been used, and with some success, on virtually all psychological disorders, but it works best, and is most commonly used as a treatment for depression. *Page 435*

13.10 Just why this has the effects that it does is not known, but as stated, this statement is true. *Page 435*

13.11 All chemicals that have an impact on psychological functioning are referred to as psychoactive drugs. *Page 436*

13.12 I typically don't like to ask questions about specific drugs because there are so many of them and because new drugs are being introduced continuously. However, I do think that it is noteworthy that chlorpromazine was the very first. *Page 436*

13.13 On an individual basis, we may find exceptions, but by and large, antipsychotic medications are more likely to suppress symptoms than cure disorders. *Page 436*

13.14 In fact, quite the opposite is true, which is one of the benefits of ECT. *Pages 436–437*

13.15 Anti-anxiety drugs do just what their name suggests: They alleviate feelings of anxiety. *Page 438*

13.16 Alternative *c* is a much better statement for a goal of behavioral therapy than for Freudian therapy. *Pages 438–440*

13.17 This statement provides a reasonable definition for the Freudian concept of transference. *Pages 439–440*

13.18 Psychoanalysis today has changed significantly from the way that Freud practiced it, but what makes it psychoanalysis is the the basic assumption that disordered symptoms reflect repressed conflict of some sort. *Page 441*

13.19 Latent content is the "hidden," symbolic content of dreams, while manifest content is the content as the person describes it. *Page 440*

13.20 Both types of therapist would agree that patients or clients may not be aware of the true source of their distress, at least at the onset of therapy. *Page 442*

13.21 Here we have a straightforward definition of empathy. *Page 442*

13.22 Behavior therapies—in general, again—are aimed at bringing about relatively permanent changes in one's behaviors following principles derived from the learning laboratory. *Page 442*

13.23 It is possible to imagine using aversion therapy to treat phobias, but each of the other alternatives was designed to treat that disorder. *Pages 444–446*

13.24 You should know this one without even having read this chapter, if you remember our discussion of Bandura and his theories about modeling from Chapter 6. *Page 446*

13.25 This one takes a bit of thought. (I like it.) Unconditional positive regard provides reinforcement for virtually everything the client says (or does). Contingency management gives conditional positive regard: One earns reinforcers only for doing what is appropriate. Hence, they are in this way opposite. *Page 445*

13.26 Cognitive therapy deals with cognitions, in particular, irrational cognitions or thoughts about oneself and the world. *Pages 446–448*

13.27 Yes, cognitive therapy can be—and has been—used for virtually all disorders, but of these choices, it is most suited for treating depression, often in conjunction with ECT or drug therapy. *Pages 446–448*

13.28 The key here, of course, is the notion of "for any particular disorder." Although it is true that *in general*, psychotherapy techniques are all about equally useful, for particular disorders, some have been found to be more effective than others. *Pages 450–452*

Chapter 14

14.1 A set of beliefs about others based on limited information and which does not allow for individual differences of those others is, by definition, a stereotype. *Page 460*

14.2 Stereotypes sometimes may be wrong, or may be used in unfortunate ways, but forming and using stereotypes helps us get along in the social world. *Pages 460–461*

14.3 As you know, there is some considerable disagreement on how to best characterize the nature of attitudes, but the one thing that all characterizations agree on is that attitudes involve some degree of evaluation. *Page 462*

14.4 Yes, attitudes often are said to have three components, but those components are the familiar affect, behavior, and cognition. The statement is therefore false. *Page 463*

14.5 What matters most to an advertiser is the behavioral component. The advertiser wants you to *do* something, i.e., purchase the advertised product or service. *Page 463*

14.6 If you act contrary to your attitude, I will have established cognitive dissonance. This will motivate you to do something, perhaps change your attitude. *Pages 464–466*

14.7 It may be helpful to have a communicator who is a celebrity delivering your message, just to get people's attention, but if that celebrity is not perceived as credible, expert, and trustworthy, it will do little good. *Pages 466–467*

14.8 Actually, alternatives *a*, *b*, and *d* are just different ways of saying the same thing. I can't imagine how learned vs. inherited factors would fit into a discussion of attribution. *Page 469*

14.9 These actions provide a good definition of the fundamental attribution error. *Pages 469–471*

14.10 Social psychologists are interested in each of these, of course, but attribution theory specifically concerns how one goes about explaining the behaviors of oneself and others. *Pages 469–471*

14.11 Here's a true piece of social psychology that conforms to common sense. *Pages 469–471*

14.12 One of the appealing aspects of attachment theory is that it views the formation of interpersonal relationships as a lifelong process and suggests that there is evidence that styles remain quite consistent. Statement *b* is the best one. *Pages 472–473*

14.13 The first statement is, in fact, quite the opposite of reality. If anything, familiarity breeds attraction. (And don't forget: We're talking "in general." Yes, there may be exceptions.) *Pages 473–475*

14.14 Sexuality is an important component of attraction for some, but compared to the others it would be rated last, or least important. *Pages 473–475*

14.15 Actually, we probably are going to like someone who likes us now, but didn't originally. *Pages 473–475*

14.16 The last alternative is the best choice here because, if Asch's subjects knew that the others in the group were confederates of Asch, the project wouldn't have worked at all. *Pages 475–476*

14.17 This is precisely what Asch found in his experiments. *Pages 475–476*

14.18 What makes obedience obedience is that it is conformity to the demands or wishes of an authority figure, real or perceived. *Pages 475–479*

14.19 Of these choices, the only justified conclusion is that the perception of authority is a strong situational force in obedience. *Pages 477–479*

14.20 He sure was. *Pages 477–478*

14.21 We must notice, interpret, and take responsibility. It matters little whether the victim knows us or not. *Pages 479–482*

14.22 Actually, the second statement (alternative *b*) provides a good statement of pluralistic ignorance. *Page 480*

14.23 Alternatives *b* and *c* are basically irrelevant. Diffusion of responsibility tells us that you are less likely to be helped if you are in a large crowd. *Page 481*

14.24 Triplett was interested in social facilitation and he demonstrated it by having children reel in fishing line, either alone or in groups. *Page 482*

14.25 When we are performing "in public," the main thing that happens is that arousal levels go up, which is okay so long as what we are doing is something simple or well-rehearsed. *Page 483*

14.26 There is an unsettling, unpleasant side of this statement, which as stated is true. The quality of our performance is—in general—more likely to be hindered by group membership than facilitated by it. *Pages 482–483*

14.27 Group polarization refers to the phenomenon that the individual attitudes of group members will tend to be strengthened (i.e., polarized) during the course of decision making. *Pages 484–485*

14.28 The problem with groupthink is not that it is pressure to reach consensus, but that it is pressure to reach consensus, right or wrong. *Page 484*

Chapter 15

15.1 I/O psychology may be associated with all of these, but it is BEST thought of as a field of applied psychology. *Page 492*

15.2 Any one of the first three statements might describe actions you would like to take, but to get things going, one first does a complete job analysis. *Page 493*

15.3 Hard criteria are objective and can be measured, while soft criteria are more subjective and call for opinions or judgments of others. *Page 493*

15.4 By definition, "soft criteria" involve making subjective judgments. *Page 493*

15.5 Unstructured interviews are notoriously poor in terms of validity as an assessment technique (which is not say that interviews have no place in the process, particularly if they are structured interviews). *Pages 494–495*

15.6 Biodata are personal, biographical information—exactly the sort of thing asked for on application forms. *Page 494*

15.7 Definitely. In fact, structured devices of any sort are usually more valid than unstructured ones. *Pages 494–495*

15.8 The very first thing that must be asked is whether or not any sort of training program is needed in the first place. *Page 496*

15.9 This is one of those "all of the above" items. Evaluation should be a constant, on-going matter during, after, and well after a training program. *Page 498*

15.10 Training programs usually are evaluated in terms of specific behavioral goals, which are what are specified in the program's training objectives. *Page 496*

15.11 As is the case in virtually all types of training or education, the more the learner, or trainee, is actually involved in hands-on experience, the more effective training will be. *Pages 497–498*

15.12 More than anything else, this theory is cognitive in its approach. *Page 499*

15.13 By definition, equity theory deals with the worker's perception of fair treatment compared to other workers at the same level within the organization. *Page 500*

15.14   This may sound reasonable, but it is, in fact false. *Page 500*

15.15   Vroom believed that workers behaved rationally and logically and on that basis constructed a very cognitive model of worker motivation. *Page 499*

15.16   The only one of these that is correlated (and positively so) is worker age. *Page 501*

15.17   Actually, quality of work life and job satisfaction are essentially the same thing, and are bound to be well correlated with each other regardless of whether either is correlated with anything else. *Page 502*

15.18   These labels for psychological space judgments are listed in order, from smallest to largest. *Page 505*

15.19   Alternative *a* provides a very good definition of the Hawthorne Effect. *Page 504*

15.20   This is a pretty good definition of a primary territory. *Page 507*

15.21   The main issue here is one of perception—feelings of distress and discomfort that accompanies overcrowding—may occur in a small town as easily as in a large city. *Page 508*

15.22   Indeed, one of the advantages of city life, not one of its stressors is that there generally tend to be many more resources available to its residents. *Page 509*

15.23   I'm not quite sure I know what the "melody" of a noise would be, and loudness does matter, but what matters most is the predictability of noise. *Pags 509–510*

15.24   By definition, they are called neurotoxins. *Page 511*

15.25   This may appear to be a picky item, but I don't think that it is. The answer is 86°F, not 106°F where the temperature is so high as to debilitate nearly everyone, i.e., it's too hot to riot. *Pages 509–510*

15.26   No, by definition, neurotoxins will indeed have a negative, poisonous effect on behavior and/or emotion. *Page 511*

15.27   Indeed, applied behavioral analysis can be thought of as a version of operant conditioning in action. *Page 512*

15.28   This is a two-parter. First, it's clear that fan support will have more of an effect (either way) in a championship game. Then, the negative effect occurs when the team is on offense, trying to execute a variety of maneuvers that are difficult with high levels of arousal. This is true, by the way, for virtually any team sport. *Page 514*

15.29   There is considerable evidence that mental practice and imaging can be beneficial in athletic training. *Page 514*

Glossary

A

abnormal statistically uncommon, maladaptive cognitions, affect, and/or behaviors that are at odds with social expectations and that result in distress or discomfort

absolute threshold the physical intensity of a stimulus that one can detect 50 percent of the time

accommodation in vision, the process in which the shape of the lens is changed by the ciliary muscles to focus an image on the retina

accommodation in Piaget's theory, the process of altering or revising an existing schema in the light of new information

acquired immune deficiency syndrome (AIDS) a deadly disease caused by a virus (HIV) that destroys the body's natural immune system, and which can be transmitted by sexual behaviors

acquisition the process in classical conditioning by which the strength of the CR increases with repeated pairings of the CS and UCS

acquisition the process in operant conditioning in which the rate of a reinforced response increases

action potential the short-lived burst of a change in the difference in electrical charge between the inside and the outside of a neuron when it fires (+40 mV)

actor-observer bias the overuse of internal attributions to explain the behaviors of others and external attributions to explain our own behaviors

addiction an extreme dependency, usually accompanied by symptoms of tolerance and painful withdrawal

adolescence the developmental period between childhood and adulthood, often begun at puberty and ending with full physical growth, generally between the ages of 12 and 20

affect the feelings or mood that accompany an emotional reaction

ageism discrimination or negative stereotyping formed solely on the basis of age

agoraphobia a phobic fear of open places, of being alone, or of being in public places from which escape might be difficult

algorithm a problem-solving strategy in which all possible solutions are generated and tested and an acceptable solution is guaranteed

alpha activity an EEG pattern associated with quiet relaxation and characterized by slow wave cycles of 8 to 12 per second

antianxiety drugs chemicals, such as the meprobamates and benzodiazepines, that alleviate the symptoms of anxiety

antidepressant drugs chemicals, such as MAO inhibitors and tricyclics, that reduce and/or eliminate the symptoms of depression

antipsychotic drugs chemicals, such as chlorpromazine, that are effective in reducing psychotic symptoms

anxiety a general feeling of apprehension or dread accompanied by predictable physiological changes

applied behavior analysis (ABA) an approach, based on operant conditioning, that attempts to find solutions to human environmental problems in the real world

aqueous humor watery fluid found in the space between the cornea and the lens that nourishes the front of the eye

arousal one's level of activation or excitement; indicative of a motivational state

assimilation the process of adding new material or information to an existing schema

association areas the areas of the frontal, parietal, and temporal lobes in which higher mental processing occurs

atonia muscular immobility, associated with REM sleep, caused by the total relaxation of the muscles

attitude a relatively stable and general evaluative disposition directed toward some object, consisting of feelings, behaviors, and beliefs

attribution the cognitions we generate when we attempt to explain the sources of behavior

audience inhibition reluctance to intervene and offer assistance in front of others

autokinetic effect the visual illusion of apparent motion in which a stationary pinpoint of light in an otherwise dark environment appears to move

autonomic nervous system (ANS) those neurons of the PNS that activate the smooth muscles and glands

aversion therapy a technique of behavior therapy in which an aversive stimulus, such as a shock, is paired with an undesired behavior

axon the long, taillike extension of a neuron that carries an impulse away from the cell body toward the synapse

axon terminals the series of branching end points of an axon where one neuron communicates with the next in a series

B

babbling speech sounds produced in rhythmic, repetitive patterns

baseline design a method in which subjects' performance with an experimental treatment is compared with performance without that treatment (the baseline)

basilar membrane a structure within the cochlea that vibrates and thus stimulates the hair cells of the inner ear

behavior what an organism does; an action of an organism that can be observed and measured

behavioral observation the personality assessment technique of drawing conclusions about one's personality based on observations of one's behaviors

behaviorism an approach to psychology emphasizing the overt, observable, measurable behavior of organisms

behavior therapy techniques of psychotherapy founded on principles of learning established in the psychological laboratory

blind spot a small region of the retina, containing no photoreceptors, where the optic nerve leaves the eye

brain stem the lowest part of the brain, just above the spinal cord, comprised of the medulla and the pons

brightness the psychological experience associated with a light's intensity or wave amplitude

British empiricists philosophers (including Locke) who claimed, among other things, that the contents of mind come from experience

C

case history an intensive, usually retrospective, detailed study of some aspects of one (or a few) individual(s)

cell body the largest mass of a neuron, containing the cell's nucleus, and which may receive neural impulses

central nervous system (CNS) those neurons in the brain and spinal cord

central tendency a measure of the middle, or average, score in a set of data

cerebellum a spherical structure at the lower rear of the brain involved in the coordination of bodily movements

cerebral cortex (or cerebrum) the large, convoluted outer covering of the brain that is the seat of cognitive functioning and voluntary action

cerebral hemispheres the two halves of the cerebral cortex, separated by a deep fissure running from front to back

chlamydia a very common STD; a bacterial infection of the genital area

chromosome literally, "colored body"; that tiny, threadlike structure found in 23 pairs in human cells that carry genes

chunk a somewhat imprecise concept referring to a meaningful unit of information as represented in memory

ciliary muscles small muscles attached to the lens that control its shape and focusing capability

classical conditioning learning in which an originally neutral stimulus comes to elicit a new response after having been paired with a stimulus that reflexively elicits that same response

client-centered therapy the humanistic psychotherapy associated with Rogers, aimed at helping the client grow and change from within

closure the Gestalt principle of organization that asserts that we tend to perceive incomplete figures as whole and complete

cochlea part of the inner ear where sound waves become neural impulses

cognitions the mental processes of knowing, perceiving, thinking, and remembering

cognitive dissonance a motivating discomfort or tension caused by a lack of balance or consonance among one's cognitions

cognitive reappraisal a rethinking of a stressful situation in a more positive light—for example, determining if a situation is real or imagined

cognitive restructuring therapy a form of cognitive therapy, associated with Beck, in which patients are led to overcome negative self-images and pessimistic views of the future

common fate the Gestalt principle of organization that says that we group together all the elements of a scene that move together in the same direction at the same speed

compulsions constantly intruding, stereotyped, and essentially involuntary acts or behaviors

conception the moment when the father's sperm cell unites with the mother's ovum to produce a zygote

concrete operations stage in Piaget's theory, from age 7 years to 12 years, when concepts can be manipulated, but not in an abstract fashion

concurrent validity the extent to which the scores on a test are correlated with other assessments made at about the same time

conditioned response (CR) in classical conditioning, the learned response (for example, salivation) evoked by the CS after conditioning

conditioned stimulus (CS) in classical conditioning, an originally neutral stimulus (for example, a tone) that, when paired with a UCS, comes to evoke a new response (a CR)

cones photosensitive cells of the retina that operate best at high levels of illumination and are responsible for color vision

conflict a stressor in which some goals can be satisfied only at the expense of other goals

conformity the changing of one's behavior, under perceived pressure, so that it is consistent with the behavior of others

consciousness our awareness or perception of the environment and of our own mental processes

conservation in Piaget's theory, an appreciation that changing the physical properties of an object does not necessarily change its essence

content validity the extent to which a test provides an adequate and fair sample of the behaviors being measured

contingency contracting establishing a token economy of secondary reinforcers to reward appropriate behaviors

contingency management bringing about changes in one's behaviors by controlling rewards and punishments

continuity the Gestalt principle of organization that claims that a stimulus or a movement will be perceived as continuing in the same smooth direction as first established

continuous reinforcement schedule (CRF) a reinforcement schedule in which each and every response is followed by a reinforcer

contrast the extent to which a stimulus is in some physical way different from other surrounding stimuli

control group participants in an experiment who do not receive any experimental treatment or manipulation

convergence the tendency of the eyes to move toward each other as we focus on objects up close

convergent thinking the reduction or focusing of many different ideas into one possible problem solution

conversion disorder the display of a severe physical disorder for which there is no medical explanation; often accompanied by an apparent lack of concern on the part of the patient

cornea the outermost structure of the eye which protects the eye and begins to focus light waves

corpus callosum a network of nerve fibers that interconnect the two hemispheres of the cerebrum

correlation a statistical technique used to determine the nature and extent of the relationship between two measured responses

correlation coefficient a number that indicates the nature (+ or −) and the strength (0 to 1) of the relationship between measured responses

cross-laterality the process of nerve fibers crossing over at the brain stem so that the left side of the body sends impulses to and receives impulses from the right side of the brain and vice versa

crowding the subjective feeling of discomfort caused by a sense of lack of space

D

dark adaptation the process by which our eyes become more sensitive to light as we spend time in the dark

death instincts (thanatos) inborn impulses, proposed by Freud, that compel one toward destruction; they include aggression

debrief to fully inform a subject about the intent and/or hypotheses of one's research once data have been collected

decibel scale a scale of experience of loudness in which 0 represents the absolute threshold and 140 is sensed as pain

defense mechanisms unconsciously applied techniques that protect the self (ego) from feelings of anxiety

dendrites branchlike extensions from a neuron's cell body where most neural impulses are received

denial refusing to acknowledge the presence of stressors

dependence a state in which drug use is either necessary or believed to be necessary to maintain functioning at some desired level

dependent variables responses measured in an experiment whose values are hypothesized to depend upon manipulations of the independent variable

depressants drugs (such as alcohol, opiates, heroin, and barbiturates) that slow or reduce nervous system activity

diagnosis the act of recognizing a disorder on the basis of the presence of particular symptoms

difference threshold the minimal difference in some stimulus attribute, such as intensity, that one can detect 50 percent of the time

diffusion of responsibility the tendency to allow others to share in the obligation to intervene

discrimination the phenomenon in classical conditioning in which an organism learns to make a CR in response to only one CS but not to other stimuli

discrimination the process in operant conditioning of differential reinforcement wherein one stimulus is reinforced while another stimulus is not

displacement directing one's motives at some substitute person or object rather than expressing it directly

dissociative disorder a disorder in which one separates from or dissociates from aspects of one's personality

divergent thinking the creation of many ideas or potential problem solutions from one idea

dominant gene a gene that carries a trait that will be expressed regardless of the gene it is paired with

Down's syndrome a condition of many symptoms, including mental retardation, caused by an extra (forty-seventh) chromosome

drive a state of tension resulting from a need that arouses and directs an organism's behavior

drug abuse a condition defined by lack of control, disruption of interpersonal relationships or difficulties at work, and a history of maladaptive drug use for at least one month

E

eardrum the outermost membrane of the ear; it is set in motion by the vibrations of a sound and transmits vibrations to the ossicles

ego the aspect of personality that encompasses the sense of "self"; in contact with the real world; operates on the reality principle

egocentric to be characterized by self; by "me" and "mine" and "my point of view"

elaborative rehearsal a mechanism for processing information into LTM that involves the meaningful manipulation of the information to be remembered

electroconvulsive therapy (ECT) a treatment, usually for the symptoms of severe depression, in which an electric current passed through a patient's head causes a seizure and loss of consciousness

electrode a fine wire used to either stimulate or record the electrical activity of neural tissue

electroencephalograph (EEG) an instrument used to measure and record the electrical activity of the brain

electromyograph (EMG) an instrument used to measure and record muscle tension/relaxation

emotion a reaction involving subjective feeling, physiological response, cognitive interpretation, and behavioral expression

empathic able to understand and share the essence of another's feelings, or to view from another's perspective

encoding the active process of representing, or putting information into memory

encoding specificity principle the hypothesis that we can retrieve only what we have stored and that retrieval is enhanced to the extent that retrieval cues match encoding cues

endocrine system a network of glands that secrete hormones directly into the bloodstream

environmental psychology the field of applied psychology that studies the effect of the general environment on organisms within it

episodic memory in LTM, the location where life events and experiences are stored

equity theory the view that workers are motivated to match their inputs and outcomes with those of fellow workers in similar positions

experiment a series of operations used to investigate relationships between manipulated events (independent variables) and measured events (dependent variables), while other events (extraneous variables) are eliminated

experimental group participants in an experiment who receive a treatment or manipulation—there may be more than one in such group in an experiment

external attribution an explanation of behavior in terms of something outside the person; a situational attribution

extinction the process in classical conditioning by which the strength of the CR decreases with repeated presentations of the CS alone (without the UCS)

extinction the process in operant conditioning in which the rate of a response decreases as reinforcers are withheld

extraneous variables factors in an experiment that need to be minimized or eliminated so as not to affect the relation between the independent and the dependent variable

F

family therapy a variety of group therapy focusing on the roles, interdependence, and communication skills of family members

fantasy an escape from stress through imagination and/or daydreaming

fetal alcohol syndrome a cluster of symptoms (*e.g.,* low birth weight, poor muscle tone, intellectual retardation), associated with a child born to a mother who was a heavy drinker of alcohol during pregnancy

figure-ground relationship the Gestalt psychology principle that stimuli are selected and perceived as figures against a ground or background

flashbulb memories particularly clear and vivid memories that are easily retrieved but not necessarily accurate in all detail

formal operations stage in Piaget's theory, ages older than 12 years, when one can generate and test abstract hypotheses, and think as an adult, where thinking follows rules

fovea the region at the center of the retina, comprised solely of cones, where acuity is best in daylight

free association the procedure in psychoanalysis in which the patient is to express whatever comes to mind without editing responses

frequency distribution an ordered listing of all *X*-values, indicating the frequency with which each occurs

frontal lobes the largest of the cerebral lobes, located in front of the central fissure and above the lateral fissure

frustration a stressor; the blocking or thwarting of goal-directed behavior

frustration-aggression hypothesis the view (now discredited) that all aggression stems from frustration

functionalism an approach to psychology emphasizing the study of the mind and consciousness as they help the organism adapt to the environment

functional fixedness the phenomenon in which one is unable to see a new use or function for an object because of experience using the object in some other function

fundamental attribution error the tendency to overuse internal attributions when explaining behavior

G

g on an intelligence test, a measure of one's overall, general intellectual abilities, commonly thought of as IQ

gate-control theory the theory of pain sensation that argues that there are brain centers that regulate the passage of pain messages from different parts of the body to the brain

gene the basic mechanism of hereditary transmission; that which gets passed from one generation to the next

general adaptation syndrome (GAS) a pattern of physiological reactions to stress, proceeding alarm to resistance to exhaustion

generalization the phenomenon in classical conditioning in which a CR is elicited by stimuli different from, but similar to, the CS

generalization the phenomenon in operant conditioning in which a response that was reinforced in the presence of one stimulus appears in response to other similar stimuli

generalized anxiety disorder persistent, chronic, and distressingly high levels of unattributable anxiety

genetics the science that studies the transmission of traits or characteristics from one generation to the next

genital herpes (Herpes type II) the most common STD; a skin infection in the form of a rash or blisters in the genital area

gestalt whole, totality, configuration; where the whole (gestalt) is seen as more than the sum of its parts

gonorrhea an STD caused by a bacterial infection of moist tissues in the genital area

group polarization the tendency for members of a group to give more extreme judgments following a discussion than they gave initially

groupthink a style of thinking of cohesive groups concerned with maintaining agreement to the extent that independent ideas are discouraged

growth spurt a marked increase in both height and weight that accompanies the onset of adolescence

H

habituation in classical conditioning, a simple form of learning in which an organism comes to ignore a stimulus of no consequence

hair cells the receptor cells for hearing, located in the cochlea, stimulated by the vibrating basilar membrane; they send neural impulses to the temporal lobe of the brain

hallucinogens drugs (such as LSD) whose major effect is the alteration of perceptual experience and mood

health psychology the field of applied psychology that studies psychological factors affecting physical health and illness

hertz (Hz) the standard measure of sound wave frequency that is the number of wave cycles per second

heuristic a problem-solving strategy in which hypotheses about problem solutions are generated and tested in a time-saving and systematic way, but that does not guarantee an acceptable solution

histogram a bar graph; a graphical representation of a frequency distribution

holophrastic speech the use of one word to communicate a number of different meanings

homeostasis a state of balance or equilibrium among internal, physiological conditions

homosexuals persons who are sexually attracted to and aroused by members of their own sex

hormones a variety of chemical compounds, secreted by the glands of the endocrine system, many of which have effects on behavior or mental states

hue the psychological experience associated with a light's wavelength

humanistic psychology an approach to psychology emphasizing the person or self as a central matter of concern

hypnosis an altered state of consciousness characterized by an increase in suggestibility, attention, and imagination

hypochondriasis a mental disorder involving the fear of developing some serious disease or illness

hypothalamus a small structure near the limbic system in the center of the brain, associated with feeding, drinking, temperature regulaion, sex, and aggression

hypothesis a tentative proposition or explanation that can be tested and confirmed or rejected

I

id the instinctive aspect of personality that seeks immediate gratification of impulses; it operates on the pleasure principle

idealistic principle the force that governs the superego; opposed to the id, it seeks adherence to standards of ethics and morality

identity crisis the struggle to define and integrate one's sense of self and what one's attitudes, beliefs, and values should be

illusion a perception that is at odds with (different from) what we know as physical reality

incentives external stimuli that an organism may be motivated to approach or avoid

independent variables events in an experiment that are manipulated by the experimenter that are hypothesized to produce changes in responses

industrial/organizational (I/O) psychology the subfield of psychology that studies the affects, behaviors, and cognitions of individuals in work settings

inferential statistics statistical tests of the significance of the results from experimental or correlational studies

inferiority complex the Adlerian notion that as children, in dealing with our environment, we develop a sense of inferiority that needs to be overcome before we can reach maturity

insanity a legal term for diminished capacity and inability to tell right from wrong

insomnia the chronic inability to get to sleep and to get an adequate amount of sleep

instincts unlearned, complex patterns of behavior that occur in the presence of particular stimuli

intelligence the capacity to understand the world and the resourcefulness to cope with its challenges; that which an intelligence test measures

interactive dualism Descartes's position that a separate body and mind influence each other and are thus knowable

intermittent reinforcement schedules reinforcement schedules in which responses are not reinforced every time they occur

internal attribution an explanation of behavior in terms of something (a trait) within the person; a dispositional attribution

interview the personality assessment technique involving a conversational interchange between the interviewer and subject to gain information about the subject

introspection a technique in which one examines one's own mental experiences and reports them in the most fundamental, basic terms

ion an electrically charged (either + or −) chemical particle

iris the colored structure of the eye that reflexively opens or constricts the pupils

J

job analysis a complete and specific description of a job, including the qualities required to do it well

job satisfaction an attitude; a collection of positive feelings about one's job or job experiences

just noticeable difference (j.n.d.) the smallest detectable change in some stimulus attribute, such as intensity

just world hypothesis the belief that the world is just and that people get what they deserve

K

kinesthetic sense the position sense that tells us the position of different parts of our bodies and what our muscles and joints are doing

L

language a collection of arbitrary symbols that follow certain rules of combination and that have significance for the language-using community

latent learning hidden learning that is not demonstrated in performance until that performance is reinforced

learning demonstration of a relatively permanent change in behavior that occurs as the result of practice or experience

lens the structure behind the iris that changes shape to focus visual images in the eye

libido the energy that activates the life (sexual) instincts (largely of the id)

life instincts (eros) inborn impulses, proposed by Freud, that compel one toward survival; these include hunger, thirst, and sex

light a radiant energy that can be represented in wave form with wavelength between 380 and 760 nanometers

limbic system a collection of structures, including the amygdala and septum, which are involved in emotionality; and the hippocampus, involved in forming long-term memories

lobotomy a psychosurgical technique in which the prefrontal lobes of the cerebral cortex are severed from lower brain centers

long-term memory (LTM) a type of memory with virtually unlimited capacity and very long, if not limitless, duration

loudness the psychological experience correlated with the intensity, or amplitude, of a sound wave

M

maintenance rehearsal a process of rote repetition (reattending) to keep information in STM

malleus, incus, and stapes (collectively, *ossicles*) three small bones that transmit and intensify sound vibrations from the eardrum to the oval window

matching phenomenon the tendency to select partners whose level of physical attractiveness matches our own

mean a measure of central tendency computed by dividing the sum of all scores by the number of observations; sometimes called the *average*

meaningfulness the extent to which information evokes associations with information already in memory

median the score above which and below which half the scores in an ordered set fall

meditation the focusing of awareness in order to arrive at an altered state of consciousness and relaxation

medulla an area of the brain stem that monitors breathing and heart rate, and where most cross laterality occurs

memory the cognitive ability to encode, store, and retrieve information

menarche a female's first menstrual period, often taken as a sure sign of the beginning of adolescence

mental retardation a condition indicated by an IQ below 70 that began during the developmental period and is associated with impairment in adaptive functioning

mental set a predisposed (set) way to perceive something; an expectation

mere exposure phenomenon the tendency to increase our liking of people and things the more we see of them

metamemory in LTM, our stored knowledge of how our own memory systems work

method of loci the mnemonic device that mentally places information to be retrieved at a series of familiar locations (loci)

Minnesota Multiphasic Personality Inventory (MMPI-2) a paper-and-pencil inventory of 567 true-false questions used to assess a number of personality dimensions, some of which may indicate the presence of a psychological disorder

mnemonic devices strategies for improving retrieval that take advantage of existing memories in order to make new material more meaningful

mode the most frequently occuring X-values in a set

modeling the acquisition of new responses through the imitation of another who responds appropriately

monochromatic literally *one-colored;* a pure light made up of light waves all of the same wavelength

mood disorders disorders of affect or feeling, usually depression; less frequently mania and depression occurring in cycles

motivation the process of arousing, maintaining, and directing behavior

motor areas the strips at the back of the frontal lobes that control voluntary movement

multiple personality the existence within one individual of two or more distinct personalities, each of which is dominant at a particular time

myelin a white, fatty covering found on some axons that serves to insulate and protect them, while increasing the speed of impulses

N

nanometer (nm) one millionth of a millimeter, the unit of measurement for the wavelength of light

narrative chaining the mnemonic device of relating words together in a story, thus organizing them in a meaningful way

naturalistic observation the method of observing and noting behaviors as they occur naturally

need a lack or shortage of some biological essential resulting from deprivation

need for affiliation the need to be with others and to form relationships and associations

need for power the learned need to be in control of events or persons, usually at another's expense

need to achieve (nAch) the learned need to meet or exceed some standard of excellence in performance

negative reinforcer a stimulus that increases the rate of a response when that stimulus is removed after the response is made

neo-Freudians personality theorists (including Adler, Jung, and Horney) who kept many basic psychoanalytic principles, but differed from a strict Freudian view, adding new concepts of their own

neonate the newborn, from birth to age 2 weeks

neural impulse a sudden and reversible change in the electrical charges within and outside the membrane of a neuron, which travels from the dendrite to the axon end of a neuron

neuron a nerve cell, the basic building block of the nervous system that transmits neural impulses

neurotoxins chemicals (poisons) that affect psychological processes through the nervous system

neurotransmitters chemical molecules released at the synapse that will, in general, either excite or inhibit neural impulse transmission

normal curve a commonly found symmetrical, bell-shaped frequency distribution

norms in the context of psychological testing, results of a test taken by a large group of subjects whose scores can be used to make comparisons or give meaning to new scores

norms in the context of social psychology, rules or expectations that guide our behavior in certain social situations by prescribing how we ought to behave

nuclei small collections or bundles of neural cell bodies

O

object permanence the appreciation that an object no longer in view can still exist and reappear later

observer bias the interference of the researcher's own motives, expectations, and past experiences with the objectivity of experimental observations

obsessions ideas or thoughts that involuntarily and persistently intrude into awareness

occipital lobes the cerebral lobes at the very back of the brain

operant referring to behavior(s) used by an organism to operate on its environment

operant conditioning changing the rate of a response on the basis of the consequences that result from that response

operational definition a definition of a concept given in terms of the methods (or operations) used to measure that concept

optic nerve a fiber composed of many neurons, which leaves the eye and carries impulses to the occipital lobe of the brain

orienting reflex the simple, unlearned response of orienting toward, or attending to, a new or unusual stimulus

overlearning the practice or rehearsal of material over and above what is needed to learn it

overregularization the excessive application of an acquired language rule (*e.g.,* for plurals or past tense) in a situation where it is not appropriate

P

panic disorder a disorder in which anxiety attacks suddenly and unpredictably incapacitate; there may be periods free from anxiety

parasympathetic division (of the ANS) those neurons involved in the maintenance of states of calm and relaxation

parietal lobes the lobes of the cerebrum found behind the frontal lobes, in front of the occipital lobes, and above the temporal lobes

peg word method the mnemonic device of forming interactive visual images of materials to be learned and items previously associated with numbers

perception the cognitive process of selecting, organizing, and interpreting stimuli

performance criteria specific behaviors or characteristics that a person should have in order to do a job as well as possible

peripheral nervous system (PNS) those neurons not found in the brain or spinal cord, but in the peripheral organs of the body

personality disorders enduring patterns of perceiving, relating to, and thinking about the environment and oneself that are inflexible and maladaptive

personal space the mobile "bubble" of space around you reserved for intimate relationships into which others may enter only by invitation

persuasion the process of intentionally attempting to change an attitude

phenomenological relating to an approach that emphasizes perception and awareness of events as being more important than the events themselves

phenomenology the study of events as they are experienced by the individual

phenylketonuria (PKU) a genetically caused disorder that produces mental retardation and that is now detectable and preventable

pheromones chemicals that produce an odor used as a method of communication between organisms

phi phenomenon the visual illusion of the apparent motion of stationary lights flashing on and off in sequence

phobic disorder an intense, irrational fear that leads a person to avoid the feared object, activity, or situation

photoreceptors light-sensitive cells (cones and rods) of the retina that convert light energy into neural energy

pinna the outer ear, which collects and funnels sound waves into the auditory canal toward the eardrum

pitch the psychological experience that corresponds to sound wave frequency and gives rise to high (treble) or low (bass) sounds

placebo an inactive substance that works because a person has come to believe that it will be effective

pleasure principle the impulse of the id to seek immediate gratification to reduce tensions

pluralistic ignorance a condition in which the inaction of others leads each individual in a group to interpret a situation as a nonemergency, thus leading to general inactivity

pons a brain stem structure forming a bridge between the brain and the spinal cord

population density a quantitative measure of the number of persons (or animals) per unit of area

positive reinforcer a stimulus that increases the rate of a response when it is presented after the response is made

posttraumatic stress disorder (PTSD) an anxiety disorder in which disruptive recollections, distressing dreams, flashbacks, and felt anxiety occur well after the experience of a traumatic event

predictive validity the extent to which a test can be used to predict future behaviors

prenatal period the period of development from conception to birth

preoperational stage In Piaget's theory, from age 2 years to 6 years, when a child begins to develop symbolic representations but cannot manipulate them; also characterized by egocentricity

primary reinforcers a stimulius (usually biologically or physiologically based) that increases the rate of a response with no previous experience required

proactive interference the inhibition of retrieval of recently learned material caused by material learned earlier

problem a situation in which there is a discrepancy between one's current state and one's desired or goal state, with no clear way of getting from one to the other

procedural memory in LTM, the storage area of stimulus-response associations and skilled patterns of responses

process schizophrenia schizophrenia in which the onset of the symptoms is comparatively slow and gradual

prognosis the prediction of the future course of an illness or disorder

projective technique a personality assessment technique requiring a subject to respond to ambiguous stimuli, thus projecting his or her self into the responses

proximity the Gestalt principle of organization that asserts that stimuli will be perceived as belonging together if they occur together in space or time

psychoactive drug a chemical that affects psychological processes and consciousness

psychoanalysis the form of psychotherapy associated with Freud, aimed at helping the patient gain insight into unconscious conflicts

psychoanalytic the approach to personality associated with Freud and his followers that relies on instincts and the unconscious as explanatory concepts

psychogenic amnesia a psychologically caused inability to recall important personal information

psychogenic fugue a condition of amnesia accompanied by unexplained travel or change of location

psycholinguistics the science that studies the cognitive processes involved in the use and acquisition of language

psychological test an objective, standardized measure of a sample of behavior

psychology the scientific study of behavior and mental processes

psychophysics the study of the relationship between physical attributes of stimuli and the psychological experiences they produce

psychosurgery a surgical procedure designed to affect one's psychological or behavioral reactions

psychotherapy the treatment of mental disorders through psychological means, effecting change in cognitions, affect, and/or behavior

puberty the stage of physical development at which one becomes capable of sexual reproduction

publicly verifiable the agreement (verifiability) of observers (public) that an event did or did not take place

punishment the administration of a punisher, which is a stimulus that decreases the rate or probability of a response that precedes it

pupil the opening in the iris that changes size in relation to the amount of light available and emotional factors

Q

quality of work life (QWL) a group of factors concerning one's work that influence one's attitude toward one's job

R

REM sleep rapid eye movement sleep during which vivid dreaming occurs, as do heightened levels of physiological functioning

random assignment the selection of members of a population in such a way that each has an equal opportunity to be assigned to any one group

range the difference between the highest and lowest scores in a distribution

rational-emotive therapy (RET) a form of cognitive therapy, associated with Ellis, aimed at changing the subject's irrational beliefs or maladaptive cognitions

rationalization generating excuses to explain one's behaviors rather than facing the real (anxiety-producing) reasons for those behaviors

reactive schizophrenia schizophrenia in which the onset of the symptoms is comparatively sudden

reality principle the force that governs the ego, arbitrating between the demands of the id, the superego, and the real world

recall a measure of retrieval in which an individual is given the fewest possible cues to aid retrieval

recessive gene a gene that carries a trait that will be expressed only if it is paired with another similar recessive gene

recognition a measure of retrieval in which an individual is required to identify as familiar material previously learned

reflex an unlearned, automatic response that occurs in the presence of specific stimuli

refractory period during the process of the human sexual response, the period following orgasm during which arousal in the male is not possible

regression a return to earlier, childish patterns of previously reinforcing behaviors as an escape from stress

reinforcement a process that increases the rate or probability of the response that it follows

reinforcers stimuli that increase the rate or probability of the responses they follow

relearning a measure of memory in which one notes an improvement in performance when material is learned for a second time

reliability consistency or dependability; in testing, consistency of test scores

repression "motivated forgetting" in which stressful events are forced from awareness into the unconscious and can no longer be remembered directly

resistance in psychoanalysis, the inability or unwillingness to freely discuss some aspect of one's life

resting potential the difference in electrical charge between the inside of a neuron and the outside when it is at rest (–70 mV)

reticular activating system (RAS) a network of nerve fibers extending from the brain stem to the cerebrum that is involved in maintaining levels of arousal

retina layers of cells at the back of the eye that contain the photosensitive rod and cone cells

retinal disparity the phenomenon in which each retina receives a different (disparate) view of the same three-dimensional object

retrieval the process of locating, removing, and using information that is stored in memory

retroactive interference the inhibition of retrieval of previously learned material caused by material learned later

rods photosensitive cells of the retina that are most active in low levels of illumination and do not respond differentially to different wavelengths of light

Rorschach inkblot test a projective technique in which the subject is asked to say what he or she sees in a series of inkblots

S

sample the portion of a larger population chosen for study

saturation the psychological experience associated with the purity of a light wave, where the most saturated lights are monochromatic and the least saturated are white light

schema a system of organized general knowledge, stored in long-term memory, that guides the encoding and retrieval of information

schizophrenia complex psychotic disorders characterized by impairment of cognitive functioning, delusions and hallucinations, social withdrawal, and inappropriate affect

science an organized body of knowledge gained through application of scientific methods

scientific methods systematic procedures of discovery that include observation, description, control, and replication

secondary reinforcers a stimulus that increases the rate of a response because of having been associated with other reinforcers; also called conditioned, or learned, reinforcer

semantic memory in LTM, the storage location for vocabulary, facts, simple concepts, rules, and the like

sensation the process of receiving information from the environment and changing that input into nervous system activity

sensorimotor stage in Piaget's theory, from birth to age 2 years, when a child learns by sensing and doing

sensory adaptation the process in which our sensory experience tends (in most cases) to decrease or diminish with continued exposure to a stimulus

sensory areas those areas of the cerebral cortex that receive impulses from our sense receptors

sensory memory the type of memory that holds large amounts of information registered at the senses for very brief periods of time

set point a normal, optimum level (or value) of equilibrium or balance among physiological or psychological reactions

sexually transmitted diseases (STDs) contagious diseases that are usually transmitted through sexual contact

shaping a procedure of reinforcing successive approximations of a desired response until that desired response is made

short-term memory (STM) a type of memory with limited capacity (7 ± 2 bits of information) and limited duration (15–20 seconds)

signal detection theory the view that stimulus detection is a matter of decision making, of separating a signal from background noise

similarity the Gestalt principle of organization that says that stimuli will be perceived together if they share some common characteristic(s)

social facilitation improved performance due to the presence of others

social interference impaired performance due to the presence of others

social learning theory the theory that learning takes place through observation and imitation of models

social loafing the tendency for a person to work less hard when part of a group in which everyone's efforts are pooled

social psychology the scientific study of how others influence the thoughts, feelings, and behaviors of the individual, and vice versa

somatic nervous system sensory and motor neurons outside the CNS that serve the sense receptors and the skeletal muscles

somatoform disorders psychological disorders that reflect imagined physical or bodily symptoms or complaints

spinal cord a mass of interconnected neurons within the spine that conveys impulses to and from the brain and is involved in some reflex behaviors

spinal reflex an automatic, involuntary response to a stimulus that involves sensory neurons carrying impulses to the spinal cord, interneurons within the spinal cord, and motor neurons carrying impulses to muscles

split-brain procedure a surgical technique of severing the corpus callosum, causing the two hemispheres to operate independently

spontaneous recovery the phenomenon in classical conditioning in which a previously extinguished CR returns after a rest interval

spontaneous recovery the phenomenon in operant conditioning in which a previously extinguished response returns after a rest interval

stage of the embryo developmental period from 2 to 8 weeks

stage of the fetus developmental period from week 8 until birth (months 3 through 9)

stage of the zygote developmental period from conception to the age of 2 weeks

standard deviation the average difference between the scores in a distribution and their mean

statistically significant differences differences in measurements that cannot be explained by chance or random factors

state-dependent memory the hypothesis that retrieval can be enhanced by the extent to which the state of one's mind at retrieval matches the state of mind at encoding

stereotype a generalized mental (cognitive) representation of someone that minimizes individual differences and is based on limited experience

stimulants drugs (such as caffeine, cocaine, and amphetamines) that increase nervous system activity

storage the process of holding encoded information in memory

strategy in problem solving, a systematic plan for generating possible solutions that can be tested to see if they are correct

stress a complex pattern of reactions to real or perceived threats to one's sense of well-being that motivates adjustment

stressors real or perceived threats to one's sense of well-being; sources of stress

subjective contours the perception of a contour (a line or plane) that is not there, but is suggested by other aspects of a scene

superego the aspect of personality that refers to ethical or moral considerations operating on the idealistic principle

survey a means of collecting observations from a large number of subjects, usually by interview or questionnaire

sympathetic division (of the ANS) those neurons involved in states of emotionality

synapse the general location where an impulse is relayed from one neuron to another by means of neurotransmitters

synaptic cleft the space between the membrane of an axon terminal and the membrane of the next neuron in a sequence

syphilis an STD caused by a bacterial infection, which may pass through four stages, ultimately resulting in death

systematic desensitization the application of classical conditioning procedures to alleviate anxiety in which anxiety-producing stimuli are paired with a state of relaxation

T

Thematic Apperception Test (TAT) a projective personality test requiring a subject to tell a series of short stories about a set of ambiguous pictures

taste buds the receptors for taste located in the tongue

temporal lobes the lobes of the cerebrum, located at the temples

territoriality the setting off and marking of a piece of territory (a location) as one's own

test-retest reliability a check of a test's consistency determined by correlating the results of a test taken by the same subjects at two different times

thalamus the last sensory relay station; it sends impulses to the appropriate area of the cerebral cortex

timbre the psychological experience related to wave purity by which we differentiate the sharpness, clearness, or quality of a tone

tolerance in using a drug, a state in which more and more of the drug is required to produce the same desired effect

training a systematic and intentional process of altering the behaviors of employees to increase organizational effectiveness

traits distinguishable, relatively enduring ways in which individuals may differ

transference in psychoanalysis, the situation in which the patient comes to feel about the analyst in the same way he or she once felt about some other important person

tremors involuntary, trembling, jerky movements

type A behavior pattern (TABP) a collection of behaviors (competitive, achievement-oriented, impatient, easily aroused, often hostile or angry) often associated with coronary heart disease

U

unconditioned response (UCR) in classical conditioning, a response (for example, salivation) reliably and reflexively evoked by a stimulus (the UCS)

unconditioned stimulus (UCS) in classical conditioning, a stimulus (for example, food powder) that reflexively and reliably evokes a response (the UCR)

V

validity in testing, the extent to which a test measures what it claims to measure

variability the extent of spread or dispersion in a set or distribution of scores

variance the square of the standard deviation

vesicles the small containers, concentrated in axon terminals, that hold neurotransmitter molecules

vestibular sense the position sense that tells us about balance, where we are in relation to gravity, and acceleration or deceleration

viability the ability to survive without interference or intervention

vicarious reinforcement (or punishment) increasing the rate (with reinforcement) or decreasing the rate (with punishment) of responses due to observing the consequences of someone else's behaviors

vitreous humor the thick fluid behind the lens of the eye that helps keep the eyeball spherical

W

wave amplitude a characteristic of wave forms (the height of the wave) that indicates intensity

wavelength a characteristic of wave forms that indicates the distance between any point on a wave and the corresponding point on the next cycle of the wave

white light a light of the lowest possible saturation, containing a mixture of all visible wavelengths

white noise a sound composed of a random assortment of wave frequencies from the audible spectrum

withdrawal a negative, painful reaction that may occur when one stops taking a drug

Z

zygote the one-cell product of the union of sperm and ovum at conception

A

Abel, E. L. (1981). Behavioral teratology. *Psychological Bulletin, 90,* 564–581.

Abel, E. L. (1984). *Fetal alcohol syndrome and fetal alcohol effects.* New York: Plenum.

Adams, G. R. (1977). Physical attractiveness, personality, and social reactions to peer pressure. *Journal of Psychology, 96,* 287–296.

Adams, G. R., & Gullotta, T. (1983). *Adolescent life experiences.* Monterey, CA: Brooks/Cole.

Adams, J. A. (1980). *Learning and memory: An introduction.* Homewood, IL: Dorsey Press.

Adams, J. L. (1974). *Conceptual blockbusting.* Stanford, CA: Stanford Alumni Association. Cited in A. L. Glass, K. J. Holyoak, & J. L. Santa (1979). *Cognition.* Reading, MA: Addison-Wesley.

Adams, J. S. (1965). *Inequity in social exchange.* In L. Berkowitz (Ed.), *Advances in experimental social psychology.* New York: Academic Press.

Adelmann, P. K., & Zajonc, R. B. (1989). Facial efference and the experience of emotion. *Annual Review of Psychology, 40,* 249–280.

Adler, T. (1989). Cocaine babies face behavior deficits. *APA Monitor, 20,* 14.

Adler, T. (1990). Does the "new" MMPI beat the "classic"? *APA Monitor, 21,* 18–19.

Agnew, H. W., Webb, W. W., & Williams, R. L. (1964). The effects of stage 4 sleep deprivation. *Electroencephalography and Clinical Neurophysiology, 17,* 68–70.

Aiello, J. R., & Aiello, T. D. (1974). The development of personal space: Proxemic behavior of children 6 through 16. *Human Ecology, 2,* 177–189.

Aiken, L. R. (1984). *Psychological testing and assessment* (4th ed.). Boston: Allyn & Bacon.

Ajzen, I., & Fishbein, M. (1980). *Understanding attitudes and predicting social behavior.* Englewood Cliffs, NJ: Prentice-Hall.

Alba, J. W., & Hasher, L. (1983). Is memory schematic? *Psychological Bulletin, 93,* 201–231.

Allen, B. P. (1987). Youth suicide. *Adolescence, 22,* 271–290.

Allen, M. G. (1976). Twin studies of affective illness. *Archives of General Psychiatry, 33,* 1476–1478.

Altman, I. (1975). *The environment and social behavior.* Monterey, CA: Brooks/Cole.

Amabile, T. M. (1985). Motivation and creativity. *Journal of Personality and Social Psychology, 48,* 393–399.

American Psychiatric Association. (1987). *Diagnostic and statistical manual of mental disorders* (3rd rev. ed.). Washington, DC: American Psychiatric Association.

American Psychological Association. (1990). Ethical principles of psychologists. *American Psychologist, 45,* 390–395.

Amoore, J. E. (1970). *Molecular basis of odor.* Springfield, IL: Thomas.

Anastasi, A. (1988). *Psychological testing* (6th ed.). New York: Macmillan.

Anderson, A. (1982). Neurotoxic follies. *Psychology Today, 16,* 30–42.

Anderson, C. A. (1987). Temperature and aggression: Effects on quarterly, yearly, and city rates of violent and nonviolent crime. *Journal of Personality and Social Psychology, 52,* 1161–1173.

Anderson, C. A. (1989). Temperature and aggression: Ubiquitous effects of heat on occurrence of human violence. *Psychological Bulletin, 106,* 74–96.

Anderson, C. A., & Anderson, D. C. (1984). Ambient temperature and violent crime: Tests of the linear and curvilinear hypotheses. *Journal of Personality and Social Psychology, 46,* 91–97.

Anderson, R., & Nida, S. A. (1978). Effect of physical attractiveness on opposite- and same-sex evaluations. *Journal of Personality, 46,* 401–413.

Anderson, J. C., Williams, S., McGee, R., & Silva, P. A. (1987). DSM-III disorders in preadolescent children. *Archives of General Psychiatry, 44,* 69–76.

Andreasen, N. C. (1982). Negative versus positive schizophrenia: Definition and validation. *Archives of General Psychiatry, 39,* 789–794.

Andreasen, N. C., Ehrhardt, J. C., Swayze, V. W., Alliger, R. J., Yuh, W. T. C., Cohen, G., & Ziebell, S. (1990). Magnetic resonance imaging of the brain in schizophrenia. *Archives of General Psychiatry, 47,* 35–44.

Andreasen, N. C., Flaum, M., Swayze, V. W., Tyrrell, G., & Arndt, S. (1990). Positive and negative symptoms in schizophrenia. *Archives of General Psychiatry, 47,* 615–621.

Andreasen, N. C., Olsen, S. A., Dennert, J. W., & Smith, M. R. (1982). Ventricular enlargement in schizophrenia: Definition and prevalence. *American Journal of Psychiatry, 139,* 292–296.

Angoff, W. H. (1988). The nature-nurture debate, aptitudes, and group differences. *American Psychologist, 43,* 713–720.

Anisfeld, M. (1984). *Language development from birth to three.* Hillsdale, NJ: Erlbaum.

Anisman, H., & Zacharko, R. M. (1982). Depression: The predisposing influence of stress. *The Behavioral and Brain Sciences, 5,* 89–137.

APA. (1987). Diagnostic and statistical manual of mental disorders (3rd rev. ed.). Washington, DC: *American Psychiatric Association.*

Aronson, E., & Linder, D. (1965). Gain and loss of esteem as determinants of interpersonal attractiveness. *Journal of Personality and Social Psychology, 1,* 156–171.

Aronson, E., Turner, J. A., & Carlsmith, J. M. (1963). Communicator credibility and communication discrepancy as a determinant of opinion change. *Journal of Abnormal and Social Psychology, 67,* 31–36.

Arvey, R. D., & Campion, J. E. (1982). The employee interview: A summary and review of recent research. *Personnel Psychology, 35,* 281–322.

Arvey, R. D., Miller, H. E., Gould, R., & Burch, P. (1987). Interview validity for selecting sales clerks. *Personnel Psychology, 40,* 1–12.

Asch, S. E. (1951). *The effects of group pressure upon the modification and distortion of judgment.* In H. Guetzkow (Ed.), *Groups, leadership, and men.* Pittsburgh: Carnegie Press.

Asch, S. E. (1956). Studies of independence and conformity: I. A minority of one against a unanimous majority. *Psychological Monographs: General and Applied, 70* (Whole No. 416), 1–70.

Aserinsky, E., & Kleitman, N. (1953). Regularly occurring periods of eye mobility and concomitant phenomena during sleep. *Science, 118,* 273–274.

Aslin, R. N., & Smith, L. B. (1988). Perceptual development. *Annual Review of Psychology, 39,* 435–473.

Atkinson, J. W., & Feather, N. T. (1966). *A theory of achievement motivation.* New York: Wiley.

Atkinson, J. W., & Litwin, G. H. (1960). Achievement motive and test anxiety conceived as motive to approach success and motive to avoid failure. *Journal of Abnormal and Social Psychology, 60,* 27–36.

Atkinson, R. C. (1975). Mnemotechnics in second-language learning. American *Psychologist, 30,* 821–828.

Auletta, K. (1984). Children of children. *Parade Magazine,* 17, 4–7.

Axelrod, S., & Apsche, J. (1983). *The effects of punishment on human behavior.* New York: Academic Press.

Azrin, N. H., & Holz, W. C. (1966). *Punishment.* In W. K. Honig (Ed.), *Operant behavior: Areas of research and application.* Englewood Cliffs, NJ: Prentice-Hall.

B

Backer, T. E., & Richardson, D. (1989). Building bridges: Psychologists and families of the mentally ill. *American Psychologist, 44,* 546–550.

Backman, C. W., & Secord, P. F. (1959). The effect of perceived liking on interpersonal attraction. *Human Relations,* 12, 379–384.

Baddeley, A. D. (1982). Domains of recollection. *Psychological Review, 89,* 708–729.

Bagozzi, R. P., & Burnkrant, R. E. (1979). Attitude organization and the attitude-behavior relationship. *Journal of Personality and Social Psychology, 37,* 913–929.

Bahrick, H. P. (1984). Semantic memory content in permastore. *Journal of Experimental Psychology:* General, 113, 1–29.

Balay, J., & Shevrin, H. (1988). The subliminal psychodynamic activation method: A critical review. *American Psychologist, 43,* 161–174.

Baley, S. (1985). The legalities of hiring in the 80s. *Personnel Journal,* 64, 112–115.

Ballenger, J. C. (1989). Toward an integrated model of panic disorder. *American Journal of Orthopsychiatry,* 59, 284–293.

Bandura, A. (1965). Influence of models' reinforcement contingencies on the acquisition of imitative responses. *Journal of Personality and Social Psychology,* 1, 589–595.

Bandura, A. (1973). *Aggression; A social learning analysis.* Englewood Cliffs, NJ: Prentice-Hall.

Bandura, A. (1974). Behavior theory and the models of man. *American Psychologist, 29,* 859–869.

Bandura, A. (1976). *Modeling theory: Some traditions, trends and disputes.* In W. S. Sahakian (Ed.), *Learning: Systems, models, and theories.* Skokie, IL: Rand McNally.

Bandura, A. (1977). *Social learning theory.* Englewood Cliffs, NJ: Prentice-Hall.

Bandura, A. (1982). Self-efficacy mechanism in human agency. *American Psychologist, 37,* 122–147.

Bandura, A., Ross, D., & Ross, S. A. (1963). Imitation of film-mediated aggressive models. *Journal of Abnormal and Social Psychology, 66,* 3–11.

Barber, T. F. X. (1972). *Suggested (hypnotic) behavior: The trace paradigm vs. an alternative paradigm.* In E. Fromm &

R. E. Shorr (Eds.), *Hypnosis: Research developments and perspectives.* Chicago: Aldine-Atherton.

Bard, P. (1934). *The neurohormonal basis of emotional reactions.* In C. A. Murchison (Ed.), *Handbook of general experimental psychology.* Worcester, MA: Clark University Press.

Barinaga, M. (1991). *Is homosexuality biological?* Science, 253, 956–957.

Barker, R. (1968). *Ecological psychology.* Stanford, CA: Stanford University Press.

Baron, R. A. (1977). *Human aggression.* New York: Plenum Press.

Baron, R. P. & Byrne, D. (1984). *Social psychology: Understanding human behavior* (4th ed.) Boston: Allyn and Bacon.

Baron, R. A., & Ransberger, V. M. (1978). Ambient temperature and the occurrence of collective violence: The "long hot summer" revisited. *Journal of Personality and Social Psychology, 36,* 351–360.

Barr, H. M., Streissguth, A. P., Darby, B. L., & Sampson, P. D. (1990). Prenatal exposure to alcohol, caffeine, tobacco, and aspirin: Effects on fine and gross motor performance in 4-year-old children. *Developmental Psychology, 26,* 339–348.

Barron, F., & Harrington, D. M. (1981). Creativity, intelligence, and personality. *Annual Review of Psychology, 32,* 439–476.

Bartus, R. T., Dean, R. L., Beer, B., & Lippa, A. S. (1982). The cholinergic hypothesis of geriatric memory dysfunction. *Science, 217,* 408–417.

Baumeister, A. A. (1987). Mental retardation: Some conceptions and dilemmas. *American Psychologist, 42,* 796–800.

Baumeister, R. F. (1985). The championship choke. *Psychology Today, 19,* 48–52.

Baumeister, R. F. (1987). How the self became a problem: A psychological review of historical research. *Journal of Personality and Social Psychology, 52,* 163–176.

Baumeister, R. F., & Steinhilber, A. (1984). Paradoxical effects of supportive audiences on performance under pressure: The home field disadvantage in sports championships. *Journal of Personality and Social Psychology, 47,* 85–93.

Bayley, N., & Schaefer, E. S. (1964). Correlations of maternal and child behaviors with the development of mental abilities: Data from the Berkeley Growth Study. *Monographs of the Society for Research in Child Development, 29,* 1–80.

Beck, A. T. (1967). *Depression: Clinical, experimental, and theoretical aspects.* New York: Harper Collins.

Beck, A. T. (1976). *Cognitive therapy and the emotional disorders.* New York: International University Press.

Beck, A. T. (1985). *Theoretical perspectives in clinical anxiety.* In A. H. Tuma & J. D. Master (Eds.), *Anxiety and the anxiety disorders.* Hillsdale, NJ: Erlbaum.

Beck, A. T., & Emery, G. (1985). *Anxiety disorders and phobias: A cognitive perspective.* New York: Basic Books.

Beckman, L. J., & Houser, B. B. (1982). The consequences of childlessness on the social-psychological well-being of older women. *Journal of Gerontology, 37,* 243–250.

Beer, M., & Walton, A. E. (1987). Organization change and development. *Annual Review of Psychology, 38,* 339–367.

Begg, I., & Paivio, A. (1969). Concreteness and imagery in sentence meaning. *Journal of Verbal Learning and Verbal Behavior,* 8, 817–821.

Bell, P. A., Fisher, J. D., & Loomis, R. J. (1978). *Environmental psychology.* Philadelphia: Saunders.

Benedict, H. (1979). Early lexical development: Comprehension and production. *Journal of Child Language,* 6, 183–200.

Bennett, T. L. (1982). *Introduction to physiological psychology.* Monterey, CA: Brooks/Cole.

Bennett, W. (1980). The cigarette century. *Science,* 80, 36–43.

Berkowitz, L. (1978). What ever happened to the frustration-aggression hypothesis? *American Behavioral Scientist,* 21, 691–708.

Berkowitz, L. (1982). Aversive conditions as stimuli to aggression. *Advances in Experimental Social Psychology,* 15, 249–288.

Berkowitz, L. (1989). Frustration-aggression hypothesis: Examination and reformulation. *Psychological Bulletin,* 106, 59–73.

Berkowitz, L. (1990). On the formation and regulation of anger and aggression. *American Psychologist,* 45, 494–503.

Berlyne, D. E. (1960). *Conflict, arousal, and curiosity.* New York: McGraw-Hill.

Berlyne, D. E. (1971). *Aesthetics and psychobiology.* Englewood Cliffs, NJ: Prentice-Hall.

Bertenthal, B. I., & Campos, J. J. (1989). *A systems approach to the organizing effects of self-produced locomotion during infancy.* In C. Rovee-Collier & L. P. Lipsett (Eds.), *Advances in infancy research.* Norwood, NJ: Ablex.

Beutler, L. E., Crago, M., & Arizmendi, T. G. (1986). *Therapist variables in psychotherapy process and outcome.* In S. L. Garfield & A. E. Bergin (Eds.), *Handbook of psychotherapy and behavior change* (3rd ed.), New York: Wiley.

Birdwhistell, R. L. (1952). *Introduction to kinesics.* Louisville, KY: University of Louisville Press.

Birnbaum, M. H., & Mellers, B. A. (1979). Stimulus recognition may mediate exposure effects. *Journal of Personality and Social Psychology,* 37, 391–394.

Block, J. (1965). *The challenge of response sets.* Englewood Cliffs, NJ: Prentice-Hall.

Bloom, F. E., Lazerson, A., & Hotstadter, L. (1985). *Brain, mind, and behavior.* San Francisco: Freeman.

Bootzin, R. R., & Acocella, J. R. (1984). *Abnormal psychology: Current perspectives* (4th ed.). New York: Random House.

Borbely, A. (1986). *Secrets of sleep.* New York: Basic Books.

Boring, E. G. (1930). A new ambiguous figure. *American Journal of Psychology,* 42, 109–116.

Bouchard, C., Tremblay, A., Després, J., et al. (1990). The response to long-term overfeeding in identical twins. *The New England Journal of Medicine,* 322, 1477–1482.

Bourne, L. E., Dominowski, R. L., & Loftus, E. F. (1983). *Cognitive process.* Englewood Cliffs, NJ: Prentice-Hall.

Bower, G. H. (1970). Imagery as a relational organizer in associative learning. *Journal of Verbal Learning and Verbal Behavior,* 9, 529–533.

Bower, G. H. (1972). Mental imagery and associative learning. In L. W. Gregg (Ed.), *Cognition in learning and memory.* New York: Wiley.

Bower, G. H. (1981). Mood and memory. *American Psychologist,* 36, 129–148.

Bower, G. H., & Clark, M. C. (1969). Narrative stories as mediators for serial learning. *Psychonomic Science,* 14, 181–182.

Bower, G. H., Monteiro, K. P., & Gilligan, S. G. (1978). Emotional mood as a context for learning and recall. *Journal of Verbal Learning and Verbal Behavior,* 17, 573–587.

Bower, G. H., & Springston, F. (1970). Pauses as recoding points in letter series. *Journal of Experimental Psychology,* 83, 421–430.

Bower, T. G. R., Broughton, J. M., & Moore, M. K. (1971). Infant responses to approaching objects: An indicator of response to distal variables. *Perception and Psychophysics,* 9, 193–196.

Bradley, D. R., & Dumais, S. T. (1975). Ambiguous cognitive contours. *Nature,* 257, 582–584.

Bradshaw, J. L., & Nettleton, N. C. (1983). *Human cerebral asymmetry.* Englewood Cliffs, NJ: Prentice-Hall.

Braine, M. D. S. (1976). Children's first word combinations. *Monographs for the Society for Research in Child Development,* 41 (Serial No. 164).

Bramel, D., & Friend, R. (1981). Hawthorne, the myth of the docile worker, and class bias in psychology. *American Psychologist,* 36, 867–878.

Bransford, J. D., & Johnson, M. K. (1972). Contextual prerequisites for understanding: Some investigations of comprehension and recall. *Journal of Verbal Learning and Verbal Behavior,* 11, 717–720.

Bratic, E. B. (1982). Healthy mothers, healthy babies coalition. *Prevention,* 97, 503–509.

Braun, P., Kochansky, G., Shapiro, R., Greenberg, S., Gudeman, J. E., Johnson, S., & Shore, M. (1981). Overview: Deinstitutionalization of psychiatric patients, a critical review of outcome studies. *American Journal of Psychiatry,* 138, 736–749.

Breckler, S. J. (1984). Empirical validation of affect, behavior, and cognition as distinct components of attitude. *Journal of Personality and Social Psychology,* 47, 1191–1205.

Bregman, J., Dykens, E., Watson, M., & Leckman, J. (1987). Fragile X syndrome: Variability in phenotype expression. Journal of the *American Academy of Child and Adolescent Psychiatry,* 26, 463–471.

Brent, D. A., Perper, J. A., Goldstein, C. E., Kolko, D. J., Allan, M. J., Allman, C. J., & Zelenak, J. P. (1988). Risk factors for adolescent suicide. *Archives of General Psychiatry,* 45, 581–588.

Brody, E. M. (1981). Women in the middle and family help to older people. *Gerontologist,* 21, 471–480.

Brody, E. M. (1985). Parent care as a normative family stress. *Gerontologist,* 25, 19–29.

Brown, J. (1958). Some tests of the decay theory of immediate memory. *Quarterly Journal of Experimental Psychology,* 10, 12–21.

Brown, J. (1976). *An analysis of recognition and recall and of problems in their comparison.* In J. Brown (Ed.), *Recall and recognition.* New York: Wiley.

Brown, J. I. (1973). *The Nelson-Denny Reading Test.* Boston: Houghton-Mifflin.

Brown, J. S. (1948). Gradients of approach and avoidances responses and their relation to motivation. *Journal of Comparative and Physiological Psychology,* 41, 450–465.

Brown, L., Durning, A., & Flavin, C. (1990). *State of the world.* New York: Norton.

Brown, R. (1973). *A first language: The early stages.* Cambridge, MA: Harvard University Press.

Brown, R., Cazden, C. B., & Bellugi, U. (1969). The child's grammar from 1 to 3. *Symposia on child language* (Vol. 2). Minneapolis: University of Minnesota Press.

Brown, R., & Kulik, J. (1977). Flashbulb memories. *Cognition,* 5, 73–99.

Browne, M. A., & Mahoney, M. J. (1984). Sport psychology. *Annual Review of Psychology,* 35, 605–626.

Bruch, H. (1980). Preconditions for the development of anorexia nervosa. *American Journal of Psychoanalysis,* 40, 169–172.

Bruner, J. S., & Goodman, C. C. (1947). Value and need as organizing factors in perception. *Journal of Abnormal and Social Psychology,* 42, 33–44.

Buck, R. (1980). Nonverbal behavior and the theory of emotion: The facial feedback hypothesis. *Journal of Personality and Social Psychology,* 38, 811–824.

Buck, R. (1985). Prime theory: An integrated view of motivation and emotion. *Psychological Review,* 92, 389–413.

Burisch, M. (1984). Approaches to personality inventory construction. *American Psychologist,* 39, 214–227.

Buss, A. H. (1966). *Psychopathology.* New York: Wiley.

Buss, A. H. (1989). Personality as traits. *American Psychologist,* 44, 1378–1388.

Buss, D., & Barnes, M. (1986). Preferences in human mate selection. *Journal of Personality and Social Psychology,* 50, 559–570.

Buss, D. M. (1984). Evolutionary biology and personality psychology. *American Psychologist,* 39, 1135–1147.

Butler, R., & Lewis, M. (1981). *Aging and mental health.* St. Louis: Mosby.

Butler, R. N., & Emr, M. (1982). SDAT research: Current trends. *Generations,* 7, 14–18.

Byrne, D. (1971). *The attraction paradigm.* New York: Academic Press.

C

Calhoun, J. B. (1962). Population density and social pathology. *Scientific American,* 206, 139–148.

Campos, J. J. (1976). *Heart rates: A sensitive tool for the study of emotional development.* In L. Lipsett (Ed.), *Developmental psychobiology: The significance of infancy.* Hillsdale, NJ: Erlbaum.

Campos, J. J., Hiatt, S., Ramsey, D., Henderson, C., & Svejda, M. (1978). *The emergence of fear on the visual cliff.* In M. Lewis & L. A. Rosenbaum (Eds.), *The development of affect.* New York: Plenum.

Cannon, T. D., Mednick, S. A., & Parnas, J. (1990). Antecedents of predominantly negative- and predominantly positive-symptom schizophrenia in a high-risk population. *Archives of General Psychiatry,* 47, 622–632.

Cannon, W. B. (1927). The James-Lange theory of emotions: A critical examination and an alternative theory. *American Journal of Psychology,* 39, 106–124.

Cannon, W. B. (1932). *The wisdom of the body.* New York: Norton.

Carey, S. (1978). *The child as word learner.* In M. Halle, J. Bresnan, & G. A. Miller (Eds.), *Linguistic theory and psychological reality.* Cambridge, MA: MIT Press.

Carson, R., Butcher, J. N., & Coleman, J. C. (1988). *Abnormal psychology and modern life (8th ed.).* Glenview, IL: Scott, Foresman.

Carson, R. C. (1989). Personality. *Annual review of psychology,* 40, 227–248.

Carson, R. L. (1962). *Silent Spring.* Boston: Houghton Mifflin.

Carson, T. P., & Carson, R. C. (1984). *The affective disorders.* In H. E. Adams & P. B. Sutker (Eds.)., *Comprehensive handbook of psychopathology.* New York: Plenum.

Cash, T. F., & Kilcullen, R. N. (1985). The eye of the beholder: Susceptibility to sexism and beautyism in the evaluation of managerial applicants. *Journal of Applied Social Psychology,* 15, 591–605.

Centers for Disease Control. (1985). *Suicide surveillance 1970–1980.* Atlanta: U.S. Department of Health and Human Resources.

Cermack, L. S., & Craik, F. I. M. (Eds.). (1979). *Levels of processing in human memory.* Hillsdale, NJ: Erlbaum.

Chaiken, S., & Stangor, C. (1987). Attitudes and attitude change. *Annual Review of Psychology,* 38, 575–630.

Chase, M. H., & Morales, F. R. (1990). The atonia and myoclonia of active (REM) sleep. *Annual Review of Psychology,* 41, 557–584.

Chasnoff, I. J., Griffith, D. R., MacGregor, S., Dirkes, K., & Burns, K. (1989). Temporal patterns of cocaine use in pregnancy. *Journal of the American Medical Association,* 261, 1741–1744.

Cheesman, J., & Merikle, P. M. (1984). Priming with and without awareness. *Perception and Psychophysics,* 36, 387–395.

Chilman, C. S. (1980). Parent satisfactions, concerns, and goals for their children. *Family Relations,* 29, 339–346.

Chilman, C. S. (1983). *Adolescent sexuality in a changing American society: Social and psychological perspectives for the human services profession* (2nd ed.). New York: Wiley.

Chomsky, N. (1965). *Aspects of a theory of syntax.* Cambridge, MA: Harvard University Press.

Chomsky, N. (1975). *Reflections on language.* New York: Pantheon Books.

Chuang, H. T., Devins, G. M., Hunsley, J., & Gill, M. J. (1989). Psychosocial distress and well-being among gay and bisexual men with immunodeficiency virus infection. *American Journal of Psychiatry,* 146, 876–880.

Clark, D. M, & Teasdale, J. D. (1985). Constraints on the effects of mood on memory. *Journal of Personality and Social Psychology,* 48, 1595–1608.

Clarkson-Smith, L., & Hartley, A. A. (1989). Relationships between physical exercise and cognitive abilities in older adults. *Psychology and Aging,* 4, 183–189.

Clore, G. L., & Byrne, D. (1974). *A reinforcement-affect model of attraction.* In T. L. Huston (Ed.), *Foundations of interpersonal attraction.* New York: Academic Press.

Cohen, S., Evans, G. W., Krantz, D. S., Stokols, D., & Kelly, S. (1980). Aircraft noise and children: Longitudinal and cross-sectional evidence on the adaptation to noise and the effectiveness of noise abatement. *Journal of Personality and Social Psychology,* 40, 331–345.

Cohen, S., Evans, G. W., Stokols, D., & Krantz, D. S. (1986). *Behavior, health, and environmental stress.* New York: Plenum.

Cohen, S., Lichtenstein, E., Prochaska, J. O., Rossi, J. S., Gritz, E. R., Carr, C. R., et al. (1989). Debunking myths about self-quitting: Evidence from 10 prospective studies of persons who attempt to quit smoking by themselves. *American Psychologist,* 44, 1355–1365.

Colby, A., & Kohlberg, L. (1984). *Invariant sequence and internal consistency in moral judgment stages.* In W. M. Kurtines & J. L. Gewitz (Eds.), *Morality, moral behavior, and moral development.* New York: Wiley.

Coles, R., & Stokes, G. (1985). *Sex and the American teenager.* New York: HarperCollins.

College Board. (1989). *College-bound seniors: 1989 SAT profile.* New York: College Entrance Examination Board.

Committee on an Aging Society. (1986). *America's aging: Productive roles in an older society.* Washington, DC: National Academy Press.

Comstock, G. A. (1980). *New emphases in research on the effects of television and film violence.* In E. L. Palmer & A. Dorr (Eds.). *Children and the Faces of Television.* New York: Academic Press.

Conger, J. J., & Peterson, A. C. (1984). *Adolescence and youth: Psychological development in a changing world.* New York: HarperCollins.

Conrad, R. (1963). Acoustic confusions and memory span for words. *Nature,* 197, 1029–1030.

Conrad, R. (1964). Acoustic confusions in immediate memory. *British Journal of Psychology,* 55, 75–84.

Cooper, J., & Croyle, R. T. (1984). Attitudes and attitude change. *Annual Review of Psychology,* 35, 395–426.

Cooper, L. A., & Shepard, R. N. (1973). *Chronometric studies of the rotation of mental images.* In W. G. Chase (Ed.), *Visual information processing.* New York: Academic Press.

Coren, S. (1972). Subjective contours and apparent depth. *Psychological Review,* 79, 359–367.

Coren, S., & Girgus, J. S. (1978). *Seeing is deceiving: The psychology of visual illusions.* Hillsdale, NJ: Erlbaum.

Corkin, S. (1984). *Lasting consequences of bilateral medial temporal lobectomy: Clinical course and experimental findings* in H. M. *Seminars in Neurology,* 4, 249–259.

Cornblatt, B. A., & Erlenmeyer-Kimling, L. (1985). Global attention deviance as a marker of risk for schizophrenia: Specificity and predictive validity. *Journal of Abnormal Psychology,* 94, 470–486.

Costa, P. T., & McCrae, R. R. (1980). *Still stable after all these years: Personality as a key to some issues in adulthood and old age.* In P. B. Baltes & O. G. Brim, Jr. (Eds.), *Life-span development and behavior.* New York: Academic Press.

Costello, C. G. (1982). Fears and phobias in women: A community study. *Journal of Abnormal Psychology,* 91, 280–286.

Coulter, W. A., & Morrow, H. W. (Eds.). (1978). *Adaptive behavior: Concepts and measurements.* New York: Grune & Stratton.

Cowan, W. M. (1979). *The development of the brain.* In *The brain* (pp. 56–69). San Francisco: Freeman.

Cowen, N. (1984). On short and long auditory stores. *Psychological Bulletin,* 96, 341–370.

Cox, R. H. (1990). *Sport psychology: Concepts and applications.* Dubuque, IA: Brown.

Coyle, J. T., Price, D. L., & DeLong, M. H. (1983). Alzheimer's disease: A disorder of central cholinergic innervation. *Science,* 219, 1184–1189.

Coyne, J. C., & Downey, G. (1991). Social factors and psychopathology: Stress, social support, and coping processes. *Annual Review of Psychology,* 42, 401–425.

Craik, F. I. M., & Lockhart, R. S. (1972). Levels of processing: A framework for memory research. *Journal of Verbal Learning and Verbal Behavior,* 11, 671–684.

Craik, F. I. M., & Tulving, E. (1975). Depth of processing and the retention of words in episodic memory. *Journal of Experimental Psychology: General,* 104, 268–294.

Creekmore, C. R. (1984). Games athletes play. *Psychology Today,* 19, 40–44.

Creekmore, C. R. (1985). Cities won't drive you crazy. *Psychology Today,* 19, 46–53.

Crews, D. J., & Landers, D. M. (1987). A meta-analytic review of aerobic fitness and reactivity to psychosocial stressors. *Medicine and Science in Sport and Exercise,* 19, 114–120.

Crockett, L. J., & Peterson, A. C. (1987). *Pubetal status and psychosocial development: Findings from the Early Adolescence Study.* In R. M. Lerner & T. T. Foch (Eds.), *Biological-psychosocial interactions in early adolescence: A life-span approach.* Hillsdale, NJ: Erlbaum.

Cronbach, L. J. (1984). *Essentials of psychological testing* (4th ed.). Cambridge, MA: HarperCollins.

Crow, T. J. (1980). Molecular pathology of schizophrenia: More than one disease process? *The British Medical Journal,* 280, 66–68.

Cunningham, S. (1984). Genovese: 20 years later, few heed stranger's cries. *APA Monitor,* 15, 30.

Curtis, R. C., & Miller, K. (1986). Believing another likes or dislikes you: Behaviors making the beliefs come true. *Journal of Personality and Social Psychology,* 51, 284–290.

Cutler, W. B., Preti, G., Krieger, A., Huggins, G. R., Ramon Garcia, C., & Lawley, H. J. (1986). Human axillary secretions influence women's menstrual cycles: The role of donor extract from men. *Hormones and Behavior,* 20, 463–473.

D

Daniel, T. C. (1990). Measuring the quality of the natural environment: A psychophysical approach. *American Psychologist,* 45, 633–637.

Darley, J. M., & Fazio, R. H. (1980). Expectancy confirmation processes arising in the interaction sequence. *American Psychologist,* 35, 861–866.

Darley, J. M., & Schultz, T. R. (1990). Moral rules: Their content and acquisition. *Annual Review of Psychology,* 41, 525–556.

Darling, C. A., & Davidson, J. K. (1986). Coitally active university students: Sexual behaviors, concerns, and challenges. *Adolescence,* 21, 403–419.

Darwin, C. (1959). *The origin of species.* London: John Murray.

Darwin, C. (1872). *The expression of emotion in man and animals.* New York: Philosophical Library [reprinted in 1955 and 1965 by the University of Chicago Press, Chicago].

Darwin, C. T., Turvey, M. T., & Crowder, R. G. (1972). An auditory analogue of the Sperling partial report procedure: Evidence for brief auditory storage. *Cognitive Psychology,* 3, 255–267.

Datan, N., Rodeheaver, D., & Hughes, F. (1987). Adult development and aging. *Annual Review of Psychology, 38,* 153–180.

Davidson, J. M., Smith, E. R., Rodgers, C. H., & Bloch, G. J. (1968). Relative thresholds of behavioral and somatic responses to estrogen. *Physiology and Behavior, 3,* 227–229.

Davis, K. (1985). Near and dear: Friendship and love compared. *Psychology Today, 19,* 22–30.

Davis, L. E., & Cherns, A. B. (1975). The quality of working life: Vol. I. *Problems, prospects and the state of the art.* New York: Free Press.

DeAngelis, T. (1989). Behavior is included in report on smoking. *APA Monitor, 20,* 3–4.

DeCasper, A. J., & Fifer, W. P. (1980). Of human bonding: Newborns prefer their mother's voice. *Science, 208,* 1174–1176.

deCuevas, J. (1990, September/October). "No, she holded them loosely." *Harvard Magazine,* pp. 60–67.

Deffenbacher, J. L. (1988). Some recommendations and directions. *Counseling Psychology, 35,* 234–236.

Dembroski, T. M., & Costa, P. T., Jr. (1987). Coronary prone behavior: Components of the Type A pattern and hostility. *Journal of Personality, 55,* 211–235.

Dement, W. C. (1960). The effect of dream deprivation. *Science, 135,* 1705–1707.

Dement, W. C. (1974). *Some must watch while some must sleep.* San Francisco: Freeman.

Dement, W. C., & Kleitman, N. (1957). The relation of eye movements during sleep to dream activity: An objective method for the study of dreaming. *Journal of Experimental Psychology, 53,* 339–346.

Deutsch, J. A. (1973). *The cholinergic synapse and the site of memory.* In J. A. Deutsch (Ed.), *The physiological basis of memory.* New York: Academic Press.

deVilliers, J. G., & deVilliers, P. A. (1978). *Language acquisition.* Cambridge, MA: Harvard University Press.

Digman, J. M. (1990). Personality structure: Emergence of the five-factor model. *Annual Review of Psychology, 41,* 417–440.

Dion, K. K., Berscheid, E., & Walster (Hatfield), E. (1972). What is beautiful is good. *Journal of Personality and Social Psychology, 24,* 285–290.

Dirkes, M. A. (1978). The role of divergent production in the learning process. *American Psychologist, 33,* 815–820.

Dixon, N. F. (1971). *Subliminal perception: The nature of a controversy.* New York: McGraw-Hill.

Dixon, N. F. (1981). *Preconscious processing.* New York: Wiley.

Dobson, K. S. (1988). *Handbook of cognitive-behavioral therapies.* New York: Guilford.

Doll, R., & Peto, R. (1981). *The causes of cancer.* New York: Oxford University Press.

Dollard, J., Doob, L., Miller, N., Mowrer, O. H., & Sears, R. R. (1939). *Frustration and aggression.* New Haven, CT: Yale University Press.

Domjan, M. (1987). Animal learning comes of age. *American Psychologist, 42,* 556–564.

Donenberg, G. R., & Hoffman, L. W. (1988). Gender differences in moral development. *Sex Roles, 18,* 701–717.

Doty, R. Y. (1986). *Gender and endocrine-related influences on human olfactory perception.* In H. Meiselman & R. S. Rivlin (Eds.), *Clinical measurement of taste and smell.* New York: Macmillan.

Dove, A. (1968). Taking the Chitling Test. *Newsweek,* July.

Drakeley, R. J., Herriot, P., & Jones, A. (1988). Biographical data, training success and turnover. *Journal of Occupational Psychology, 61,* 145–152.

Duffy, E. (1962). *Activation and behavior.* New York: Wiley.

Duncan, J. (1985). Two techniques for investigating perception without awareness. *Perception and Psychophysics, 38,* 296–298.

Duncker, K. (1945). On problem solving. *Psychological Monographs, 58* (Whole No. 270).

Dunnette, M. D., & Borman, W. C. (1979). Personnel selection and classification systems. *Annual Review of Psychology, 30,* 477–525.

Dweck, C. S. (1986). Motivational processes affecting learning. *American Psychologist, 41,* 1040–1048.

E

Ebbinghaus, H. E. (1885/1964). *Memory: A contribution to experimental psychology.* New York: Dover.

Edwards, C. P. (1977). *The comparative study of the development of moral judgment and reasoning.* In R. L. Munroe, R. Munroe, & B. B. Whiting (Eds.), *Handbook of cross-cultural human development.* New York: Garland.

Eich, J. E., Weingartner, H., Stillman, R. C., & Gillan, J. C. (1975). State-dependent accessibility of retrieval cues in the retention of a categorized list. *Journal of Verbal Learning and Verbal Behavior, 14,* 408–417.

Eisdorfer, C. (1983). Conceptual models of aging. *American Psychologist, 38,* 197–202.

Ekman, P. (1972). *Universals and cultural differences in facial expression of emotion.* In J. K. Cole (Ed.), *Nebraska symposium on motivation.* Lincoln: University of Nebraska Press.

Ekman, P. (1973). *Cross-cultural studies in facial expression.* In P. Ekman (Ed.), *Darwin and facial expressions: A century of research in review.* New York: Academic Press.

Ekman, P., Friesen, W. V., O'Sullivan, M., Diacoyanni-Tarlatzis, I., Krause, R., et al. (1987). Universals and cultural differences in the judgment of facial expressions of emotion. *Journal of Personality and Social Psychology, 53,* 712–717.

Ekman, P., Levenson, R. W., & Friesen, W. V. (1983). Autonomic nervous system activity distinguishes among emotions. *Science, 221,* 1208–1210.

Elkind, D. (1967). Egocentrism in adolescence. *Child Development, 38,* 1025–1034.

Elkind, D. (1981). *Children and adolescents: Interpretive essays on Jean Piaget.* New York: Oxford University Press.

Elkind, D. (1984). *All grown up and no place to go.* Reading, MA: Addison-Wesley.

Elkind, D., & Bowen, R. (1979). Imaginary audience behavior in children and adolescents. *Developmental Psychology, 15,* 38–44.

Elliott, J. (1977). *The power and pathology of prejudice.* In P. G. Zimbardo & F. L. Ruch, *Psychology and life* (9th ed., Diamond Printing). Glenview, IL: Scott, Foresman.

Ellis, A. (1970). *Reason and emotion in psychotherapy.* Secaucus, NJ: Stuart.

Ellis, A. (1973). *Humanistic psychotherapy: The rational-emotive approach.* New York: McGraw-Hill.

Ellis, A. (1987). The impossibility of achieving consistently good mental health. *American Psychologist, 42,* 364–375.

Ellis, A. (1991). *How can psychological treatment aim to be briefer and better?* The rational-emotive approach to brief therapy. In K. N. Anchor (Ed.), *Handbook of medical psychotherapy.* Toronto: Hogrefe & Huber.

Ellis, L., & Ames, M. A. (1987). Neurohormonal functioning and sexual orientation: A theory of homosexuality-heterosexuality. *Psychological Bulletin,* 101, 233–258.

Entwistle, D. (1966). *Word Associations of Young Children.* Baltimore: Johns Hopkins University Press.

Epstein, S. M. (1967). *Toward a unified theory of anxiety.* In B. A. Maher (Ed.), *Progress in experimental personality research.* New York: Academic Press.

Erez, M., & Zidon, I. (1984). Effect of goal acceptance on the relationship of goal difficulty to performance. *Journal of Applied Psychology,* 69, 69–78.

Erikson, E. H. (1963). *Childhood and society.* New York: Norton.

Erikson, E. H. (1965). *The challenge of youth.* Garden City, NY: Doubleday (Anchor Books).

Erikson, E. H. (1968). *Identity: Youth and crisis.* New York: Norton.

Erlenmeyer-Kimling, L. (1968). *Studies on the offspring of two schizophrenic parents.* In D. Rosenthal & S. S. Kety (Eds.), *The transmission of schizophrenia.* Elmsford, NY: Pergamon Press.

Erlenmeyer-Kimling, L., & Jarvik, L. F. (1963). Genetics and intelligence: A review. *Science,* 142, 1477–1479.

Eron, L. D. (1982). Parent-child interaction, television violence, and aggression in children. *American Psychologist,* 37, 197–211.

Erwin, E. (1980). Psychoanalytic therapy: The Eysenck argument. *American Psychologist,* 35, 435–443.

Evans, G. W., & Howard, R. B. (1973). Personal space. *Psychological Bulletin,* 80, 334–344.

Eysenck, H. J. (1952). The effects of psychotherapy: An evaluation. *Journal of Consulting Psychology,* 16, 319–324.

Eysenck, H. J. (1960). *Behavior Therapy and the Neuroses.* London: Pergamon Press.

Eysenck, H. J. (1973). *The inequality of man.* London: Temple Smith.

Eysenck, H. J., & Eysenck, S. B. G. (1976). *Psychoticism as a dimension of personality.* London: Hodder & Stoughton.

F

Falbo, T., & Peplau L. A. (1980). Power strategies in intimate relationships. *Journal of Personality and Social Psychology,* 38, 618–628.

Fantz, R. L. (1961). The origin of form perception. *Scientific American,* 204, 66–72.

Fantz, R. L. (1963). Pattern vision in newborn infants. *Science,* 140, 296–297.

Farrell, M. P., & Rosenberg, S. D. (1981). *Men at midlife.* Boston: Auburn House.

Fast, J. (1970). *Body language.* New York: M. Evans.

Fazio, R. H. (1989). *On the power and functionality of attitudes: The role of attitude accessibility.* In A. R. Pratkanis, S. J. Breckler, & A. G. Greenwald (Eds.), *Attitude structure and function.* Hillsdale, NJ: Erlbaum.

Feeney, J. A., & Noller, P. (1990). Attachment style as a predictor of adult romantic relationships. *Journal of Personality and Social Psychology,* 58, 281–291.

Fein, G. G., Schwartz, P. M., Jacobson, S. W., & Jacobson, J. L. (1983). Environmental toxins and behavior development. *American Psychologist,* 38, 1188–1197.

Fenker, R. M., & Lambiotte, J. G. (1987). A performance enhancement program for a college football team: One incredible season. *The Sport Psychologist,* 1, 224–236.

Festinger, L. (1957). *A theory of cognitive dissonance.* Stanford, CA: Stanford University Press.

Festinger, L., & Carlsmith, J. M. (1959). Cognitive consequences of forced compliance. *Journal of Abnormal and Social Psychology,* 58, 203–210.

Festinger, L., Schachter, S., & Back, K. (1950). *Social processes in informal groups: A study of human factors in housing.* New York: HarperCollins.

Finnegan, L. P. (1982). *Outcome of children born to women dependent upon narcotics.* In B. Stimmel (Ed.), *The effects of maternal alcohol and drug abuse on the newborn.* New York: Haworth.

Fischhoff, B. (1990). Psychology and public policy: Tool or toolmaker? *American Psychologist,* 45, 647–653.

Fishbein, M., & Ajzen, I. (1975). *Belief, attitude, intention, and behavior: An introduction to theory and research.* Reading, MA: Addison-Wesley.

Fisher, A. C. (1977). Sport personality assessment: Facts, fallacies, and perspectives. *Motor Skills: Theory into Practice,* 1, 87–97.

Fisher, S., & Greenberg, R. P. (1977). *The scientific credibility of Freud's theories and therapy.* New York: Basic Books.

Fishman, J. (1987). Type A on trial. *Psychology Today,* 21, 42–50.

Flament, M. F., Rapoport, J. L., Berg, C. J., Sceery, W., Kilts, C., Mellstrom, B., & Linnoila, M. (1985). Clomipramine treatment of childhood obsessive-compulsive disorder: A double-blind study. *Archives of General Psychiatry,* 42, 977–983.

Flament, M. F., Whitaker, A., Rapoport, J. L., Davies, M., Berg, C. Z., Kalikow, K., Sceery, W., & Shaffer, D. (1988). Obsessive-compulsive disorder in adolescence: An epidemiologic study. *Journal of the American Academy of Child and Adolescent Psychiatry,* 27, 289–296.

Flavell, J. H. (1982). On cognitive development. *Child Development,* 53, 1–10.

Flexser, A. J., & Tulving, E. (1982). Priming and recognition failure. *Journal of Verbal Learning and Verbal Behavior,* 21, 237–248.

Folkman, S. (1984). Personal control and stress and coping processes: A theoretical analysis. *Journal of Personality and Social Psychology,* 46, 839–852.

Ford, M. R., & Lowery, C. R. (1986). Gender differences in moral reasoning: A comparison of justice and care orientations. *Journal of Personality and Social Psychology,* 4, 777–783.

Forisha-Kovach, B. (1983). *The experience of adolescence.* Glenview, IL: Scott, Foresman.

Fowler, C. A., Wolford, G., Slade, R., & Tassinary, L. (1981). Lexical access with and without awareness. *Journal of Experimental Psychology: General,* 110, 341–362.

Fowles, D. G. (1990). *A profile of older Americans:* 1989. Washington, DC: American Association of Retired Persons.

Frank, E., Kupfer, D. J., Perel, J. M., Cornes, C., Jarrett, D. B., et al. (1990). Three-year outcomes for maintenance therapies in recurrent depression. *Archives of General Psychiatry,* 47, 1093–1099.

Frankenburg, W. K., & Dodds, J. B. (1967). The Denver Developmental Screening Test. *Journal of Pediatrics,* 71, 181–191.

Frazier, T. M., David, G. H., Goldstein, H., & Goldberg, I. D. (1961). Cigarette smoking and prematurity. *American Journal of Obstetrics and Gynecology,* 81, 988–996.

Free, M. L., & Oei, T. P. S. (1989). Biological and psychological processes in the treatment and maintenance of depression. *Clinical Psychology Review,* 9, 653–688.

Freedman, D. X. (1984). Psychiatric epidemiology counts. *Archives of General Psychiatry,* 41, 931–934.

Freedman, J. L. (1975). *Crowding and behavior.* New York: Viking Press.

Freedman, J. L. (1988). Television violence and aggression: What the evidence shows. *Applied Social Psychology Annual,* 8, 144–162.

Freeman, J. L. (1984). Effect of television violence on aggressiveness. *Psychological Bulletin,* 96, 227–246.

Freud, A. (1958). *Adolescence: Psychoanalytic study of the child.* New York: Academic Press.

Fribourg, S. (1982). Cigarette smoking and sudden infant death syndrome. *Journal of Obstetrics and Gynecology,* 142, 934–941.

Friedman, H. S., & Booth-Kewley, S. (1987). The "disease-prone personality": A meta-analytic review of the construct. *American Psychologist,* 42, 539–555.

Friedman, M., & Rosenman, R. (1959). Association of specific overt behavior patterns with blood and cardiovascular findings. *Journal of the American Medical Association,* 169, 1286.

Friedman, M. I., & Stricker, E. M. (1976). The physiological psychology of hunger: A physiological perspective. *Psychological Review,* 83, 409–431.

Friedman, S. (1972). Habituation and recovery of visual response in the alert human newborn. *Journal of Experimental Child Psychology,* 13, 339–349.

Frijda, N. H. (1988). The laws of emotion. *American Psychologist,* 43, 349–358.

Furstenberg, F. F., Brooks-Gunn, J., & Chase-Lansdale, L. (1989). Teenaged pregnancy and childbearing. *American Psychologist,* 44, 313–320.

G

Gabrielli, W. F., & Plomin, R. (1985). Drinking behavior in the Colorado adoptee and twin sample. *Journal of Studies on Alcohol,* 46, 24–31.

Gagné, R. M. (1984). Learning outcomes and their effects: Useful categories of human performance. *American Psychologist,* 39, 377–385.

Galanter, E. (1962). *Contemporary psychophysics.* In R. Brown et al. (Eds.), *New directions in psychology.* New York: Holt, Rinehart and Winston.

Garbarino, J. (1985). *Adolescent development: An ecological perspective.* Columbus, OH: Merrill.

Gardner, E. (1963). *Fundamentals of neurology.* Philadelphia: Saunders.

Gardner, L., & Neu, R. (1972). Evidence linking an extra Y chromosome to sociopathic behavior. *Archives of General Psychiatry,* 26, 220–222.

Garfield, S. L. (1981). Psychotherapy: A 40-year appraisal. *American Psychologist,* 36, 174–183.

Garner, D. M., Olmsted, M. P., Davis, R., Rockert, W., Goldbloom, D., & Eagle, M. (1990). The association between bulimic symptoms and reported psychopathology. *International Journal of Eating Disorders,* 9, 1–15.

Gazzaniga, M. S., & LeDoux, J. E. (1978). *The integrated mind.* New York: Plenum.

Geen, R. G., & Thomas, S. L. (1986). The immediate effects of media violence on behavior. *Journal of Social Issues,* 42, 7–28.

Geller, E. S. (1985). The behavior change approach to litter management. *Journal of Resource Management,* 14, 117–122.

Geller, E. S. (1986). Prevention of environmental problems. In B. A. Edelstein & L. Michelson (Eds.), *Handbook of prevention.* New York: Plenum.

Geller, E. S., Bruff, C. D., & Nimmer, J. G. (1985). "Flash for life": Community-based prompting for safety belt promotion. *Journal of Applied Behavioral Analysis,* 18, 309–314.

Geller, E. S., & Lehman, G. R. (1986). Motivating desirable waste management behavior: Applications of behavioral analysis. *Journal of Resource Management,* 15, 58–68.

Geller, E. S., & Nimmer, J. G. (1985). *Social marketing and applied behavior analysis: An integration for quality of life intervention.* Blacksburg: Virginia Polytechnic Institute and State University.

Geller, E. S., Rudd, J. R., Kalsher, M. J., Sreff, F. M., & Lehman, G. R. (1987). Employer-based programs to motivate safety belt use: A review of short-term and long-term effects. *Journal of Safety Research,* 18, 1–17.

Gellhorn, E. (1964). Motion and emotion: The role of proprioception in the physiology and pathology of the emotions. *Psychological Review,* 71, 457–472.

Gelman, R. (1978). Cognitive development. *Annual Review of Psychology,* 29, 297–332.

Gelso, C. J., & Fassinger, R. E. (1990). Counseling psychology: Theory and research on interventions. *Annual Review of Psychology,* 41, 355–386.

Geracioti, T. D., & Liddle, R. A. (1988). Impaired cholecystokinin secretion in bulimia nervosa. *New England Journal of Medicine,* 319, 683–688.

Gerow, J. R., & Murphy, D. P. (1980). The validity of the Nelson-Denny Reading Test as a predictor of performance in introductory psychology. *Educational and Psychological Measurement,* 40, 553–556.

Gibson, E. J. (1987). Introductory essay: What does infant perception tell us about theories of perception? *Journal of Experimental Psychology: Perception and Performance,* 13, 515–523.

Gibson, E. J. (1988). Exploratory behavior in the development of perceiving, acting, and the acquiring of knowledge. *Annual Review of Psychology, 39,* 1–41.

Gibson, E. J., & Walk, R. D. (1960). The visual cliff. *Scientific American, 202,* 64–71.

Gillam, B. (1980). Geometrical illusions. *Scientific American, 242,* 102–111.

Gilligan, C. (1982). *In a different voice.* Cambridge, MA: Harvard University Press.

Glasgow, R. E., & Lichtenstein, E. (1987). Long term effects of behavioral smoking cessation interventions. *Behavior Therapy, 18,* 297–324.

Glass, A. L., Holyoak, K. J., & Santa, J. L. (1979). *Cognition.* Reading, MA: Addison-Wesley.

Glass, D. C., & Singer, J. E. (1972). *Urban stress.* Hillsdale, NJ: Erlbaum.

Glass, D. C., Singer, J. E., & Friedman, L. N. (1969). Psychic cost of adaptation to an environmental stressor. *Journal of Personality and Social Psychology, 12,* 200–210.

Glenn, N. D., & Weaver, C. N. (1981). The contribution of marital happiness to global happiness. *Journal of Marriage and the Family, 43,* 161–168.

Glueck, S., & Glueck, E. (1950). *Unraveling Juvenile Delinquency.* New York: Commonwealth Fund.

Glueck, S., & Glueck, E. (1956). *Physique and Delinquency.* New York: Harper & Row.

Golbus, M. S. (1980). Teratology for the obstetrician: Current status. American Journal of Obstetrics and Gynecology, 55, 269.

Gold, P. E. (1987). Sweet memories. *American Scientist, 75,* 151–155.

Goldfried, M. R., Greenberg, L. S., & Marmar, C. (1990). Individual psychotherapy: Process and outcome. *Annual Review of Psychology, 41,* 659–688.

Goldstein, I. L. (1980). Training in work organizations. *Annual Review of Psychology, 31,* 229–272.

Goldstein, I. L. (1986). *Training in organizations.* Monterey, CA: Brooks/Cole.

Goleman, O. (1980). 1,528 little geniuses and how they grew. *Psychology Today, 14,* 28–53.

Goodwin, D. W., Powell, B., Bremer, D., Hoine, H., & Stein, J. (1969). Alcohol and recall: State-dependent effects in man. *Science, 163,* 1358–1360.

Gorenstein, E. E. (1984). Debating mental illness. *American Psychologist, 39,* 50–56.

Gottesman, I. I., & Bertelsen, A. (1989). Confirming unexpressed genotypes for schizophrenia. *Archives of General Psychiatry, 46,* 867–872.

Gottlieb, B. H. (1981). *Social networks and social support.* Beverly Hills, CA: Sage.

Gough, H. G. (1985). A work orientation scale for the California Psychological Inventory. *Journal of Applied Psychology, 70,* 505–513.

Gracely, R. H., Lynch, S., & Bennett, G. J. (1991). *The central process responsible for AßLTM-mediated allodynia in some patients with RSD is sensitive to perfusion of the microenvironment of nociceptor terminals.* Paper presented at the 21st Annual Meeting of the Society for Neuroscience. New Orleans.

Graf, P., & Schacter, D. A. (1985). Implicit and explicit memory for new associations in normal and amnesic subjects. *Journal of Experimental Psychology: Learning, Memory, and Cognition, 11,* 501–518.

Green, D. M., & Swets, J. A. (1966). *Signal detection theory and psychophysics.* New York: Wiley.

Greenberg, J., & Cohen, R. L. (1982). *Equity and justice in social behavior.* New York: Academic Press.

Greenberg, L. S., & Safran, J. D. (1987). *Emotion in psychotherapy.* New York: Guilford.

Greenberg, L. S., & Safran, J. D. (1989). Emotion in psychotherapy. *American Psychologist, 44,* 19–29.

Greenough, W. T. (1984). Structural correlates of information storage in mammalian brain. *Trends in Neurosciences, 7,* 229–233.

Greer, S. (1964). Study of parental loss in neurotics and sociopaths. *Archives of General Psychiatry, 11,* 177–180.

Gregory, R. L. (1977). *Eye and brain: The psychology of seeing (3rd ed.).* New York: New World Library.

Grinspoon, L. (1977). *Marihuana reconsidered (2nd ed.).* Cambridge, MA: Harvard University Press.

Gross, R. T., & Duke, P. M. (1980). The effect of early and late maturation on adolescent behavior. *The Pediatric Clinics of North America, 27,* 71–77.

Grossman, H. J. (Ed.). (1973). *Manual on terminology and classification in mental retardation.* Washington, DC: American Association on Mental Deficiency.

Grossman, H. (Ed.) (1983). *Classification in Mental Retardation (3rd Ed.).* Washington, DC: American Association of Mental Deficiency.

Guilford, J. P. (1959a). *Personality.* New York: McGraw-Hill.

Guilford, J. P. (1959b). *Traits of creativity.* In H. H. Anderson (Ed.), *Creativity and its cultivation.* New York: Harper-Collins.

Guion, R. M., & Gibson, W. M. (1988). Personnel selection and placement. *Annual Review of Psychology, 39,* 349–374.

Gur, R. E., Resnick, S. M., Alavi, A., Gur, R. C., Caroff, S., Dann, R., et al. (1987). Regional brain function in schizophrenia. *Archives of General Psychiatry, 44,* 119–125.

Gurman, A. S., Kniskern, D. P., & Pinsof, W. M. (1986). *Research on the process and outcome of marital and family therapy.* In S. L. Garfield & A. E. Bergin (Eds.), *Handbook of psychotherapy and behavior change (3rd ed.).* New York: Wiley.

H

Haas, R. G. (1981). *Effects of source characteristics on cognitive responses and persuasion.* In R. E. Petty, T. M. Ostrom, & T. C. Brock (Eds.), *Cognitive responses in persuasion.* Hillsdale, NJ: Erlbaum.

Hake, D. F., & Foxx, R. M. (1978). Promoting gasoline conservation: The effects of reinforcement schedules, a leader, and self-recording. *Behavior Modification, 2,* 339–369.

Hall, E. T. (1966). *The hidden dimension.* Garden City, NY: Doubleday.

Hall, W. G., & Oppenheim, R. W. (1987). Developmental psychology. *Annual Review of Psychology, 38,* 91–128.

Hammen, C., Burge, D., Burney, E., & Adrian, C. (1990). Longitudinal study of diagnoses in children of women with unipolar and bipolar affective disorder. *Archives of General Psychiatry, 47,* 1112–1117.

Harding, C. M. (1988). Course types in schizophrenia: An analysis of European and American studies. *Schizophrenia Bulletin, 14,* 633–642.

Hare, R. D. (1970). *Psychopathology: Theory and Research.* New York: Wiley.

Harkins, S. (1987). Social loafing and social facilitation. *Journal of Experimental Social Psychology, 23,* 1–18.

Harkins, S., & Petty, R. E. (1981). Effects of source magnification of cognitive effort in attitudes: An information-processing view. *Journal of Personality and Social Psychology, 40,* 401–413.

Harkins, S. G. & Petty, R. E. (1982). Effects of task difficulty and task uniqueness on social loafing. *Journal of Personality and Social Psychology, 43,* 1214–1229.

Harlow, H. F. (1932). Social facilitation of feeding in the albino rat. *Journal of Genetic Psychology, 41,* 211–221.

Harris, B. (1979). What ever happened to Little Albert? *American Psychologist, 34,* 151–160.

Harris, D. V. (1973). *Involvement in sport: A somatopsychic rationale for physical activity.* Philadelphia: Lea & Febiger.

Harris, L., & Associates. (1975, 1981, 1983). *The myth and reality of aging in America.* Washington, DC: The National Council on Aging.

Harrow, M., Goldberg, J. F., Grossman, L. S., & Meltzer, H. Y. (1990). Outcome in manic disorders. *Archives of General Psychiatry, 47,* 665–671.

Harter, S. (1978). Effectance motivation reconsidered: Toward a developmental model. *Human Development, 21,* 34–64.

Hartman, S., Grigsby, D. W., Crino, M. D., & Chhokar, J. (1986). The measurement of job satisfaction by action tendencies. *Educational and Psychological Measurement, 46,* 317–329.

Harvey, J. H., & Weary, G. (1984). Current issues in attribution theory. *Annual Review of Psychology, 35,* 427–459.

Hastorf, A. H., & Cantril, H. (1954). They saw a game: A case study. *Journal of Abnormal and Social Psychology, 49,* 129–134.

Hatfield, E., & Sprecher, S. (1986). *Mirror, mirror . . . The importance of looks in everyday life.* Albany: State University of New York Press.

Havighurst, R. J. (1972). *Developmental tasks and education (3rd ed.).* New York: McKay.

Hayduk, L. A. (1983). Personal space: Where we now stand. *Psychological Bulletin, 94,* 293–335.

Hayes, C. D. (Ed.). (1987). *Risking the future (Vol. 1).* Washington, DC: National Academy Press.

Haynes, S. G., McMichael, A. J., & Tyroler, H. A. (1978). Survival after early and normal retirement. *Journal of Gerontology, 33,* 872–883.

Hazan, C., & Shaver, P. (1987). Romantic love conceptualized as an attachment process. *Journal of Personality and Social Psychology, 52,* 511–524.

Hearold, S. (1986). A synthesis of 1043 effects of television on social behavior. In G. Comstock (ed.). *Public Communication and Behavior.* New York: Academic Press.

Hebb, D. O. (1955). Drives and the C.N.S. (conceptual nervous system). *Psychological Review, 62,* 243–254.

Heffernan, J. A., & Albee, G. W. (1985). Prevention perspectives. *American Psychologist, 40,* 202–204.

Hellige, J. B. (1990). Hemispheric asymmetry. *Annual Review of Psychology, 41,* 55–80.

Hellige, J. B. (Ed.). (1983). *Cerebral hemisphere asymmetry: Method, theory, and application.* New York: Praeger.

Helzer, J. E., Robins, L. N., & McEnvoy, L. (1987). Post-traumatic stress disorder in the general population. *New England Journal of Medicine, 317,* 1630–1634.

Hilgard, E. R. (1975). Hypnosis. *Annual Review of Psychology, 26,* 19–44.

Hilgard, E. R. (1978, January). Hypnosis and consciousness. *Human Nature,* pp. 42–49.

Hilgard, E. R., & Hilgard, J. R. (1975). *Hypnosis in the relief of pain.* Los Altos, CA: W. Kaufman.

Hilgard, J. R. (1970). *Personality and hypnosis: A study of imaginative involvement.* Chicago: University of Chicago Press.

Hill, W. F. (1985). *Learning: A Survey of Psychological Interpretations (4th ed.).* New York: Harper & Row.

Hinrichs, J. R. (1976). *Personnel training.* In M. Dunnette (Ed.), *Handbook of industrial and organizational psychology.* Skokie, IL: Rand McNally.

Hinsz, V. B., & Davis, J. H. (1984). Persuasive arguments theory, group polarization, and choice shifts. *Personality and Social Psychology Bulletin, 10,* 260–268.

Hobfoll, S. E. (1986). *Stress, social support, and women.* Washington, DC: Hemisphere.

Hobfoll, S. E. (1988). *The ecology of stress.* Washington, DC: Hemisphere.

Hobfoll, S. E. (1989). Conservation of resources: A new attempt at conceptualizing stress. *American Psychologist, 44,* 513–524.

Hobson, J. A. (1977). *The reciprocal interaction model of sleep cycle control: Implications for PGO wave generation and dream amnesia.* In R. R. Drucker-Colin & J. L. McGaugh (Eds.), *Neurobiology of sleep and memory.* New York: Academic Press.

Hobson, J. A., & McCarley, R. W. (1977). The brain as a dream state generator: An activation-synthesis hypothesis of the dream process. *American Journal of Psychiatry, 134,* 1335–1348.

Hofferth, S. L., & Hayes, C. D. (Eds.). (1987). *Risking the future: Adolescent sexuality, pregnancy, and childbearing.* Washington, DC: National Academy Press.

Hoffman, D. D. (1983). The interpretation of visual illusions. *Scientific American, 245,* 154–162.

Hogan, J. (1989). Personality correlates of physical fitness. *Journal of Personality and Social Psychology, 56,* 284–288.

Hogan, R., & Nicholson, R. A. (1988). The meaning of personality test scores. *American Psychologist, 43,* 621–626.

Holden, C. (1980). A new visibility for gifted children. *Science, 210,* 879–882.

Holmes, T. H., & Rahe, R. H. (1967). The social readjustment rating scale. *Journal of Psychosomatic Research, 11,* 213–218.

Holmes, T. S., & Holmes, T. H. (1970). Short-term intrusions into the life-style routine. *Journal of Psychosomatic Research, 14,* 121–132.

Horn, J. L. (1976). Human abilities: A review of research and theories in the early 1970s. *Annual Review of Psychology, 27,* 437–485.

Horowitz, F. D., & O'Brien, M. (Eds.). (1985). The gifted and talented: Developmental perspectives. Washington, DC: *American Psychological Association.*

Hostetler, A. J. (1987). Alzheimer's trials hinge on early diagnosis. *APA Monitor,* 18, 14–15.

Hovland, C. I., & Weiss, W. (1951). The influence of source credibility on communication effectiveness. *Public Opinion Quarterly,* 15, 635–650.

Howard, K. I., Kopata, S. M., Krause, M. S., & Orlinsky, D. E. (1986). The dose-effect relationship in psychotherapy. *American Psychologist,* 41, 159–164.

Howell, W. C., & Dipboye, R. L. (1982). *Essentials of industrial and organizational psychology.* Homewood, IL: Dorsey Press.

Hsia, J. (1988). Limits on affirmative action: Asian American access to higher education. *Educational Policy,* 2, 117–136.

Hubel, D. H. (1979). The brain. *Scientific American,* 241, 45–53.

Hughes, F. P., & Noppe, L. D. (1985). *Human development.* St. Paul, MN: West.

Hughes, J., Smith, T. W., Kosterlitz, H. W., Fothergill, L. A., Morgan, G. A., & Morris, H. R. (1975). Identification of two related peptides from the brain with potent opiate agonist activity. *Nature,* 258, 577–579.

Hulin, C. L., & Smith, P. C. (1964). Sex differences in job satisfaction. *Journal of Applied Psychology,* 48, 88–92.

Hull, C. L. (1943). *Principles of behavior.* Englewood Cliffs, NJ: Prentice-Hall.

Hunt, M. (1987, August 30). Navigating the therapy maze. *The New York Times Magazine,* pp. 28–31, 37, 44, 46, 49.

Huston, A. C., Watkins, B. A., & Kunkel, D. (1989). Public policy and children's television. *American Psychologist,* 44, 424–433.

Huston, T. L., Ruggiero, M., Conner, R., & Geis, G. (1981). Bystander intervention into crime: A study based on naturally occurring episodes. *Social Psychology Quarterly,* 44, 14–23.

I

Iaffaldano, M. T., & Muchinsky, P. M. (1985). Job satisfaction and job performance: A meta-analysis. *Psychological Bulletin,* 97, 251–273.

Ilgen, D. R., & Klein, H. J. (1989). Organizational behavior. *Annual Review of Psychology,* 40, 327–351.

Insko, C. A. (1965). Verbal reinforcement of attitude. *Journal of Personality and Social Psychology,* 2, 621–623.

Isenberg, D. J. (1986). Group polarization: A critical review and meta-analysis. *Journal of Personality and Social Psychology,* 50, 1141–1151.

J

Jacobs, B. L. (1987). How hallucinogenic drugs work. *American Scientist,* 75, 386–392.

Jacobs, B. L., & Trulson, M. E. (1979). Mechanisms of action of LSD. *American Scientist,* 67, 396–404.

Jacobson, D. S. (1984). Neonatal correlates of prenatal exposure to smoking, caffeine, and alcohol. *Infant Behavior and Development,* 7, 253–265.

James, W. (1890). *Principles of psychology.* New York: Holt, Rinehart and Winston.

James, W. (1892). *Psychology: Briefer course.* New York: Holt, Rinehart and Winston.

James, W. (1904). Does consciousness exist? *Journal of Philosophy,* 1, 477–491.

Janis, I. L. (1972). *Victims of groupthink.* Boston: Houghton Mifflin.

Janis, I. L. (1983a). *Groupthink: Psychological studies of policy decisions and fiascos (2nd ed.).* Boston: Houghton Mifflin.

Janis, I. L. (1983b). The role of social support in adherence to stressful decisions. *American Psychologist,* 38, 143–160.

Janoff-Bulman, R. (1979). Characterological versus behavioral self-blame: Inquiries into depression and rape. *Journal of Personality and Social Psychology,* 37, 1798–1809.

Jeffery, R. W. (1989). Risk behaviors and health: Contrasting individual and population perspectives. *American Psychologist,* 44, 1194–1202.

Jenkins, C. D. (1976). Recent evidence supporting psychological and social risk factors for coronary disease. *New England Journal of Medicine,* 294, 1033–1038.

Jenkins, J. G. & Dallenbach, K. M. (1924). Oblivescence during sleep and waking. *American Journal of Psychology,* 35, 605–612.

Jensen, A. R. (1969). How much can we boost IQ and scholastic achievement? *Harvard Educational Review,* 39, 1–123.

Jensen, A. R. (1973). *Educability and group differences.* London: Methuen.

Jensen, A. R. (1980). *Bias in mental testing.* New York: Free Press.

Jensen, A. R. (1981). *Straight talk about mental tests.* London: Methuen.

Johnson, D. L. (1989). Schizophrenia as a brain disease. *American Psychologist,* 44, 553–555.

Johnson, J., Weissman, M. M., & Klerman, G. L. (1990). Panic disorder, comorbidity, and suicide attempts. *Archives of General Psychiatry,* 47, 805–808.

Johnson, M. K., & Hasher, L. (1987). Human learning and memory. *Annual Review of Psychology,* 38, 631–668.

Jones, E. E. (1979). The rocky road from acts to dispositions. *American Psychologist,* 34, 107–117.

Jones, E. E., & Nisbett, R. E. (1971). *The actor and the observer: Divergent perceptions of behavior.* Morristown, NJ: General Learning Press.

Jones, K. L., Smith, D. W., Ulleland, C. N., & Streissgoth, A. P. (1973). Patterns of malformation in offspring of chronic alcoholic mothers. *Lancet,* 3, 1267–1271.

Jones, M. C. (1957). The careers of boys who were early or late maturing. *Child Development,* 28, 113–128.

Joyce, P. R., & Paykel, E. S. (1989). Predictors of drug response in depression. *Archives of General Psychiatry,* 46, 89–99.

Julien, R. M. (1985). *A primer of drug action (4th ed.).* San Francisco: Freeman.

Jussim, L., Coleman, L. M., & Lerch, L. (1987). The nature of stereotypes: A comparison and integration of three theories. *Journal of Personality and Social Psychology,* 52, 536–546.

K

Kagan, J. (1988). The meanings of personality predicates. *American Psychologist,* 43, 614–620.

Kagan, J., & Lamb, S. (1987). *The emergence of morality in young children.* Chicago: University of Chicago Press.

Kahn, S., Zimmerman, G., Csikzentmihalyi, M., & Getzels, J. W. (1985). Relations between identity in young adulthood and intimacy at midlife. *Journal of Personality and Social Psychology, 49*, 1316–1322.

Kalish, R. A. (1976). *Death and dying in a social context.* In R. H. Binstock & E. Shanas (Eds.), *Handbook of aging and the social sciences.* New York: Van Nostrand Reinhold.

Kalish, R. A. (1985). *Death, grief, and caring relationships.* Monterey, CA: Brooks/Cole.

Kamiya, J., Barber, T. X., Miller, N. E., Shapiro, D., & Stoyva, J. (1977). Biofeedback and Self-control. Chicago: Aldine.

Kamin, L. (1968). "Attention-like processes in classical conditioning." In M. Jones (Ed.), *Miami symposium on the prediction of behavior: Aversive stimulation.* Miami: University of Miami Press.

Kamin, L. (1969). *Predictability, surprise, attention, and conditioning.* In R. Church & B. Campbell (Eds.), *Punishment and aversive behaviors.* Englewood Cliffs, NJ: Prentice-Hall.

Kandel, E. R., & Schwartz, J. H. (1982). Molecular biology of learning: Modulation of transmitter release. *Science, 218*, 433–443.

Kanizsa, G. (1976). Subjective contours. *Scientific American, 234*, 48–52.

Kaplan, G. M. (1991). The use of biofeedback in the treatment of chronic facial tics: A case study. *Medical psychotherapy, 4*, 71–84.

Kaplan, R. M. (1984). The connection between clinical health promotion and health status. *American Psychologist, 39*, 755–765.

Kaplan, S. (1987). Aesthetics, affect and cognition: Environmental preference from an evolutionary perspective. *Environment and Behavior, 19*, 3–32.

Karoum, F., Karson, C. N., Bigelow, L. B., Lawson, W. B., & Wyatt, R. J. (1987). Preliminary evidence of reduced combined output of dopamine and its metabolites in chronic schizophrenia. *Archives of General Psychiatry, 44*, 604–607.

Katzell, R. A., & Guzzo, R. A. (1983). Psychological approaches to productivity improvement. *American Psychologist, 38*, 468–472.

Katzell, R. A., & Thompson, D. E. (1990). Work motivation: Theory and practice. *American Psychologist, 45*, 144–153.

Kay, S. R., & Singh, M. M. (1989). The positive-negative distinction in drug-free schizophrenic patients. *Archives of General Psychiatry, 46*, 711–717.

Kazdin, A. E., Esveldt-Dawson, K., French, N. H., & Unis, A. S. (1987). Problem-solving skills training and relationship therapy in the treatment of antisocial child behavior. *Journal of Consulting and Clinical Psychology, 55*, 76–85.

Keating, D. P. (1980). Thinking processes in adolescents. In J. Adelson (Ed.) *Handbook of adolescent psychology.* New York: Wiley.

Keesey, R. E., & Powley, T. L. (1975). Hypothalamic regulation of body weight. *American Scientist, 63*, 558–565.

Keesey, R. E., & Powley, T. L. (1986). The regulation of body weight. *Annual Review of Psychology, 37*, 109–133.

Keith, P. M. (1983). A comparison of the resources of parents and childless men and women in very old age. *Family Relations, 32*, 403–409.

Kelly, H. H. (1967). Attribution theory in social psychology. In D. Levine (Ed.), *Nebraska symposium on motivation.* Lincoln: University of Nebraska Press.

Kelley, H. H. (1973). The process of causal attribution. *American Psychologist, 28*, 107–128.

Kelley, H. H., & Michela, J. L. (1980). Attribution theory and research. *Annual Review of Psychology, 31*, 457–501.

Kelley, H. H., & Thibault, J. W. (1978). *Interpersonal relations: A theory of interdependence.* New York: Wiley.

Kempler, D., & Van Lanker, D. (1987). The right turn of phrase. *Psychology Today, 21*, 20–22.

Kermis, M. D. (1984). *The psychology of human aging.* Boston: Allyn & Bacon.

Kershner, J. R., & Ledger, G. (1985). Effect of sex, intelligence, and style of thinking on creativity: A comparison of gifted and average IQ children. *Journal of Personality and Social Psychology, 48*, 1033–1040.

Kessler, S. (1980). *The genetics of schizophrenia: A review.* In S. J. Keith & L. R. Mosher (Eds.), *Special report: Schizophrenia.* Washington, DC: U.S. Government Printing Office.

Kett, J. F. (1977). *Rites of passage: Adolescence in America from 1790 to the present.* New York: Basic Books.

Kientzle, M. J. (1946). Properties of learning curves under varied distributions of practice. *Journal of Experimental Psychology, 36*, 187–211.

Kiesler, C. A. (1982). Mental hospitals and alternative care. *American Psychologist, 37*, 349–360.

Kiesler, C. A., & Sibulkin, A. (1987). *Mental hospitalization: Myths and facts about a national crisis.* Beverly Hills, CA: Sage.

Kiester, E. (1984a). The playing fields of the mind. *Psychology Today, 18*, 18–24.

Kiester, E. (1984b). The uses of anger. *Psychology Today, 18*, 26.

Kiester, E., Jr. (1980). Images of the night: The physiological roots of dreaming. *Science 80, 1*, 36–43.

Kimble, G. A. (1981). *Biological and cognitive constraints on learning.* In L. Benjamin (Ed.), *The G. Stanley Hall Lecture Series* (Vol. 1). Washington, DC: American Psychological Association.

Kimble, G. A. (1989). Psychologist from the standpoint of a generalist. *American Psychologist, 44*, 491–499.

Kimmel, D. C. (1988). Ageism, psychology, and public policy. *American Psychologist, 43*, 175–178.

Kimmel, H. D. (1967). Instrumental conditioning of autonomically-mediated behavior. *Psychological Bulletin, 67*, 337–345.

Kimmel, H. D. (1974). Instrumental conditioning of autonomically-mediated responses in human beings. *American Psychologist, 29*, 325–335.

King, M., Murray, M. A., & Atkinson, T. (1982). Background, personality, job characteristics, and satisfaction with work in a national sample. *Human Relations, 35*, 119–133.

Kinsbourne, M. (1982). Hemispheric specialization and the growth of human understanding. *American Psychologist, 37*, 411–420.

Kinsey, A. C., Pomeroy, W. B., & Martin, C. E. (1948). *Sexual behavior in the human male.* Philadelphia: Saunders.

Kinsey, A. C., Pomeroy, W. B., Martin, C. E., & Gebhard, P. H. (1953). *Sexual behavior in the human female.* Philadelphia: Saunders.

Kirkpatrick, D. L. (1976). *Evaluation of training.* In R. L. Craig (Ed.), *Training and development handbook* (2nd ed.) New York: McGraw-Hill.

Kirscht, J. P. (1983). Preventive health behavior: A review of research and issues. *Health Psychology, 2,* 277–301.

Kisker, E. (1985). Teenagers talk about sex, pregnancy, and contraception. *Family Planning Perspectives, 17,* 83–90.

Kleitman, N. (1963a). Patterns of dreaming. *Scientific American, 203,* 82–88.

Kleitman, N. (1963b). *Sleep and wakefulness.* Chicago: University of Chicago Press.

Klerman, G. L. (1990). Treatment of recurrent unipolar major depressive disorder. *Archives of General Psychiatry, 47,* 1158–1162.

Knapp, S., & VandeCreek, L. (1989). What psychologists need to know about AIDS. *The Journal of Training and Practice in Professional Psychology, 3,* 3–16.

Knittle, J. L. (1975). *Early influences on development of adipose tissue.* In G. A. Bray (Ed.), *Obesity in perspective.* Washington, DC: U.S. Government Printing Office.

Knowles, E. S. (1983). Social physics and the effects of others: Tests of the effects of audience size and distance on social judgments and behavior. *Journal of Personality and Social Psychology, 45,* 1263–1279.

Kobasa, S. C. (1979). Stressful life events, personality, and health: An inquiry into hardiness. *Journal of Personality and Social Psychology, 37,* 1–11.

Kobasa, S. C. (1982). *The hardy personality: Toward a social psychology of stress and health.* In G. S. Sanders & J. Suls (Eds.), *Social Psychology of Health and Illness.* Hillsdale, NJ: Erlbaum.

Kohlberg, L. (1963). Moral development and identification. In H. W. Stevenson (Ed.), *Child psychology.* Chicago: University of Chicago Press.

Kohlberg, L. (1969). *Stages in the development of moral thought and action.* New York: Holt, Rinehart and Winston.

Kohlberg, L. (1981). *Philosophy of moral development.* New York: HarperCollins.

Kohlberg, L. (1985). *The psychology of moral development.* New York: HarperCollins.

Kohler, W. (1969). *The task of Gestalt psychology.* Princeton, NJ: Princeton University Press.

Kolata, G. (1987). What babies know, and noises parents make. *Science, 237,* 726.

Kolb, B. (1989). Brain development, plasticity, and behavior. *American Psychologist, 44,* 1203–1212.

Korchin, S. J., & Scheldberg, D. (1981). The future of clinical assessment. *American Psychologist, 36,* 1147–1158.

Kosslyn, S. M. (1987). Seeing and imagining in the cerebral hemispheres: A computational approach. *Psychological Review, 94,* 148–175.

Kraeplin, E. (1883). *Compendium der psychiatrie.* Leipzig: Abel.

Kraeplin, E. (1919). *Dementia praecox and paraphrenia.* Edinburgh, Scotland: E & S Livingstone.

Krantz, D. S., & Glass, D. C. (1984). *Personality, behavior patterns, and physical illness: Conceptual and methodological issues.* In W. D. Gentry (Ed.), *Handbook of behavioral medicine.* New York: Guilford.

Krantz, D. S., Grunberg, N. E., & Braum, A. (1985). Health psychology. *Annual Review of Psychology, 36,* 349–383.

Krueger, W. C. F. (1929). The effect of overlearning on retention. *Journal of Experimental Psychology, 12,* 71–78.

Krupat, E. (1985). *People in cities: The urban environment and its effects.* New York: Cambridge University Press.

Kübler-Ross, E. (1969). *On death and dying.* New York: Macmillan.

Kübler-Ross, E. (1981). *Living with death and dying.* New York: Macmillan.

Kunst-Wilson, W. R., & Zajonc, R. B. (1980). Affective discrimination that cannot be recognized. *Science, 207,* 557–558.

Kupfer, D. J., Frank, E., & Perel, J. M. (1989). The advantage of early treatment intervention in recurrent depression. *Archives of General Psychiatry, 46,* 771–775.

L

Lafferty, P., Beutler, L. E., & Crago, M. (1989). Differences between more and less effective psychotherapists: A study of select therapist variables. *Journal of Consulting and Clinical Psychology, 57,* 76–80.

Laird, J. (1984). The real role of facial response in the experience of emotion: A reply to Tourangeau and Ellsworth, and others. *Journal of Personality and Social Psychology, 47,* 909–917.

Laird, J. M. A., & Bennett, G. J. (1991). *Dorsal horn neurons in rats with an experimental peripheral mononeuropathy.* Paper presented at the 21st Annual Meeting of the Society for Neuroscience. New Orleans.

Landers, D. M. (1982). Arousal, attention, and skilled performance: Further considerations. *Quest, 33,* 271–283.

Landers, S. (1987a). AIDS: Behavior change yes, test no. *APA Monitor, 18,* 28–29.

Landers, S. (1987b). Panel urges teen contraception. *APA Monitor, 18,* 6.

Landers, S. (1989). High school seniors' illicit drug use down. *APA Monitor, 20,* 33.

Landers, S. (1990). Sex, condom use up among teenage boys. *APA Monitor, 21,* 25.

Landesman, S., & Butterfield, E. C. (1987). Normalization and deinstitutionalization of mentally retarded individuals. *American Psychologist, 42,* 809–816.

Landesman, S., & Ramey, C. (1989). Developmental psychology and mental retardation: Integrating scientific principles with treatment practices. *American Psychologist, 44,* 409–415.

Lanetto, R. (1980). *Children's conceptions of death.* New York: Springer.

Lang, P. J. (1985). *The cognitive psychophysiology of emotion: Fear and anxiety.* In A. H. Tuma & J. D. Maser (Eds.), *Anxiety and the anxiety disorders.* Hillsdale, NJ: Erlbaum.

Lashley, K. S. (1950). *In search of the engram.* Symposia of the Society for Experimental Biology, 4, 454–482.

Latané, B., & Darley, J. M. (1968). Group inhibition of bystander intervention in emergencies. *Journal of Personality and Social Psychology, 10,* 215–221.

Latané, B., & Darley, J. M. (1970). *The unresponsive bystander: Why doesn't he help?* Englewood Cliffs, NJ: Prentice-Hall.

Latané, B., & Nida, S. (1981). Ten years of research on group size and helping. *Psychological Bulletin, 89,* 308–324.

Latané, B., Williams, K., & Harkins, S. (1979). Many hands make light work: The causes and consequences of social loafing. *Journal of Personality and Social Psychology, 37,* 822–832.

Latham, G. P. (1988). Human resource training and development. *Annual Review of Psychology, 39,* 545–582.

Lawler, E. E. (1982). Strategies for improving the quality of work life. *American Psychologist, 37,* 486–493.

Lazarus, R. S. (1981). Little hassles can be hazardous to your health. *Psychology Today, 15,* 58–62.

Lazarus, R. S. (1991a). Progress on a cognitive-motivational-relational theory of emotion. *American Psychologist, 46,* 819–834.

Lazarus, R. S. (1991b). *Emotion and Adaptation.* New York: Oxford University Press.

Leahey, T. H., & Harris, R. J. (1989). *Human learning (2nd ed.).* Englewood Cliffs, NJ: Prentice-Hall.

Lehrer, P. M., & Woolfolk, R. L. (1984). *Are stress reduction techniques interchangeable, or do they have specific effects? A review of the comparative empirical literature.* In L. Woolfolk & P. M. Lehrer (Eds.), *Principles and practice of stress management.* New York: Guilford.

Lempers, J. D., Flavell, E. R., & Flavell, J. H. (1977). The development in very young children of tactile knowledge concerning visual perception. *Genetic Psychology Monographs, 95,* 3–53.

Lenneberg, E. H. (1967). *Biological foundations of language.* New York: Wiley.

Lenneberg, E. H., Rebelsky, F. G., & Nichols, I. A. (1965). The vocalizations of infants born to deaf and hearing parents. *Human Development, 8,* 23–27.

Lenzenweger, M. F., Dworkin, R. H., & Wethington, E. (1989). Models of positive and negative symptoms in schizophrenia: An empirical evaluation of latent structures. *Journal of Abnormal Psychology, 98,* 62–70.

Leon, G. R., & Roth, L. (1977). Obesity: Psychological causes, correlations and speculations. *Psychological Bulletin, 84,* 117–139.

Leonard, J. (1970, May 8), Ghetto for blue eyes in the classroom. *Life,* p. 16.

Lerner, M. J. (1965). The effect of responsibility and choice on a partner's attractiveness following failure. *Journal of Personality, 33,* 178–187.

Lerner, M. J. (1980). *The belief in a just world.* New York: Plenum.

LeVay, S. (1991). A difference in hypothalamic structure between heterosexual and homosexual men. *Science, 253,* 1034–1037.

Leventhal, H., & Cleary, P. D. (1980). The smoking problem: A review of the research and theory in behavioral risk modification. *Psychological Bulletin, 88,* 370–405.

Levine, J. D., Gordon, N. C., & Fields, H. L. (1979). Naloxone dose dependently produces analgesia and hyperalgesia in post-operative pain. *Nature, 278,* 740–741.

Levine, J. M., & Moreland, R. L. (1990). Progress in small group research. *Annual Review of Psychology, 41,* 585–634.

Levine, M. F., Taylor, J. C., & Davis, L. E. (1984). Defining quality of work life. *Human Relations, 37,* 81–104.

Levinson, D. J. (1978). *The seasons of a man's life.* New York: Ballantine Books.

Levinson, D. J. (1986). A conception of adult development. *American Psychologist, 41,* 3–13.

Levinson, D. J., Darrow, C. M., Klein, E. B., Levinson, M. H., & McKee, B. (1974). *The seasons of a man's life.* New York: Knopf.

Levinthal, C. F. (1983). *Introduction to physiological psychology (2nd ed.).* Englewood Cliffs, NJ: Prentice-Hall.

Lewinsohn, P. M., Zeiss, A. M., & Duncan, E. M. (1989). Probability of relapse after recovery from an episode of depression. *Journal of Abnormal Psychology, 98,* 107–116.

Ley, P. (1977). Psychological studies of doctor-patient communication. In S. Rachman (Ed.), *Contributions to medical psychology (Vol. 1).* Elmsford, NY: Pergamon Press.

Lidz, T. (1973). *The origin and treatment of schizophrenic disorders.* New York: Basic Books.

Lieberman, M. A. (1983). The effects of social support on response to stress. In L. Goldbert & D. S. Breznitz (Eds.), *Handbook of stress management.* New York: Free Press.

Lindsley, D. B., Bowden, J., & Magoun, H. W. (1949). Effect upon EEG of acute injury to the brain stem activating system. *Electroencephalography and Clinical Neurophysiology, 1,* 475–486.

Litt, M. D. (1988). Self-efficacy and perceived control: Cognitive mediators of pain tolerance. *Journal of Personality and Social Psychology, 54,* 149–160.

Locke, E. A. (1968). Toward a theory of task motivation and incentives. *Organizational Behavior and Human Performance, 3,* 157–189.

Locke, E. A. (1976). The nature and causes of job satisfaction. In M. D. Dunnette (Ed.), *Handbook of industrial and organizational psychology.* Skokie, IL: Rand McNally.

Locke, E. A., & Latham, G. P. (1984). *Goal setting: A motivational technique that works.* Englewood Cliffs, NJ: Prentice-Hall.

Locke, E. A., Shaw, K. N., Saari, L. M., & Latham, G. (1981). Goal-setting and task performance: 1969–1980. *Psychological Bulletin, 90,* 124–152.

Locke, J. (1690/1964). *An essay concerning human understanding.* New York: New American Library (Meridian Books).

Loftus, E. F., & Loftus, G. R. (1980). On the permanence of stored information in the human brain. *American Psychologist, 35,* 409–420.

Long, P. (1986). Medical mesmerism. *Psychology Today, 20(1),* 28–29.

Lord, C. G. (1980). Schemas and images as memory aids. *Journal of Personality and Social Psychology, 38,* 257–269.

Lorenz, K. (1969). On aggression. New York: Bantam Books.

Lott, A. J., & Lott, B. E. (1974). *The role of reward in the formation of positive interpersonal attitudes.* In T. L. Huston (Ed.), *Foundations of interpersonal attraction.* New York: Academic Press.

Lozoff, B. (1989). Nutrition and behavior. *American Psychologist, 44,* 231–236.

Lubin, B., Larsen, R. M., & Matarazzo, J. D. (1984). Patterns of psychological test usage in the United States: 1935–1982. *American Psychologist, 39,* 451–454.

Lucas, E. A., Foutz, A. S., Dement, W. C., & Mittler, M. M. (1979). Sleep cycle organization in narcoleptic and normal dogs. *Physiology and Behavior, 23,* 325–331.

Luh, C. W. (1922). The conditions of retention. *Psychological Monographs,* Whole No. 142.

Lykken, D. T. (1957). A study of anxiety in the sociopathic personality. *Journal of Abnormal and Social Psychology, 55,* 6–10.

Lykken, D. T. (1982). Fearlessness: Its carefree charm and deadly risks. *Psychology Today, 16,* 20–28.

Lynch, G., & Baudry, M. (1984). The biochemistry of memory: A new and specific hypothesis. *Science, 224,* 1057–1063.

Lynn, R. (1977). The intelligence of the Japanese. *Bulletin of the British Psychological Society, 30,* 69–72.

Lynn, R. (1982). IQ in Japan and the United States shows a greater disparity. *Nature, 297,* 222–223.

Lynn, R. (1987). The intelligence of the Mongoloids: A psychometric, evolutionary and neurological theory. *Personality and Individual Differences, 8,* 813–844.

Lynn, R. (1991). Educational achievements of Asian Americans. *American Psychologist, 46,* 875–876.

Lynn, S. J., & Rhue, J. W. (1986). The fantasy-prone person: Hypnosis, imagination, and creativity. *Journal of Personality and Social Psychology, 51,* 404–408.

M

MacDonald, M. R., & Kuiper, N. A. (1983). Cognitive-behavioral preparations for surgery: Some theoretical and methodological concerns. *Clinical Psychology Review, 3,* 27–39.

Mace, N. L., & Rabins, P. V. (1981). *The 36-hour day.* Baltimore: Johns Hopkins University Press.

MacFarlane, A. C. (1988). The longitudinal course of posttraumatic morbidity. *Journal of Nervous Disorders, 176,* 30–39.

Mackenzie, B. (1984). Explaining race differences in IQ: The logic, the methodology, and the evidence. *American Psychologist, 39,* 1214–1233.

Mackintosh, N. J. (1986). The biology of intelligence? *British Journal of Psychology, 77,* 1–18.

MacMillan, J., & Kofoed, L. (1984). Sociobiology and antisocial personality: An alternative perspective. *Journal of Mental Disorders, 172,* 701–706.

Maddi, S. R., & Kobasa, S. C. (1984). *The Hardy Executive: Health and Stress.* Homewood, IL: Dorsey Press.

Magid, K. (1988). *High Risk: Children Without a Conscience.* New York: Bantam.

Mahowald, M. W., & Schenck, C. H. (1989). *REM sleep behavior disorder.* In M. H. Krygr, T. Roth, & W. C. Dement (Eds.), *Principles and practice of sleep medicine.* Philadelphia: Saunders.

Maier, N. R. F. (1931). Reasoning in humans II: The solution of a problem and its appearance in consciousness. *Journal of Experimental Psychology, 105,* 181–194.

Malatesta, C. A., & Isard, C. E. (1984). *The ontogenesis of human social signals: From biological imperative to symbol utilization.* In N. A. Fox & R. J. Davidson (Eds.), *The psychobiology of affective development.* Hillsdale, NJ: Erlbaum.

Mandler, G. (1980). Recognizing: The judgment of previous occurrence. *Psychological Review, 87,* 252–271.

Manning, M. L. (1983). Three myths concerning adolescence. *Adolescence, 18,* 823–829.

Marengo, J. T., & Harrow, M. (1987). Schizophrenic thought disorder at follow-up. *Archives of General Psychiatry, 44,* 651–659.

Markowitz, J. S., Weissman, M. M., Ouellete, R., Lish, J. D., & Klerman, G. L. (1989). Quality of life in panic disorder. *Archives of General Psychiatry, 46,* 984–992.

Marks, I. M. (1986). Epidemiology of anxiety. *Social Psychiatry, 21,* 167–171.

Marschark, M., Richmond, C. L., Yuille, J. C., & Hunt, R. R. (1987). The role of imagery in memory: On shared and distinctive information. *Psychological Bulletin, 102,* 28–41.

Martin, G. B., & Clark, R. D. (1982). Distress crying in neonates: Species and peer specificity. *Developmental Psychology, 18,* 3–9.

Martin, R. J., White, B. D., & Hulsey, M. G. (1991). The regulation of body weight. *American Scientist, 79,* 528–541.

Martindale, C. (1981). *Cognition and consciousness.* Homewood, IL: Dorsey Press.

Marx, J. (1990). Alzheimer's pathology explored. *Science, 249,* 984–986.

Marziali, E. (1984). Prediction of outcome of brief psychotherapy from therapist interpretive interactions. *Archives of General Psychiatry, 41,* 301–304.

Maslow, A. H. (1943). A theory of human motivation. *Psychological Review, 50,* 370–396.

Maslow, A. (1954). *Motivation and personality.* New York: Harper.

Maslow, A. H. (1970). *Motivation and personality (2nd ed.).* New York: HarperCollins.

Massaro, D. W. (1975). *Experimental psychology and information processing.* Skokie, IL: Rand McNally.

Masters, W., & Johnson, V. (1979). *Homosexuality in perspective.* Boston: Little, Brown.

Masters, W., Johnson, V., & Kolodny, R. C. (1987). *Human sexuality* (3rd ed.). Glenview, IL: Scott, Foresman/Little, Brown.

Matarazzo, J. D. (1980). Behavioral health and behavioral medicine: Frontiers for a new health psychology. *American Psychologist, 35,* 807–817.

Matlin, M. W. (1983). *Perception.* Boston: Allyn & Bacon.

Matsumoto, D. (1987). The role of facial response in the experience of emotion: More methodological problems and a meta-analysis. *Journal of Personality and Social Psychology, 52,* 769–774.

Matthews, K. A. (1982). Psychological perspectives on the Type A behavior pattern. *Psychological Bulletin, 91,* 293–323.

Matthews, K. A. (1988). Coronary heart disease and Type A behavior: Update on an alternative to the Booth-Kewley and Friedman (1987) quantitative review. *Psychological Bulletin, 104,* 373–380.

Matthies, H. (1989). Neurobiological aspects of learning and memory. *Annual Review of Psychology, 40,* 381–404.

Mattson, S. N., Barron, S., & Riley, E. P. (1988). *The behavioral effects of prenatal alcohol exposure.* In K. Kuriyama, A. Takada, & H. Ishii (Eds.), *Biomedical and social aspects of alcohol and alcoholism.* Tokyo: Elsevier.

Mayer, R. E. (1983). *Thinking, problem solving, cognition*. San Francisco: Freeman.

Mayer, W. (1983). Alcohol abuse and alcoholism. *American Psychologist, 38*, 1116–1121.

McCann, I. L., & Holmes, D. S. (1984). Influence of aerobic exercise on depression. *Journal of Personality and Social Psychology, 46*, 1142–1147.

McCarthy, B. W., Ryan, M., & Johnson, F. (1975). *Sexual awareness*. San Francisco: Boyd & Fraser.

McClelland, D. C. (1958). *Risk-taking in children with high and low need for achievement*. In J. W. Atkinson (Ed.), *Motives in fantasy, action, and society*. New York: Van Nostrand Reinhold.

McClelland, D. C. (1982). The need for power, sympathetic activation, and illness. *Motivation and Emotion, 6*, 31–41.

McClelland, D. C. (1985). *Human motivation*. Glenview, IL: Scott, Foresman.

McClelland, D. C., Atkinson, J. W., Clark, R. A., & Lowell, E. L. (1953). *The achievement motive*. Englewood Cliffs, NJ: Prentice-Hall.

McClelland, D. C., & Winter, D. G. (1969). *Motivating economic development*. New York: Free Press.

McCloskey, M., Wible, C., & Cohen, N. J. (1988). Is there a special flashbulb-memory mechanism? *Journal of Experimental Psychology: General, 117*, 171–181.

McCormick, D. A., Clark, G. A., Lavond, D. G., & Thompson, R. F. (1982). *Initial localization of the memory trace for a basic form of learning*. Proceeding: National Academy of Sciences, 79, 2731–2735.

McCrae, R. R., & Costa, P. T. (1984). *Emerging lives, enduring dispositions: Personality in adulthood*. Boston: Little, Brown.

McCrae, R. R., & Costa, P. T. (1986). Clinical assessment can benefit from recent advances in personality psychology. *American Psychologist, 41*, 1001–1002.

McCrae, R. R., & Costa, P.T. (1987). Validation of the five-factor model of personality across instruments and observers. *Journal of Personality and Social Psychology, 52*, 81–90.

McDougall, W. (1908). *An introduction to social psychology*. London: Methuen.

McGaugh, J. L. (1983). Hormonal influences on memory. *Annual Review of Psychology, 34*, 297-323.

McGinnis, J. M. (1985). Recent history of federal initiatives in prevention policy. *American Psychologist, 40*, 205–212.

McGlashan, T. H., & Fenton, W. S. (1992). The positive-negative distinction in schizophrenia: Review of natural history indicators. *Archives of General Psychiatry, 49*, 63–72.

McGlynn, T. J., & Metcalf, H. L. (1989). Diagnosis and treatment of anxiety disorders: A physician's handbook. *American Psychiatric Press*, 80.

McGuire, W. J. (1985). *Attitudes and attitude change*. In G. Lindzey & E. Aronson (Eds.), *Handbook of social psychology*. New York: Random House.

McKim, W. A. (1986). *Drugs and behavior*. Englewood Cliffs, NJ: Prentice-Hall.

McNaughton, B. L., & Morris, R. G. M. (1987). Hippocampal synaptic enhancement and information storage within a distributed memory system. *Trends in Neuroscience, 10*, 408–415.

McNeil, D. (1970). *The acquisition of language: The study of developmental psycholinguistics*. New York: HarperCollins.

Mednick, M. T. (1989). On the politics of psychological constructs: Stop the bandwagon, I want to get off. *American Psychologist, 44*, 1118–1123.

Mednick, M. T. S. (1979). *The new psychology of women: A feminist analysis*. In J. E. Gullahorn (Ed.), *Psychology and women: In transition*. New York: Wiley.

Mednick, S. A., Moffitt, T. E., & Stack, S. (1987). *The Causes of Crime: New Biological Approaches*. New York: Cambridge University Press.

Meer, J. (1986). The reason of age. *Psychology Today, 20*, 60–64.

Meichenbaum, D. (1977). *Cognitive-behavior modification: An integrative approach*. New York: Plenum.

Meichenbaum, D., & Turk, D. C. (1987). *Facilitating treatment adherence*. New York: Plenum.

Melzack, R. (1973). *The puzzle of pain*. Baltimore: Penguin Books.

Melzack, R., & Wall, P. D. (1965). Pain mechanisms: A new theory. *Science, 150*, 971–979.

Meredith, N. (1986). Testing the talking cure. *Science 86, 7*(5), 30–37.

Mervis, J. (1986). NIMH data points the way to effective treatment. *APA Monitor, 17*, 1, 13.

Michael, J. L. (1985) *Behavior analysis: A radical perspective*. In B. L. Hammonds, (Ed.), *Psychology and learning*. Washington, DC: American Psychological Association.

Middlemist, R. D., & Peterson, R. B. (1976). Test of equity theory by controlling for comparison of workers' efforts. *Organizational Behavior and Human Performance, 15*, 335–354.

Milgram, S. (1963). Behavioral studies of obedience. *Journal of Abnormal and Social Psychology, 67*, 371–378.

Milgram, S. (1965). Some conditions of obedience and disobedience to authority. *Human Relations, 18*, 57–76.

Milgram, S. (1970). The experience of living in cities. *Science, 167*, 1461–1468.

Milgram, S. (1974). *Obedience to authority*. New York: HarperCollins.

Milgram, S. (1977). *The individual in a social world*. Reading, MA: Addison-Wesley.

Miller, B. C., & Sollie, D. L. (1980). Normal stress during the transition to parenthood. *Family Relations, 29*, 459–465.

Miller, D. T., & McFarland, C. (1987). Pluralistic ignorance: When similarity is interpreted as dissimilarity. *Journal of Personality and Social Psychology, 53*, 298–305.

Miller, D. T., & Ross, M. (1975). Self-serving biases in the attribution of causality: Fact or fiction? *Psychological Bulletin, 82*, 213–225.

Miller, G. A. (1956). The magical number seven plus or minus two: Some limits on our capacity for processing information. *Psychological Review, 63*, 81–96.

Miller, G. A., Galanter, E., & Pribram, K. H. (1960). *Plans and the structure of behavior*. New York: Holt, Rinehart and Winston.

Miller, J. G. (1984). Culture and the development of everyday social explanation. *Journal of Personality and Social Psychology, 46*, 961–978.

Miller, N. E. (1944). Experimental studies of conflict. In J. M. Hunt (Ed.), *Personality and the behavior disorders*. New York: Ronald Press.

Miller, N. E. (1959). *Liberalization of basic S-R concepts: Extensions to conflict behavior, motivation, and social learning.* In S. Koch (Ed.), *Psychology: A study of a science* (Vol. 2.). New York: McGraw-Hill.

Miller, N. E. (1978). Biofeedback and visceral learning. *Annual Review of Psychology, 29,* 373–404.

Miller, N. E. (1983). Behavioral medicine: Symbiosis between laboratory and clinic. *Annual Review of Psychology, 34,* 1–31.

Miller, R. C., & Berman, J. S. (1983). The efficacy of cognitive behavior therapies: A quantitative review of the research evidence. *Psychological Bulletin, 94,* 39–53.

Miller, R. R., & Spear, N. E. (Eds.). (1985). *Information processing in animals: Conditioned inhibition.* Hillsdale, NJ: Erlbaum.

Millstein, S. G. (1989). Adolescent health: Challenges for behavioral scientists. *American Psychologist, 44,* 837–842.

Milner, B. (1959). The memory deficit in bilateral hippocampal lesions. *Psychiatric Research Reports, 11,* 43–52.

Milner, B. (1965). *Memory disturbances after bilateral hippocampal lesions.* In B. Milner & S. Glickman (Eds.), *Cognitive processes and the brain.* New York: Van Nostrand Reinhold.

Milner, B., Corkin, S., & Teuber, H. L. (1968). Further analysis of the hippocampal amnesic syndrome: 14-year follow-up study of H. M. *Neuropsychologica, 6,* 215–234.

Minami, H., & Dallenbach, K. M. (1946). The effect of activity upon learning and retention in the cockroach. American *Journal of Psychology, 59,* 682–697.

Minuchin, S., & Fishman, H. C. (1981). *Family therapy techniques.* Cambridge, MA: Harvard University Press.

Mishkin, M., & Appenzeller, T. (1987). The anatomy of memory. *Scientific American, 256,* 80–89.

Mobley, W. H. (1977). Intermediate linkages in the relationship between job satisfaction and employee turnover. *Journal of Applied Psychology, 62,* 237–240.

Money, J. (1972). *Man woman/Boy girl.* Baltimore: Johns Hopkins University Press.

Money, J. (1987). Sin, sickness, or status? Homosexual gender identity and psychoneuroendocrinology. *American Psychologist, 42,* 384–399.

Monson, T. C., & Snyder, M. (1977). Actors, observers, and the attribution process. *Journal of Experimental Social Psychology, 13,* 89–111.

Moore, K. L. (1982). *The developing human (3rd ed.).* Philadelphia: Saunders.

Morgan, W. P. (1980). The trait psychology controversy. *Research Quarterly for Exercise and Sport, 51,* 50–76.

Morris, C. W. (1946). *Signs, language, and behavior.* Englewood Cliffs, NJ: Prentice-Hall.

Morrison, D. M. (1985). Adolescent contraceptive behavior: A review. *Psychological Bulletin, 98,* 538–568.

Moruzzi, G., & Magoun, H. W. (1949). Brain stem reticular formation and activation of the EEG. *Electroencephalography and Clinical Neurophysiology, 1,* 455–473.

Moscovici, S., Lage, E., & Naffrechoux, M. (1969). Influences of a consistent minority on the response of a majority in a color perception task. *Sociometry, 32,* 365–380.

Moscovici, S., Mugny, G., & Van Avermaet, E. (1985). *Perspectives on minority influence.* New York: Cambridge University Press.

Mowday, R. T. (1983). *Equity theory prediction of behavior in organizations.* In R. M. Steers & L. W. Porter (Eds.), *Motivation and work behavior* (3rd ed.). New York: McGraw-Hill.

Muchinsky, P. M. (1987). *Psychology applied to work* (2nd ed.). Homewood, IL: Dorsey Press.

Muchinsky, P. M., & Tuttle, M. L. (1979). Employee turnover: An empirical and methodological assessment. *Journal of Vocational Behavior, 14,* 43–77.

Mulac, A., Incontro, C. R., & James, M. R. (1985). Comparison of gender-linked language effect and sex role stereotypes. *Journal of Personality and Social Psychology, 49,* 1098–1109.

Munn, N. L. (1956). *Introduction to Psychology.* Boston: Houghton-Mifflin.

Murray, D. J. (1983). *A history of western psychology.* Englewood Cliffs, NJ: Prentice-Hall.

Murray, D. M., Johnson, C. A., Leupker, R. F., & Mittlemark, M. B. (1984). The prevention of cigarette smoking in children: A comparison of four strategies. *Journal of Applied Social Psychology, 14,* 274–288.

Murray, H. A. (1938). *Explorations in personality.* New York: Oxford University Press.

N

Nakazima, S. (1962). A comparative study of the speech developments of Japanese and American English in children. *Studies in Phonology, 2,* 27–39.

Nash, M. (1987). What, if anything, is regressed about hypnotic age regression? *Psychological Bulletin, 102,* 42–52.

Nathan, P. E. (1983). Failures in prevention: Why we can't prevent the devastating effect of alcoholism and drug abuse. *American Psychologist, 38,* 459–467.

National Council on Alcoholism. (1979). *Facts on alcoholism.* New York: Author.

National Institute on Drug Abuse. (1987). *National household survey on drug abuse: Population estimates 1985.* Rockville, MD: Author.

National Institute of Mental Health. (1984). The NIMH epidemiologic catchment area program. *Archives of General Psychiatry, 41,* 931–1011.

National Institutes of Health, *Review Panel on Coronary Prone Behavior and Coronary Heart Disease.* (1981). *Coronary-prone behavior and coronary heart disease: A critical review.* Circulation, 63, 1199–1215.

Nemeth, C. (1986). Differential contributions of majority and minority influence. *Psychological Review, 93,* 23–32.

Neugarten, B. L., & Neugarten, D. A. (1986). *Changing meanings of age in the aging society.* In A. Piter & L. Bronte (Eds.), *Our aging society: Paradox and promise.* New York: Norton.

Neugarten, B. L., & Neugarten, D. A. (1989). *Policy issues in an aging society.* In M. Storandt & G. R. VandenBos (Eds.), *The adult years: Continuity and change.* Washington, DC: American Psychological Association.

Newby, R. W. (1987). Contextual areas in item recognition following verbal discrimination learning. *Journal of General Psychology, 114,* 281–287.

Newcomb, M. D., & Bentler, P. M. (1989). Substance abuse among children and teenagers. *American Psychologist, 44*, 242–248.

Newcomb, N., & Dubas, J. S. (1987). *Individual differences in cognitive ability: Are they related to timing of puberty?* In R. M. Lerner & T. T. Foch (Eds.), *Biological-psychosocial interactions in early adolescence: A life-span approach.* Hillsdale, NJ: Erlbaum.

Newell, A., Shaw, J. C., & Simon, H. A. (1962). *The process of creative thinking.* In H. E. Gruber, G. Terrell, & M. Wertheimer (Eds.), *Contemporary approaches to creative thinking.* New York: Atherton Press.

Newman, B. M., & Newman, P. R. (1984). *Development through life: A psychosocial approach.* Homewood, IL: Dorsey Press.

Nickerson, R. S., & Adams, M. J. (1979). Long-term memory for a common object. *Cognitive Psychology, 11*, 287–307.

Nicol, S. E., & Gottesman, I. I. (1983). Clues to the genetics and neurobiology of schizophrenia. *American Scientist, 71*, 398–404.

Nisbett, R. E. (1972). Hunger, obesity, and the ventromedial hypothalamus. *Psychological Review, 79*, 433–453.

Norcross, J. C. (1986). *Handbook of eclectic psychotherapy.* New York: Brunner/Mazel.

O

Oden, M. H. (1968). The fulfillment of promise: 40-year follow-up of the Terman gifted group. *Genetic Psychology Monographs, 77*(1), 3–93.

Oetting, E. R., & Beauvais, F. (1990). Adolescent drug use: Findings of national and local surveys. *Journal of Consulting and Clinical Psychology, 58*, 385–394.

Offer, D., & Offer, J. (1975). *From teenage to young manhood: A psychological study.* New York: Basic Books.

Offermann, L. R., & Gowing, M. K. (1990). Organizations of the future: Changes and challenges. *American Psychologist, 45*, 95–108.

Offord, D. R., Boyle, M. H., Szatmari, P., Rae-Grant, N. I., Links, P. S., et al. (1987). Ontario child health study. *Archives of General Psychiatry, 44*, 832–836.

Ogilvie, B. C., & Howe, M. A. (1984). Beating slumps at their game. *Psychology Today, 18*, 28–32.

Oller, D. K. (1981). *Infant vocalization.* In R. E. Stark (Ed.), *Language behavior in infancy and early childhood.* New York: Elsevier.

Orne, M. (1969). *Demand characteristics and the concept of quasi-controls.* In R. Rosenthal & R. Rosnow (Eds.), *Artifact in behavioral research.* New York: Academic Press.

Ortony, A., Clore, G. L., & Collins, A. (1988). *The cognitive structure of emotions.* New York: Cambridge University Press.

Ortony, A., & Turner, T. J. (1990). What's basic about basic emotions? *Psychological Review, 97*, 315–331.

P

Paivio, A. (1971). *Imagery and verbal processes.* New York: Holt, Rinehart and Winston.

Paivio, A. (1986). *Mental representations: A dual coding approach.* New York: Oxford University Press.

Parker, E. S., Birnbaum, I. M., & Noble, E. P. (1976). Alcohol and memory: Storage and state dependency. *Journal of Verbal Learning and Verbal Behavior, 15*, 691–702.

Parsons, H. M. (1974). What happened at Hawthorne? *Science, 183*, 922–932.

Pavlov, I. (1927). *Conditioned reflexes.* New York: Oxford University Press.

Pavlov, I. (1928). *Lectures on conditioned reflexes: The higher nervous activity of animals* (Vol. I) (H. Gantt, Trans.). London: Lawrence and Wishart.

Pavlovich, M., & Greene, B. F. (1984). A self-instructional manual for installing low-cost/no-cost weatherization material: Experimental validation with scouts. *Journal of Applied Behavior Analysis, 17*, 105–109.

Pearce, J. M., & Hall, G. (1980). A model for Pavlovian conditioning: Variations in the effectiveness of conditioned but not of unconditioned stimuli. *Psychological Review, 87*, 532–552.

Peck, M. (1982). Youth suicide. Death Education, 6, 29–47.

Perls, F. S. (1967). Group vs. individual psychotherapy. *ETC: A Review of General Semantics, 34*, 306–312.

Perls, F. S. (1971). *Gestalt Therapy Verbatim.* New York: Bantam Books.

Perls, F. S., Hefferline, R. F., & Goodman, P. (1951). *Gestalt Therapy.* New York: Julian Press.

Peters, W. A. (1971). *A class divided.* Garden City, NY: Doubleday.

Peterson, A. C. (1988). Adolescent development. *Annual Review of Psychology, 39*, 583–607.

Peterson, A. C., & Ebata, A. T. (1987). *Developmental transitions and adolescent problem behavior: Implications for prevention and intervention.* In K. Hurrelmann (Ed.), *Social prevention and intervention,* New York: de Gruyter.

Peterson, L. R., & Peterson, M. J. (1959). Short-term retention of individual verbal items. *Journal of Experimental Psychology, 58*, 193–198.

Petty, R. E., & Cacioppo, J. T. (1981). *Attitudes and persuasion: Classic and contemporary approaches.* Dubuque, IA: Brown.

Petty, R. E., & Cacioppo, J. T. (1986). The elaboration likelihood model of persuasion. *Advances in Experimental Social Psychology, 19*, 123–205.

Petty, R. E., Harkins, S. G., Williams, K. D., & Latané, B. (1977). The effects of group size on cognitive effort and evaluation. *Personality and Social Psychology Bulletin, 3*, 579–582.

Piaget, J. (1932/1948). *The moral judgment of the child.* New York: Free Press.

Piaget, J. (1954). *The construction of reality in the child.* New York: Basic Books.

Piaget, J. (1967). *Six psychological studies.* New York: Random House.

Piner, K. E., & Kahle, L. R. (1984). Adapting to the stigmatizing label of mental illness: Foregone but not forgotten. *Journal of Personality and Social Psychology, 47*, 805–811.

Plawin, P., & Suied, M. (1988, December). Can't get no satisfaction. *Changing Times,* p. 106.

Plomin, R. (1990). The role of inheritance in behavior. *Science, 248*, 183–188.

Pola, J., & Martin, L. (1977). Eye movements following autokinesis. *Bulletin of the Psychonomic Society, 10*, 397–398.

Pope, H. G., & Hudson, J. I. (1986). Antidepressant therapy for bulimia: Current status: *Journal of Clinical Psychiatry, 47*, 339–345.

Pope, H. G., Hudson, J. I., Jonas, J. M., & Yurgelun-Todd, D. (1985). Antidepressant treatment of bulimia: A two-year follow-up study. *Journal of Clinical Psychopharmacology, 5*, 320–327.

Porter, L. W., & Steers, R. M. (1973). Organizational, work, and personal factors in employee turnover and absenteeism. *Psychological Bulletin, 80*, 151–176.

Posner, M. I. (1973). *Cognition: An introduction.* Glenview, IL: Scott, Foresman and Company.

Posner, M. I., & Keele, S. W. (1970). Retention of abstract ideas. *Journal of Experimental Psychology, 83*, 304–308.

Post, R.B., & Leibowitz, H. W. (1985). A revised analysis of the role of efference in motion perception. *Perception, 14*, 631–643.

Powers, S. I., Hauser, S. T., & Kilner, L. A. (1989). Adolescent mental health. *American Psychologist, 44*, 200–208.

Pressley, M., Levin, J. R., & Delaney, H. D. (1982). The mnemonic keyword method. *Review of Educational Research, 52*, 61–91.

Pyle, R. L., Mitchell, J. E., & Eckert, E. D. (1981). Bulimia: Report of 34 cases. *Journal of Clinical Psychiatry, 42*, 60–64.

Q

Quay, H. C. (1965). Psychopathic personality as pathological stimulation seeking. *American Journal of Psychiatry, 122*, 180–183.

Quayle, D. (1983). American productivity: The devastating effect of alcoholism and drug abuse. *American Psychologist, 38*, 454–458.

R

Rachlin, H. C., & Green, L. (1972). Commitment, choice, and self-control. *Journal of the Experimental Analysis of Behavior, 17*, 15–22.

Rahe, R. H., & Arthur, R. J. (1978). *Life changes and illness reports.* In K. E. Gunderson & R. H. Rahe (Eds.), *Life stress and illness.* Springfield, IL: Thomas.

Reich, J. (1986). The epidemiology of anxiety. *The Journal of Nervous and Mental Disease, 174*, 129–136.

Reilly, R. R., & Chao, G. T. (1982). Validity and fairness of some alternative employee selection procedures. *Personnel Psychology, 35*, 1–62.

Reinke, B. J., Ellicott, A. M., Harris, R. L., & Hancock, E. (1985). Timing of psychological changes in women's lives. *Human Development, 28*, 259–280.

Reis, H. T., Nezlek, J., & Wheeler, L. (1980). Physical attractiveness in social interaction. *Journal of Personality and Social Psychology, 38*, 604–617.

Reis, S. M. (1989). Reflections on policy affecting the education of gifted and talented students: Past and future perspectives. *American Psychologist, 44*, 399–408.

Rescorla, R. A. (1968). Probability of shock in the presence and absence of CS in fear conditioning. *Journal of Comparative and Physiological Psychology, 66*, 1–5.

Rescorla, R. A. (1987). A Pavlovian analysis of goal-directed behavior. *American Psychologist, 42*, 119–129.

Rescorla, R. A. (1988). Pavlovian conditioning: It's not what you think it is. *American Psychologist, 43*, 151–160.

Rescorla, R. A., & Wagner, A. R. (1972). *A theory of Pavlovian conditioning: Variations in the effectiveness of reinforcement and nonreinforcement.* In A. H. Black & W. F. Prokasy (Eds.), *Classical conditioning II: Current research and theory.* Englewood Cliffs, NJ: Prentice-Hall.

Rest, J. R. (1983). *Morality.* In J. Flavell & E. Markman (Eds.), *Handbook of child development: Cognitive development.* New York: Wiley.

Reveley, M. A., Reveley, A. M., & Baldy, R. (1987). Left cerebral hemisphere hypodensity in discordant schizophrenic twins. *Archives of General Psychiatry, 44*, 624–632.

Reynolds, A. G., & Flagg, P. W. (1983). *Cognitive psychology.* Boston: Little, Brown.

Rhodes, S. R. (1983). Age-related differences in work attitudes and behaviors: A review and conceptual analysis. *Psychological bulletin, 93*, 328–367.

Rice, M. L. (1989). Children's language acquisition. *American Psychologist, 44*, 149–156.

Richardson-Klavehn, A., & Bjork, R. A. (1988). Measures of memory. *Annual Review of Psychology, 39*, 475–543.

Riggio, R. E. (1990). *Introduction to industrial/organizational psychology.* Glenview, IL: Scott, Foresman.

Robins, L. N., Helzer, J. E., Weissman, M. M., Orvaschel, H., Guenberg, E., Burke, J. D., & Regier, D. A. (1984). Lifetime prevalence of specific psychiatric disorders in three sites. *Archives of General Psychiatry, 41*, 949–958.

Roche, A. F., & Davila, G. H. (1972). Late adolescent growth in stature. *Pediatrics, 50*, 874–880.

Rock, I. (1986). *The description and analysis of object and event perception.* In K. R. Boff, L. Kaufman, & J. P. Thomas (Eds.), *Handbook of perception and human performance:* Vol. 2. Cognitive processes and performance. New York: Wiley.

Rodin, J. (1981). Current status of the internal-external hypothesis of obesity: What went wrong? *American Psychologist, 36*, 361–372.

Rodin, J., & Salovey, P. (1989). Health psychology. *Annual Review of Psychology, 40*, 533–579.

Roediger, H. L. (1990). Implicit memory: Retention without remembering. *American Psychologist, 45*, 1043–1056.

Roethlisberger, F. J., & Dickson, W. J. (1939). *Management and the Worker.* New York: Wiley.

Rook, K. S. (1987). Social support versus companionship: Effects of life stress, loneliness, and evaluation by others. *Journal of Personality and Social Psychology, 52*, 1132–1147.

Rose, A. S., & Blank, M. (1974). The potency of context in children's cognition: An illustration through conservation. *Child Development, 45*, 499–502.

Rosenbaum, M. E. (1986). The repulsion hypothesis: On the nondevelopment of relationships. *Journal of Personality and Social Psychology, 51*, 1156–1166.

Rosenman, R. H., Brand, R. J., Jenkins, C. D., Friedman, M., Strauss, R., & Wurm, M. (1975). Coronary heart disease in the Western Collaborative Group Study: Final follow-up experience of 8 years. *Journal of the American Medical Association, 233*, 872–877.

Rosenman, R. H., Friedman, M., Strauss, R., Wurm, M., Kositcheck, R., Hahn, W., & Werthessen, N. T. (1964). A predictive study of coronary heart disease. *Journal of the American Medical Association,* 189, 15–22.

Rosenthal, D. (1970). *Genetics of psychopathology.* New York: McGraw-Hill.

Ross, C. A., Heber, S., Norton, G. R., & Anderson, G. (1989). Differences between multiple personality disorder and other diagnostic groups on structured interview. *Journal of Nervous and Mental Disorders,* 177, 487–491.

Ross, L. D. (1977). *The intuitive psychologist and his shortcomings:* Distortions in the attributional process. In L. Berkowitz (Ed.), *Advances in experimental social psychology (Vol. 10).* New York: Academic Press.

Rossi, A. S. (1980). *Aging and parenthood in the middle years.* In P. B. Baltes & O. G. Brim, Jr. (Eds.), *Lifespan development and behavior* (Vol. III). New York: Academic Press.

Roth M., & Argyle, N. Anxiety, panic and phobic disorders: An overview, *Journal of Psychiatric Research,* 22, (Suppl. 1), 33–54.

Rotton, J., & Frey, J. (1985). Air pollution, weather, and violent crimes: Concomitant analysis of archival data. *Journal of Personality and Social Psychology,* 49.

Rowe, J. W., & Kahn, R. L. (1987). Human aging: Usual and successful. *Science,* 237, 143–149.

Roy, A., DeJong, J., & Linnoila, M. (1989). Extraversion in pathological gamblers. *Archives of General Psychiatry,* 46, 679–684.

Rubenstein, E. A. (1983). Television and behavior. *American Psychologist,* 38, 820–825.

Rubin, Z. (1973). *Liking and loving: An invitation to social psychology.* New York: Holt, Rinehart and Winston.

Rutter, M., Graham, P., Chadwick, O., & Yule, W. (1976). Adolescent turmoil: Fact or fiction? *Journal of Child Psychology and Psychiatry,* 17, 35–56.

Ryan, E. D., & Kovacic, C. R. (1966). Pain tolerance and athletic participation. *Journal of Personality and Social Psychology,* 22, 383–390.

S

Saal, F. E., & Knight, P. A. (1988). *Industrial/organizational psychology.* Monterey, CA: Brooks/Cole.

Sadalla, E. K., & Oxley, D. (1984). The perception of room size: The rectangularity illusion. *Environment and Behavior,* 16, 394–405.

Saegert, S., & Winkel, G. H. (1990). Environmental psychology. *Annual Review of Psychology,* 41, 441–477.

Salthouse, T. A. (1989). *Age-related changes in basic cognitive processes.* In M. Storandt & G. R. VandenBos (Eds.), *The adult years: Continuity and change.* Washington, DC: American Psychological Association.

Samuelson, F. J. B. (1980). Watson's Little Albert, Cyril Burt's twins, and the need for a critical science. *American Psychologist,* 35, 619–625.

Satir, V. (1967). *Conjoint family therapy.* Palo Alto, CA: Science and Behavior Books.

Sauser, W. J., & York, C. M. (1978). Sex differences in job satisfaction: A reexamination. *Personnel Psychology,* 31, 537–547.

Schacter, D. L. (1987). Implicit memory: History and current status. *Journal of Experimental Psychology: Learning, Memory, and Cognition.* 13, 501–518.

Schacter, S., & Gross, L. P. (1968). Manipulated time and eating behavior. *Journal of Personality and Social Psychology,* 10, 98–106.

Schacter, S., & Singer, J. (1962). Cognitive, social, and physiological determinants of emotional states. *Psychological Review,* 69, 379–399.

Schaie, K. W., & Willis, S. L. (1986). *Adult development and aging* (2nd ed.). Boston: Little, Brown.

Scharf, B. (1978). *Loudness,* In E. C. Carterette & M. P. Friedman (Eds.), *Handbook of perception.* New York: Academic Press.

Scheerer, M. (1963). Problem solving. *Scientific American,* 208, 118–128.

Schmitt, N., & Robertson, I. (1990). Personnel selection. *Annual Review of Psychology,* 41, 289–319.

Schroeder, S. R., Schroeder, C. S., & Landesman, S. (1987). Psychological services in educational settings to persons with mental retardation. *American Psychologist,* 42, 805–808.

Schultz, D. P., & Schultz, S. E. (1990). *Psychology and industry today.* New York: Macmillan.

Schultz, R., & Alderman, D. (1974). Clinical research on the "stages of dying." *Omega,* 5, 137–144.

Schultz, R., & Decker, S. (1985). Long-term adjustment to physical disability: The role of social support, perceived control and self-blame. *Journal of Personality and Social Psychology,* 48, 1162–1172.

Scott, K. G., & Carran, D. T. (1987). The epidemiology and prevention of mental retardation. *American Psychologist,* 42, 801–804.

Scott, M. D., & Pelliccioni, L., Jr. (1982). *Don't choke: How athletes become winners.* Englewood Cliffs, NJ: Prentice-Hall.

Sears, P. S., & Barbee, A. H. (1977). *Career and life satisfaction among Terman's gifted women.* In J. Stanley et al. (Eds.), *The gifted and the creative: Fifty year perspective.* Baltimore: Johns Hopkins University Press.

Seligman, M. E. P. (1975). *Helplessness: On depression development and death.* San Francisco: Freeman.

Selkoe, D. J. (1990). Deciphering Alzheimer's disease: The amyloid precursor protein yields new clues. *Science,* 248, 1058.

Selye, H. (1956). *The stress of life.* New York: McGraw-Hill.

Selye, H. (1974). *Stress Without Distress.* Philadelphia: Lippincott.

Shadish, W. R. (1984). Policy research: Lessons from the implementation of deinstitutionalization. *American Psychologist,* 39, 725–738.

Shaffer, M. (1982). *Life after stress.* New York: Knopf.

Shaver, P., Hazan, C., & Bradshaw, D. (1988). *Love as attachment: The integration of three behavioral systems.* In R. J. Sternberg & M. L. Barnes (Eds.), *The psychology of love.* New Haven, CT: Yale University Press.

Shedler, J., & Block, J. (1990). Adolescent drug use and psychological health: A longitudinal study. *American Psychologist,* 45, 612–630.

Sheehy, R. N. (1976). *Passages: Predictable Crises from Adult Life.* New York: Dutton.

Shekelle, B., Hulley, S. B., Neaton, J. D., Billings, J. H., Borhani, N. O., et al. (1985). The MRFIT behavior pattern study II: Type A behavior and the incidence of coronary heart disease. *American Journal of Epidemiology,* 122, 559–570.

Sheldon, W. H. (1940). *The Varieties of Human Physique: An Introduction to Constitutional Psychology.* New York: Harper.

Sheldon, W. H. (1942). *The Varieties of Temperament: A Psychology of Constitutional Differences.* New York: Harper.

Sheldon, W. H. (1944). Constitutional factors in personality. In J. McV. Hunt (Ed.) *Personality and Behavior Disorders.* New York: Ronald Press.

Sheldon, W. H. (1954). *Atlas of Men: A Guide for Somatotyping the Adult Male at All Ages.* New York: Harper.

Shertzer, B. (1985). *Career planning* (3rd ed.). Boston: Houghton Mifflin.

Shimamura, A. P. (1986). Priming effects in amnesia: Evidence for a dissociable memory function. *Quarterly Journal of Experimental Psychology, 38A,* 619–644.

Shipley, T. (1961). *Classics in psychology.* New York: Philosophical Library.

Shippee, G., & Gregory, W. L. (1982). Public commitment and energy conservation. *American Journal of Community Psychology, 10,* 81–93.

Shotland, R. L. (1985). When bystanders just stand by. *Psychology Today, 19,* 50–55.

Shulman, H. G. (1971). Similarity effects in short-term memory. *Psychological Bulletin, 75,* 399–415.

Shulman, H. G. (1972). Semantic confusion errors in short-term memory. *Journal of Verbal Learning and Verbal Behavior, 11,* 221–227.

Siegler, R. S. (1983). Five generalizations about cognitive development. *American Psychologist, 38,* 263–277.

Siegler, R. S. (1989). Mechanisms of cognitive development. *Annual Review of Psychology, 40,* 353–379.

Skinner, B. F. (1956). A case history in the scientific method. *American Psychologist, 11,* 221–233.

Skinner, B. F. (1957). *Verbal behavior.* Englewood Cliffs, NJ: Prentice-Hall.

Skinner, B. F. (1983). Intellectual self-management in old age. *American Psychologist, 38,* 239–244.

Skinner, B. F. (1984). *A matter of consequence.* New York: Knopf.

Skinner, B. F. (1987). What ever happened to psychology as the science of behavior? *American Psychologist, 42,* 780–786.

Skinner, B. F. (1989). The origins of cognitive thought. *American Psychologist, 44,* 13–18.

Skinner, B. F. (1990). Can psychology be a science of mind? *American Psychologist, 45,* 1206–1210.

Skolnick, A. (1979). *The intimate environment* (2nd ed.). Boston: Little, Brown.

Slobin, D. I. (1979). *Psycholinguistics.* Glenview, IL: Scott, Foresman.

Small, J. G., Klapper, M. H., Kellams, J. J., Miller, M. J., Milstein, V., Sharpley, P. H., & Small, I. F. (1988). Electroconvulsive treatment compared with lithium in the management of manic states. *Archives of General Psychiatry, 45,* 727–732.

Smith, A., & Stansfield, S. (1986). Aircraft noise exposure, noise sensitivity, and everyday errors. *Environment and Behavior, 18,* 214–226.

Smith, D. (1987). Conditions that facilitate the development of sport imagery training. *The Sport Psychologist, 1,* 237–247.

Smith, M. L., Glass, G. V., & Miller, T. I. (1980). *The benefits of psychotherapy.* Baltimore: Johns Hopkins University Press.

Smith, P. C. (1976). *Behavior, results, and organizational effectiveness: The problem of criteria.* In M. D. Dunnette (Ed.), *Handbook of industrial and organizational psychology.* Skokie, IL: Rand McNally.

Smith, S. (1979). Remembering in and out of context. *Journal of Experimental Psychology: Human Learning and Memory, 5,* 460–471.

Snarey, J. (1987). A question of morality. *Psychology Today, 21,* 6–8.

Snyder, S. H. (1980). *Biological aspects of mental disorder.* New York: Oxford University Press.

Snyder, S. H. (1984, November). Medicated minds. *Science 84,* pp. 141–142.

Snyderman, M., & Rothman, S. (1987). Survey of expert opinion on intelligence and aptitude testing. *American Psychologist, 42,* 137–144.

Solomon, R. L. (1980). The opponent-process theory of acquired motivation: The costs of pleasure and the benefits of pain. *American Psychologist, 35,* 691–712.

Solomon, R. L., & Corbit, J. D. (1974). An opponent-process theory of motivation. I. Temporal dynamics of affect. *Psychological Review, 81,* 119–145.

Sorenson, R. C. (1973). *Adolescent sexuality in contemporary America.* New York: Abrams.

Spanos, N. P., & Barber, T. F. X. (1974). Toward convergence in hypnosis research. *American Psychologist, 29,* 500–511.

Spear, N. E., Miller, J. S., & Jagielo, J. A. (1990). Animal learning and memory. *Annual Review of Psychology, 41,* 169–211.

Sperling, G. (1960). The information available in brief visual presentation. *Psychological Monographs, 74,* (Whole No. 498).

Sperling, G. (1963). A model for visual memory tasks. *Human Factors, 5,* 19–31.

Sperry, R. (1968). Hemispheric disconnection and unity in conscious awareness. *American Psychologist, 23,* 723–733.

Sperry, R. (1982). Some effects of disconnecting the cerebral hemispheres. *Science, 217,* 1223–1226.

Spitz, H. (1986). *The raising of intelligence: A selected history of attempts to raise retarded intelligence.* Hillsdale, NJ: Erlbaum.

Springer, J. P., & Deutsch, G. (1981). *Left brain, right brain.* San Francisco: Freeman.

Squire, L. R. (1982). The neuropsychology of human memory. *Annual Review of Neuroscience, 5,* 241–273.

Squire, L. R. (1986). Mechanisms of memory. *Science, 232,* 1612–1619.

Squire, L. R. (1987). *Memory and the brain.* New York: Oxford University Press.

Squire, L. R., & Slater, P. C. (1978). Bilateral and unilateral ECT: Effects on verbal and nonverbal memory. *American Journal of Psychiatry, 135,* 1316–1320.

Stagner, R. (1982). The importance of historical context. *American Psychologist, 37,* 856.

Stagner, S. F., & Burke, P. J. (1982). A reexamination of body build stereotypes. *Journal of Research in Personality, 16,* 435–446.

Standing, L. (1973). Learning 10,000 pictures. *Quarterly Journal of Experimental Psychology, 25,* 207–222.

Standing, L., Canezio, J., & Haber, R. N. (1970). Perception and memory for pictures: Single-trial learning 2500 visual stimuli. *Psychonomic Science,* 19, 73–74.

Stechler, G., & Halton, A. (1982). *Prenatal influences on human development.* In B. B. Woolman (Ed.), *Handbook of developmental psychology.* Englewood Cliffs, NJ: Prentice-Hall.

Stein, B. A. (1983). Quality of work life in action: Managing for effectiveness. New York: *American Management Association.*

Stenchever, M. A., Williamson, R. A., Leonard, J., Karp, L. E., Ley, B., Shy, K., & Smith, D. (1981). Possible relationship between in utero diethylstibestrol exposure and male infertility. *American Journal of Obstetrics and Gynecology,* 140, 186–193.

Stevenson, H. W., Lee, S. Y., & Stigler, J. W. (1986). Mathematics achievement of Chinese, Japanese, and American children. *Science,* 231, 693–696.

Stiles, W. B., Shapiro, D. A., & Elliot, R. (1986). "Are all psychotherapies equivalent?" *American Psychologist,* 41, 165–180.

Stokols, D. (1972). On the distinction between density and crowding: Some implications for future research. *Psychological Review,* 79, 275–277.

Stokols, D. (1990). Instrumental and spiritual views of people-environment relations. *American Psychologist,* 45, 641–646.

Stoner, J. A. F. (1961). *A comparison of individual and group decisions involving risk.* Unpublished master's thesis, Massachusetts Institute of Technology, Cambridge, MA.

Storandt, M. (1983). Psychology's response to the graying of America. *American Psychologist,* 38, 323–326.

Strupp, H. H. (1986). Psychotherapy: Research, practice, and public policy (How to avoid dead ends). *American Psychologist,* 41, 120–130.

Strupp, H. H., & Binder, J. L. (1984). *Psychotherapy in a new key.* New York: Guilford.

Stunkard, A. J. (1988). Some perspectives on human obesity: Its causes. *Bulletin of the New York Academy of Medicine,* 64, 902–923.

Stunkard, A. J., Harris, J. R., Pederson, N. L., & McClearn, G. E. (1900). The body-mass index of twins who have been reared apart. *New England Journal of Medicine,* 322, 1483–1487.

Stunkard, A. J., Sorensen, T. I. A., Hanis, C., et al. (1986). An adoption study of human obesity. *New England Journal of Medicine,* 314, 193–198.

Sue, S., & Okazaki, S. (1990). Asian-American educational achievements: A phenomenon in search of an explanation. *American Psychologist* 45, 913–920.

Suinn, R. M. (1980). *Psychology in sports: Methods and applications.* Minneapolis: Burgess.

Surwit, R. S., Feinglos, M. N., & Scovern, A. W. (1983). Diabetes and behavior. *American Psychologist,* 38, 255–262.

Swedo, S. E., Rapoport, J. L., Leonard, H., Lenane, M., & Cheslow, D. (1989a). Obsessive-compulsive disorder in children and adolescence. *Archives of General Psychiatry,* 46, 335–341.

Swedo, S. E., Schapiro, M. B., Grady, C. L., Cheslow, D. L., et al. (1989b). Cerebral glucose metabolism in childhood-onset obsessive-compulsive disorder. *Archives of General Psychiatry,* 46, 518–523.

Szasz, T. S. (1960). *The myth of mental illness.* New York: HarperCollins.

Szasz, T. S. (1982). The psychiatric will: A new mechanism for protecting persons against "psychosis" and psychiatry. *American Psychologist* 37, 762–770.

T

Tandon, R., & Greden, J. F. (1989). Cholinergic hyperactivity and negative schizophrenic symptoms. *Archives of General Psychiatry* 46, 745–753.

Tanner, J. M. (1973). Growing up. *Scientific America,* 135, 34–43.

Tanner, J. M. (1981). Growth and maturation during adolescence. *Nutrition Review,* 39, 43–55.

Tanner, J. M., Whitehouse, R. H., & Takaishi, M. (1966). Standards from birth to maturity for height, weight, height velocity, and weight velocity: British children, 1965. *Archives of Diseases in Childhood,* 41, 457–471, 613–635.

Taylor, S. E. (1990). Health psychology: The science and the field. *American Psychologist,* 45, 40–50.

Taylor, W., Pearson, J., Mair, A., & Burns, W. (1965). Study of noise and hearing in jute weaving. *Journal of the Acoustical Society of America,* 4, 144–152.

Tenopyr, M. L. (1981). The realities of employment testing. *American Psychologist,* 36, 1120–1127.

Terenius, L. (1982). Endorphins and modulation of pain. *Advances in Neurology,* 33, 59–64.

Thackwray-Emmerson, D. (1989). The effect of self-motivation on headache reduction through biofeedback training. *Medical Psychotherapy,* 2, 125–130.

Thayer, W. P. (1983). *Industrial/organizational psychology: Science and application.* In C. J. Scheirer & A. M. Rogers (Eds.), *The G. Stanley Hall lecture series* (Vol. 3). Washington, DC: American Psychological Association.

Thibault, J. W., & Kelley, H. H. (1959). *The social psychology of groups.* New York: Wiley.

Thompson, C. I. (1980). *Controls of eating.* Jamaica, NY: Spectrum.

Thompson, C. P. (1982). Memory for unique personal events: The roommate study. *Memory and Cognition,* 10, 324–332.

Thompson, J. W., & Blaine, J. D. (1987). Use of ECT in the United States in 1975 and 1980. *American Journal of Psychiatry,* 144, 557–562.

Thompson, R. (1969). Localization of the "visual memory system" in the white rat. *Journal of Comparative and Physiological Psychology,* 2, 1–17.

Thompson, R. (1981). Rapid forgetting of spatial habit in rats with hippocampal lesions. *Science,* 212, 959–960.

Thompson, R. (1986). The neurobiology of learning and memory. *Science,* 233, 941–947.

Thorndike, A. L., Hagen, E. P., & Sattler, J. M. (1986). *The Stanford-Binet Intelligence scale, Fourth edition: Technical manual.* Chicago: Riverside.

Thorndike, E. L. (1911). *Animal intelligence.* New York: Macmillan.

Thornton, G. C., III, & Cleveland, J. N. (1990). Developing managerial talent through simulation. *American Psychologist,* 45, 190–199.

Tilley, A. J., & Empson, J. A. C. (1978). REM sleep and memory consolidation. *Biological Psychology*, 6, 293–300.

Tobin-Richards, M., Boxer, A., & Peterson, A. C. (1984). *The psychological impact of pubertal change: Sex differences in perceptions of self during early adolescence.* In J. Brooks-Gunn & A. C. Peterson (Eds.), *Girls at puberty: Biological, psychological, and social perspectives.* New York: Plenum.

Tohen, M., Waternaux, C. M., & Tsuang, M. T. (1990). Outcome in mania. *Archives of General Psychiatry*, 47, 1106–1111.

Tolman, C. W. (1969) Social feeding in domestic chicks: Effects of food deprivation of non-feeding companions. *Psychonomic Science*, 15, 234.

Tolman, E. C. (1932). *Purposive behaviorism in animals and men.* Englewood Cliffs, NJ: Prentice-Hall.

Tolman, E. C., & Honzik, C. H. (1930). Introduction and removal of reward and maze performance in rats. *University of California Publication in Psychology*, 4, 257–275.

Tomkins, S. S. (1962). *Affect, imagery, consciousness: Vol. I. The positive affects.* New York: Springer.

Torrey, T. W., & Feduccia, A. (1979). *Morphogenesis of the vertebrates.* New York: Wiley.

Triplett, N. (1898). The dynamogenic factors in pacemaking and competition. *American Journal of Psychology*, 9, 507–533.

Tucker, D. M. (1981). Lateral brain function, emotion, and conceptualization. *Psychological Bulletin*, 89, 19–46.

Tulving, E. (1972). *Episodic and semantic memory.* In E. Tulving & W. Donaldson (Eds.), *Organization of memory.* New York: Academic Press.

Tulving, E. (1985). How many memory systems are there? *American Psychologist*, 40, 385–398.

Tulving, E. (1986). What kind of a hypothesis is the distinction between episodic and semantic memory? *Journal of Experimental Psychology: Learning, Memory, and Cognition*, 12, 307–311.

Tulving, E., & Thompson, D. M. (1973). Encoding specificity and retrieval processes in episodic memory. *Journal of Experimental Psychology: Learning, Memory, and Cognition*, 8, 336–342.

Turkington, C. (1985). Computer unlocks secrets in folds, functions of brain. *APA Monitor*, 16, 12–13.

Turner, C. W., Hesse, B. W., & Peterson-Lewis, S. (1986). Naturalistic studies of the long-term effects of television violence. *Journal of Social Issues*, 42, 7–28.

Turner, J. S., & Helms, D. B. (1987). *Contemporary adulthood.* New York: Holt, Rinehart, and Winston.

Tuttle, T. C. (1983). Organizational productivity: A challenge for psychologists. *American Psychologist*, 38, 479–486.

U

Ulrich, R. E., Stachnick, T. J., & Stainton, N. R. (1963). Student acceptance of Generalized Personality Inventory. *Psychological Reports*, 13, 831–834.

Underwood, B. J. (1957). Interference and forgetting. *Psychological Review*, 64, 49–60.

V

Valenstein, E. S. (1980). *The psychosurgery debate: Scientific, legal, and ethical perspectives.* San Francisco: Freeman.

Valenstein, E. S. (1986). *Great and desperate cures.* New York: Basic Books.

Valliant, G. E., & Valliant, C. O. (1990). Natural history of male psychological health, XII: A 45-year study of predictors of successful aging at age 65. *American Journal of Psychiatry*, 147, 31–37.

VandenBos, G. R. (1986). Psychotherapy research: A special issue. *American Psychologist*, 41, 111–112.

Varca, P. E. (1980). An analysis of home and away game performance of male college basketball teams. *Journal of Sport Psychology*, 2, 245–257.

Vaughn, B. E., & Langlois, J. H. (1983). Physical attractiveness as a correlate of peer status and social competence in preschool children. *Developmental Psychology*, 19, 561–567.

Ventura, J., Nuechterlein, K. H., Lukoff, D., & Hardesty, J. P. (1989). A prospective study of stressful life events and schizophrenic relapse. *Journal of Abnormal Psychology*, 98, 407–411.

Verillo, R. T. (1975). *Cutaneous sensation.* In B. Scharf (Ed.), *Experimental sensory psychology.* Glenview, IL: Scott, Foresman.

Vinacke, W. E. (1974). *The psychology of thinking* (2nd ed.). New York: McGraw-Hill.

Vitz, P. C. (1990). The use of stories in moral development. *American Psychologist*, 45, 709–720.

Vokey, J. R., & Read, J. D. (1985). Subliminal messages: Between the devil and the media. *American Psychologist*, 40, 1231–1239.

Vroom, V. (1964). *Work and motivation.* New York: Wiley.

W

Walker, L. J. (1989). A longitudinal study of moral reasoning. *Child Development*, 601, 157–166.

Wallace, P. (1977). Individual discrimination of humans by odor. *Physiology and Behavior*, 19, 577–579.

Walsh, B. T., Kissileff, H. R., Cassidy, S. M., & Dantzic, S. (1989). Eating behavior of women with bulimia. *Archives of General Psychiatry*, 46, 54–58.

Walster, E., Aronson, V., Abrahams, D., & Rottman, L. (1966). Importance of physical attractiveness in dating behavior. *Journal of Personality and Social Psychology*, 4, 508–516.

Walster, E., & Festinger, L. (1962). The effectiveness of "overheard" and persuasive communications. *Journal of Abnormal and Social Psychology*, 65, 395–402.

Walster, E., & Walster, G. W. (1969). The matching hypothesis. *Journal of Personality and Social Psychology*, 6, 248–253.

Walster, E., Walster, G. W., & Berschied, E. (1978). *Equity: Theory and research.* Boston: Allyn & Bacon.

Walters, G. C., & Grusec, J. E. (1977). *Punishment.* San Francisco: Freeman.

Warrington, E. K., & Weiskrantz, L. (1968). New method of testing long-term retention with special reference to amnesic patients. *Nature*, 217, 972–974.

Warrington, E. K., & Weiskrantz, L. (1970). Amnesic syndrome: Consolidation or retrieval? *Nature, 228,* 629–630.

Watkins, L. R., & Mayer, D. J. (1982). Organization of endogenous opiate and nonopiate pain control systems. *Science, 216,* 1185–1192.

Watkins, M. J. (1990). Mediationism and the obfuscation of memory. *American Psychologist, 45,* 328–335.

Watson, C. J. (1981). An evaluation of some aspects of the Steers and Rhodes model of employee attendance. *Journal of Applied Psychology, 66,* 385–389.

Watson, J. B. (1919). *Psychology from the standpoint of a behaviorist.* Philadelphia: Lippincott.

Watson, J. B. (1925). *Behaviorism.* New York: Norton.

Watson, J. B. (1926). What is behaviorism? *Harper's Monthly Magazine, 152,* 723–729.

Watson, J. B., & Raynor, R. (1920). Conditioned emotional reactions. *Journal of Experimental Psychology, 3,* 1–14.

Weaver, C. N. (1980). Job satisfaction in the United States in the 1970s. *Journal of Applied Psychology, 65,* 364–367.

Wechsler, D. (1958). *The measurement and appraisal of adult intelligence* (4th ed.). Baltimore: Williams & Wilkins.

Wechsler, D. (1975). Intelligence defined and undefined: A relativistic reappraisal. *American Psychologist, 30,* 135–139.

Wechsler, D. (1981). Manual for the Wechsler Adult Intelligence Scale—Revised. New York: *The Psychological Corporation.*

Weiner, B. (1985). An attributional theory of achievement motivation and emotion. *Psychological Review, 92,* 548–573.

Weisberg, R. W. (1986). *Creativity: Genius and other myths.* San Francisco: Freeman.

Weissman, M. M. (1988). The epidemiology of anxiety disorders: Rates, risks and familial patterns. *Journal of Psychiatric Research, 22,* (Suppl. 1), 99–114.

Weissman, M. M., Klerman, G. L., Markowitz, J. S., & Ouellette, R. (1989). Suicidal ideation and suicide attempts in panic disorders and attacks. *The New England Journal of Medicine, 321,* 1209–1214.

Weldon, E., & Gargano, G. M. (1988). Cognitive loading: The effects of accountability and shared responsibility on cognitive effort. *Personality and Social Psychology Bulletin, 14,* 159–171.

Wertheimer, M. (1961). Psychomotor coordination of auditory and visual space at birth. *Science, 134,* 1692.

Wheeler, R. J., & Frank, M. A. (1988). Identification of stress buffers. *Behavioral Medicine, 14,* 78–89.

Whitehurst, G. (1982). Language development. In B. Wolman (Ed.), *Handbook of developmental psychology.* Englewood Cliffs, NJ: Prentice-Hall.

Wickens, D. D. (1973). Some characteristics of word encoding. *Memory and Cognition, 1,* 485–490.

Wiesner, W. H., & Cronshaw, S. F. (1988). A meta-analytic investigation of the impact of interview format and degree of structure on the validity of the employment interview. *Occupational Psychology, 61,* 275–290.

Wilkes, J. (1986). Conversation with Ernest R. Hilgard: A study in hypnosis. *Psychology Today, 20*(1), 23–27.

Williams, K., Harkins, S., & Latané, B. (1981). Identifiability as a deterrent to social loafing: Two cheering experiments. *Journal of Personality and Social Psychology, 40,* 303–311.

Williams, K., Nida, S. A., Baca, L. D., & Latané, B. (1989). Social loafing and swimming: Effects of identifiability of individual and relay performance of intercollegiate swimmers. *Basic and Applied Social Psychology, 10,* 73–82.

Williams, R. L. (1972). *The BITCH Test (Black Intelligence Test of Cultural Homogeneity).* St. Louis: Williams and Associates.

Wilson, G. T. (1982). *Adult disorders.* In G. T. Wilson & C. M. Franks (Eds.), *Contemporary behavior therapy: Conceptual and empirical foundations.* New York: Guilford Press.

Winett, R. A., Leckliter, I. N., Chinn, D. E., Stahl, B., & Love, S. Q. (1985). Effects of television modeling on residential energy conservation. *Journal of Applied Behavior Analysis, 18,* 33–44.

Winter, D. G. (1987). Leader appeal, leader performance, and the motive profiles of leaders and followers: A study of American presidents and elections. *Journal of Personality and Social Psychology, 52,* 196–202.

Winter, D. G. (1988). The power motive in women—and men. Journal of Personality and Social Psychology, 54, 510–519.

Winter, D. G., & Stewart, A. J. (1978). *The power motive.* In H. London & J. E. Exner (Eds.), *Dimensions of personality.* New York: Wiley.

Winters, K. C., Weintraub, S., & Neale, J. M. (1981). Validity of MMPI code types in identifying DSM-III schizophrenics. *Journal of Consulting and Clinical Psychology, 49,* 486–487.

Witmer, J. F., & Geller, E. S. (1976). Facilitating paper recycling: Effects of prompts, raffles, and contests. *Journal of Applied Behavior Analysis, 9,* 315–322.

Wollen, K. A., Weber, A., & Lowry, D. H. (1972). Bizarreness versus interaction of mental images as determinants of learning. *Cognitive Psychology, 3,* 518–523.

Wolpe, J. (1958). *Psychotherapy by reciprocal inhibition.* Stanford, CA: Stanford University Press.

Wolpe, J. (1969). Basic principles and practices of behavior therapy of neuroses. *American Journal of Psychiatry, 125,* 1242–1247.

Wolpe, J. (1981). Behavior therapy versus psychoanalysis. *American Psychologist, 36,* 159–164.

Wolpe, J. (1982). *The practice of behavior therapy* (3rd ed.). New York: Pergamon Press.

Wood, C. (1986). The hostile heart. *Psychology Today, 20,* 10–12.

Woodworth, R. S., & Schlosberg, H. (1954). *Experimental Psychology.* New York: Holt, Rinehart and Winston.

Wright, L. (1988). The Type A behavior pattern and coronary artery disease. *American Psychologist, 43,* 2–14.

Wurtman, R. J. (1985). Alzheimer's disease. *Scientific American, 247,* 62–74.

Wysowski, D. K., & Baum, C. (1989). Antipsychotic drug use in the United States, 1976–1985. *Archives of General Psychiatry, 46,* 929–932.

Y

Yates, A. J. (1980). *Biofeedback and the Modification of Behavior.* New York: Plenum.

Yates, A. (1989). Current perspectives on the eating disorders: I. History, psychological and biological aspects. *Journal of the American Academy of Child and Adolescent Psychiatry, 28,* 813–828.

Yates, A. (1990). Current perspectives on eating disorders: II. Treatment, outcome, and research directions. *Journal of the American Academy of Child and Adolescent Psychiatry, 29*, 1–9.

Yates, F. A. (1966). *The art of memory.* Chicago: University of Chicago Press.

Z

Zajonc, R. B. (1965). Social facilitation. *Science, 149*, 269–274.

Zajonc, R. B. (1968). Attitudinal effects of mere exposure. *Journal of Personality and Social Psychology,* Monograph Suppl. 9, 1–27.

Zajonc, R. B., & Markus, H. (1982). Affective and cognitive factors in preferences. *Journal of Consumer Research, 9*, 123–131.

Zedeck, S., Tziner, A., & Middlestadt, S. E. (1983). Interviewer validity and reliability: An individual analysis approach. *Personnel Psychology, 36*, 230–237.

Zelnik, M., & Kantner, J. F. (1980). Sexual activity, contraceptive use, and pregnancy among metropolitan-area teenagers: 1971–1979. *Family Planning Perspectives, 12*, 230–237.

Zigler, E. & Hodapp, R. M. (1991). Behavioral functioning in individuals with mental retardation. *Annual Review of Psychology, 42*, 29–50.

Zimmerman, M., & Coryell, W. (1989). DSM-III personality disorder diagnoses in a nonpatient sample. *Archives of General Psychiatry, 46*, 682–689.

Zuckerman, M. (1978). Sensation seeking and psychopathology. In R. D. Hare & D. Schalling (Eds.). *Psychopathic Behavior.* New York: Wiley.

Zuckerman, M., Eysenck, S., & Eysenck, H. J. (1978). Sensation seeking in England and America: Cross-cultural, age, and sex comparisons. *Journal of Consulting and Clinical Psychology, 46*, 139–149.

Zuckerman, M., Buchsbaum, M. S., & Murphy, D. L. (1980). Sensation seeking and its biological correlates. *Psychological Bulletin, 88*, 187–214.

Credits

▲▲▲▲▲▲▲▲

Chapter 1

13 Luis Villota/The Stock Market. 17 (b) Giraudon/Art Resource, NY. 18 (t) The Granger Collection, New York; (b) Darwin Museum, Down House, Kent/Royal College of Surgeons of England. 19 (t) The Granger Collection, New York; (b) Archives of the History of American Psychology. 20 (both) The Granger Collection, New York. 21 UPI/Bettman. 22 (t) Historical Pictures Service; (b) Joe McNally. 23 (t,c) The Bettmann Archive; (b) UPI/Bettmann. 34 Martin Rogers/Tony Stone Worldwide. 38 Figure 1.4(B) D. G. Boring (1930) "A New Ambiguous Figure." AMERICAN JOURNAL OF PSYCHOLOGY, 42, 109–116; Figure 1.4(C) *Ascending and Descending* by M.C. Escher. © M. C. Escher Heirs c/o Cordon Art, Baarn, Holland. Collection Haags Gemeente-museum, The Hague. 40 Hangarter/The Picture Cube.

Chapter 2

47 Steve Chen/West Light. 48 Henley & Savage/Picturesque. 51 Fritz Goro, *Life* Magazine © 1971 Time Warner Inc. 63 Don Carroll/The Image Bank. 71 Oscar Palmquist/Lightwave. 72 Eunice Harris/The Picture Cube.

Chapter 3

79 Tom McCarthy/The Picture Cube. 81 Per Sundstrom/ © 1982 *Discover* Magazine. 83 Courtesy American Cancer Society. 84 Charles Gupton/Picturesque. 86 Michael Siluk/The Image Works. 87 Figure 3.4 Enrico Ferorelli. 89 Enrico Ferorelli. 90 Yves De Braine/Black Star. 91 Figure 3.5 George Zimbel/Monkmeyer Press Photo Service. 92 Figure 3.6 Marcia Weinstein. 94 Bonnie Schiffman/Onyx. 100 Tony Freeman/PhotoEdit. 101 Bob Daemmrich/The Image Works. 102 Ken Kaminsky/The Picture Cube. 106 (t) Skjold/PhotoEdit; (b) Melanie Carr/Zephyr Pictures. 108 Elizabeth Crews. 110 Sidney Harris. 111 Dave Schaefer/PhotoEdit. 113 (1) Allan Carey/The Image Works; (r) Bob Daemmrich/Stock, Boston.

Chapter 4

121 Lawrence Manning/West Light. 134 Joe McDonald/Tom Stack & Associates. 138 Richard Hutchings/InfoEdit. 145 Tony Freeman/PhotoEdit. 149 Stanley Rowin/The Picture Cube. 150 REPRINTED FROM PSYCHOLOGY TODAY MAGAZINE Copyright © 1987 American Psychological Association.

Chapter 5

159 Tom Doody/The Picture Cube. 162 Therese Frape/The Picture Cube. 169 Figure 5.5(B) D. G. Boring (1930) "A New Ambiguous Figure." AMERICAN JOURNAL OF PSYCHOLOGY, 42, 109–116. 170 Figure 5.7 Tony Stone Worldwide. 171 Figure 5.9 Joe Sohm/The Image Works; Figure 5.10 Dennis Kucharzak; Figure 5.11 Francis de Richemond/The Image Works. 172 Figure 5.12 Murray & Assoc./Picturesque; Figure 5.13 Frank Whitney/The Image Bank. 176 Christopher Springmann. 178 From DREAMSTAGE Scientific Catalog,

Copyright © 1977 J. Allan Hobson and Hoffmann-La Roche Inc. 179 Louis Psihoyos. 180 Mimi Forsyth/Monkmeyer Press Photo Service. 185 Melanie Carr/Picturesque. 186 (1) Rick Friedman/The Picture Cube; (r) Bob Daemmrich/Tony Stone Worldwide.

Chapter 6

195 Eastcott-Momatiuk/The Image Works. 197 (b) Tass from Sovfoto. 202 Bob Higbee/Berg & Associates. 203 Vloo/Stockphotos, Inc. 204 Courtesy of Professor Benjamin Harris, University of Wisconsin-Parkside. From Watson's 1919 film, *Experimental Investigation of Babies.* 207 (t) The Granger Collection, New York; Figure 6.4 Richard Wood/The Picture Cube. 208 Maxwell MacKenzie/Tony Stone Worldwide. 218 Hank Morgan/© 1984 *Discover* Magazine. 219 Courtesy Department of Psychology, University of California, Berkeley. 221 REPRINTED FROM PSYCHOLOGY TODAY MAGAZINE Copyright © 1986 American Psychological Association. 222 Figure 6.9 Courtesy Dr. Albert Bandura.

Chapter 7

229 Willie Hill, Jr./The Image Works. 234 Richard Hutchings/InfoEdit. 235 (both) Bob Daemmrich/The Image Works. 237 Ken Heyman. 239 (t) Tony Freeman/PhotoEdit; (b) Charles Gupton/Picturesque. 240 Keith Gunnar/Bruce Coleman Inc. 246 Hugh Rogers/Monkmeyer Press Photo Service. 250 Tass from Sovfoto. 251 (both) From *Congestorium Artificia Memoriae* by Johannes Romberch, Venice, 1553.

Chapter 8

263 Richard Hutchings/PhotoEdit. 265 Bob Daemmrich/Tony Stone Worldwide. 266 (t) Bob Daemmrich/The Image Works; (b) Don Smetzer/Tony Stone Worldwide. 273 Reprinted with special permission of King Features Syndicate, Inc. 274 (t) Burk Uzzle/Magnum; (b) Milt & Joan Mann/Cameramann International. 278 Elizabeth Crews/The Image Works. 282 (t) Historical Pictures Service; (b) Courtesy Stanford University News and Publications Service. 283 Riverside Publishing Company, Chicago, IL. 285 Ray Stott/The Image Works.

Chapter 9

301 John Coletti/Tony Stone Worldwide. 303 Jeff Foott/Tom Stack & Associates. 304 (1) Anthony Jalondi/Monkmeyer Press Photo Service; (r) Francis de Richemond/The Image Works. 305 Bob Daemmrich/Stock, Boston. 308 Ellis Herwig/Stock, Boston. 309 (t) Douglas Corry/Uniphoto; (b) Brian Parker/Tom Stack & Associates. 311 Lawrence Migdale/Stock, Boston. 313 John Anderson/Tony Stone Worldwide. 314 William Thompson/The Picture Cube. 316 John Coletti/Stock, Boston. 318 Catherine Allport/The Image Works. 321 Figure 9.5 © Diana O. Rasche. 323 (t) Jon Riley/Tony Stone Worldwide; (b) David Strickler/The Picture Cube. 324 (l) Peter Marlow/Magnum; (r) Ellis Herwig/Stock, Boston. 326 Jon Riley/Picturesque 329 Figure 9.6 (t) George Harrison; Figure 9.6 (b) John Chellman/Animals Animals. 330 Figure 9.7 Photos Courtesy Dr. Paul Ekman. From UNMASKING THE FACE by Paul Ekman and Wallace V. Friesen. 331 Figure 9.8 From DARWIN AND FACIAL EXPRESSION: A CENTURY OF RESEARCH IN REVIEW, edited by Paul Ekman. Academic Press, 1973. By permission of Dr. Paul Ekman.

Chapter 10

337 Jeffry W. Myers/Stock, Boston. 343 Historical Pictures Service. 344 (t) The Bettmann Archive; (c) Association for the Advancement of Psychoanalysis of the Karen Horney Psychoanalytic Institute and Center, New York; (b) Charles Gupton/Tony Stone Worldwide. 346 (t) Elizabeth Crews. 348 (l) Independence Historical Park Collection/Eastern National Parks and Monuments Association; (r) The Franklin D. Roosevelt Library. 349 Courtesy Harvard University News Office. 356 Michal Heron/Monkmeyer Press Photo Service. 359 Stacy Pickerell/Tony Stone Worldwide.

Chapter 11

369 Michael Beasley/Tony Stone Worldwide. 371 Tony Freeman/PhotoEdit. 375 Michael Grecco/Stock, Boston. 377 Richard Pasley/Stock, Boston. 378 Harold Chapman/The Image Works. 383 © Joel Gordon 1983. 385 (t) Courtesy American Cancer Society; (b) Patrick Watson/The Image Works.

Chapter 12

393 D. & I. MacDonald/Unicorn. 395 (t) Rick Smolan; (b) Victor Englebert. 396 (t) AP/Wide World; (b) The Granger Collection, New York. 397 AP/Wide World. 398 Sygma. 400 (t) Charles Harbutt/Actuality; (b) Dagmar Fabricius/Stock, Boston. 403 Owen Franken/Sygma. 406 Susan Greenwood/Gamma-Liaison. 407 (both) Courtesy Cornelia B. Wilbur, M. D. 408 Tony Freeman/PhotoEdit. 410 Brookhaven National Laboratory and NYU Medical Center. 416 Al Vercoutere, Atascadero, CA. 417 (both) Al Vercoutere, Atascadero, CA. 420 NIMH.

Chapter 13

427 Robin Forbes/The Image Bank. 429 Scala/Art Resource, NY. 430 By Courtesy of the Trustees of Sir John Soane's Museum. 431 (l) Rob Nelson/Picture Group; (r) Paul L. Meredith/Tony Stone Worldwide. 435 James D. Wilson/Woodfin Camp & Associates. 439 Historical Pictures Service. 442 Hugh L. Wilkerson. 445 Courtesy Dr. Joseph Wolpe. 446 (All) Courtesy Dr. Albert Bandura. 447 UPI/Bettmann.

Chapter 14

459 Eastcott/Momatiuk/The Image Works. 460 (both) Courtesy Mrs. Jane Elliott and ABC Television. 462 Margo Granitsas/The Image Works. 463 Courtesy Evan-Picone Inc. 466 Bill Bachmann/The Image Works. 467 © Jeffrey Henson Scales. 473 Mary Kate Denny/PhotoEdit. 474 Frank Siteman/The Picture Cube. 475 © Ethan Hoffman/Picture Project. 476 William Vandivert. 477 (t) Courtesy World Federation of Bergen-Belsen Associations; Figure 14.6 Copyright 1965 by Stanley Milgram. From the film OBEDIENCE, distributed by the Pennsylvania State University, PCR. 479 Terry McKay/The Picture Cube. 483 Jean-Claude Lejeune. 484 Lawrence Manning/Tony Stone Worldwide.

Chapter 15

491 REPRINTED FROM PSYCHOLOGY TODAY MAGAZINE Copyright © 1986 American Psychological Association. 495 Jim Pickerell/Tony Stone Worldwide. 499 Brian Seed/Tony Stone Worldwide. 501 David Young-Wolff/PhotoEdit. 506 (l) Robert Brenner/PhotoEdit; (c) David R. Frazier Photolibrary. 507 (l) Alan Carey/The Image Works; (c) M. Dwyer/Stock, Boston; (r) Marty Heitner/The Picture Cube. 511 (l) Jettmar/Allstock/Picture Group; (r) Courtesy Nancy Gerow. 514 Dan McCoy/Rainbow.

Literary, Figures, and Tables

Chapter 2

54 Fig. 2.4 "Action Potentials Recorded from Inside a Nerve Fiber" by A.L. Hodgkin and A.F. Huxley. Reprinted by permission from NATURE, Volume 144, No. 3651, October 1939. Copyright © 1939 by Macmillan Magazine, Ltd.

Chapter 3

99 Fig. 3.10 Figure 8 from "Standards from Birth to Maturity for Height, Weight, Height Velocity, and Weight Velocity: British Children, 1956" by J.M. Tanner, R.H. Whitehouse, and M. Takaishi from *Archives of Disease in Childhood*. Vol. 41, October 1966. Copyright © 1966 by the British Medical Association. Reprinted by permission of the British Medical Journal and the authors.

Chapter 4

124 Fig. 4.2 From "Contemporary Psychophysics" by Eugene Galanter from *New Directions in Psychology*. Copyright © 1962 by Holt, Rinehart, and Winston, Inc. Reprinted by permission of the author. 151 Fig. 4.23 "The gate-control theory of pain" from *Psychology: Boundaries and Frontiers* by William Buskit and David Gerbing. Copyright © 1990 by Scott, Foresman and Company. Reprinted by permission of Scott, Foresman and Company.

Chapter 5

179 Fig. 5.19 "Typical sleep pattern of a young adult" from *Current Concepts™: The Sleep Disorders* by Peter Hauri, PhD. Copyright © 1982 by The Upjohn Company, Kalamazoo, Michigan. Reprinted by permission.

Chapter 6

220 Fig. 6.8 "Introduction and Removal of Reward, and Maze Performance in Rats" by E.C. Tolman and C.H. Honzik from *University of California Publications in Psychology* Volume IV 1928–1931. Reprinted by permission.

Chapter 7

234 Fig. 7.2 "Short-term Retention of Individual Verbal Items" by Lloyd R. Peterson and Margaret J. Peterson, from *Journal of Experimental Psychology* (September, 1959), the American Psychological Association. Reprinted by permission of the authors. 245 Fig. 7.4 From "Long-term Memory for a Common Object" by Raymond S. Nickerson and Marilyn Jager Adams, *Cognitive Psychology*, 11. Copyright © 1979 Academic Press. Reprinted by permission. 248 Fig. 7.5 from "Narrative Stories as Mediators for Serial Learning" by Gordon H. Bower and Mical C. Clark, from *Psychonomic Science*, 1969, Volume 14(4). Copyright © 1969 by Psychonomic Journals, Inc. Reprinted by permission. 249 Fig. 7.6 From "Mnemotechnics in Second-Language Learning" by Richard C. Atkinson, from *American Psychologist* Volume 30, August 1975, Number 8. Published by the American Psychological Association. Reprinted by permission of the author. 249 Fig. 7.7 From "Bizarreness versus Interaction of Mental Images as Determinants of Learning" by Keith A. Wollen, Andrea Weber, and Douglas H. Lowry, from *Cognitive Psychology*, 1972. Copyright © 1972 by Academic Press, Inc. Reprinted by permission. 250 Fig. 7.8 From *Plans and the Structure of Behavior* by George A. Miller, Eugene Galanter, and Karl H. Pribram (Holt, Rinehart and Winston 1960). Reprinted by permission of the authors. 252 Fig. 7.10

From "The Conditions of Retention," by C. W. Luh, from *Psychological Monographs*. Psychological Review, Co., 1922. **253** Fig. 7.11 From "Properties of Learning Curves under Varied Distribution of Practice" by Mary J. Kientzle, from *Journal of Experimental Psychology* 36 (June, 1946). Published by the American Psychological Association, Inc. Reprinted by permission of the author.

Chapter 8
267 Fig. 8.2 From Newell and Simon (1972), cited in COGNITION by Arnold Glass, Keith Holyoak, and John Santa. New York: Random House, 1979. **286** Fig. 8.10 Wechsler Intelligence Scale. Copyright © 1955 by the Psychological Corporation. Reproduced by permission. All rights reserved. **295** Fig. 8.11 From "Problem-Solving" by Martin Scheerer, from *Scientific American*, Vol. 208, 1963.

Chapter 9
330 Fig. 9.7 "Cross-Cultural Studies of Facial Expressions" from *Darwin and Facial Expression: A Century of Research in Review* edited by Paul Ekman. Copyright © 1973 by Academic Press, Inc. Reprinted by permission of Academic Press, Inc. and the author.

Chapter 10
351 Fig. 10.3 From *The Inequality of Man* by H.J. Eysenck. Copyright © 1973 by Hans J. Eysenck. Reprinted by permission of Educational & Industrial Testing Services.

Chapter 12
404 Fig. 12.3 McGlynn TJ, Metcalf HL: Diagnosis and Treatment of Anxiety Disorders: A Physician's Handbook. Washington DC, American Psychiatric Press, 1989, p. 80. Copyright © 1989 American Psychiatric Press, Inc. **419** Fig. 12.8 From "Clues to the Genetics and Neurobiology of Schizophrenia" by Susan E. Nicol and Irving I. Gottesmann, *American Scientist*, Vol. 71, No. 4 July–August 1983. Copyright © 1983 by Sigma Xi. The Scientific Research Society, Inc. Reprinted by permission.

Chapter 13
447 Fig. 13.2 From *Reason and Emotion in Psychotherapy* by Albert Ellis (New York: Citadel, 1962) and *A New Guide to Rational Living* by Albert Ellis and Robert A. Harper (North Hollywood, CA: Willshire Books, 1975). Copyright © by the Institute for Rational-Emotive Therapy. **450** Fig. 13.3 From "The Dose-Effect Relationship in Psychotherapy" by Kenneth I. Howard, S. Mark Kopta, Merton S. Krause and David E. Orlinsky, *American Psychologist*, Volume 41, February 1986, Number 2. Copyright © 1986 by the American Psychological Association, Inc. Reprinted by permission **451** Fig. 13.4 From table 5.1 from *The Benefits of Psychotherapy* by Mary Lee Smith, Gene V. Gloss, and Thomas I. Miller. Copyright © 1980 by The Johns Hopkins Press. Printed by permission.

Chapter 15
496 Fig. 15.1 Adapted from *Training in Organizations: Needs Assessment, Development, and Evaluation*, Second Edition by I.L. Goldstein. Copyright © 1986, 1974 by Wadsworth, Inc. Adapted by permission of Brooks/Cole Publishing Company, Pacific Grove, CA 93950. **512** Fig. 15.3 "Workers At Risk from Neurotoxins" from NEUROTOXIC FOLLIES by Alan Anderson from PSYCHOLOGY TODAY, July 1982. Reprinted with permission from PSYCHOLOGY TODAY magazine. Copyright © 1982 (Sussex Publishers, Inc.).

Name Index

Jenkins, C., 383
Jenkins, J., 254
Jensen, A., 290–291
Johnson, D. L., 420
Johnson, J., 400
Johnson, M. K., 239, 250, 257
Johnson, V., 318
Jones, A., 494
Jones, E., 471
Jones, K. L., 84
Jones, M. C., 100
Jordan, M., 395
Joyce, P., 435
Julien, R., 184, 189
Jung, C., 343, 344
Jussim, L., 461

Kagan, J., 97, 349
Kahle, L., 397
Kahn, R., 113
Kahn, S., 108
Kalish, R. A., 114
Kamin, L., 206, 219
Kamiya, J., 381
Kandel, E., 243
Kanizsa, G., 167
Kanter, J. F., 105, 106
Kaplan, G., 381
Kaplan, R. M., 382
Kaplan, S., 511
Karoum, F., 419
Karpov, A., 250
Kasparov, G., 250
Katzell, R., 494–495, 501
Kay, S., 417
Kazden, A., 452
Keating, D. P., 101
Keesey, R., 312
Keith, P. M., 108
Kelley, H., 469, 472
Kempler, D., 71
Kermis, M. D., 112
Kershner, J., 271, 288
Kessler, S., 418
Kett, J. F., 98
Kientzle, M., 253
Kiesler, C., 428, 433
Kiester, E., 178, 514, 515
Kilcullen, R., 494
Kilner, L. A., 98
Kimble, G., 36, 37, 212
Kimmel, D. C., 112
Kimmel, H., 381
King, M., 502
Kinsbourne, M., 69
Kinsey, A., 317
Kirkpatrick, D., 497
Kirscht, J. P., 385
Kisker, E., 106
Klein, H., 499
Kleitman, N., 178
Klerman, G., 400, 411, 452
Knapp, S., 320
Knight, P., 502
Knittle, J., 312
Knowles, E., 476
Kobasa, S. C., 376
Kofoed, L., 409
Kohlberg, L., 88, 96–97

Kolata, G., 84, 87
Kolb, B., 51, 52
Koop, C. E., 185
Korchin, S., 358, 361
Kosslyn, S. M., 72
Kovacic, C., 514
Kraepelin, E., 396, 417
Krantz, D., 383, 384
Kreuger, W., 252
Krupat, E., 509
Kübler-Ross, E., 113–114
Kuiper, N., 380
Kulik, J., 246
Kunkel, D., 468
Kunst-Wilson, W., 474
Kupfer, D., 451

Laborit, H., 436
Lafferty, P., 451
Laird, J. M., 151, 330
Lamb, S., 97
Lambiotte, J., 515
Landers, D., 381, 514
Landers, S., 102, 106, 320
Landesman, S., 292, 293, 294
Landis, D., 318
Lanetto, R., 114
Lang, P., 324
Lange, C., 325
Langlois, J., 474
Lashley, K., 242
Latané, B., 479–482
Latham, G., 496, 497, 500
Lawler, E., 502
Lazarus, R., 327, 375
Leahey, T., 246
Ledger, G., 271, 288
LeDoux, J. E., 70
Lee, S., 290, 291
Lehman , G., 513
Lehrer, P., 381
Leibowitz, H., 175
Lempers, J. D., 94
Lenneberg, E., 275, 277
Lenzenweger, M., 417
Leon, G., 313
Leonard, J., 459
Lerner, M. J., 470
LeVay, S., 65, 318
Leventhal, H., 385
Levine, J. M., 461, 484
Levine, M. F., 502
Levinson, D. J., 107, 108, 109–110
Levinthal, C., 311
Lewinsohn, P., 411
Lewis, M., 114
Ley, P., 385
Lichenstein, E., 385
Liddle, R., 315
Lidz, T., 420
Lieberman, M. A., 381
Liebert, R. M., 468
Linder, D., 473
Lindsley, D. B., 64
Linoila, M., 308
Linz, D., 468
Litt, M., 151
Little Albert, 203–204, 206, 346

Litwin, G., 322
Locke, E., 500, 501
Locke, J., 18, 23, 37
Lockhart, R., 239
Loftus, E., 238
Loftus, G., 238
Long, P., 182
Lord, C., 250
Lott, A. J., 472
Lott, B. E., 472
Lowery, C. R., 97
Lowry, D., 249
Lozott, B., 83
Lucas, E., 181
Luh, C., 241
Lykken, D. T., 408
Lynch, G., 243
Lynch, S., 151
Lynn, R., 290, 291
Lynn, S., 182

MacDonald, M., 380
Mace, N., 414
MacFarlane, A., 403
Mackenzie, B., 291
Mackintosh, N., 291
MacMillan, J., 409
Maddi, S., 376
Magid, K., 410
Magoun, H. W., 64
Mahoney, M., 514
Mahowald, M., 180
Maier, N., 270, 271
Malatesta, C. A., 89
Mandler, G., 241
Manning, M. L., 98
Marengo, T., 415
Markowitz, J., 400
Marks, I., 208
Markus, H., 462
Marmar, C., 449, 450, 452
Marschark, M., 248
Martin, G. B., 87
Martin, R. J., 312, 313
Martindale, C., 236
Marx, J., 415
Marziali, E., 452
Maslow, A., 23, 304–305, 348, 500
Massaro, D., 231
Masters, W., 318, 320
Matarazzo, J., 385
Matin, L., 175
Matsumoto, D., 330
Matthews, K., 383
Matthies, H., 243
Mattson, S. N., 84
Mayer, D. J., 56
Mayer, R., 250
Mayer, W., 186
Mayo, E., 504–505
McCann, I. L., 108, 381
McCarley, R., 180
McClelland, D., 321–322
McCloskey, M., 246
McCormick, D., 242
McCrae, R. R., 107, 110, 352
McDougall, W., 303
McEvoy, L., 403

McFarland, C., 480
McGaugh, J., 246
McGinnis, J., 385
McGlashan, T., 417
McGlynn, T., 404
McGuire, W., 461
McKim, W., 185, 186
McNaughton, B., 243
McNeil, D., 277
Mednick, M. T. S., 97
Mednick, S., 409, 417
Meichenbaum, D., 380, 385
Mellers, B., 474
Melzack, R., 150, 151
Mendel, G., 48
Meredith, N., 428
Merikle, P., 147
Mervis, J., 452
Metcalf, H., 404
Michael, J., 212
Michela, J., 469
Middlemist, R., 500
Milgram, S., 477–479, 509
Miller, B. C., 108
Miller, D. T., 471, 480
Miller, G., 235, 249
Miller, J. G., 470
Miller, K., 473
Miller, N. E., 346–347, 353, 373, 381, 385
Miller, R., 206, 452
Miller, T. I., 452
Millstein, S. G., 102, 106
Milner, B., 242, 243
Minami, H., 254
Minuchin, S., 449
Mishkin, M., 242, 243
Mitchell, J., 315
Mobley, W., 503
Moffitt, T., 409
Money, J., 318
Moniz, E., 434
Monson, T., 471
Moore, K. L, 81, 83, 87
Morales, F., 180
Moreland, R., 461, 484
Morgan, W., 514
Morris, C., 243, 273
Morrison, D. M., 107
Morrow, H., 292
Moruzzi, G., 64
Moscovici, S., 476, 484
Mother Theresa, 395
Mowday, R., 500
Muchinsky, P., 494, 502, 503
Mulac, A., 323
Munn, N., 337
Murphy, D. P., 29
Murray, D. J., 429
Murray, D. M., 385
Murray, H., 321, 362

Nakazima, S., 275
Nash, M., 183
Nathan, P., 186
Nemeth, C., 476
Nettleton, N. C., 72
Neugarten, B. L., 112–113
Neugarten, D. A., 112–113
Newby, R., 244

Tolman, E., 219–221
Tomkins, S., 329
Torrey, T. W., 81
Triplett, N., 482
Tsuang, M., 411
Tucker, D., 328
Tulving, E., 239, 244
Turk, D., 385
Turner, C., 468
Turner, J., 109
Turner, T. J., 327
Tuttle, T., 502, 503

Ulrich, R., 337
Underwood, B., 255

Valenstein, E. S., 434
Valliant, C. O., 113
Valliant, G. E., 113
Van Lancker, D., 71
Vance, James, 146–147
Vandecreek, L., 320
VandenBos, G. R., 450
Varca, P., 514
Vaughn, B., 474
Ventura, J., 420

Verillo, R., 149
Vinacke, W., 271
Vitz, P. C., 96
Vokey, J., 146
Vroom, V., 499

Wagner, A., 206
Walk, R., 87
Walker, L. J., 97
Walker, T., 262
Wall, P., 150
Wallace, P., 144
Walsh, B., 315
Walster, E., 467, 472, 474
Walster, G., 474
Walters, G., 217
Walton, A., 502
Warrington, E. K., 244
Washington, G., 188
Waternax, C., 411
Watkins, B., 468
Watkins, L. R., 56
Watkins, M., 238
Watson, C., 502
Watson, J. B., 22, 23,
    203–204, 345–346, 353
Weary, G., 471

Weaver, C. N., 108, 502
Weber, A., 249
Wechsler, D., 278, 284–286
Weiner, B., 327
Weisberg, R., 289
Weiskrantz, L., 244
Weiss, W., 466
Weissman, M., 399, 400
Weldon, E., 482
Wertheimer, M., 23, 87, 171
Wethington, E., 417
Wheeler, R., 381
White, B. D., 312, 313
White, J., 147
Whitehouse, R. H., 99
Whitehurst, G., 276
Wible, C., 246
Wickens, D., 237
Wiesner, W., 495
Wilkes, J., 182
Williams, K., 482
Williams, R., 264
Willis, S. L., 108
Wilson, G., 209
Winett, R., 512
Winkel, G. H., 40, 503
Winter, D. G., 322, 323
Winters, K., 417

Witmer, J., 513
Wollen, K., 249
Wolpe, J., 444–445, 452
Wood, C., 383
Woolfolk, R., 381
Wright, F. L., 395
Wright, L., 383, 384
Wundt, W., 19–20, 21, 22, 23
Wurtman, R., 414, 415
Wysowski, D., 436

Yates, A. J., 314, 315, 381
Yates, F. A., 249
York, C., 501
Young, T., 136, 137

Zacharko, R., 412
Zajonc, R., 329, 330, 462,
    474, 483
Zedeck, S., 494
Zeiss, A., 411
Zelnick, M., 105, 106
Zidon, I., 500
Zigler, E., 292, 294
Zimmerman, M., 408
Zuckerman, M., 308, 409

Subject Index

▲▲▲▲▲▲

A

Ability, types of, 282–283, 288–289
Abnormality
    defined, 395–396
    inappropriateness of value judgments
        about, 395–396
    types of, 396–398
Academic aptitude, 289
Accommodation
    Piagetan, 90
    visual, 131, 170
Acetylcholine (ACh), 56
    and memory, 243, 415
Achievement motivation, 321–322
Acoustic coding, 236
Acquired immune deficiency syndrome
    (AIDS), 319–320
Acquisition, 200, 210, 211
Acrophobia, 399
Action potential, 53
Actor-observer bias, 471
Adaptation, sensory, 126
Addiction, 185
Adolescence
    adjustment during, 98
    defined, 97–98
    difficulties in, 98, 101–102
    drug use in, 102–103
    egocentrism in, 102
    identity formation in, 101
    physical development in, 99–100
    sexuality in, 104–105
Adulthood
    early, 107–109
    late, 112–114
    middle, 109–111
Advertising, as classical conditioning,
    202–203, 463–464
Affect, 324
    abnormalities of, 395
    and attitude, 462
    defined, 16
    flat, 415
Affiliation, as motivation, 323
Age, chronological and mental, 283
Ageism, 112
Aggression
    induction of, 221–222
    stress and, 378
    temperature and, 510–511
    violence as, 468
Agoraphobia, 399, 400
Alarm, stress and, 379
Alcohol
    adolescent use of, 102–103
    abuse of, 186–187
    effect on fetus, 83–84
Algophobia, 399
Algorithm, defined, 268

Alienation, 479
Alpha waves, 176
Alzheimer's disease, 56, 414–415
American College Testing Program
    (ACT), 287
American Psychological Association
    (APA), 24
Amnesia, 242–243
    psychogenic, 406
Amphetamines, 185–186, 419
Amplitude, 129
    defined, 127
Amygdala, 64
    and emotion, 328
Anal stage, 342–343
Analgesics, 187
Animal experiments, ethics in, 36
Anorexia nervosa, 314–315
Anterograde amnesia, 243
Antianxiety drugs, 438
Antidepressants, 437–438
Antipsychotic drugs, 419
Antisocial personality disorder, 408–410
Anvil, 141, 142
Anxiety, 399
    basic, 344
    behavior therapy for, 444
    drug therapy for, 438
    tests of, 360–361
Anxiety disorders
    generalized, 401
    obsessive–compulsive disorder,
        401–403
    panic disorder, 400
    phobic disorder, 399–400
    posttraumatic stress disorder, 403–404
    stress and, 378
Anxious/ambivalent style of interaction,
    473
Apathy, 479–482
Apnea, 181
Application, job, 494
Applied behavior analysis (ABA), 512
Applied psychology
    environmental psychology, 503–513
    industrial-organizational (I/O)
        psychology, 25, 492–503
    sports psychology, 513–515
Approach-approach conflict, 372–373
Approach-avoidance conflict, 373–374
Aptitude, 289
    tests of, 287
Aqueous humor, 132
Archetypes, Jungian, 344
Armed Forces Qualification Test, 287
Army Alpha Test, 287
Army Beta Test, 287
Army General Classification Test, 287
Arousal, 302

to accomplish task, 498
    in athletics, 514
    as motivation, 307–308
Assessment, 356–357
    behavioral observation, 357–358
    interviews, 358–359
    projective techniques, 360–361
    tests, 359–360
Assignment, random, 35
Assimilation, 90
Association areas, of brain, 66, 68–69
Astraphobia, 399
Atonia, 180
Attachment theory of interpersonal
        attraction, 472–473
Attitude
    cognitive dissonance and, 464–466
    components of, 462
    defined, 461
    formation of, 469–483
    object of, 462
    persuasion and, 466–467
Attraction, interpersonal, 471–475
Attractiveness, physical, perceptions
        of, 474
Attribution error, 469–470, 478
Attribution theory, 469–471
Audience
    facilitation by, 482–483
    inhibition by, 480, 483, 514
Audition. See Hearing
Auditory canal, 142
Auditory nerve, 142
Authority, obedience to, 477–479
Autokinetic effect, 175
Autonomic nervous system (ANS), 58
    divisions of, 58
    and emotion, 327
    stress and, 379
Autophobia, 399
Average, defined, 523
Aversion therapy, 445
Avoidance, 373, 377
Avoidance–avoidance conflict, 373
Avoidant personality disorder, 409
Avoidant style of interaction, 472–473
Axis, X- and Y-, 522
Axon, 51
    myelinated, 52
    structure of, 54
Axon terminal, 52

B

Babbling, 275
Bar graph, 522
Barbiturates, 187
Base rate, 208
Baseline design, 35
Basic anxiety, 344

Basic hostility, 345
Basilar membrane, 142
Bedlam, 429–430, 432
Behavior
  abnormalities of, 395
  attitudes and, 462
  defined, 15
  emotion and, 324
  goal–oriented nature of, 370
  and health, 382
  learning and, 197
  modifying
    for environmental reasons, 511–513
    for health reasons, 385–386
Behavior disorder. *See* Psychological
  disorder
Behavior therapy, 444–446
Behavioral observation, 357–358
Behavioral/learning approach to personality, 345–347, 353
Behaviorism, 22, 345–347
  purposive, 221
  See also Operant conditioning
Benzodiazepines, 438
Bias
  actor-observer, 471
  ageism as, 112
  in favor of physical attractiveness, 474
  fundamental attribution error,
    469–470, 478
  of intelligence tests, 290
  just world hypothesis as, 471
  prejudice as, 458–459
  sampling, 27
  self-serving, 471
  stereotype as, 461
Binocular cues, 169
Biodata, 494
Biofeedback, 381
Biogenic amines, 412
Bipolar mood disorder, 410, 411
Blindspot, 133
Blocking, 206
Blood, glucose in, 312
Body language, 329
Brain
  anatomy of, 66
  association areas, 66, 68–69
  cerebellum, 63
  cerebrum, 65–72
  hypothalamus, 65
  limbic system, 64
  lower, 61–65
  medulla, 62
  memory and, 242–243
  motor areas, 66, 67
  neurons in, 52
  organic mental disorders of, 414
  psychosurgery on, 434
  sensory areas, 66–67
  thalamus, 65
Brain stem, 61–62
Brightness
  constancy of, 172
  defined, 127
British empiricists, 18

Bulimia, 314–315
Bystander apathy, 479–482

C

Caffeine, 184
Calcium deficiency, effect on fetus, 83
California Personality Inventory (CPI), 360
Cannon–Bard theory of emotion,
  325–326
Cardinal traits, 349
Career
  satisfaction in, 501–503
  stages of, 109
  See also Job
Case history, 27–28
Catatonic schizophrenia, 417
Causality, 90
Cause and effect, 31
Cell body, 51
Central nervous system (CNS), 57
Central tendency, 523
  measures of, 523–525
Central traits, 349–350
Cephalocaudal sequencing, 86
Cerebellum, 63
Cerebral cortex, 65
  and emotion, 328
  functions of, 66–69
  hemispheres of, 70–72
  lobes of, 66
Cerebrotonia, 354
Cerebrum. *See* Cerebral cortex
Chemical senses
  smell (olfaction), 143, 144–145
  taste (gustation), 143–144
Childhood
  cognitive development in, 88–94
  defined, 85
  language acquisition in, 275–278
  motor development in, 85–86
  perceptual development in, 87–88
  physical development in, 85–86
  Piagetan view of, 90–94
  sensory development in, 87–88
  social development in, 94–97
Chlamydia, 319
Chlorofluorocarbons (CFCs),
    discouraging use of, 512
Chlorpromazine, 436
Cholecystokinin (CCK), 315
Chromosomes, 80
  defined, 48
Chunking, 235
Ciliary muscles, 131
Cities
  advantages of, 509
  crowding in, 508
  stressors in, 508
Classical conditioning, 197–200
  in attitude formation, 463
  modern view of, 205–206
  phenomena of, 200–202
  in psychotherapy, 444
  significance of, 202–205
  stages of, 201
Claustrophobia, 399

Client-centered psychotherapy, 442, 443
Clinical psychology and psychologists,
    24–25, 430–431
Closure, as principle of organization, 167
Clozapine, 436
Cocaine, 102, 185
  effect on fetus, 84
Cochlea, 142
Codeine, 187
Coding
  acoustic, 236
  in long-term memory, 238–239
  methods of, 244–246
  in short-term memory, 236–237
Cognition
  abnormalities of, 395
  as aspect of attitude, 462
  as aspect of emotion, 324, 328
  defined, 16
  and depression, 413
  in neonate, 88–89
Cognitive development, 88–94
  concrete operations stage, 92, 93
  criticisms of, 93–94
  formal operations stage, 93
  preoperational stage, 91–92, 93
  sensorimotor stage, 90–91, 93
Cognitive dissonance, 308, 309
  in attitude change, 464–466
Cognitive maps, 219–220
Cognitive processes, 16
Cognitive psychology, 25
Cognitive psychotherapies, 446
  cognitive restructuring, 448
  rational-emotive (RET), 447–448
Cognitive reappraisal, 380
Cognitive restructuring therapy, 448
Cognitive-behavioral therapies, 446
Collective unconscious, 344
Color
  discrimination of, 134
  experiencing, 137–138
  physics of, 127–129
  primary, 136
  receptors for, 136–137
Colorblindness, 137–138
  in animals, 218
Common fate, as principle of
    organization, 167
Common traits, 349
Communication
  credibility of, 466–467
  doctor-patient, 385
  in family, 449
Community mental health centers, 432–433
Complexity of sound, 140
Compulsions, 402
Conception, 80
Concrete operations stage, 92, 93
Concurrent validity, of tests, 281
Conditioned response (CR), 199
Conditioned stimulus (CS), 199
Conditioning, 197
  classical, 197–206
  operant, 206–218
Cones, 132, 134–135

sensitivity of, 136–137
Confidentiality, 36
Conflict
  approach-approach, 372–373
  approach-avoidance, 373–374
  avoidance-avoidance, 373
  multiple approach-avoidance, 374
Conformity, 475–476
Consciousness, 16, 160, 339
  characteristics of, 161
  drug-altered, 183–189
  in hypnosis, 180–183
  levels of, 339
  sleep and, 176–180
Consensus, 469
Conservation, 92, 94
  of energy, 512–513
Constancies, perceptual, 171–175
Constitutional theories, 354
Content validity, of tests, 281
Context, as memory cue, 244
Contingency contracting, 44, 213,
    445–446
Contingency management, 44
Continuity, as principle of organization,
    166–167
Continuous reinforcement (CRF)
    schedule, 214, 215
Contrast, and selectivity, 162
Control group, 34
Conventional morality, 96
Convergence, 170
Convergent thinking, 271–272
Conversion disorder, 405, 406
Cornea, 130
Corpus callosum, 70
Correlation coefficient, 29
Correlation
  in inferential statistics, 527–529
  methods of, 28–31
  pitfalls in using, 31
Counseling psychology and psychologists,
    25, 431
Counselors, licensed, 431
Counterirritation, pain relief from, 152
Countertransference, 441
Creativity, 271–272, 273
  as gift, 288
Credibility, 466–467
Crime
  blaming victim of, 471
  as stressor, 403
  temperature and incidence of,
    510–511
Criterion-referenced test, 360
Critical thinking, 3–4
Cross-laterality, 62, 67, 70
Crowding, 508
Crystallized ability, 282
Cutaneous senses, 145–148

D

Dark adaptation, 126, 134–135
Data
  describing, 523–52
  evaluating, 527–529

organizing, 521–522
DDT, banning of, 512
Death, preparing for, 113–114
Death instincts, Freudian concept of, 339
Debriefing, 36
Decibel scale, 139, 140
Decision making, 484–485
Deep sleep, 177
Defense mechanisms, 340
  types of, 341–342
Definition, operational, 16
Degenerative dementia, 414–415
Deinstitutionalization, 432
  evaluation of, 433
Delta waves, 177
Dendrite, 51
Denial, as defense mechanism, 341
Dependent personality disorder, 409
Dependent variable, 32, 33
Depressants, 186–187
Depression
  biological factors in, 411–412
  chronic nature of, 410–411
  drug therapy for, 437–438
  panic disorder and, 400
  psychological factors in, 412–413
Depth perception, 169–171
DES (diethylstilbestrol), effect on fetus, 84
Descriptive statistics, 523–527
Development, 80
  cognitive, 88–94
  Erikson's view of, 94–95
  Kohlberg's view of, 96–97
  language, 275–278
  motor, in childhood, 85–86
  perceptual, in childhood, 87–88
  physical
    in adolescence, 99–100
    in childhood, 85–86
  Piaget's view of, 90–94
  prenatal, 80–81
    environmental influences on, 83–84
    physical aspects of, 81–82
  psychosocial, 94–95
  sensory, in childhood, 87–88
  social, in childhood, 94–97
Developmental psychology, 24
Deviance, 395
Diagnosis, 396–398
*Diagnostic and Statistical Manual of
    Mental Disorders (DSM–III–R),*
    396–398
Dichromatism, 137–138
Diethylstilbestrol (DES), effect on fetus,
    84
Difference, statistically significant, 528
Differential reinforcement, 218
Diffusion of responsibility, 481
Discrimination (prejudice), 458–459,
    460–461
Discrimination (psychological term), 201,
    218
Disorganized schizophrenia, 417
Displacement, as defense mechanism, 342
Disposition, 461
Dispositional attribution, 469

Dissociative disorders, 405
  multiple personality disorder, 406–407
  psychogenic amnesia, 406
  psychogenic fugue, 406
Distance perception, 169–171
Distraction, and performance levels,
    509–510
Distributed practice, 252
Divergent thinking, 271, 272
Doctor-patient relationship, 385
Dominant gene, 49
Dopamine, 56, 185
  and depression, 412
  and schizophrenia, 417, 418–420
Down's syndrome, 293
Dreams, 178
  Freudian interpretation of, 440
Drinking
  of alcohol, 102–103, 186–187
  as behavior, 311
Drive state, 303
Drives, 303–304, 308
  physiologically-based, 309–320
  psychologically-based, 321–330
Drug abuse, 184
  in adolescence, 102–103
  effect on fetus, 83–84
  pharmacology of, 183–189
Drug therapy
  antidepressants, 437–438
  antipsychotics, 436–437
  tranquilizers, 438
*DSM-III-R (Diagnostic and Statistical
    Manual of Mental Disorders),*
    396–398
Dual-center theories of hunger, 312
Dualism, interactive, 18
Dysthymia, 413

E

Ear, anatomy of, 141–142
Eardrum, 141, 142
Eating
  as behavior, 312–313
  disorders of, 314–315
ECT (electroconvulsive therapy),
    435–436, 438
Ectomorph, 354–355
Educational-instructional psychology, 24
EEG (electroencephalograph), 176
Ego, Freudian concept of, 340
Egocentrism, 91, 94
  adolescent, 102
Elaborative rehearsal, 239
Electra complex, 343
Electroconvulsive therapy (ECT),
    435–436, 438
Electroencephalograph (EEG), 176
Electromagnetic spectrum, 128
Electromyograph (EMG), 176
Embryo, 81–82
Emergencies, reaction to, 479–482
EMG (electromyograph), 176
Emotions
  amygdala and, 64
  components of, 324

conditioned response and, 202–203
defined, 324
expressions of, 329–331
motivational role of, 327
mother's, effect on fetus, 84
physiology of, 327–329
septum and, 64
theories of, 325–327
Empathic, defined, 442
Empiricism, British, 18
Employment
application, 494
fairness in, 500
interview, 494–495
training for, 495–498
Encapsulated nerve endings, 145
Encoding
defined, 231
in long-term memory, 238–239
methods of, 244–246
in short-term memory, 236–237
specificity of, 245–246
Endocrine system, nervous system and, 58
Endomorph, 354–355
Endorphins, 56
gate-control theory on, 150
Energy conservation, 512–513
Environment
and intelligence, 290
noise in, 509–510
personal space as, 504–508
and prenatal development, 83–84, 293
preservation of, 39, 511–513
temperature as, 510–511
toxins in, 511
Environmental concerns, 39, 511–513
Environmental frustration, 371
Environmental psychology, 503
behavior modification in, 511–513
and environmental variables, 509–511
and personal space, 504–506
and territoriality, episodic memory, 240
Equity model of interpersonal attraction, 472
Equity theory, 500
Eros, Freudian concept of, 339
Escape, 377
Esteem, need for, 304–305
Ethical Principles of Psychologists (APA), 35
Ethics, in research, 34, 35–36
Excitatory neurotransmitter, 54
Exercise, to combat stress, 381
Exhaustion, 382
Expectancy theory, 499
Experience, importance of, 18, 37
learning and, 197
Experiment
controlled, 34–35
defined, 31
procedures for, 31–33
Experimental group, 34
External attribution, 469
Extinction, 200, 210, 211
Extraneous variable, 32, 33
Extroversion-introversion, 350–351

Eye, anatomy of, 130–133
light receptors in, 132, 134–135

F

Facial expression, 329–331
Facilitation, social, 482–483
Factor analysis, 350
Family therapy, 449
Fantasy, as defense mechanism, 341
Farsightedness, 131
Fear, treatment of, 208–209
Feedback, 3
at work, 500
Fetus, 82–83
Fight or flight response, 328
Figure-ground relationship, 165
Fixation, 377
Fixed-interval (FI) schedule, 214
Fixed-ratio (FR) schedule, 214
Flashbulb memories, 246
Flattened affect, 415
Flavor, 143
Flooding, 444–445
Fluid-analytic ability, 282
Fluoxetine, 437
Formal operations stage, 93
Fovea, 133
Fragile X syndrome, 293–294
Free association, 439
Free nerve endings, 145
Frequency distributions, 521–522
Frequency theory, 142
Freudian
approach to personality, 338–343
psychoanalysis, 439–441
Frontal lobes, 66
Frustration, 370–372
environmental, 371
personal, 372
social, 371
Frustration-aggression hypothesis, 378
Fugue, psychogenic, 406
Functional fixedness, 270
Functionalism, 20, 22
Fundamental attribution error, 469–470, 478

G

G (general intellectual ability), 282
Gate-control theory of pain, 150–151
Gender
genetics and, 50
moral development and, 97
physical growth and, 99
Gene
defined, 48
delayed expression of, 50
dominant, 49
recessive, 49
General adaptation syndrome (GAS), 378–382
Generalization, 201, 204, 217–218
excessive, 448
Generalized anxiety disorder, 401
Generate-test strategy, defined, 268
Generativity, 108

Genetics
and body size, 313
fundamentals of, 48–49
importance of, 50, 72
and intelligence, 290–291
and mental illness, 418, 419, 420
Genital herpes, 319
Genital stage, 343
Gestalt, defined, 165, 442
Gestalt
psychology, 23–24, 165
psychotherapy, 442–444
Giftedness
as predictor of success, 289
types of, 288–289
Glove anesthesia, 405
Glucose, blood levels of, 312
Goals
behavior and, 370–371
growth and, 377
setting, 2
in employment, 500–501
Gonorrhea, 319
Graduate Record Examination (GRE), 288
Grammar, development of, 275–277
Graphs
bar, 522
line, 523
Group decision making, 484–485
Group polarization, 484
Group therapy, 448–449
Groupthink, 484
Growth spurt, 99–100
Gustation, 143–144

H

Habituation, 198
Hair cells, 142
Hallucinogens, 187–188
Hammer, 141, 142
Handedness, 70
Hardy personality, 376
Hawthorne Effect, 26, 504–505
Health
psychological factors affecting, 383–384
psychological interventions and, 384–386
Health psychology, 25, 382
functions of, 384–386
Hearing, 138
anatomy of, 141–143
discrimination, 140
physics of, 139–141
sound localization, 87
thresholds of, 124
Heart disease, psychological factors in, 383–384
Helping behavior, 480–482
Hematophobia, 399
Hemispheres, brain, 70–72
Heredity
importance of, 37, 48
and intelligence, 290–291
and mental illness, 418, 419, 420

Heroin, 102, 187
  effect on fetus, 84
Herpes type II, 319
Hertz (Hz), 140
Heuristic, defined, 269
Hierarchy of needs, 304–305
Hippocampus, 64
  and memory, 242
Histogram, 522
Histrionic personality disorder, 409
Holophrastic speech, 275
Home-field advantage, 514
Homeostasis, 306–307, 309
Homosexuality, 317–318
Hormones, 58
  and emotion, 328
  puberty and, 100, 104
  sex and, 316
Hostility, basic, 345
Hue
  defined, 127
  primary, 136
Human immunodeficiency virus (HIV),
    319–320
Human relations movement, 505
Humanistic
  psychology, 23
  psychotherapies
    client–centered, 442, 443
    Gestalt, 442–444
Humanistic/phenomenological approach
    to personality, 347–348, 353
Hunger, 312
  stimuli for, 312–313
  theories of, 312
Hyperphagia, 312
Hypnosis, 180, 182–183
  pain relief from, 151
Hypochondriasis, 404–405
Hypothalamus, 64
  and emotion, 328
  functions of, 65
  and hunger drive, 312
  location of, 310
  and sexuality, 318
  and temperature regulation, 310
Hypothesis, 33
  defined, 15

I

I/O (industrial–organizational) psychol-
    ogy, 25, 492
  job analysis, 493–494
  job motivation, 498–501
  job satisfaction, 501–503
  personnel selection, 494–495
  personnel training, 495–498
Id, Freudian concept of, 340
Idealistic principle, 340
Identity, formation of, 101
Illusions, optical, 165, 168, 169, 172–175
Imaginary audience, 102
Incentives, 305–306, 322
Incus, 141, 142
Independence, 107
Independent variable, 32, 33

Industrial-organizational (I/O)
    psychology, 25, 492
  job analysis, 493–494
  job motivation, 498–501
  job satisfaction, 501–503
  personnel selection, 494–495
  personnel training, 495–498
Infant. See Neonate
Infectious disease, effect on fetus, 83
Inferential statistics, 527–529
Inferiority complex, 344
Informed consent, 36
Inheritance. See Heredity
Inhibitory neurotransmitter, 55
Insane asylums, 429–430
Insanity, defined, 398
Insomnia, 176, 181
Instincts, 302–303, 308
  Freudian view of, 339
Institutions, 429–430
  deinstitutionalization from, 432–433
Intellectual giftedness, 289
Intelligence, 72
  definitions of, 16, 17, 278–279
  extremes of, 289, 292–293
  tests of, 282–288
Intelligence quotient (IQ), 283
  of gifted children, 289
  graph of, 530–531
  racial and ethnic factors in, 290–291
  of retardates, 292–293
  tests of, 287
Intelligence tests
  group, 286–288
  Stanford–Binet, 282–284
  Wechsler, 284–286
  value of, 285–286
Intensity, and selectivity, 162
Interactive dualism, 18
Interdependence, 107
Interference, 253–254
  proactive, 255
  retroactive, 254–255
  social, 483
Intermittent reinforcement schedules, 214
Internal attribution, 469
Interpersonal attraction, 471
  factors affecting, 473–475
  theories of, 472–473
Interposition, 170, 171
Interview, 358–359
  employment, 494–495
Intimacy, vs. isolation, 108
Intimate distance, 506
Introspection, 20
Ion, 53
Iris, 130
Isolation, vs. intimacy, 108

J

James-Lange theory of emotion, 325
Job
  analysis of, 493–494
  application for, 494
  fairness in, 500
  goals at, 500

hiring for, 494–495
matching personnel to, 501–503
motivation for, 498–501
training for, 495–498
Jungian theory, 344
Just noticeable difference (j.n.d.),
    124–125
Just world hypothesis, 470–471

K

Key words, as memory cue, 249
Kinesthetic sense, 149
Knee jerk reflex, 60

L

Language
  acquisition of, 274–278
  biology-oriented theory of, 277–278
  body, 329
  defined, 272–273
  learning–oriented theory of, 276–277
  in memory, 239–240
  memory and, 236–237
  Piaget and, 94
  purpose of, 273–274
  symbols in, 273
Latency stage, 343
Latent content, of dreams, 440
Latent learning, 219–220
Law of effect, 207
Leadership ability, as gift, 288
Learning
  classical conditioning and, 197–206
  classroom, 5–6
  cognitive approaches to, 219–223
  defined, 196–197
  factors affecting, 2–4
  frustration and, 377
  language, 275–278
  latent, 219–220
  observational, 463
  operant conditioning and, 206–218
  optimizing, 4, 39, 240–253
  permanence of, 197
  textbook study in, 7–8
Learning theory, 346
Lens, 130
Life change, as stressor, 374–375
Life instincts, Freudian concept of, 339
Lifestyle, defined, 384–385
Light
  detection of, 123, 124
  physics of, 127–129
  sensing, 134
  white, 129
Limbic system, 64
  and emotion, 328
Line graph, 523
Listening, skills for, 6
Lithium, 437
Little Albert experiment, 203–205
Lobotomy, 434
Loci, method of, 249–250, 251
Long-term memory (LTM), 237
  information encoding in, 238–239
  permanence of, 238

defined, 413
process, 416
prognosis of, 421
reactive, 416
symptoms of, 413–416, 417
types of, 416–417, 418
Scholastic Aptitude Test, 287
Science
defined, 14
psychology's debt to, 18–19
Scientific method, 15
Secondary drives, 303
Secondary reinforcement, 213
Secondary territories, 507
Secondary traits, 350
Secure style of interaction, 472
Selectivity
factors affecting, 162–163
personal aspects of, 163–164
Self-actualization, 348
need for, 305
Self-esteem, 95
Self-image, 95, 353
physiology and, 50, 100
restructuring of, 448
Self-serving bias, 471
Selye's general adaptation syndrome
(GAS), 378–382
Semantic memory, 239–240
Semicircular canals, 142, 149
Sensation-seekers, 308
Senses and sensation, 122
brain and, 67
chemical, 143–144
cutaneous, 145–148
hearing, 87, 124, 138–143
in neonate, 87–88
nervous system and, 58
physiology of, 68–69
position, 148–149
sight, 72, 87, 124, 127–138
smell, 87–88, 124, 143–144, 145
taste, 87–88, 124, 143–144
thalamus and, 65
touch, 145–148
vestibular, 149
Sensitivity, sensory, 123
Sensorimotor stage, 90–91, 93
Sensory adaptation, 126
Sensory areas, of brain, 66–67
Sensory development, in childhood, 87–88
Sensory memory, 232
capacity of, 231
duration of, 231
Sensory neuron, 57
Sensory thresholds, 122–125, 146
Sentence completion tests, 361
Septum, 64
Serotonin, 188
and depression, 412
and memory, 243
Set point, 306
Sex
cues for, 316–317
diseases transmitted by, 318–320
as drive, 314–316

pheromones and, 144
See also Gender
Sexuality, 314–316
adolescent, 104–105
Sexually transmitted diseases (STDs),
318–320
Shading, 171, 172
Shape, constancy of, 172
Shaping, 210
Short-term memory (STM), 232
capacity of, 235–236
duration of, 233–235
information encoding in, 236–237
intelligence and, 282
Sight. See Vision
Sightedness, 131
Signal detection, 125–126
Significance, statistical, 528–529
Silent Spring (Carson), 511
Similarity
and interpersonal attraction, 474–475
as principle of organization, 166
Situational attribution, 469
16 PF, 360
Size
and selectivity, 162
relative, 170–171, 171–172
and selectivity, 162
Skin, 145–147
anatomy of, 148
Skinner box, 207
Sleep apnea, 181
Sleep
deep, 177
dreams in, 178
EEG of, 177
REM, 178–180
stages of, 176–178
Sleep spindles, 177
Smell, 143, 144–145
in neonate, 87–88
thresholds of, 124
Smoking
cognitive dissonance and, 308
effect on fetus, 83
efforts to curb, 385
pharmacology of, 185
Social development, in childhood, 94–97
Social distance, 506
Social exchange model of interpersonal
attraction, 472
Social facilitation, 482–483
Social frustration, 371
Social group, membership in, 95
Social influence
apathy, 479–482
conformity, 475–476
facilitation, 482–483
loafing, 482
obedience, 477–479
Social interference, 483
Social learning theory, 221–223
Social loafing, 482
Social psychology, 25, 460
issues in, 462–465, 468, 471, 473–475
perspective of, 460–461

research in, 466–467, 475–485
theories of, 464–466, 469–472
Social support, to combat stress, 381
Social workers, clinical, 431
Social Readjustment Rating
Social Readjustment Rating Scale
(SRRS), 374
as predictor of physical illness, 375
Somatic nervous system, 58
Somatoform disorders, 404
conversion disorder, 405, 406
hypochondriasis, 404–405
Somatotonia, 354
Sound
amplitude of, 139–140
frequency of, 140
purity of, 140–141
Sound localization, 87
Source traits, 350
Spectrum, visible, 128
Speech
brain and, 70, 71
holophrastic, 275
telegraphic, 276
See also Language
Spinal cord
function of, 60–61, 68–69
structure of, 59–60
Spinal reflex, 60, 69
Split-brain procedure, 70
Spontaneous recovery, 200, 211
Sports psychology, 513
and peak performance, 514–515
SQ3R method, 10
Stability-instability, 350–351
Standard deviation, 526
Standardized tests, 279
Stanford-Binet Intelligence Scale
abilities evaluated on, 282–284
score distribution of, 284
Stapes, 141, 142
State-dependent memory, 246
Statistically significant differences, 528
Statistics, 520–521
descriptive, 523–527
frequency distributions, 521–522
graphs in, 522
inferential, 527–529
normal curve in, 529–531
STDs (sexually transmitted diseases),
318–320
Stereotype, 461
physical attractiveness, 474
Stimulants, 184–186
Stimulus, neutral, 198
Stirrup, 141, 142
Storage, defined, 231
Strategy, defined, 268
Stress, 370
conflict-induced, 372–374
crowding and, 508
dealing with, 376–377
strategies for, 380–381
frustration-induced, 370–372
life-induced, 374
mental illness and, 420